The Junior Encyclopedia of Canada

James H. Marsh
Editor in Chief

VOLUME V

S – Z

(Index)

Hurtig Publishers

Hurtig Publishers Ltd.
1302, Oxford Tower
10235 - 101 Street
Edmonton, Alberta
Canada T5J 3G1

Every attempt has been made to identify and credit sources for
photographs. The publisher would appreciate receiving
information as to any inaccuracies in the credits for
subsequent editions.

Canadian Cataloguing in Publication Data

Main entry under title:
The Junior Encyclopedia of Canada

Editor in Chief: James H. Marsh

ISBN 0-88830-334-3 (set) —ISBN 088830-335-1
(v. 1). —ISBN 0-88830-336-X (v. 2). —ISBN
0-88830-337-8 (v. 3). —ISBN 0-88830-338-6
(v. 4). —ISBN 0-88830-339-4 (v. 5).

1. Canada—Dictionaries and encyclopedias—
Juvenile literature   I. Marsh, James H.

FC23.J86 1990   j971'.003   C90-090120-9
F1006.J86 1990

Designed, typeset, and manufactured
in Canada

Cover photo by Hans Blohm/Masterfile

Scorpion

Scorpions, like spiders, belong to the Class Arachnid, Phylum Arthropoda.

Their elongated body consists of a cephalothorax and an abdomen with a poisonous stinger at the tip. The largest species measure 15 cm long. Two appendages in front of the head end in pincers used by the scorpion to catch and handle its prey. There are eight feet used for walking. Two comb-like appendages under the abdomen — the *pectins* — unique to scorpions, are probably sensory organs.

Though they may have up to 12 eyes, scorpions can only see changes in degree of light.

There are more than 1000 species of scorpion in the tropics and sub-tropics. They hide by day under rocks or in burrows, emerging at night to catch insects or other invertebrates for food. They slowly tear apart their prey with their pincers, having paralysed even the largest with the poisonous stinger. To humans, the sting of a scorpion feels much like a bee sting.

At birth, young scorpions are fully formed and cling to the mother's back for protection during their first few days. There is only one species (*Paruroctonus boreus*) in Canada. It is found in southern Alberta, Saskatchewan, and British Columbia.

▷ SUGGESTED READING: Charlene W. Billings, *Scorpions* (1983).

Scorpionfish

Scorpionfish are marine fish that usually live near the bottom of the ocean, especially where the seabed is rocky. There are more than 300 species worldwide. They are found on both the Atlantic and Pacific coasts of Canada.

Scorpionfish have a large spiny head, a large mouth, and a stocky body. They are primarily red or brown in colour (many are called redfish) and they range in size from 15 cm to 91 cm. The fin spines are poisonous in most species.

Most scorpionfish are *ovoviviparous*: that is, the eggs develop inside the female's body and she spawns 10 000 live little fish. The young float with the currents, living on plankton. Scorpionfish are highly regarded as food fish. Some are caught by hook and line, others by nets dragged along the ocean bottom. The Atlantic redfish is particularly important in the Atlantic fishery. Scorpionfish are sold fresh or frozen under the name "ocean perch."

Scotian Shelf

The Scotian Shelf is a large, shallow section of the underwater seabed off the coast of Nova Scotia. During the ice age, when water levels in the oceans were lower, some of the shelf was dry land. Today, Sable Island is the only part of the shelf above water. The shelf is a rich fishing ground, and recently natural gas deposits were discovered.

▷ RELATED ARTICLE: **Grand Banks.**

Scots

Nearly 865 500 Canadians are of Scottish origin, and over 3 million more are partly Scottish. The Scots have been coming to Canada for more than three and a half centuries, and they have been a major influence in Canada's development.

Early Arrivals In the 1620s, a few Scots started settlements in Nova Scotia. The settlements were short lived and the territory was soon returned to France. The first regular movement of Scots to Canada dates from around 1720, when the Hudson's Bay Company began recruiting men from the Orkney Islands for work in the fur trade.

During the 18th century, too, soldiers from the Scottish Highlands arrived as members of the British army. Highland regiments fought during the Seven Years' War of 1756-63. Although many of the Highlanders and Orkneymen returned home after their tour of duty, some stayed on as settlers. Other Scots moved into Montreal and Quebec City to set up businesses when New France became British territory at the end of the Seven Years' War.

Immigration The first large wave of Scottish immigration took place between 1770 and 1815. About 15 000 settlers arrived directly from Scotland during this period. Most were Highlanders and most came as family groups. As well, there were Scots among the Loyalists who fled to British North America after the American Revolution. Nova Scotia, Prince Edward Island, and Upper Canada [Ontario] were the main centres of Scottish settlement, though Scots could be found in all regions.

Notable settlements included Pictou, N.S., which was started by Highlanders who arrived on their ship *Hector* in 1773. Three settlements were launched by Lord Selkirk: Prince Edward Island (1803), Baldoon (1804), and the Red River Colony (1812). There were also numerous settlements in the eastern districts of what is today called Ontario.

Piper at Peggy's Cove, N.S. (photo by Sherman Hines/Masterfile).

Scottish Band at the Antigonish games, Nova Scotia (photo by Sherman Hines/ Masterfile).

The second wave of Scottish migration took place from 1815 to 1870. During this period, about 170 000 Scots moved to British North America. They included Lowlanders as well as Highlanders, and they came from a wide range of backgrounds. Some were very poor, such as the tenant farmers who were forced from their homes when the landlords took over the land for sheep farming. Others were working-class families from the cities who felt they would do better in North America. There were also business people, engineers, doctors, lawyers, teachers, and clergy. Some of the immigrants paid their own way. Many came with the help of settlement schemes which were sponsored by the government or by colonization companies.

The third wave of immigration, which began in 1870, saw the arrival of more Lowlanders than Highlanders, and a smaller proportion of rural families. They were mostly skilled workers and professionals. They tended to find jobs in Canadian cities, especially in the large urban centres. This trend continued during the 20th century. Today Scottish immigrants to Canada come from all backgrounds, but most are from the Scottish Lowlands and most make their life in Canada in the cities.

The Scots in Canada In the early years, Scots played a leading role in the fur trade

and in exploration connected with the fur trade. Simon Fraser, Simon McTavish, Sir Alexander Mackenzie, Sir George Simpson, the McGillivrays, and many many more were of Scottish origin. Similarly, Scots often took the lead in politics. Canada's first two prime ministers, Sir John A. Macdonald and Alexander Mackenzie, were both born in Scotland; so was George Brown, the powerful politician and newspaperman. Education, religion, and business were other areas in which the Scots had particularly strong influence. In many ways, they shaped the Canada that exists today, whether they did so physically by building railways or intellectually by designing a school system.

In regions where large numbers of Scots settled, Scottish traditions have remained particularly strong. Each of the Maritime provinces has its own tartan and many of the towns have Scottish names. In many communities in Canada, Highland Games are held annually, accompanied by Highland dancing and pipe bands. Canadians from other ethnic backgrounds enjoy these events, just as many enjoy playing golf, which originated in Scotland. Scottish festivals such as St Andrew's Day (November 30) and Burns Night (January 25) are celebrated throughout Canada. Meanwhile, Canadians of Scottish origin continue to make a strong contribution in all areas.

▷ RELATED ARTICLES: **Baldoon; Ethnic Origin; Fur Trade; Hector; Hudson's Bay Company; North West Company; Orkneymen; Red River Colony; Lord Selkirk.**

▷ SUGGESTED READING: Allen Andrews, *The Scottish Canadians* (1981); John Kenneth Galbraith, *The Scotch* (1985); Stanford Reid, editor, *The Scottish Tradition in Canada* (1976).

■ Scott, Barbara Ann

Figure skater (*born in 1928 at Ottawa, Ont.*). Scott was Canada's favourite woman sports star of the 1940s, sparking admiration throughout the country with her exquisite figure skating. She inspired thousands of girls to take up the sport.

Scott practised seven hours a day from the time she was nine years old. In 1940, she won the Canadian junior championship. In 1944 she won the senior championship, holding the title until she retired from figure-skating competitions in 1948. Meanwhile, she won the North American championship in 1945, holding that too until 1948. In 1947 and 1948 she won both the European and the world championships. In 1948 she also won the

Barbara Ann Scott was Canada's favourite woman sports star in the 1940s. She was honoured when she was chosen to be one of the two athletes who carried the Olympic flame on the first part of its journey from St John's, Nfld, to Calgary in 1988 (courtesy Canada's Sports Hall of Fame).

gold medal in figure skating at the Olympic Games. When she returned home to Ottawa after this triumph, she was greeted with a victory parade and cheering crowds. In 1945, 1947, and 1948 she was awarded the Lou Marsh Trophy as Canada's outstanding athlete of the year.

On giving up competitive skating, Scott joined the Hollywood Ice Revue in New York.

▷ SUGGESTED READING: Barbara Ann Scott, *Skate With Me* (1950).

■ Scott, Duncan Campbell

Poet (*born in 1862 at Ottawa, Canada West [Ont.]; died there in 1947*). Though he would have liked to become a doctor, family poverty forced Scott to join the Department of Indian Affairs in Ottawa in 1879. He became deputy superintendent of the department in 1913 and stayed at the job until his retirement in 1932. His work gave him the chance to visit many Indian reserves and to understand their way of life. This helped him write some of his finest poems, such as *The Forsaken* and *On the Way to the Mission*. These show the pain suffered by Indians when tempted by or forced into the "white man's world." Scott also wrote nature poems, short stories, and essays. But he is best remembered for his "Indian poems."

▷ SUGGESTED READING: K.P. Stich, *The Duncan Campbell Scott Symposium* (1980).

■ Scott, Francis Reginald

Lawyer, poet (*born in 1899 at Quebec City, Que.; died in 1985 at Montreal, Que.*). Scott had a privileged childhood, but he was taught early to believe that his privileges carried with them the responsibility to help those less fortunate than himself. As a young student at Oxford University in England, he began to study the theories of socialism. He returned to Canada in 1923, and began to study law the next year. In 1928 he became a professor of law at McGill University. His social ideas found expression principally in his poetry during these years, until the onset of the Great Depression prompted him to become politically active. In 1931-32, he and several other academics founded the League for Social Reconstruction, to study how socialist ideas might be used to solve some of Canada's problems. In 1932 the league became part of the socialist party, the Co-operative Commonwealth Federation (CCF). Despite the disapproval of McGill University, Scott remained a leading member of the CCF

and its successor, the New Democratic Party, until he retired from politics in 1962. Thereafter he concerned himself with the problem of strengthening Canadian unity.

As a teacher, Scott had considerable influence on the ideas of young intellectuals such as Pierre Elliott Trudeau. As a lawyer, he became known as a defender of civil rights. In one of his most famous cases, in 1957, Scott persuaded the Supreme Court of Canada to declare Quebec's notorious Padlock Act to be unconstitutional. In the early 1980s, he acted as an unofficial legal adviser to the Cree Indians of northern Quebec in their successful effort to gain recognition for their land claims in the territory affected by the James Bay Project.

Scott was also a great poet. He experimented with new poetic forms, and encouraged others to do the same. Much of his poetry deals with social issues and is written in what is called a "satiric" vein. That is, he would, in his poetry, criticize Canadian attitudes and institutions by poking fun at them, making them seem ridiculous. His serious poetry often deals with the human spirit and its kinship with nature. His *Collected Poems* won a Governor General's Award in 1981.

▷ RELATED ARTICLE: **Padlock Act.**

▷ SUGGESTED READING: Sandra Djwa, *F.R. Scott and His Works* (1989).

■ Scott, Robert

Painter (*born in 1941 at Melfort, Sask.*). Scott is one of Canada's most inventive abstract painters and he is represented in many public collections.

Most of his paintings are very large. They are done in a distinctive, energetic style. The surfaces of his paintings appear turbulent and result from the thick build-up of many layers of paint. Scott uses all kinds of tools to create his pictures. He even uses his fingers to plow through the surface of paint to reveal underlying layers of many different colours. In effect, he draws at the same time that he paints.

Scott has been influenced by many important painters in the history of art. He has learned to emphasize the all-over expanse of the flat surface of the canvas on which he works. His paintings are full of rhythm and feeling.

▷ RELATED ARTICLE: **Painting.**

■ Scott, Thomas

Adventurer (*born about 1842 at Clandeboye, Ireland; died in 1870 at Fort Garry, Red River Colony [Man.]*). Thomas Scott

F.R. Scott *was one of the leading Canadian intellectuals of his day. He was active in politics and law and was also one of Canada's best poets (courtesy Canapress Photo Service).*

Duncan Campbell Scott *wrote some of his finest poems about the Indian Reserves he visited in the course of his job with the Department of Indian Affairs (courtesy NAC/ C-3187).*

Scouts Canada Badge
(courtesy Boy Scouts of Canada).

Beaver Badge *(courtesy Boy Scouts of Canada).*

T.W. Scott *was the first premier of Saskatchewan (courtesy Saskatchewan Archives Board/ R-A2470).*

was executed by a Metis firing squad during the Red River Rebellion. This caused him to be viewed as a martyr in Ontario, though he was far from saintly. He was a violent and boisterous Orangeman (who, among other things, was fiercely anti-Catholic). He had immigrated to Canada in 1863 and then drifted west. In 1869 he arrived at the Red River Colony, where he found work as a labourer.

Scott soon became known as a trouble maker, and in 1869-70 he allied himself with the most extreme anti-Metis group. Arrested by Louis Riel's followers, he was so insulting and unruly that early in March 1870 the Metis held a trial and condemned him to death for insubordination. This was a capital offence among Metis buffalo hunters, and Scott was duly executed on March 4, 1870. His death caused a storm of protest in Ontario. Most of the anger was directed against Louis Riel, who was held responsible for Scott's death.

▷ RELATED ARTICLE: **Red River Rebellion.**

▷ SUGGESTED READING: Robert Robertson, *The Execution of Thomas Scott* (1968).

■ Scott, Thomas Walter

Premier of Saskatchewan (*born in 1867 in London Township, Ont.; died in 1938 at Guelph, Ont.*). Walter Scott was the first premier of Saskatchewan. He headed a Liberal government from 1905 to 1916. Like many other politicians of his period, Scott started out as a journalist, having apprenticed as a printer in Portage la Prairie in 1885. He moved to Regina the following year and gained experience on several papers. In 1895 he bought the Regina *Leader*, which he used to promote Liberal views.

At this time, Regina was still capital of the North-West Territories, and in 1900 Scott was elected as one of the four members of Parliament to represent the territories in Ottawa. He took part in the debates leading to the formation of the province of Saskatchewan. He then returned to Regina to be the new province's premier, defeating his powerful rival, Frederick Haultain, in the first provincial elections. As premier, Scott oversaw construction of the university, the founding of a government telephone system, and many other measures, including granting women the vote (1916).

■ Scouts Canada

Scouting was founded in Great Britain in 1907 by Robert Baden-Powell. Several groups were started in Canada, and in

1914 the Canadian General Council was formed. In 1976, the organization became known as Scouts Canada. The national headquarters, which includes a museum, is in Ottawa, Ont. Every governor general since Earl Grey has been Chief Scout.

In 1989, 205 000 youths aged 5 to 26 were enroled, and there were 66 886 adult leaders. Scout programs for both boys and girls are divided by age: Beavers (5-7), Cubs (8-10), Venturers (14-17), and Rovers (17-26). Scout groups work closely with sponsors such as churches, schools, and service clubs in their community.

Members are encouraged to become good citizens and leaders with a knowledge and understanding of other cultures. They can earn badges for skill in many areas, such as computer studies, law awareness, sailing, and religion. Respect for nature, wood lore, and camping continue to be important to the scouting movement. The scout motto is "Be Prepared." Camporees and jamborees are held so that scouts from all over Canada can meet each other, and sometimes scouts from other nations.

▷ SUGGESTED READING: Boy Scouts of Canada National Council, *Fieldbook for Canadian Scouting* (1986); Robert E. Milks, *75 Years of Scouting in Canada* (1981).

■ SCTV

SCTV was a television comedy series that was written, produced, and performed primarily by Canadian artists from 1976 to 1983. The letters of the title were the call letters of an imaginary television station, Second City TV. Most of the sketches satirized popular American television programs and personalities, exaggerating situations and behaviour until they seemed ridiculous. There was some Canadian content. From the McKenzie brothers, two Canadian hick characters created by Rick Moranis and Dave Thomas, the world learned that Canadians lived in The Great White North, drank lots of beer, and said "eh?" at least once in every sentence.

Most of the material used in the show was written by the performers themselves. These included John Candy, Rick Moranis, Andrea Martin, Eugene Levy, Joe Flaherty, Catherine O'Hara, Dave Thomas, and Martin Short. All but Martin and Flaherty were Canadians, and most have gone on to successful careers in Hollywood.

SCTV grew out of a live comedy revue that originated in Chicago in 1959. In 1973, a Canadian entertainment entrepreneur, Andrew Alexander, bought the Canadian rights to the idea. The first Canadian Second City shows were also live productions, in Toronto. In 1976 SCTV was adapted to television. Although it was broadcast briefly on the CBC and NBC networks, it was, for the most part, sold to individual television stations for broadcast. It was received with critical acclaim, winning two Emmy Awards in the United States and two ACTRAS in Canada. It is still seen in syndicated broadcasts in countries around the world.

■ Sculpin

The cottids, or sculpins (Family Cottidae), are usually marine fish, though some species live in fresh water. They are all cold-water fish, usually found at less than 100 m deep. The large head may bear various appendages. The eyes are large and prominent. The pectoral fins look like huge fans. The pelvic fins often consist of nothing more than a few soft rays and a spine.

Sculpins are spiny fish that live in cold water (artwork by Karen Klitz).

Sculpins are usually scaleless. Some species are covered with plate-like scales or little hairs that give them a furry appearance. All these characteristics add up to an unusual appearance, well represented by the Atlantic sea raven (*Hemitripterus americanus*). Another unusual characteristic is that, when taken from the water, sculpins blow themselves up to such an extent that they are unable to sink back beneath the surface. Solitary by nature, they rarely live in schools. They feed on bottom-dwelling invertebrates and small fish. They are in turn prey for other species. They are not usually fished by humans.

■ Sculpture

The native people of Canada, particularly the Inuit and the Haida, have excelled in sculpture. In the European tradition in Canada, however, sculpture has always trailed behind the other arts, and there have been few professional sculptors. The lack of patrons who commission works of sculpture, the absence of foundries and stonecutters, and the high cost of materials and large studio space have all discouraged artists from becoming sculptors.

Time (1973) by Kosso Eloul (courtesy of the sculptor).

Nevertheless sculpture has flourished at various times in Canada — in Quebec in the 18th and 19th centuries, in the decade following the World War I, and as part of the contemporary art scene.

Sculpture can be created in three different ways: by carving, by modelling, or by construction. In choosing one method over another, the sculptor is influenced by individual preference, and may also be limited by the materials available and the technology of the period in which he or she lives.

SCULPTURE FROM 1700 TO 1880

Sculpture was one of the earliest European art forms to be practised in Canada. In New France in the late 17th century, the Roman Catholic Church needed religious statues for its chapels; shipyards wanted figureheads to decorate their ships; and merchants ordered signboards for their shops. These objects were too large to transport from France. It was easier and quicker to import sculptors from Europe to train local woodworkers in the art of sculpting.

In this way, three important traditions were established that were to hold true for the next 200 years in Quebec: sculpture would be almost always in wood; it would follow European models in style; and sculptors would be trained in workshops as apprentices.

In the 18th and 19th centuries, certain families excelled as sculptors. The Levasseur and Baillairgé families, for example, produced many famous artists over several generations. Between 1732 and 1737, the cousins Noël and Pierre-Noël Levasseur decorated the Ursuline chapel in Quebec City. They covered the entire altar wall with relief sculptures, statues in the round, and columns, all carved in wood, gilded with gold, and

Angel With a Trumpet in the Ursuline Chapel in Quebec City (courtesy Old Monastery of the Ursulines, Quebec).

Apostle St Simon by Louis-Philippe Hébert (courtesy Musée du Québec).

Noon Hour *(1918-19) by Florence Wyle (courtesy Canadian War Museum/ NMC).*

Young Indians Hunting, *1905, by Alfred Laliberté, who was one of Canada's most active sculptors. Known for his flowing lines, he produced over 900 statues and 200 smaller bronzes (photo by Malak, Ottawa).*

Figurehead Design *for the ship,* Earl of Moira. *Shipbuilders were one of the main customers for sculpture in 19th-century Canada (courtesy NAC/C-15227).*

painted in rich colours. The chapel was "restored" and considerably altered in 1902. The Levasseurs also carved figureheads for vessels built in the French royal shipyards in the colony. Many of these ships were named after Canadian animals (beaver, caribou) or native groups (Algonquin, Iroquois), and, although none of the carvings has survived, we know that they illustrated the name of the particular ship they decorated. Around 1727 one of the Levasseurs was commissioned to carve the royal arms over the doors of official buildings in Quebec.

Until the 1880s, the Roman Catholic Church, local merchants, and shipyards — now stretching from present-day Niagara-on-the-Lake through Kingston and Quebec City to several ports in the Maritime provinces — remained the major customers for sculpture in Canada. In the 19th century alone, probably 10 000 figureheads were carved in Canada. But the age of wood sculpture was over. After 1850, the church increasingly ordered plaster statues (statues cast in a mold from a figure modelled in clay or some other pliable material). At the same time, wooden sailing ships gave way to metal steamships, and decorative figureheads were no longer required.

SCULPTURE FROM 1880 TO 1950

Modelling, compared with carving, gives the sculptor more freedom of expression. This technique was well suited to the lifelike sculpture that was popular in Canada towards the end of the 19th century. The major commissions were for historical monuments commemorating events and leaders of the past, or for sculptures portraying the native people, who, it was feared, were a vanishing race. In Toronto between 1896 and 1910, for example, Walter Allward completed memorials for the North-West Rebellion, the South

African War and statues of the political figures John Graves Simcoe, Oliver Mowat, and J.S. Macdonald.

World War I greatly increased the demand for memorials. Over 60 000 Canadians had died in the war and, in addition to Ottawa and the major battlefields of Europe, hundreds of towns and cities throughout the country commissioned their own memorials. Allward won the competition for the monument at Vimy Ridge, France, which was the site of a great battle. Emanuel Hahn won the competition for Fort William [Thunder Bay, Ont.], and Alfred Howell for Saint John, N.B., and Guelph, Ont. Canadian sculptor R. Tait McKenzie, who was also an orthopedic surgeon and director of physical education at the University of Pennsylvania in the United States, erected many memorials in Britain and the U.S., as well as at home. Most war memorials were sculptures of the human form such as soldiers in uniform, groups of women and children, or figures representing ideas such as Peace and Victory.

By 1928, Canadian sculptors felt confident enough to establish their own association, the Sculptors' Society of Canada. They felt that existing organizations ignored their needs. There were no foundries in Canada specializing in bronze casting, for example, and sculptors had to send their fragile plaster molds to the U.S. or Europe to be cast, an awkward and expensive arrangement when the sculpture was large. By banding together, they hoped to promote co-operation among Canadian sculptors, to encourage public interest in sculpture through exhibitions and lectures, and to have an influence over the selection of public art. Though the sculptors had some success in achieving their aims, they suffered during the Depression of the 1930s when there were few commissions for their art.

They had an ally in architect John Lyle, however, who in the 1930s and 1940s led a crusade to integrate sculpture with architecture, particularly sculpture depicting Canadian themes. Many sculptors

Reef and Rainbow *(around 1927-35), cast tin, by Elizabeth Wyn Wood (courtesy AGO).*

were commissioned to produce relief panels and murals for banks and other public buildings constructed at this time.

In the years between the wars, Canadian sculptors were influenced by European modernism, an art style that broke away from the realism of the previous generation. They still concentrated on the human figure, but in a stylized simple form where line and mass and the arrangement of light and shade were considered more important than anatomically correct detail. While Europeans were experimenting with many different new styles, "sculpture" still meant carved or modelled figures to most Canadian sculptors.

Transart (1973-74). In this sculpture Walter Redinger uses abstract shapes created from fibreglass (photo by Malak, Ottawa).

CONTEMPORARY SCULPTURE

Since the end of World War II, sculpture in Canada has changed from being very conservative to perhaps the most innovative art form. Sculptors now work in different styles, different materials, and different techniques. A sculpture may still be an object, or it may be part of an installation you walk through. It may even be a process, where the idea in the artist's mind or the reaction it evokes in the viewer is more important than the object itself. Sculptors use a variety of materials, such as wood, bronze, steel, aluminum, concrete, fibreglass, plastic, fibre, and neon tubing. They cut and weld metal, mold plastic, hammer nails, construct in wood, assemble assorted objects in new ways, weave and knot fabric, and sometimes colour their creation with glossy industrial paint.

In making this change, Canadian sculptors have been influenced by European artists such as Pablo Picasso and Julio Gonzàlez, by British sculptors Henry Moore and Anthony Caro, and by the American David Smith. Assisted by

grants from the Canada Council, Canadian artists have been able to travel abroad and within Canada to view important sculpture exhibits. The most significant customers (or patrons) for contemporary sculptors are corporations and government agencies, many of which commission large sculptural works for the outside of their buildings and smaller pieces for their art collections. Monumental sculptures by Kosso Eloul, Sorel Etrog, and Robert Murray, for example, can be found in public spaces in many Canadian cities. At the same time, the number of private collectors is increasing, and art dealers are becoming more willing to represent sculptors and show their work.

▷ RELATED ARTICLES: **Baillairgé Family; Kosso Eloul; Sorel Etrog; Indian Art; Inuit Art; Frances Loring; Robert Murray; Florence Wyle.**

▷ SUGGESTED READING: Christine Boyanoski, *Loring and Wyle: Sculptures Legacy* (1987); Dorothy Cameron, *Sculpture 67* (1968); Bruce Ferguson and Sandy Naune, *Space Invaders* (1985); George Swinton, *Sculpture of the Eskimo* (1982); Mathew Teitelbaum and Peter White, *Joe Fafard: Cows and Other Luminaries 1977-1987* (1987).

Sculpture outside Quebec National Assembly (photo by Sherman Hines/ Masterfile).

Study *for head of Sir Robert Borden, painted plaster by Frances Loring. If a more durable sculpture is desired, the plaster model can be sent to a foundry to be cast in bronze (courtesy AGO).*

The Candidate *by Saskatchewan sculptor Joe Fafard, who uses a unique method of painting his bronze statues (courtesy Woltjen/Udell Gallery).*

Sculpture *is often used to complement or contrast with architecture. This metal sculpture sits outside the Toronto Dominion Centre in Toronto (photo by James Marsh).*

Sea Ice in Eclipse Sound in the Canadian Arctic (photo by Barbara Brundege and Eugene Fisher).

Range of Northern
Sea Lion ●

California Sea Lion (artwork by Pieter Folkens).

Northern Sea Lions are the largest eared seals. They may weigh more than 1000 kg. Unlike earless seals, sea lions can move their hind limbs under their bodies, which helps them move about on land (artwork by Pieter Folkens).

■ Scurvy

Scurvy is a disease that killed many of the early explorers and settlers of Canada. It is caused by a lack of vitamin C, which is found primarily in fresh food. The food these people ate was mostly salted or dried; fresh food did not last on the long voyages or over the winters.

Jacques Cartier's expedition, wintering where Quebec City now stands in 1535-36, suffered an outbreak of scurvy. With little fresh food in their diet, victims grew weak. Their breath smelled foul. Their gums bled and their teeth fell out. Twenty-five sailors died. Following instructions from the native people, the rest of the expedition was saved by drinking a

tea made from the bark and needles of the white cedar tree.

Today fresh food and vitamins are easily available to most Canadians and scurvy has become very rare.

▷ SUGGESTED READING: Kenneth J. Carpenter, *The History of Scurvy and Vitamin C* (1986).

■ Sea Ice

Sea ice is frozen sea water. It occurs in the oceans of both the Northern and Southern Hemispheres.

Sea ice covers about three-quarters of the Arctic Ocean in summer, and virtually all of it in winter. The ice is about 3 m thick, on average. It presents a barrier and a grave danger to ships attempting to travel through it.

How Salt Water Freezes Salt lowers the freezing point of sea water below that of fresh water. The greater the salt content of the water, the lower its freezing temperature.

In September or October, needles and crystals of ice begin to form in northern water near the coastline, gradually spreading farther into the sea. These form a sludge which hardens into thin plates of ice, which bend with the ocean swells on which they float. These plates gradually thicken and turn opaque. By spring, this ice, called *first-year ice*, can range from 30 cm to 2 m thick.

If this ice does not melt completely the following year, it grows harder and thicker in subsequent winters. Old ice is found in the northernmost passages of the Queen Elizabeth Islands, for instance, and in the central core of polar ice in the Arctic Ocean.

Old sea ice contains less salt than the sea water from which it forms. The salt gathers in tiny pockets of brine when the ice partially melts in summer, and these drain down, leaving the ice quite fresh.

▷ RELATED ARTICLE: **Ice.**

■ Sea Lion

The northern sea lion (*Eumetopias jubata*) is the largest eared seal. Large males are as big as a walrus. They may weigh more than 1000 kg and be more than 3 m long. Females weigh about 300 kg and are about 2 m long. Except for a thick growth of longer hair on the neck of adult males, the body is covered with short, coarse brown fur. Northern sea lions inhabit the northern Pacific Ocean from Japan to California. They spend most of their lives in the ocean feeding on marine invertebrates and fish. Sea lions can dive at least 180 m.

During the breeding season between May and August, they form colonies on rocky coasts. The pregnant females are the first to come ashore, forming groups of 10 to 30 individuals. The males arrive later, with the strongest ones claiming an area of beach and driving off any competitors. The females soon give birth, and then mate again. The harem master does not feed during the entire breeding period. Typically females return annually to give birth on the same beach.

Mothers nurse their young for most of a year and teach the young to swim. Females become sexually mature at about three years. Males become sexually mature at six or seven years, but they are not large enough to successfully defend a territory and breed with the resident females until they are nine or ten years old. Northern sea lions are killed by humans, killer whales, and a few large sharks. In the wild they may live for 17 years.

▷ SUGGESTED READING: Mark Shawver, *Sea Lions* (1986).

■ Sea Otter

The sea otter (*Enhydra lutris*) is a member of the weasel family (Mustelidae). It is the smallest marine mammal, weighing up to 39 kg and reaching up to 1.5 m in length. It has very thick fur: as many as 18 hairs emerge from a single hair follicle. The fur traps a layer of air which insulates the sea otter from the cold sea water. This is a necessity since sea otters do not have the layer of insulating blubber found in all other marine mammals. The sea otter takes great care of its fur, cleaning and grooming it frequently.

It eats sea urchins, molluscs, crustaceans, and fish. It breaks the shells of invertebrates with a rock it brings up from the ocean floor. The otter floats on its back, balances the rock on its chest, and pounds the shell on the rock until the shell breaks.

Mating occurs in spring and summer, and the young are born the following spring. Sea otters were once abundant on the Pacific coast as far south as California, but they were nearly exterminated in the 19th century by hunters coveting their fur. Protective international laws in the early 1900s, and also the creation of refuges, helped the sea otter recover. In some places, the populations have recovered to the point that they have seriously reduced populations of sea urchins, abalones, and clams. Now that humans harvest few sea otters, killer whales and sharks are its chief natural predators.

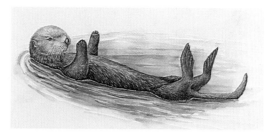

▷ RELATED ARTICLES: **Otter; Weasel.**
▷ SUGGESTED READING: Ralph Buxton, *Nature's Water Clowns: The Sea Otters* (1974).

■ Sea Urchin

Sea urchins are echinoderms belonging to the same order as starfish (Echinodermata). The sea urchin is shaped like a half-circle, covered with spines. The spiny skeleton (called the test) protects the internal organs. It is made up of many tiny interlocking plates of calcium carbonate (the same material that makes up seashells) and is covered with skin. It has five holes through which five pairs of tube feet protrude. The tube feet are used for moving and to sense for food. The spines are movable and are also used for locomotion. The mouth is located on the underside. It is surrounded by a five-sided jaw-like structure with five teeth called Aristotle's lantern. Urchins live on the ocean bottom in shallow water and use the Aristotle's lantern to scrape algae and small organisms from rock surfaces. In Canada, sea urchins can often be found in puddles at low tide.

■ Seal

Seals are sea mammals, beautifully adapted to their life in the water. Unlike whales, seals must return to land or ice floes to bear their young. Seals dive to feed and return to the surface for air at breathing holes.

Seals belong to the order of mammals called Pinnipedia, which also includes sea lions and the walrus. True seals, unlike sea lions, do not have external ears. This is why they are also called earless seals. Also unlike sea lions, true seals cannot move their hind limbs under their body. This makes it very difficult for them to move about on land, where they are in danger from predators. The seal swims effortlessly by undulating its body, like a fish, and by using its webbed hind limbs for propulsion.

Seals are well protected from the cold arctic water by thick, waterproof fur and a layer of fat (blubber). Many seals are highly sociable, moving and hunting together. Seals feed on a variety of sea life, from microscopic plankton to crabs, octopus,

Sea Otters almost continuously groom themselves (artwork by Todd Telander).

Sea Urchin (courtesy NMNS).

Range of Sea Otter ●

The Hooded Seal is so named for the large nasal cavity of the male, which can be inflated to form a rounded hood.

Harbour Seals are the most widespread seals. They utter a variety of sounds, from grunts, snorts, and snuffles to a high-pitched yap.

Bearded Seals have a large moustache. This seal is sometimes called the "square flipper" because of the shape of the foreflippers.

Grey Seals breed and molt in dense colonies. They crawl far inland on deserted islands during the breeding season.

Harp Seals are the basis of the sealing industry in eastern Canada. In some years, over 300 000 were slaughtered, but the hunt has declined because of worldwide protests.

Ringed Seals are the smallest seals. They are primarily solitary, though they warn one another of danger (all artwork by Pieter Folkens).

squid, and bottom-dwelling fish. When diving for food, their nostrils close and their heart beat slows to only 10 to 20 beats per minute.

The largest of the seven species found in Canada is the northern elephant seal (*Mirounga angustirostris*). It is a rare visitor to the Pacific coast. Adult males may weigh more than 3500 kg and may be longer than 6 m. It can dive deeper than 300 m. Other large seals native to Canada include the bearded seal (*Erignathus barbatus*) and the hooded seal (*Cystophora cristata*). These weigh no more than 400 kg and are no more than 3 m long. The grey seal (*Halichoerus grypus*) may also reach 3 m but weighs no more than 290 kg. The harp seal (*Phoca groenlandica*) is

up to 2 m long and weighs up to 180 kg. The ringed seal (*P. hispida*) and the harbour seal (*P. vitulina*) have maximum lengths of 1.6 and 1.7 m and maximum weights of 100 and 150 kg, respectively.

Ringed seals and bearded seals live in arctic waters. Harp seals, hooded seals, and grey seals are found along the Atlantic coast. The harbour seal is found along both the Atlantic and Pacific coasts and enters the Arctic Ocean, but does not range into the arctic islands. Small populations of harbour seals are found in some rivers and freshwater lakes along the eastern side of Hudson Bay. Polar bears, killer whales, and some sharks are natural enemies.

▷ SUGGESTED READING: Anne Bardoo, *Seals of Eastern Canada: Educational Games and Activities for Ages 6-12* (1987); Fred Bruemmer, *Season of the Seal* (1988); Merebeth Switzer, *Seals* (1985).

■ **Sealing**

Sealing has gone on along Canada's coastline for thousands of years. Native people hunted seals long before the first Europeans arrived. They used the skins, meat, and oil from the blubber. Inuit still hunt seals in the Arctic. European colonists took up the hunt as a business in the 1700s, producing skins for clothing and oil for lighting.

Today, conservation groups oppose the hunt. They say it is cruel, and threatens to wipe out the seal populations. Sealers argue that they rely on the hunt for part of their income. Since the 1960s, the government has set quotas on the number of seals that may be killed.

North Pacific The northern fur seal follows a long migration route around the North Pacific Ocean. Each spring the animals return to the same group of small, rocky islands in the Bering Sea to breed. For a long time hunters have taken advantage of the breeding season to visit the islands and kill the seals. Then, after 1867, hunters began shooting the animals from boats on the high seas.

To protect the fur seal from extinction, four countries signed an agreement in 1911. The United States, Japan, Russia, and Canada agreed to stop hunting seals in open water and to regulate the kill on land. Even though no Canadians take part in the hunt any longer, Canada takes a share of the profits from the sale of the pelts.

Atlantic Coast Two species of seals arrive in the waters off Newfoundland and in the Gulf of St Lawrence early each spring. The harp and hooded seals breed at the edge of the ice that extends down the coast from the north. When warmer weather comes, the seals return towards the Arctic.

In the 18th century, hunters caught the seals by laying nets beneath the water in narrow channels. Then they began going out to the ice in small boats. Boats were replaced by large sailing ships, and by 1830 thousands of hunters were involved each season.

Hunters carried long poles with metal hooks at one end, called gaffs. As they walked across the ice, they struck the seal on the head, then skinned it in a matter of seconds using sharp knives. The gaff was banned in 1967, and hunters now use shorter wooden clubs. Many of the dead animals were young harp seals, valued for their snow-white pelts.

The seal hunt was dangerous work. Many ships sank in the ice. Hunting parties easily got lost when heavy weather set in. Newfoundland's worst season occurred in 1914, when 77 seal hunters failed to return to their ship in a storm, and another 174 perished when a second vessel vanished.

Sealers continued to take advantage of new technology. In the 1870s most of the sailing ships added steam engines. Each of these famous "Wooden Walls," as they were called, carried as many as 300 men to the ice. Then, in the years before World War I, wooden vessels gave way to ones made of steel.

Controversy Between the two world wars the hunt declined as petroleum replaced seal oil as a lamp fuel. After World War II, however, profits from the hunt grew as demand grew for seal skins for clothing.

Hundreds of thousands of seals were killed each year, and the population began to decline. The government began to restrict the hunt by issuing licences, shortening the hunting season, and setting quotas on the number of animals that could be killed.

During the 1960s and 1970s, the seal hunt raised a storm of controversy. Conservationists claimed that the hunt was a slaughter of innocent baby animals and should be stopped. Sealers argued that they were just trying to make a living following a centuries' old tradition. The two sides met in several angry confrontations on the ice.

The controversy led to a decline in the hunt. Countries in Europe began to boy-

Inuit with a seal catch, near Broughton Island, N.W.T. (photo by Karl-Heinz Raach).

cott the sale of seal products, and the market collapsed. The hunt continues, but on a reduced scale. In 1989 only a few thousand animals were killed.

▷ RELATED ARTICLES: **Bering Sea Dispute; Fur Trade; Seals.**

▷ SUGGESTED READING: Cassie Brown and Harold Horwood, *Death on the Ice* (1972); Farley Mowat, *Wake of the Great Sealers* (1973); Guy David Wright, *Sons and Seals: A Voyage to the Ice* (1984).

■ Seashell

Seashells are rigid structures made out of calcium carbonate that is secreted by molluscs. The shells provide the creature with protection, with something for the muscles to be connected to, or in some cases, with a means of flotation (when filled with air).

Shells take a wide range of shapes and colours. Most have three layers. The middle layer is the thickest part of the shell. It is made up of several layers of calcium carbonate crystals. The inner layer is made up of flat plates of crystals often called mother-of-pearl. The outer layer consists of organic matter that may be glossy, flaky, or spiny. The inner layer is secreted by the mantle as a whole; the other layers are secreted by cells located on the edges of the mantle.

If a tiny particle of material is caught between the mantle and the shell, it will be covered by several iridescent layers, transforming it into a pearl. Various species of molluscs produce pearls, but only a few of them produce the pearls used in jewellery.

It is easy to collect seashells along the shoreline. Even discarded ones, broken by the waves, allow you to identify the types of species living in that region. For a collection with scientific or commercial value, however, you must gather living organisms.

Shell fossils help to date the sedimentary rocks in which they are found and to establish the environmental conditions in which they lived. Shells have long been

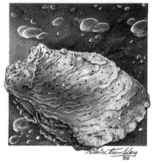

Seashells from a snail (above), clam (centre), and oyster (below). The shell is a hard covering secreted by these animals (artwork by Claire Tremblay).

used for decoration and for money, dishes, and musical instruments.

▷ SUGGESTED READING: Peter S. Dance, *The World's Shells: A Guide for Collectors* (1976); Julius Gordon, *Seashells of the North East Coast* (1981); Dean Morris, *Animals that Live in Shells* (1977); Graham D. Saunders, *Shells: An Introduction to Seashells of the World* (1979).

Seaweed *Some seaweed occurs in beds 30 to 40 metres deep (courtesy NMNS).*

■ Seaweed

Seaweeds are plant-like algae found on ocean shorelines. Some live in beds 30 to 40 m deep but most live in the intertidal zone where they are exposed at low tide. Some seaweeds float in the water. Others have a root-like anchor that does not absorb nutrients. Seaweeds are red, yellow, or brown because of pigments. Combined with chlorophyll, these pigments mean they can carry out photosynthesis despite the low level of light penetrating the water. Seaweeds provide cover for innumerable small animals. Though seldom found on our dinner tables, several species are edible and very nutritious. In fact, we do eat them without knowing it, because the food industry uses them as thickeners in ice cream, salad dressing, and so on. Their extracts are also used in the creation of many products including cloth, printing ink, and cosmetics. The seaweed thrown up on shore after a storm is the most complete natural fertilizer imaginable. Irish moss, a red algae, is harvested for commercial use off the East Coast.

▷ RELATED ARTICLE: **Irish Moss.**

■ Sechelt Peninsula

The Sechelt Peninsula lies north of Vancouver on the so-called "Sunshine Coast" of southern British Columbia. The name comes from an Indian word meaning "place of shelter from the sea." Its beautiful coastline makes it a popular summer vacation spot.

■ Second-Language Education

A person's first language is the language that he or she grew up speaking naturally, without even thinking about it. A second language is any other language that is learned, whether in a school or elsewhere. A few children, in perfectly bilingual homes, may grow up speaking two languages fluently, but this is unusual. Second-language education in Canada received a boost in 1971 when the federal government declared that Canada was officially bilingual and multicultural.

There are a number of types of second-language education in Canada. One form, which has been available to most children, is when a second language, such as French, English, German, or Latin, is taught as a subject in school.

Since the 1960s, second-language education in Canada has increasingly taken the form not of studying a language as though it were just another subject, but of learning other subjects through the medium of a second language. This is called immersion education. Everything is taught and learned in the second language, which is supposed to be used even in the playground and during breaks. "Partial immersion" allows for some use of the first language. In 1965 a group of anglophone parents at St-Lambert, Que., began a French-immersion kindergarten. By 1986-87, over 184 000 students in 1400 schools across Canada were involved in immersion schools. French-immersion education receives support and funding from the federal government.

The success of French-immersion education has created a demand for similar programs in other languages. Some cities offer Hebrew, Ukrainian, and German immersion. Some native schools also operate wholly or partly in a native language, especially in the early grades. The aim of all such programs is to produce students who will be fluent in one of Canada's official languages and in another, usually ancestral, language.

Another form of second-language education is the teaching of immigrants to speak either English or French. Outside of Quebec, this usually takes the form of English-as-a-Second Language (E.S.L.). The aim always is to teach immigrant children to read and write English fluently enough so that they can work comfortably in the language. In Quebec, there has been some controversy over this issue, but today immigrants who settle in Quebec enrol their children in French-language, not English-language, schools.

In the 1970s another form of second-language education emerged as ethnic groups began to demand that their children should be taught their ancestral language. This form of second-language education was known as "heritage language" teaching. It usually consists of devoting a certain amount of each school day to teaching a heritage language. Heritage-language teaching has been demanded both by recently arrived immigrants and by established ethnic groups. Since 1977 it has received government funding in Ontario, Manitoba, Alberta, British Columbia, and the Northwest Territories.

Both bilingualism and multiculturalism have created an obvious demand for second-language education, and an increasing number of Canadian students are learning a second language. In 1986-87, of roughly 4 938 000 students in Canadian schools, over 1 800 000 were learning a second language.

▷ SUGGESTED READING: Hector Hammery, *French Immersion: Myths and Reality* (1989); Marita Moll and Geraldine Gilliss, *Teaching French as a Second Language in Canada* (1979).

■ Secord, Laura

Heroine of the War of 1812 (*born Laura Ingersoll in 1775 at Great Barrington, Massachusetts; died in 1868 at Chippawa [Niagara Falls], Ont.*). Laura Ingersoll immigrated to Upper Canada [Ontario] with her family when she was 20, and in 1797 she married James Secord, a merchant at Queenston on the Niagara River. During the War of 1812, Laura overheard some Americans talking of a surprise attack on the British post at Beaver Dams. Since her husband was too sick to go and warn the British, she took the message herself. Slipping out early on the morning of June 22, 1813, she walked from Queenston to Beaver Dams. She took a roundabout route to avoid the American posts. She arrived late at night, having walked 30 km, and gave her message to Lieutenant James FitzGibbon, the commanding officer. Two days later, when the Americans made what they thought was a "surprise" attack, they were ambushed by a British force of Mohawk and other native soldiers, and surrendered.

At the time, she was not hailed as a heroine. It was only later that the story of her walk became widely known — because she publicized it. After her husband died in 1841, she was not well off, so she asked the government for a pension, describing her heroism with great drama. FitzGibbon gallantly supported the petitions, testifying to the usefulness of the news she had brought him. (Some historians believe that he already knew.) She was 85 when she at last received a reward — £100, sent her by Queen Victoria's oldest son, the Prince of Wales.

▷ RELATED ARTICLE: **War of 1812.**

▷ SUGGESTED READING: John Bassett, *Laura Secord* (1981); Ruth McKenzie, *Laura Secord: The Legend and the Lady* (1971).

■ Sedge

Sedge is a grass-like plant that is common

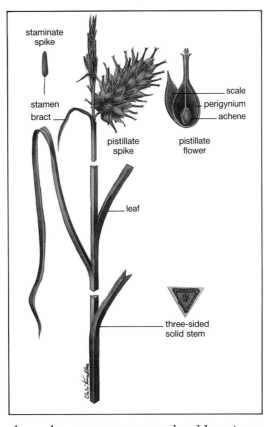

Sedges can be told from grasses by their three-sided stems (artwork by Claire Tremblay).

throughout temperate and cold regions. The largest group belongs to the genus *Carex* (Family Cyperaceae), which refers to the sharp leaf margins. Sedges look like tall grasses but are readily distinguished from grasses by their three-sided solid stems. The male (stamenate) and female (pistillate) flowers are usually clustered in separate spikes. Within the spikes, the flowers are sometimes solitary on the ends of the shoots. The female flowers are characterized by the presence of a membranous sac that envelopes the pistil and later the seed. The seed may be lens shaped or three-angled.

More than 270 species of sedge exist in Canada, none of them of any economic importance. They are not suitable for humans or livestock to eat. The value of sedge is most evident in its native habitat, bordering sloughs and other wet places where it provides food and cover for waterfowl. In milder climates, *C. pendula*, grown as a garden ornamental (usually near water), is prized for its bold effect (up to 1.5 m tall) and long, drooping spikes.

■ Sedimentary Rock, *see* Rock

■ Sedna

Sedna is the Inuit goddess of the sea. She is one of the most dreaded figures in Inuit myths. One tale describes how she created the animals of the sea.

The story of Sedna is typical of myths

Sedna

Sedna lived with her father in an igloo near the seashore. She was very beautiful and many men wanted to marry her, but she refused. One day a handsome young hunter appeared in his kayak and promised her many riches if she would be his wife. She left with the stranger, but then he changed into a bird and took her to a cold, barren place where she was miserable. Next year, when her father came to visit, she begged him to take her away in his boat. But the sea gods were angry and caused a great storm.

The father was frightened, so he threw Sedna overboard into the swirling waters.

The first time she clutched the boat he cut off her fingers. They became seals. The second time he cut off her hands. They became walruses. The third time he cut off her arms. They became whales. Sedna sank to the bottom of the ocean, and the sea animals followed her. She is bitter and full of vengeance, and will only let hunters catch her animals when it suits her mood. At other times she sends them home hungry or sweeps them out to sea.

all over the world which tell how the animals were created.

■ Séguin, Richard

Musician (*born in 1952 at Montreal, Que.*). Richard and his sister, Marie-Claire, recorded in the 1970s under the name "Les Séguin." Seguin then hooked up with Serge Fiori in a new duo called "Fiori-Seguin." The project yielded only one album, *200 Nuits à l'heure*, a landmark in Quebec rock that was awarded three Félix trophies at the 1977 L'Adisq Awards.

Richard Séguin officially began his solo career in 1980 with the release of *La Percée*, an album that was largely unnoticed. However, his second solo set, *Trace et contraste*, featured the songwriting co-operation of poet Louky Bersianik. "Chanson pour durer" from that album won three awards at the prestigious Festival de Spa. The highly acclaimed album *Double vie* earned him acclaim as "Quebec's Best Rock Singer/Songwriter" by the public. His fifth solo album, *Journée d'amérique*, rapidly reached platinum status (100 000 copies sold).

■ Seigneurial System

The seigneurial system was the name for the way land was held in New France. The government in France gave large blocks of land in New France to French nobles, army officers, merchants, and government officials, who became known as *seigneurs* (meaning lords or landlords). Land was also given to the Roman Catholic Church. The aim was to get the colony of New France settled as quickly as possible so that it could raise enough produce to feed its people.

The seigneurs were required either to farm their land themselves or lease much of it to farmers (known as *habitants*). Most seigneurs brought poor people from France to be habitants. Others found their farmers within the colony.

Both seigneurs and habitants had certain duties toward each other. The seigneur was required to clear his land and find settlers for it. He also had to maintain a house to which the habitants came to pay their rents and to settle minor disputes. Seigneurs had to build a mill where the habitants could grind the grain they grew. Local leadership was provided by a "Captain of the Militia," who was selected from among the habitants by the governor. A few seigneurs tried to make habitants work for them for a few days each year without pay, though this was against the law. If the seigneur failed to carry out his duties, his seigneury could be taken from him and given to someone else.

The habitants' duties included building themselves houses, ploughing their land, and starting farms. They had to pay their seigneur various forms of taxes, which might include some of their grain and other produce as well as a little money. In return, the habitants became virtual owners of their farms, which they could leave to their children. If they sold the land outside the family, they had to pay the seigneur a part of the money they received.

The average seigneury was 5 km by 15 km in area. Since there were no roads at first, the seigneuries were situated alongside the St Lawrence and other rivers, which served as highways. As many as possible of the habitants' farms also had access to a river (or, later, to a road). The typical farm was thus a long, thin strip about 175.5 m by 1755 m, which became thinner still when a habitant divided his farm among his children.

After the conquest of 1760, the new British rulers of the colony kept on the seigneurial system. It was not abolished

Seigneurial System Since there were no roads when the land was first settled, as many farms as possible had to have access to the river. The typical farm was thus a long, narrow strip (artwork by Michael Lee).

Seigneurial System

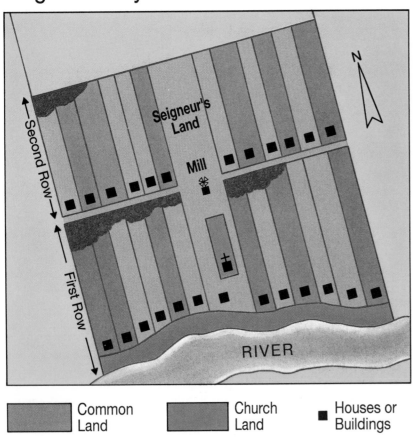

Second Row

First Row

Seigneur's Land

Mill

N

RIVER

| | Common Land | | Church Land | ■ | Houses or Buildings |

until 1854. Today, its pattern is still visible in the shape of the strip farms alongside rivers and roads in Quebec.

▷ RELATED ARTICLE: **Corvée; New France.**

▷ SUGGESTED READING: R. Cole Harris, *The Seigneurial System in Early Canada: A Geographical Survey* (1966); Rosemary Neering and Stan Garrod, *Life in New France* (1976).

■ Selkirk

Selkirk, Man., is on the west bank of the Red River north of Winnipeg. A farm settlement, it was seized by an economic boom in 1875 when the Canadian Pacific Railway made plans to put its rail line through the town. As it turned out, the railway was built through Winnipeg, but Selkirk continued to grow as a river port. In 1913 a steel mill opened and it remains the major employer. Lower Fort Garry, a stone fort dating from the fur-trade days, is nearby. The town is named for Lord Selkirk, founder of the Red River Colony. The population in 1986 was 10 013.

For further information, contact the Town Secretary, 200 Eaton Avenue, Selkirk, Man., R1A 0W6.

■ Selkirk, Thomas Douglas, 5th Earl of

Scottish noble and colonizer (*born in 1771 at St Mary's Isle, Scotland; died in 1820 at Pau, France*). Lord Selkirk made three attempts to establish colonies of poor Scottish farmers in Canada. The last, the Red River Colony, was the origin of the province of Manitoba.

First Colonies Thomas Douglas was the youngest of seven sons and did not expect to inherit the wealth and title of his father. But all his brothers died tragically, and he became the 5th Earl of Selkirk in 1799. The new Lord Selkirk became interested in the plight of Scottish farmers who were forced from their lands when landowners decided to use the fields for raising sheep. He decided to help the dispossessed farmers make a new start in British North America.

Selkirk's first colony was in Prince Edward Island, where he sent 800 settlers in 1803. His second was at Baldoon in Upper Canada (Ontario). The Prince Edward Island settlement was a success, but the Baldoon settlement failed. Selkirk, however, was not discouraged. After buying enough stock in the Hudson's Bay Company to give him a voice in its activities, he persuaded the company to grant him a large parcel of land in Rupert's Land where he intended to plant another colony.

Red River Selkirk's colony, located on the Red River in what is now Manitoba, was called Assiniboia. It began in 1812 with the arrival of an advance party under the command of Miles Macdonell; two months later, the first 120 settlers and their families arrived. From the beginning, the colony was plagued by difficulties. The North West Company, with its Metis allies, believed that the colony was a challenge to its business. Twice, the Nor'Westers drove the colonists away, only to have them return.

In 1816 Selkirk himself came west, at the head of a force of retired soldiers. He captured Fort William from the Nor'Westers, then moved on to Red River in the summer of 1817 to organize the colony. He returned to Montreal to fight in court against the North West Company's attacks on his settlers.

By this time Selkirk was ill with tuberculosis. He had to leave Canada before the court case was finished. He died in France while travelling to a warmer climate for his health.

The original Red River Colony was handed over to the HBC by Selkirk's heirs. In 1870 it was sold to the Canadian government. Today the centre of Selkirk's colony forms part of Winnipeg.

▷ RELATED ARTICLES: **Baldoon; Red River Colony.**

▷ SUGGESTED READING: John Morgan Gray, *Lord Selkirk of Red River* (1963); Grant MacEwan, *Cornerstone Colony: Selkirk's Contribution to the Canadian West.* (1977).

■ Selkirk Mountains

The Selkirk Mountains are one of the ranges of the Columbia Mountains in the southeast corner of British Columbia. Car and rail traffic cross the mountains via Rogers Pass. In 1989, North America's longest railway tunnel (14.7 km) was opened through Rogers Pass. In the Kootenay region, mining and logging have been important to the economy of the province.

The Selkirks are older than the Rocky Mountains. They were named for Lord Selkirk, the founder of the Red River Colony in what is now Manitoba.

▷ SUGGESTED READING: J.F. Garden, *The Selkirks: Nelson's Mountains* (1984).

■ Selye, Hans

Pioneer of research on stress (*born in 1907 at Vienna, Austria; died in 1982 at Montreal, Que.*). Dr Hans Selye made a lifelong study of stress. After joining the staff of McGill University in 1932, he set out to

Thomas Douglas, *Earl of Selkirk (courtesy NAC/ C-1346).*

investigate the harm that strain and worry could do to people and how it could affect their physical health. In 1945 he became the first director of the Institute of Experimental Medicine and Surgery at the University of Montreal. In 1977, after his retirement, he founded the International Institute of Stress.

Selye vastly increased the world's knowledge of stress: what it is, how it affects people, and how one can cope with it. He wrote more than 1700 scientific papers on the subject, as well as popular books for the general public. These included *The Stress of Life* (1956) and *Stress Without Distress* (1974).

▷ SUGGESTED READING: Hans Selye, *The Stress of My Life: A Scientist's Memoirs* (1977).

■ Semple, Robert
Governor of Rupert's Land 1815-16 (*born in 1777 at Boston, Massachusetts; died in 1816 at the Red River Colony*). Semple was a businessman and writer of travel books. He also became governor of the Red River Colony in 1815 at the height of the troubles between the colonists, the North West Company, and the local Metis. The following June, he and 20 of his men were killed in a skirmish with the Metis at Seven Oaks.

▷ RELATED ARTICLES: **Red River Colony; Seven Oaks Incident.**

■ Senate
The Senate is one branch of the Parliament of Canada. Senators are appointed by the governor general, on the advice of the prime minister (this advice is never refused). Senators must be at least 30 years old, be a subject of the queen, and they must retire at age 75. They must hold residence in the province that they represent. There are 104 senators. They are distributed as follows: 24 each from Ontario and Quebec, ten each from Nova Scotia and New Brunswick, six each from the western provinces and Newfoundland, four from P.E.I., and one each from the two territories.

Unlike the House of Commons, the Senate cannot propose a law to raise or spend public money. In theory, no bill can become law without the Senate's consent. In practice, however, the Senate has not vetoed a bill from the House of Commons since 1936. It has delayed some bills that it has opposed, and it has suggested changes to others.

Meanwhile, the Senate continues to debate and approve bills. Senators provide valuable help in going over laws clause by clause. Senate committees produce studies of issues such as unemployment, poverty, and so on. In one extreme case, in 1988, the Senate delayed a bill (the free-trade bill) on the instructions of the Leader of the Opposition. The government claimed that this was interference in the democratic process and called an election (which it won).

The Senate was created at the time of Confederation in 1867. Its role was to represent less populous regions and to balance the power of the House of Commons. (The voters were often thought to be too fickle.) Because the Senate is appointed, while the House is elected by the people, many people object to the idea that the Senate could block laws proposed by the people's representatives.

Over the years, there have been many proposals to reform or to abolish the Senate. Recent suggestions are that senators should be elected and that the Senate should be given more power to defend the interests of the provinces.

▷ RELATED ARTICLES: **Government; House of Commons; Parliament.**

▷ SUGGESTED READING: John Bejermi, *How Parliament Works* (1985); Colin Campbell, *The Canadian Senate: A Lobby from Within* (1978); C.E.S. Franks, *The Parliament of Canada* (1987).

■ Separate Schools

Some Canadian provinces have two systems of education: a system of non-religious public schools and a "separate" system of Roman Catholic schools. Both systems are supported by the public through taxes. Catholic parents may choose to pay their taxes to support the separate system and to send their children to a separate school.

The dual system dates back to the 19th century, when schools were largely operated by the churches. Section 93 of the Constitution Act, 1867, guaranteed the rights of people to send their children to these schools.

Separate schools exist in Alberta, Saskatchewan, and Ontario. In Quebec, the provincial government wishes to separate school systems based on language (French and English) rather than on religion. In Newfoundland, a combination of public schools and a variety of different religious schools are all publicly supported. In the remaining provinces — New Brunswick, Nova Scotia, Prince Edward Island, Manitoba, and British Columbia — separate schools are treated as private schools. These schools receive some funding from the provincial government, but they must also charge fees.

Separate schools continue to be a political issue. In Manitoba, the Roman Catholic community is pressing the government to create a separate school system. Ontario decided in 1984 to extend funding of separate schools through high school. Human-rights experts also suggest that to limit funding to only Catholic and Protestant schools is contrary to the Canadian Charter of Rights and Freedoms, especially in view of the very large number of other ethnic and religious groups in Canada.

▷ RELATED ARTICLES: **Education; Education History; Private Schools; Schools.**

■ Separatism

Separatism is a political movement of part of a political unit towards independence. The term is most often used to describe political movements in Quebec in the 1960s.

The first separatist movement actually emerged in Nova Scotia shortly after Confederation in 1867, but it was quickly defeated.

The separatist movement emerged in Quebec in the late 1950s and 1960s as a result of great social and political changes. A number of organizations were active in politics. The Parti Québécois, formed in 1968, became the focus for all these groups. In 1970 an extremist group, called the FLQ turned to violence in order to push the separatist cause. Their actions during the October Crisis shocked the people of Quebec. In 1976 the PQ swept to power in Quebec. In 1980 it offered its proposal for independence to the voters of Quebec in a referendum, which was defeated by 60% of the voters. The people of Quebec showed a declining interest in separation and the PQ put aside their plans.

Nevertheless, after René Lévesque's death, the new PQ leader Jacques Parizeau brought the party back to a separatist position. Separatism flared again in 1990 when the Meech Lake Accord, recognizing Quebec as a "distinct society," was rejected. It then appeared that all political parties in Quebec favoured some form of separatism.

Separatist sentiment has emerged from time to time in western Canada as a protest against policies that westerners believe favour Quebec and Ontario.

▷ RELATED ARTICLES: **October Crisis; Parti Québécois; Political History; Quebec.**

▷ SUGGESTED READING: Bruce W. Hodgins, Richard P. Bowler, James L. Hanky and George A. Rawlyk, *Canadiens, Canadians and Québecois* (1974); Jane Jacobs, *The Question of Separatism: Quebec and the Struggle over Sovereignty* (1980).

■ Sept-Îles

Sept-Îles, Que., lies far out on the north shore of the St Lawrence River at the eastern end of the province. Jacques Cartier, the 16th-century French explorer, named it after the seven islands at the entrance to the bay. The site was long visited by Montagnais people, who still occupy the area. Settlement began in 1651 and for many years the community was a small

Iron Ore *facilities at Sept-Îles, Que. (photo by Hans Blohm/Masterfile).*

Poet Robert Service in front of his famous cabin in Dawson (courtesy Yukon Archives).

Some Service Clubs in Canada

Active 20-30 Clubs
Association of
  Kinsmen Clubs
Canadian Progress
  Clubs
International
  Association of Lions
  Clubs
Kiwanis International
Optimist International
Rotary International

Some Fraternal Societies in Canada

Ancient and Free
  Accepted Masons
Associated Canadian
  Travellers
Benevolent and
  Protective Order of
  Elks of Canada
Benevolent Irish
  Society, Inc.
Canadian Woodmen of
  the World
Independent Order of
  Foresters
Independent Order of
  Oddfellows
Knights of Columbus
Knights of Pythias
Loyal Orange
  Association

fishing and trading post. In the 1950s, however, a mining boom in the region led to rapid expansion of the city. It emerged as one of Canada's most important seaports, shipping huge cargoes of ore brought down from the interior by rail. The population in 1986 was 25 637.

For further information, contact the Greffier, 546 avenue Dequen, Sept-Îles, Que., G4R 2R4.

Service, Robert William

Poet and novelist (*born in 1874 at Preston, England; died in 1958 at Lancieux, France*). With such poems as "The Shooting of Dan McGrew," "The Cremation of Sam McGee," and "The Spell of the Yukon," Robert Service brilliantly captured the spirit of the Klondike gold rush of 1897-99. Yet he was nowhere near the Yukon during the heady years of the gold rush. He was on his way to Mexico.

Service immigrated to Canada in 1896 in the hope of becoming a cowboy. He led a wandering life until 1903, when he joined the Canadian Bank of Commerce in British Columbia. In 1904 the bank sent him to its Whitehorse branch in the Yukon, and it was then he wrote his first gold rush poems. Published in 1907 as *Songs of a Sourdough*, they were an instant success. The following year, the bank transferred Service to Dawson, the town that had been the centre of the gold rush ten years earlier. Living there quietly in a small cabin, he wrote more poems about the gold rush and a novel, *The Trail of '98* (1910). And then, having permanently identified himself with the Yukon, he left forever in 1912 and resumed a life of travelling and writing.

After further adventures and many more books, Service settled in France, where he lived quietly. Few people knew he was the world-famous author who had interpreted so vividly "the stillness, the moonlight, the mystery" of the Canadian North.

▷ Suggested Reading: Carl F. Klinck, *Robert*

Service: A Biography (1976); Robert W. Service, *The Cremation of Sam McGee* (1986) and *The Shooting of Dan McGrew* (1988).

Service Clubs

Service clubs are organizations founded specifically for the purpose of service to the community. Most originated in the United States in the early 20th century, and spread into Canada. They draw their members mainly from among business and professional people, and prefer as members people who have demonstrated qualities of leadership. Local clubs are linked to national or international organizations, but in their charitable activities they are concerned exclusively with projects in their own communities. Much of their work is intended to supplement the efforts of existing social-welfare agencies. Service clubs may, for instance, operate summer camps for underprivileged children, or raise money to build a new hospital wing, or to equip a specialized medical facility.

Service clubs differ from fraternal societies in that they do not offer their members any financial advantages, like group insurance. Nor do they have secret ceremonies or rituals to distinguish them from the rest of the community. Members of service clubs benefit only from the satisfaction derived from their community work, from new friendships, and from the strengthening of business and professional ties among themselves.

Fraternal societies may engage in charitable work in the community, but most exist mainly to provide good fellowship and financial advantages to their members. They originated in Britain and the United States, and most were brought to Canada by immigrants in the 19th century. Membership is open to all classes of society, but they are particularly attractive to those who might benefit from the sickness, funeral, and other insurance programs that are provided. There are several kinds of fraternal societies. Some are based on ethnic origins; others are restricted to members of a particular religion; and yet others are based on their members' work. Those fraternal societies that engage actively in social and charitable work differ from service clubs principally in the retention of symbolism and ritual in their meetings.

Service Industries

A service industry produces services rather than manufactured products. The term covers an extremely wide variety of

Tourism supports a large service industry, as can be seen by the shops, motels, and entertainment in Niagara Falls (photo by J.A. Kraulis/Masterfile).

Restaurants are a growing area of the service industry (courtesy Take Stock Inc.).

Radio Announcer at a control board at a radio station in Ottawa (photo by Jim Merrithew).

activities, but can be grouped into four major areas. Commercial services include restaurants, hotels, retail trade, recreation, amusement, and personal care. Financial and legal services include banking, insurance, real estate, and investment. Transportation and communication include television, radio, automobile services, and airlines. Finally, health care, education, social services, and religion are grouped as non-commercial.

The enormous growth in the service industries has been one of the major changes in the economies of all developed nations in the 20th century. In 1911 it accounted for about 33% of the working population. Today it is 70%.

Three major reasons are given for this growth. First is the higher efficiency of manufacturing and agriculture, which now require far fewer workers to produce the same goods. Second is the large growth in the economy, which has created more wealth. More money is therefore available for activities such as travelling and eating out. Finally, new technologies have created new jobs in services. For example, computers have greatly increased the need for operators, repairs, and sales.

▷ Related Articles: **Economics; Industry.**

■ Seton, Ernest Thompson

Author, illustrator, naturalist (*born in 1860 at South Shields, County Durham, England; died in 1946 at Seton Village near Santa Fe, New Mexico, U.S.*). Born Ernest Evan Thompson, he came to Canada in 1866. He changed his name because he believed he had claim to a Scots title. Seton moved to the U.S. in 1896 and later became an American citizen. A graduate of the Ontario School of Art, he was a successful book illustrator. He was also Manitoba's official naturalist and won respect

for his studies of wildlife. In addition, he was a founder of two youth groups, the League of Woodcraft Indians (1902) and the Boy Scouts of America (1910).

He is best known, however, as the first successful writer of realistic animal stories. His books include *Wild Animals I Have Known* (1898), *Lives of the Hunted* (1910), and *Animal Heroes* (1905). Although Seton's stories are sometimes sentimental, the animal behaviour he describes is based on close observation.

■ Seven Oaks Incident

The Seven Oaks Incident was a violent clash on the banks of the Red River between Red River colonists and a party of Metis. It was the worst incident in a long rivalry between the Hudson's Bay Company and the North West Company. HBC traders were trying to stop the export of pemmican supplies from the colony, and the Metis, working for the NWC, seemed to pose a threat to this policy.

On June 19, 1816, Governor Robert Semple led a group of armed settlers out to confront the Metis, led by Cuthbert Grant. Shooting began and Semple and 20 other colonists died. Temporarily, all colonists left the country.

▷ Related Article: **Red River Colony.**
▷ Suggested Reading: Joanne Pelletier, *Skirmish at Seven Oaks* (1985).

Firefighters pour foam on pools of gasoline (photo by Jim Merrithew).

Ernest Thompson Seton (courtesy NAC/C-9485).

Death of General Wolfe
This painting by Benjamin West was one of the most famous of its day, for it portrayed a great victory far away. Nevertheless, it is historically inaccurate. Only one of the men grouped around General Wolfe (who was killed at the battle) was actually there. Similar French paintings show Montcalm dying on the battlefield. In fact, he died later, in the town (courtesy NGC).

Map of the St Lawrence River and Quebec This map, drawn around the time of the Seven Years' War, shows how Wolfe led the British past the fortress of Quebec, where they climbed the cliff to engage the French on the Plains of Abraham (courtesy NAC/NMC/ 2716).

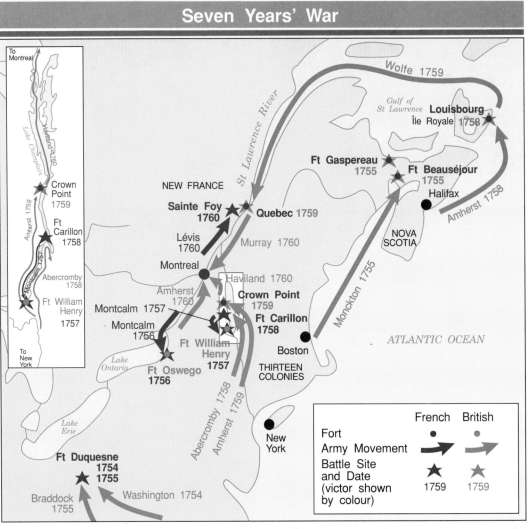

Seven Years' War

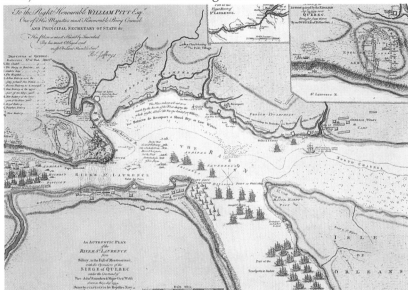

■ Seven Years' War

The Seven Years' War was the final struggle between France and Britain for control of North America. Lasting from 1756 to 1763, it resulted in the British conquest of New France and the beginning of British rule along the St Lawrence River.

The war in North America was part of a worldwide conflict that included major campaigns in Europe and India. On one side were Great Britain and Hanover in alliance with Prussia. On the other side were France, Austria, Sweden, Saxony, Russia, and eventually Spain.

The fighting in North America started in 1754, two years before the official declaration of war. At first the French won most of the victories, fighting with a combination of French soldiers from France, native people who were allies of the French, and *Canadiens* (Canadian-born French). The British forces were a similar mix: professional soldiers, native people, and American colonists. But the British also had the Royal Navy, which dominated the seas and prevented French ships from arriving from Europe with reinforcements and supplies. This was a vital factor in turning the war in Britain's favour. The main developments are shown in the table.

▷ RELATED ARTICLES: **Jeffery Amherst; François-Gaston de Lévis; Robert Monckton;**

Louis Joseph Montcalm; Plains of Abraham, Battle of; Paris, Treaty of; Sainte-Foy, Battle of; Pierre de Rigaud Vaudreuil; James Wolfe.

▷ Suggested Reading: J.B. Brebner, *Canada: A Modern History* (1960); Gordon Donaldson, *Battle for a Continent: Quebec 1759* (1973); Desmond Morton, *Sieges of Quebec* (1984); G.F.G. Stanley, *New France* (1968).

■ Seventy-two Resolutions, *see* Quebec Resolutions

■ Severn River

The Severn River, 982 km long, flows north out of the wooded Canadian Shield country of northwest Ontario into Hudson Bay. Occupied by the Cree, it was an important canoe route to the interior during the days of the fur trade.

■ Sexually Transmitted Disease

Sexually transmitted diseases are a group of some 20 or so infections that are spread by intimate sexual contact, particularly by intercourse. The sexually transmitted diseases (STD) include the diseases once known as venereal disease, or VD. (The word "venereal" comes from the name of Venus, the Roman goddess of Love, and means "relating to sexual intercourse.") Three of the most common sexually transmitted diseases are genital herpes, gonorrhoea, and syphilis. Though none of these diseases now kills very many people, some of them, especially syphilis, can. The true incidence of STD in Canada is unknown.

AIDS (Acquired Immunodeficiency Syndrome), a disease first recognized in 1981, can also spread by sexual contact. Caused by a virus which attacks the immune system by which the body defends itself against disease, AIDS is a deadly and incurable disease. (*See* separate article on **AIDS.**)

What Causes the Sexually Transmitted Diseases? Certain germs — tiny bacteria, even tinier viruses, and other micro-organisms — cause the sexually transmitted diseases. These germs can only survive in warm, moist parts of the body, such as the vagina. Outside of such areas they soon die. This is why it is almost impossible to get syphilis or other sexually transmitted diseases from a toilet seat or door knob.

Who Gets Sexually Transmitted Diseases? Sexually transmitted diseases are the most common of all the diseases that humans pass among themselves. In Canada, as in other industrialized countries, they are the most common diseases among young people. One of every eight or nine adolescents, in fact, has a sexually transmitted disease. The majority of these people have a minor disease, such as genital herpes.

Genital Herpes A virus similar to the one that causes cold sores on the lips is the cause of genital herpes. The virus is passed during direct physical contact with the open sores of an infected person. This virus produces itching sores and blisters on the genitals. These sores appear in times of stress or poor health. After a week or so, they become dormant, only to reappear later. There is, as yet, no cure for herpes.

Gonorrhoea is a relatively common and not very dangerous disease, though it can cause sterility in both men and women and blindness in infants infected by their mothers at birth. The disease often has no visible symptoms. Penicillin and other antibiotics kill the gonorrhoea bacteria. Some disease-causing bacteria, however, and particularly those that cause gonorrhoea, are becoming resistant to antibiotics. In 1986 there were 35 290 cases of gonorrhoea reported in Canada.

Syphilis (also known as "the clap") is a relatively rare and dangerous disease. Effective treatment has been available only since the discovery of antibiotics in the middle of this century. If left untreated, syphilis produces nasty complications. In the long term, after many years without unique symptoms, syphilis produces heart disease, insanity, paralysis, and death. Syphilis is particularly dangerous for pregnant women, for it may deform or kill their children. Today, syphilis can always be cured. In 1986 there were 2199 cases of syphilis reported in Canada.

Preventing the Spread of Sexually Transmitted Diseases If you are sexually active, avoiding casual sexual encounters and using a condom will help to avoid infection.

Abstaining from sex dramatically reduces one's chances of getting these diseases.

▷ Suggested Reading: Donna Cherniak, *Sexually Transmitted Diseases* (1983); Alan Meitzer, *The ABC's of S.T.D.: A Guide to Sexually Transmitted Diseases* (1983).

■ Seymour, Bertha Lynn

Ballet dancer (*born in 1939 at Wainwright, Alta*). Seymour is one of the world's great dramatic ballerinas. She studied ballet in Vancouver, competed in local festivals and competitions, and won a scholarship to the Sadler's Wells School (now the Royal Ballet School) in England

Time Line: Seven Years' War

- **1756** Britain declares war on France
- **1756** Fort Oswego (on Lake Ontario) captured by the French, led by General Montcalm
- **1757** Fort William Henry (on Lake George) taken by the French under Montcalm
- **1758** After a 7-week siege, the French fortress of Louisbourg is captured by the British
- **1758 (July)** Fort Carillon (on Lake Champlain) besieged by a large British force under General Abercromby. Beaten off by the French
- **1759 (from June to Sept)** Siege of Quebec, led by General Wolfe, is withstood by French **(July & Aug)** From the south shore, British cannon pound Quebec with shellfire, reducing much of the town to rubble. On the north shore, an attempted crossing of the Montmorency River (July 31) by the British is beaten off by General Lévis **(Sept 13)** Battle of the Plains of Abraham, followed by surrender of Quebec to the British on Sept 18
- **1760 (Apr)** Ste-Foy (near Quebec). The French under Lévis rout the British forces under Murray
- **1760 (Sept)** Montreal falls to the British after the armies led by Amherst, Murray, and Haviland converge on the city. On Sept 8, Vaudreuil surrenders New France to Amherst
- **1763** Treaty of Paris formally ends the war. France gives up all its territories in North America, except for the islands of Saint-Pierre and Miquelon off Newfoundland

Guardian, *1972, acrylic on paper by artist Jack Shadbolt. The painting shows the influence of Northwest Coast native art on Shadbolt's work (courtesy of the artist).*

■ Shadbolt, Jack Leonard

Painter (*born in 1909 at Shoeburyness, England*). Shadbolt is one of Canada's most versatile painters. He has a thorough understanding of primitive and modern art styles, and he uses techniques from both these traditions in his own work. Although he has made several series of paintings on different subjects, one recurring theme is the native art of British Columbia. He admires the design and decoration in Northwest Coast Indian art, particularly the way it shows the outside shape and internal structure of an object at the same time. Shadbolt taught for many years in schools and at the art college in Vancouver. He is a poet, and has written three books about art. He has also painted murals, theatre posters, and has done stage, ballet, and costume designs.

▷ SUGGESTED READING: Marjorie M. Halpin, *Jack Shadbolt and the Coastal Indian Image* (1983).

■ Shadd, Alfred Schmitz

Western Canada's first Black doctor (*born in 1870 near Chatham, Ont.; died in 1915 at Winnipeg, Man.*). Shadd came from a remarkable family. His grandfather, Abraham Shadd (1801-82), had escaped slavery in the United States and was the first Canadian Black to be elected to public office (in 1859, to the Raleigh Town Council). One of Abraham's daughters, Mary Shadd (1823-93), was probably the first Canadian woman to run a newspaper, the *Provincial Freeman*. Some of the Shadd family became preachers. Others became lawyers.

Alfred chose medicine. He left his home in Chatham in 1896 and went to Kinistino, in what is now Saskatchewan, to take a teaching job. Soon he found himself also acting as doctor, for there was no local doctor and he had some medical training. He returned to Ontario to complete his medical degree, and by 1898 he was back in Kinistino, fully qualified. For the rest of his life he served as the region's doctor, moving to nearby Melfort in 1904.

Shadd helped found the Melfort hospital and was owner of the local newspaper. Shadd died suddenly of appendicitis and was sadly mourned by thousands. His funeral procession was more than 3 km long.

■ Shaman

A shaman is a religious figure in Indian and Inuit society. The shaman could be either a man or a woman, and was the link between the spirit world and the

when she was only 14 years old. By 1959, she was a principal dancer with the Royal Ballet in London, which she had joined in 1956. She danced with the Deutsche Opern Ballet in Berlin (1966-70), and was director of the Bavarian States Opera Ballet in Munich (1978-79). She has also performed in Canada as a guest artist with the National Ballet of Canada.

As a ballerina, Seymour has extraordinary emotional power. Britain's most talented choreographers created roles especially for her. She has also choreographed ballets herself. Her last public appearance was in 1981.

▷ SUGGESTED READING: R. Austin, *Lynn Seymour: An Authorized Biography* (1980); Anthony Crickmay, *Lynn Seymour: A Photographic Study* (1980).

community. He or she was expected to foretell the future, control the weather, locate fish or game, provide leadership in religious celebrations, heal the sick, and expel evil spirits.

The powers of the shaman were believed to come from a supernatural force. A spirit entered the chosen person, usually during a trance, and gave the shaman powers of healing and knowledge. Depending on the particular native group, the shaman practised his or her craft in different ways. The rituals might include singing, dancing, wearing special costumes and masks, and playing music on the drum or tambourine. Most shamans worked for the well-being of the community, but some were believed to use their powers for sorcery. For this reason, shamans were also feared. *See* various entries under **Native People**.

▷ SUGGESTED READING: Marius Barbeau, *Medicine Men on the North Pacific Coast* (1958); Spencer Lee Rogers, *The Shaman: His Symbols and his Healing Power* (1982); Luke Wallin, *Ceremony of the Panther* (1987).

■ Shandro

Shandro, Alta, northeast of Edmonton, is a centre of Ukrainian settlement in the province. It is named for Nikon Shandro (1886-1942), the first settler and the first Ukrainian elected to a provincial legislature (1913). A museum recreates the life of pioneer Ukrainians.

■ Shark

Sharks are primitive marine fishes that have existed for 350 million years. They are commonly known by their high tail fin. Their crescent-shaped mouth has several rows of triangular teeth which constantly replace themselves. The skeleton is made of soft cartilage.

Twenty-six species in nine families are found in Canada, some only in summertime because sharks generally prefer warmer waters. Only 13 species are to be found in Canada year-round. Adult size varies greatly by species, from 15 cm to 18 m, and male sharks are generally 25% smaller than females. The whale shark is the world's largest fish. In most sharks, the eggs develop inside the female's body and the baby is identical to adults when born. Some hunting sharks can conserve muscle heat to improve the efficiency of their chase. These fish can endure long periods without food.

Movies have greatly exaggerated the danger that sharks pose to humans. Some species only eat crustaceans. Others eat fish, invertebrates, and marine mammals. The whale shark eats only microscopic plankton.

▷ SUGGESTED READING: Wyatt Blassingame, *Wonder of Sharks* (1984); Rhoda Blumberg, *Sharks* (1976); Jacques-Yves Cousteau and Philippe Cousteau, *The Shark: Splendid Savage of the Sea* (1970); David Taylor, *Sharks* (1986).

■ Shatner, William, *see* Canadian International Stars

■ Shaw Festival

The Shaw Festival was founded in 1962 at Niagara-on-the-Lake, Ont. It is the only festival in the world that showcases the plays of Irish dramatist George Bernard Shaw (1856-1950). For many years, the Festival has also produced plays by other dramatists who were contemporaries of Shaw.

Peter Pan production at the Shaw Festival, with Tom McCamus as Peter Pan (photo by David Cooper/Shaw Festival).

The Shaw Festival has three stages: the historic Court House, which seats 345; the new Festival Theatre, which opened in 1973 and was designed by architect Ron Thom to seat 861; and the smaller Royal George, which seats 353. Under directors Paxton Whitehead (1967-77) and Christopher Newton (since 1980), the Festival has broadened its repertoire to include popular comedies, musicals, farces, and Canadian plays, as well as music, mime, and dance events. In 1984 George

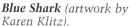

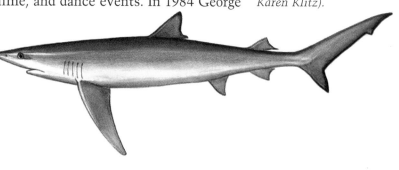

Shaman's Drum (courtesy NMC/CMC/S77-264).

Blue Shark (artwork by Karen Klitz).

Orwell's novel *1984* was performed as a one-day workshop event which took the whole town for its stage and involved the entire Shaw Festival company. Altogether there are about 70 actors in the ensemble, most of whom return year after year to work together. Heath Lamberts is just one of the actors who made his name at Shaw. The Festival has also fostered a remarkable group of stage and costume designers.

Many Shaw Festival productions have toured Canada and the United States. And, since 1983, the Shaw Festival has co-produced plays with various Toronto theatres during the winter season.

▷ SUGGESTED READING: Brian Doherty, *Not Bloody Likely: The Shaw Festival 1962-1973* (1974).

■ Shawinigan

Shawinigan, Que., lies beside the St-Maurice River north of Trois-Rivières. It began in 1899 at the site of a power dam on the river. Because electricity was freely available, several large manufacturers moved to the community, including pulp, textiles, and chemicals. The power plant, now owned by Hydro-Québec, began providing electricity to Montreal in 1903. Since the 1960s, however, the pace of growth has slowed as the number of jobs in the industry has declined. Politician Jean Chrétien is from Shawinigan. The population in 1986 was 21 470.

For further information, contact the Greffier, 550 avenue de I'Hôtel-de-Ville, C.P. 400, Shawinigan, Que., G9N 6V3.

■ Shebib, Donald

Filmmaker (*born in 1938 at Toronto, Ont.*). Shebib is best known as the director of *Goin' Down the Road* (1970), the story of two Maritime friends in Toronto. Other films include *Between Friends* (1973), the story of a marriage breakdown, and *The Climb* (1986), a mountaineering adventure. He has also directed episodes of the television series "Night Heat" and "Danger Bay."

■ Shediac

Shediac, N.B., is a town in the southeast corner of the province looking across Northumberland Strait to Prince Edward Island. Originally a timber and shipbuilding centre, it is now a summer tourist resort with some of New Brunswick's best beaches. Fishing is also important; the town is called "the lobster capital of the world." Shediac's population in 1986 was 4370.

For further information, contact the Greffier, C.P. 969, Shediac, N.B., E0A 3G0.

■ Sheep Farming

Sheep are raised in Canada for their meat and milk. They were first brought to Canada by the French settlers in the 17th century and used as a source of wool as well as meat. In 1965 there were over one million sheep in Canada, but the number has decreased since then. Breeders at the Agriculture Canada research station at Lennoxville, Que., have crossbred several breeds to produce a unique Canadian breed, called DLS.

Sheep Farm, *Manora, Ont. (photo by Jim Merrithew).*

■ Shelburne

Shelburne, N.S., is a fishing harbour on the Atlantic coast of Nova Scotia, 208 km southwest of Halifax. At the end of the American Revolution, about 3000 Loyalists arrived in 30 ships from New York. In the next few years the town grew to a population of over 16 000. A sizeable number were Black refugees who settled in their own community, Birchtown. Shelburne was briefly the largest town in British North America. The Loyalists gradually moved elsewhere. Many Loyalist-era buildings have survived, however, and many residents still trace a connection to the Loyalist refugees. The population in 1986 was 2312.

For further information, contact the Municipal Clerk, P.O. Box 280, Shelburne, N.S., B0T 1W0.

■ Sherbrooke

Sherbrooke, Que., is the major city in the Eastern Townships of south-central Quebec. It lies 147 km east of Montreal at the junction of the Magog and St François rivers. Situated in a district of lakes and rivers, Sherbrooke is known for the beauty of the surrounding countryside. The city takes its name from Sir John Sherbrooke, who was governor-in-chief of British

Shawinigan Falls *on the St-Maurice River (photo by John deVisser).*

North America, 1816-18. Sherbrooke's population in 1986 was 74 438.

HISTORY

Beginnings During the 17th and 18th centuries, Sherbrooke was the site of a portage at the foot of the falls on the Magog River. It was known as the Grandes Fourches (The Forks). Following the American Revolution, a large number of Loyalists settled in the area that became known as the Eastern Townships. The first to settle at The Forks were pioneers from Vermont in the United States. They built mills beside the river, and in 1818 they named their settlement for Governor Sherbrooke.

Growth of the City Sherbrooke developed as a centre of the textile industry. Canada's first cotton mill was built there in 1844, and a woollen mill was opened in 1867. Other businesses, such as stores and banks, were established to serve the factory workers. In 1852, Sherbrooke's population was 3000. By 1891, the population had grown to 10 000. At first, the majority of inhabitants were English-speaking, but many French Canadians moved to Sherbrooke to work in the mills and factories, and after the 1870s they outnumbered the English Canadians.

Sherbrooke was among the first communities in Canada to be served by a railway, which was completed in 1853. The city soon became a major transportation centre, the hub of a network of railway lines that connected with the Maritimes and with the United States, as well as

Sherbrooke from the air (photo by Michel Gagné/ SSC Photocentre).

with several major cities in Quebec.

By the 1950s, Sherbrooke's population was over 50 000. Although little new industry has been added since then, Sherbrooke continues to develop as a centre of education and government. The university, founded in 1954, provides many jobs, as did provincial government offices.

THE MODERN CITY

Population The city's population has dropped since 1971, when it was 80 700. One reason for this is that many people have moved to suburbs outside the city limits. The percentage of French-speakers has risen over the years. By 1986, almost 94% of Sherbrooke's population was French-speaking.

Education The University of Sherbrooke has more than 8600 full-time students. Sherbrooke also has two community colleges, Collège Régional Champlain and the CÉGEP de Sherbrooke.

Transportation Sherbrooke lies at the intersection of two major highways. One runs west to Montreal; the other goes north towards Trois-Rivières and south to the United States. The passenger rail service stopped in 1981 but was started up again in 1985.

Communications Sherbrooke has two daily newspapers, the *Record* (English) and *La Tribune* (French). It also has a weekly French-language paper, *La Nouvelle*. There are three television stations and four radio stations.

Culture Much of Sherbrooke's cultural activity centres on the university. The city has a symphony orchestra and several theatre groups. The principal museums are the Musée des beaux-arts (artworks, principally on the Eastern Townships re-

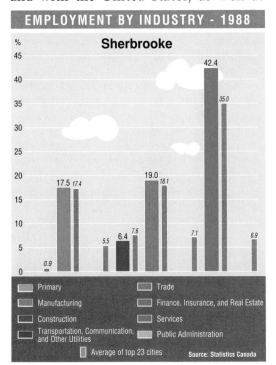

EMPLOYMENT BY INDUSTRY - 1988

Sherbrooke

%

45		
		42.4
40		35.0
35		
30		
25		
20	17.5 17.4	19.0 18.1
15		
10		7.1
5	5.5 6.4 7.6	6.9
0	0.9	

■ Primary   ■ Trade
■ Manufacturing   ■ Finance, Insurance, and Real Estate
■ Construction   ■ Services
■ Transportation, Communication, and Other Utilities   ■ Public Administration

■ Average of top 23 cities   Source: Statistics Canada

Sherbrooke, Que., is located in a region of lakes and mountains near Mount Orford Provincial Park (courtesy City of Sherbrooke).

gion) and the Musée des sciences naturelles du Séminaire de Sherbrooke (natural sciences, ethnology, and fine arts). There are a number of other museums, archives, and art galleries. A major arts centre and music camp are located just west of Sherbrooke in Mount Orford Provincial Park. Nearby is a lakeside recreation centre at Magog.

For further information, contact the Greffier, 145 rue Wellington nord, C.P. 610, Sherbrooke, Que., J1H 5C1.

■ **Shield,** *see* **Canadian Shield**

■ **Shilling, Arthur**
Painter (*born in 1941 at Rama Indian Reserve, Orillia, Ont.; died there in 1986*). Although he was proud of his Ojibwa heritage, Shilling did not join any particular school of native art. He is best known for his portraits and self-portraits, which are impressionistic rather than detailed in style. He also liked to paint colourful scenes of life on the Rama Reserve because, he said, "there is no other way to express the beauty of my people." He built an art gallery on the reserve to encourage local artists and to show their work. The National Film Board made a documentary film about his life, and Shilling himself wrote a book, *The Ojibwa Dream* (1986), which was published after his death. His works are popular with collectors in both Canada and the United States.

Clothesline, 1982, oil on masonite by artist Arthur Shilling (courtesy DIAND/Mrs M. Shilling).

■ **Shilo,** *see* **Canadian Forces Bases**

■ **Shiners' Wars**
The Shiners' Wars, between 1837 and 1845, were outbreaks of fighting in the Ottawa Valley between lumbermen of Irish and French-Canadian origin. They were sparked by the arrival of large numbers of Irish in the lumbering region around Bytown (Ottawa) after the Rideau

Canal was completed in 1832. The Irish soon came to dominate the timber trade, displacing many of the French Canadians. This led to tensions and then to brawling.

The name "Shiners" has three possible origins: the French word *cheneur* (oakman); the shiny hats worn by the Irish; or the kind of coin paid to lumbermen.
▷ RELATED ARTICLE: **Timber Trade.**

■ **Shinplasters**
Shinplasters were bills worth 25 cents, issued three times by the Canadian government (1870, 1900, and 1923). The term may date to the American Revolution when soldiers used similar bills to pad their shoes.

Ships being serviced at yards in Halifax, N.S. (photo by Sherman Hines/Masterfile).

■ **Shipping Industry**
Shipping is the movement of goods by water. Shipping services have always been an economic lifeline for Canada. For the first settlers, ships were the source of essential supplies from Europe. They also carried fish, fur, and timber to overseas markets.

In the 19th century, Canada was one of the world's foremost ship-owning nations. (It ranked fourth in 1878.) Samuel Cunard, a Maritimer, founded the famous Cunard Company, one of the largest shipping companies in the world.

Although there are few Canadian-owned deep-sea ships today, vessels from abroad require a number of services in Canadian ports, including pilots and tugs to bring them to dock, repairs, and supplies. About 2000 workers, called longshoremen, load and unload cargoes on the docks.

Today, about one-third of Canada's exports and one-quarter of its imports move by water. Traffic on the East Coast consists mainly of fuel, salt, gypsum, and general cargo. West Coast shipping includes forest products and other natural resource products. By far the most impor-

Canada's Ports and Harbours	
Ports Canada*	
Place	*Thousands of Tonnes*
Vancouver	70 317
Sept-Îles	23 043
Montreal	21 831
Quebec	17 852
Halifax	14 780
Saint John	14 696
Prince Rupert	12 658
Trois-Rivières	2038
Port Colborne	1214
St John's	999
Belledune	446
Chicoutimi and Baie de Ha! Ha!	416
Prescott	287
Churchill	77

* administered by the federal government

Harbours**	
Thunder Bay	17 311
Hamilton	12 855
Fraser River	5779
North Fraser	5432
Windsor	4170
Nanaimo	2662
Toronto	1621
Port Alberni	1006
Oshawa	187

** under control of local commissions appointed by federal and local governments

Harbours and Ports***	
Baie-Comeau	6974
Sault Ste-Marie	5895
Goderich	2201
Dalhousie	917
Mulgrave	459
Charlottetown	450
Newcastle	313
Pugwash	300
Gros-Cocouna	292
Rimouski	289

*** administered by Canadian Coast Guard. There are over 570 in Canada

Ferry Boats *crossing the ice-covered St Lawrence River at Quebec City (photo by Jim Merrithew).*

tant route is the St Lawrence Seaway, where outgoing cargoes include iron ore, fuel, wheat, and numerous manufactured products.

Other important shipping services include ferry services on the East and West coasts and barge services up the Mackenzie River. There are 23 000 people employed in shipping in Canada.

Canadian ships and foreign operating in Canadian waters must follow rules laid down by the federal Department of Transport. The Canadian Coast Guard makes sure that ships meet these requirements and that they follow pollution-preventing procedures.

▷ RELATED ARTICLES: **Ferries; Transportation.**

■ **Ships and Shipbuilding**

The word "ship" is usually reserved for a vessel large enough to go on the open sea. Egyptians were likely the first people to build ships, about 5000 years ago. They were also the first to use sails and to make ships from planks of wood.

Until the 19th century, there were only two ways of powering a ship: by paddle and by sail. Canada's Northwest Coast Indians built impressive whaling ships that used both oars and sail. Around the year 1000 AD, Norse sailors crossed the North Atlantic Ocean in broad, roomy ships called *knorrs*. These were powered by a single, large sail, and could also be rowed.

Age of Discovery In the mid-1400s, Europeans developed a new kind of sailing ship. It was built by fastening wooden planks to a skeleton, made up of a keel running the length of the ship and ribs. It was steered by a rudder in the stern. This sailing ship carried a variety of sails. Large square sails worked well when the wind was blowing from behind. Triangular sails, called *lateens*, helped the ship sail into the wind. This was the type of ship that carried the Portuguese, French, and

English explorers across the ocean in the 1400s and 1500s. It was small and very uncomfortable. Only the captain and officers had cabins. The crew slept on the deck. Though the ships were seaworthy, many went down in storms. John Cabot, Sir Humphrey Gilbert, and Gaspar Corte-Real were just a few of the explorers lost at sea. Nevertheless, the main danger on long sea voyages was not sinking but the disease scurvy, which is caused by a lack of vitamin C.

The sailing ship increased in size in the 1600s and 1700s, though it changed little in design. Sailing ships hauled fish and furs back to Europe. They brought settlers and supplies to Canada. They also took part in wars. In one famous naval battle, the French adventurer d'Iberville ran into three English warships in James Bay. His single ship, *Pélican*, sank two, captured and sank another, and drove the third away. Nevertheless, the English navy was supreme and this sealed Canada's fate. English ships captured and destroyed Louisbourg in 1758 and then carried British troops to Quebec, which fell in 1759.

Canada's Golden Age of Sail By the mid-19th century, Canada was one of the major seafaring nations of the world. The ports of Halifax, Saint John, Quebec, Montreal, and others were crowded with sailing ships. Canadian ships sailed every ocean and visited every major port.

Between 1786 and 1920, over 4000 large, wooden ships were built in Canada. By 1878, Canada's sailing fleet ranked fourth in the world. Sailing ships were built in numerous locations, on creeks, rivers, and coves all over Canada. Shipyards were set up wherever there was a ready supply of timber, especially pine, which was used for masts.

The first small sailing ships were likely built at Port-Royal in 1606. The first ship built in New France, the *Galiote*, was launched in 1663. The shipyards near

Fishing Ship *off the coast of Newfoundland. The fish were so plentiful that they could be hauled in with baskets (courtesy NAC/92348).*

Battle at Sea, *1813. The British ship HMS Shannon (right) is victorious over the American ship Chesapeake (courtesy NAC/C-41825).*

Marco Polo

The *Marco Polo* was launched in 1851 at Marsh Creek in Saint John, N.B. The ship had a unique design, combining the underwater body of a clipper and the midship of a cargo carrier. It carried timber to England and cotton from Alabama. In 1852, gold was discovered in Australia. The *Marco Polo* was converted to a passenger ship. In July 1852 it set sail for Australia with 930 passengers, making it in a record 76 days. Previous voyages had taken at least 100 days. On its return to Liverpool, England, the *Marco Polo* was hailed "the fastest ship in the world." It continued to make the voyage for 15 years. Finally, weakened and held together by chains, the ship was sold to carry timber and coal. It ran ashore in July 1883 off the coast of P.E.I., and sank a month later (*photo courtesy New Brunswick Museum*).

Quebec City produced numerous vessels, including a large warship for the French navy. In 1677-78, La Salle built four vessels on Lake Ontario, including the *Frontenac*. Later, in 1697, he built the *Griffon* on the Niagara River to carry trade goods on the Upper Great Lakes.

The War of 1812 brought a flurry of shipbuilding. In 1814, HMS *St Lawrence* was launched in Kingston. It carried over 100 cannon and 1000 men. After the war, the demand for ships grew with the timber trade. In 1824 the *Columbus* was built at Quebec City. It was the largest ship in the world at the time, but it only made one trip. It sailed to England and was dismantled for its timber.

Canadian ships were fast and well built and were in demand in other countries. At a time when the exploits of the great "Clipper" ships were famous around the world, the *Marco Polo*, launched in Saint John in 1851, was the fastest ship in the world. The *W.D. Lawrence*, launched in 1874 in Maitland, N.S., was the largest full-rigger ship built in Canada.

Age of Steam Canada also helped pioneer the use of steam power. In 1809, the steam-powered *Accommodation* was launched in Montreal. It carried passengers between Montreal and Quebec City.

The *Royal William* was built near Quebec City in 1831. It was a paddle steamer, but also carried sails. In 1833 it became the first merchant ship to cross the Atlantic Ocean largely under steam.

Despite these promising beginnings, Canada could not compete with others in building iron ships. Nations such as Britain, Germany, and Denmark could produce these ships cheaper and faster. By the mid-1890s, no more large sailing ships were built in Canada. The "golden age of sail" had passed.

Nevertheless, Maritime shipyards continued to build smaller fishing schooners and coasters. The *Bluenose*, launched in Lunenburg, N.S., in 1921, was the foremost racing schooner of its day.

Postage Stamp *celebrating the Tall Ships (courtesy Canada Post Corporation).*

Shipyard *in Lunenburg, N.S., around 1900, with three fishing schooners under construction. The famous* Bluenose *was launched here in 1921 (courtesy NAC/C-8599).*

Shipyards were opened at Collingwood, on Georgian Bay, and at Thunder Bay, on Lake Superior, in order to build ships to travel the Great Lakes. These included passenger ships, such as the *Cayuga* and *Noronic*, as well as long, narrow lake carriers designed to carry wheat and ore through the Great Lakes canals.

World War II created a huge demand for ships, especially during the Battle of the Atlantic. Ships were being sunk by German U-boats almost as fast as they could be replaced. Almost 800 merchant ships and warships were built in Canada during the war.

Since 1945, Canadian shipyards have concentrated on small, specialized ships. Canada has excelled at making vessels that can handle icy waters. These include the ice-breaking ferry *Abegweit*, built to cross the Northumberland Strait to P.E.I. and the large icebreaker *Terry Fox*, launched in 1983.

Canada has also developed oceanographic research ships, offshore drilling platforms, fishing vessels, tugs, dredges, and self-dumping log barges.

Canada also continues to build a small

Halifax Shipyard, *with a modern fishing vessel under construction (photo by Barrett & MacKay/Masterfile).*

number of naval and coast-guard vessels. Twelve new "Tribal Class" destroyers are being built for anti-submarine duties with the Canadian navy. The shipbuilding and ship-repair industries employ about 7500 workers in Canada today.

▷ RELATED ARTICLES: **Bluenose; Ferries; Ice-breakers; Shipping Industry.**

▷ SUGGESTED READING: Peter Carnahan, *Schooner Master: A Portrait of David Stevens* (1989); Esther Clark Wright, *Saint John Ships and their Builders* (1976); Michael Custode, *Ancient Ships on American Shores* (1986); Claude K. Darrach, *Race to Fame: The Inside Story of the Bluenose* (1985); Diane Dutton, *From Sail to Steam: Ships and Shipbuilding in the Regions of Quebec and Montreal* (1982); Skip Gillham, *Ships Along the Seaway* (1986); Keith R. McLaren, *Bluenose and Bluenose II* (1981); Hugh L. Pullen, *Atlantic Schooners* (1967); Nicholas Tracy, *Canadian Shipbuilding and Shipping Business: The State of Scholarship* (1985); Frederick William Wallace, *Wooden Ships and Iron Men* (1937).

■ Shippagan

Shippagan, N.B., lies at the farthest north-eastern point of mainland New Brunswick. Jesuit missionaries arrived here in 1634. They were followed by traders, fishermen, and farmers. Fishing and peat moss are still the main industries. The name comes from a Micmac word, *Sepagunchiche*, which means "passageway for ducks." Shippagan's population was 2801 in 1986.

For further information, contact the Greffier, C.P. 280, Shippagan, N.B., E0B 2P0.

■ Shooting Star

Shooting stars are plants belonging to the genus *Dodecatheon*, of the primrose (Primulaceae) family. The name "dodecatheon," bestowed by Swedish botanist Linnaeus in 1751, means "12 gods" in Greek. The English name is "Indian chief," because the flower looks like a plumed native headdress.

There are 13 species of shooting star native to western North America; one to Siberia. Canada has six species, which may be seen in wet prairie lands, near the ocean, or in the mountains.

The few-flowered shooting star (*D. pulchollum*) is a perennial herb-like plant which flowers in spring and decorates the sides of streams, wet fields, clearings, and salty bogs, from Alaska to Manitoba. Its leaves are arranged in a circle at ground level. From this rose emerges a floral stalk (60 cm high) crowned with a bouquet of three to 25 flowers. The flower has the

unusual shape of a half-opened umbrella. Its five backward-turning petals, of a lovely pinkish purple, form a cone with the stamens.

The broad-leaved shooting star (*D. hendersonii*) of southern British Columbia was used on a five-cent Canadian postage stamp (1978).

Shooting stars come in many cultivated varieties, known for their vigour and floral beauty. The *D. integrifolium*, a native of Colombia, is used as an ornamental flower.

■ Short Story

A short story is a piece of narrative fiction that is short enough to be read at one sitting. It is one of the classical literary genres, along with the play, the novel, and the poem. Because it is brief, the short story usually develops one central idea, and every sentence is crafted to reveal a unifying theme. Edgar Allan Poe, an American short story writer of the 19th century, said: "A short story deals with a single character, a single event, a single emotion, or the series of emotions called forth by a single situation." While a novel contains a chain of situations, the short story is usually limited to one event which is revealed in plot format. The short story often begins very close to the climax.

Because of its development in the 20th century, the short story is said to be a modern art form, but early types of short fiction include the parable, the fable, and the folk tale. Stories passed from generation to generation in the oral tradition are also ancestors of the literary short story.

Early Canadian forms of the short story include the animal stories of Ernest Thompson Seton (*Wild Animals I Have*

HMCS **Fraser** *is a Canadian-built "St Laurent Class" destroyer. A Sea King helicopter, which aids in submarine searches, approaches the deck (Canadian Forces Photo).*

***Shooting Star** (photo by Tim Fitzharris).*

Known, 1898) and Charles G.D. Roberts (*The Kindred of the Wild, 1902*).

Collections of stories connected by setting were introduced by Duncan Campbell Scott's *In the Village of Viger* (1896) and Stephen Leacock's *Sunshine Sketches of a Little Town* (1912).

Of the modern Canadian short story writers, Morley Callaghan was one of the first to explore human moral issues in an urban setting. His stories are collected in *Morley Callaghan's Stories* (1959). Sinclair Ross, Hugh Garner, and W.O. Mitchell are other moral realists. Ethel Wilson's short fiction influenced the work of writers from the late 1940s to the early 1960s, including Margaret Laurence's *The Tomorrow-Tamer and Other Stories* (1963) and Alice Munro's *Dance of the Happy Shades* (1968). The story cycles of Margaret Laurence (*A Bird in the House*, 1963) and Alice Munro (*Who Do You Think You Are?*, 1978) contain short stories unified by recurring characters and settings.

Canada boasts short story writers of international reputation, including Alice Munro and expatriates Mavis Gallant and Clark Blaise. Other writers known mainly for their short stories are Leon Rooke, Hugh Hood, W.P. Kinsella, Ken Mitchell, and Guy Vanderhaeghe.

Recent short story collections include Morley Callaghan's *The Lost and Found Stories of Morley Callaghan* (1985), Alice Munro's *The Progress of Love* (1986), and W.P. Kinsella's *The Fencepost Chronicles* (1987).

▷ RELATED ARTICLES: **Fiction; Novel.**

▷ SUGGESTED READING: Martha Brooks, *Paradise Cafe and Other Stories* (1988); Children's Writers Workshop, *Shivers in Your Nightshirt: Eerie Stories to Read in Bed* (1986).

Water Shrew The water shrew is a secretive mammal. It spends most of its time under the cover of overhanging banks by forest streams. It is seldom seen (artwork by Jan Sovak).

■ Shoyama, Thomas Kunito

Economist, public servant (*born in 1916 at Kamloops, B.C.*). After graduation from the University of British Columbia in 1938, Shoyama worked as a journalist and publisher until 1945. During 1945-46 he worked for the Canadian Army Intelligence Corps, and then he became a research economist for the government of Saskatchewan. In that position, and subsequently as an economic adviser to the government during 1950-64, he helped set up the machinery for the social programs introduced by the Co-operative Commonwealth Federation (CCF) administration of Premier T.C. Douglas. In 1964 he moved to the federal civil service, first as a senior economist with the Economic Council of Canada, and subsequently in other senior positions. He was a member of the Royal Commission on Canada's Economic Prospects, which recommended the adoption of free trade with the United States. Since 1980 he has been a visiting professor at the University of Victoria.

■ Shrew

Shrews are members of the Soricidae family. They are all small and have long, pointed snouts, tiny eyes, and ears that do not project above the fur. Glands on some shrews produce a disgusting odour.

Fourteen species of shrews are found in Canada. They do not occur in the arctic islands. Most eat a variety of invertebrates. A few eat some vegetation, and others prey on small mammals, amphibians, or fish. The pygmy shrew (*Sorex hoyi*) is Canada's smallest mammal. Fully adult pygmy shrew males may weigh not much more than a dime.

Shrews do not hibernate. Because of their small size they lose heat quickly and often must eat their own weight or more in food each day. A shrew may starve to death in less than a day if it cannot eat enough food. Periods of intense feeding and searching activity alternate around the clock with short intervals of deep sleep during which the body temperature drops. Several species have poisonous saliva, which can paralyse prey weighing more than the shrew. Most shrews spend their lives beneath loose vegetation. They are not very good at burrowing.

Shrews typically have one to three litters annually, each with two to ten young. Shrews are generally considered to be beneficial to humans because they eat so many insects.

▷ RELATED ARTICLE: **Mammals.**

▷ Suggested Reading: Gun Bjork, *Shrews* (1977); Aileen Fisher, *Valley of the Smallest: The Life Story of a Shrew* (1966).

■ Shrike

Two species of shrike nest in Canada: the Loggerhead Shrike (*Lanius ludovicianus*) and the Northern Shrike (*L. excubitor*). They are black, grey, and white birds with a black mask around the eyes and a hooked black bill with a tooth-shaped notch in it (like a falcon's bill).

The shrike inhabits open or shrubby sites where there are trees and fenceposts. It has superb eyesight and only hunts by day. It lives on insects, small mammals, and small birds. The shrike usually impales its prey on a sharp tree branch or barbed wire, and then eats it at leisure. The Northern Shrike winters in southern Canada. The Loggerhead Shrike winters in the central and southern United States.

▷ Suggested Reading: Arthur Cleveland Bent, *Life Histories of North American Wagtails, Shrikes, Vireos and Their Allies* (1965).

■ Shrimp

Shrimp are crustaceans. Their well-developed legs, called *pleopods*, make them excellent swimmers and burrowers. More than 100 species are known to exist in Canadian waters, 85 of them in the Pacific. The northern pink shrimp (*Pandalus borealis*), one of the most widely fished, is found in both the northern Atlantic and Pacific. It is pink or light red and can reach 16 cm in length, the size depending on the water depth (larger ones are in deeper waters).

Shrimp live on soft, muddy bottoms. Northern pink shrimp migrate from one area of the sea to another and from deeper to shallower water. Shrimp spend the day on the ocean bottom where they eat small worms and tiny crustaceans. At night many move upwards to eat small swimming crustaceans, returning to the ocean bottom in the morning. Some species, including the northern pink shrimp, begin life as males and become females as they grow older. Reproduction occurs in summer and fall, with the eggs remaining attached to the female's abdomen all winter. An average-sized female shrimp carries over 2000 eggs.

▷ Related Article: **Crustaceans.**
▷ Suggested Reading: T.H. Butler, *Shrimps of the Pacific Coast of Canada* (1980).

■ Siamon, Sharon

Writer and editor (*born in 1942 at Saskatoon, Sask.*). Siamon is one of author Max Braithwaite's children. After receiving an English degree from the University of Toronto, she travelled in Europe and East Africa — where she taught English and history in the king of Uganda's palace school. She lives in Toronto. Her writing for children includes short stories and about 12 family and mystery-adventure novels, including *Amy Made Hats* (1979), *The Girl Who Hated Dinner* (1979), *A Puli Named Sandor* (1981), *Fishing For Trouble* (1987), and *A House for Josie* (1988).

■ Siberry, Jane

Singer and songwriter (*born in 1955 at Toronto, Ont.*). Siberry worked as a waitress while establishing her singing career in Toronto. She released her first album, *Jane Siberry*, in 1981. Her two albums, *The Speckless Sky* (1985) and *The Walking* (1987), sold over 100 000 copies each and helped to establish her reputation abroad. Her most recent album is *Bound by the Beauty* (1989), which includes the single "Everything Reminds me of my Dog." Siberry is known for her unique style and impressive stage performances.

■ Sidney

Sidney, B.C., is on the Saanich Peninsula on the east coast of Vancouver Island, 30 km north of Victoria. It is named for an officer in the Royal Navy. Farm settlement began in 1873 and the growth of agriculture and the subsequent need for better transportation prompted the inauguration in 1895 of the Victoria and Sidney Railway. The town is the business hub of the Northern Peninsula. Main occupations include boat building, ocean sciences, and commercial fishing. Ferries from the United States and from the British Columbia mainland arrive nearby. Sidney's population in 1986 was 8982.

For further information, contact the Town Clerk, 2440 Sidney Avenue, Sidney B.C., V8L 1Y7.

Breeding Range of Northern Shrike Loggerhead Shrike

Northern Shrike winters in southern Canada (courtesy Macmillan Illustrated Animal Encyclopedia).

Jane Siberry (courtesy Duke Street Records/ photo by George Whiteside).

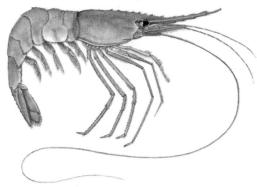

Northern Pink Shrimp is one of the most widely fished species (artwork by Kendal Morris).

Arthur Sifton was one of the men who helped create the province of Alberta (courtesy Glenbow Archives).

■ Sifton, Arthur Lewis

Premier of Alberta (*born in 1858 at St Johns, Canada West [Ont.]; died in 1921 at Ottawa, Ont.*). Arthur Sifton not only served as premier of Alberta (1910-17), but he was one of the men who helped create Alberta in the first place. Like his brother Clifford Sifton, he had a major impact on life in the West.

During the early 1880s, Arthur practised law with Clifford in Brandon, Man. In 1885 he moved to the western prairies, which were then part of the region called the North-West Territories. He was elected to the legislative assembly of the North-West Territories in 1899, and over the next few years he worked hard to get Alberta and Saskatchewan made into provinces. By the time this was achieved in 1905, Arthur Sifton had been made a judge, and in 1907 he became the first chief justice of Alberta. In 1910 he resigned from the position to become Liberal premier of Alberta.

During Sifton's premiership, women made important gains in Alberta. In 1916 they were given the vote, and two women — Emily Murphy and Alice Jamieson — were made magistrates, the first female magistrates in the British Empire. In 1917 Sifton moved to federal politics, serving in the Union government of Prime Minister Robert Borden. He was secretary of state and minister of public works from 1919 to 1921. He was one of two Canadians to sign the Treaty of Versailles on behalf of Canada in 1919.

■ Sifton, Sir Clifford

Politician (*born in 1861 near Arva, Canada West [Ont.]; died in 1929 at New York City, U.S.*). It was largely because of Clifford Sifton that western Canada was settled by people from Ukraine, Poland, Germany, and many other European countries. His immigration program brought Europeans flocking to the prairies.

Sifton had moved West in 1875. In the early 1880s, he practised law in Brandon, Man., with his brother Arthur, and from 1888 to 1896 he was a member of the Manitoba legislature. He served as a Liberal cabinet minister in the legislature 1891-96.

Moving to federal politics in 1896, Sifton was appointed minister of the interior in Prime Minister Laurier's government. As such, he was in charge of Canada's immigration policy. At the time, English-speaking people were the most favoured immigrants, since Canadians of

Clifford Sifton launched a vigorous campaign to bring immigrants to settle the western prairie (courtesy NAC/PA-27943).

British origin wanted Canada to be overwhelmingly British. But Sifton believed that farming people from eastern and central Europe would make excellent homesteaders.

Besides seeking settlers in Britain and the United States, Sifton launched a vigorous program to attract farmers from continental Europe. Begun in 1896-97, this program was so well organized and so successful that it continued long after Sifton left politics.

Sifton resigned his Cabinet post in 1905, since he was strongly against some of Laurier's policies. Having broken with the Liberal party, he retired from Parliament altogether in 1911. He was knighted in 1915 and continued to play a powerful role in public affairs, especially through his newspaper; since 1898 he had been owner of the *Manitoba Free Press*.

▷ SUGGESTED READING: D.J. Hall, *Clifford Sifton* (1976); Jan Truss, *The Judgement of Clifford Sifton* (1979).

■ Signal Hill

The mighty rock named Signal Hill guards the northern shore of the narrow entrance to the harbour at St John's, Nfld. The harbour was used by fishermen by the 1500s, and signal flags and guns were mounted on the hill from early times. A signal house built on the hill in 1796 used a complicated series of flags to guide ships and warn them of danger.

Britain began to fortify Signal Hill in the early 1800s during the Napoleonic Wars. By the 1840s forts, barracks, and gun batteries defended the town, but it was never attacked. In 1897-1900 the Cabot Tower was built, and in 1901 Guglielmo Marconi received the first transatlantic radio signal on the hill. Always popular for tourists and citizens to visit, Signal Hill became a National Historic Park in 1958.

Signal Hill lies at the entrance to the harbour of St John's (photo by Lorraine Parrow/First Light).

Sikhs

Sikhs are a cultural and religious group from the Punjab in northern India. Since the early 1900s, many have made their home in Canada. It is estimated that there are about 130 000 Sikhs in Canada.

The name Sikh comes from a word meaning disciple or follower. Sikhs are followers of Guru Nanak, who founded the Sikh faith in the 16th century. Sikh men all have the name Singh, meaning lion, and most observe the "five K's" of their religion:

● *kes*, to keep their hair uncut and their beards unshaven,

● *kangha*, to wear a comb, a reminder that they must live clean lives,

● *kara*, to wear a steel bracelet on the right wrist, a sign of humility,

● *kuchha*, to wear a pair of short pants, a soldier's clothing,

● *kirpan*, to carry a dagger or sabre, a sign that they are spiritual soldiers.

The emphasis on being a soldier is a result of the experience of Sikhs in the Punjab. They were surrounded by people of other religions who were likely to attack them. Thus, although they were farmers, they also had to be warriors. Over the centuries, they kept up the warrior tradition. The Sikh regiments of the Indian army were among the most respected in the days of the British Empire. Their uniform incorporated the five K's, along with the traditional turban.

In Canada, some Sikh men, especially those born in Canada, have cut their hair and shaved their beards. Others observe the five K's and wear the turban, even though the rest of their clothing may be western in style. Canadian Sikhs also keep up traditions such as taking care of the needy. Above all, Sikhs keep up the religious observances, with daily prayers in the home and with Sunday services in a Sikh temple. Most of the larger Canadian cities have at least one temple.

Some Canadian Sikhs have been involved in a movement to form an independent Sikh state in northern India. A few have taken to violence to achieve this aim. But the great majority of Sikhs in Canada live peaceably, working in a wide variety of jobs.

▷ RELATED ARTICLE: **South Asians.**

▷ SUGGESTED READING: Mohinder Singh, *Basics of Sikhism* (1989).

Silver

Silver is a white, lustrous metal. The familiar tarnishing occurs because the metal reacts with hydrogen sulphide present in the air. Silver has many useful properties. It is highly malleable, so it is used in dental fillings, jewellery, and by artists. Silver conducts heat and electricity more easily than any other metal. This makes it very useful in electrical and electronics industries. Automobile manufacturers, for instance, use it in heated window shields. Silver crystals are sensitive to light, so silver is used extensively in photography. Silver is also used in coins.

Silver is rarely found in its pure state. It is present in ore bodies, particularly with other metals. It must, therefore, be extracted from the ore by refining and smelting processes.

The area around Cobalt, Ont., was the site of a silver rush in the early 20th century. In 1903 two railway workers, while looking for lumber along the shores of Long Lake, found silver. A larger find was made by a blacksmith not long after, on the north shore of the lake. This find led to the development of the mining town of Cobalt. Today, Ontario is the largest producer of silver in Canada followed by B.C., New Brunswick, and Quebec. In 1987, $424 million worth of silver was mined in Canada.

Silver was valued highly by early French colonists, who brought it with them from France. They kept their worn-out silver coins and objects, melted them down, and made new items. As a result, apart from church pieces, little silver from early times survives today.

Church Silver Because they believed that precious metals honoured God, colonists supplied their churches with silver objects as soon as they could afford to. At first the silver objects came from France. The Huron Indians of Lorette, Que., have a silver monstrance that was brought to Canada in 1664.

About 1700, when New France was

Sikh Kirpan (photo by Chris Buck).

Mool Mantra

The basic belief of the Sikhs is given in the *Mool Mantra*:

There is One God
He is the supreme truth.
He, The Creator,
Is without fear and without hate.
He, The Omnipresent,
Pervades the universe.
He is not born,
Nor does He die to be born again.
By his grace shalt thou worship Him.

Before time itself
There was a truth.
When time began to run its course
He was the truth.
Even now, He is the truth
And
Evermore shall truth prevail.

Characteristics of Silver

Formula: Ag
Appearance: a brilliant white, lustrous metal
Properties: a melting point of 962°C; highest electrical and heat conductivity of all metals; very malleable
Atomic Weight: 107.870
Uses: in photographic films and papers, electrical products, silverware, jewellery, ornaments, silver plating, brazing and soldering, alloys, and mirrors

Sikh "Ceremony of Bliss" weds the couple in the presence of the Guru (courtesy Provincial Museum of Alberta).

Silver Monstrance *A monstrance is used to display the Host in a small glass container surrounded by rays (courtesy Royal Ontario Museum).*

Silver *teapot, sugar bowl, and creamer (courtesy NGC).*

The Silver Dart *was the first airplane to fly in Canada. The wingspan was 14.9 m; the weight (including pilot), 390 kg (courtesy Library of Congress).*

well established, French silversmiths started to come to the colony. They taught their skills to Canadian apprentices. At first, Canadian silversmiths copied French models, but they soon developed their own, simpler styles. The greatest early Canadian silversmith was Quebec City's François Ranvoyzé.

Domestic and Trade Silver Wealthy settlers had silver cups, spoons, forks, ladles, and other tableware, which might be plain, decorated with simple patterns, or engraved with the owner's initials or coat of arms. Objects might also be stamped with a symbol or initials — the silversmith's "signature."

Most of Canada's early silver jewellery was made for Indians. During the colonial wars, gifts of silver were given to celebrate military alliances. Brooches, bracelets, and other ornaments were traded for furs. The Hudson's Bay Company stopped using Indian trade silver in 1821.

In the 1850s, the process of electroplating was invented. This meant that less silver was needed, because silver was used only to coat objects made of cheaper metals. Many more people could afford "silverplate" than "sterling" silver (which is 92.5% silver, 7.5% copper). Mass production became profitable.

Hendery and Leslie of Montreal was responsible for much of the Canadian silver manufactured from 1850 to 1899. In 1899 the company was taken over by Henry Birks and Sons. Birks became Canada's most important silver seller and silversmith. It produced tableware and tea services, as well as special presentation pieces. The most famous of these is the Grey Cup (1909).

Silver tableware is not as popular now as it once was. Many people prefer stainless steel tableware, which does not require cleaning.

▷ SUGGESTED READING: Doug Baldwin, *Cobalt: A Pictorial History of the Development of Silver Mining* (1978); Mike Macbeth, *Silver Threads Among the Gold: The Rags to Riches Saga of a Man and his Mines* (1987).

■ Silver Dart

The *Silver Dart* was the first airplane to fly in Canada and in the British Empire. It was designed and piloted by J.A.D. McCurdy and was powered by a 40 horsepower engine built by American engineer Glenn Curtiss.

The *Silver Dart's* historic flight took place on February 23, 1909, over the frozen Bras d'Or Lake at Baddeck Bay on Cape Breton Island, N.S. The plane was towed onto the ice by a one-horse sleigh, and the propeller was turned by hand to start the engine. McCurdy then flew the plane about a kilometre at a maximum speed of 65 km per hour and a height of 9 m, before making a perfect landing. He later flew this silver-winged "heavier-than-air-machine" more than 200 times. But he damaged it beyond repair when landing on soft sand in August, 1909.

The *Silver Dart* was one of the world's earliest planes. Only six years had passed since the Americans, Wilbur and Orville Wright, had made their first flight. Only one year had passed since Casey Baldwin, piloting the *Red Wing* at Hammondsport, U.S. became the first Canadian to fly a plane and the seventh person in the world to do so. Like McCurdy and Curtiss, Baldwin was a member of the Aerial Experiment Association, a group of enthusiasts recruited by Alexander Graham Bell to build flying machines.

A full-scale model of the *Silver Dart* can be seen at the National Aviation Museum, Ottawa.

▷ RELATED ARTICLES: **Aviation; Alexander Graham Bell; J.A.D. McCurdy.**

▷ SUGGESTED READING: John Melady, *Pilots: Canadian Stories From the Cockpit From First Flight to the Jet Age* (1989).

■ Silver Islet

Silver Islet is a small island of rock at the west end of Lake Superior, across the harbour from Thunder Bay, Ont. Between 1869 and 1884 it was one of the richest silver mines in the world. The buildings and mine are now in ruins. More than $3 million worth of silver was mined before the ore ran out.

■ Silverheels, Jay

Actor (*born Harold Jay Smith in 1919 on the Six Nations Indian Reserve, Ont.; died in 1980 at Woodland Hills, California, U.S.*). Silverheels is best known for his role as Tonto on the "Lone Ranger" series, both the films (1956, 1958) and the television series (1949-57). He was a great athlete as a youth and enjoyed sports all his life. In 1938 he was "discovered" and went to Hollywood. Starting as an extra (an actor in crowd scenes), he became a star in more than 30 films, including *Broken Arrow* (1950) and *The Man Who Loved Cat Dancing* (1973). Silverheels helped many young actors, and in 1963 founded the Indian Actors Workshop in Hollywood.

■ Simard, René

Singer (*born in 1961 at Chicoutimi, Que.*). Simard was the most popular child-star in the history of Canadian popular music. He won his first major talent show at the age of nine, released his debut single the following year, and quickly outsold the Beatles and Elvis Presley in Quebec. In the mid-1970s he performed in films and was the host of "The René Simard Show" on CBC television. He has continued to perform into the 1990s.

■ Simcoe

Simcoe, Ont., is a town located in southwestern Ontario, 10 km north of Lake Erie. Named for John Graves Simcoe, the first governor of Upper Canada [Ontario], it was founded by Aaron Culver in 1795. The Great Western Railway reached Simcoe in 1872. Incorporated as a town in 1888, Simcoe is now a business centre for the surrounding tobacco-growing region. Simcoe's population in 1986 was 14 290.

For further information, contact the Town Clerk, 50 Colborne Street South, P.O. Box 545, Simcoe, Ont., N3Y 4N5.

■ Simcoe, Elizabeth Posthuma

Diarist (*baptized Elizabeth Gwillim in 1762 at Aldwinkle, England; died in 1850 at Devon, England*). She was given her second name because she was a *posthumous* baby (born after her father's death)

and was only a few hours old when her mother died. Brought up by an aunt, she married John Graves Simcoe in 1782 and accompanied him to Upper Canada ten years later, on his appointment as lieutenant-governor.

In Upper Canada, Elizabeth Simcoe sketched the scenery and kept a diary, which gives a fascinating picture of day-to-day life in the newly formed colony. There were few settlers at first and not many houses: the Simcoes lived part of their time in a tent. "We have a very large bower, composed of oak boughs, in which we dine, it being greatly cooler than the tent," she wrote the first summer. In winter she was bitterly cold, in summer far too hot; and she lived in constant fear of the many rattlesnakes. Yet she played the role of "governor's lady," even holding formal balls.

▷ SUGGESTED READING: Mary Beacock Fryer, *Elizabeth Simcoe 1762-1850: A Biography* (1989); Mary Quayle Innis, editor, *Mrs Simcoe's Diary* (1965).

■ Simcoe, John Graves

First lieutenant-governor of Upper Canada (*born in 1752 at Cotterstock, England; died in 1806 at Exeter, England*). Simcoe joined the British army as a young man. He first came to North America during the American Revolution. In 1777 he took command of a Loyalist regiment, the Queen's Rangers, and soon proved himself to be one of the best commanders in the British army. Wounded three times, he was sent home sick in 1781.

In 1791 Simcoe was appointed lieutenant-governor of Upper Canada [Ontario]. He arrived in June 1792 after wintering at Quebec. He governed Upper Canada until 1796. This was a daunting task, for in all Upper Canada there were barely 10 000 settlers. They were mainly recently arrived Loyalists. Most of them lived in the eastern part of the colony along the lakes and rivers that served as highways. Simcoe established his first capital city at the small settlement of Newark [Niagara-on-the-Lake]. But this was dangerously near the American border. Simcoe would have preferred to establish his capital at what he called New London, on the Thames River, but he lacked the resources at that time. Meanwhile, in 1793, he began to build a temporary capital, York, on the northwest shore of Lake Ontario. This was the beginning of today's Toronto.

To get the country settled quickly, Simcoe gave large grants of land to promi-

Portrait *of Elizabeth Simcoe, 1799 (courtesy NAC/C-81931).*

A Loyal British Town

"There was to be one Church, one university to guard the constitution ... there at every street corner was to be a sentry, there the very stones were to sing, 'God Save the King.'"

John Graves Simcoe describing York (later Toronto)

nent Loyalists and to anyone else who promised to organize settlement. He also advertised for settlers in the United States. So many Americans took up his offer that by 1812 about 60% of the population were American-born non-Loyalists. Meanwhile, Simcoe had roads cut through the forest. A major route was Yonge Street, which was begun in 1793 and ran from York to Lake Simcoe by 1796.

Simcoe later went on to be governor of Santo Domingo in the Caribbean (1797).

▷ RELATED ARTICLES: **Loyalists; Toronto; Upper Canada.**

■ Siminovitch, Louis

Scientist and professor (*born in 1920 at Montreal, Que.*). Siminovitch is a leading world figure in medical genetics and molecular biology. His research studies have added much to the understanding of genes and have had great impact on cancer research. He is regarded by many as Canada's chief biologist. He has encouraged and promoted numerous younger Canadian researchers as well as making his own outstanding contributions as a medical scientist.

In 1947, as a young graduate from McGill University, Siminovitch won a fellowship to the Institut Pasteur in France. There he did important new research on bacterial viruses. He returned to Canada in 1953 and he worked in Toronto. There in 1966 he was appointed professor of medical genetics at the University of Toronto. From 1970 to 1985, he was also geneticist-in-chief at the Hospi-

tal for Sick Children, where he and his team did research into hereditary conditions, such as muscular dystrophy. Since 1983, he has been director of one of Canada's leading multi-disciplinary research centres, the Research Institute at Mount Sinai Hospital in Toronto.

■ Simmie, Lois

Author and poet (*born in 1932 at Edam, Sask.*) Simmie grew up in Mervin and Livelong, Sask. Her writing career began when she was in her late thirties. She published two collections of short stories and a novel before she began writing for children. A visit to an aunt who was knitting a bonnet for an expected grandchild led to Simmie's writing some "Auntie" poems, which eventually became two collections, *Auntie's Knitting a Baby* (1984) and *An Armadillo is Not a Pillow* (1986). The poems are about the funny, sad, scary, and ordinary things of childhood. *What Holds Up the Moon?* (1988) is a picture book based on a single long poem. It features Roberta Muldoon, a little girl seeking the answer to the title's question. She gets different answers from everyone she asks.

■ Simon Fraser University

Simon Fraser University is located in Burnaby, B.C. It offers over 60 programs through the faculties of arts, business administration, education, applied sciences, and science. It also offers co-operative education programs and correspondence courses. Graduate courses are offered at the master's and doctoral levels. SFU was founded in 1963. Its main campus, designed by architects Arthur Erickson and Geoffrey Massey, is a spectacular site on top of Burnaby Mountain. A satellite campus is located in downtown Vancouver. There are about 6300 full-time undergraduate and graduate students. For further information, write the Registrar's Office, Simon Fraser University, Burnaby, B.C., V5A 1S6.

■ Simonds, Guy Granville

Army officer (*born in 1903 at Bury St Edmunds, England; died in 1974 at Toronto, Ont.*). Guy Simonds was a graduate of the Royal Military College in Kingston, Ont. In April 1943, when he was almost 40 years old, he became Canada's youngest general. This was during World War II, in which Simonds held a series of senior appointments and served in North Africa, Italy, and northwestern Europe. In October-November 1944, he led the First Canadian Army at the Battle of the

General Guy Simonds taking the salute of the Canadian soldiers in Germany, May 31, 1945 (courtesy NAC/PA-159557).

Scheldt. He had been given command of the army while General Crerar was sick. The Battle of the Scheldt was a bitterly tough campaign, in which the Canadians captured the strategically important Scheldt estuary between Antwerp, Belgium, and the sea. Simonds received much praise for his tactics and leadership in this victory. After the war he was appointed commandant of Canada's National Defence College (1949-51) and chief of general staff (1951-55).

■ Simoneau, Léopold

Tenor, teacher (*born in 1918 near Quebec City, Que.*). Simoneau was widely recognized as the best Mozart tenor of his time, but he sang other areas of opera as well. He made his debut in 1941 and first sang in a Mozart opera in 1943. He often sang with his wife Pierrette Alarie, who was a soprano. His beautiful voice, with its clear, precise tone, has been preserved in several recordings, notably in *Cosi fan tutte*, with Herbert von Karajan conducting. He and his wife have taught singing extensively in Canada.

■ Simpson, Sir George

Governor of the Hudson's Bay Company (*born about 1787 at Lochbroom, Scotland; died in 1860 at Lachine, Canada East [Que.]*). From 1821 to his death he was the most important figure in the Canadian fur trade.

Early Life There was nothing in Simpson's humble beginnings to indicate that he would become one of Canada's business leaders. Born illegitimate in northern Scotland, he was raised by relatives and went to London as a boy to work in his uncle's sugar business. There he impressed one of the leading partners in the Hudson's Bay Company (HBC) and in 1820 he came out to Canada as deputy governor-in-chief of the company.

Simpson arrived in Rupert's Land at the end of the great competition between the HBC and the North West Company. When the two rivals merged in 1821, he was put in charge of the trade in most of the Northwest. A tireless worker and a skilled diplomat, Simpson was successful in convincing rival traders to work peaceably together in the new company. In 1826 he was named governor of all the HBC territories in Canada.

"The Little Emperor" Since the HBC controlled all of Rupert's Land, Simpson was virtual dictator of the country. His word was law in the fur trade and he earned the nickname "Little Emperor."

He travelled across the West in a large canoe paddled by a crack team of the best voyageurs, and he prided himself on the great distances he covered each day.

The governor was an efficient, even ruthless, administrator. He reorganized the transportation network and drove many of the company's rivals from the field. He also cut costs by laying off traders, lowering wages, and dealing strictly with the Indians. People who crossed him usually found themselves sent to remote, unattractive posts, if they had a job at all. But his efforts resulted in a period of great success for the HBC. In 1841 he was knighted by Queen Victoria.

Simpson had several native mistresses, and at least six illegitimate children. Simpson paid for the support of these children, but took no responsibility for raising them. In 1830 he married his cousin, Frances, who came to live with him at Red River. From 1833 he made his headquarters at Lachine, near Montreal, where he entertained royalty, business people, and politicians. Frances, suffering from ill health, did not like life in Canada and spent much of her time in England.

Later in his life, Simpson expanded his business activities by investing in banks, railways, and shipping projects. His death marked the passing of the fur-trade era. Farm settlers and railway builders were preparing to move into the West and no other fur trader ever enjoyed the same power that Sir George had wielded.

▷ RELATED ARTICLES: **Fur Trade; Hudson's Bay Company.**

▷ SUGGESTED READING: Keith Wilson, *George Simpson and the Hudson's Bay Company* (1977).

■ Simpson, Thomas

Explorer (*born in 1808 in Scotland; died in 1840 south of the Red River Colony*). Educated as a clergyman, he was given a job as a fur trader by his cousin, George Simpson, governor of the Hudson's Bay Company. Between 1837 and 1840 Thomas took part in three boat expedi-

Sir George Simpson's Canoe, *painting by William Armstrong. Simpson travelled across the West in a canoe paddled by a team of the best voyageurs (courtesy Royal Ontario Museum).*

Sir George Simpson *(artwork by Irma Coucill).*

tions to survey the then-unknown Arctic coast of America.

A vain, moody person, he was mysteriously shot while on his way to England to get support for another expedition.

■ Sinclair, Gordon Allan

Journalist and broadcaster (*born in 1900 at Toronto, Ont.; died there in 1984*). Sinclair began work as a journalist with the *Toronto Star* in 1922. During the Depression of the 1930s he travelled through India, China, and Africa reporting on these distant and largely unknown countries. He also wrote several books based on his experiences. On June 6, 1944, he gave his first radio broadcast over CFRB in Toronto, when he was invited to break the news of the D-Day invasion. Before long he had his own radio program on the station, so he resigned from the newspaper. In 1957 he became a regular panellist on the popular and long-lasting Canadian Broadcasting Corporation show "Front Page Challenge," where he won a following for his crusty, forthright manner. In later life he wrote two autobiographies, *Will the Real Gordon Sinclair Please Stand Up* (1966) and *Will Gordon Sinclair Please Sit Down* (1975).

▷ SUGGESTED READING: Scott Young, *Gordon Sinclair: A Life and Then Some* (1987).

■ Sir George Williams University, *see* Concordia University

■ Sissons, John Howard

Judge (*born in 1892 at Orillia, Ont.; died in 1969 at Edmonton, Alta*). Sissons was the first person to serve as judge of the Territorial Court of the Northwest Territories when the court was established in 1955. He had previously been a judge in Alberta. The Inuit called him Ekoktoegee, which means "the one who listens to things." Sissons always took great trouble to understand the native viewpoint. He was determined to administer justice in a way that all would find fair, taking into account native customs as well as Canadian law. This was especially important, for many of the Inuit were still living according to their age-old traditions and knew little of Canadian ways farther south.

Twice each year, Sissons travelled a circuit by aircraft and dog sled so that he could hold court in remote Arctic communities (though his "court" might be an igloo or the cabin of his plane). He retired in 1966 and then wrote up his experiences in the book *Judge of the Far North* (1968).

Judge John Sissons *(courtesy N.W.T. Archives).*

▷ SUGGESTED READING: Jack Sissons, *Judge of the Far North: The Memoirs of Jack Sissons* (1968).

■ Sitting Bull

Sioux chief (*born about 1834 in Dakota Territory, U.S.; died in 1890 at Standing Rock, North Dakota, U.S.*). Between 1877 and 1881, Sitting Bull and some 5000 Sioux camped on the Canadian prairies, having fled across the border after defeating Colonel Custer's force at the Battle of Little Bighorn (1876). The battle was the climax of Sioux efforts to protect their territory from incoming settlers and gold miners. Although the Sioux had signed a treaty with the U.S. government in 1868, the terms were disregarded when rumours of gold brought fortune hunters thronging to their lands. This led to fierce warfare between the Sioux and the U.S. army.

Sitting Bull knew he was safe from American attack in Canada. Major James Walsh of the North-West Mounted Police personally assured the chief that the Mounties would protect him, provided he and his followers behaved peacefully. But the Canadian government did not want the Sioux as permanent residents, for their presence could cause political problems with the United States. The Blackfoot and other prairie people also hoped the Sioux would leave, for there were not enough bison left to feed everyone.

Persuaded to return to the United

Sitting Bull, chief of the Sioux Indians (courtesy NAC/PA-39334).

States in 1881, Sitting Bull agreed to tour for a while with Buffalo Bill's Wild West Show. He was a major attraction because of his fearsome reputation as the chief whose men had cut down Custer and the 7th Cavalry at Little Bighorn. He died in an exchange of gunfire when soldiers and Indian police, still nervous of his influence, tried to arrest him on his reserve at Standing Rock.

▷ RELATED ARTICLE: **James M. Walsh.**

▷ SUGGESTED READING: Terry Leeder, *White Forehead of the Cypress Hills* (1979); C.R. Stein, *The Story of the Little Bighorn* (1983).

■ Skate, *see* Ray

■ Skating, *see* Ice Skating; Speed Skating

■ Skeena River

The Skeena River, 579 km long, is the second-largest river entirely in British Columbia. It begins in the mountainous northwest interior of the province and flows into the Pacific Ocean near Prince Rupert. An important waterway for Indian people, it is the homeland of the Tsimshian and Gitskan.

Skeena River, in the Hazelton Mountains of B.C. (photo by Tom W. Parkin/Pathfinder).

Fur traders were active in the Upper Skeena in the 19th century, followed by gold prospectors. The salmon fishery was flourishing by the 1890s and several canneries were built near the river mouth. Fishing and logging continue to be important. The river valley provides a major highway and rail link between the interior and the Pacific coast.

■ Skelton, Oscar Douglas

Scholar and public servant (*born in 1878 at Orangeville, Ont.; died in 1941 at Ottawa, Ont.*). After studying at Queen's University and the University of Chicago, he was a professor of political economy at Queen's from 1909 to 1925. During that time, he wrote a book on socialism, and biographies of Alexander

Tilloch Galt and Wilfrid Laurier. In 1925 Prime Minister King asked him to join the public service as undersecretary of state for external affairs. Skelton became one of the most powerful officials in the government, advising the prime minister on domestic affairs as well as on foreign policy. He is considered the founder of the modern Department of External Affairs, and one of the most able public servants Canada has known.

■ Ski Jumping, *see* Skiing

■ Skiing

Skiing is the sport of gliding across snow on skis. There are two main types of skiing: alpine and nordic. Alpine skiing is racing down the slopes of mountains or hills. Downhill racing takes place on steep courses, and the test is one of speed and nerves. Slalom also takes place on an alpine course, but it includes many more gates, and therefore tests the skiers' ability to turn and control the skis.

Nordic skiing includes cross-country skiing and ski jumping. Nordic skiing began about 5000 years ago in Scandinavia as a form of travel in winter. Ski jumping likely began with a few daredevil skiers. Freestyle skiing is the most recent form of skiing. It includes aerials, ballet, and moguls (skiing over bumps). The first skier to flip in mid-air was reported about 80 years ago, but it only became an organized sport in the 1950s.

Skiing in Canada Skiing was brought to Canada by Scandinavians in the mid-19th century. Many early skiers were gold miners and lumbermen in British Columbia. Ski jumping was so thrilling to watch that it quickly became a popular spectator sport. The first ski-jumping club in Canada was formed at Revelstoke, B.C.

Alpine skiing began in Canada when some members of Canada's snowshoeing clubs put on skis. They were ridiculed at first, but the new sport was exciting and soon became popular. In a few years, skiers packed open hills near Canadian

Anne Heggtveit

(born in Ottawa in 1939). She started skiing at age two and at age 15 won a giant slalom race in Norway. She won Canada's first Olympic gold medal in skiing in 1960.

Pierre Harvey

(born in Rimouski, Que. in 1957). He began competing as a swimmer and was a champion cyclist before taking up cross-country skiing. He has become Canada's top cross-country skier. He has won all four gold medals at the Canadian championship twice.

He was the first Canadian to win a World Cup cross-country ski race.

Cross-country Skier
Pierre Harvey at the 1988 Winter Olympic Games (courtesy Athlete Information Bureau/ Canadian Olympic Association).

"Jackrabbit" Johannsen at age 90 (courtesy Canadian Ski Museum).

cities. They packed snow by climbing the hills sideways in the morning and spent the rest of the day practising. New clubs sprang up. In 1917 Canada's first ski resort opened in Ste-Marguerite, Que. In 1932 Alex Foster jacked up his car and used it to run the world's first rope tow.

Better and safer equipment, tows and chair lifts greatly increased the popularity of alpine skiing. Today, 2 million Canadians take part in alpine skiing. There are about 650 resorts in the mountains of Alberta and B.C., the Laurentians and Gatineau hills of Quebec, and near Collingwood, Ont.

Cross-country skiing also increased in popularity when new equipment, especially toe plates, allowed the skier to go faster. Simple waxes helped the skis to grip the snow. "Jackrabbit" Johannsen, who was born in Norway, blazed many new ski trails in the Laurentian Mountains of Quebec. Today, some four million Canadians take part in the sport.

Canadian Ski Champions Skiing competition began in Revelstoke, B.C., with the ski jump. Nearby Rossland had an in-

ternational carnival of skiing which attracted thousands of spectators. They came to watch local hero Olaus Jeldness win the ski jump. New world records were set by Canadians for the length of jumps by Nels Nelson in 1925 and Bob Lymbourne in 1933. More recently, Horst Bulau (1979) and Steve Collins (1980) won the junior world championship in jumping.

Canadians had little success competing in alpine skiing until 1958. In that year, Lucile Wheeler unexpectedly won the world championship in downhill and slalom.

Anne Heggtveit won Canada's first Olympic gold medal in skiing in 1960. Nancy Greene won the world championship in 1967 and a gold medal in the 1968 Olympics. In the mid-1970s Canadian men skiers burst onto the world scene. Concentrating on downhill skiing, the fastest and most exciting event, Ken Read, Steve Podborski, Dave Irwin, and Dave Murray earned the nickname "Crazy Canucks" for their aggressive attacks on European courses. They won 14 World Cup races, and in 1982 Podborski won the downhill World Cup trophy, the first North American to do so. In 1988 Karen Percy won two bronze medals at the Calgary Olympics.

Downhill skiing is a dangerous sport

Freestyle skiing at Olympic Park, Calgary (photo by Rick Rudnicki/Take Stock Inc.).

Steve Podborski on a downhill ski run. He was the World Cup champion in 1982 (courtesy Canapress Photo Service).

and many Canadians have been injured. In 1989, Brian Stemml suffered serious injuries after a spectacular fall at a course in Austria.

Canadian success has been slower to come in cross-country skiing. However, Canadians have been leaders in the younger sport of freestyle skiing. Marie-Claude Asselin won the women's aerial World Cup in 1981, 1982, and 1983. She also won the women's combined World Cup in 1981 and 1982.

▷ Related Articles: **Nancy Greene; Steve Podborski.**

▷ Suggested Reading: Edward R. Baldwin, *The Cross-Country Skiing Handbook* (1983); Erwin A. Bauer, *Cross-Country Skiing and Snowshoeing* (1975); Michael Keating, *Cross Country Canada* (1977); Steve Podborski, *The Skier's Sourcebook* (1988).

■ Skinners Pond

Skinners Pond, P.E.I., is situated on the west coast of the island, 165 km northwest of Charlottetown. It was first settled by Acadians, who were joined by Irish immigrants in the mid-1800s. Fishing is the main activity, along with collecting Irish moss. Country singer "Stompin'" Tom Connors is the most famous native son. Its population in 1986 was 119.

■ Skunk

Skunks are members of the Mustelidae family. These cat-sized mammals are easily recognized by their bushy tails and the white stripes or spots on a black background. They are best known for their method of self-defence. When threatened, they will shoot a jet of stinking fluid from their anal glands in the direction of the enemy. If this fluid enters the eyes it stings and can also cause temporary blindness.

Both the striped skunk (*Mephitis mephitis*) and the western spotted skunk (*Spilogale gracilis*) are found in Canada. They occupy forests, prairies, farms, and suburbs. They are nocturnal (active at night) and eat invertebrates, small mammals, eggs and young birds, reptiles, amphibians, fruit, seeds, nuts, and garbage. Great Horned Owls and carnivores such as the lynx and fox may attack skunks.

From December to March most skunks sleep in a communal den, using stored fat for energy. Striped skunks mate in February or March but at least some spotted skunks mate in late summer. Both species give birth to one annual litter of two to ten young. Skunks are helpful to humans because they eat many harmful insects and rodents. Nevertheless, they are

Habitat of the Skunk Skunks have one litter of two to ten young in May (artwork by Jan Sovak).

also sometimes a nuisance, stealing poultry and spraying pets with their foul odour. Skunks also have a tendency to carry and transmit rabies. Wild skunks often live three or four years.

▷ Suggested Reading: Laima Dingwall, *Skunks* (1985).

■ Škvorecký, Josef

Writer (*born in 1924 at Nachod, Czechoslovakia*). He grew up in Czechoslovakia under both the Nazi and communist regimes. When his first novels were published in the 1950s, they were banned because they did not give the official com-

Range of Striped Skunk

Range of Western Spotted Skunk

Striped Skunk (courtesy *Macmillan Illustrated Animal Encyclopedia*).

Writer Josef Škvorecký came to Canada after the Soviet invasion of his native Czechoslovakia (photo by Andrew Danson).

munist point of view. In 1968, after the Soviet invasion of Czechoslovakia, he came to Canada with his wife, Zdena Salivarova. Together, Škvorecký and his wife founded a book company in Toronto to publish the work of other Czech exiles.

Škvorecký's best-known novels, which have been translated into English, are *The Cowards* (1958), *The Bass Saxophone* (1963), *The Swell Season* (1975), *The Engineer of Human Souls* (1977) and *Dvořák in Love* (1983). He is a keen jazz musician, and music plays an important role in his writing.

A professor at the University of Toronto, Škvorecký has won several honours, including a Governor General's Award (1984). In 1982 he was nominated for the Nobel Prize, the world's highest literary honour.

Slavery

Slavery dates back to ancient Greece and Rome. Canada has instances of slavery in its past. The native people of the Northwest Coast enslaved the enemies they captured in battle. In New France, some of the wealthier French families kept slaves, though there were never very many. The total between 1608 and the British Conquest of 1760 amounted to 3604. The majority were native people, but about 1032 were Blacks brought from Africa or New England. Most worked as household servants and were fairly well treated.

Slavery continued after the Conquest, and the Loyalists who came to Canada in the wake of the American Revolution brought Black slaves with them. But already British reformers were calling for the abolition of slavery. In 1793 Lieutenant-Governor John Simcoe passed a law against slavery in Upper Canada [Ontario], though his legislation did not free those who were already slaves. There was also a vigorous attack on slavery in New Brunswick, led by the lawyer and politician Ward Chipman. Such measures led to a decline in slavery, but it remained legal until 1834, when slavery was abolished throughout the British Empire. British North America then became a refuge for escaped slaves from the United States. Before all slavery in the United States ended in 1865, some 30 000 American slaves escaped to Canada.

▷ RELATED ARTICLE: **Underground Railroad.**

▷ SUGGESTED READING: Linda Bramble, *Black Fugitive Slaves in Early Canada* (1988); Barbara Smucker, *Underground to Canada* (1982).

Slocum, Joshua

The first person to sail alone around the world (*born in 1844 in Wilmot Township, N.S.; lost at sea in 1909*). Joshua Slocum went to sea at 16, and by the age of 25 he was a ship's captain. During the following years, he commanded many large ocean-going sailing ships, which carried cargoes throughout the world.

Slocum's first wife Virginia lived on board ship with him, along with their children, all of whom were born at sea. Virginia died in 1884, and though Slocum married again, his second wife was not such an eager seafarer.

In the 1890s, Slocum decided to tackle a solo trip around the world — something that had not yet been achieved. He bought an old hulk and spent more than a year building it into a seaworthy sailboat called the *Spray*. The *Spray* was 12 m long. In it, Slocum set sail from Boston, Massachusetts, in April 1895. He completed his around-the-world voyage three years and two months later, when he arrived in Newport, Rhode Island, in June 1898. This epic voyage is described in Slocum's book, *Sailing Alone Around the World* (1900).

Slocum made other solo voyages in the *Spray*, and in 1909 he set out on a one-man voyage to the Amazon River. On the way there, he ran into a severe gale, and neither he nor the *Spray* was ever seen again. Slocum was presumed drowned.

Slug

Land slugs are gastropod (snail-like) molluscs, generally without a shell. They are widely distributed around the world. Slugs are extremely variable in size and form, which makes them difficult to both describe and identify. They range in size from 2 cm to 26 cm in length. Some slug species retain a tiny remnant shell internally, while others are completely shell-less both inside and out.

Slugs spend their lives wrapped in a coat of slime, which protects them from drying out and contracting infection. It enables movement by assisting a slug's strong, muscular foot to glide over and grip surfaces. Slugs feed on a variety of plant and animal material, using a tongue-like *radula*. Slugs damage important crops and serve as the intermediate hosts of numerous parasites that attack both wildlife and humans. Slugs are generally more active at night or after a rain.

The largest slug found in Canada is the native Pacific bananaslug (*Ariolimax columbianus*), which is found in forested areas. These slugs are generally considered beneficial as they recycle dead leaves, trees, and sometimes animals. Other common slug species found in Canada, which are often introduced species, prefer to eat fruit, vegetables, and plants.

As well as land slugs, there are over 3000 species of sea slugs. They can have interior or exterior shells. Some sea slugs have brilliant arrays of often fluorescent colours, while others blend into their surroundings. Many of the colourful sea slugs secrete toxic chemicals such as sulphuric acid.

▷ Related Article: **Mollusc.**

▷ Suggested Reading: Jennifer Coldrey, *Discovering Slugs and Snails* (1987).

■ Smallpox, *see* Epidemics

■ Smallwood, Joseph Roberts

Premier of Newfoundland (*born in 1900 at Gambo, Nfld*). Smallwood brought Newfoundland into Confederation and was the province's first premier (1949-72). He began his career as a journalist, first in Newfoundland and Nova Scotia and then in the United States, where for five years he worked for a socialist newspaper in New York. He returned to Newfoundland in 1925 to become a union organizer, trying to get decent wages and working conditions for railwaymen, fishermen, and other workers. In the late 1930s, he also became a broadcaster; as "Joe the Barrelman," he hosted a daily radio show about Newfoundland history and traditions. This made him well known throughout the island.

In 1946 Smallwood was elected as one of the delegates to a convention held in St John's to discuss the future of Newfoundland — whether it should remain a British colony, become an independent nation, or become a province of Canada. Smallwood favoured the latter, and for the next three years he led the campaign for Confederation. It was largely because of his energies that a majority of Newfoundlanders came to support Confederation and thus caused Newfoundland to join Canada in 1949. Smallwood became the new province's premier, heading a Liberal government.

Smallwood began his premiership with great energy and introduced a number of popular measures, such as expanded medical and social services. He also launched some impressive large-scale projects, including iron ore development in Labrador and the mammoth hydroelectric project

Joseph Smallwood signing the agreement that brought Newfoundland into Canada (courtesy NAC/ PA-1280 80).

at Churchill Falls. These projects were popular, for they benefited Newfoundlanders by improving their lives and providing jobs. Less popular among the workers was Smallwood's handling of unions. He crushed a loggers' strike in 1959, and he sided more and more with the business leaders than with the workers.

Over the years, Smallwood gradually lost popularity, and after losing the 1971 election to the Conservatives, he resigned as premier early in 1972. In 1977 he resigned his seat in the legislature. He had brought out *The Book of Newfoundland* in 1937, and in his later life he devoted much of his energies to producing *The Encyclopedia of Newfoundland and Labrador*, the first two volumes of which were published in 1981 and 1984.

▷ Suggested Reading: Harold Horwood, *Joey: The Life and Political Times of Joey Smallwood* (1989).

■ Smallwood Reservoir

Smallwood Reservoir is a large, artificial lake in the interior of Labrador, near the Quebec border. Made between 1966 and 1974 by damming the Churchill River, it was created to produce hydroelectric power. It is named for Newfoundland premier, Joseph Smallwood. At 6527 km², it is the third-largest man-made lake in the world.

■ Smellie, Elizabeth Lawrie

Nurse (*born in 1884 at Port Arthur [Thunder Bay], Ont.; died in 1968 at Toronto, Ont.*). Smellie was the first woman to hold the rank of colonel in the Canadian Army. She served in the Canadian Army Medical Corps in World War I, during which she received the Royal Red Cross (1917). From 1924 to 1947, she was chief superintendent in Canada of the Victorian Order of Nurses (VON). Taking a leave of absence from the VON during World War II, she helped form the Canadi-

Donald Smith risked his fortune in backing the construction of the Canadian Pacific Railway. In 1873 he infuriated Prime Minister Sir John A. Macdonald by withdrawing his support for the government during the Pacific Scandal. "I could lick that man Smith quicker than hell could frizzle a feather," Macdonald shouted (courtesy NAC/ C-3841).

an Women's Army Corps in 1941. Until 1944 she served as matron-in-chief of the Royal Canadian Medical Corps. Her promotion to colonel was in 1944.

▷ RELATED ARTICLE: **Nursing.**

■ Smelt

There are nine species of smelt, a predatory fish, in Canada. They belong to the family Osmeridae. They have long bodies, somewhat silvery in colour, and small, round scales. They give off a characteristic, cucumber-like odour when first out of the water. They usually have many teeth on their jaws, tongue, and palate. Like the Salmonids, they have a small, fatty, and boneless fin just in front of the tail. Depending on the species, they may be marine, freshwater, or anadromous (living in the ocean but reproducing in freshwater).

Important members of the food chain, these fish live on plankton, shrimp, and small fish. They are prey to several fish prominent in human diet, including the Atlantic cod, and to whales and other marine mammals and seabirds. In spring and summer, the rainbow smelt (*O. mordax*) is subject to commercial and amateur fishing when they come to shore to spawn.

■ Smith, Arthur James Marshall

Poet and scholar (*born in 1902 at Montreal, Que.; died in 1980 at East Lansing, Michigan, U.S.*). While students at McGill University in Montreal in 1925, A.J.M. Smith and F.R. Scott started a magazine called the *McGill Fortnightly Review*. It was the first literary magazine in Canada to publish modern poetry, and it gave a start to many new poets. Smith also made Canadian poetry available to many new readers by putting together several fine collections of poetry. These collections are still used by many university students. In addition to all that, Smith wrote a great deal of poetry on Canadian themes, one of them being "The Lonely Land," which many critics feel is one of the best descriptions ever written of the wild Canadian northland.

▷ RELATED ARTICLE: **F.R. Scott.**

▷ SUGGESTED READING: John Ferns, *A.J.M. Smith* (1979).

■ Smith, Donald Alexander, 1st Baron Strathcona and Mount Royal

Fur trader and railway financier (*born in 1820 at Forres, Scotland; died in 1914 at London, England*). Smith joined the Hudson's Bay Company in 1838 and began a

hardship post in Labrador. Gifted with both shrewdness and compassion, he moved steadily upward in the company. In December 1869, during the Red River Rebellion, Sir John A. Macdonald sent him to the Red River Colony to find a peaceful solution to the problem there. Smith went as a Hudson's Bay Company official, but he had private authority to act for the Canadian government. At first, Riel was suspicious of him and kept him in Fort Garry under surveillance. Smith bore it patiently and he successfully persuaded the Red River people to begin negotiations with Canada.

Smith's political career followed. He was a member of Parliament from 1871 to 1880. A good Conservative, he nevertheless felt obliged to speak against the Pacific Scandal in Parliament in 1873. Macdonald viewed this as treachery, for it helped bring down his government, but Smith felt his conscience came before his political party.

In 1880 Smith was part of the Montreal group that created the Canadian Pacific Railway Company. During the tumultuous years of 1881-85, when the railway was being built and was more than once on the edge of bankruptcy, he backed the project stoutheartedly. Like his cousin George Stephen, he risked his fortune by doing so.

After the railway was completed, Smith was knighted and then created Baron Strathcona. He was Canadian High Commissioner to Great Britain from 1896 until his death.

▷ RELATED ARTICLES: **Canadian Pacific Railway; Pacific Scandal; Red River Rebellion.**

■ Smith, George Isaac

Premier of Nova Scotia 1967-70 (*born in 1909 at Stewiacke, N.S.; died in 1982 at Truro, N.S.*).

A veteran of World War II, Smith got involved in Conservative Party politics after the war. He helped to bring Robert Stanfield into the party as provincial leader in 1948, then won election to the legislature himself the next year.

After serving in several Cabinet posts, Smith followed Stanfield as leader of the Nova Scotia Conservatives, and premier of the province in 1967. But after more than a decade in power, the Conservatives were losing their appeal. They lost the election of 1970. Although Smith kept his seat, he resigned as party leader.

Smith remained in the Nova Scotia legislature until 1974, then was appointed to the Senate in Ottawa.

George Isaac Smith was premier of Nova Scotia (courtesy Nova Scotia Information Centre).

Smith, Goldwin

Professor and publicist (*born in 1823 at Reading, England; died in 1910 at Toronto, Ont.*). Smith was probably the most informed and versatile writer of his age, the envy of many lesser journalists. Sharp, acid, vigorous, he went to the United States in 1868 to teach at Cornell University. From there he moved to Canada in 1871. In 1875 he married a rich Toronto widow, Mrs Henry Boulton, owner of a large house called The Grange (now the site of the Art Gallery of Ontario). There Smith settled down to write and enjoy whatever literary and social possibilities Toronto offered. He wrote for a variety of journals, including the *Week* and the *Bystander*, which he founded.

Goldwin Smith was a Canadian nationalist in the 1870s; by the 1880s he had come to the conclusion that Canada should join the United States. To this end he published in 1891 *Canada and the Canadian Question*.

Smith and his wife held a literary "salon" at The Grange, where important visitors from abroad were entertained.

▷ RELATED ARTICLE: **Canada First.**

Smith, Lois

Ballet dancer (*born in 1929 at Vancouver, B.C.*). Smith was Canada's first principal ballerina. She had some ballet training in Vancouver, but worked mainly in musicals and operettas. In 1949 she married David Adams, then a dancer-choreographer at the Winnipeg Ballet. When the National Ballet of Canada was formed in 1951, Celia Franca asked Adams to join the company. He agreed, and suggested she might hire his wife as well. Franca accepted Smith on the strength of a photograph, and hired her as a principal dancer. Together, Adams, the company's lead male dancer, and Smith performed the great classical roles. She retired from the National Ballet in 1969 and opened her own school in Toronto.

Smith, Titus

Botanist (*born in 1768 at Granby, Massachusetts; died in 1850 at Dutch Village, near Halifax, N.S.*). The son of Loyalists who moved to Nova Scotia in 1783, Titus Smith was the first to make a botanical study of Nova Scotia. In 1801-02 he travelled through the interior, which was little known at the time, making a survey of the colony's resources and listing its trees, plants, and shrubs. His reports were of great value, and he followed them up with articles in the newspapers and lectures on botany, which made him well known throughout Nova Scotia. From 1841 until his death, he served as secretary to the Central Board of Agriculture.

Smithers

Smithers, B.C., is a town beside the Bulkley River in the west-central interior of the province. It was named for an official of the Grand Trunk Pacific Railway (now Canadian National Railways) when the townsite was laid out in 1913. Forestry and mining have been the main economic activities. Tourism is also important to the area. Smithers offers excellent skiing facilities on nearby Hudson Bay Mountain. The population in 1986 was 4713.

For further information, contact the Town Clerk, P.O. Box 879, Smithers, B.C., V0J 2N0.

Smiths Falls

Smiths Falls, Ont., lies beside the Rideau River in eastern Ontario, south of Ottawa. It is named for pioneer settler Major Thomas Smyth and grew as an important locksite on the Rideau Canal. The falls provided power for several early mills and factories. Today the town is a tourist centre for the Rideau Lakes. Industry is also important. The population in 1986 was 9163.

For further information, contact the Town Clerk, 77 Beckwith Street North, P.O. Box 695, Smiths Falls, Ont., K7A 4T6.

Smoking

Smoking is a major cause of death and disease. It is estimated that some 30 000 deaths per year in Canada are related to smoking. Smoking has been linked to heart disease and lung cancer and a large number of other diseases.

Why Smoking Causes Disease Cigarette smoke contains several thousand different chemicals. One of these chemicals, *nicotine*, is a strong stimulant. People who smoke cigarettes become highly addicted to nicotine. This makes it very hard to stop smoking. Those who try to stop suffer changes in heart rate, high blood pressure, high temperature, irritability, anxiety, and sleep disturbance.

Cigarette smoke also contains acids, alcohols, cyanide, nitrogen oxide, and poisonous carbon monoxide. These substances irritate the lungs and greatly increase the risk of lung cancer, a very deadly disease. Smoking has also been linked to emphysema and chronic bronchitis, two very disabling diseases.

Carbon monoxide makes up about 4%

Goldwin Smith (*courtesy NAC/C-26215*).

How Dangerous is Smoking?

The poisons and chemicals contained in cigarette smoke have been linked to shorter lifespans and to a number of serious health problems for smokers.

These include:
- Up to 10 times the risk of death as a result of lung cancer
- Cancer of the throat, mouth, lips, pancreas, kidneys, and bladder
- An increased chance — from three to 20 times — of developing serious lung diseases
- A 50% to 70% higher rate of heart disease
- Strokes, ulcers, sinus, and circulation problems, teeth and gum disease, and wrinkles
- Heavy smokers between 40 and 69 years of age are twice as likely to be hospitalized than non-smokers
- Reduced life-span averaging eight years for smokers who smoke over two packs of cigarettes a day, and four years for those who smoke a half pack a day
- Increased risk to the health of unborn children. Pregnant women who smoke expose their babies to greater risks from blood disease, birth defects, and premature births.

Tobacco Death Chart

Tobacco is linked to the deaths of 30 000 Canadians every year.

For every 100 000 15-year old smokers, tobacco will kill 18 000.

The following table compares the causes of death from future causes for the average 15-year-old smoker.

Cause of Death		Tobacco
Car Accidents	1200	15x more
Suicides	900	20x more
Murders	130	135x more
AIDS	70	250x more
Drug Abuse	10	1800x more
	2310 total	8x more

Barbara Smucker
(courtesy Penguin Books Canada).

of the smoke of an average cigarette. This gas reduces the capacity of blood to carry oxygen. Thus, while nicotine causes the heart to work harder, carbon monoxide reduces the oxygen needed to do this work. As a result, smoking reduces the ability to hear or see. It also leads to heart disease. As nicotine enters the bloodstream, the arteries become more narrow. Blood platelets become sticky and cluster together, causing the heart rate to increase. Since the heart is beating faster, it is pumping more blood through narrower openings. This leads to strokes and heart attacks.

Why Do People Smoke? Most young people begin to smoke through "peer pressure" or perhaps rebelliousness. Once they start, they continue because smoking is addictive. They are far more likely to smoke if their parents smoke.

Many people get sick when they first try to smoke, but smoking often produces a relaxing effect in others. With repeated use, smokers become tolerant of the disagreeable effects. They also become addicted to nicotine. The dependence on nicotine causes smokers to persist in the habit, even though close to 75% of all smokers say they want to quit.

Who Smokes? In 1986, about 28% of the population age 15 and over smoked regularly. Of this total, 3 million were men and 2.5 million were women. These figures are lower than 20 years ago. In 1966, 54% of males and 32% of females smoked. In 1986, these figures were 31% for males and 26% for females. Despite this decrease in percentages, a great many people still smoke, increasing their risk of disease.

The province of Quebec has the highest smoking rate in Canada. In 1986, 34% of people in Quebec were regular smokers, compared to 29% in Atlantic Canada, 28% in the Prairie provinces, 26% in Ontario, and 22% in British Columbia.

Of great concern today is the fact that people are smoking at a younger age. A generation ago people started at age 16. Today, the age has fallen to between 12 and 14. About 40% of teenage girls between ages 15 and 19 smoke. Although it is against the law to sell cigarettes to minors, not one retailer has been convicted in the last 40 years.

Second-hand Smoke It has been proven that people who smoke are also threatening the health of others. The children of parents who smoke have increased rates of colds and lung disorders. Smoke that streams from a smoker's cigarette to someone sitting next to the smoker contains 50 times the dangerous chemicals that are inhaled by the user. Thus people who live with or work with smokers are also at risk.

Quitting Quitting smoking is difficult. Nevertheless, every year thousands of people succeed, usually for health reasons. Since nicotine creates a permanent tolerance in the body, an ex-smoker cannot take a cigarette now and then. He or she is very quickly addicted again.

▷ RELATED ARTICLE: **Drugs.**

▷ SUGGESTED READING: Margaret O. Hyde, *Know About Smoking* (1983); Bobbie Jacobson, *The Ladykillers* (1983); Rob Stephey, *Tobacco* (1987).

■ Smucker, Barbara

Writer (*born Barbara Claassen in 1915 at Newton, Kansas, U.S.*). Smucker earned a BSc and a teaching certificate from Kansas State University (1936). She has been a high-school teacher, a journalist and, after a library science degree (1965), a children's and reference librarian. She moved to Canada in 1969.

Smucker's Mennonite heritage is present in most of her eight children's books. *Henry's Red Sea* (1955) and *Cherokee Run* (1957) provide Mennonite children with stories about their heritage. *Wigwam in the City* (1966, also published as *Susan*, 1972) explore the problems of young Indians leaving the reservation to seek city employment. Two historical novels deal with escaping persecution. *Underground to Canada* (1977) tells of two Black girls who followed the Underground Railroad to Ontario to escape slavery in Mississippi. *Days of Terror* (1979) tells the story of a Mennonite family's flight from Russia at the time of the 1917 Revolution. It won the Canadian Council Children's Literature Prize.

A car accident brings a boy into contact with the lifestyle of an Amish community near Kitchener, Ont., in *Amish Adventure* (1983). The time fantasy, *White Mist* (1985), has the twin themes of environmental pollution and racial prejudice. Seven-year-old Jacob Snyder has the responsibility of guarding a pair of nesting Canada Geese in *Jacob's Little Giant* (1987). In 1988, the Canadian Authors' Association recognized Smucker's entire body of writings by giving her the Vicky Metcalf Award.

■ Smuggling

Smuggling refers to the hidden, illegal

transfer of goods or people across a border. It is carried on because the items are banned, or because people want to avoid paying customs charges or taxes.

Canada has many kilometres of coastline and a long border with the United States. Since it is impossible to guard all of this frontier, smugglers have always thrived. In colonial times, when Britain or France wanted to control the import of goods into Canada, settlers simply smuggled goods in from the American colonies or the West Indies. Traders routinely smuggled furs to New York to get around trading regulations.

Smuggling reached a peak in the 1920s and early 1930s when the United States banned all imports of liquor during Prohibition. Canadian "rum runners" made fortunes sneaking liquor into the United States, either by truck or in boats.

Today it is not unusual for travellers returning to Canada from the United States to try to smuggle goods through the border to avoid paying duty. A more serious problem is the smuggling of illegal drugs into the country. And in late 1989 a scandal erupted about fuel trucks from the United States apparently smuggling loads of hazardous wastes to dump in Canada. As a result, the government increased its vigilance at border crossings.

▷ RELATED ARTICLE: **Prohibition.**

■ Snag

Snag, Y.T., is a tiny Indian village situated 465 km northwest of Whitehorse just off the Alaska Highway. On February 3, 1947 a weather station there recorded a temperature of -63°C.

This is the lowest official temperature ever measured in Canada.

■ Snail

Snail is the common name for several groups of gastropod molluscs. Although some are found on land in the world's humid regions and in fresh water, most are marine. In Canada, the freshwater species are particularly abundant in the area around the Great Lakes. Several species have been introduced from Europe.

The snail's body is covered with a spiral shell. The common snail (*Helix pomatia*) has a pair of long tentacles on the top of the head. The eyes are at the top of the tentacles.

During their larval development, the body takes on a twist which brings the tail end up over the head. The mouth has a sort of tongue (the *radula*), covered with tiny rasping teeth. Depending on the species, they eat other animals, plants, or filter water for their food. Most species have gills but those found on land have developed a lung covered by the mantle. Several species other than the common terrestrial snail are also edible, such as the whelk and the periwinkle.

As "escargot" (the French word for snail), these molluscs are considered a delicacy.

▷ RELATED ARTICLES: **Molluscs; Seashells.**

▷ SUGGESTED READING: Sylvia A. Johnston, *Snails* (1982),

Common Snail *(artwork by Kendal Morris).*

■ Snake

Snakes are reptiles. Their skin is covered with scales. They are long and legless and have 100 to several hundred vertebrae. Snakes have a forked tongue which enables them to smell. They lick particles from the air and when flicking it onto the roof of their mouth they sense what is in the air. Some snakes lay eggs; others give birth to live young.

Some Snakes of Canada
Black Rat Snake (top), Northern Red Belly (second row, right), Western Rattlesnake (second row, left), Red-Sided Garter, and Northern Water Snake (bottom) (artwork by Jan Sovak).

*Bullsnake (courtesy
Macmillan Illustrated
Animal Encyclopedia).*

*Rat Snake (courtesy
Macmillan Illustrated
Animal Encyclopedia).*

*Common Garter Snake
(courtesy Macmillan
Illustrated Animal
Encyclopedia).*

Breeding Range of
Common Snipe ●

All snakes prey on other animals. Most have special jaws that allow them to swallow prey much larger than their body diameter. Some snakes such as boas and pythons wrap themselves around their prey to suffocate it. There is one species of boa in Canada. The rubber boa (*Charina bottae*) is found in southern British Columbia. It eats birds and small mammals. Other snakes subdue their prey by injecting it with poisonous venom. There are only two species in Canada that are poisonous to humans; both are rattlesnakes. The massasauga (*Sistrurus catenatus*) is found in some areas of southern Ontario, and the western rattlesnake (*Crotalus viridis*) is found in dry areas of southern Saskatchewan and the interior of B.C. Rattlesnakes eat small rodents (such as mice) and some birds and frogs.

Of the 24 species of snakes that can be found in Canada, the most abundant and widespread is the common garter snake (*Thamnophis sirtalis*). It eats mostly frogs and worms. Snakes are eaten by mammals and birds of prey.

▷ RELATED ARTICLE: **Reptiles.**

▷ SUGGESTED READING: Nina Leen, *Snakes* (1978); Mike Linley, *The Snake* (1984); Janet Stewart, *Snakes and Other Reptiles* (1989); Merebeth Switzer and Katherine Grier, *Snakes* (1986).

■ Snipe

There are 16 species of snipe, a shorebird of the sandpiper family (Scolopacidae). One species, the Common or Wilson's

Snipe (*Gallinago gallinago*), nests all over Canada. It is a stocky shorebird with short legs, long bill, and plumage splashed with bright flecks of brown, black, yellow, and chamois. The snipe's head is horizontally striped and its eyes are set far back on its skull so it can see both forwards and backwards. It nests in swamps, bogs, or prairie fields. The nest is on the ground, in a small hole lined with bits of grass. Usually it is the female who sits on the three or four eggs for about 20 days.

The snipe eats earthworms, the larvae of aquatic insects, and small crustaceans. It winters in southern British Columbia, and from the southern United States to Brazil. It has a distinctive zig-zag flight. During mating season, it flies in a circle and then plunges towards Earth, causing a strange bleating sound as air rushes through the feathers of its tail.

▷ SUGGESTED READING: Leslie M. Tuck, *The Snipes: A Study of the Genus Capella* (1972).

Common Snipe (courtesy Macmillan Illustrated Animal Encyclopedia).

■ Snively, Mary Agnes

Nurse (*born in 1847 at St Catharines, Canada West [Ont.]; died in 1933 at Toronto, Ont.*). Mary Agnes Snively was superintendent at Toronto General Hospital and head of its school of nursing for 25 years. She led the Nightingale movement in Canada, which brought a radical improvement to nursing, dramatically raising standards and making nursing a recognized profession. She trained at Bellevue Hospital, New York, and in 1884 she was appointed to head the Training School for Nurses at Toronto General Hospital. Until 1910 she headed the nursing staff, training nurses with her strict and challenging regime. She was the moving force behind the organization of the Canadian National Association of Trained Nurses (later the Canadian Nurses Association), of which she was elected first president in 1911.

■ **Snow,** *see* Precipitation

■ **Snow, Clarence Eugene "Hank"**
Country singer, songwriter (*born in 1914 at Liverpool, N.S.*). Snow began playing the guitar as a child. By the time he was 16 he was singing professionally. By the mid-1930s, he had his own program on a Halifax radio station, and had begun to write and record his own songs. Over the next ten years he established himself as one of Canada's most popular entertainers, touring widely and appearing regularly on the Canadian Broadcasting Corporation national network. Snow's efforts to break into the American market were not successful until 1950, when his recording of his own composition, "I'm Moving On," was released. It was one of the most successful country records ever made. By 1985, it had been played on radio more than one million times, more often than any other country music record. Other hits, like "Golden Rocket" in 1950, and "I Don't Hurt Any More" in 1954, followed, and during the 1950s Snow was one of the top stars in American country music. He moved permanently to the United States in 1950, and became an American citizen in 1958. He has received numerous awards, and is recognized as one of the founders of Canadian country and western music.

▷ RELATED ARTICLE: **Popular Music.**

■ **Snow, Michael James Aleck**
Artist, filmmaker, musician (*born in 1929 at Toronto, Ont.*). Snow is one of Canada's most prominent contemporary artists. He is well known at home and in the United States and Europe. His main interest is in ideas about art; for example, in the relationship between one kind of art and another. He has worked in many media, including drawing, printmaking, painting, sculpture, photography, holography, film, and music, and he has written three books. He is always experimenting with different techniques in his work, exploring the meaning of art and its relationship to life. He moved to New York in 1962 and returned to Toronto in 1972.

▷ RELATED ARTICLE: **Painting.**
▷ SUGGESTED READING: Regina Cornwell, *Snow Seen: The Films and Photographs of Michael Snow* (1980).

■ **Snowmobile**
A snowmobile is a motor vehicle with tracks which travels on snow and ice. It gives almost the same kind of freedom of movement over snow as that given by skis, snowshoes, or sleds. Snowmobiles

Early Snowmobile *designed by J.A. Bombardier (courtesy Bombardier Inc.).*

are used by many Canadians for sport, by farmers for odd jobs, and by native people for hunting.

After the invention of the automobile, many inventors tried to make a motor vehicle that could travel on snow. In 1922, Joseph-Armand Bombardier, a mechanic from Valcourt, Que., made his sled pushed by a propeller; it did not work well. He persisted, and eventually came up with the first practical snowmobile. Two key inventions allowed the vehicle to move over the snow: the two endless tracks, one on each side of his automobile, and the mechanism for driving these tracks.

In 1937 Bombardier sold 50 of his machines. They were used as buses and as ambulances.

In the 1950s, small, air-cooled engines came into use. This made possible the small familiar snowmobile, which is used for sport. The number of snowmobiles in use began to increase rapidly, especially in Quebec.

Bombardier made many improvements to his basic invention, and the company

Venus Simultaneous, *1962, oil on canvas by Michael Snow (courtesy AGO).*

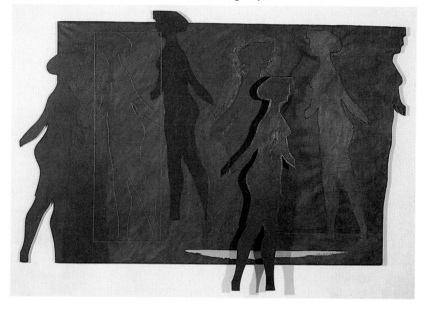

Inuit hunting by snowmobile on the frozen Arctic Ocean (photo by Barbara Brundege and Eugene Fisher).

he founded flourished. In the 1960s it produced about half of all the snowmobiles in North America and coined the name Ski-Doo. Led by Bombardier Inc., the snowmobile industry grew rapidly during that decade.

By the 1970s, North Americans were buying some 250 000 snowmobiles every year. Many of these machines were noisy. As governments began to require quieter machines, many manufacturers went out of business. Today only four companies make snowmobiles: Bombardier, Yamaha, Arctic Cat, and Polaris.

▷ Related Article: **J.A. Bombardier.**

▷ Suggested Reading: June Maxam, *Complete Guide to Snowmobiling* (1970); Julie Morgan, *Snowmobiles* (1971).

■ Snowshoeing

Snowshoeing was a common means of moving in deep snow among the native people. It was taken up by the French fur traders and later became a popular form of recreation. In the mid-to-late-19th century, members of clubs went on long-distance "tramps" in single file. These outings were accompanied by food and song. Snowshoeing races were held as early as 1843 and included hurdles and a steeplechase. It was a vigorous sport considering the distances (up to 20 km) and the threat of bleeding feet and frostbite.

Snowshoeing fell in popularity as the

Strapping on a Snowshoe, *from a painting by R. Rutherford, 1884 (courtesy NAC/C-98974).*

Snowshoeing is still a popular recreation in Canada (photo by John Foster/Masterfile).

new winter sports of skating and skiing grew in the 1890s. These are 70 clubs in Canada today.

▷ Suggested Reading: Kirk Wipper, *Snowshoeing is Fun* (1978); Gerry Wolfram, *Walk Into Winter: A Complete Snowshoeing and Winter Camping Guide* (1977).

■ Soccer

Soccer is the most popular sport in the world, played in at least 150 countries. It is played on a grassy field, called a "pitch," with a goal at each end. The round ball may be kicked or hit with the chest, head, or other parts of the body. Only the goalkeeper may use his hands. Soccer is known throughout the world as "football." It was named soccer in England to avoid confusion with rugby. The name "soccer" is used in North America, where the name football refers to another sport.

The first recorded game of soccer took place in England in 217 AD. In the 19th century, the sport spread to Europe and then to South America, Asia, and Africa. Soccer became an Olympic sport in 1900. The first soccer game in Canada likely took place in Toronto in 1876, although variations of the sport go back to 1859. Soon the sport spread across the country. In 1914 Canada joined the International Soccer Association (FIFA). The national championship began in 1913, and teams played international matches during the 1920s and 1930s.

Soccer changed with the influx of immigrants to Canada after World War II. European groups brought their own traditions to Canada. By the 1970s, Canada was producing more of its own players and its results in competition have improved steadily. In 1986 Canada finally qualified for the World Cup, losing close matches with soccer powers France, Hungary, and the Soviet Union. A Canadian team reached the quarter-final at the Olympic Games in 1984.

Soccer enjoyed a brief popularity at the professional level in the late 1970s and early 1980s. Canada had five teams in the North American Soccer League. Toronto Metros-Croatia and Vancouver Whitecaps won the league championship. There were few Canadian players in the league, which collapsed in 1985. In 1987 a new, all-Canadian league began play. In 1990 the Canadian Soccer League had teams in Victoria, Vancouver, Edmonton, Winnipeg, Montreal, Kitchener-Waterloo, London, Hamilton, Toronto, Ottawa, and North York. Soccer continues to grow in popularity in Canada and now ranks first in participants among all summer sports.

▷ SUGGESTED READING: Colin Jose, *The Story of Soccer in Canada* (1982); Bruce Kidd, *Who's a Soccer Player?* (1986); James Rothaus, *Defence and Goal Tending* (1980).

■ Social Credit

Social credit began as an economic theory. An English engineer, Major C. Douglas, argued that there is not enough money to purchase all the goods and services produced. He therefore suggested that money be distributed to the people. The idea inspired the Alberta evangelist William Aberhart. He used his radio program to promote social credit as a cure for the Great Depression. He formed a party called Social Credit and led it to power in 1935. The party won nine more elections under Aberhart and Ernest C. Manning. It was never able to put its main principle into effect (because money is a federal responsibility).

In 1952 a Social Credit government was formed under W.A.C. Bennett in B.C. Bennett actually paid no attention to the ideas of social credit, but he governed in its name for 20 years. He was followed by his son, William, and then by Bill Vander Zalm as premier.

The Social Credit Party has also been active in federal politics. It won 15 seats in 1935. In 1962, the party won 26 seats in Quebec under the leadership of Réal Caouette. The national leader, Robert Thompson captured only four seats in English Canada. The two split in 1963, with Caouette forming his own group, the Créditistes. The party disappeared by the early 1980s.

▷ RELATED ARTICLE: **William Aberhart.**

▷ SUGGESTED READING: Joseph A. Boudrea, editor, *Alberta, Aberhart and Social Credit* (1975); Alvin Finkel, *The Social Credit Phenomenon* (1990).

■ Social Insurance Number

Every Canadian who pays money to or receives money from the federal government has a social insurance number (or SIN).

A SIN is a nine-digit number which makes it easy for computers to keep track of Canadians. The number system, which came into existence in April 1964, was intended for use in Unemployment Insurance and Canada Pension transactions, and for increased efficiency. Its use has been expanded to include income tax, family allowance transactions, and government business at the provincial and municipal levels. The SIN number is not required for use in other transactions, and although such use has never been declared illegal, it may be considered improper. A person can refuse to give this number, but in so doing runs the risk of not being able to use the service for which the number is requested.

■ Social Security

Social Security is the network of government programs aimed at protecting the living standards of Canadians during periods of illness, accident, old age, and unemployment. Since the 1920s, government has also set a minimum wage below which employers may not pay their workers.

History Government has not always provided aid for the poor and disadvantaged. In New France, the Catholic Church cared for the needy. Nuns fed the homeless, ran hospitals for the elderly and the sick, sheltered orphans and extended a helping hand to the penniless. Many families and neighbours looked after the needs of their own, less-fortunate members.

The Maritime colonies introduced the "poor law," the beginning of the modern welfare system. Local governments raised tax money to pay for the care of the poor. Often, people who could not support themselves were lodged in poorhouses. Squalid poorhouses sheltered the sick, the mentally ill, orphans, and the unemployed — the destitute of all ages. They became so overcrowded and neglected that only people with no other choice would live there. In New Brunswick, where small communities could not even afford a poorhouse, the poor were sold into servitude at public auctions.

During the 19th century, government funding for social policies was modest. Most aid still came from private charity. In colonial society, the majority of people lived in rural settings where they were largely self-sufficient, growing their own food and looking after their own needs. Neighbours helped each other when times were bad.

At that time, people blamed the poor for their own poverty. They thought that charity should be harsh and meagre so as not to encourage the poor to depend on it.

Industrial Society As industrialization drew people to the large cities in search of work, it removed them from the support network of friends and family in the smaller communities. For a while the old attitudes towards charity prevailed. Poverty was blamed on personal laziness or drinking. However, attitudes slowly changed. The government began to take a larger role in providing help for people threatened by sickness, age, injury, or unemployment.

Workers' Compensation was the earliest example of a modern social policy. Originally, workers tried to finance their own schemes for helping their fellows who were unable to work owing to illness or accident. As the number of work accidents rose, the government of Ontario stepped in with the first Workers' Compensation Act, in 1914. It promised a regular income for workers injured on the job. Other provinces soon followed suit.

During World War I, Manitoba became the first province to pass a Mothers' Pension Act. This measure gave a small income to widowed, divorced, or deserted women with children to support. Once again, other provinces passed similar laws. Canadians were realizing that in industrial society workers faced threats to their livelihood that were not always their own fault. Since private charity could not fill the need, government assistance was necessary.

The old-age pension was the next social policy to appear. The federal government introduced the plan in 1927, under pressure from J.S. Woodsworth and a small group of Labour MPs. The pension of $20 per month was paid to Canadians aged 70 and over whose incomes were low enough. This proof that recipients were poor enough to qualify for help was called a means test. The cost of the scheme was shared with provincial governments.

The Great Depression The terrible suffering of the Great Depression emphasized the need for governments to do something about the problem of unemployment. Early in 1935 Prime Minister R.B. Bennett announced his "New Deal," a program of income-support policies that tried to ease the suffering of the Depression. Bennett's policies never became law, but they showed that government was more willing to ensure economic security for its citizens.

During World War II, experts feared that another depression was likely when peace returned. Hoping to ward off such a downturn, the federal government created an unemployment insurance plan in 1940 for workers who temporarily lost their jobs. In 1944 the government followed with a family allowance plan which paid benefits to mothers with children below the age of 16. This was Canada's first *universal* social policy, meaning it was paid regardless of the income of the recipient and did away with the means test. The expected depression did not follow the war. But unemployment insurance and family allowances are still important social policies today. So, too, is the old-age pension, which was made universal in 1951.

Medicare Many Canadians still lacked good health care because of their inability to pay for it. During the 1950s, the expense of a hospital stay was covered by an insurance plan financed by the provinces and the federal government. Then, in 1962, Saskatchewan pioneered a tax-supported medicare system which paid for doctors' bills as well. After a storm of controversy, the system was accepted. Later in the decade, the federal government offered to add its funds to any provincial medicare scheme. By 1971, Canada had a nation-wide medicare system.

Other programs have added to the network of social policies protecting Canadians from falling into destitution. Taken together, these social assistance programs make up what is called the welfare state.

But they have not succeeded in ridding the country of poverty. Joblessness, and the gap between rich and poor, remain. In the 1980s, the creation of many food banks, which distribute free food to needy people, showed that many Canadians still lacked a minimum income to provide for their needs.

In 1985, governments spent $61.6 billion on social security programs in Canada. As politicians have begun to worry about government overspending, they have tried to find ways of reducing this amount. One suggestion is to end universality by making social programs available only to those who truly need them. In other words, this would be a return to the means test.

Another idea is the guaranteed minimum income concept. Under this plan, wage earners would receive assistance whenever their incomes fall below a certain level.

Whether cost-cutting changes can be made fairly, without putting the well-being of some Canadians at risk, was a question much debated in the late 1980s and early 1990s.

▷ Related Articles: **Bennett's New Deal; Medicare; Poverty; Workers' Compensation.**

■ Social Work

Social workers try to help people to understand and solve their personal and social problems.

Until the 20th century, social work meant relief of the poor. Because most people believed that poverty was the result of weaknesses of character, little thought was given to helping people help themselves. Relief took the form of providing food, clothing, and shelter.

The understanding that poverty is a problem of society as a whole came slowly. Social critics pointed out that family violence, alcoholism, and poverty were byproducts of our economic system. The idea emerged that society had a responsibility to help people help themselves, for example, through job training. The hardship of the Great Depression of the 1930s showed clearly how economic hardship created social problems. As a result, the government brought in numerous social security measures, such as old-age pensions, unemployment insurance, and welfare. The need for social workers to help administer these programs grew rapidly. In 1941 there were about 1700 social workers in Canada. By 1986 there were more than 43 900.

Some of Canada's best-known social reformers were connected to social programs. These include J.S. Woodsworth, founder of the Co-operative Commonwealth Federation (which later became the NDP); Charlotte Whitton, child welfare activist and later mayor of Ottawa; Leonard Marsh, author of an important book on social security; and Harry Cassidy, director of University of Toronto's School of Social Work for many years.

Social workers deal with individuals and families suffering problems such as marital breakdown, child abuse, alcoholism, sexual assault, and so on. Many social workers contribute to the care of the physically and mentally ill. They counsel students and work in community centres, homes for the aged, and hostels. Some are also employed in industry and government to assist with work-related problems. Some counsel prisoners and those on parole from prison.

▷ RELATED ARTICLE: **Social Security.**

▷ SUGGESTED READING: Employment and Immigration Canada, *Careers in Social Work and Social Welfare* (1978).

■ Socialism

There are many different varieties of socialism, both in practice and in theory. It can be an economic theory, which prefers public to private ownership and which favours economic planning. In practice, this has meant that the central government controls the economy. However, another socialist tradition describes this as "state capitalism," since nothing really changes for workers except that their employer is the state rather than a private capitalist. These socialists favour a system where workers control industry.

Other socialists favour social equality and social justice, so that there are no extremes of wealth or poverty or of power and influence. Thus, they support all measures of social security (medicare, pensions, daycare, and so on) and of taxation systems which tax the rich in proportion to their wealth. Some socialists favour co-operation rather than competition, which they see as leading to inequality and injustice. Internationally, they favour measures of international co-operation, peace, and disarmament.

Opponents of socialism often compare it to the Soviet economic and political system, especially since the Soviet Union officially describes itself as socialist. However, most western socialists do not admire the Soviet Union. To emphasize the difference between themselves and Soviet socialists, they call themselves democratic socialists or social democrats.

Socialists insist that real democracy is possible only with socialism. In their view, parliamentary democracy does not go far enough. It deals only with the political rights (such as freedom and the right to vote) but not with such economic rights as the right to a job, the right to democracy in the workplace, the right to a decent wage. In this regard, socialists argue that parliamentary democracy should go beyond the right to elect one's representative in Parliament, and should instead stress direct participation by all citizens. They wish to go beyond "representative democracy" to "participatory" democracy.

Although it has never been supported by the majority of Canadians, socialism has been an influential political force in Canada. In the early 1900s, revolutionary socialism was the philosophy of the Socialist Party of Canada and of some labour groups. The Communist Party of Canada (founded in 1921) also championed this philosophy. The main supporters of democratic socialism in Canada have been some unions, the Co-operative Commonwealth Federation (founded in 1932) and its successor the New Democratic Party.

▷ RELATED ARTICLES: **Communist Party of Canada; Co-operative Commonwealth Federation; New Democratic Party.**

▷ SUGGESTED READING: Ivan Avakumovic, *Socialism in Canada* (1978); Richard Evans, *Socialism* (1977).

■ Sociology

Sociology is the study of human relationships and the rules that guide them. Sociologists focus on how societies change, or resist change, and on the roles of institutions such as churches and schools in society. On a very broad level, sociology attempts to describe the *social structure*, that is, the whole network of relationships among individuals and groups.

Sociology uses the scientific method to test and verify theories. It makes widespread use of questionnaires, public opinion polls, and historical records. It may also use controlled experiments to compare the behaviour of two similar groups. By changing one feature of one group, called a *variable*, the sociologist may learn if that variable makes a difference in how the group behaves.

Branches of Sociology Some of the major areas of study today are family, work, education, politics, economics, labour, law, ethnic relations, sport, and aging.

Historical Development The study of sociology emerged in France. It was given its name by Auguste Comte. The French sociologist Émile Durkheim was one of the first to combine research and theory in his study of suicide. Two German social thinkers developed theories that have led to two quite different traditions. Karl Marx's approach emphasized the importance of *class* in society. He described three social classes: the small business owners (such as farmers and shopkeepers), workers who sell their labour for wages, and the capitalists, who own the means of production and acquire wealth from the surplus provided by the worker's labour. Marx developed a grand theory about how these classes are in conflict. The theory greatly influenced the development of communism, one of the powerful political movements of the 20th century.

Another tradition is based on the work of Max Weber and others. It sees that social classes can be defined in many ways, such as inequalities in income, education, power, prestige, and so on.

Sociology in Canada Programs in sociology emerged in Canadian universities in the 1920s, despite opposition from other fields of study. Important early work was done by S.D. Clark, who studied the role of the church in Canadian society. French-Canadian sociologists focused on the survival of French culture in Canada. Sociologists from other countries made contributions. French sociologist Marcel Giraud studied the Metis. American sociologist S.M. Lipset wrote an important book on the rise of socialism in Canada.

Many of the works of sociology have a revolutionary air to them. This is because they often challenge commonly held views about society. For example, John Porter's book, *The Vertical Mosaic* (1965), challenged the view of equality in Canadian society. He showed that wealth and power are in the hands of a few and are passed on through families. Later studies by sociologists such as Wallace Clement have confirmed Porter's findings.

Sociology underwent a spectacular expansion in Canada in the 1960s. In 1960, there were 61 sociologists in Canada. By 1990 this had increased dramatically. Sociology is now one of the largest departments at every major Canadian university.

▷ RELATED ARTICLE: **Anthropology.**

▷ SUGGESTED READING: Alexander Himelfarb and James C. Richardson, *Sociology for Canadians: A Reader* (1984).

■ Sod House

Sod houses were a common sight on the prairies during the peak period of western settlement, from 1897 to 1914. They were made from pieces of turf (sod) cut from the ground. Homesteaders built houses out of sod because they lacked other building materials such as wood or brick. The sod was turned grass-side down and was used like brick to build walls. Inside, the walls were plastered over or covered with cloth or paper, and the floor was usually just packed earth. The roof was made with poplar poles covered with hay. A thin layer of sod was sometimes placed over the hay.

Pioneers outside a sod shack in Alberta, around 1907 (courtesy Glenbow Archives/ NA-474-7).

Although most sod houses leaked after rainstorms, they were warm and snug in winter and cool in summer.

▷ Suggested Reading: T.B. Dennis, *Albertans Built* (1986).

■ Soil

Soil is the thin layer of organic and mineral material that covers much of the land. Soil is more than just "dirt." Its complex mixture of ingredients supports all plant life on the land. Without soil, there would be no forests or agriculture.

Composition Soil is made up of particles of gravel, sand, silt, clay, minerals, and salts. It also contains decaying plant and animal remains. The decaying process is caused by tiny micro-organisms. Therefore, this material is called *organic*. Soil also contains countless millions of insects, worms, fungi, molds, and bacteria. Finally, all soil contains air and water.

How Soil Forms Soil begins to form when rock and other debris are broken down into tiny particles (called *parent material*) by weathering. Ice, rain, and wind wear down the rock. Water dissolves the minerals. The organic material builds up slowly over time.

Soil may form at the place it weathered, or it may be moved to new locations by wind, water, or glaciers.

Fertile soil may develop in as little as 1000 years or it may take 5000 years.

Soil Profiles Because soil contains so many different ingredients, it varies greatly from place to place. The kind of soil that develops depends on climate, vegetation, how much water is available, and other factors.

Because soil develops at different rates, it forms layers, called *horizons*. Most soils contain three horizons, A, B, and C. These horizons are also called topsoil, subsoil, and parent material. The topsoil varies in depth from less than 1 cm to several centimetres. It is usually dark brown

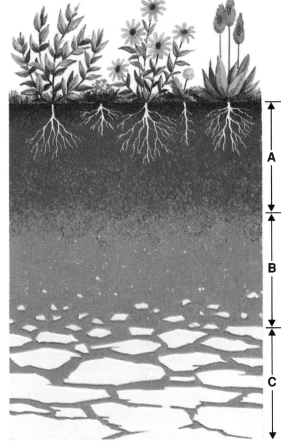

Horizons

Topsoil contains a high percentage of humus, which forms from leaf litter, decaying animal remains, and so on — A

Subsoil receives minerals carried down by water through the topsoil — B

Parent Material is the weathered particles of rocky material from which soil is formed — C

Soil Profile (artwork by Michael Lee).

or black because of its high content of organic material.

The subsoil is usually brownish and may be a few centimetres to a metre deep. The parent material consists of rock, clay, silt, sand, or gravel.

Soil scientists classify soils by their texture, colour, and chemical condition. The amount of acid or alkali in a soil affects the kinds of plants that can grow. Highly acidic or alkaline soils are harmful to many plants.

SOIL REGIONS OF CANADA

Soil covers about 80% of Canada's land surface. (The rest is bare rock or water.) Much of the soil is thin, or poor. Only about 7% of Canada's land contains soil suitable for agriculture. Because Canada is so vast, this 7% still represents a large area. Canada may be divided into five major regions.

Canadian Shield This region covers nearly half of Canada's land area. It includes most of Quebec and Ontario and the northern sections of Manitoba and Saskatchewan. Most of the soil is too poor for farming, although it supports a vast, valuable forest.

Western Mountain Region The mountainous areas of B.C. and western Alberta

Spring Tilling near Poltimore, Que. Soil is one of our most precious and fragile natural resources (photo by J.A. Kraulis/Masterfile).

Rush Lake *area of Saskatchewan. About three-quarters of Canada's farming soil is found in western Canada (photo by Bill Brooks/Masterfile).*

Water Erosion *occurs when water creates rills or gullies, carrying away the topsoil (courtesy Agriculture Canada).*

have a variety of soils. The southern, sheltered areas, such as the Okanagan Valley, are suitable for fruit. The coastal areas of B.C. are excellent for vegetables and grain.

Interior Plains About 75% of Canada's farming soil is found in the southern areas of Alberta, Manitoba, and Saskatchewan. Prairie soils are alkaline and are usually black, dark brown, and brown. They are suitable for grain production and rangeland. Because there is little rain in the summer, these soils may suffer drought and wind erosion.

St Lawrence Region The soils of southern Ontario and Quebec support various agricultural activities, depending on the local conditions. The soils are acidic and in most regions lime must be added for good crops.

Appalachian Region Parts of the Atlantic Provinces and Gaspé region of Quebec support mixed farming, potatoes, and orchard crops. For good crops, lime is often required because the soil is acidic.

SOIL AT WORK

Soil is fertile because of its organic matter and nutrients. When the soil is not cultivated, most of the materials from decaying plants are returned to the soil. When crops are harvested, the amount of organic material and nutrients returning to the soil is reduced. These essential ingredients are depleted over time.

To keep soils fertile, farmers add organic material (such as manure) and chemical fertilizers. Although these methods continue to produce excellent crops in Canada, there are increasing concerns that the quality of soil is deteriorating. For example, the organic content of soils on prairie farmland has declined by over 40% since farming began and by over 30% in the St Lawrence region. Soil nutrients have also greatly declined in all areas. There is also growing concern that herbicides and pesticides are threatening to destroy soils. These chemicals are used to kill insects and weeds, but they also kill many other organisms in the soil. They are also absorbed in the crops, where they may pose a risk to wildlife and to people.

Soil is also threatened by salt, which evaporates from water used to irrigate crops. The build-up of salts is an especially serious problem in the prairie region. Salt build-up is very difficult and very expensive to reverse.

Soil Erosion is the most serious threat to soil in Canada. The more frequently soil is turned by the plough, the more easily it is washed or blown away.

Water erosion occurs when the supply of rain and melted snow exceeds the capacity of the soil to absorb it. Water then flows down slopes and creates rills or gullies, often removing organic matter.

Wind Erosion *can swiftly carry away the soil if it is dry and unprotected (courtesy Ontario Ministry of Agriculture and Food).*

Wind erosion is most serious on the prairies, where the wind speeds are high and soils are dry. It is made worse when farming practices leave the soil unprotected. Much of the prairie topsoil was blown away during the drought years of the 1930s.

Today, it is estimated that the value of soil lost to erosion is well over $500 million every year.

Farming Methods Canada is fortunate in having so much fertile soil. With proper management, the soil could likely continue to produce crops indefinitely.

However, poor farming practices are destroying much of Canada's farmland. These practices include overuse of heavy machinery, poor manure management, planting the same crop year after year, too much ploughing, removing wind breaks, and many other activities.

As these activities are changed, the prospect for the future brightens. Rotating corn with hay and oats, for example, can reduce losses. In the prairie region, rotations of wheat, oats, barley, and hay have greatly reduced erosion losses.

▷ SUGGESTED READING: W.A. Andrews, editor, *A Guide to the Study of Soil Ecology* (1973); Grant MacEwan, *Charles Noble: Guardian of the Soil* (1983).

■ Sointula

Sointula, B.C., is a small fishing village on Malcolm Island in the strait between North Vancouver Island and the mainland. It began in 1900 when a group of socialist miners from Finland arrived to establish a colony. Sointula is Finnish for "harmony." Led by Matti Kurikka, the colony lasted five years. After it collapsed, many of the settlers stayed on and their descendants still live there today in the small, rural community. Sointula's population in 1986 was 692.

For information, contact the Regional District of Mount Waddington, Box 729, Port McNeill, B.C., V0N 2R0.

■ Solandt, Omond McKillop

Research director (*born in 1909 at Winnipeg, Man.*). Early in the 1930s, Solandt did research in physiology under Charles Best in Toronto, and during World War II he ran a blood bank in London, England. Asked to investigate why army tank crews were fainting in action, he discovered that it was because the gases from the gun went back into the tank when the gun was fired. This research led to further work for the army, and by the end of the war Solandt was superintendent of the British Army Operational Research Group. He worked on military research for the Canadian government after the war, and in 1947 became founding chairman of the Defence Research Board. Solandt has since served Canada in several other capacities, including chairman of the Science Council of Canada (1966-72). In his retirement, he has been especially concerned with environmental studies and with agricultural research in developing countries.

■ Solar Energy

Solar energy consists of sunlight and other kinds of radiation. It is produced by nuclear fusion reactions in the Sun and floods the Earth with energy.

All life depends on sunshine. It provides the energy without which nothing could grow and nothing could feed. As well, it is the original source of most of the energy that powers Canada.

Indirect Uses of Solar Energy A very small fraction of all the solar energy that falls on Earth is absorbed by living plants in the process known as photosynthesis. We draw on the energy so absorbed in the form of wood, peat, coal, and petroleum. About one-fifth of the total amount of solar energy that falls on Earth is absorbed by evaporating water. The absorbed energy returns to the Earth as precipitation, which ends up in rivers and we harness it as hydroelectricity. Most of the remaining energy drives the winds, waves, and ocean currents. We harness this flow of energy in forms such as wind energy. Of the forms of energy used in Canada, only nuclear and geothermal energy do not originate in solar energy.

DIRECT USES OF SOLAR ENERGY

The term "solar energy" is often used to refer only to the energy that can be harnessed directly from the Sun's rays. This supply of energy is often unreliable and, in a northern country like Canada, relatively weak in the winter. Using it directly, however, reduces the need to rely on expensive energy transmission and delivery systems such as electric power grids and pipelines. Furthermore, solar energy is free and inexhaustible.

Solar Heating Solar heating systems, which directly convert the energy of sunshine into heat, are classified as "active" or "passive" devices.

Passive solar heating systems are features designed as an integral part of buildings, such as south-facing windows, that take advantage of sunlight for light and heat in the winter. Over-hanging eaves shade the windows in summer. Experiments have demonstrated that, compared to classic construction techniques, well-

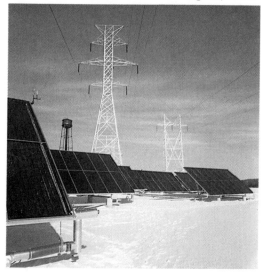

Solar Panels *used to heat water at a pulp and paper plant in Quebec (photo by Jim Merrithew).*

designed passive solar features can increase the cost of building a home by 5% or less, while greatly reducing the energy needed to heat such a home.

Active solar systems, as the name suggests, have mechanical devices. Basically, they consist of a roof-top collector, a heat-storage unit to store energy for use at night or on a cloudy day, and a heat distribution system. The first solar-heated home in Canada was built by an engineer in Surrey, B.C., in 1970. Since then, a number of houses have been built by individuals or the federal government. Active solar systems have also been used to dry crops and lumber.

Solar Electricity Another technology which directly captures solar energy, converting it into electricity, is the photovoltaic cell. These cells are made of materials such as silicon, whose intimate structure can be engineered so that when sunlight falls on it electrons flow through it, creating an electric current. Solar cells work for many years without needing to be repaired or replaced. They are relatively expensive, however, and so in Canada they are used mostly in places which are not reached by the electricity grids, and where fairly small amounts of power are needed. For instance, solar cells power recording instruments and radio transmitters at remote weather stations scattered through the North. Photovoltaic cells are increasingly used to power watches and calculators and also to power satellites.

▷ RELATED ARTICLE: **Energy.**

▷ SUGGESTED READING: Franklyn M. Branley, *Solar Energy* (1975); Shawn Buckley, *Sun Up to Sun Down: Understanding Solar Energy* (1979); Steve L. Gadler, *Sun Power: Facts About Solar Energy* (1978).

■ Solomon's Seal

Solomon's Seal (genus *Polygonatum*) belongs to the lily family (Liliaceae). Two species (*P. biflorum*, *P. pubescens*) are found in Canada, from southeast Saskatchewan to the Maritimes. They grow in wet forests. The Latin name *Polygona-*

tum means "several knees," because of the appearance of the rhizome (underground stem). The name Solomon's Seal comes from the resemblance to the inside of the sliced rhizome to the object used to personalize sealing wax on letters. Native people used both species as a source of food, cosmetics, and medicine.

■ Somers, Harry

Composer (*born in 1925 at Toronto, Ont.*). After studies in Toronto and Paris, he worked in Toronto as a taxicab driver, music copyist, and broadcaster to support himself while saving his best energies for composing. He became one of the outstanding figures in Canadian music.

Somers's best works are clear, forceful, and moving. Somers learned to use various techniques of other composers by recreating it in his own image. He went on often to invent not just a particular musical work but also his way of composing it. As a result, his forms have been his own, even when he composed under the classic titles: fugue (*12 X 12: Fugues for Piano*, 1951); song cycle (*Five Songs for Dark Voice*, 1956); suite (various); sonata (several); symphony (two); and concerto (two extraordinary piano concertos, 1947 and 1956). In each of these, Somers reinvestigates the form and reaches conclusions that are his own. In many other works — *Lyric for Orchestra*, 1960; *Twelve Miniatures*, 1964; *Voiceplay*, 1971; *Music for Solo Violin*, 1973 — he invented forms as well as music. Somers's opera *Louis Riel* (1967) is still the pre-eminent work in its genre, and is remarkably unlike any other operas that come to mind.

▷ SUGGESTED READING: Brian Cherney, *Harry Somers* (1975).

■ Somerset Island

Somerset Island, 24 786 km², lies in the central Arctic Archipelago. It is a high plateau with little plant life. Animal life includes caribou, muskoxen, and hordes of seabirds. It was named in 1819 by the naval explorer, William Edward Parry, after a county in England.

■ Somme, Battle of the

The Battle of the Somme was one of the longest, bloodiest battles of World War I. It began on July 1, 1916 north of the Somme River in northern France. On the first day of battle a regiment from Newfoundland was virtually wiped out. Canadians did not enter the battle until the end of the summer, when tanks were first used on the Western Front. They fought brave-

Solomon's Seal is a member of the lily family (artwork by Claire Tremblay).

ly and suffered heavy casualties before rain, snow and sleet stopped the battle near the end of November. The Allies lost almost 624 000 dead and wounded at the Somme, of whom 24 713 were Canadians and Newfoundlanders. The battle is often referred to as an example of the horror and futility of war.

▷ RELATED ARTICLE: **World War I.**

■ Sorel

Sorel, Que., is a city on the south shore of the St Lawrence River, at the mouth of the Richelieu River, about halfway between Montreal and Trois-Rivières. It was founded in 1781 as a Loyalist settlement, but had been a seigneury since 1672. Both the St Lawrence and the Richelieu rivers were important trade routes, and Sorel grew as a port handling commercial traffic. Today, shipbuilding and heavy industry are the major employers. The city is a business centre for farming in the Richelieu Valley. Its population in 1986 was 19 522.

For further information, contact the Greffier, 71 rue Charlotte, C.P. 368, Sorel, Que., J3P 7K1.

■ Souris

Souris, P.E.I., lies on Northumberland Strait in the northeast corner of the island. It was originally an Acadian farming centre. In the mid-1800s, shipbuilding was important, and though this industry has declined, the town remains an important fishing port. The name comes from the French word for "mouse." It refers to the plagues of mice that are documented as early as 1724. Its population in 1986 was 1379. In recent years Souris has staged the biggest Christmas parade in Canada (based on the number of floats).

For further information, contact the Town Administrator, P.O. Box 628, Souris, P.E.I., C0A 2B0.

■ Souris

Souris, Man., is a town situated at the junction of Plum Creek and the Souris River in the southwest corner of the province. Long occupied by Plains Indians, the first settlers arrived in 1881. Today it is a business centre for the surrounding farm district. As well, it is known as a source of agate stones, used in costume jewellery. The town boasts Canada's longest suspension bridge. The population in 1986 was 1751.

For further information, contact the Town Secretary, P.O. Box 518, Souris, Man., R0K 2C0.

■ Souris River

The Souris River, 720 km long, winds through the wheat fields of southeast Saskatchewan down into North Dakota and up into Manitoba where it joins the Assiniboine River. It was a minor route in the fur-trade era and several posts were built along its banks. The Saskatchewan government is building two dams (one on the tributary Moose Mountain Creek) for flood control and to produce hydroelectricity. The name Souris is French for "mouse."

■ Sourkes, Theodore Lionel

Biochemist (*born in 1919 at Montreal, Que.*). Dr Sourkes is known throughout the world for his research on nutrition and the nervous system, especially the role of vitamins in the nervous system. Based in Montreal, he has been a McGill University professor of psychiatry since 1965 and professor of biochemistry since 1970. His work at McGill included studies that led to the use of the drug L-DOPA to treat Parkinson's disease. He has written more than 300 scientific articles on the nervous system and mental disease, including the landmark study "Biochemistry of Mental Disease" (1962). He is also the author of "Nobel Prize Winners in Medicine and Physiology" (1966).

■ Souster, Raymond

Poet (*born in 1921 at Toronto, Ont.*). Except for service in the Royal Canadian Air Force during World War II, Souster has lived in Toronto all his life and has had a career in banking for 45 years. *When We Were Young* (1946), his first book of poetry, reflects his sympathy for urban workers. *The Colour of the Times* (1964) received the Governor General's Award. *Extra Innings* (1977) looks back to Toronto of the early 20th century. An experimental poet, he helped many new poets get into print when he edited the magazine *CONTACT* (1952-54) and the anthology *New Wave Canada: the New Explosion in Canadian Poetry* (1966).

▷ SUGGESTED READING: Bruce Whiteman, *Raymond Souster and his Works* (1984).

■ South African War

The South African War (Boer War), 1899-1902, pitted forces of the British Empire against the independent Afrikaner republics of South Africa and the Orange Free State. About 8000 Canadian volunteers took part. They were the first significant body of Canadian soldiers to serve overseas.

The direct cause of the war was a dispute over political rights in the republic of South Africa. Gold had been discovered there, and a large population of prospectors had gathered from around the world. They wanted political rights that the government refused to grant them. The Afrikaners, or Boers (the people of Dutch origin who were the first settlers in the area), were afraid that they would lose control of their countries. Among the prospectors were a few very wealthy British adventurers and empire-builders who saw a war as an opportunity to conquer the Boers and annex their republics into the British Empire. They promoted the war vigorously, and it ended as they wished.

Canadians were divided in their reaction to the war. Most English Canadians supported the war enthusiastically. Canada, they felt, should rally to the support of "Queen and Empire." They followed the course of the war avidly, and celebrated with great pride when Canadians helped to win victories, as at the Battle of Paardeberg. The success of the Canadian soldiers, contrasted with the inadequacies of British generalship, fed English-Canadian self-confidence.

Most French Canadians, and a few English Canadians, were critical of the war. French Canadians tended to sympathize with the Afrikaners. French-Canadian nationalist leaders such as Henri Bourassa criticized the federal government's decision to send troops. They argued that Canada should not participate in any war that did not threaten Canada itself. By participating in the South African War, they warned, Canada was committing itself to providing similar support to Britain in future, perhaps larger, wars. The debate over the issue became extremely bitter, and left lasting scars on English-French Canadian relations.

▷ RELATED ARTICLES: **Henri Bourassa; Political History; Wilfrid Laurier.**

▷SUGGESTED READING: Desmond Morton, *Canada at Paardeberg* (1986).

■ South Asians

South Asia encompasses India, Pakistan, Bangladesh, and Sri Lanka. There are 266 800 people of South Asian origin living in Canada, and another 47 235 are partly South Asian.

Some South Asians have come directly from South Asia. Others have come from different parts of the world, such as Africa and the Caribbean, where their ancestors settled and where their families have lived for generations.

THE PIONEERS

The first South Asians to migrate to Canada were Sikhs, who settled in British Columbia at the beginning of the 20th century. Sikhs are a distinct religious and cultural group based in northern India. They heard about Canada because some Sikh soldiers travelled across Canada in 1902 on their way to Edward VII's coronation ceremonies in England. The first group of Sikhs set out for Vancouver the following year, arriving on a Canadian Pacific steamship from Hong Kong. Between 1904 and 1908, more than 5000 South Asians arrived in British Columbia. At least half of them soon moved on to the United States.

These early migrants were mainly single young men. Their aim was to work hard, earn money, and eventually return to their families in India. Most of them found work in sawmills in B.C. From the first, they met strong opposition in Canada. English Canadians considered them unfit to be part of Canadian society.

As a result of the strong prejudice against the Sikhs, in 1908 the federal government passed a law to prevent Sikhs from entering Canada. The law stated that future migrants must come to Canada by "continuous passage." Since there was no steamship service between India and Canada, this meant that no residents of India could enter Canada, even though they held British passports. In 1914, 376 South Asians, most of them Sikhs, attempted to challenge the "continuous passage" law. They chartered a freighter, the *Komagata Maru*, which brought them to Vancouver from Hong Kong. However, they were not allowed to land. For two months the ship sat in Vancouver harbour. It was finally forced to leave, with almost all of its passengers still on board.

In the following years, the laws were changed slightly to allow in a few more South Asians, mainly women and children. However, the total population remained very small, consisting almost entirely of the men who had arrived before 1908. Most worked in British Columbia's forest industries, living together in bunkhouses. In the Sikh tradition, they helped those in need. They housed and fed others who could not find work. It was not always easy for Sikhs to get work. By British Columbian law, they were barred from many jobs. Until 1947, Asians were not allowed to vote in provincial elections.

THE MODERN ERA

After 1951, changes in Canada's immigration laws gradually made it easier for South Asians to enter the country. Many Sikhs came to join relatives in Canada. As well, large numbers of South Asians who were not Sikhs began to immigrate. Among them were many from Pakistan. Increasingly, South Asians came by air rather than by sea, arriving in the eastern provinces and making their home there. A large proportion were professional people, highly educated men and women who joined the staff of universities, hospitals, and businesses.

Since the late 1960s, large numbers of South Asians have entered Canada from countries that are not part of the Indian subcontinent. Several thousand have come from Fiji, where half the population is of South Asian origin. Others have come from Trinidad and Guyana. Between 1968 and 1976, over 20 000 South Asians arrived as refugees from Kenya, Uganda, and Tanzania. The 1980s saw the arrival of other refugees. These included Sikhs who felt threatened by their neighbours in India, and Tamils who fled from Sri Lanka because of the fighting there.

As a rule, South Asians have quickly found work in Canada or have started their own businesses. Most live in Ontario, British Columbia, and Alberta. Most dress in western clothes, though many of the Sikh men continue to wear a turban as prescribed by their religious traditions. The Sikhs follow the Sikh religion. Pakistanis are Muslims. Most other South Asians are either Muslims or Hindus, though a few are Buddhists or Christians.

South Asians are proud of their ancient culture and try to retain some part of it in Canada. Despite this, the younger people, especially children born in Canada, tend to be more Canadian than Asian in outlook and habits.

The National Association of Canadians of Origins in India was founded in 1976 as one of the major organizations for South Asian Canadians.

▷ RELATED ARTICLES: **Ethnic Group; Immigration; Komagata Maru; Prejudice and Discrimination; Refugees.**

▷ SUGGESTED READING: Norman Buchignani, and others, *Continuous Journey: A Social History of South Asians in Canada* (1985).

■ South Moresby National Park Reserve

South Moresby National Park Reserve covers 1470.4 km² of the Queen Charlotte Islands, a spectacular forest wilderness off the west coast of British Columbia. When Europeans arrived, the area was inhabited by the Haida who today claim to own the island. Whaling, mining, and logging have all taken place. It was set aside in 1987 as a national park because of its wild beauty and historical importance. Rare mosses and unusual animals are native to the island, which was likely a refuge during the last glaciation.

■ South Nahanni River

The South Nahanni River, 563 km long, is one of the most spectacular waterways in Canada. It rises in the mountains near the border between the Yukon and the Northwest Territories and flows across the southwest corner of the territories to the Liard River. The remote river features all kinds of exotic landforms, from hot springs to bottomless sinkholes and towering hoodoos. It plunges through three awesome canyons before tumbling over Virginia Falls, a waterfall taller than Niagara. The lower two-thirds of the river is in Nahanni National Park.

■ South Saskatchewan River, *see* Saskatchewan River

■ South Sea Company

The South Sea Company was a large British trading company organized in 1711. In law, it was the only company allowed to trade on the Pacific coast of America. Until 1833, British ships doing business on the coast had to carry licences from the company.

■ Southampton Island

Southampton Island, 41 214 km², lies at the top of Hudson Bay, separating the bay from Foxe Basin to the north. The barren island was home to the Sadlermiut, a group of Inuit who were wiped out by disease in 1902-03. It is named for a British noble, the Earl of Southampton. During World War II there was a major airfield at Coral Harbour.

■ Southern Indian Lake

Southern Indian Lake lies in the forest wilderness of north-central Manitoba. A widening of the Churchill River, the lake is 2247 km². It was part of an important fur-trade canoe route. Manitoba Hydro has diverted the Churchill River from the southern shore of the lake into the Rat River to produce hydroelectricity.

■ Sovereign Council

The Sovereign Council was the governing council in New France. Established after

South Nahanni River *flows through some of North America's most spectacular scenes (courtesy Environment Canada, Parks).*

Louis XIV took charge of the colony in 1663, it consisted of the governor, intendant, and bishop, along with five councillors. In 1703 the council was renamed the Superior Council and the number of councillors was increased to a total of 12. The council served as a court of appeal as well as a governing body, and was the senior law court in the colony.

▷ RELATED ARTICLE: **New France.**

■ Sovereignty

Sovereignty describes a state's control over its own territory. Under international law, a country such as Canada has a right to govern itself, to exclude others from its territory, from the waters around the territory, and from its air space. A state also has the power to represent the claims of its citizens in dealings with other states. A sovereign state also sends its own representatives to international organizations, such as the United Nations. Canada's control over its relations with other nations was gained gradually, beginning with Confederation in 1867.

The sovereignty of states has eroded in the 20th century. Huge multinational companies may wield great economic power across national boundaries. The power of a single nation to control communications and the media may have a strong effect on a nation's values. In Canada, the presence of the world's most powerful nation, the United States, along its border is a challenge to its independence.

ARCTIC SOVEREIGNTY

A country's claim to sovereignty over land or sea depends on international law. Among accepted proofs of sovereignty are discovery, conquest, and administration.

Canada's claim to the mainland in the North, up to the Arctic coast, has never been challenged. Doubts have been raised, however, over Canada's claim to the arctic islands. Some of the first explorers were English (for example, Martin Frobisher and John Davis). However, many of the islands were discovered by Scandinavians or Americans.

In 1880 Great Britain transferred its rights to all the islands in the Arctic to Canada, "whether discovered or not." Some people claimed that this was a feeble basis for sovereignty, since the British had little right to turn over islands that were not yet discovered.

Meanwhile, American explorers were active around Ellesmere Island in the 1880s and 1890s. A greater danger to Canada's claims, however, came from Otto Sverdrup of Norway. Between 1898 and 1902 he discovered Axel Heiberg, Ellef Rignes, and Amund Rignes islands, claiming them all for Norway.

Canada tried to support its claims over the islands with a series of patrols. In 1904 A.P. Low mapped and claimed Ellesmere Island. J.E. Bernier carried out several voyages. In 1909 he set up a plaque on Melville Island, claiming all lands from the mainland to the North Pole for Canada. Vilhjalmur Stefansson discovered and claimed the last of the arctic islands for Canada.

In 1903 the Canadian government moved to assert sovereignty over the western Arctic by setting up a Mounted Police post on Herschel Island. In 1919 the Danish government stated that Ellesmere Island belonged to no one. The Canadians met this challenge in 1922 by setting up RCMP posts at Pond Inlet on Baffin Island, and on the east coast of Ellesmere Island. The police established Canadian law, strengthening Canada's claims. In 1930 Norway finally abandoned its claims to the Sverdrup Islands.

Today, Canada's claim to the arctic islands is secure. However, all nations do not recognize the waterways among the islands as Canadian. Canada regards the channels and straits as its own waters. It requires that foreign vessels request permission to pass. The United States has ignored these claims, believing the seas open to all. It has sent tankers and a submarine into the Arctic without Canada's permission.

Canada's national anthem refers to the "True North strong and free." If it is to support its claim to the Far North, many people believe that Canada will have to be more active in that area.

▷ RELATED ARTICLES: **Canadian-American Relations; External Affairs.**

■ Space Industry

Canada entered the space age in 1962, when the satellite *Alouette I* was sent in-

Raising the Canadian Flag at Canada Point on Bylot Island. Captain Joseph-Elzéar Bernier is second from the left (courtesy NAC/ PA-139394).

to orbit by an American rocket. Canada was the third country to have a satellite in orbit. In 1972 Canada became the first nation to have its own commercial satellite communications system. The satellite *Anik A-1* provided coast-to-coast telephone services. Today, satellites provide radio and television signals to all parts of Canada, including the Far North.

Canada's best-known contribution to space technology was *Canadarm*, a robotic arm used on the space shuttle in 1981. Finally, in 1984, astronaut Marc Garneau was the first Canadian to conduct experiments in space.

Space technology is particularly important to Canada, because of its great land area. Satellites greatly improve communications over these distances and help map remote regions. Space industries also provide many "high tech" jobs.

Nevertheless, ventures into space are enormously expensive. Most space projects require the co-operation of several nations. Thus, the United States has invited several nations to work on various projects. In Canada, the government spends a great deal of money supporting the space industry. For example, it will spend about $1.2 billion over 17 years on the space station alone.

The Canadian Industry The Canadian space industry consists of about 50 companies. The largest company is Spar Aerospace Ltd, which accounts for one-half of the sales and employment. In 1987 the industry employed about 3700 people and sold about $400 million in products and services. Most of these sales are to other countries. For example, Spar built

Canada in Space This painting shows highlights of Canada's involvement in space, from the launch of the satellite Alouette I in 1962 to the use of Canadarm and the experiments of astronaut Marc Garneau aboard the space shuttle (artwork by Paul Fjeld).

communications satellites for Brazil, which were launched in 1985 and 1986.

Canadian Astronaut Program Canada currently has a team of six astronauts, who were selected in 1983. Marc Garneau was the first to enter space, aboard the space shuttle *Challenger* in 1984. Steve MacLean has been assigned to fly the next mission. The other members of the team are Ken Money, Bob Thirsk, Roberta Bondar, and Bjarni Tryggvason.

The astronauts were chosen from more than 4000 applicants and have a wide range of scientific expertise, from laser physics to aviation medicine. When the space station goes into operation in the late 1990s, there will be a Canadian astronaut aboard for a six-month period every two years.

CANADIAN SPACE PROJECTS

Space is a very hostile environment to machines and humans, which are subject to extreme temperatures, intense and dangerous radiation, and very low gravity. Producing equipment that can survive and operate there is an enormous engineering challenge.

RADARSAT is a satellite scheduled for launch in 1994 or 1995. It will use radar to obtain valuable images of Earth even in darkness and through cloud cover. It will use a powerful microwave instrument to send and receive signals from space. It will be used to look for resources, monitor ice conditions in the Arctic, and many other purposes.

MSAT is a mobile communications satellite that is scheduled for launch in 1992. It will provide a communications link for mobile users, such as doctors, firefighters, police, oil rigs at sea, and ships.

Space Station The space station is the largest international development project in history. Canada's main contribution

Two Astronauts working outside the space shuttle, using Canadarm (courtesy SSC Photocentre).

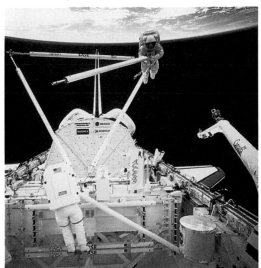

White-throated Sparrow.
Sparrows can be identified by their cone-shaped bills (artwork by Claire Tremblay).

Chipping Sparrow
(courtesy Macmillan Illustrated Animal Encyclopedia).

will be the Mobile Servicing System (MSS). It is a more advanced version of Canadarm and will be used to move equipment and astronauts around the space station. It will release and capture satellites and help to dock the space shuttle. The Canadian government is investing $1.2 billion in this project.

Space Science in Canada began in the 1930s, with instruments to study the Northern Lights. Satellites have greatly helped collect information about space. For example, *Alouette I* and others collected data on the electrically charged gases in the upper atmosphere. Telescopes in space are able to penetrate much farther into the universe, without interference from the Earth's atmosphere. There were two in orbit in 1990.

Space science is also conducted in space. Because of the very low gravity, space could be used to perfect new drugs and more perfect crystals for use in electronics. Astronaut Marc Garneau conducted experiments to find out why astronauts lose track of their legs and arms in space. By performing a space-age version of the game Pin the Tail on the Donkey, Garneau provided data on how the human body's nervous system adapts to space. An interesting side-effect of Garneau's experience in space concerned space sickness. This serious problem affects about 40% of astronauts, and could be fatal. All tests indicated that Garneau would be sick, but he was not. Dr Douglas Watt of McGill University has used Garneau's experience to propose a theory of what causes space sickness. He believes it is related to the ability of the eyes to focus despite movements in the head — the process that allows a baseball player to keep his eyes on the ball as he runs.

Space science is also supported in Canada by earthbound laboratories. The David Florida Laboratory, near Ottawa, is one of the most advanced in the world. It provides rigorous tests for space equipment before it is launched.

▷ Related Articles: **Astronaut; Canadarm; John Herbert Chapman; Remote Sensing; Robot; Satellite.**

▷ Suggested Reading: Lydia Dotto, *Canada in Space* (1987); Christopher Trump, *Canada in the Twentieth Century: Space* (1987).

■ Sparrow

Sparrows belong to the Emberizidae family. They are often confused with the House Sparrow, which belongs to the Passeridae family. There are 34 species of sparrow in Canada. Most of them eat grain (except in summer when they feed larvae and insects to their young). Sparrows, along with buntings, form a subfamily of small birds which have cone-shaped bills.

Both sexes usually have similar plumage. It is usually the male sparrow that sings, and it is usually the subtle differences in song, size, and plumage that help to set the various subspecies apart from one another. In forests the song is often whistled (for example, the White-throated Sparrow, *Zohotrichia albicollis*). In open spaces, it is often warbled or quite unmelodious (for example, the Song Sparrow, *Melospiza melodia*, or the Grasshopper Sparrow, *Ammodramus savannarum*).

Some sparrows winter in Canada (such as the American Tree Sparrow, *Spizella arborea*, which nests on the Arctic coast or in open tundra). There are more than 20 sub-species of Song Sparrows, eight of them in Canada.

▷ Suggested Reading: Kathleen Pohl, *Sparrows* (1987).

■ Speaker

The Speaker is the official who presides over debates in the House of Commons or in provincial legislatures. There is also a Speaker of the Senate whose job, although similar to those of the other Speakers, is less demanding. The Speaker must have a good knowledge of parliamentary rules and must show no bias towards any one political party. This is difficult, since the Speaker is chosen from the elected representatives and therefore does belong to one of the political parties.

Traditionally, the Speaker was selected by the prime minister who usually consulted with the opposition parties. Nowadays, however, in the House of Commons the Speaker is selected by the members of Parliament voting by secret ballot before the opening of Parliament.

Jeanne Sauvé, the newly elected Speaker, pretends to be reluctant to take office. She is escorted by Prime Minister Pierre Trudeau (right) and leader of the Opposition Joe Clark (left) (courtesy Canapress Photo Service).

The position of Speaker is very demanding, since he or she has to be present at most debates, to make decisions on complicated rules of order, to keep order even when tempers are high, and to treat all parties equally and fairly. For these reasons, the position of Speaker is usually treated with much respect. To attack or criticize the Speaker is considered to be very serious, although it is always possible to challenge the Speaker's ruling in a debate.

The Speaker is assisted by a Deputy Speaker and by a small staff of advisers and administrators. As well as presiding over debates, he or she is also responsible for the day-to-day running of the buildings of Parliament or the legislature. Thus, for example, the Speaker is responsible for maintenance, repairs, and cleaning; the parliamentary library and restaurants; security; and all that has to be done to ensure that elected representatives can carry out their duties.

The word "Speaker" dates back to the mid-1300s in England when the Speaker was the spokesperson of parliament to the king or queen, and took royal messages back to Parliament. This could be a dangerous job. Even today, the person elected Speaker pretends not to want the position and has to be escorted to the Speaker's chair. In French, the Speaker can be referred to as Monsieur (or Madame) L'Orateur, but the more common term is *le Président*.

▷ SUGGESTED READING: John Bejermi, *How Parliament Works* (1985); James Jerome, *Mr. Speaker: The Man in the Middle* (1985).

■ Speech from the Throne

The Speech from the Throne is read by the governor general at the beginning of a new Parliament. It is actually written by the prime minister and Cabinet. It reviews the current state of the country and announces the government's plans for the new session of Parliament, outlining what topics will be dealt with and what laws will be passed. Thus, it is of interest because it describes what the government intends to do. At the very next sitting of Parliament, the leaders of the opposition parties reply to the Speech from the Throne and then lead off a general debate on the government's plans. It is called the Speech from the Throne because in Britain the speech is read by the king or queen from a throne in the House of Lords. In medieval times, the monarch would announce from the throne what Parliament was expected to do. The Speech from the Throne also exists at the provincial level, except that in Quebec an Inaugural Address is read not by the lieutenant-governor but by the premier.

■ Speed Skating

Speed skating takes place on indoor or outdoor oval tracks. For men, there are races of 500, 1500, 5000, and 10 000 m. Women race distances of 500, 1000, 1500, and 3000 m. A fifth race is added for the Olympic Games: 1000 m for men and 5000 m for women.

In speed skating, two competitors race in separate lanes against the clock, changing lanes on each lap. In "short track racing," many skaters start together and race against each other. Speed skating has been dominated by Dutch and Scandinavian skaters. However, Canada has produced several outstanding speed skaters. A new $39 million oval was built in Calgary for the 1988 Olympic Games.

■ Spence Bay

Spence Bay, N.W.T., lies on the west coast of Boothia Peninsula on the eastern Arctic mainland. The hamlet was created in 1947 when the government settled several Inuit families there because animal resources were more plentiful. Inuit residents still rely on carving, hunting, and

Governor General Edward Schreyer reading the Speech from the Throne (courtesy SSC Photocentre).

Some Canadian Speed Skaters

- **1897** Jack McCulloch of Winnipeg won the world championship in Montreal
- **1932** Jean Wilson of Toronto won gold and silver medals at the Olympic Games
- **1952** Gordon Audley won an Olympic bronze medal in the 500 m
- **1976** Cathy Priestner won an Olympic silver medal
- **1976** Sylvia Burka was women's world champion
- **1977** Sylvia Burka was world sprint champion
- **1984** Gaëtan Boucher won two gold medals and one bronze at the Olympics

Gaëtan Boucher is the greatest speedskater in Canada's history. He won two gold medals at the 1984 Olympic Games (courtesy Canapress Photo Service).

Sphagnum Moss *leaves contain living green cells and larger water-storage cells (artwork by Claire Tremblay).*

Black Widow Spider *The poison of the black widow causes severe pain in humans (photo by Stephen J. Krasemann/DRK Photo).*

fishing. The population in 1986 was 488.

For further information, contact the Town Clerk, General Delivery, Spence Bay, N.W.T., X0E 1B0.

■ Sphagnum

The genus *Sphagnum* belongs to the Phylum Bryophyta and consists of "peat" or "bog moss." Well adapted to acidic aquatic life, *Sphagnum* is found in marshes and bogs where it forms a thick carpet. Its stems are erect and bear a group of branches. To multiply it releases spores from sphericals at the end of a stock. The leaves consist of two alternating groups of cells: living green cells and much larger dead water-storage cells with many pores. The latter can fill with water so efficiently that *Sphagnum* can retain more than 20 times its own weight in water. This capability is put to several uses. Moist turf or *Sphagnum* is placed as a protective wrapping around the roots of living plants or vegetables being sent long distances. When dug into the soil, *Sphagnum* improves its texture and increases its ability to retain moisture. In World War I, *Sphagnum* became a popular and effective absorbent bandage. Canadian *Sphagnum* may have taken 10 000 years to develop — it is thus quite wrong to talk about peat or turf as a "renewable resource."

■ Spider

Spiders belong to the Class Arachnida of Phylum Arthropod. While 30 000 species have been identified, their true number is much larger. Some 1300 species live in Canada. Several species are found as far north as Ellesmere Island.

Almost all spiders are solitary ground dwellers. Their body consists of a cephalothorax and an abdomen, with the cephalothorax bearing up to eight eyes, two pairs of appendages about the mouth used to manipulate prey, and four pair of locomotive legs. They have no antenna. The spinnerets that make their webs are at the end of the abdomen. The web is used to catch and cover their prey, and the silk is used to protect their eggs. Some species spin a new web daily and eat the old one. Some spiders often move about by spinning a thread and letting themselves be carried on the breeze.

Spiders live primarily on insects, but the larger ones can catch small vertebrates. Many spiders can absorb only liquids. Once they have caught a victim, they first suck its blood and then inject it with digestive enzymes that reduce it to a broth-like consistency they can ingest.

Wolf Spider *(photo by Tim Fitzharris).*

All spiders are poisonous, but few pose any danger to human beings. The venom of the black widow spider, which is found in some southern regions of Canada, produces severe and painful symptoms but is rarely fatal. Spiders play an important role in controlling insect populations.

▷ Suggested Reading: Adrian Forsyth, editor, *The Architecture of Animals* (1990); Alice Hopf, *Spiders* (1990); Herbert W. Levi, *Spiders and Their Kin* (1987).

■ Spiraea

Spiraea is a shrub which belongs to the rose family (Rosaceae). The name spiraea may come from the spiral shape of the berries in some species. The meadowsweet spiraea (*S. latifolia*) is found throughout the eastern Canadian temperate zone as far north as James Bay — and on Vancouver Island, where it was accidentally introduced with some cranberry plants. This shrub usually grows in wet, open locations, but can also be found in very dry spots with poor soil, such as sand banks. It can overwhelm blueberry patches and become a real problem. Since it spreads via underground shoots, one plant can quickly become a thick colony.

During the lengthy flowering season, tiny white or pale pink flowers are clustered in dense "bouquets" that, thanks to the many long stamens, have a downy appearance. The hardhack spiraea (*S. tomentosa*), which grows in southeastern Canada from the Maritimes to Ontario, has pink flowers and a generous covering of down on the branches and the underside of the leaves. The most widespread species, the white meadowsweet (*S. Alba*), grows from Alberta to Newfoundland.

■ Spiritualism

Spiritualism is the belief that some people are able to communicate with the spirits of the dead. The belief has been found in one form or another in almost all the world's cultures. Today, the belief is held in many developing countries, especially in Latin America, where it is known as Spiritism. Most religions strongly oppose the practice.

In trying to communicate with spirits, spiritualists turn to especially sensitive or gifted people called *mediums*. Since the 1970s, this term has given way to the term *channeller*. A channeller contacts a spirit to "channel" information for the benefit of the "sitter." Today thousands of Canadians call themselves spiritualists. They regularly attend seances, circles, or services in the spiritualist churches found in the larger cities.

Spiritualism in its modern form dates from the mid-19th century. It follows the practice of the Fox sisters, two young farm girls who were the first of the "spirit-rappers." They popularized the practice of rapping and knocking on tables (two knocks for yes, one for no) to communicate with the spirits of the dead. Margaretta (Maggie) was born in 1833 and Catherine (Katie) in 1837 in a farming community near Belleville in what is now Ontario.

Today, spiritualists still claim that the Fox sisters were natural mediums, even though they confessed that they faked the knocks and raps. Nevertheless, all agree that the Fox sisters began the modern practice of "spirit communication."

The most famous medium in the United States in the 1920s was known as Margery the Medium. Her real name was Mina Stinson Crandon (1888-1941). She was born on a farm near Princeton, Ont. Her husband, Dr LeRoy G. Crandon, encouraged her to hold seances in their Boston residence. In the darkened parlour, bells rang, objects appeared and disappeared, fingerprints appeared on smooth tablets, and voices spoke. These phenomena were caused, she explained, by her spirit guide who was named Walter. Walter was the spirit of Marjery's brother, Walter Stewart Stinson, who had been killed in 1911 in a railway accident near Princeton.

The best-known evidence supplied by a Canadian for the existence of the spirit world is the "spirit photography" of Dr T. Glendenning Hamilton (1873-1935). A respected doctor in Winnipeg, Dr Hamilton combined two hobbies into a single interest: spiritualism and photography. Between 1918 and 1934, he hosted seances in his home. When the mediums produced "physical" effects, he photo-

graphed them. He took black and white photographs of mediums producing "ectoplasm." Although unknown to scientists, "ectoplasm" is considered by spiritualists to be a souvenir of the spirit realm. It is a gauze-like, white substance. Some 300 of his spirit-photographs are preserved in a library at the University of Manitoba.

W.L. Mackenzie King, who was prime minister longer than anyone else in Canada's history, attended a sitting of the Hamilton circle on August 20, 1933. King was a practising spiritualist. He believed in the mystic power of numbers and in the importance of coincidences. He attended numerous seances. He conducted his own table-rapping sessions at his residence in Ottawa. (His spirit guide was named Myers.) He erected mystical ruins at his estate Kingsmere in Gatineau Park. King's beliefs gave him comfort. In the spirit world his efforts were praised by Queen Victoria, Sir Wilfrid Laurier, and many other famous people.

▷ SUGGESTED READING: John Robert Colombo, *Mysterious Encounters: Personal Accounts of the Supernatural in Canada* (1990); Kathleen Kilgore, *The Ghost-Maker* (1984).

■ Spohr, Arnold Theodore

Ballet dancer and director (*born in 1927 at Rhein, Sask.*). Spohr is one of the most respected people in Canadian dance. He was a star athlete in his youth and trained as a ballet dancer in England and the United States. He danced with the Royal Winnipeg Ballet from 1943 to 1954, and rose to be principal dancer. In 1958 he was appointed artistic director of the company. Under his leadership, the Royal Winnipeg Ballet became extremely popular in Canada and won great international acclaim. He selected ballets that would show off the dancers to advantage, and was constantly looking for new choreographers. He took the company on several foreign tours, and frequently performed across Canada. In 1970 he established a division of the Royal Winnipeg Ballet School to train professional dancers, and he also taught in the dance program at the Banff Centre. He retired in 1988. He has received many honours and awards for his work in dance.

▷ RELATED ARTICLE: **Royal Winnipeg Ballet.**

■ Sponge

Sponges (Phylum Porifera) have a very primitive structure and were thought to be plants until 1765, when they were recognized as animals. Some 10 000 species

The Fox Sisters

To while away the evening of March 31, 1848, Maggie (then 15) and Katie (only 11) began to play games to amuse themselves and to annoy their parents.

They threw around string and began to rap and knock on the furniture. Katie cried out the popular name for the devil, "Here, Mr Splitfoot, do as I do!"

Katie then knocked and to her astonishment, there was a knock in return. Soon the family heard stories that their cottage was haunted by the restless spirit of a murdered pedlar whose body was buried in the cellar.

Maggie and Katie became a local sensation. In 1850 they moved to New York and became the world's best-known mediums. In 1888 Maggie confessed that her spiritualism was a fraud. Katie confessed to fraud three years later. They admitted that the raps were produced by toe movements.

The Crandons

Problems arose when the Crandons tried to claim *Scientific American*'s offer of $2500 to anyone who could produce psychic effects under close observation. They had to satisfy the magazine's panel of experts. The panel sat through a series of Margery's seances in July and August 1924.

Some of the judges were sympathetic to Margery, but the majority were hostile — especially when it was discovered that the fingerprint (said to be Walter's) on the wax tablet was really that of the Crandons' dentist! The offer was never awarded.

are known. They are aquatic organisms, almost all of them marine and permanently attached. They take different forms (flattened, tubular, branching, or fanning); their size varies from 1 mm to more than 1 m in length.

Sponges have no distinct organs. If a sponge is cut into pieces, each piece will still function perfectly. Strong stimulus may also cause some cells to separate from the body and join together in a new organism. Tiny fibres made of calcium or silica and called *spicules* are found throughout the sponge body, giving it a degree of rigidity.

Sponges feed by pumping water through surface pores; the water circulates through canals where tiny food particles are absorbed before the water is ejected through large openings. Sponges have few enemies. Some small animals seek protection by living in the sponge's canals. Some crabs camouflage themselves with a bit of sponge on their shell. The sponges humans use are actually the skeleton of the animal, made up of a material called *spongin*.

▷ SUGGESTED READING: Arthur Myers, *Sea Creatures do Amazing Things* (1981).

Hurdles at the Western Canada Games (photo by Pat Price/Take Stock Inc.).

Cycling is one of many sports taken up recently for fitness as well as competition (photo by Pat Price/Take Stock Inc.).

■ Sports

Sports are games of skill that are played according to rules. All sports are contests requiring physical skill. They are played indoors or out, between individuals or teams. Sports are played for fun, for fitness, for money, or for glory.

Sports are an important part of modern culture. They are followed passionately by millions of people. In Canada, many people attend sports events. Many more watch sports on television. About 1 billion people around the world watched the summer Olympic Games in 1988. Sports heroes receive as much attention in our society as movie stars or political leaders.

Sports appeal to people on many levels. For those who participate, they are a test of skill, courage, or power. Those who watch can enjoy the contest as a display.

Boys Choosing Sides for a hockey game on Sarnia Bay, December 1908 (courtesy NAC/ PA-60732/John Boyd).

PARTICIPATION IN PHYSICAL RECREATION ACTIVITIES - 1988

(Percentage of Population Age 10 and Over)

Walking
Gardening
Swimming
Bicycling
Social Dancing
Home Exercises
Ice Skating
Alpine Skiing
Jogging/ Running
Golf
Baseball/Softball
Bowling
Cross Country Skiing
Tennis
Ice Hockey
Volley ball

0 10 20 30 40 50 60 70

Source: 1988 Campbell's Survey, Well-being in Canada

They experience the victories and defeats of athletes as if they were their own. Many people are loyal to athletes or teams that represent their town, city, or country.

The sport most identified with Canada is hockey. It is loosely based on the British games of bandy, shinty, and rugby. Being played on ice, it is appropriately Canadian. Canadians invented the sport and excel at it. In the 1950s and 1960s, the Soviets challenged Canada's supremacy in hockey. The best Soviet and Canadian players met in a dramatic series in 1972. The entire nation was crushed when the Canadian team lost the first game and was jubilant when it won the series. Hockey's continuing importance to Canadians was shown when Wayne Gretzky was traded from the Edmonton Oilers. The mayor of Edmonton said that the heart had been torn out of the city.

The great importance attached to winning has put athletes under great pressure. In the 1988 Olympic Games, millions of Canadians rejoiced when Ben Johnson won the 100 m dash. A day later, they felt disgraced when he was disqualified for using drugs. An inquiry into sports held in 1989 heard testimony of how many athletes took drugs to win.

Because of television, sports generate a great deal of money. Ordinary people find it harder to identify with athletes who

Curling Match at *Montreal, 1855 (courtesy NAC/C-40148).*

make millions of dollars for playing a game. They may turn to sports in order to escape from everyday cares. But sports now seem as troubled as other aspects of society.

Most modern sports developed gradually over time. It is often impossible to say exactly when or where a sport was first played. Canadians have played a role in the development of several major sports. Ice hockey, lacrosse, and football were all at least partly invented in Canada. The sport of basketball was invented by Canadian James Naismith. Canadians have excelled in many sports, from baseball to yachting, from horse racing to bobsledding.

SPORTS HISTORY

The native people played a wide variety of games and sports. Many of these games were played for pleasure or gambling, such as ring and pole, dice, and birch-bark cards. Some games helped young warriors or hunters to develop useful skills, such as wrestling, archery, spear throwing, and canoe racing. Dog sled races, drum dances, ball games, hand wrestling, high kick, and finger pull were popular among the Inuit. Many of these games are still played during the Arctic Winter Games.

The game of baggattaway (the modern game of lacrosse) was played by at least 40 different tribes. It likely had political and religious importance. Matches were played among tribes and between villages. Sometimes they were played to settle a territorial dispute. In a famous incident, the Ottawa chief Pontiac used a game of baggattaway as a trick to capture an English fort. The ball was thrown into the fort. The warriors charged in after it and captured the fort.

The Europeans inherited the toboggan, snowshoe, lacrosse, and canoe from the native people. The French Canadians added sleigh racing, wrestling, and horse racing to the sporting life.

Colonial Times Pioneer farmers had little time for sports, but they did compete in ploughing, horse racing, and canoeing. They held regattas in which they competed with the Indians and voyageurs in canoeing.

The Scots brought several organized sports to Canada. They introduced curling around 1807 and golf as early as the 1860s. Golf did not catch on at first because it required considerable land for the course. However, ice is abundant in Canada and available to everyone. Thus curling became popular. Other winter sports, such as tobogganing, sleighing, and ice skating were natural in Canada's climate. The British army officers stationed in Canada introduced their two favourite sports: cricket and equestrian sports. The officers also played a kind of stick and ball game on the ice which later developed into hockey.

Weight Thrower at *the Antigonish Highland games (photo by Sherman Hines/Masterfile).*

Other sports, such as gymnastics, swimming, and track and field, were promoted for health reasons. Rowing was the first sport in which Canadians excelled. In 1867, a rowing crew from Saint John, N.B., won the world championship at Paris, France.

Sports in the Industrial Age In the 19th century, most athletes came from the well-to-do classes of society, or they were officers in the military. Working people had little time for sports. Their only day off was Sunday and many of them were prohibited by religious beliefs to play sports on Sunday. In the 1860s, the factory hours were shortened. Working people had more time for sports, but were often excluded. The upper classes called them "rowdies," and tried to keep them out of the race tracks, for example, by putting up fences and charging admission. Women were also prevented from participating in sports. They were, however, encouraged to watch and admire the men.

Lacrosse was a very popular sport in Canada in the late 19th century. Today it has a limited following (photo by Toby Rankin/Masterfile).

Cross-country Skiing is a popular winter sport in Canada (courtesy Athlete Information Bureau/Canadian Olympic Assn).

Sports Medicine

Sports medicine identifies and treats the kinds of injuries that athletes get.

Typical injuries include torn muscles, twisted knees, and sprained ankles.

The term "sports medicine" came into common use several decades ago, when some doctors began to specialize in treating competitive athletes. Today sports medicine is not just concerned with top athletes. It also deals with the needs of ordinary people, for Canadians are more physically active than they were 20 years ago.

The professionals in sports medicine include physicians, physical therapists, exercise physiologists, coaches, and other sports scientists. They help athletes plan training programs, treat injuries of both professional and amateur athletes, and educate people on how to avoid injuries when exercising.

The major sports medicine clinics are in Canada's universities.

Olympic Stadium, Montreal (photo by J.A. Kraulis).

CIAU University Football Canadian football developed around the same time as American football and has very similar rules (photo by Jim Merrithew).

The growth of industry changed sports radically. Steamboats and railways made it possible to move teams from place to place, making wider competition possible. Shorter working hours gave workers more time to participate. The upper classes began to see sports as a healthy diversion for the workers. Furthermore, sports played a part in the new national feeling in Canada after Confederation. All Canada rejoiced when the Saint John rowers won the world championship.

The key to the spread of sports was organization. Numerous clubs and organizations were established all over Canada. Sports rules were standardized so that athletes could compete under the same conditions.

While more people of different classes began to participate in sports, they continued to be run by "gentlemen." The true sportsman, they believed, played for the sake of the game, not for money. This was the origin of the controversy between amateur and professional sports. The sports organizers held professionals in very low regard. Ned Hanlan contributed most to overcoming this attitude. He was the world rowing champion. Thousands paid to see him row against the best in the world. His feats were a source of national pride.

As sports grew in popularity, the pressure to win increased. Team owners began to pay the best athletes to play for them. Those who saw sports as a gentlemanly pursuit violently opposed the paying of athletes. At first the athletes were forced to take payment in secret. If they were caught, they and their teams were disqualified.

While most team sports became professional, the amateur tradition lived on above all in the Olympic Games. The Games were resurrected in 1896 under a strict code of amateurism.

Over the years of the early 20th century, some sports grew in popularity while others declined. Lacrosse dropped in popularity as football and baseball grew. In winter, hockey emerged as the premier game. It became the sport most identified with Canada. As more of the best players became professionals, smaller towns could no longer compete. In the early days of hockey, towns such as Renfrew, Ont., Dawson City, Yukon, and Victoria, B.C., could challenge for the Stanley Cup. As salaries went up, only the largest cities could support teams and build arenas of sufficient size. By the late 1940s, Canada had only two professional hockey teams.

Today's sports are a mixture of the two sporting traditions: amateur and professional. Hockey, for example, has numerous amateur leagues, with strict rules against paying players. Once they are a certain age, the best players move on to the professional league.

The ideals of amateur sport are carried on in the Olympic Games. Canada entered the Olympic Games in 1908. It still competes in the Olympic and Commonwealth Games, among others. However, in place of commercial rivalries, these games have become political. Athletes are thought of as representatives of their nations. Their success or failure is experienced as the success or failure of the whole nation.

In 1961 the federal government began to provide money to support amateur sport. The government of Canada now spends about $50 million a year in direct funding of amateur sport. Most of the money (about $33 million) goes to the organizations that run amateur sport in

Canada. The money is used to provide better coaching for talented Canadian athletes. As a result, Canadians have been much more successful in international competition. In the 1980s, Canadians were world champions or held world records in alpine skiing, speed skating, figure skating, yachting, track and field, equestrian sports, swimming, shooting, boxing, wrestling, and pentathalon. In June 1990, the Dubin Inquiry (which investigated the Johnson drug scandal) criticized this "win-at-all-costs" attitude. The Inquiry's report stated that Canadians should change their view of sport and that "government funding should not enshrine victory as the sole worthy objective of participation in sport."

▷ SUGGESTED READING: Trent Frayne, *The Best of Times: Fifty Years of Canadian Sports* (1988); Alan Metcalf, *Canada Learns to Play: The Emergence of Organized Sport in Canada 1807-1914* (1987); Don Morrow, Wayne Simpson, Mary Keyes, Frank Cosentino, and Ron Lappage, *A Concise History of Sport in Canada* (1989).

■ Spring

A spring is a place where water rises naturally from the ground.

Some springs in the mountain regions of western Canada produce warm water. Examples include the Cave and Basin Springs in Banff National Park, Alta. Some, such as Harrison Hot Springs in British Columbia, produce water at a temperature over 37°C. In both cases, the water has been heated by geothermal energy, that is, by hot rocks below the surface of the Earth.

Spring water contains minerals dissolved from rocks. Springs whose water contains less than 1 gram of minerals per litre are called *freshwater springs*. Those with more minerals are called *mineral springs*. Very salty water is produced by what are called *brine springs*.

Mineral deposits produce spectacular displays of colour and form at some springs such as the Paint Pots, in Kootenay National Park, B.C.

■ Springfield

Springfield, Man., is a regional municipality on the eastern edge of Winnipeg. Farm settlement began in the 1870s and farming remains important to the local economy. Many residents now commute to Winnipeg. Springfield's population in 1986 was 9836.

For further information, contact the Secretary, 628 Main Street, Oakbank, Man., R0E 1J0.

■ Springhill

Springhill, N.S., lies in northern Nova Scotia, not far from the New Brunswick border. Settled by Loyalists in 1790, it became a mining centre after coal was found in the 1830s. After a terrible mining disaster in 1958, when 74 people died, the largest mines were closed. No other industry has taken the place of mining and Springhill's economy is not healthy. The singer Anne Murray is from Springhill. The population in 1986 was 4712.

For further information, contact the Town Clerk, Box 1000, Springhill, N.S., B0M 1X0.

■ Spruce

Spruce trees belong to the pine family (Pinaceae). Seven species are found in Canada, only five of which are native. Black spruce and white spruce are the most widespread, growing across the country and north to the treeline. Spruce trunks can be up to 90 m long; for instance, the Sitka spruce (*Picea sitchensus*). Many spruce trees have flexible branches which often grow right from ground level. All of the species are evergreen.

The balsam fir (*Abies balsamea*) and the white and black spruce are the most widely used species in the pulp and paper industry, because of the strong quality of their fibre and because their logs float, making it easy to transport them from forest to plant. Spruce is the preferred tree for sawn timber, and, since it vibrates well, for musical instruments (for example, pianos, guitars, and violins). The Norway spruce (*P. abies*) comes from Europe and is often planted as an ornamental. The main enemies of the spruce are in-

Skater Kurt Browning is one of many Canadians who won world championships in the 1980s (courtesy Canapress Photo Service).

White Spruce is one of seven species of spruce found in Canada (artwork by Claire Tremblay).

sects (especially the spruce budworm), porcupines, and forest fires.

▷ SUGGESTED READING: Sherman G. Brough, *Wild Trees of British Columbia* (1989).

■ Spruce Budworm, *see* Ontario

■ Spruce Grove

Spruce Grove, Alta, is a city in the centre of an agricultural district just west of Edmonton. It is named for the spruce trees once common in the area. Many residents commute to Edmonton. The population in 1986 was 11 918.

For further information, contact the City Manager, 410 King Street, Spruce Grove, Alta, T7X 2Z1.

■ Spry, Graham

Journalist, political organizer, businessman, and diplomat (*born in 1900 at St Thomas, Ont.; died in 1983 at Ottawa, Ont.*). Spry had four quite different careers in the course of his long life. After studying at Oxford University in England on a Rhodes Scholarship, he worked for the *Manitoba Free Press* as a reporter and editorial writer (1920-22). In 1930 he founded the Canadian Radio League with his friend Alan Plaunt, an organization which played a major role in the establishment of public broadcasting in Canada. As a left-wing political activist, he and Plaunt published the *Farmers' Sun* (later the *New Commonwealth*), 1932-37. Spry also helped to write *Social Planning for Canada* (1935) for the League for Social Reconstruction, and was chairman of the Co-operative Commonwealth Federation (CCF) in Ontario (1934-36). He then turned to his business career, joined Standard Oil and became a director of the company in the United Kingdom (1940-46). From 1946 to 1968 he was agent general for Saskatchewan in Britain, and in 1962 he helped defeat that province's doctors' strike against medicare by recruiting British doctors and nurses to go to the province. On his return to Canada, he continued to work for public broadcasting, and was chairman of the Canadian Broadcasting League (1968-73).

■ Spying

Spying or espionage takes place whenever one government wishes to obtain information secretly about another, or about its own citizens. Typically, espionage is used to gather information about the military and economic power of foreign states and about threats of extreme political change or terrorism at home.

In colonial times, there was no organized spy network in Canada. However, both French and English spied on each other to gain useful military information during their long conflict for control of North America.

The first actual use of a network of government agents was by Prime Minister John A. Macdonald in the 1860s. Fearing the activities of Fenian agitators (Irish nationalists based in the U.S.), he sent several spies undercover to report on Fenian plans to invade Canada.

During World War I, government spies were on the alert against possible sabotage by German agents in Canada. During and after the war, a radical labour movement grew stronger in the country. Fearing a threat to public order, the government began spying on the leaders of this movement. Most secret work was carried out by the Royal Canadian Mounted Police.

Several Canadians served overseas during World War II as agents in "the secret war" against Germany. These volunteers worked behind enemy lines sabotaging the war effort and sending out valuable information. On the homefront, agents kept an eye on pro-Nazi groups and tracked down enemy saboteurs at work in Canada.

The most important development in espionage during World War II was the use made of signals intelligence. This involved intercepting and decoding enemy radio messages. Canada created a secret agency, the Examination Unit, to perform such work in 1941. The Examination Unit listened in, for example, on secret Japanese radio messages broadcast in the Pacific and so gained important information on the Japanese war effort. Also the Canadian Navy used signals intelligence to track the movements of German submarines ("U-boats") in the Atlantic Ocean and to warn the convoys that sailed between Halifax and Great Britain.

After the war, the Examination Unit continued its secret work as the Canadian Security Executive (CSE). The CSE exchanges information with some of Canada's allies, such as the United States and Great Britain. Canada itself operates no spy satellites or spy planes but relies on its allies for information from these sources.

Canada has not developed a modern organization to spy on foreign countries, like the American CIA or the Soviet KGB. However, the government has used secret agents to report on political activity with-

---

Notable Canadian Spies

Thomas Pichon (1700-81) was a French official at Fort Beauséjour in southern New Brunswick. He passed information to the British which allowed them to capture the fort from the French in 1755.

De Grassi Sisters spied for the government during the rebellion in Upper Canada in 1837. Because of their ages, Charlotte, 15, and Cornelia, 13, passed unnoticed in and out of the rebel camp gathering information. Finally Cornelia was suspected, but she raced to safety on horseback in a hail of gunfire. On her final mission, her sister Charlotte suffered a bullet wound.

Gilbert McMicken (1813-91) was a merchant turned spy who was in charge of the secret agents Prime Minister John A. Macdonald used against the Fenians.

Gustave Bieler (1904-44) was one of several Canadians working secretly in occupied France during World War II, blowing up trains and disrupting German troop movements. Early in 1944 he was captured by the enemy, tortured, and shot.

in the country and to counter foreign spies active in Canada. Such efforts were increased after 1945, when a Soviet embassy official, Igor Gouzenko, defected in Ottawa and revealed the existence of a Soviet spy ring operating in Canada.

For many years the Security Service of the RCMP carried out this job. Following a government investigation of the performance of the RCMP Security Service, a new Canadian Security Intelligence Service (CSIS) was created in 1984 to take over the role of chief Canadian spy agency. The government also established, at the same time, a Security Intelligence Review Committee (SIRC) to monitor the work of CSIS and to report to Parliament. SIRC acts as a public watchdog, to prevent abuses of power by the new Canadian spy agency.

▷ RELATED ARTICLES: **Fenians; Igor Gouzenko; Royal Canadian Mounted Police; William Stephenson.**

▷ SUGGESTED READING: Leo Heaps, *Hugh Hambleton, Spy: Thirty Years With the K.G.B.* (1983); H. Montgomery Hyde, *The Quiet Canadian* (1962); Roy MacLaren, *Canadians Behind Enemy Lines 1939-1945* (1981); John Sawatsky, *Gouzenko: The Untold Story* (1984); Sir William Stephenson, *A Man Called Intrepid* (1976); James R. Sweeney, *True Spy Stories* (1981).

■ Squamish

Squamish, B.C., is a district municipality at the head of Howe Sound, 70 km north of Vancouver. With a spectacular setting of sea and mountains, it is a popular outdoor recreation area. The ski hills at Whistler Mountain are among the best in British Columbia. Squamish is the winter home of the American Bald Eagle. The name comes from a Salish Indian word meaning "mother of the wind." The population in 1986 was 10 157.

For further information, contact the District Municipal Clerk, P.O. Box 310, Squamish, B.C., V0N 3G0.

■ Squid

Squid, along with other cephalopods, are considered to be the most advanced group of all molluscs, and the most highly developed of all the invertebrates. One squid species, *Architeuthis*, the giant squid, is both the world's largest mollusc and the world's largest invertebrate. It can be 20 m long and weigh close to 2000 kg. Early mariners' tales of gigantic sea monsters may be based on encounters with giant squid. There have been numerous documented accounts of struggles be-

Squid are swift swimmers, creating a sort of jet propulsion by squirting water out through a narrow funnel opening (artwork by Kendal Morris).

tween giant squid and sperm whales, and whales have been found with huge sucker marks and tears in their flesh which researchers attribute to battles with giant squid.

Most squid are much smaller. Like all other cephalopods, squid are restricted to marine environments. They are worldwide in distribution and their habitats range from shallow coastal waters to the depths of the open ocean. Some species occur in huge schools while others, like the giant squid, are thought to be rather solitary creatures.

Squid lack an external shell but they have an internal shell, called the *gladius* or *pen*, located just under the skin in the centre of their back. Unlike the rather bulbous-shaped octopus, squid are shaped like torpedoes. They are swift, long-distance swimmers. They create a sort of jet propulsion by rapidly squirting the water filling their mantle cavity out through their narrow funnel opening. Squid have ten appendages (eight arms and two tentacles). Their arms bear rows of suckers (many of which are hooked) along their inside length, while their tentacles, which are generally longer, only have suckers at their enlarged tips. Squid have strong, beak-like jaws, and a many-toothed ribbon-like, rasping tongue called the *radula*. Many species are equipped with light organs which produce a greenish blue luminescence. Nearly all squid squirt ink as a defence to confuse their attackers and to provide themselves with cover to escape.

The most common squid in Canadian waters are *Loligo pealei* and *Illex illecebrosus*, which are found off the East Coast. These and other species are commercially fished in many parts of the world including Canada. While *Loligo* and *Illex* are heavily fished by foreign squid-fishing fleets, Canadian fisherman have traditionally regarded them as bait. As most Canadians are unfamiliar with squid as food, most of the squid caught by Canadian fishermen today are exported. This is a shame, for squid are delicious when properly prepared and offer consumers excellent nutritional value and flavour at moderate cost.

▷ RELATED ARTICLE: **Molluscs.**

▷ SUGGESTED READING: Joseph J. Cook, *The Phantom World of the Octopus and Squid* (1965); Jacques Cousteau, *Octupus and Squid: The Soft Intelligence* (1973); Gwynne Vevers, *Octopus, Cuttlefish and Squid* (1977).

■ Squires, Sir Richard Anderson

Politician (*born in 1880 at Harbour Grace, Nfld; died in 1940 at St John's, Nfld*). Squires was twice prime minister of Newfoundland before Newfoundland joined Canada. He was in power 1919-23 and 1928-32. Squires was first elected to the Newfoundland Assembly in 1909. After being defeated in 1913, he was appointed to the Legislative Council and the Cabinet, in which he served until 1918.

In 1919 Squires founded the Liberal Reform Party, which won the election that year; but he had to resign four years later because of charges of corruption. Although he rebounded to win the 1928 election, his second period in power was also brought to an end because he was charged with corruption. Squires's ineffectual leadership, coupled with the deepening economic crisis, caused Newfoundland to take a step backwards politically; in 1934 Newfoundland was so desperate that it had to give up responsible government and return to being a colony of Britain.

▷ RELATED ARTICLE: **Commission of Government.**

■ Squirrel

Squirrels are members of the rodent family Sciuridae. These mammals are found throughout most of the world; 22 species occur in Canada.

Because many squirrels are active during the day, they are among the best known and most frequently seen wild mammals. They are found in forests, prairies, mountains, and even in the tundra.

The squirrels can be divided into two groups: ground squirrels and tree squirrels. Ground squirrels, chipmunks, prairie dogs, and marmots have long front claws which they use to dig tunnels. Almost all are true hibernators. Tree squirrels, with their long, bushy tails and sharp curved claws that help them climb, are active year-round. Tree squirrels found in Canada include southern and northern flying squirrels (*Glaucomys volans, G. sabrinus*), the grey squirrel (*Sciurus carolinensis*), the fox squirrel (*S. niger*), the red squirrel (*Tamiasciurus hudsonicus*), and the Douglas squirrel (*T. douglasii*).

Squirrels feed mainly upon vegetation, and many species accumulate piles of food. They eat insects, eggs, young birds, and dead animals. A few squirrels are occasionally cannibalistic. Mating occurs in the spring with gestation lasting 22 to 44 days. Depending upon the species, the single annual litter has three to eight young. Squirrels may damage cereal crops and electrical and telephone lines. Their tunnels and hillocks can be a hazard to animals and farm machinery.

Squirrels are members of the rodent family. There are 22 species in Canada, of which four are shown here: northern flying squirrel (top), thirteen-lined ground squirrel (left), least chipmunk (right), and hoary marmot (artwork by Jan Sovak).

Northern Flying Squirrel in mid flight (courtesy Macmillan Illustrated Animal Encyclopedia).

▷ Suggested Reading: George Peck, *Squirrels* (1985); S.P.E. Woods Jr, *The Squirrels of Canada* (1988).

■ Stadacona

Stadacona was an Iroquois village on the St Lawrence River at the present site of Quebec City. Jacques Cartier discovered Stadacona on his second expedition to Canada in 1535. The village was not fortified and was occupied by about 500 people who lived by farming, fishing, and hunting. The villagers were eager to trade. Cartier visited Hochelaga, another village farther upstream, and wintered near Stadacona.

After several Frenchmen had died of scurvy during the winter, Cartier learned of a cure made from the bark of white cedar. Cartier kidnapped Chief Donnacona, his two sons, and seven others so they could tell the French king about precious metals they had described in their country. The king was impressed, but all the captives died before Cartier returned with Jean-François Roberval in 1541 to found a colony. This time the Stadaconans were not friendly, the metals proved worthless, and the settlement was abandoned.

When Samuel de Champlain arrived at the site in 1603, the St Lawrence Iroquois and their villages had disappeared. They were probably victims of European diseases and of warfare with rival native groups to the south and west.

▷ Related Articles: **Jacques Cartier; Exploration; Hochelaga; New France; Scurvy.**

■ Stamps, *see* Postage Stamps

■ Standard of Living

A standard of living is the state of welfare of the average person in a society. It is a difficult thing to define because many factors that affect welfare cannot be measured. Such factors as a clean environment, safe streets, social harmony, a sense of peace and security, human rights, and access to public services all play a part in the individual's well-being. Yet, these factors cannot be reduced to numbers.

A second problem in defining standard of living is that in all societies there is a wide gap between the highest income and the lowest. Thus, an average standard of living hides this difference. The same standard of living figure could be given for two very different societies: one with the benefits spread quite evenly among its residents and one with most of the benefits flowing to a few.

One way in which the standard of living is measured in Canada is to divide the total output of the economy by the population. This figure is called *real output per person*, and it has risen most years as a result of a growing economy.

Another way to judge standard of living is to compare Canada to other major economies. This also presents serious difficulties because each country reports its output in its own currency. Also average prices in different countries vary greatly. The best comparison of standards of living among various countries is that produced by the Organization for Economic Co-operation and Development. This measurement takes account of different price levels in various countries. According to this method, Canada's standard of living stood second only to that of the United States in 1987. Furthermore, Canada's standard of living has risen to close much of the gap between it and that of the U.S. In 1970 Canada's standard of living was approximately 80% of the U.S. figure. In 1987 the Canadian standard was about 93% of the U.S. figure.

■ Stanfield, Robert Lorne

Premier of Nova Scotia and leader of the federal Progressive Conservative Party (*born in 1914 at Truro, N.S.*). Stanfield first became active in politics in the late 1940s, when he built up Nova Scotia's Conservative Party, which at the time had no members elected to the legislature. He became leader of the Nova Scotia Conservatives in 1948 and was elected to the legislature in 1949. He led the Conservatives to victory in the 1956 provincial election and remained premier of Nova Scotia until 1967.

Stanfield was a popular premier. Known for his common sense and moderation, he tried to make Nova Scotia more self-reliant. He is regarded as one of the province's most successful premiers. He resigned in 1967 to become leader of the federal Conservative Party. It was hoped that he could bring the federal Conservatives to power as he had the Nova Scotia Conservatives. But Stanfield remained leader of the opposition and never became prime minister. He had a formidable opponent in the accomplished Liberal leader, Pierre Trudeau, who won three successive elections against Stanfield and the Conservatives. Stanfield resigned as party leader in 1976. He has since continued to serve Canada in a number of public capacities, such as chairman of the Commonwealth Foundation.

Robert Stanfield was premier of Nova Scotia and federal leader of the Progressive Conservative Party (courtesy Canapress Photo Service).

▷ RELATED ARTICLE: **Progressive Conservative Party.**

▷ SUGGESTED READING: E.D. Haliburton, *My Years With Stanfield* (1973); Geoffrey Stevens, *Stanfield* (1973).

■ Stanley, Frederick Arthur, Baron Stanley of Preston

Governor general (*born in 1841 at London, England; died in 1908 at Holwood, England*). The Stanley Cup is named after Lord Stanley, who presented it to Canada in 1893 to encourage amateur hockey. Lord Stanley was a son of the British prime minister Lord Derby, and he sat in the British Parliament before being appointed to Canada as governor general. He served as governor general from 1888 to 1893.

■ Stanley Cup

The Stanley Cup is the oldest trophy in professional sports in Canada. It was donated by Governor General Lord Stanley in 1893 to be awarded to the amateur hockey champions of Canada. It was first awarded to Montreal AAA in 1893. Except for 1919, when the playoffs were cancelled because of an influenza epidemic, it has been awarded every year since.

The first professional team to win the cup was the Ottawa Senators in 1909. In 1926 the Stanley Cup became the exclusive property of the National Hockey League.

The original silver bowl is on permanent display in the Hockey Hall of Fame. A replica of the original sits atop the present trophy. The names of all the players on the winning teams since 1930 are engraved on the base. The cup itself has a colourful history. It has been lost, misplaced, dented, and stolen. Jean Beliveau started the tradition of the captain skating around the arena with the cup held high. It is now passed around from player to player.

By far the most successful team in the Stanley Cup playoffs is the Montreal Canadiens, with 23 victories, followed by the Toronto Maple Leafs, with 13. The Edmonton Oilers won the cup five times from 1980 to 1990.

▷ SUGGESTED READING: Frank Orr, *The Stanley Cup: The World Series of Hockey* (1976).

■ Staple Thesis

The staple thesis examines the effect on Canada's economic, social, and political development, of this country's historical reliance on the export of natural resources, or *staples*, for its prosperity. The thesis was first expressed in the 1920s by two Canadian economic historians, H.A. Innis and W.A. Macintosh. It is basically a theory to explain economic growth.

Macintosh argued that reliance on staple exports was merely a stage in economic development. Innis took a more negative view. He believed that continued reliance on staple exports weakened Canada. Consequently, rather than evolving into a mature economy, Canada would concentrate on finding new kinds of staples to export. Historians are generally agreed that Innis's view is the correct one.

■ Star of Courage

The Star of Courage is the second-highest Canadian medal for bravery, the other two being the Cross of Valour (first) and the Medal of Bravery (third). All three bravery awards were introduced in 1972. Any person or group can recommend someone for a medal by writing to Government House in Ottawa, Ont.

▷ RELATED ARTICLE: **Decorations for Bravery.**

■ Starfish

Starfish have five sides, are symmetrical, usually have five arms attached to a central body, and are covered with tiny spines. The mouth is centrally placed on the underside. The starfish can regenerate a lost arm. The underside of an arm has a furrow containing the tube feet, which are activated, as with all echinodermata, by a water vascular system. The tip of each arm bears a photoreceptive organ.

Starfish eat crustaceans, molluscs, or worms. Some species eat by catching particles suspended in the water with a mucus secreted by the body that carries the prey to the mouth.

Starfish are found from the shoreline to very great ocean depths. Some 1500 species are known worldwide. The giant *Pycnopodia helianthoides* is found all along

The Stanley Cup

The Stanley Cup has been presented annually since 1915. Prior to then, any team could challenge the cup holder to a playoff. The winner would be the Stanley Cup champion.

This could happen more than once in any given year. Including these championships, the Ottawa Hockey club (the Silver Seven and the Senators) won 20 championships.

Captain Mark Messier raises the Stanley Cup after the Edmonton Oilers' victory in 1990 (courtesy Reuters/Bettmann Newsphotos).

Ochre Sea Star *is one of 1500 species of starfish (photo by Thomas Kitchin).*

Canadian coastlines: it may measure 1 m in diameter and have up to 24 arms.

▷ SUGGESTED READING: Philip Lambert, *The Sea Stars of British Columbia* (1981).

■ Starling

Starling is the name of a large Old World family of birds (Sturnidae), which has 111 species worldwide. Only two have been introduced to Canada: the European Starling (*Sturnus vulgaris*), living in the southern part of the country, and the Crested Myna (*Acridotheres cristatellus*), living in Vancouver where it was introduced in the 1890s.

The European Starling is slightly larger than a blackbird. Black with a yellow bill during nesting season, it gets beige spots and the bill turns black in the fall and winter. It lives primarily on open ground, in cities and farmland. It is very friendly except in mating season: in the fall you see it in huge bands in the fields, often accompanied by grackles, cow blackbirds, and cowbirds. The Crested Myna is also black with a yellow bill, but its wings sport white patches. Unlike the European Starling, the Crested Myna has barely spread in its 90 years in Canada.

Starlings nest in tree hollows, eaves-troughing, birdhouses, and even postbox-

European Starling *(courtesy Macmillan Illustrated Animal Encyclopedia).*

es. The four to five eggs take 11 to 14 days to hatch. In 1890 and 1891, 100 birds were introduced to New York; they prospered so well that they spread throughout the U.S. and into southern Canada. Tough and quarrelsome, starlings take nesting spots away from native species, particularly swallows and the Blue Rock Thrush. Though it eats grains, the starling relieves us of a large quantity of insects as well.

■ Stars

Stars are balls of gases glowing intensely. The glow is caused by radiation from nuclear reactions in the stars. The spectacle of the stars, of which about 2500 are visible to the naked eye from Canada, has long fascinated people. Our Sun is a star.

Supernova A supernova is the violent explosion of a massive star.

Stars are born when gas, mostly hydrogen, congeals into massive balls.

Squeezed by the force of its own gravity, a star gets so hot it turns into a nuclear furnace. Nuclear fusion reactions, like those in a hydrogen bomb, turn its hydrogen into helium. The star shines until it has used up all its fuel. Massive stars then blow themselves apart. They become, for a few days or weeks, inconceivably brighter than the Sun. Stars like the Sun die in a gentler way.

Most of the elements of which our bodies and the planets are made are created within the stars. The supernovae spew these elements into space. A supernova is the closest thing to the creation of the universe that we can observe.

Star Gazing Only a few of the brighter stars are visible from cities. Over cities the sky glows with artificial light — from street lamps among other sources — which masks the light from fainter stars. Hence many more stars can be seen far from the city. The best time for star gazing is a cloudless, moonless night.

Constellations are groups of stars that form recognizable patterns. They serve as landmarks in the sky. With the help of a star chart, they will guide you through the stars. Of the constellations in the northern sky, one of the easiest to recognize is the Big Dipper. It is part of a larger constellation called Ursa Major, Latin for the great bear.

Imagine a straight line drawn between the two stars on the end of its bowl. Following this line outward you will find Polaris, the pole star. Polaris appears to remain fixed in the sky (because it is in line with the Earth's axis of rotation). All other stars appear to move around it. When

Breeding Range of European Starling ●

Discovery of a Star

On the night of February 24, 1987, Ian Shelton, a young Canadian astronomer, was working at an observatory operated by the University of Toronto on a mountain top in northern Chile. He noticed a peculiar bright spot on a photograph he had just taken through an antique telescope.

Stepping outside to look up at the sky with his eyes, he saw a new star in a galaxy known as the Large Magellanic Cloud.

Shelton was the first to recognize this very rare event. The object was quickly identified as a supernova, and officially named Supernova Shelton 1987A.

AVERAGE INCOME RELATED TO LEVEL OF EDUCATION—1987

Thousands of Dollars

Education Level	Male	Female
Grades 0 to 8	23.3	12.3
Some or Completed High School	23.7	13.5
Some Post-secondary	22.9	13.7
Post-secondary Certificate or Diploma	28.8	18.3
University Degree	42.6	26.5

■ Male ■ Female   Source: Statistics Canada

you face Polaris, you face due north.

Other easy constellations to recognize are Orion, Cassiopeia, Leo, and Scorpius.

Of the stars visible in the night skies over Canada, the brightest is Sirius. It is bright because it is so close. Light travels at 300 000 km per second. It takes only 1.3 seconds for light to get to Earth from its neighbour, the Moon. Light reaches Earth from the planets in minutes or hours. It takes 8.6 years for light to get here from Sirius. However, the brightest object of all in the night sky, next to the Moon, is the planet Venus.

Stars and planets are very different. Stars generate their own light. Planets reflect light from the Sun. The planets Mercury, Venus, Mars, Jupiter, and Saturn are visible to the naked eye. They are bright because they are so close to Earth. Planets are not always shown on a chart of the sky because they move relative to the stars. Unlike stars, they do not twinkle.

Images of the stars in the night skies are projected on the domed ceiling of a planetarium. Stars are viewed through binoculars or telescopes. The Royal Astronomical Society of Canada includes both professional and amateur astronomers. It has branches across Canada. There is also an Association des groupes d'astronomes amateurs in Quebec.

▷ Related Articles: **Astronomy; Meteorite.**
▷ Suggested Reading: Necia H. Apfel, *Nebulae: The Birth and Death of Stars* (1988); Franklyn Mansfield Branley, *Journey into a Black Hole* (1986); Heather Couper, *Galaxies and Quasars* (1986); Terence Dickinson, *Exploring the Night Sky* (1987); Roy Gallant, *Private Lives of the Stars* (1986).

■ Statistics

The science of statistics deals with the analysis of information from any given

"population." The population might be all the students in one province who take a particular course. The information might be their scores on a provincial exam in that subject. The population might just as easily be the weekly output of automobiles from a particular factory. The information in this case might deal with various models produced and time needed to produce a particular model.

Descriptive Statistics deals with the information collected from an entire population. For example, if seven students write an exam, and obtain scores of, respectively, 60, 40, 52, 71, 80, 52, and 84, then one can compute the *average* (or *mean*) score: the sum of the seven scores, divided by the number (7) of scores. You should check that it is approximately 62.7.

One can also compute the *variance*, which measures how widely dispersed are the marks from the average. For example, if the scores had been 5, 5, 5, 5, 90, 90, 90, the average would have been approximately 41.4. In this second case, the variance is much higher, which tells the statistician that the scores are more widely dispersed from the average.

In addition, statisticians compute the *median* by arranging the data in increasing order: for example, 40, 52, 52, 60, 71, 80, 84. The number at the midpoint of the list is the median (the fourth number, 60).

One more important number is the *mode*, which is the number occurring most often in the data (52). For the second set of scores above (5, 5, 5, 5, 90, 90, 90), the median is 5 and so is the mode. All of these data can be used to form a good picture of the population under study.

Descriptive statistics is used in industry and in sports. In hockey the statistics may be goals against, average shots on goal and so on. A common statistic in baseball is batting average.

Descriptive statistics is used extensively by the government, using census data, to form an accurate picture of the Canadian population.

Inferential Statistics uses a *sample* from a population to make predictions about the make-up of that population. One of the widest uses of inferential statistics is in the prediction of election results. It is fairly common now to predict the outcome in a particular riding as soon as 10% (or less!) of the votes are counted.

Politicians count inferential statisticians (called "pollsters" because they take written or telephone polls of randomly selected samples of the voting public) among their most important campaign tools. The techniques of inferential statistics are also used in testing new drugs before allowing them to be marketed, in the evaluation of alleged health hazards, and also in taking inventory at large factories and on tree farms (no one wants to actually count 3 million trees, so they use a random sample and a statistical estimate).

One of the more interesting applications of statistics is in the analysis of health-related issues, such as smoking. The conclusion that smoking causes lung cancer was not based on asking people to smoke and then checking to see if they got the disease — this conclusion was reached from the statistical analysis of the information on lung cancer cases among smokers and non-smokers.

Often graphs, charts, and other tables are used to show statistical information. These are sometimes easier to understand than raw data and usually make it very easy to see the information at a glance. Pie and circle graphs are just two of many ways to show statistics. Graphs, charts, and tables are often produced by a computer, which is a useful tool for statisticians when they are dealing with large amounts of data or complicated statistics. By using a computer, statisticians get both the speed and accuracy necessary in dealing with data.

Statistics Canada

This is the agency which collects, analyses and publishes facts and figures which have to do with the business of Canada and being a Canadian. This agency came into being under the name Dominion Bureau of Statistics in 1918. It publishes the *Canada Handbook* and the *Canada Yearbook* every second year. Copies of this publication are available in libraries, including your school library.

The people in Statistics Canada work with others in various departments of the government to gather and present the facts and figures. Often different departments are involved in the compiling of a single set of figures. For instance, one of the agency's responsibilities is to compile and publish the Consumer Price Index which, in turn, is an indicator of the cost of living and inflation. To do this, people within Statistics Canada consult with several other departments. Once the Consumer Price Index is completed, the results are used by almost every government department as well as by many agencies and organizations outside government. Other important activities of Statistics Canada have to do with the census of the population, the Labour Force Survey, and the Gross National Product.

▷ SUGGESTED READING: Statistics Canada, *Canada: A Portrait* (1989).

Statute of Westminster

The Statute of Westminster, dated December 11, 1931, was a British law that made clear Canada's power to make its own laws.

The Imperial Conference of 1926 declared that Canada and the other British dominions were no longer colonies but free and equal partners with Great Britain under the king. That declaration led directly to the Statute of Westminster, which removed all remaining legal limits on independence except where Canadians chose to keep them. The federal and provincial governments disagreed about the written part of Canada's constitution (the British North America Act). Therefore any changes to it remained a responsibility of the British Parliament until the Constitution Act, 1982.

Staunton, Edward Stewart (Ted)

Writer (*born in 1956 at Toronto, Ont.*). Staunton was educated at the University of Toronto. While completing his education degree, he wrote a children's story for a class assignment. It became the picture book *Puddleman* (1983), which was republished in 1988 with new illustrations. A second picture book, *Taking Care of Crumley* (1984), introduced two characters, Maggie and Cyril, who have continued their humorous friendship through three juvenile novels. Maggie "the Greenapple Street Genius" must constantly create ingenious plans to rescue her friend Cyril. *Maggie and Me* (1986), *Greenapple Street Blues* (1987), and *Mushmouth and the Marvel* (1988) each contain five of their funny adventures. A little boy told by his parents that he is too small to wash the family car decides to prove them wrong in the picture book *Simon's Surprise* (1986).

Steel, *see* Iron and Steel

Steele, Sir Samuel Benfield

North-West Mounted Police officer (*born in 1849 at Purbrook, Canada West [Ont.]; died in 1919 at London, England*). Sam Steele was one of the first to join the North-West Mounted Police on its formation in 1873. Though still in his early twenties, he was an experienced soldier,

Sir Sam Steele saw action as a Mountie and a soldier from South Africa to the Yukon (courtesy NAC/PA-28146).

Vilhjalmur Stefansson preparing to leave on a hunting trip in the Canadian Arctic (courtesy NAC/C-71050).

having enlisted in the militia during the 1866 Fenian invasions and taken part in the Red River Expedition in 1870. Between then and joining the Mounties, he served in the artillery.

He was made a sergeant-major in the NWMP and five years later was commissioned an officer. This was the beginning of an action-packed career, in which Steele usually managed to be wherever the going was toughest. He brought order to the rowdy camps of construction workers who built the railway to the Pacific in the 1880s, and in 1898-99 he was NWMP superintendent in the Yukon. He often worked a 19-hour day to enforce Canadian law among the Klondike gold miners. In 1900 he went overseas as commander of Strathcona's Horse, a regiment formed to fight in the South African War. After that he served with the South African Constabulary.

Steele was back in action again during World War I when, as a major-general in the army, he trained the 2nd Canadian Division and took it to England. He was knighted in 1918 and retired at the end of the war, dying a few months later.

▷ SUGGESTED READING: Stan Garrod, *Sam Steele* (1979).

■ Stefansson, Vilhjalmur

Arctic explorer (*born in 1879 at Arnes, Man.; died in 1962 at New Hampshire, U.S.*). The son of Icelandic immigrants to Canada, Stefansson was raised in the

United States where his family moved when he was a baby. As a young man he studied to become an anthropologist. Shortly after finishing university, he made his first trip to the Arctic in 1906 where he passed a winter living with an Inuit family in their driftwood lodge.

Returning to the North in 1908, Stefansson trekked toward Victoria Island where he was the first non-native to meet the Copper Inuit, an isolated group of seal hunters living in the central Arctic. He touched off a huge debate by claiming that these fair-haired people, who he called the "Blond Eskimos," were descendants of the Vikings. This theory is now thought unlikely.

Stefansson's third expedition was in command of the Canadian Arctic Expedition (1913-18), a large-scale study of life in the North. He quarrelled with other scientists and the expedition divided. Stefansson travelled by dog sled far to the north over the sea ice where he found four new islands (the last sizeable pieces of land to be discovered anywhere in the world). When asked about the dangers of exploration in the frozen North, Stefansson said that "one gets used to danger and one gets tired of staying scared."

Stefansson believed that Canada should develop the North and he came up with schemes to raise reindeer like cattle, and to send submarines under the North Pole. He even tried to seize control of a remote arctic island that belonged to the Soviet Union.

Stefansson quarrelled with many of his fellow scientists in Canada who believed he was more interested in seeking publicity than in science. The government also lost patience with the explorer when his schemes failed, and he spent the last part of his life in the United States.

As much as for his explorations, Stefansson was known for his belief that the Arctic was a "friendly" place where nonnatives could learn to live in comfort. More than that, he argued that the North was a land of great potential wealth. Stefansson lectured and wrote books about the Arctic and its people, and earned for himself the name "Prophet of the North."

▷ SUGGESTED READING: Alexander D. Gregor, *Vilhjalmur Stefansson and the Arctic* (1978); William R. Hunt, *Stef: A Biography of Vilhjalmur Stefansson* (1986).

■ Steinbach

Steinbach, Man., lies in a farm district southeast of Winnipeg. It was founded in 1874 as part of a large migration of Men-

Steinbach, Man. (courtesy Steinbach Chamber of Commerce).

nonite settlers into Manitoba from Russia. Steinbach is an important centre for the surrounding farms. Its population in 1986 was 7473.

For further information, contact the Town Secretary, P.O. Box 1090, Steinbach, Man., R0A 2A0.

■ Stellarton

Stellarton, N.S., lies beside the East River, south of Pictou near the province's North Shore. First settled by Scots immigrants in 1774, it was a coal-mining centre from 1827 until the mines closed in 1957. The Nova Scotia Museum of Transportation is scheduled to open in 1990. The population in 1986 was 5259.

For further information, contact the Town Clerk, P.O. Box 2200, Stellarton, N.S., B0K 1S0.

■ Stephen, George, 1st Baron Mount Stephen

Banker and railway president (*born in 1829 at Dufftown, Scotland; died in 1921 at Hatfield, England*). Stephen was head of the company that built the Canadian Pacific Railway (CPR), serving as its president from 1880 to 1888. This mighty enterprise called on all the Scottish grit and determination that had made Stephen a successful businessman.

He had first come to Canada in 1850 to join his uncle's clothing and drapery business; within ten years he was its owner. His business interests spread to banking and railways, and by 1873 he was a director of the Bank of Montreal. He was the bank's president from 1876 to 1881.

Stephen was always attracted by bold ventures: one was buying an ailing, half-finished Minnesota railway, the St Paul and Pacific, which he did with his cousin Donald Smith, J.J. Hill, and Norman Kittson. Through their skilful handling of the project they made $1 million each and emerged with a well-run railway (re-

named the St Paul, Minneapolis and Manitoba in 1879).

While this money was not yet invested, the Canadian government asked Stephen's group if it would build the Canadian Pacific Railway. Stephen agreed, but it proved far more difficult and costly than had been anticipated. As president of the CPR, Stephen shouldered the burden of raising the vast sums of money needed for construction. To get the required loans, he risked losing his own fortune. It was a great triumph when the railway was completed in November 1885.

After eight years with the CPR, Stephen retired to England in 1888. He was made Baron Mount Stephen in 1891.

▷ SUGGESTED READING: David Cruise and Alison Griffiths, *Lords of the Line: The Men Who Built the CPR* (1988).

■ Stephenson, Sir William Samuel

Businessman, intelligence officer (*born in 1896 at Winnipeg, Man.; died in 1989 at Paget, Bermuda*). Stephenson's adventures began in World War I, during which he survived a gas attack in the trenches, then became a fighter pilot. He shot down eight enemy planes before being shot down and taken prisoner.

After the war, while at the University of Manitoba, Stephenson began his research on radio which led to his invention of the wirephoto. In 1921 he moved to England where he teamed up with a British photo-telegraphy researcher, Professor T. Thorne Baker. By 1922 they were able to send pictures instantly over long distances without the use of telephone or telegraph wires. The first such photo officially sent by this method was of two skiers, which was printed in the London *Daily Mail* on December 27, 1922. This invention, together with the radio company Stephenson formed in England, made him a millionaire before he was 30.

During World War II, he took on his most famous role. He directed Britain's intelligence operations in North and South America. At an old farmhouse near Oshawa, Ont., he set up Special Training School 103 ("Camp X"). There, recruits received basic training in security and intelligence techniques. Some of them went on to advanced training before being parachuted by plane or landed by submarine in Nazi-occupied Europe.

Stephenson once more concentrated on his business interests after the war, and in 1968 he retired to Bermuda. He received many honours and awards, and in 1982, at the age of 86, he was appointed honorary colonel commandant of the intelligence branch of the Canadian Armed Forces.

▷ RELATED ARTICLE: **Spying.**

▷ SUGGESTED READING: H. Montgomery Hyde, *The Quiet Canadian* (1962).

■ Stephenville

Stephenville, Nfld, lies at the head of St George's Bay on the southwest coast of the island. It began in 1846 as an Acadian fishing and farming community. During World War II, the construction of an American air base brought rapid growth, but when the base closed in 1966 the economy suffered. Since 1981 a large paper mill has provided many jobs for the town, which is an important business centre for the surrounding region. The Stephenville Festival theatre company was founded in 1979. Stephenville's population in 1986 was 7994.

For further information, contact the Town Clerk, P.O. Box 420, Stephenville, Nfld, A2N 2Z5.

■ Sternberg, Charles Mortram

Paleontologist (*born in 1885 at Lawrence, Kansas, U.S.; died in 1981 at Ottawa, Ont.*). Sternberg was a dinosaur hunter; he searched for the fossils of dinosaurs, especially in Alberta. Sternberg came from an American family of fossil collectors, who in 1912 made their first expedition to Alberta's fossil fields in the Badlands along the Red Deer River. The expedition was on behalf of the Geological Survey of Canada. Sternberg worked for the Geological Survey and the National Museum of Canada for the rest of his career, and became a world-famous authority on dinosaurs. His main finds were in Alberta, but he also collected fossils in Saskatchewan, British Columbia and Nova Scotia. After retiring in 1950, Sternberg helped set up Dinosaur Provincial Park in Alberta.

▷ SUGGESTED READING: L.S. Russell, *Dinosaur Hunting in Western Canada* (1966).

■ Stewart

Stewart, B.C., is a district municipality in the isolated northwest interior next to the Alaska Panhandle, 880 km northwest of Vancouver. It is named for two brothers who began prospecting there in 1902 and touched off a mining boom in the area. Mining and forest-based industries are the major employers. Stewart's population in 1986 was 858.

For further information, contact the District Municipal Clerk, P.O. Box 460, Stewart, B.C., V0T 1W0.

Stikine Territory

Stikine Territory was created in July 1862 in the extreme northwest corner of British Columbia next to Alaska. Gold had been found on the Stikine River, and the British wanted to impose orderly government before a rush of prospectors began. A year later, most of the territory became part of British Columbia.

***Writer Kathy Stinson** (courtesy Annick Press Ltd).*

■ Stickleback

Sticklebacks are small fish up to 5 cm long. There are five species in Canada, some freshwater and some oceangoing. Their main characteristic, the one that gives them their name, is the presence of three spines, one before the dorsal fin, one along the side, and one by the pelvic fin. Their colour ranges from green to black. Male three-spine sticklebacks (*Gasterosteus aculeatus*) bear a large red spot during mating season.

Sticklebacks live on small crustaceans and insects, and are themselves prey to fish and birds. The male plays an important role in reproduction; he builds the nest where the female lays the eggs, fertilizes them, and protects them. Biologists study this fish because of its large numbers and wide varieties. It has distinctive behaviour patterns. For example, certain species dislike salty water. Its value therefore is scientific; it has no economic importance.

■ Stikine River

The Stikine River, 539 km long, flows through the scenic wilderness of northwestern British Columbia to empty into the Pacific Ocean near Wrangell, Alaska. It has long been home to the Tlingit and Tahltan peoples, whose word for "great river" gives the Stikine its name. A deep, narrow stretch of canyon separates the upper and lower sections of the river. The fur trade reached the area in the 1820s, and in the 1860s there was a small gold rush. Steamboats plied the river and it became an important route to the interior. Today salmon fishing is the mainstay of the people of Telegraph Creek, B.C., one of the two communities on the river.

▷ RELATED ARTICLE: **River.**

■ Stinson, Kathy

Writer (*born in 1952 at Toronto, Ont.*). Stinson has used her childhood memories and her experiences as a teacher and mother to write several short books for preschool-aged children. *Red is Best* (1982), *Big or Little?* (1983), *Those Green Things* (1985), and *The Bare Naked Book* (1986) use simple, rhythmic language which captures little children's responses to the world around them. She has also written *Seven Clues in Pebble Creek* (1987), a mystery novel, and *Teddy Rabbit* (1988).

■ Stocks and Bonds

Stocks and bonds are sold (issued) by companies to raise money for ongoing business activity and expansion. Bonds are also issued by all levels of government (federal, provincial, municipal) when tax revenues are less than the amount the government is spending. Once issued, the stocks and bonds are traded (bought and sold) among investors.

Bonds differ from stocks in one basic way. A bond provides evidence of a loan made to the issuer by the bondholder. The loan must be paid back to whoever owns the bond at a stated date, known as the *bond maturity date*. A stock represents a *share* of ownership, and thus stocks are often called shares. A stockholder is a part-owner of the company.

Because bonds are a loan, interest is paid to the bondholder as payment for lending the money. The interest payable is stated as a percentage of the amount borrowed, known as the *par value* of the bond. A bond with a par value of $1000 and an interest rate of 10%, promises to pay $100 a year interest. The issuer is obliged to pay at the agreed time. Only in the case of bankruptcy can the bondholder not receive the payments promised by a company.

Although a bond has a fixed par value, the prices at which it trades through time in the financial market may be higher or lower than par value. If for a certain class of bonds the market interest rate is 8% and a bond of that type also has an interest rate of 8%, it will sell for par value. But when the market rate rises to 9%, no investors will pay par value for the 8% bond because nearly identical bonds are available at the higher 9% rate. The price of the bond will fall until the interest payable plus the gain to be received at maturity from the difference between par value and the lower price paid, yields an investor a return of 9% a year. When the

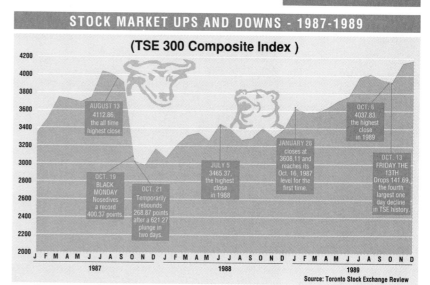

STOCK MARKET UPS AND DOWNS - 1987-1989

(TSE 300 Composite Index)

AUGUST 13 4112.86, the all time highest close.

OCT. 19 BLACK MONDAY Nosedives a record 400.37 points.

OCT. 21 Temporarily rebounds 268.87 points after a 621.27 plunge in two days.

JULY 5 3465.37, the highest close in 1988

JANUARY 26 closes at 3608.11 and reaches its Oct. 16, 1987 level for the first time.

OCT. 6 4037.83, the highest close in 1989

OCT. 13 FRIDAY THE 13TH Drops 141.69, the fourth largest one day decline in TSE history.

1987   1988   1989

Source: Toronto Stock Exchange Review

market rate falls, for the same reason bond prices increase. Because market interest rates change frequently, bond prices fluctuate over time. While such fluctuations may be less than with stocks, the risk of loss is very real if the bond is sold prior to maturity.

An exception to the general behaviour of bonds is Canada Savings Bonds. These bonds are issued once a year by the federal government and can be sold back to the government, and no one else, at any time for par value. Consequently their price is fixed at par value.

Of the two types of stocks — *common* and *preferred* — the most widely held type is common stock. Common stockholders are the firms' residual owners and as such have the right to vote in the affairs of the company and to share in the profits through *dividends*. Dividends are a share of profits and of the growing value of the firm. A company is not obliged to pay dividends. This remains the decision of the board of directors, who are elected by the stockholders. While dividends are important to shareholders, it is having the business do well and selling the stock at a profit that is most important.

Prices of common shares change according to current and expected future earnings of the firm. Because earnings are related to industry-wide events and general business conditions, in addition to events unique to the firm, prices are very variable. Historically, stockholders have realized higher returns than bondholders but at a greater risk of having to sell at a loss.

Preferred stock also represents ownership of the firm, but preferred takes preference over common. That is, preferred dividends are paid before common divi-

Toronto Stock Exchange on Black Monday, October 19, 1987 (courtesy Canada Wide Feature Services).

Stocks

Most stock is traded on stock exchanges where members (brokers) buy and sell shares on behalf of clients (investors).

Trading results are carried in most newspapers. A typical line in a stock table for a day's trading might look like this:

Stock:	ABC
Div Rate:	0.36
High:	8
Low:	7 1/2
Close:	7 7/8
Net Chge:	-1/4
Vol 100s:	79

The name of the imaginary company is ABC which has paid 36 cents in dividends in the past 12 months. The highest price at which the stock sold during the day is $8.00, the lowest price is $7.50 and the last trade of the day, the closing price, went through at $7.875. The closing price is -1/4 or 25 cents lower than the closing trade of the day before. A total volume of 7900 shares were traded.

dends. In return, preferred dividends are restricted to a fixed rate.

Stone Angel

The Stone Angel (1964) is a novel by Margaret Laurence. Ninety-year-old Hagar Shipley, suffering from a fatal disease, remembers her earlier life and fights to keep her dignity as her son and daughter-in-law prepare to send her to an old-age home. She had been a very proud girl, and she had disobeyed her father when she married a poor and lazy farmer. She realizes that she had never allowed herself to love other people. In many ways, she is like the statue of a stone angel in the cemetery: blind and cold. She did not understand other people or feel kindly toward them. In the novel, Laurence used her memories of growing up in Neepawa, Man. The character of Hagar has been called the finest portrayal of an old person in Canadian literature.

▷ SUGGESTED READING: Lillian Perigoe, editor, *The Stone Angel* (1983).

Stonefly

Stonefly is a name for insects belonging to Order Plecopiera (they fold the rear wings over their bodies while at rest). The body is long and flattened, and the antennae are long and thread-like. Two long filaments ("cerci") are often found at the end of the abdomen. Larvae develop in water; adults live near water. Stoneflies live on lichen, algae, and leaves; many species do not eat in the adult stage. Larvae resemble adults, but have no wings. Larvae feed on aquatic plants, detritus, and small aquatic organisms; in turn, they are eaten by fish. Stoneflies belong to one of the rare groups of insects that are more diversified in temperate and cold regions (such as Canada) than in the tropics. They like cool, well-aerated, and unpolluted water, which explains their preference for running water, especially high in the mountains. The larvae are therefore good indicators of water quality. Some 300 species are known in Canada.

Stoney Creek

Stoney Creek, Ont., lies on the eastern edge of Hamilton, in the Niagara Peninsula. First settled by Loyalists in the 1780s, it grew as a farming and fruit-growing centre. During the War of 1812, British troops won an important victory over American invaders here. A re-enactment of the Battle of Stoney Creek (June 6, 1813) takes place every year. The population in 1986 was 43 554.

For further information, contact the City Clerk, 777 Highway 8, P.O. Box 9940, Stoney Creek, Ont., L8G 4N9.

Stoney Creek, Battle of

The Battle of Stoney Creek was a decisive battle in the War of 1812 because it turned back the American invasion in the Niagara Peninsula. An American army of some 3500 men had penetrated as far as Stoney Creek, near present-day Hamilton, Ont. But Billy Green, a 19-year-old who lived nearby, discovered the Americans' password and reported it, together with the army's position, to the British officer Colonel Harvey. On the night of June 5-6, 1813, Green guided Harvey and 700 British and Canadian soldiers to the American camp, where they crept forward silently and then launched a surprise attack in the dark. The battle was confused and bloody, and losses on both sides were high. Among the more than 100 American prisoners taken were the two American generals and numerous other officers.

▷ RELATED ARTICLE: **War of 1812.**

Storm-Petrel

Petrels are small seabirds (14 to 25 cm) of the Hydrobatidae family, whose erratic flight resembles that of the swallow. Since they drag their feet while fluttering just above the surface, they appear to be walking on the waves. They were named Storm-petrels because their presence during gusty weather was thought by sailors to be a warning of a storm.

Three species live in Canada: the Fork-tailed Storm-petrel (*Oceanodroma furcata*), Leach's Storm-petrel (*O. leucorhoa*), and Wilson's Storm-petrel (*Oceanites oceanicus*). The Fork-tailed Storm-petrel is ash grey; the others are rusty brown with a white spot on the rump. Petrels nest in colonies on isolated islands, coming to land only to reproduce. The single egg is laid in a burrow, where it is safe from seagulls but vulnerable to rats and cats. The parental changing of the guard takes place at night; by day the colony seems deserted, but one parent remains hidden near the nest while the other is fishing far out at sea.

Petrels have a peculiar defence strategy: the stomach contains an oily, smelly liquid which the bird can vomit on its adversary. This liquid, which is rich in fat and vitamin A, is also used to feed the young.

Stornoway

Stornoway is the name of the official residence of the Leader of the Opposition in

Stonefly (artwork by Jan Sovak).

Breeding Range of Leach's Storm-petrel

Breeding Range of Fork-tailed Storm-petrel

the House of Commons. It was built in 1913-14 by a wealthy merchant, Asconi J. Major, as a two-storey stucco house in the village of Rockcliffe Park near Ottawa, Ont. During World War II, Crown Princess Juliana of the Netherlands and her family lived in the house. In 1950 it was purchased by a private trust to provide a residence for the Leader of the Opposition, and George Drew was the first such leader to occupy the house. In 1970 the Government of Canada took over responsibility for Stornoway and its spacious grounds. Except for interior decoration, the house has not been changed very much since it was built.

▷ SUGGESTED READING: Maureen McTeer, *Residences: Homes of Canada's Leaders* (1982).

■ Stowe, Emily Howard

Suffragette and first Canadian woman doctor *(born Emily Jennings in 1831 at Norwich, Upper Canada [Ont.]; died in 1903 at Toronto, Ont.)*. Both as a doctor and a suffrage worker, Emily Stowe was a leading force in the 19th-century struggle for women's rights. Having started out as a school teacher, she decided to become a doctor in the 1860s. She found her way blocked by laws and regulations which made it impossible for women to study medicine in Canada. Determined to pursue her chosen career, Stowe enrolled at New York Medical College for Women, graduating in 1867. But her path was still blocked. By Ontario law, all graduates from the United States had to take a course at an Ontario medical school, followed by an exam, before they could be licensed to practise in the province. In effect, this prevented any woman from getting a licence, because no Ontario medical school would admit women.

Since Stowe could not comply with the regulations, she decided to ignore them, and she opened a doctor's office in Toronto late in 1867. She was eventually granted a licence in 1880, though she still had not fulfilled all the required conditions. To make things easier for other women, Stowe organized the Woman's Medical College in Toronto in 1883. This was one of two women's medical colleges founded that year, the other being at Kingston.

Meanwhile, she campaigned to get more opportunities for women, and especially the vote. In 1876 she helped found Canada's first suffrage group, the Toronto Women's Literary Club, and she was a founder and first president of the Dominion Women's Enfranchisement Associa-

tion (1889). Stowe's continual campaigning made her unpopular in some circles, and she often had to withstand scathing criticism.

In 1896 she wrote, "My career has been one of much struggle characterized by the usual persecution which attends everyone who pioneers a new movement." Yet generations of Canadian women have been grateful to her. She opened the way for women in medicine, and she pioneered the movement which led to women getting the vote.

▷ RELATED ARTICLE: **Woman's Suffrage.**

▷ SUGGESTED READING: Janet Ray, *Emily Stowe* (1978).

■ Stowe-Gullen, Ann Augusta

Suffragette and doctor *(born in 1857 at Mount Pleasant, Canada West [Ont.]; died in 1943 at Toronto, Ont.)*. The daughter of Emily Stowe, Stowe-Gullen was the first woman to gain a medical degree in Canada. Having been permitted to study at the Toronto School of Medicine together with the male students from Victoria College, Cobourg, she graduated in 1883. She then joined the staff of the newly formed Woman's Medical College, where she taught for many years. She also ran a practice for women and children, and was closely associated with Toronto Western Hospital, of which her husband, Dr John Gullen, was a founder.

Although Stowe-Gullen's way into medicine was far easier than her mother's, she was just as committed to widening the scope for other women. In 1903 she succeeded her mother as president of the Dominion Women's Enfranchisement Association, remaining president after it became the Canadian Suffrage Association in 1907. She retired from the position in 1911 but continued to agitate vigorously for "votes for women" until this was granted during World War I.

▷ RELATED ARTICLES: **Emily Stowe; Woman's Suffrage.**

▷ SUGGESTED READING: Carlotta Hacker, *The Indomitable Lady Doctors* (1974).

■ Strachan, John

Anglican bishop *(born in 1778 at Aberdeen, Scotland; died in 1867 at Toronto, Ont.)*. John Strachan, first bishop of Toronto, was one of the strong voices in Canadian religion. He was also a powerful conservative influence in education and politics.

Strachan immigrated to Upper Canada in 1799, and in 1803 he was ordained an Anglican priest and appointed rector of

Emily Stowe *(courtesy NAC/C-9480).*

Bishop John Strachan *believed that it was his destiny to keep Upper Canada British (courtesy NAC/C-7432).*

Cornwall. There he established a school to which the powerful Loyalist families sent their sons. He became rector of York [Toronto] at the beginning of the War of 1812. When the Americans captured York in 1813, he emerged the leader of those people left in the town. By his strong authority, he protected the interests of the people and prevented the worst effects of looting.

From then on, Strachan gained political as well as religious influence. He became an important member of the Family Compact, a group of men who then ruled Upper Canada. In 1817 he was appointed to the Executive Council and in 1820 to the Legislative Council. Strachan's religious and educational careers advanced with his political career. Made archdeacon of York in 1825, he became first bishop of Toronto in 1839. He was first president of King's College, which he helped found in 1827. When King's was secularized in 1850 (made a non-religious body called the University of Toronto), he founded a new Anglican university, Trinity College (1851).

Much of Strachan's power lay in the fact that leading members of the Family Compact had been students of his, early in the century. It was appropriate that he died in the year of Confederation when the old Tory ideals of Upper Canada were vanishing into history and a new age was dawning.

▷ RELATED ARTICLES: **Family Compact; Upper Canada.**

■ Strait of Anian

The Strait of Anian was a legendary passage out of the Pacific Ocean across the top of America. The name came from the Chinese province of Ania. The strait was believed to begin somewhere along the coast of British Columbia or Alaska. Many explorers sought the passage, which appeared on maps in the 16th century. At the end of the 18th century, a number of land and sea expeditions proved that no such strait existed.

■ Strait of Belle Isle

The Strait of Belle Isle is the northern outlet of the Gulf of St Lawrence. It separates the Great Northern Peninsula of Newfoundland from the mainland of southern Labrador. It is about 14.4 km wide at its narrowest point, with an average width of 17.6 km. Navigation through the strait is often extremely hazardous, because of frequent dense fogs, severe variations in ocean currents, and the common presence of icebergs. The strait is often blocked by ice for as much as eight to ten months of the year.

■ Strait of Canso

The Strait of Canso is a deep, narrow channel dividing Cape Breton Island from mainland Nova Scotia. It is 1.2 km wide. In 1955 the strait was spanned by the Canso Causeway. The causeway created a year-round ice-free harbour, and ports were expanded at Port Hawkesbury and Mulgrave. The area is an important paper milling centre.

■ Strait of Georgia

The Strait of Georgia separates Vancouver Island from the southern mainland of British Columbia. The shores of the strait have been occupied by Coast Salish people for over 5000 years. The Spanish explored the area in 1791, followed the next year by British sea captain George Vancouver. He named the strait for his king, George III. Vancouver is the largest city on the strait. There are several deep-sea shipping ports open year round, and the mild climate and many sheltered harbours make the strait an ideal place for boating.

■ Stratas, Teresa

Soprano (*born Anastasia Stratakis in 1938 at Toronto, Ont.*). This remarkable singing actress was born to Greek parents who operated a restaurant in Toronto. She sang Greek songs on the radio at 13. At 16 she began four years of voice lessons at the Royal Conservatory. She made her professional debut at age 20 as Mimi in Puccini's *La Bohème* with the Toronto Opera Festival (later Canadian Opera Company). She made her Metropolitan Opera debut as Poussette in Massenet's *Manon* in 1959.

In the 1960s Stratas took many of the major lyric-soprano roles at the Metropolitan Opera. In 1967 she returned to Canada to sing Desdemona in the Expo 67 World Festival production of Verdi's *Otello* in Montreal.

In the 1970s, Stratas branched out into television and films, starring in Norman Campbell's 1972 CBC TV production of Puccini's *La Rondine*, and Franco Zeferelli's film productions of Leoncavallo's *I Pagliacci* in 1981 and Verdi's *La Traviata* in Rome in 1983.

In over 30 years onstage and before the cameras, Stratas has established herself as one of the foremost singing actresses of her generation. She is also a fiercely independent person who lives her offstage life with disregard for the pampered lifestyles of most opera stars. She spent the summer of 1981, for instance, working as a volunteer in the children's hospitals of Mother Teresa.

Stratas' singing is preserved on a number of recordings, including *Lulu* under Boulez, *I Pagliacci* under Prêtre, *La Traviata* under Levine (film soundtrack), and *The Merry Widow* under Karajan. She also made two recordings of the songs of Kurt Weill.

▷ SUGGESTED READING: Harry Rasky, *Stratas* (1978).

■ Stratford

Stratford, Ont., is the highest city in Ontario (364 m). It lies in the heart of southwestern Ontario, 50 km northeast of London. Founded in the 1830s by the Canada Company, it grew quickly during the railway-building boom of the 1850s when several railways passed through town. Today the economy relies on a mix of light manufacturing as well as several auto-related industries. Stratford is well known as the home of the Stratford Festival. The population in 1986 was 26 451.

For further information, contact the City Clerk, City Hall, Stratford, Ont., N5A 2L1.

The Stratford Festival Theatre *sits in a park setting by a pond. It seats over 2000 (courtesy Stratford Festival).*

■ Stratford Festival

The Stratford Festival is Canada's best-known theatre. It was founded by a local journalist, Tom Patterson, in Stratford, Ont., in 1953. Its first play opened in a huge tent. The first director was Tyrone Guthrie, from Britain, and the designer was Tanya Moiseiwitsch. In his three seasons, Guthrie set the tone for the Stratford Festival: it would feature plays by Shakespeare and other famous dramatists, the actors would be international stars and promising Canadians, and the stage would be a modified Elizabethan

thrust stage. In 1957 the tent was replaced by the Festival Theatre. It seats 2276 people on three sides of the open stage and looks rather like a tent itself.

By 1971 the Stratford Festival had two more stages: the Avon Theatre, which seats 1100 in front of a conventional proscenium arch stage, and the Third Stage, a 500-seat space generally used for experimental theatre and for training young actors.

The Stratford Festival has always had a strong music program, including symphony, jazz, and pop concerts, and opera and musicals. In the early 1980s, choreographer Brian Macdonald directed a dazzling series of Gilbert and Sullivan operettas; *The Mikado* later toured Britain and the United States. The main company also toured the U.S., Europe, the Soviet Union, and Australia. Several Stratford productions have been made into films and videotapes for television. In 1989 the season ran for six months, with 525 performances and a company of 100 actors.

The Stratford Festival is often called Canada's national theatre. It has produced over 35 original Canadian plays. As Canadian theatre became more nationalistic in the 1970s and 1980s, there were many bitter disputes over the appointment of British directors to run the festival. Many of Canada's best actors have trained and worked at Stratford, including Martha Henry, William Hutt, Christopher Plummer, and Kate Reid. The Stratford Festival has also set superb standards in stage and costume design.

▷ SUGGESTED READING: Tom Patterson and Allan Gould, *First Stage: The Making of the Stratford Festival* (1989); John Pettigrew and Jamie Portman, *Stratford: The First Thirty Years 1953-1983* (1985); Grace Lydiatt Shaw, *Stratford Under Cover: Memories on Tape* (1977).

■ Strathcona Provincial Park

Strathcona Provincial Park (2225 km²) is a mountain wilderness area in central Van-

Scene from The Merry Wives of Windsor, *1967, at the Stratford Festival (courtesy Stratford Festival).*

Oedipus Rex, *performed at the Stratford Festival, 1955 (courtesy Stratford Festival).*

Directors of the Stratford Festival
Tyrone Guthrie 1953-55
Michael Langham 1956-67
Jean Gascon 1968-74
Robin Phillips 1975-80
John Hirsch 1981-85
John Neville 1986-89
David William 1990-

couver Island in British Columbia. It was established in 1911. The park features several towering peaks, including the Golden Hinde (2200 m), the highest mountain on the island. Small glaciers are present on a few of these peaks.

Strathcona Provincial Park was named for Donald Smith, Baron Strathcona, an early official of the Canadian Pacific Railway. It is popular with campers, hikers, and skiers.

■ Strawberry

Strawberries (*Frageria*) belong to the rose family (Rosaceae). In Canada there are three native species and several cultivated varieties. The plant is low and has a short stem from which grow the leaves, white flowers, and berries. The common strawberry (*Fragaria virginiana*) grows wild in open fields and woods. Its berry is much smaller than commercially grown strawberries, which come from a crossbreed of different species.

The actual fruits of the strawberry plant are the tiny granules found on the berry's surface, each of which contains a seed. The fleshy part is the receptacle, that is, the support for the fruit. Strawberries reproduce by their seeds, and also by *stolons*, a kind of stem lying along the surface of the soil from which new plants grow at intervals. These new plants then take root and become independent of the parent.

Strawberries have been used as medicine for many centuries. The leaves, for example, are said to cure diseases of the stomach and kidney, and the berry relieves fevers and ulcers.

▷ RELATED ARTICLE: **Berries, Wild.**

Wild Strawberry (photo by Mary W. Ferguson).

■ Stren, Patti

Writer, illustrator (*born in 1949 at Brantford, Ont.*). After graduating from the University of Toronto, she worked with autistic children in Israel before studying at the Ontario College of Art and the New York School of Visual Arts. Illustrated with unique cartoon-like drawings, her books are serious in theme, but simple and humorous in presentation. All explore friendship or self-acceptance. In *Hug Me* (1977), for example, a porcupine longs for a friend to hug. A similar theme appears in *Bo, the Strictor That Couldn't* (1978) and *Sloan & Philamina; Or How To Make Friends With Your Lunch* (1979).

A related theme, that of accepting being different from others, is dealt with in *I'm Only Afraid of the Dark (at Night!!)* (1982) and *Mountain Rose* (1982). Stren's novels, *There's a Rainbow in My Closet* (1979) and *I Was a 15-Year-Old Blimp* (1985) explore this same theme of being different from others and searching for an identity.

■ Strikes and Lockouts

Strikes and lockouts are two kinds of work stoppages. A *strike* occurs when workers leave their jobs in order to shut down their workplace. The purpose of a strike is to pressure employers to deal with their employees, either to negotiate with them or to grant their demands.

A *lockout* is an action taken by an employer to lock workers out of the workplace. Employers resort to lockouts when they believe workers are being unreasonable, or because they expect a strike. In Canada, lockouts occur far less frequently than strikes.

A strike is one of the few tactics that workers can use in conflicts with their employers. From time to time other methods are used (for example, sabotage, where workers damage their machines; sit-ins, where they occupy the workplace and refuse to move; or work-to-rule, where they follow the operating rules of the workplace in every detail in order to slow the work down).

Strikes and lockouts are controlled by legislation. For example, a strike or lockout cannot legally occur if a collective agreement is in force. Likewise, a strike cannot be called until workers have held a democratic vote. Nonetheless, workers can ignore the legal restrictions. If they do, the resulting strike is described as illegal, unofficial, or wildcat.

When workers go on strike they set up pickets around the workplace. Picketers carry signs announcing the strike. Other unions are expected to honour the picket by not crossing the line. In law, pickets are for information only and picketers are not supposed to stop anyone trying to enter the workplace. In the heat of a strike, however, picketers do sometimes block

Marchers demonstrating during the Hamilton Steel Strike (courtesy NAC/PA-120506).

gates and roads, especially if the employer has hired strike-breakers to fill the jobs of striking workers. This is when violence may flare on the picket line. Quebec has dealt with this problem by banning the use of strike-breakers, but no other province has followed suit.

▷ RELATED ARTICLES: **Cape Breton Strikes; Estevan Coal Miners' Strike; Fraser River Fishermen's Strike; Oshawa Strike; Windsor Strike.**

▷ SUGGESTED READING: Irving Abella, editor, *On Strike: Six Key Labour Struggles in Canada 1919-1949* (1974); David Jay Bercuson, *Confrontation at Winnipeg: Labour, Industrial Relations and the General Strike* (1974); Geoffrey Bilson, *Goodbye Sarah* (1981); Claire MacKay, *One Proud Summer* (1981) and *Pay Cheques and Picket Lines* (1987).

■ Strom, Harry Edwin

Premier of Alberta (*born in 1914 at Burdett, Alta; died in 1984 at Edmonton, Alta*). Strom was the last Social Credit premier of Alberta, ending the party's 35-year hold on power in the province. The child of Swedish immigrants to Canada, he grew up in rural Alberta and became a farmer himself. He first won election to the legislature for the Socreds in 1955, and was re-elected four times.

Under Premier E.C. Manning, Strom served in the Cabinet as minister of agriculture. When Manning retired at the end of 1968, Strom followed him as party leader and premier. He was the first premier of Alberta who was born in the province.

After three decades in office, the Social Credit Party was losing its appeal with voters. Strom was unable to win back public support, and in the election of 1971 the Socreds lost to a surging Conservative Party.

Strom remained leader of the party until 1973, and retired from politics completely in 1975.

■ Strong, Maurice Frederick

Businessman, environmentalist (*born in 1929 at Oak Lake, Man.*). Strong went to work at a Hudson's Bay Company trading post in the Arctic in 1944 when he was just a teenager. Over the next 20 years, he built a successful career in business.

In the late 1960s, he got involved in international aid, first as head of the Canadian International Development Agency (CIDA), then in jobs with the United Nations.

As world concerns for the future of the environment grew, Strong held key posts with the UN, including secretary-general of the UN Conference on the Human Environment.

Strong returned to business in 1976-78 as head of the government-owned oil company, Petro-Canada. After holding senior government jobs in Canada during the 1980s, he returned to work at the UN.

Strong has been recognized with many awards for his work to save the environment. An officer of the Order of Canada, he has received more than 25 honorary degrees.

■ Sturgeon

Sturgeons are primitive fish whose characteristics resemble those of fossils dating from 100 million years ago. Sturgeons belong to Family Acipenseridae. We have five species in Canada, some freshwater and some anadromous (living in the sea but reproducing in fresh water). Their body, flat on the underside, has a shield of scales, called scutes, along the top. The snout is long and flat, and four barbels lie on the underside, in front of the mouth.

These fish have long lives, growing slowly and reaching impressive lengths. They use their mouth to vacuum the bottom for insect larvae, molluscs, worms, and crustaceans. They have great economic value since their flesh is delicious and their eggs are sold for caviar. The sturgeon begins to reproduce late in life. Unfortunately, pollution and commercial and sport fishing have caused a significant decline in the population of several species which cannot grow and reproduce fast enough to replace the losses.

▷ SUGGESTED READING: Canada Department of Fisheries, *Freshwater Fishes of Canada* (1985).

■ Sturgeon Falls

Sturgeon Falls, Ont., lies beside the Trans-Canada Highway between North Bay and Sudbury in central Ontario. It began with the arrival of Canadian Pacific Railway in 1881 and grew along with the lumber and pulp and paper industries. The town is 75% French-speaking and is a centre of French culture in Ontario. Its population in 1986 was 5895.

For further information, contact the Town Clerk, 17 Holditch Street, P.O. Box 270, Sturgeon Falls, Ont., P0H 2G0.

■ Subway, *see* Transportation

■ Sucker

There are 17 members in Canada of Family Catostomidae. These usually elongated freshwater fish have a forked tail, single dorsal fin, and mouth on the underside of the head whose thick lips are covered in tiny sensitive bulbs. This distinctive mouth enables them to bottom-feed by sucking in insect larvae and small crustaceans. The most common suckers are silver in colour, with brownish backs. Suckers reproduce in spring in gravelly waterbeds.

Suckers are not an important commercial or sport fish, but sometimes the white sucker (*Catostomus commersonnii*) and the longnose sucker (*C. catostomus*) are caught in the spring using nets. Their flesh is sweet but bony. Tolerant of a variety of conditions, suckers are found in both stony streams and deep lakes.

■ Sudbury

Sudbury is Canada's most important mining centre. It lies on the Trans-Canada Highway in central Ontario, 390 km north of Toronto. The city itself had a population of 88 717 in 1986, but it is part of a regional municipality with 152 476 residents. One-third of the people are French-speaking.

Ojibwa Indians were the first occupants of the area. Permanent settlement began in 1883 with the arrival of the Canadian Pacific Railway. The site was named for the English birthplace of the wife of one of the railway builders.

Mining Town While digging for the railway, labourers discovered deposits of nickel and copper. Soon, large mines were in production. Two of the most important are the International Nickel Company (Inco Ltd) and Falconbridge Ltd. Mines in the Sudbury area are still the largest source of nickel in the world, and they produce more copper than anywhere else in Canada. It is believed that the minerals formed when a giant meteorite struck the Earth, leaving a crater 74 km across known as the Sudbury Basin.

Because of the mining, the forest around Sudbury was destroyed. For many

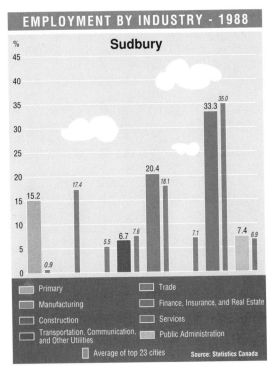

EMPLOYMENT BY INDUSTRY - 1988

Sudbury

Legend	
Primary	Trade
Manufacturing	Finance, Insurance, and Real Estate
Construction	Services
Transportation, Communication, and Other Utilities	Public Administration
Average of top 23 cities	Source: Statistics Canada

Values shown: 15.2, 0.9, 17.4, 5.5, 6.7, 7.6, 20.4, 18.1, 33.3, 35.0, 7.1, 7.4, 6.9

ONTARIO

Sudbury ●

Toronto ●

years the city was famous for its barren, rocky, landscape. However, successful attempts were made to restore vegetation in the area.

Mining is still important to the economy of Sudbury, but more and more people are finding jobs in other industries. Tourists can visit an underground mine at the Big Nickel Mine, and the Anderson Farm Museum and the Flour Mill Heritage Museum.

Sudbury is the site of Laurentian University, opened in 1960, and an impressive new museum of science and technology, Science North.

For further information, contact the City Clerk, 200 Brady Street, Bag 5000, Sudbury, Ont., P3A 5P3.

■ Suicide

Suicide is the act of taking one's own life. It is among the ten leading causes of death in Canada. For young people (five to 19 years old), suicide is second only to accidents as the leading cause of death.

Suicide Rates Compared to other countries, Canada has a moderate rate of suicide. About 15 in every 100 000 Canadians take their own life. The rate of suicide in Canada has been increasing since World War II.

More men than women kill themselves. Men tend to use deadly certain means of suicide, such as guns. Women, on the other hand, tend to use less certain means of suicide, such as overdoses of drugs. Many more women than men attempt suicide and survive.

Science North in *Sudbury, Ont. (photo by Malak, Ottawa).*

The rate of suicide in young people has been increasing, particularly in young men between 10 and 19 years old. People in this age group face demands to be strong and independent, which they might find difficult. Some have problems at school; others cannot find work, or have been rejected by a friend or lover.

Other people who are likely to kill themselves include those suffering from certain mental illnesses, alcoholics, and prisoners. The suicide rate of native people is more than twice as high as the Canadian average.

Many communities in Canada have a crisis centre with trained volunteers who will discuss problems over the phone with troubled people.

Since 1972, suicide has not been a crime in Canada.

▷ Suggested Reading: Marion Cook, *Teenagers Talk about Suicide* (1988); Jane Mersky Leder, *Dead Serious* (1987); Brenda Rabkin, *Growing up Dead: The Tragedy of Adolescent Suicide* (1978).

Sulphur Pit, *Pincher Creek, Alta. Sulphur is extracted from sour natural gas and pumped outside, where it turns solid (photo by Harry Savage).*

■ Sulphur

Sulphur is a bright yellow non-metallic element. It is common in most rock types. The most important source of sulphur is hydrogen sulphide (H_2S), which is present in sour natural gas. H_2S is extracted by chemical means from the gas and fed to a furnace. Gas from the furnace is then converted to liquid and pumped outside, where it turns solid.

Sulphur is widely used for fertilizer, the pulp and paper industry, and metal refining. Canada ranks third in the world in sulphur production.

Sulphur dioxide (SO_2) is a byproduct of producing metals. It is very difficult to control and is one of the causes of acid rain.

▷ Related Article: **Acid Rain.**

Sumac (artwork by Claire Tremblay).

■ Sumac

Sumacs (*Rhus*) belong to the cashew family (Anacardiaceae). Several sumacs are highly poisonous: poison ivy (*Rhus radicans*), poison sumac (*R. vernix*), and poison oak (*R. diversilobum*). Simple skin contact with any part of these plants causes blisters and intense itching. The non-poisonous species are the staghorn sumac (*R. typhina*) and the smooth sumac (*R. glabra*). The staghorn sumac is a small tree with a generally twisted trunk, whose branches are spread in a way that exposes all their leaves to the light. The leaves are very large and consist of a number of folioles each. The numerous flowers are grouped in long panicles. Almost every part of the plant — flowers, berries, branches, and leaves — is covered with tiny reddish and very acidic hairs. The smooth sumac, however, is hairless and less common. Sumac berries remain on the tree until the next spring. Sumacs are used as ornamental plants. In fall their leaves turn every shade from yellow to deep reddish purple.

■ Summerside

Summerside, P.E.I., is situated in Bedeque Bay on the south coast of the island, 60 km from Charlottetown. The first settlers were Acadians, followed by Loyalists. In the 1800s, the town grew as a shipbuilding centre after Joseph Pope opened a shipyard. When that industry collapsed late in the century, Summerside relied on trade with the surrounding farmers.

Following World War I, the town became the centre of silver fox breeding in Canada. This business also collapsed, but Summerside prospered as a port and business centre. The local economy was

Characteristics of Sulphur

Formula: S
Appearance: a bright yellow to yellowish brown, brittle
Properties: non-metallic, not soluble in water, used by plants in the form of sulphate ions
Atomic Weight: 32.07
Uses: fertilizers, drugs, plastics, paper, steel, insecticides, and photographic and leather processing

Sun Maiden

In the long-ago time there lived a beautiful girl, the daughter of a chief. All the young braves wanted to marry her, but she refused because she felt she belonged to the Sun.

In the same camp lived a young man with a crooked back and a twisted face. Everyone called him Scarface. The only people who were kind to him were an old medicine woman and the Sun Maiden. Before long, Scarface too fell in love with the Sun Maiden, but she explained that he would have to visit the Sun and get his permission before she could marry him.

So Scarface travelled east in search of the Sun. He asked the Wolf, the Bear, the Beaver, and then the Fox to help him find his way, and at last the Moon Woman took pity and brought him to the Sky Country where the Sun lived.

The Sun straightened Scarface's back and cleared his face, and soon he stood tall and handsome as any brave. Then the Sun took him to the edge of the Sky Country where they looked out over the Earth. "Without me," said the Sun, "there would be no light, no warmth, no food or healing." He told Scarface to go back to his people and teach them respect for the Sun. They should build a lodge round as the Sun, painted red for day and black for night, and decorate it with beaver fur, eagle feathers, and a buffalo robe. There they should celebrate a special dance in his honour. Scarface returned to the camp, where he married the Sun Maiden and taught the people the ritual of the Sun Dance.

threatened recently by the closing of Canadian Forces Base Summerside, which is estimated to have cost the area over 1500 jobs.

The town has hosted a number of national sports events and a world softball championship (1989). The lovely climate attracts many summer visitors. Summerside's population in 1986 was 8020.

For further information, contact the Town Administrator, P.O. Box 1510, Summerside, P.E.I., C1N 4K4.

■ Sun Dance

The Sun Dance was the most important festival of the Plains native people. It was held in the summer when many bands were gathered together. The ceremony lasted for several days. A buffalo hunt was organized to provide food for the people who watched the dance. Then a sacred pole and a sacred lodge were erected on the site. The dancers hoped that the Great Spirit would give them special guidance, power, and success in hunts. They often danced until they were exhausted and seeing visions. Like many native ceremonies, the Sun Dance was misunderstood and was declared illegal between 1885 and 1951.

The Sun Maiden was a legend told by the Blackfoot people about the origin of the Sun Dance (*see* box).

▷ SUGGESTED READING: Dianne Lynn Common, *Little Loon and the Sun Dance* (1982); Thomas E. Mails, *Sundancing At Rosebud and Pine Ridge* (1978); Fred W. Voget, *The Shoshoni-Crow Sun Dance* (1984).

■ Sunday Closing

The issue of whether retailers should be open on Sunday has created controversy because Sunday has traditionally been the Christian day of rest. Up to the mid-1980s, the law in Canada prohibited stores from opening on Sunday. In 1985 the Supreme Court of Canada struck down the federal Lord's Day Act because the Act made Christian religious values into a law binding on Christians and non-Christians alike. However, this ruling did not resolve the issue because it did not apply to provincial Sunday-closing laws intended to promote family activities or set uniform holidays for retail workers. In 1986, the Supreme Court upheld such a provincial law. Since then some municipalities have enacted by-laws prohibiting Sunday shopping, and some of these continue to be challenged in the courts.

■ Sunday Schools

Sunday schools are special classes of religious education held primarily for children and young adults. They are taught by members of a church or parish. They were started in England in 1780 by Robert Raikes, a newspaper publisher and prison reformer who was concerned about the children who were required to work every day but Sunday. He felt that Sunday classes in religion could keep these children from a life of crime. After he wrote about them in his newspaper, the idea spread across the country. When Raikes died in 1811, it was reported that 500 000 children in the British Isles were attending Sunday schools.

Sunday schools are primarily a Protestant movement. Roman Catholics have provided religious instruction mainly through their own church-affiliated schools or catechism classes, but some, along with a number of Eastern Orthodox, Jewish, Moslem, Hindu, Buddhist, and Sikh communities have adapted Sunday schools as a method of providing extra religious education.

Although there are early reports of Sunday schools in Nova Scotia and Lower Canada [Quebec] around 1800, the first official one on record in Canada was begun in Brockville, Upper Canada [Ontario], by a Presbyterian minister, Rev. William Smart, in 1811. The movement rapidly spread.

For many years the Bible was the only book used in the classes and children were required to memorize long passages of scripture. Gradually other material from England and the United States was added to the curriculum. In 1963 the United Church of Canada published its "New Curriculum," which was the first entirely Canadian Sunday school course.

While the 1940s and 1950s showed very high enthusiasm for Sunday school classes, attendance has declined dramatically since the mid-1960s. It is estimated that only one in three Canadian parents exposes children to religious education in the churches.

■ Sunflower

Sunflower is the common name for several plants of the family Compositae. It was native to Central America and was introduced to Canada in 1875. Sunflowers grow up to 1.75 m tall. The flowers grown for oilseed have dark seeds, which contain about 50% oil. The flowers grown for eating seeds have larger, lighter seeds, with less oil content.

Sunflower oil is low in fat content and is popular for cooking. It is also used in margarine and mayonnaise. Over 90% of Canada's crop comes from Manitoba.

■ Sunshine Sketches of a Little Town

Sunshine Sketches of a Little Town, published in 1912, is a book of stories by Stephen Leacock. It is set in Mariposa, a fictional town by the shores of a fictional lake – Lake Wissanotti – in southern Ontario. The people who live there are often very foolish because they wish they were as important as people who live in big cities. The most important person in town is Josh Smith, who owns the hotel and becomes a member of Parliament.

Leacock based his sketches on the town of Orillia, Ont. In them he gently pokes fun at human character weaknesses. Although some of the residents of Orillia were angry because they thought Leacock was laughing at them, the book became very popular. It is considered one of the best books of Canadian humour ever written.

▷ RELATED ARTICLE: **Stephen Leacock.**

■ Supernova, *see* Stars

■ Supreme Court of Canada

The Supreme Court is located in Ottawa and is the highest court in Canada. It is the final court of appeal for cases arising from all other courts. It rules mainly on constitutional disputes, including cases involving the Canadian Charter of Rights and Freedoms.

The Constitution Act of 1982 made the Supreme Court very important. The inclusion of the Charter in the Constitution means that the courts decide cases involving people's guaranteed rights, and some of these cases end up in the Supreme Court. In addition, the Supreme Court can be asked to make rulings to settle disputes about the meaning of the Charter and the Constitution. Thus the Supreme Court's decisions can affect everyone. For example, its decisions and rulings have dealt with such issues as freedom of speech, women's rights, store opening hours, and language rights.

The Supreme Court has nine judges, one of whom is the Chief Justice. (In 1990 Antonio Lamer was Chief Justice.) Of the nine, three must be from Quebec, in order to ensure knowledge of Quebec's civil law system, which is different from that of other provinces. The other six judges are usually appointed to represent the other regions of Canada, though this is a custom, not a strict requirement. Judges must be qualified lawyers with at least ten years experience and are appointed by the federal government. If the Meech Lake Accord had passed the federal government would have made appointments from lists provided by the provinces. In 1982, the first woman was appointed to the Supreme Court. By 1990 three of the nine justices were women.

Supreme Court justices must retire at age 75. Once appointed, they can be dis-

Sunflower *(photo by Tim Fitzharris).*

Brian Dickson

Chief Justice of Canada (born in 1916 at Yorkton, Sask.). After graduating from the University of Manitoba law school in 1938, he established a legal practice in Winnipeg. During World War II he was seriously wounded at the invasion of Normandy. He became a judge in Manitoba in 1963, and a member of the Supreme Court in 1973. He was Chief Justice from 1984 to 1990.

Justices of the Supreme Court *entering the House of Commons for the opening of Parliament. Of the nine judges, three must be from Quebec. One of the nine is chosen to be Chief Justice (courtesy Canapress Photo Service).*

Gerald LeDain

Lawyer and judge (born in 1924 in Montreal). A prominent lawyer, he also taught at McGill University in Montreal and York University in Toronto. From 1967 to 1972 he was Dean of the Osgoode Hall Law School at York. In 1969 the federal government appointed him chairman of an important inquiry into the non-medical use of drugs in Canada. He became a justice on the Supreme Court in 1984, serving until he retired for health reasons in 1989.

Bertha Wilson

Lawyer and judge (born in 1923 in Kirkcaldy, Scotland). After coming to Canada, she studied law at Dalhousie University in Halifax. For several years a partner in a major Toronto law firm, she became a judge on the Ontario Court of Appeal in 1975. In 1982 she made legal history by becoming the first woman appointed to the Supreme Court of Canada.

Kiefer Sutherland

Actor (born in 1967 at London, England). He grew up in California and moved to Canada at the age of eight. He is the son of Donald Sutherland and the grandson of the politician T.C. Douglas.

Sutherland's first big part was the title role in Daniel Petrie's *Bay Boy* (1983), about a nice boy growing up in Cape Breton.

He now lives in California, where he continues to make films. He was a delinquent in *Stand By Me* (1986), a city slicker in *Bright Lights, Big City* (1988), a gunslinger in *Young Guns* (1989), and a vampire in *Lost Boys* (1987).

missed only for good reasons by a joint decision of the Senate and House of Commons. This is to ensure their independence and to protect them from possible political interference.

Besides hearing appeals in important civil and criminal law cases, the Supreme Court also makes decisions on constitutional issues. When the federal and provincial governments disagree on their rights and powers, or a law is challenged as unconstitutional, or a decision is required as to what the Constitution means, it is the Supreme Court that is asked to make a final ruling.

The Supreme Court was established in 1875. At first it was unpopular with provincial governments which thought that it would be used by the federal government to weaken them. Despite the creation of the Supreme Court, important constitutional and legal decisions continued to be made in Britain, by the Judicial Committee of the Privy Council. This was because in its early years Canada was a British colony and thus accepted Britain's legal authority. In 1949 this authority was ended and the Supreme Court became the final authority for all Canadian legal decisions.

Since the Constitution Act of 1982, the Supreme Court has become increasingly important. Its authority to interpret the Constitution and the Charter of Rights and Freedoms has made it in some ways even more important than Parliament, since it can declare laws and government decisions to be unconstitutional or in violation of the Charter, as it did with the federal government's law on abortion in 1988. This represents a basic change in Canada's political tradition by which Parliament was considered to be the supreme authority. Some critics have argued that the new importance of the Supreme Court brings Canada closer to the constitutional process of the United States than to that of Britain. Whether this is true or not, most Canadians have accepted the new role of the Supreme Court. By the end of the 1980s, there were concerns that the amount and importance of the work of the Supreme Court were creating many problems for the justices, who found it increasingly difficult to handle all the work that faced them.

As the highest court in the land and the interpreter of the Canadian Constitution, the Supreme Court is one of the most important institutions in the country. It has an impact on the lives of all Canadians.

▷ SUGGESTED READING: Howard A. Doughty, *Our Legal Heritage* (1978); Frederick B. Sussman, *The Law in Canada: A Citizens' Introduction* (1976).

■ Surrey

Surrey, B.C., is a district municipality lying between the Fraser River and the American border, east of Vancouver. Originally, logging and farming were the main activities, and growth was slow. Since the 1960s, Surrey has grown rapidly; it is now the second-largest municipality in British Columbia after Vancouver. It is a residential area where industry and farming are also important. Its population in 1986 was 181 447.

For further information, contact the District Municipal Clerk, 14245 56 Avenue, Surrey, B.C., V3W 1J2.

■ Surveying, *see* Maps and Mapping

■ Sutherland, Donald

Actor (*born in 1935 at Saint John, N.B.*). After studying at the University of Toronto and training in Britain, Sutherland started his acting career on stage in London, England. He soon switched to films and has won international fame.

Most of his work has been done for Hollywood, in such films as *M*A*S*H* (1970), *Klute* (1971), *Day of the Locust* (1975), *Ordinary People* (1980), and *Eye of the Needle* (1981). In 1976 he was chosen to act in the films of two great Italian directors: Bertolucci's *1900* and the title role in Fellini's *Casanova*.

Sutherland's Canadian films include *Act of the Heart* (1970), *Murder by Decree* (1979), and *Threshold* (1981). In 1987-88 he went to China to make the film *Bethune: The Making of a Hero*. He first

Actor Donald Sutherland

acted the role of the great Canadian doctor in the television play "Bethune" (1977). Sutherland is the subject of a National Film Board documentary called *Give Me Your Answer True* (1987).

■ Suzor-Coté, Marc-Aurèle de Foy

Painter and sculptor (*born in 1869 at Arthabaska, Que.; died in 1937 at Daytona Beach, Florida, U.S.*). Suzor-Coté began his career as a painter in the village church, as an assistant to the church decorator. In 1890 he went to Parish to study, first in the Académie Julian, and then in the Académie Colarossi and the École des beaux-arts. Although he visited Canada and the United States frequently, both to paint and exhibit, he did not return permanently to Quebec until 1908. By that time he had come under the influence of the French Impressionist painters. Some of his finest works are small landscape paintings, depicting his beloved Laurentian countryside in the Impressionist style. He was also a skilful painter of portraits and historical subjects, and by 1918 had become an accomplished sculptor. His career ended in 1927, when he became paralysed.

▷ SUGGESTED READING: Hugues de Jouvancourt, *Suzor-Coté* (1978).

■ Suzuki, David Takayoshi

Scientist and broadcaster (*born in 1936 at Vancouver, B.C.*). A third-generation Japanese Canadian, David Suzuki has gained world fame for his work in genetics. He is also known throughout Canada for his science programs on radio and television. From 1963 on, he was on the staff of the University of British Columbia, where in 1969 he was promoted to full professor of zoology. With the aim of controlling pests, he conducted a major research project on the common fruit fly. This genetic study resulted in him being able to breed a strain of fly that died in hot weather. This was of great significance, and not only as a form of pest control; it also meant that such defects could be used to probe the development and behaviour of insects. For three years in a row (1969-72), Suzuki was awarded the E.W.R. Steacie Memorial Fellowship as Canada's outstanding research scientist.

Meanwhile, Suzuki had also begun to write and broadcast for the public. He believes that it is important that people understand and appreciate science. His popular television programs included "Suzuki on Science" (1971-72), which was followed by "Science Magazine"

(1974-79), and "The Nature of Things" (launched in 1979). Recent programs include "A Planet for the Taking" (on television) and "It's a Matter of Survival" (on radio).

▷ SUGGESTED READING: Ron Wideman, *David Suzuki* (1987); David Suzuki, *Metamorphosis* (1988).

■ Sverdrup, Otto

Arctic explorer (*born in 1854 at Bindal, Norway; died in 1930 at Oslo, Norway*). An experienced sea-captain, Sverdrup was a colleague of the celebrated explorer Fridtjof Nansen. In 1988 Sverdrup went with Nansen across Greenland on skis, and 1893-96 he was captain of Nansen's ship, the *Fram*, on its famous voyage across the top of the world.

In 1898 Sverdrup took his own expedition into the Arctic to survey the north coast of Greenland. When bad weather foiled his plans, he and his crew turned their attention to Ellesmere Island. They spent four years exploring parts of that island and several others to the west. Sverdrup claimed the area for Norway, but the islands became Canadian territory.

■ Sverdrup Islands

The Sverdrup Islands are three mountainous, heavily glaciated islands in the High Arctic. Ellef Ringnes, Amund Ringnes, and Axel Heiberg islands were all visited in 1901 and 1902 by a Norwegian expedition led by Otto Sverdrup. Each of the islands was named for supporters of the expedition.

■ Swallow

Of the 60 species of swallow worldwide, seven nest in Canada. Their pointed wings are important in the rapid and elegant flight that enables them to catch insects. Insects fly less when it is cold, and swallows then have difficulty finding food, since they do not walk very well on their short legs.

Bank Swallow (courtesy *Macmillan Illustrated Animal Encyclopedia*).

Purple Martin (courtesy *Macmillan Illustrated Animal Encyclopedia*).

Barn Swallows *A swallow's rapid, elegant flight helps it catch insects on the fly (courtesy NMNS/artwork by Jean-Luc Grondin).*

Trumpeter Swan *is the largest swan in Canada (photo by Wayne Lankinen/DRK Photo).*

Swallows have distinctive plumage, song, and nesting habits. Three species live in colonies: Purple Martins (*Progne subis*) live in sectioned birdhouses; Cliff Swallows (*Hirundo pyrrhonata*) build gourd-shaped mud nests under roof eaves; Bank Swallows (*Riparia riparia*) dig holes in sandbanks. The other species are solitary. Rough-winged Swallows (*Stelgidopteryx serripennis*) follow the Bank Swallow example. Tree Swallows (*Tachycineta bicolor*) use birdhouses or tree hollows where they compete with the Blue Rock Thrush and the sparrow; Barn Swallows (*H. rustica*) build mud and straw nests in covered places such as barns. Violet-green Swallows (*T. thalassina*), found only in the West, nest either alone or in loose colonies, choosing a cliff crevice, birdhouse, or building cavity. When swallows come together in the fall, they can number in the thousands. During migration they stick close to the shoreline and never cross large open stretches of water.

■ Swan

Swans are large white aquatic birds with long flexible necks and a patch of naked skin in front of the eyes. Of the seven known species, three nest in Canada: the Tundra Swan (*Cygnus columbianus*) has a melodious song and a yellow spot under the eye; the Trumpeter Swan (*C. buccinator*), our largest swan (2.5 m wingspread); and the Mute Swan (*C. olor*), which can be easily recognized from the black lump on its forehead. The Mute Swan was imported from Eurasia to add beauty to our public gardens. Some escaped into the wild and can be found in Ontario and a few places in the United States. The man-

ufacture of powder puffs and feather boas in the 19th century nearly caused the extinction of the Trumpeter Swan; 1200 summer in Alberta now, mainly in the Grande Prairie area. The total continental population is about 9000 birds, nesting primarily in Alaska and wintering in British Columbia and the U.S. Trumpeter and Whistling Swans nest near water or grassy shores, which teem with the insects they use to feed their young. The adults mate for life.

▷ SUGGESTED READING: Jay Featherly, *Ko-Huh: The Call of the Trumpeter Swan* (1986); Deborah King, *Swan* (1985).

■ Swan, Anna

The "Nova Scotia giantess" (born in 1846

Anna Swan *toured with her husband Martin Bates, who was slightly shorter than she. They called themselves "the largest married couple in the world" (courtesy NAC/PA-51546).*

Breeding Range of
Tundra Swan ●
Trumpeter Swan ●

at Mill Brook, N.S.; died in 1888 at Seville, Ohio, U.S.). Unlike Angus McAskill, the "Cape Breton giant," Anna Swan was exceptionally tall even as a child. By the time she was five, she was already 142 cm (4 ft 8 in). She grew to be 228 cm (7 ft 6 in).

When Anna was 16, she joined P.T. Barnum's American museum in New York, where she was paid $1000 a month to let people look at her. During an overseas tour in 1871, she met and married Martin Van Buren Bates, the "Kentucky giant." He was smaller than she, only 220 cm (7 ft 2 1/2 in).

In England, the newlyweds gave a performance for Queen Victoria, who presented Anna with a gold watch. They then toured Europe, billing themselves "the largest married couple in the world." On returning to North America, they settled in Ohio. They farmed during the winter and travelled with a circus in the summer. They had two abnormally large babies, but both died at birth.

▷ RELATED ARTICLE: **Angus McAskill.**

■ Swede, George

Writer (born in 1940 at Riga, Latvia). He moved to Canada when he was seven and grew up in Vancouver. Educated at the University of British Columbia and Dalhousie University, he now teaches psychology at Ryerson Polytechnical Institute.

His best-known children's books are the "Sherlock the Bloodhound Detective" series, which began with *The Case of the Moonlit Gold Dust* (1979). Sherlock and Watson the cat can think but cannot talk. Nevertheless, in each of these simple mysteries, they help their owner, Inspector Holmes of the Halifax Police Department, solve a theft.

Swede's poetry was not originally written for children. *Tick Bird* (1983), *Time is Flies* (1984), and *High Wire Spider* (1986) contain simple poems, most often connecting human life and nature. Swede rejects rhyme and tends to avoid traditional poetic devices like similes and metaphors. Instead, he tries for the suggestive descriptions of his favourite form, the haiku.

■ Swift

Swifts are members of the Apodidae family. They have narrow wings and small feet with claws for clinging to cliff faces. They resemble swallows but are different because of their dull, grey colour and their flight pattern. Four species nest in Canada: the Black Swift (*Cypseloides niger*), the Chimney Swift (*Chaetura pelagica*), Vaux's Swift (*C. vauxi*), and the White-throated Swift (*Aeronautes saxatalis*).

Swifts eat insects and their small bills and large mouths are well adapted to feeding only in flight. Swifts nest in barns, hollow tree trunks, cracks in rock faces, and chimneys. All four species winter in South America.

■ Swift Current

Swift Current, Sask., is a city in southwest Saskatchewan, on a creek of the same name. The Canadian Pacific Railway reached the site in 1882 and a town began to take shape. It is now the business centre of a ranching and farming region. The oil, gas, and chemical industries also provide many jobs. The population in 1986 was 15 666.

For further information, contact the City Clerk, City Hall, P.O. Box 340, Swift Current, Sask., S9H 3W1.

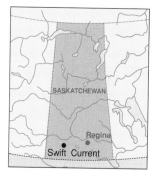

■ Swimming

Competitive swimming is one of the most popular and successful sports in Canada. There are four styles in competitive swimming: freestyle, breaststroke, backstroke, and butterfly. In medley events, the swimmer uses all four strokes in a pre-arranged order.

Swimming clubs began to organize meets in the 1870s in Toronto and Montreal. Races were often held in open waters, over courses marked by floats and booms. Long-distance swimming was very popular.

George Hodgson of Montreal was Canada's outstanding swimmer of the early days of competition. He won the 400 m and 1500 m events at the 1912 Olympic Games, setting world records that stood for 12 years. George Vernot, also of Montreal, placed second in the 1500 m race and third in the 400 m race at the 1920 Olympics.

After 1930, Canadian swimmers began to excel at shorter distances. Phyllis Dewar of Moose Jaw, Sask., won five gold medals at the British Empire Games in 1934 and 1938.

In 1966 Elaine Tanner set world records and won two silver medals at the Olympic Games. In 1973 Bruce Robertson became the first Canadian man to win a world championship since George Hodgson. The improvements in Canadian swimming can be measured by the achievements in the Commonwealth Games after World War II: 1 gold in 1950,

Breeding Range of Vaux's Swift ●

Breeding Range of Black Swift ●
Chimney Swift ●

White-throated Swift (courtesy Macmillan Illustrated Animal Encyclopedia).

2 in 1962, 15 in 1978. Outstanding swimmers of this era were Nancy Garapick (Halifax), Donna-Marie Gurr (Vancouver), and Graham Smith (Edmonton).

Canada enjoyed its greatest Olympic success at the 1984 Olympic Games. Alex Baumann won two gold medals, Victor Davis a gold and silver, and Anne Ottenbrite a gold and silver. As well, the men's team took a silver in the 400 m medley and the women's team a bronze in the same event.

Marathon Swimming takes place on open water for long distances. Marathon swimmers try to win races or set records. Many are professionals who swim for prize money. Long-distance swims go in and out of favour. At certain times, they have captured the public enthusiasm, as when Marilyn Bell became the first person to swim across Lake Ontario (64 km). In 1955 she became the youngest person to swim the English Channel (34 km). In 1956 she crossed the dangerous Juan de Fuca Strait in record time.

The Canadian National Exhibition championship swims were held in the 1930s and cancelled until 1948. Cliff Lumsdon of Toronto, likely the greatest swimmer of his day, won this event in 1949, 1950, 1952, 1953, and 1955.

Marathon swimming fell in popularity in the 1970s and 1980s. Nevertheless, Cindy Nicholas of Scarborough, Ont., was the outstanding swimmer. She made a record crossing of Lake Ontario in 1974. She made ten crossings of the English Channel, setting the round-trip speed record. In 1987 Vicki Keith swam across Lake Ontario, and back, in 56 hours.

▷ Laurence Clark, *Synchronized Swimming: 60 Years to Celebrate* (1985); Glynn Leyshon, *Swimmers* (1989); Jeno Tihanyl and Alex Baumann, *Swimming with Alex Baumann* (1989).

■ Swordfish

The swordfish's "sword" is a long extension of the bones of the upper jaw. It uses the sword to stun or kill fish. Only one genus and species is found in Canadian waters (*Xiphias gladius*).

The swordfish travels the oceans, entering Canadian waters about June and leaving in October or November. They move to deep waters in daylight hours and rise to the surface at night. Fishermen and whalers have long been aware of the aggressive nature of the swordfish. They have attacked wooden vessels, submarines, and whales.

Swordfish may grow to a very large size. The largest fish recorded in Canadian waters weighed 415 kg. It was caught off Cape Breton in 1961. The world record for sportfishing was a 536 kg swordfish caught off Chile in 1953. Swordfish have been fished in Canada at least since 1900. In 1970 some $3.6 million worth were landed in Atlantic Canada. However, the fishery ceased in that year because very high levels of mercury were found in some specimens. Very few have been landed since then. Swordfish flesh is greatly prized and is very expensive.

■ Sydney

Sydney is the second-largest city in Nova Scotia and the largest on Cape Breton Island. Its population in 1986 was 27 754. The city overlooks a deep harbour at the eastern end of Cape Breton Island and is the centre of a group of mining towns. Surrounded by the richest coalfields in eastern Canada, Sydney is known for the huge steel mill that has been its main industry since 1900.

HISTORY

Beginnings In 1784, when Cape Breton Island was made a separate colony from Nova Scotia, Sydney was chosen as the site for its capital. It was named after Lord Sydney, a British statesman. The townsite was laid out in 1785 by the first lieutenant-governor, Joseph DesBarres. He had already sent in 129 settlers. There was also a small military garrison at Sydney. But the population remained small. In 1820, when Cape Breton once again became part of Nova Scotia, Sydney had only a few hundred residents.

Although Sydney was no longer a capital, it continued to be the administrative centre of Cape Breton Island. But there

Swordfish (artwork by Pieter Folkens).

was little activity on the island.

Although the French had mined coal there during the early 18th century, the British did not develop the industry at first. They feared that it might compete with British coal. Only in the mid-19th century, when there was an increased demand for coal in North America, did mining in the Sydney region begin on a large scale. In 1877, a rail line was built between Sydney and Louisbourg, providing the village with a winter port through which it could export its coal. In 1891 the Intercolonial Railway linked the area with the rest of Cape Breton Island.

Growth of the City In 1899 a steel mill was built at Sydney; this caused the city to boom. When the mill opened in 1900, it was the largest self-contained steel plant in North America.

Thousands of newcomers flocked to Sydney to take jobs in the steel mill and related businesses. Some came from Cape Breton farms. Many came from Europe. In 1904 Sydney was incorporated as a city. To service the growing population, hospitals and schools were built. New shops sprang up along the waterfront.

Since World War II, steelmaking and coal mining have been in decline at Sydney. As a result, the local economy has struggled to provide enough jobs for the population. The recent history of the city has been dominated by attempts to breathe new life into the twin industries.

THE MODERN CITY

Today, as in the past, Sydney is both the economic and administrative centre of Cape Breton Island and its principal city. It lies at the heart of the Cape Breton coal-mining area, which includes the nearby communities of Reserve Mines, Glace Bay, Dominion, New Waterford, North Sydney, and Sydney Mines.

The view of Sydney is dominated by the steel mill, which occupies most of the south side of the outer harbour. The mill is surrounded by frame houses, which the steel company built for its workers. The oldest portions of the city are alongside the waterfront.

Population Most of Sydney's population arrived during the early years of the 20th century, when the city was experiencing its boom. The people came from many different countries, including the coal-mining valleys of Wales. Between 1899 and 1901, the population is said to have increased from 3000 to 10 000.

Education The University College of Cape Breton is situated in Sydney. There

Sydney, N.S. (photo by John deVisser).

are also two regional colleges, the Cape Breton Regional Vocational School and the Cape Breton Adult Vocational Training Centre.

Transportation Sydney Airport is east of the city, on the road to Glace Bay. It is served by Air Canada and Canadian Airlines International. Sydney was connected to central Canada by railway in the 1890s. It is now served by VIA Rail and CN. The CN East Coast Marine and Ferry Service to Newfoundland is located at North Sydney, at the end of the Trans-Canada Highway. An arterial highway connects Sydney with North Sydney.

Communications Sydney's daily newspaper is the *Cape Breton Post*. The *Micmac News* is published weekly. The city has two television stations and five radio stations.

Culture Cossit House, on Charlotte Street, is the oldest house in Sydney. Built in 1787, it is a provincial museum. St Patrick's Church, on the Esplanade near the government wharf, is a historical museum. Wentworth Park, near the centre of the city, has duck ponds and picnic areas.

Each summer, during the first week of August, Sydney celebrates its heritage with Action Week, during which there is a festival of music, special events, and sports.

▷ RELATED ARTICLES: **Cape Breton Island; Cape Breton Strikes; Coal; Joseph DesBarres.**

■ Sydney Mines

Sydney Mines, N.S., is a coal-mining town on the north side of Sydney Harbour at the east end of Cape Breton Island. The site has been mined since 1724, though it was 1826 before large-scale operations began. Mining faltered after 1920, the last mine closed in 1975, and today the town suffers high unemployment. The population in 1986 was 8063.

For further information, contact the City Clerk, P.O. Box 730, Sydney, N.S., B1P 6H7.

Grain Elevators, Taber, Alta (photo by J.A. Kraulis).

Sir Étienne Taché served in the government of the Province of Canada from 1841 to 1865, serving briefly as premier (artwork by Irma Coucill).

Bishop Taché was a strong advocate of the Metis people in their dispute with the government (courtesy NAC/PA-74103).

■ Taber

Taber, Alta, is a town 50 km east of Lethbridge. It was settled by Mormons beginning in 1903. Ranching and wheat farming were important activities. As the area was irrigated, sugar beets became an important crop. The food-processing and petroleum industries are Taber's main employers. The population in 1986 was 6382.

For further information, contact the Town Manager, P.O. Box 2229, Taber, Alta, T0K 2G0.

■ Table Tennis

Table tennis is played with racquets and a ball over a 15 cm net placed on a wooden table. The hollow sound of the ball gives the game its other name, "ping pong." Table tennis was invented in the late 19th century as an attempt to miniaturize tennis for indoor play. The pimpled rubber racquet was added in 1903, allowing for the player to put a spin on the ball.

Canada has had a number of outstanding players. In the 1970s, Violette Nesukaitis of Toronto won four North American championships. Ed Lo won the gold medal in singles at the 1979 Pan-American Games. Mariana Domontos of Quebec won nine straight national championships from 1976 to 1985, as well as many international titles. Table tennis was an Olympic sport for the first time in 1988.

■ Taché, Alexandre-Antonin

First Catholic archbishop of St-Boniface (*born in 1823 at Rivière-du-Loup, Lower Canada [Que.]; died in 1894 at St-Boniface, Man.*). Taché was a member of the Oblate order of priests. He worked in the West for almost 50 years following his arrival at the Red River in 1845. During the late 1840s, he served at Île-à-la-Crosse [Sask.] and then returned to the Red River Colony, where he was made bishop (1853) and then archbishop (1871) of St-Boniface.

As a longtime resident of the region, Taché understood the problems of the Metis. Before the Red River Uprising (1869-70), he warned the federal government that trouble was brewing. But the government ignored his advice. Unfortunately, Taché was away in Rome when the rebellion started, but he later helped restore calm. By acting as a go-between for the government, he persuaded Louis Riel to leave Canada. Taché had known Riel for years and had sponsored his schooling in Montreal. He later fell out with Riel, finding him too extreme and unpredictable, but he remained a strong advocate for the Metis people. He spoke up on their behalf and tried to get the government to attend to their problems.

▷ RELATED ARTICLES: **Metis; Northwest Rebellion; Louis Riel.**

■ Taché, Sir Étienne-Paschal

Politician (*born in 1795 at Montmagny, Lower Canada [Que.]; died there in 1865*). Taché was a leading politician in the Province of Canada in the mid-19th century.

Trained as a doctor, Taché practised medicine for more than 20 years before moving into politics when the Province of Canada was formed in 1841. He was elected to the Legislative Assembly, and in the famous LaFontaine-Baldwin government of 1848-51, he was commissioner of public works. He continued to be a member of every government until 1857. By then he was in the Legislative Council, the appointed body that was an early equivalent of the Senate.

In June 1864, Taché was called upon to be the premier in the coalition government of Tories and Reformers who had agreed to work together to bring about Confederation. Thus it was Taché who presided as chairman of the Quebec Conference of October 1864; and it was he who defended the resulting 72 Resolutions in the Province of Canada's Legislative Council in the early spring of 1865. His death in July 1865 deprived the Canadian government of a judicious and fair-minded premier.

▷ RELATED ARTICLES: **Great Coalition; Province of Canada.**

■ Tadoussac

Tadoussac, Que., overlooks the mouth of the Saguenay River on the north shore of the St Lawrence River, 210 km northeast of Quebec City. Now a small village, it once was an important fur-trade centre during the French regime. French traders chose the site, long popular with native groups, for the first attempt to plant a colony in Canada in 1600. After the fur trade ended, logging and tourism were the mainstays of the economy. The population in 1986 was 838.

For further information, contact the Secretary, 162 rue des Jesuites, Tadoussac, Que., G0T 2A0.

■ Tahltan

The Tahltan live in a dry, rugged plateau between the Coast and Rocky mountains in northern B.C. They speak Athapaskan. They moved into the Stikine River valley about 300 years ago and depended on the river's salmon run for their food.

The Tahltan were active traders, acting as go-betweens for the peoples on the coast and in the interior. The gold rush to the Yukon disrupted their lives and brought new diseases. The Tahltan population dwindled. In 1988 they numbered 1370. Many worked in sport hunting, fishing, prospecting, and mining. *See* **Native People: Northwest Coast.**

■ Taiga

Taiga is the Russian term used for the belt of evergreen forest that circles around the northern part of the globe. This zone is also known as the boreal forest. Canada's portion of this, the largest forest in the world, is about 2000 km wide in places. It extends from the Atlantic Ocean to the Pacific and covers one-quarter of the country. Taiga also covers most of Alaska, a good deal of the Soviet Union, and much of Scandinavia. The southern limit of the taiga is a line where trees have about 160 days a year in which to grow. Its northern limit is the treeline, the line north of which life for trees is not possible. *See* **Boreal Forest; Natural Regions; Tundra.**

■ Tait, Douglas

Illustrator (*born in 1944 at Medicine Hat, Alta*). Tait studied art at the University of Chile and the Vancouver School of Art before accepting a position as graphic designer at Simon Fraser University. In 1970, he illustrated his first children's book, Paul St Pierre's *Chilcotin Holiday*. *Secret of the Stlalakim Wild* (1972) was the first of eight books by Christie Harris that he has illustrated. For his pictures in *The Trouble with Princesses* (1980), a collection of native legends, he earned the Howard-Gibbon Medal. Other books he has illustrated include Lois McConky's

Boardwalk at Tadoussac, Que. (photo by Barrett & MacKay/Masterfile).

Sea and Cedar: How the Northwest Coast Indians Lived (1973) and Maria Campbell's *People of the Buffalo: How the Plains Indians Lived* (1976). Tait's pen and ink drawings portray native villages and artifacts very accurately. In the pictures for the legends, he also communicates a feeling of mystery and wonder through his use of light and shade.

A Child in Prison Camp, *illustrated by Shizuye Takashima (courtesy Tundra Books Inc./ Toronto Public Library).*

■ Takashima, Shizuye

Artist, writer (*born in 1928 at Vancouver, B.C.*). Takashima, with thousands of other Japanese Canadians, was moved to a prison camp in central British Columbia during World War II. After the war, she moved with her family to Ontario, studied at the Ontario College of Art, and became a well-known painter.

A Child in Prison Camp (1971), winner of the Howard-Gibbon Medal, is the story of her life during the war. She vividly describes events and emotions: the fear of standing in the train station in Vancouver, waiting to be moved from her home; the terror of a house fire; the joys of celebrating the sacred Japanese O-ban festival; and the calmness of experiencing the grandeur of nature. The book's theme is the power of family love and co-operation. Eight watercolour pictures sensitively depict several of the major events of these difficult years.

■ Talbot, Thomas

Soldier and settlement promoter (*born in 1771 at Malahide, Ireland; died in 1853*

Colonel Thomas Talbot *brought settlers to southwestern Ontario and did much to develop the whole region (courtesy McIntosh Art Gallery/University of Western Ontario).*

at London, Canada West [Ont.]). Colonel Thomas Talbot settled large parts of what is now southwestern Ontario, south of London along the north shore of Lake Erie. He served his early years in the British army. From 1791 to 1794, he was private secretary to Governor Simcoe of Upper Canada. In 1803, with the help of Simcoe and other influential men in Britain, Talbot obtained a land grant of about 2000 ha, the basis of his Talbot Settlement. For each family he settled, he was to be granted further land for himself.

During the next 50 years, Talbot not only brought in settlers, but he also built mills and highways and did much to develop the whole region. Despite this, he was not popular with everyone. He behaved like an old-time aristocrat who believed that he had the right to rule the people on his land. He never married and lived with his servants in his castle at Port Talbot, becoming very eccentric as he grew older. The town of St Thomas and other places in the region take their names from this energetic and unusual colonizer who did so much to develop this part of Ontario.

▷ SUGGESTED READING: Fred Coyne Hamil, *Lake Erie Baron: The Story of Colonel Thomas Talbot* (1955).

■ Talon, Jean

Intendant of New France (*born about 1625 at Châlons-sur-Marne, France; died in 1694 in France*). Jean Talon arrived in New France in 1665. This was just two years after Louis XIV took over the running of the colony. As intendant, it was Talon's job to reorganize New France according to the king's wishes. His official title said he was intendant of justice, police, and finance "in Canada, Acadia, and Newfoundland," but he concentrated most of his energies on "Canada" — the settlements along the St Lawrence River. He served two terms of office in North America: 1665-68 and 1669-72.

When Talon arrived at Quebec in 1665, New France was on the brink of ruin. The fur trade was virtually at a standstill, and the colony's scattered population stood at barely 3200. Many more settlers were needed if New France was to prosper. Besides recruiting immigrants in France, Talon persuaded more than 800 French soldiers to stay on as settlers when their term of duty was over. He brought young women from France (the "filles du roi") to marry the soldiers and other single men. He penalized settlers who refused to marry by forbidding them to fish, hunt, or

Jean Talon completely reorganized New France, changing it from a small fur-trading outpost to a thriving colony (courtesy NAC/C-7100).

take part in the fur trade. And he encouraged people to have children by giving rewards to large families. As a result of these efforts, the population more than doubled to over 7500 by the time he left in 1672.

Meanwhile, Talon started industries based on farming so that the settlers could support themselves, rather than relying on supply ships from France. He encouraged people to grow hemp and flax so that thread and cloth could be made. Rope was also made, and the wool from sheep was carded and woven. A brewery was built to make beer from locally grown barley and hops. A shoe-making industry was started, using leather from the hides of cattle, deer, and other animals. Most important was the shipyard Talon established, hoping to build ships for the French navy as well as for the people of New France.

Few matters were too large or too small to escape Talon's interest. He completely reorganized New France, changing it from a small missionary and fur-trading outpost into a thriving colony. But his efforts had few lasting benefits, because the French government and later intendants did not follow up on his work. Talon's own career had a happier ending. After returning to France, he was made secretary to the king and given the title of Count d'Orsainville.

▷ RELATED ARTICLES: **Intendant; New France.**

▷ SUGGESTED READING: Thomas Chapais, *The Great Intendant: A Chronicle of Jean Talon in Canada, 1665-1672* (1914, reprint 1964).

■ Tamarack

The tamarack (*Larix laricina*) is a larch that belongs to the pine family (Pinaceae). Its range extends from Newfoundland to northeastern British Columbia and as far north as the Yukon. Since it cannot grow well in the shade, it is found mixed with other widely spaced trees in usually damp and poorly drained places such as swamps and bogs. Leaves are single on the year's new growth, but are grouped in bundles of ten to 20 on older sections of the branch. Like other larches, the tamarack loses its needles in the fall. Its rot-resistant wood is still sometimes used to make posts and railway ties.

Tamarack is important to wildlife: deer nibble on the young trees, and squirrels and chipmunks save its cones for winter. Porcupines can kill tamaracks by ripping off their bark to get at the sweet sap in the inner layer.

▷ RELATED ARTICLE: **Larch.**

■ Tanager

The often vividly coloured tanager belongs to the sub-family Thraupinae, a family of some 240 species found only in the Americas, primarily in the tropics. It lives in forests, feeding on insects and fruit.

Only two species nest in Canada: the Western Tanager (*Piranga ludoviciana*) and the Scarlet Tanager (*P. olivacea*). Both species have a notch at the base of the bill. The females of both species are a greenish olive; in mating season the male Western Tanager has a red head, a black back and wings, a partly black tail, and the rest is yellow. The male Scarlet Tanager is entirely red, except for black wings and tail. For the rest of the year, the males resemble the females. The nests are built in trees, and incubation of the three to five eggs lasts 13 to 14 days. Tanagers winter in South America. The Summer Tanager (*P. rubra*) is an occasional visitor to southern Ontario, New Brunswick, and Nova Scotia.

▷ SUGGESTED READING: Morton L. Isler and Phyllis R. Isler, *The Tanagers: Natural History, Distribution and Identification* (1987).

■ Tanner, Elaine

Swimmer (*born in 1951 at Vancouver B.C.*). Nicknamed "Mighty Mouse," Elaine Tanner attracted world attention at the 1966 Commonwealth Games when she won four gold medals and three silver, setting a world record in the 220-yard butterfly stroke. Nobody before had ever won four gold medals at the Commonwealth Games. She was awarded the Lou Marsh Trophy as Canada's outstanding athlete of the year, thus setting another record: at 15 years old, she was the youngest person to have won the trophy.

At the 1967 Pan-American Games, Tanner again swam to victory. Again she

Elaine Tanner was nicknamed "Mighty Mouse" for her heroic swimming feats (photo by Bill Cunningham).

set world records, in the 110-yard backstroke and the 440-yard individual medley. In 1968 she won two silvers and a bronze at the Olympic Games, and the following year she retired from competitive swimming.

▷ RELATED ARTICLE: **Swimming.**

▷ SUGGESTED READING: Glynn Leyshon, *Swimmers* (1989).

■ Tantramar Marsh

Tantramar Marsh is an area of bogs, rivers, and marshes lying at the head of Chignecto Bay where New Brunswick and Nova Scotia join. The area is flooded by the high tides of the Bay of Fundy. Beginning in the 1670s, the Acadians built dikes to drain the marshes and reclaim the land for farming. The marshes turned out to be very good soil for growing hay, and a successful industry developed. More recently, haying went into decline and the marshes are being reclaimed as a habitat for many kinds of waterbirds. *See* photo, Volume III, page 338.

■ Tarte, Joseph-Israël

Journalist and politician (*born in 1848 at Lanoraie, Canada East [Que.]; died in 1907 at Montreal, Que.*). Israël Tarte was a caustic and outspoken journalist who vigorously supported the power of the Roman Catholic Church in Quebec. He edited several newspapers, including *Le Canadien* (1874-93). He was also an elected politician, first in the Quebec Assembly (1877-81) and then in the House of Commons in Ottawa (1891-1902).

Tarte's politics were basically Conservative, but various factors, including the Manitoba Schools Question of the early 1890s, eventually drove him over to the Liberals. His strong support of the Liberals in the 1896 election helped bring Wilfrid Laurier to power as prime minister. Tarte served as a Cabinet minister in Laurier's government until 1902, when a dispute over their views on the tariff policy caused Laurier to dismiss him.

Tarte then returned to journalism. As editor of his newspaper, *La Patrie*, he proved to be a powerful critic of Laurier and the Liberals.

Scarlet Tanager The male is almost entirely vivid red (courtesy Macmillan Illustrated Animal Encyclopedia).

Breeding Range of:
Western Tanager ●
Scarlet Tanager ●

Elzéar-Alexandre Taschereau was the first Canadian to be made cardinal of the Roman Catholic Church (courtesy NAC/C-23565).

■ Taschereau, Elzéar-Alexandre

Roman Catholic cardinal and archbishop (*born in 1820 at Ste-Marie-de-la-Beauce, Lower Canada [Que.]; died in 1898 at Quebec City, Que.*). Taschereau was the first Canadian to be made a cardinal of the Roman Catholic Church (in 1886). A brilliant scholar, he first made his name as an educator. Having taught at the Séminaire de Québec and served on its council of directors, he helped found Laval University in 1852. He was twice rector of Laval (1860-66 and 1869-71).

In 1870 Taschereau was made archbishop of Quebec. In this position he showed great moderation, in contrast to the more rigid churchmen of his day, such as Bishop Bourget of Montreal. Bourget believed that the church should forbid Catholics to vote for members of the Liberal Party (whom he viewed as godless revolutionaries), but Taschereau felt that it was up to individuals to decide such matters. This made the future far more promising for Catholic Liberals, such as the young Wilfrid Laurier, who later became prime minister. Nevertheless, Taschereau was a strong supporter of the role of the Catholic church and he worked hard to strengthen its religious influence in Canada.

■ Task Force

A task force is a group set up by government to gather information and make recommendations on a particular matter. For example, a Task Force on Canadian Unity was established in 1977 and reported in 1979. A government is not bound to follow the advice of a task force.

■ Tatamagouche

Tatamagouche, N.S., is a scenic village looking onto Northumberland Strait from the north shore of Nova Scotia. Originally an Acadian village, it was burned during the expulsion of the Acadians in 1755, then resettled as a farm colony in 1770. For many years, shipbuilding was a major industry. Today the community relies on farming, fishing, and lumbering. The population in 1986 was 58.

For further information, contact the Village Clerk, P.O. Box 192, Tatamagouche, N.S., B0K 1V0.

■ Taxation

The word "tax" refers to a payment that an individual or business is required to make to the government. The person who pays the tax is called a *taxpayer*.

Purposes of Taxes The government uses taxes for several reasons, the most important of which is to raise money to pay for government activities. Tax payments may be used by the government to build and repair schools, to pay teachers' salaries, to pay for social programs such as welfare, to buy military equipment, to pay police salaries, and to pay for many other government activities; or to attempt to create a fairer distribution of wealth in society. Most tax systems require wealthier members of society to pay higher taxes than the poor. A government may decrease taxes to encourage people to spend money or invest and thus stimulate economic growth and economic stability. Decreases in taxes have been used to stimulate business activity and cause the economy to grow more rapidly. Increases in taxes tend to reduce business activity and to slow both economic growth and price increases.

TYPES OF TAXES

There are many different types of taxes. The types of taxes that are probably most familiar to Canadians are the personal income tax, the retail sales tax, and the property tax.

Personal Income Tax Most Canadians are required to pay a portion of the money they earn — from working, from investments, or from renting their property out to others — to the government. This is called *income tax*. All provincial governments and the federal government impose income taxes. In 1987-88 about 46% of the federal government's revenue came from personal income taxes.

Retail Sales Tax Most provinces require that a person who purchases goods in that province pay a portion of the purchase price to the government. Usually goods that are considered to be essential, for example milk and other basic food products, are exempt from the tax.

Property Taxes Owners of land and buildings are usually required to pay taxes based on the value of their property to the local government in the area where the land and buildings are located. Local governments raise much of their revenue from property taxes.

Other Taxes Tariffs or *duties* are taxes on the value of goods entering or leaving Canada. Tariffs have been used to protect Canadian industry from foreign competition. *Excise taxes* are sales taxes that are imposed on the sale of a specific item. If the excise tax is imposed on a good that is considered to be a luxury, this is sometimes called a *luxury tax*. *Corporate in-*

come tax is a tax paid by corporations on the income they earn. *Estate taxes* arise if the government takes some portion of the wealth of a person who has died. *Inheritance taxes* arise if the person who receives something from a person who has died is required to pay part of the inheritance to the government.

Goods and Services Tax (GST) The federal government has proposed to replace its existing sales tax with a tax that would apply to the sale of most goods and the provision of many services. This general Goods and Services Tax will commence on January 1, 1991.

PRINCIPLES OF TAXATION

Canadians expect the tax system to be fair. In part, this means that we expect people in identical circumstances to pay the same amount of tax. This principle is referred to as *equity*. Equity is another word for fairness. It is generally considered fair also for persons who are in different circumstances to pay different amounts of tax.

Canada's system of personal income tax requires individuals with greater incomes to pay a larger percentage of their income in tax. This type of tax is called a *progressive tax*. A *regressive tax* is one which requires lower income individuals to pay a larger proportion of their income in tax.

In some cases, people pay more taxes if they receive greater benefits from the government. The taxes on gasoline were originally designed so that those who used the roads the most would pay most of the taxes used for road repair.

▷ SUGGESTED READING: Mary Austin Millard and Alison Kemp Mitchell, *Economics: A Search for Patterns* (1971).

■ Taylor, Cora

Writer (*born in 1936 at Fort Qu'Appelle, Sask.*). Taylor's interest in writing began to develop after she read W.O. Mitchell's *Who Has Seen the Wind?* While a student at the University of Alberta, she wrote a short story, which later became the beginning of her first novel, *Julie* (1985). *Julie* won the Canada Council prize and the Canadian Association of Children's Librarians award. The heroine of *Julie* is a girl who can foresee the future. She has difficulty accepting her strange ability, especially because her family thinks she is lying. A wise old lady tells her she must take responsibility for her ability to see into the future. Julie does and saves her father's life.

In *The Doll* (1987), Meg suffers from rheumatic fever and her parents are getting divorced. She is sent to her grandmother's farm and discovers that, when she holds an old doll she finds, she can travel into the past. In the past, she learns about the courage of pioneer families and about where she really belongs.

Although they are both fantasies, Taylor's novels realistically present prairie landscapes and sensitively describe the difficulties of growing up.

■ Taylor, Edward Plunket

Businessman and racehorse owner (*born in 1901 at Ottawa, Ont.; died in 1989 at Lyford Cay, the Bahamas*). Together with his colleagues Wallace McCutcheon and Colonel W. Eric Phillips, Taylor was founder of Argus Corporation, a giant investment company which controlled businesses ranging from farm machinery to grocery stores. Taylor was president of this multimillion-dollar enterprise from its formation in 1945 until 1969. He then served as chairman (1969-71).

As well as being one of Canada's foremost business tycoons, E.P. Taylor was spectacularly successful as a racehorse breeder. In 1950, at stables near Oshawa, Ont., he established his National Stud Farm (which he renamed Windfields Farm in 1968). There he bred and trained racehorses. By the late 1980s, Taylor's stables had produced 19 winners of Canada's most prestigious horse race, the Queen's Plate. His most famous horse was Northern Dancer, which in 1964 became the first Canadian-bred horse to win the Kentucky Derby and which also won the Queen's Plate that same year.

▷ SUGGESTED READING: Richard Rohmer, *E.P. Taylor: The Biography of Edward Plunket Taylor* (1978).

■ Taylor, Kenneth Douglas

Diplomat (*born in 1934 at Calgary, Alta*). A veteran member of Canada's foreign service, Taylor was appointed Canadian ambassador to Iran in 1977. The country was in turmoil as opponents of the government of the shah of Iran tried to overthrow it. In January 1979 they succeeded.

The shah left Iran and the Ayatollah Khomeini returned to form a very conservative and very anti-American government. The turmoil increased over the summer of 1979. It reached a climax when, in November, about 500 Iranian revolutionaries seized the American embassy in the capital, Tehran. They took about 90 hostages, including 66 Ameri-

Cover illustration by Oni for the novel Julie, by Cora Taylor (courtesy Western Producer Prairie Books).

cans. Six Americans evaded capture and were hidden by the Canadian embassy for over two months. Finally, in January 1980, they were smuggled out of the country posing as Canadians. The exploit startled and gratified Americans. Taylor became an instant celebrity. After a term as Canadian consul-general in New York, Taylor left the public service and accepted an executive position with an American corporation.

■ Teacher

In a general sense, a teacher is someone who teaches anything (for instance, dancing or golf). In the formal sense, a teacher is a person who is officially licensed to teach in a school or college. University professors do not need a licence to teach, since universities are independent and appoint their own staffs.

In 1987, there were more than 276 000 elementary and secondary teachers in Canada.

Licensing Teachers are licensed by the provincial departments of education, which award teaching certificates. These certificates recognize that a person: 1) has reached an approved educational level, usually at least a bachelor's degree, 2) has completed an approved course of training, and 3) is personally suitable for the work of teaching. A certificate can be revoked for incompetence or misconduct. Teaching certificates are a modern version of the custom in medieval Europe whereby teachers had to be approved by the church.

Teacher Training In Canada until about the late 1800s, anyone could set up a school and advertise as a teacher. Teaching was often something that people did when they could not find other work. With the establishment of a government-funded public school system, the authorities considered it important to control who could teach. Thus, teacher-training programs were established and a system of certificates was created.

Most teacher training was done in teachers' colleges or colleges of education. These were sometimes called "normal schools," because they established the "norm," or model of good teaching. Only a few teachers went to university and they usually taught in high schools. In 1950 only 15% of teachers had university degrees. In 1985 over 81% of teachers held degrees and all teacher training was done in universities. Teacher training consists of a program of academic studies in both subject matter (history, science,

physical education, and so on) and in teaching (psychology, methods of teaching, and so on), accompanied by on-the-job training in schools.

By 1920, teachers had created professional associations in all provinces. That year they created a national organization, the Canadian Teachers' Federation. Teachers' associations worked to improve teachers' pay and working conditions, which, until the 1950s, were generally poor. Salaries were low, women were paid less than men, classes were very large, and there was little or no job security. These conditions sometimes led teachers to take strike action. The first teachers' strike anywhere in the British Empire took place in Victoria, B.C., in 1919. More often, however, teachers turned to negotiations in order to improve their working conditions. By the 1950s, the growing public awareness of the importance of education, the increasing qualifications of teachers, and the shortage of trained teachers led to improvements in salaries and working conditions.

In the early years of the teaching profession, most teachers were women, although principals and administrators were usually men. The 20th century saw more men entering the profession. Today 43% of Canadian teachers are men. Both men and women are now paid equally, but men still greatly outnumber women in administrative positions. In 1960, 34% of principals were women. By 1987 the figure had dropped to 7%.

In recent years, teachers' unions have become increasingly militant. Teacher strikes have occurred in most Canadian provinces, though in some provinces (for example, Manitoba) teachers are not allowed to strike. However, except in Quebec, teachers have not worked closely with the labour movement, nor have they officially supported any particular political party. Teachers see themselves as professionals, along the lines of doctors or lawyers, rather than as unionists.

▷ Suggested Reading: Sybil Shack, *Armed With a Primer: A Canadian Teacher Looks at Children, Schools and Parents* (1965); Vivian Martin Smith, *Faces Along My Way* (1970).

■ Technology

What is Technology? Technology is often simply thought of as human skills, tools, and machines. But it is much more than that. Technology is a process, a system, a part of ourselves. It is a *way* of doing something as well as the tools we use.

CN Tower, *Toronto (photo by J.A. Kraulis).*

Soaring *Technology has enabled mankind to conquer the skies and even move into space (photo by David Lissy/Take Stock Inc).*

Hydroelectric *Generators Electrical technology is of great importance to Canada. It enables Canadians to take advantage of the power of its rivers. It has supported many industries, such as pulp and paper, and metal refining (photo by Jim Merrithew).*

Technology and Science These two terms are often confused. In fact, science and technology are two very different things. The confusion arises because much of our technology is based on scientific research. For example, the plastics and electronics industries would not be possible without the sciences of chemistry and physics. The laser was based on a scientific idea of Albert Einstein.

Nevertheless, much of our technology has developed without any scientific basis. It came from human ingenuity in solving practical problems. For example, Japanese craftsmen put edges on their swords that are still unsurpassed in their strength and sharpness. Yet they had no scientific knowledge of metallurgy.

Technology, in fact, has often led science to new discoveries. For example, in the 1930s Bell Labs in the U.S. built an instrument to investigate the cause of noise interfering with radio transmissions. They discovered that the source of much of this "noise" came from far in outer space. This accidental discovery led to a whole new science, which is called radio astronomy.

Technology and Culture Radio astronomy made discoveries that changed our ideas of the universe. Often technology has an effect on our culture far beyond its application to a particular task. The Canadian communications expert Marshall McLuhan argued that television has a profound effect on how we think and interact with one another. Technology can make something easier to do, but it may also make things easier to control. For example, computers make tasks such as typing or calculating easier. They may also make it easier to keep track of and control workers.

Technology is often credited with improving our lives. Medicine, cars, airplanes, plastics, televisions, microwave ovens, and hundreds of other items are sold to us with promises that they will make our lives easier and more comfortable. Nevertheless, this very technology is also blamed for many evils in our society, including pollution, rapid loss of our resources, unemployment, and deterioration of our diet and education.

The development of nuclear energy was one of the greatest scientific and technical achievements of the 20th century. After the atomic bomb was dropped on Hiroshima in 1945, one of the scientists who developed the bomb remarked that it was the tragedy of science that its discoveries should be used for destruction. Another replied that it was not the tragedy of science, but of mankind.

Research and Development The development of technology has become of great importance to modern economies. Technology contributes to economic growth by creating new products and making industry more efficient.

The best means of developing new technology, however, remains a puzzle. The link between scientific research and new technology is not well understood. Furthermore, many scientists object to the view that every scientific insight is only valuable if it leads to some new gadget.

Technology *provides powerful means to exploit our natural resources (courtesy Smoky River Coal Ltd).*

Telidon

Telidon is a technology for communicating information. Canadian scientists developed and launched it in the late 1970s. Its name comes form the Greek words meaning "to know at a distance." Telidon is a combination of computers that store, manipulate, and retrieve information, telephone lines that transmit it, and televisions or computer screens that display it in the form of words and colour pictures.

The Telidon system has many possible uses. You could, for instance, use it to study weather maps, pay bills, shop, read electronic magazines, or learn from electronic textbooks that test your knowledge, answer your questions, and correct your mistakes. Bell Canada Enterprises Inc. currently offers an electronic telephone number directory using Telidon technology.

Although Telidon is a technical success, the number of Canadians now using it, and the rate at which this number is growing, is less than was originally expected.

In Canada, much research is done in universities. A few industries, such as the aerospace, chemical, and electronic industries, spend heavily on research. The federal government set up scientific agencies in the 19th century to support research that would help the mining and forestry industries as well as agriculture. The National Research Council was set up in 1916. Today, most provinces have their own research councils.

In 1966, the federal government set up the Science Council of Canada as a result of a concern over the lack of technological development in Canada.

In 1987, about $7.4 billion was spent on research and development in Canada. About one-third of this was funded by the federal government. This represents a lower percentage than many other nations and is of concern to many experts.

HISTORY OF TECHNOLOGY

The native people developed a wide variety of technology. Each group's technology was adapted to local conditions. This can be easily illustrated by comparing the tipi of the Plains people to the wooden longhouses of the Huron. The tipi was easily dismantled and moved, making it suitable for a migratory people. The longhouse is a more permanent structure, suited to a farming people. Some of the technology of the native people was complex. The harpoon, for example, had a special tip to stay embedded in the animal, and a line and float to prevent the animal from sinking.

The Early Fishery in Canada shows how the way of doing something can have far-reaching effects. French and Portuguese fishermen had cheap supplies of salt. They hauled the fish on board, salted it, and headed home. The English, on the other hand, did not have supplies of salt. They took their catch ashore and hung it on racks to dry it out. Thus they had to spend time on land, which led to Newfoundland being settled by the English.

Pioneer Technology The early stage of settling Canada was one of survival. The settlers brought familiar technology and adapted it to local conditions and materials. They cleared the land with metal axes and saws. Yet they also learned a great deal from the native people. They learned to plant corn, beans, and squash from the Huron. They adopted the birchbark canoe and snowshoe for travelling in the wilderness.

Mill of Philemon Wright on the Ottawa River. *Mills ground the wheat and sawed lumber (courtesy NAC/C-608).*

Grinding grain and sawing timber were the pioneers' two biggest chores, after ploughing. They quickly put up mills, modelled on European mills, on Canada's many fast-moving rivers.

Shipbuilding illustrates how technology must have fertile ground on which to grow. The colonists took up building wooden sailing ships. They excelled at it and Canada was one of the great sea-going nations during the age of sail. Ships such as the *Marco Polo* were among the finest and fastest in the world.

Canada also pioneered the development of the steamship. John Molson financed construction of the *Accommodation* in 1809, one of the first steamships anywhere. Later, the *Royal William* was the first ship to cross the Atlantic mostly under the power of steam.

Yet, when the age of steam arrived, Canada did not have strong enough industries to support it. By the mid-1880s, few

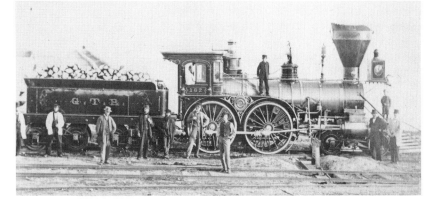

oceangoing ships were built in Canada.

Railways are a good example of how a new technology can transform a whole society. Railways brought increased trade and gave rise to new industries. They had powerful social effects, concentrating commerce in the large cities, opening whole new areas to settlement. They also had political consequences. Most historians agree that Canada would not exist as a nation if it had not been joined by the railway.

The first major railways were built in the 1840s and 1850s. By 1900 Canada had one of the largest railway networks in the world.

Industrialization Steam power could be applied to industry as well as transportation. Steam-powered machines could be placed near labour or markets, unlike waterpower, which had to be near a waterfall. The growth of industry resulted in the growth of cities in the 19th century, a trend that continues today.

Agriculture Steam-powered tractors were awkward but helpful on farms. They were soon replaced by gasoline-powered tractors. Numerous other machines, such as harvesters, made farming faster and eliminated the need for many workers. New strains of wheat, such as Marquis, developed in Canada, made farming possible farther north. Pasteurization, refrigeration, processed cheese, and other developments led to a great increase in food production.

Automobiles revolutionized the way individuals could move around. Like railways, they led to new industries. The auto industry is the largest industry in Canada. Cars transformed the cities as people moved to suburbs.

Communications technology emerged after science developed an understanding of electricity. The telephone was invented by Alexander Graham Bell in Canada in the 1870s. In 1906 Reginald Fessenden, a Canadian, made the first "wireless" broadcast. Radio, television, and the computer followed.

Pace of Change The settlement of Canada was made possible by the sailing ship in the 1600s and 1700s. These ships became larger over the years, but they basically remained unchanged for 400 years. It took about 100 years for steamships to replace sailing ships. The automobile was invented in the 1860s and there were millions on the roads only 40 years later.

The pace of technological change has increased rapidly. In the 1940s, for exam-

Communications Technology has had a powerful effect on many aspects of society, from entertainment to our understanding of the universe (photo by Mike Keller/Take Stock Inc.).

ple, few people outside science fiction writers thought about satellites. Within 30 years, satellites were common tools for relaying television signals around the world.

The very speed of change has raised concerns about technology. The discovery of the structure of the atom in the early 20th century and Albert Einstein's theory of how mass and energy are related are still changing our view of the universe. These discoveries also led to the splitting of the atom and the atomic bomb. Within 40 years, humans had invented a technology that could destroy the world. It is this pace of change together with the power of technology that have led to the feeling that such changes are out of control.

The negative effects of technology, such as pollution, loss of jobs, military danger, and others have led some people

Bucketwheel Reclaimer is part of the massive technology needed in the conversion of oil sands to oil (photo by Victor Post Photography).

to suggest that the future of the human race depends on our understanding and tolerance keeping pace with our technological advances.

▷ SUGGESTED READING: David Evans, *Technology and Change in Canada* (1989); Michael Folsom and Marcia Folsom, *The Macmillan Book of How Things Work* (1987); Ursula Franklin, *The Real World of Technology* (1990).

■ Tecumseh

Shawnee chief and hero of the War of 1812 (*born in 1768 in the Ohio Valley; died in 1813 near Moraviantown [present-day Thamesville, Ont.]*). "A more ... gallant Warrior does not I believe exist," wrote General Isaac Brock of Tecumseh. The American-born Tecumseh was Brock's friend and ally during the War of 1812. Tecumseh had allied himself with the British because of his struggle against the American authorities, who had taken over more and more of his people's land in the Ohio Valley. Tecumseh dreamed of forming a large-scale confederacy of tribes that would be strong enough to defend native lands from American settlers and from the U.S. troops that supported them. He hoped that a British victory would help achieve this.

Tecumseh met Brock early in the war, and they formed an immediate friendship. Co-operating well together, they captured Detroit in August 1812. But after Brock's death at Queenston Heights, Tecumseh had a less compatible ally — General Henry Proctor. Proctor was a more cautious campaigner than Brock

and far less courageous. At the Battle of Moraviantown in October 1813, Proctor and his British troops fled as soon as the Americans attacked, leaving Tecumseh and his 500 followers to face a 3000-strong invasion force. Yet Tecumseh stood his ground, fighting on until he was killed.

▷ RELATED ARTICLE: **War of 1812.**

▷ SUGGESTED READING: David C. Cooke, *Tecumseh: Destiny's Warrior* (1959); Luella Bruce Creighton, *Tecumseh* (1965); Betty Wylie, *Tecumseh* (1982).

■ Tekakwitha, Kateri

"The Lily of the Mohawks" (*born in 1656 at Ossernenon [Auriesville, New York, U.S.]; died in 1680 at St-François-Xavier Mission (near Montreal), New France*). For more than three centuries, Kateri Tekakwitha has been revered by Roman Catholics as an exceptionally pure and saintly person. There is a shrine to her at the St-François-Xavier Mission at Caughnawaga, near Montreal, Que.

The daughter of an Algonquin mother and a Mohawk father, she was converted to Christianity by French missionaries, and in 1676 she was baptized. This caused her to be persecuted by the non-Christian Mohawks, so she took refuge at the mission. There she gained her reputation for purity, for she lived very austerely and took a vow not to marry.

Never strong in health, she died at the early age of 24, but her reputation for saintliness grew. In 1943, she was declared venerable (the first step in becoming a saint). Over the years, many pilgrims visited her shrine and some claimed that she had performed miracles by answering their prayers. In 1980 the pope beatified Kateri Tekakwitha. Beatification is the second of three steps towards being officially recognized a saint of the Roman Catholic Church.

▷ RELATED ARTICLE: **Saints.**

■ Telecommunications

Telecommunications are the communication of information such as sound or images over long distances. "Tele" comes from the Greek for "far." Canada's telecommunication systems also include an elaborate radio and television system, telephones, networks for computer data transmission, and more.

Telecommunications technology is ushering us into a new era, the Information Age. About half of all jobs in Canada now require people to digest and communicate information. This proportion has

Tecumseh was an ally of the British in the War of 1812 (courtesy Metropolitan Toronto Library).

doubled in the past 40 years. *See* **Communications; Radio; Satellites; Telephone; Telegraph; Television.**

■ **Telefilm Canada,** *see* **Film**

■ **Telegraph**

A telegraph is a method of sending messages over a distance by means of electrical signals flowing through wires. The word "telegraph" comes from the Greek for "writing at a distance."

The telegraph communicates words letter by letter. In the telegraph system, each letter of the alphabet is represented in a code made up of long and short bursts of electrical current. These bursts of current are formed simply by opening and closing a switch. A telegraph receiver writes the signal in the form of dots and dashes on slowly winding paper tape.

The telegraph was the first of the modern methods for telecommunication. It began to remove the classic barriers to communication, time, and distance. By allowing great quantities of information to move at great speed over great distances, the telegraph bound the different regions of Canada together. It then spread across the Atlantic and Pacific oceans to put the country in touch with the rest of the world.

History In December 1846, barely two years after American inventor Samuel Morse sent the first message by telegraph, a telegraph company had been formed in Canada and the first telegraph messages to be exchanged in Canada were flowing between Toronto, Hamilton, Niagara, and St Catharines, Ontario.

People like news that is fresh. News communicated by telegraph wire was considerably fresher than that communicated by steamboat or stage-coach, the fastest means of travel in the Canada of the 1840s. With the telegraph, people could learn what was happening elsewhere within hours, whereas before it was days or even weeks after an event had happened before they heard news of it. The very word "telegraph" came to suggest up-to-the-minute news and many newspapers, such as *The Evening Telegraph* of Montreal, included it in their names. The telegraph had many other uses too. For instance, you could use it to "wire" not only news but also money — that is, you could send money from one bank to another by wire.

There was strong demand for such services and telegraph wires began to spread along roads and the new railways.

Wiring the World In 1852, Frederick Gisborne, a Canadian telegraph engineer, completed the first submarine telegraph line in North America. It was a link between New Brunswick and Prince Edward Island. Gisborne went on to direct the dominion government telegraph and signal service, which provided telegraph service to frontier regions of Canada.

By this time, networks of telegraph wires spread over much of the continents of North America and Europe. In 1866, by linking Valencia, Ireland to Heart's Content, Newfoundland, the first transatlantic cable linked these two networks.

In 1886, electronic messages first crossed Canada through telegraph wires strung alongside the just-completed Canadian Pacific Railway. It took about three minutes for the messages to get from Nova Scotia to British Columbia.

In 1902, a telegraph cable spanned the Pacific Ocean for the first time, linking British Columbia with New Zealand and Australia. Using it, it was possible to send a message to Australia in 18 minutes.

Today, telegraph cables link six continents and form part of a great integrated network of telecommunications. The telegraph has evolved into the Telex, a system in which typewriter-like keyboards send coded electrical pulses to distant typewriter-like printers. The main organizations providing telegraph service in Canada, the Canadian National and the Canadian Pacific railway companies, combined to form CNCP Telecommunications (renamed Unitel in 1990).

■ **Telephone**

A telephone is an electronic device for sending sound or other forms of information over distance.

There are hundreds of millions of telephones in the world, linked together in an enormous network. In Canada, where great distances separate relatively few people, there are more telephones per household than in any other country in the world. Canadians make about 37 billion telephone calls per year.

The largest telephone company in Canada is Bell Canada. A privately owned enterprise, it links most of the telephones in Ontario, Quebec, and the eastern Northwest Territories. Bell Canada Enterprises runs telephone companies in the Atlantic Provinces. In Manitoba, Saskatchewan, and Alberta, the provincial governments own the main telephone companies. British Columbia Telephone is a subsidiary of a United States company. All

Signals

The electrical currents travelling through a telephone wire form a continuous, smoothly varying stream of electricity. This kind of signal is known as an *analogue signal*.

Like the pulses of electricity that flow through a computer, the pulses of light in an optical fibre are *digital signals*. A digital signal is a signal that jumps abruptly between only two values. Such signals carry information with much less chance of error than analogue signals.

these companies are regulated by the federal government.

The word *telephone* comes from Greek words meaning "distant sound." As well as carrying sound, today's telephone systems also carry computer data, pictures (coded in the form of electrical signals) and other kinds of information. The technology of the telephone is merging with that of other telecommunication systems, such as communication satellites, cable television, and computers.

Invention of the Telephone Alexander Graham Bell first got the idea for the telephone while staying with his family near Brantford, Ont., in 1874. "Of this you may be sure," he said later, "the telephone was invented in Canada." In 1876, on another visit to his family in Canada, Bell made the first long-distance telephone call over the telegraph lines linking Brantford with Paris, Ont., some 16 km away. This demonstration proved that his invention worked.

Improvements in the Telephone System Today's telephones work on the same principle as the telephones into which Bell spoke more than a century ago. Both consist of a *transmitter* and a *receiver*. The transmitter changes the vibrations of the air, caused by a voice, into vibrations in electrical currents. The receiver changes vibrating electrical current back into sound, recreating the voice of the person speaking at the other end of the line. The major changes in telephone technology have not been in the telephones themselves, but in the network that links them. Researchers, for instance, have been continually increasing the distances over which telephone sys-

tems can carry voice signals. People everywhere want telephones, it seems, and so telephone wires have spread within cities and towns, and across continents and oceans.

Microwave Relays By the end of World War II (1939-45), it was possible to make a telephone call from one side of Canada to the other. This feat was made possible by repeaters, devices that boost electrical signals, spaced out along the transcontinental telephone lines.

After World War II, the telephone companies built a new long-distance system. Instead of wires, the telephone messages in the new system were carried by radio beams of the kind known as microwaves, so-called because their wavelengths are extremely short. The first microwave link in Canada, between Prince Edward Island and Nova Scotia, began working in 1948. By 1958 a chain of microwave relay towers spaced 30 to 50 km apart stretched across Canada.

Each of these towers can receive a signal from the tower to the east, and relay it to the tower to the west, or vice versa. Microwave relay towers, therefore, have four antennae, two for receiving, facing in opposite directions, and two for transmitting, which also face in opposite directions.

As well as carrying telephone signals, this trans-Canada telephone network made it possible to send television signals from coast to coast for the first time.

Cables Under the Sea The only way to send a telephone signal across an ocean such as the Atlantic was, until the middle of the 20th century, by means of short-wave radio. This could not be done reliably, because conditions in the *iono-sphere* (the uppermost layer of the atmosphere, used to reflect short-wave radio beams back to Earth) often interfered with the transmissions.

The solution was to lay a telephone cable on the ocean floor. Such a long cable requires electronic repeaters which have to work for at least 25 years under difficult conditions. It would be very expensive to fish them off the ocean floor and replace them if they wore out more frequently than this. In 1956, the development of such repeaters allowed two trans-Atlantic telephone cables to link Newfoundland with Scotland. It became possible for Canadians to talk on the phone to people in Europe at any time.

Some of the many telephone cables that now rest on the floors of the world's

British Columbia Telephone microwave site, Dog Mountain, B.C. (photo by Graeme Stuart/British Columbia Telephone Company).

oceans link Canada with the United Kingdom and with Bermuda. The 15 000 km long ANZCAN cable, the longest underwater telecommunications cable in the world, links Canada with Australia and New Zealand.

Satellites As well as flowing through submarine cables, telephone calls from Canada can get to countries overseas by bouncing off satellites. Communication satellites, the first of which were launched in the 1960s, act like microwave relay stations high in the sky. Communication satellites swing around the Earth at an altitude of 35 888 km. In orbit at this height they keep pace precisely with the Earth's rotation, and so appear to remain fixed in the sky. It takes about one-quarter of a second for a signal to make the round trip from Earth to a satellite and back to Earth. Because of this delay, satellites are not as ideal for long distance voice communications as landbased systems.

Cellular Telephones are portable telephones that allow people to speak to each other from moving cars. These phones are linked to telephone exchanges in many cities by means of radio. The system was created in 1986, and by 1990 linked all major Canadian cities and over 200 cities in the U.S.

The Canadian communication satellite known as MSAT (for Mobile Satellite), planned for launch in early 1992, will allow telephone messages to be exchanged between cars, airplanes, and ships moving almost anywhere within Canada, no matter how remote.

Optical Fibres and Computers Until the 1980s, when you made a telephone call the sound of your voice was converted into an electrical signal which flowed through a wire. Now the sound of your voice is converted into a signal formed by pulses of light from a laser. These pulses flow through a kind of "light wire" called optical fibres — flexible strands of glass, each one the diameter of a hair, down the centre of which light is channelled with very little loss of power.

Telephone companies are replacing their conventional copper wires by optical fibres. Optical fibres have linked Halifax and Toronto since 1988, for instance, and stretched across Canada to Vancouver in March 1990. By 1992-93 it will extend to Newfoundland and Prince Edward Island. CNCP Telecommunications is building a rival transcontinental network constructed partly of optical fibres.

The advantage of optical fibres is that they can handle a far heavier flow of information than wires can, and can handle far more kinds of information — not just sounds, but also images and computer data. This is because the signals optical fibres carry are of the kind called digital.

Canadian engineers have pioneered the development of fibre optics, and of ways of using these fibres to make it as easy for computers to communicate with other computers over the telephone as it is for people. For instance, Northern Telecom, a company based in Ontario, traces its roots back to Alexander Graham Bell's father, who launched the first telephone company in Canada. It became a manufacturer of telephones for the Bell system, and then became one of the first companies in the world to build telephone equipment that worked in the digital language of computers, such as the exchanges that switch calls from one telephone to another. When telephone messages travelled in the form of analogue signals, telephone exchanges used physical switches. As more and more telephone messages are carried by digital signals, computers are replacing these switches and the telephone system — the phones, the exchanges, and the complex networks — are themselves beginning to resemble giant computers.

▷ RELATED ARTICLES: **Alexander Graham Bell; Satellites.**

▷ SUGGESTED READING: David Carey, *The Telephone: How it Works* (1981); Len Darwin, *What Makes a Telephone Work?* (1970).

■ Television

The word "television" means "to see at a distance." Today, watching television is Canada's major leisure activity. Over 98% of Canadian households have at least one television. The average Canadian watches television over three hours a day. Many Canadian children spend more time in front of a television than in the classroom.

How Television Works Television relies on a characteristic of human vision called *persistence*. An image lasts in the brain for 0.1 second after it disappears. By using a series of single pictures, which are flashed on the screen faster than the eye can see, television creates the illusion of a flowing picture.

Television cameras record these images by *scanning*. That is, they break down a scene into a series of horizontal lines. The camera records along each line, left to right, producing electrical signals.

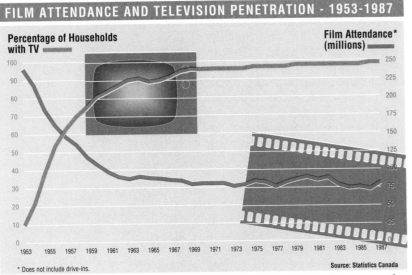

FILM ATTENDANCE AND TELEVISION PENETRATION - 1953-1987

Percentage of Households with TV

Film Attendance* (millions)

* Does not include drive-ins.

Source: Statistics Canada

These signals are sent through space or by cable to television sets, where a picture tube recreates the series of lines.

Television was developed in England and the U.S. in the 1920s and 1930s. Regular broadcasting began in the U.S. in the late 1940s and by 1949 there were over 1 million sets in the U.S.

Television in Canada Television came later to Canada than many other countries. The size of Canada, the costs, and a desire of the government to ensure good programming all played a part in this delay.

The Canadian Broadcasting Corporation (CBC) began broadcasting television in French and English on September 4-6, 1952. The first English telecast ran for three hours in the evening.

Television soon was more popular than radio. In 1954, 22% of Canadian households had television sets. This increased to over 90% by 1965.

At first, television was broadcast by lo-

Cast of "Degrassi Jr High," an acclaimed television drama that deals with contemporary problems (CBC Photo/ Fred Phipps).

cal stations to local regions. For nine years, the CBC was the only network in Canada. Private stations bought programs from the CBC and from American networks. In 1958, there were 50 television stations. In that same year, a string of microwave towers made it possible to send signals across Canada. In 1961, Canada's second network, CTV, began to broadcast.

In 1972, Canada became the first country in the world to use a satellite (ANIK A-1) to relay television signals. As a result, most of Canada's people, including those in the Far North receive television signals.

Cable Television Cable television began in an effort to improve reception. However, it was soon used to distribute more and more stations. As a result, Canadians watched more and more television, most of it American.

Pay Television Cable also allowed the cable companies to sell packages of television channels to subscribers. These signals are scrambled and decoded for those who pay the cable company. The first pay TV services began in Canada in 1983.

Educational Television A number of Canadian provinces, notably Quebec, Ontario, and Alberta support networks that present educational programs without commercials.

Programming Although Canada has built one of the most sophisticated television systems in the world, it has not been able to fill that system with the products of its own culture.

The first decade of television in Canada (1952-62) is now seen as a "Golden Age" for Canadian programs. Regular newscasts began in 1954. There were talk shows, political shows, concerts, operas, drama, and sports. Telecasts of NHL hockey began in 1952. Many of these programs were successful, especially in Quebec. In the 1960s the CBC faced increasing competition from American programs beamed across the border or shown on the private network, CTV. Drama, concerts, and opera disappeared. The exciting "This Hour Has Seven Days" was cancelled as being too controversial.

The CBC continued to produce public affairs shows, such as "Man Alive," "Take 30," and "the fifth estate." News, public affairs, and sports remain the most popular forms of Canadian television. Nevertheless, the audience share of the CBC and Radio-Canada (the French-language network) has fallen from one-half of the national audience to one-quarter.

Television Family in 1956, when TV was still a relative novelty. Today it is part of almost every home (courtesy NAC/PA-111390).

THE IMPACT OF TELEVISION

The Canadian communications critic Marshall McLuhan was one of the first to draw attention to the impact of television. He noted how a single broadcast could hold the attention of millions or even billions of viewers. The question of whether this brings people closer together in a "global village" or simply isolates them more and more is hotly debated.

Critics of television point out that television's *main* purpose is to sell products. Over $1 billion is spent on TV advertising every year. Critics argue that the actual programs are simply the "package" for the commercials. Programs are not made to sell to audiences. They are made to attract audiences. It is the audiences who are sold — to the advertisers.

Television has had a huge influence on politics. Many people believe that the influence is all bad, reducing election campaigns to media events.

In Canada, television is so dominated by advertising and programs from the U.S. that many people see it as a threat to

Actor Donald Sutherland plays Norman Bethune in a television drama (courtesy NAC/CBC Collection/26417).

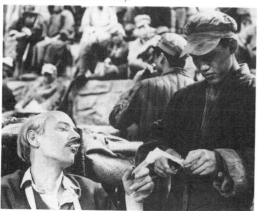

the very existence of Canada as a nation. Canadians spend over 65% of their viewing time watching American programs.

Finally, the impact of television on children is of growing concern. Critics of television point out that a child of three or four is at the stage of the greatest emotional development that human beings undergo. This development can only take place through touching, doing, testing, and learning social skills. If children spend 35 hours or more per week watching television, they may not develop emotionally and socially. As the most powerful technology in our lives, television is one of the least understood.

▷ SUGGESTED READING: Clive Dobson, *Fred's TV* (1989); Barbara Hehner, editor, *Making It: The Business of Film and Television Production in Canada* (1987); Marie-Claude Hecquet and David McNicoll, editors, *A Guide to Film and Television Courses in Canada* (1979); Knowlton Nash, *Prime Time at Ten: Behind the Camera Battles of Canadian TV Journalism* (1989); Paul Rutherford, *When Television was Young: Prime Time Canada 1952-1967* (1990).

■ Tell, Diane

Singer and songwriter (*born in 1957 at Quebec City, Que.*). Tell grew up in Quebec and Paris. She studied music and then moved to Montreal in the 1970s where she hoped to sell her own brand of folk-pop. After her second album, *Entre Nous*, she moved to New York City in 1979. In 1980 she was awarded two Félix trophies at the L'Adisq Awards. Six more albums were released in the 1980s. They included such smash singles as "Manhattan Monotone," which was the most popular French song in 1985. Tell has lived in France since 1983 and she is equally popular in that country.

■ Témiscaming

Témiscaming, Que., lies on the Ontario border at the south end of Lake Timiskaming where it joins the Ottawa River. It began in 1917 as a company town built by a pulp and paper company to house workers from a nearby paper mill. The mill closed in 1972, but the laid-off employees set up a co-operatively owned company, called Tembec, which has become very successful. The town's economy still relies on the mill. The name Témiscaming comes from an Algonquian phrase meaning "deep water," a reference to the lake. The population in 1986 was 2071. For further information, contact the Secretary, 451 rue Kipawa, C.P. 730, Témiscaming, Que., J0Z 3R0.

Temperance Movement

The Temperance movement of the 19th and early 20th centuries consisted of people and organizations opposed to the drinking of alcoholic beverages. The Canadian movement began around 1827, when temperance societies were formed in Nova Scotia and in Montreal, Lower Canada [Quebec]. The movement reached its climax during World War I, when the production and sale of liquor were banned by law.

▷ RELATED ARTICLE: **Prohibition.**

Tennant, Veronica

Ballet dancer (*born in 1947 at London, England*). Tennant is one of Canada's most admired ballerinas. She trained at the National Ballet School and joined the National Ballet Company in 1965. She rose rapidly as a principal dancer, and has performed in a wide range of classical and contemporary ballets. She also starred in two prize-winning films produced by Norman Campbell for CBC television, *Cinderella* (1968) and *The Sleeping Beauty* (1972). She is known for her dramatic flair and her superb technique. In 1989 she retired from the National Ballet amid great acclaim. Tennant has also written books for children. She has received many honours and awards for her contribution to dance in Canada.

▷ SUGGESTED READING: Veronica Tennant, *The Nutcracker* (1985).

Tennis

Tennis began as a game called "court tennis," which was invented about 700 years ago in France. It was played on indoor courts and was very popular among the upper classes and even royalty. It was originally a form of handball. The racquet was introduced by 1500.

The modern, outdoor version of the game began with an Englishman, Major Walter Wingfield, who devised a set of rules. He introduced the game at a garden party in Wales in 1873. By the time the first championship was held in Wimbledon, England, in 1877, the game was very similar to the one we play today. Wimbledon is still the site of the most prestigious tennis tournament in the world.

In its early years tennis was a society sport, played mostly on private courts. By the early 20th century, it had spread to playgrounds and public courts. It came to Canada only a few years after it spread in England. A club was formed in Toronto in 1875. By the time the first Canadian championship was held in Toronto, in

Veronica Tennant in the National Ballet production of Onegin *(courtesy National Ballet of Canada/photo by Barry Gray).*

1890, there were clubs in most major cities. Today, over 2 million people play tennis in Canada, making it the third most popular sport, after swimming and ice skating.

The major tennis tournaments in Canada are the Canadian Open Men's championship and the Canadian Open Women's championship. They are held alternately in Toronto and Montreal and attract the world's best players (hence the name "open"). The Canadian Nationals tournament is restricted to Canadian players only. There are also various provincial championships. In addition, Canada participates in the international Davis Cup.

Canadians have participated in international events since around 1913, with few successes. Carling Bassett-Seguso was at one time ranked eighth in the world among women, and Helen Kelesi has been in the top 25. The highest-ranked male player was Glen Michibata, who was 48th in 1986. Fine indoor courts and improved coaching programs may bring a more promising future. In June 1990, Sebastien LeBlanc and Sebastien Lareau won the junior doubles title at the French Open in Paris. It was the first Grand Slam victory by Canadians.

▷ SUGGESTED READING: Lucie Arvisais and Joseph Brabenec, *Child's Play* (1982) and Josef Brabenec, *Tennis: The Will to Win* (1980).

■ Termite

Termite is the common name for insects belonging to the order Isoptera. Thanks to micro-organisms in their digestive tube, termites can digest wood. This permits them to recycle dead trees and plants, which is useful, but they can also damage crops and the wooden framework of buildings.

There are about 2000 species worldwide, but only four species in Canada. One species lives in southern Ontario, two are in British Columbia, and one is in southern Alberta and British Columbia. The Canadian species do some damage. Though termites are sometimes called "white ants," they are not related to ants, and are not always white. These social insects live in colonies with four distinct *castes*.

The first caste consists of the king, queen, and other winged individuals (future kings and queens of new colonies), all of them dark-coloured. They shed their wings after starting a new colony. The queen has a huge abdomen and produces thousands of eggs. Most of the eggs are given to the white, blind males and females of the second caste, the workers. The last two castes are composed of soldiers, with their large heads armed with huge jaws, and nymphs, which could replace the king or queen should either die. Termite young go through six stages prior to adulthood. Tropical species can build huge nests, or termitaria, that may stand taller than a human being.

▷ SUGGESTED READING: Francis L. Behnke, *A Natural History of Termites* (1977); Peter R. Limbury, *Termites* (1974).

■ Tern

Terns, like gulls, belong to the Laridae family. The plumage is white and grey, the head largely black, and the feet black, orange, or yellow. Twelve species have

Common Tern *(courtesy Macmillan Illustrated Animal Encyclopedia).*

Breeding Range of Arctic Tern ●

been found in Canada, six of them nesting here. The Common Tern (*Sterna hirundo*) nests from Alberta to Newfoundland; the Black Tern (*Chlidonias niger*), from British Columbia to Quebec; Forster's Tern (*S. forsteri*) in Manitoba, Saskatchewan, and Alberta; and the Arctic Tern (*S. paradisaea*) in the North. The Caspian Tern (*S. caspia*) nests on coastal islands and islands in large lakes, and the Roseate Tern (*S. dougallii*), in southern Nova Scotia. Terns lay two to four eggs, and the young develop rapidly. The nest is placed on a raft of aquatic plants or on sandy or pebbly beaches, depending on the species.

An aggressive bird, the tern attacks anyone entering its nesting colony. The Arctic Tern is known for its exceptionally long migration — it leaves eastern Canada for Europe, then flies southward to South Africa and finally the Antarctic, for a trip of more than 17 000 km.

▷ SUGGESTED READING: John P.S. Mackenzie, *Seabirds* (1987).

Termite *of the soldier caste (artwork by Jan Sovak).*

■ Terra Nova National Park

Terra Nova National Park (396 km²) is situated on the rocky shores and deeply indented coastline of Bonavista Bay on the east coast of Newfoundland. Sea stacks, arches, and caves are some of the features of the rocky headlands. The boreal forest of the park is dominated by black spruce and is home to moose, black bear, beaver, and pine marten. Ducks and geese overwinter in Newman Sound estuary. The Bald Eagle, ospreys, and shorebirds are all regular visitors. The park, established in 1957, features hiking trails; camping, fishing, and swimming facilities; and an 18-hole golf-course.

Arctic Tern *in flight. These birds migrate some 35 000 km to Antarctica and back (photo by G.J. Harris).*

For further information, contact the Superintendent, Terra Nova National Park, Glovertown, Nfld, A0G 2L0.

▷ SUGGESTED READING: David M. Baird, *Rocks and Scenery of Terra Nova National Park* (1966).

■ Terrace

Terrace, B.C., is a city on the Skeena River in the northwest interior, 160 km east of Prince Rupert. It was originally a Tsimshian village. Settlement began in 1910 with the arrival of the Grand Trunk Pacific Railway. Since that time, the forest industry has been the biggest employer.

The population in 1986 was 10 532.

For further information, contact the District Municipal Clerk, 3215 Ebony Street, Terrace, B.C., V8G 2X8.

■ Terrorism

Terrorism is the act of using terror to frighten people in order to achieve a political goal. Terrorist acts include kidnapping, killing, bombing, taking hostages, and other kinds of violence. Terrorists also hope to show people that the authorities are not in control and thus to weaken peoples' confidence in their government.

Terrorism is also sometimes used to attract publicity. If, for example, an organization cannot get reported in the media, it can draw attention to itself by creating a spectacular incident. In recent years, terrorism has created problems for the media. If the media do not report a terrorist act, then they are suppressing news. On the other hand, if they do report it, they might be helping to create the very effect that the terrorists wanted. To be effective, terrorism needs publicity.

Terrorists turn to violent actions for several different reasons: some fight for nationalism, some for religion, some for language, some for land, and so on. Such terrorism is sometimes described as revolutionary or insurgent terrorism because it involves people fighting against some system which they see as unjust.

Governments can also use terrorist methods to put down a rebellion, for example, or to frighten people into submission. Throughout history, conquering armies have used massacre and destruction in order to crush resistance.

Terrorism became prominent in the 1970s. The main centre of terrorist activity was in the Middle East, where various Palestinian groups turned to terrorism in their struggle to win a homeland in Palestine. Their particular target was Israel and its supporters. Besides being active in the Middle East, Palestinian groups launched attacks around the world: hijacking aircraft, bombing buildings, and shooting civilians.

Whether someone is or is not a terrorist can be a matter of interpretation. Terrorists often see themselves as freedom fighters or as part of a struggle for liberation. They see themselves as being in a state of war and entitled to attack those they see as their enemy, especially when they cannot obtain their goals peacefully.

Terrorism has never played a major part in Canadian history, though there have been cases where violence has been used to intimidate opposition, as when James Wolfe moved up the St Lawrence River to attack Quebec in 1759.

In the 1960s, the Front de libération du Québec (FLQ) used terrorism. The FLQ wanted Quebec to be an independent country and it turned to attacking symbols of Canadian federal authority, such as mailboxes, armouries, and government buildings. In 1970 the FLQ murdered a Quebec Cabinet minister, Pierre Laporte, and kidnapped a British diplomat, James Cross. Those responsible were allowed to leave the country in return for Cross's life, but they later returned and were sentenced to jail. In 1985 an Air India flight from Montreal blew up over the Atlantic Ocean, killing everyone on board, most of whom were Canadians. Though never proved, it was generally suspected that Indian terrorists who were fighting the Indian government were responsible.

▷ RELATED ARTICLE: **October Crisis.**

▷ SUGGESTED READING: George Jonas, *Vengeance* (1984); Edgar O'Ballance, *Terrorism in the 80's* (1989); Bonnie Szumski, editor, *Terrorism: Opposing Viewpoints* (1986).

■ Teslin

Teslin, Y.T., overlooks Teslin Lake on the Alaska Highway near the Yukon-B.C. border. During the Klondike gold rush, Teslin Lake was one of the routes into the Yukon. In 1903 a trading post opened on the site. Today it is a service centre for travellers on the Alaska Highway. The population in 1986 was 181.

For further information, contact the Manager, Village of Teslin, Y.T., Y0A 1B0.

■ Texada Island

Texada Island, 301 km², lies in the Strait of Georgia just north of Vancouver, near Powell River, B.C. Iron and copper-gold mining began in 1883 and lasted until

1976. Logging and limestone quarrying are now important activities. The island was named after a Spanish naval officer.

Thatcher, Wilbert Ross

Premier of Saskatchewan (*born in 1917 at Neville, Sask.; died in 1971 at Regina, Sask.*). Ross Thatcher was educated in Saskatchewan and at Queen's University in Kingston, Ont., then went into business. He entered politics as a member of the Co-operative Commonwealth Federation (CCF), and was elected to the federal House of Commons in 1945, 1949, and 1953. He left the CCF in 1955 and ran unsuccessfully as a Liberal in 1957 and 1958. In 1959 he switched to provincial politics, and was elected leader of the Saskatchewan Liberal party.

Thatcher won the provincial election in 1964 and became premier. He was strongly critical of the socialist policies of the provincial CCF government, especially the way in which the crown corporations were managed. As premier he spoke strongly for free enterprise, but followed a moderate program. He quarrelled with the federal Liberal party, which was more interested in social programs than he was. Thatcher lost the provincial election of 1971 to the New Democratic Party, and he died a month later.

▷ SUGGESTED READING: Dale Eisler, *Rumours of Glory: Saskatchewan and the Thatcher Years* (1987).

The Box

The Box is a musical group with five members. All draw on a wide range of musical influences such as folk, European progressive rock, and pop. As a group, The Box succeeds in turning these different musical influences into a very cohesive sound that some have labelled "pop poetry." The Box began as a group called Check Point Charlie, formed in 1983. It caught the attention of record executives when it finished second at a Montreal talent show. Signed to Alert Records in 1984 as The Box, the group released its debut album that same year. The Box began to receive cross-Canada attention and accolades from fans and critics alike, with its second album, *All the Time, All the Time, All the Time*. While that record earned The Box a 1985 Félix Trophy at L'Adisq for "Band of the Year," its third and fourth LPs, *Closer Together* and *The Pain and the Pleasure* (1990), solidified its base across Canada.

The Pas

The Pas, Man., is an important economic centre in west-central Manitoba. Overlooking the Saskatchewan River, it was the site of a fur-trade post from the 1750s. In 1906 local Cree sold the actual townsite and moved across the river. As mining, logging, and fishing flourished in the north in the early 1900s, The Pas grew and prospered. A sawmill and pulp and paper complex owned by the government is the town's major employer. Agriculture and tourism are also important. The population in 1986 was 6283.

For further information, contact the Town Administrator, P.O. Box 870, The Pas, Man., R9A 1K8.

Theatre

Canadian theatre has closely followed the European tradition. Until the early 20th century, most theatre in Canada was performed by touring companies from abroad. Theatre in Canada began to develop its own identity in the 1920s. Today, talented playwrights, actors, directors, and designers work in theatres and festivals from coast to coast.

EARLY THEATRE, 1600-1920

In 1606 a group of French explorers was welcomed back to Port-Royal from their voyages along the New England coast by the performance of a play. This celebration is the first recorded performance in Canada. As more military officers and settlers arrived in the colony, a few other plays were performed. These were usually classical plays brought from France. The church feared that these entertainments would corrupt the population. In 1694 the bishop banned a performance of Molière's play *Tartuffe* because it poked fun at religion.

The church put an end to all theatrical performances in Quebec City and Montreal until after the Conquest in 1760.

In English Canada, British military officers put on shows in Halifax, Saint John, York [Toronto], Kingston, Montreal, Quebec City, and Victoria. Their performances quickly became events attended by the "best" society in town. They used whatever makeshift stage they could find in taverns and other public buildings. In 1853, for example, naval officers performed plays on the deck of a British ship anchored in Esquimalt Harbour while their guests watched from shore. At first the female roles were played by men.

Theatre began to attract enthusiastic audiences in the mid-19th century. Theatre criticism was often quite direct as the audience pelted an actor with eggs or sticks. As always, there were people who

---

Ambrose Small

Ambrose Small (1863-unknown) was a theatre impresario and a millionaire. Small and his wife Theresa owned a chain of theatres, including the Grand Opera House on Adelaide Street in Toronto. On December 2, 1919, they sold the theatres for $1.7 million to Trans-Canada Theatres Ltd, who gave them a down payment of $1 million. Theresa immediately deposited the cheque into their bank. Later that day, Small had a meeting with his lawyer, who left him on the steps of the Grand Opera House around 5:30 PM. That was the last known sighting of Ambrose Small. He did not arrive home that night. He was not seen by any of his girlfriends or gambling associates. He did not show up at any of the race courses he normally visited. Nor did he draw any money from his bank.

Before long, the disappearance of Ambrose Small was a major news story throughout North America. Was he murdered? He had many enemies. No trace of him has ever been found.

William Hutt, as the pompous Lady Bracknell in The Importance of Being Earnest *(1976) (courtesy Stratford Festival Archives).*

Théâtre du Nouveau Monde (TNM)

Théâtre du Nouveau Monde was founded in 1951 in Montreal by graduates of the Compagnons de Saint-Laurent theatre group, including Jean Gascon and Jean-Louis Roux. At first it concentrated on the French classics, especially works by Molière.

Over the years the theatre expanded to include plays by well-known international writers as well as by contemporary Quebec playwrights. In 1952 the Théâtre du Nouveau Monde established a theatre school,

---

disapproved of the theatre as a "house of sin."

One of the first theatre buildings in Canada was built by the military in Halifax in 1789. Similar modest buildings followed in other cities. In 1825 John Molson and a group of Montreal businessmen put up the splendid Theatre Royal. It seated about 1500 spectators and cost $30 000. The Royal Lyceum opened in Toronto in 1848. By the 1890s, there were grand opera houses in London, Toronto, and Vancouver. Several prairie towns also had theatres. The most impressive was the Walker Theatre in Winnipeg. It was built in 1907 with a marble lobby, beaded glass chandeliers, and plush seats for 1800 patrons.

With a few exceptions, the actors and plays were all imported from Britain, the United States, and France. As transportation by rail, canal, and ocean liner improved, it became easier to add Canada to the North American circuit.

The few Canadian actors who did emerge were usually forced to go abroad to establish their reputation. Julia Arthur, whom one critic called "the most gifted, beautiful and versatile actress that this country has produced," worked first in the United States and then in London before she returned to found her own American touring company. The seven Marks Brothers, however, were a huge success on the Canadian circuit for over 30 years. Together with their families, they presented melodramatic favourites such as *Uncle Tom's Cabin* in every town they visited.

By 1920, the golden age for the touring companies was over. World War I had made travelling difficult. Radio and films were attracting audiences in large numbers. The Depression of the 1930s dealt the final blow to this imported commercial theatre. Fortunately, just at this time,

---

Poster for the Marks Brothers, 1905 (courtesy Metropolitan Toronto Library).

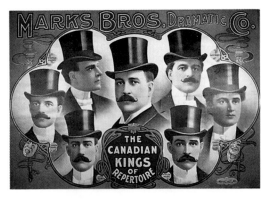

---

new groups of amateur players began to form in various cities across Canada.

THE LITTLE THEATRE MOVEMENT, 1920-50

The first amateur theatre clubs were formed in the 1870s, in Hamilton, Ont., and in Montreal. In 1907 Governor General Earl Grey announced a Musical and Dramatic Competition for small theatre groups. It was held each year in Ottawa, Toronto, Montreal, and Winnipeg. Within a year, a French amateur festival, the Concours de l'Île, began in Montreal. Although the Grey Competition lasted only until 1911, it boosted the growth of amateur theatre in Canada.

Within a few years, there were hundreds of community theatres in every large town and many smaller centres across Canada. They often worked in cramped spaces and had few props and little scenery. They were daring and imaginative in their performances, and they experimented with new Canadian plays. The best-known theatre was Hart House Theatre at the University of Toronto. Built in 1919 to seat 500 people, it was superbly equipped with the latest technology. It had workshops and wardrobe rooms, and special effects for making smoke, rain, lightning, and flowing water. Many of Canada's most successful actors, directors, designers, technicians, and playwrights began their careers at Hart House.

In Montreal, it was a priest, Émile Legault, who organized the most influential group, the Compagnons de Saint-Laurent (1937-52). Legault worked for a year in French theatre. He trained his actors in new stage methods, in mime and dance, and made their work fresh and magical. Many of them went on to lead Quebec theatre for the next 30 years. Among the most talented of his troupe were Jean Gascon and Jean-Louis Roux, who founded the Théâtre du Nouveau Monde in 1951. Like most theatre companies in Quebec at the time, however, Legault's group performed only European dramas.

During the Depression in the 1930s, political plays that were closely related to current events were also performed in large cities, especially in Toronto. Called "agitprop" (from the words "agitation" and "propaganda"), this theatre was organized by people who wanted to transform society. The actors were often unemployed workers. They performed short plays and skits in church basements, labour halls, as well as in theatres such as

Hart House Theatre. The best-known political play, *Eight Men Speak*, was based on the trial and imprisonment of eight Canadian communists. After a few performances, however, it was banned by the police in both Toronto and Winnipeg.

With so much activity going on all over the country, a new governor general, Lord Bessborough, set up the Dominion Drama Festival (DDF) in 1932 to showcase amateur theatre. The week-long finals were held in a different city each year. Prizes were awarded in several categories: for playwrights, directors, actors, designers, and technicians. The DDF changed its name to Theatre Canada in 1970 and disbanded in 1978. For more than 30 years, it had trained a whole generation of drama lovers.

PROFESSIONAL THEATRE, 1950 TO THE PRESENT

By 1950 it was obvious that enthusiastic amateurs could no longer compete against experienced professionals in the theatre. The Canada Council was established in 1957 and it was keen to promote a strong professional theatre in every region of the country. The next 30 years saw a flourishing of all kinds of theatrical activity in Canada.

Summer theatre festivals are popular in Canada. Many are held in picturesque towns close to large cities where visitors can picnic near the water or stroll around the old town square before they settle down for the performance. Some festivals perform dramas by famous international writers. Others are committed to developing Canadian plays. All have given opportunities to actors and designers in Canada. They have also helped to develop enthusiastic theatre audiences among all age groups, both through regular performances and special school previews. Two of the largest are the Stratford Festival in

"Thrust Stage" of the Stratford Festival Theatre (courtesy Stratford Festival/photo by Jane Edmonds).

The Max Bell Theatre, *Calgary, is an example of a proscenium stage (photo © Bilodeau/Preston/Take Stock Inc.).*

Stratford, Ont., and the Shaw Festival in Niagara-on-the-Lake, Ont.

The Charlottetown Summer Festival has been held in the Confederation Centre of the Arts every year since 1965. It specializes in spectacular Broadway-style Canadian musical plays. The most popular has been *Anne of Green Gables*, which has been performed every summer since 1965.

Festival Lennoxville began at Bishop's University in the Eastern Townships of Quebec in 1972. The organizers hoped to celebrate Canadian playwrights. Despite a varied series of Canadian plays and excellent casts, however, the festival was forced to close in 1982.

The Blyth Festival in rural Ontario has relied since it was founded in 1975 on strong community support. It presents new Canadian plays, especially those dealing with local history or farm issues. Some plays have been adapted from stories written by authors such as Alice Munro who have lived in the area.

REGIONAL THEATRES

In the 1960s the federal, provincial, and municipal governments provided money to build theatres across Canada.

The Canada Council took the lead in encouraging the development of strong regional theatres. In 1962 the council selected the newly founded Manitoba Theatre Centre (MTC) as the model for all other regions to follow when they established their own civic theatres.

The results of this enthusiasm and financing were impressive. In less than ten years, regional theatres were established in most provinces: the Vancouver Playhouse and the Neptune Theatre in Halifax in 1963; the Saidye Bronfman Centre in Montreal in 1967; Theatre Calgary and Theatre New Brunswick in 1968; the National Arts Centre in Ottawa and the

The Stage

Canadian theatre stages come in a variety of shapes and sizes.

The most common is the *proscenium stage*, which is separated from the audience by an arch with curtains hung on it. When the curtain is open, the arch forms a kind of picture-frame around the set on the stage. An example is Theatre Calgary (left).

The *thrust stage* is a platform surrounded by the audience on three sides. It is modelled after the open stage used by Shakespeare at the Globe Theatre in London. The thrust stage encourages a special relationship to develop between the actors and the nearby audience. The best example is the Stratford Festival.

Many small theatres are located in old factory buildings. Because of the large open space, they often have *flexible stages* and seating which can be changed with each new production. An example is Theatre Passe Muraille in Toronto.

Rock and Roll *poster designed for the Grand Theatre, London, Ont. (courtesy Grand Theatre).*

Joseph Shoctor

Joseph Shoctor (born in 1922), lawyer and theatre enthusiast, was the driving force behind Edmonton's first professional theatre. It began in an old Salvation Army citadel in 1965. It concentrated on plays with famous directors and casts that were likely to be a commercial success. In 1976 the Citadel Theatre moved into a magnificent new building in downtown Edmonton (*photo by Dwayne Brown*).

Tamara

John Krizanc's play *Tamara* was first staged at an international festival in Toronto in 1981. It is Canada's most successful theatrical export. The play is set in a large country home where different scenes are acted in different rooms at the same time. Members of the audience are free to follow whichever actors they choose from room to room. In this way they can create their own storyline. *Tamara* has been a great hit in Los Angeles, Mexico City, and New York. Further productions are planned in London, Paris, and Australia.

Centaur Theatre in Montreal in 1969; and the St Lawrence Centre in Toronto in 1970. In addition, the Grand Theatre in London, Ont., and the Bastion Theatre in Victoria, B.C., went professional in 1971.

These new theatres provided work for Canadian actors and designers. However, with a few exceptions, the regional theatres in their first few years did not produce many Canadian plays.

ALTERNATE THEATRE

Small Spaces In the 1970s a group of small theatres opened across Canada as alternatives to the large regional theatres. These theatres were committed to developing and performing Canadian plays. They could afford to experiment because their overhead expenses were low. They occupied spaces carved out of old factory and warehouse buildings. They worked with young and often unknown playwrights and gave premieres to their works. As a result, dozens of Canadian writers who began their careers at the alternate theatres in the 1970s are now regularly performed in large and small theatres. These include David Freeman, David French, John Murrell, Sharon Pollock, Michel Tremblay, and George Walker.

Quebec In Quebec, the new theatre was closely associated with political and cultural developments in the province. Quebec's Ministry of Cultural Affairs and Montreal's Arts Council gave large grants to theatre, and a number of new companies were founded. For many years, the only theatre that made a serious effort to present Canadian plays was Gratien Gélinas's Comédie-Canadienne (1958). Gélinas was a successful actor and writer in Montreal who had created two extremely popular characters for the stage, Fridolin and Tit-Coq. When he produced plays by other Quebec writers he could not fill the hall, and the theatre closed in 1972. The Théâtre du Nouveau Monde and other theatres still concentrated on traditional plays from abroad.

Just at this time, however, a number of talented Quebec dramatists began to write plays about political and social conflicts in the province. Françoise Loranger wrote a political satire, *Chemin du roy comédie patriotique*, which presented the confrontation between Ottawa and Quebec in the form of a hockey game. Robert Gurik used bitter satire in his *Hamlet, prince du Québec* (1968). Politicians such as Pierre Trudeau, and members of the church and the English-speak-

ing community were presented as characters in William Shakespeare's play *Hamlet*.

Michel Tremblay had the greatest impact of all. In *Les Belles-Soeurs* ("The Step-Sisters," 1968), for example, he wrote about the frustrations of working-class women in east-end Montreal, letting the characters speak in the street language *joual*. Later, Quebec dramatists also questioned the role of the church and traditional family ties.

The 1970s saw expansion in all kinds of theatrical activity. By mid-decade, there were over 100 theatre groups in Quebec, more than in all the other provinces combined.

There were also radical groups that hoped to reform society by rousing the public to a sense of injustice. They created their own plays around issues they thought were important. The "scripts" for these plays were often only a series of stage directions. The actors improvised their parts as they went along. Among the best-known of these troupes was the Théâtre du Meme Nom (TMN, 1969), a parody of the conservative Théâtre du Nouveau Monde (TNM). It ridiculed political, social, and cultural institutions in Quebec, including the church. By the early 1980s, many of these troupes had disbanded.

Collectives are plays developed by a director and a group of actors through improvisation (the actors making up words and actions as they go along). The idea began in Europe, and was taken up by radical theatre troupes in Quebec.

The Farm Show (1972) is the most successful of these collective creations. Paul Thompson, director of Toronto's Theatre Passe Muraille, took a group of actors to Clinton, Ont., where they worked for a summer with local farmers while they developed their play. In a series of skits and songs, they described familiar personalities and incidents.

In Newfoundland, the Mummers Troupe used collective techniques to investigate injustice in the outports. Their 1978 play *They Club Seals, Don't They?* was a spirited defence of the local sealing industry. In Saskatoon, 25th Street Theatre developed *Paper Wheat* (1977), a vivid description of prairie farm life that later went on national tour and television. In *Ten Lost Years* (1974), Toronto Workshop Productions investigated the hardships suffered by people during the Depression. It was one of the most popular plays ever performed in Canada. Despite these great successes, however, the collective spirit seemed burned out by the early 1980s.

THEATRE FOR EVERY GROUP

In recent years, there has been an extraordinary growth of theatrical activity in Canada. Toronto, for example, is now the third-largest centre in the world for English-language theatre. In addition to the main theatres and festivals and the smaller alternate stages, there are also theatre groups for women and for senior citizens. Two of the largest areas of growth have been in children's theatre and in multicultural theatre. Some ethnic groups perform in their traditional languages, but most perform Western-style dramas. Native groups sometimes combine European traditions with their own ceremonies and rituals. In 1986 playwright and director Tomson Highway brought great acclaim to modern native drama when he won an award for his play *The Rez Sisters*.

In the economic recession of the early 1980s, many theatre companies had to find ways around rising production costs. One-person plays became common, and some were surprisingly effective. Linda Griffiths, for example, played both Prime Minister Trudeau and his wife in *Maggie and Pierre*. Eric Peterson performed John Gray's *Billy Bishop Goes to War*, a play about Canada's World War I flying ace, in theatres across Canada as well as in London and New York.

In Edmonton, Brian Paisley organized Canada's first Fringe Festival in 1982 to give small theatre companies a chance to perform before an audience. The companies paid their own way and, in return, they got the total box-office receipts. In the first eight years, companies booked in from as far away as Europe, Australia, and the United States as well as Canada. In 1985 Vancouver began its own "On the Fringe" Festival, which followed directly from the Edmonton event. Victoria and Winnipeg have also taken up the idea.

Some blockbuster shows and other types of commercial theatre are financially successful. The musical *Cats* ran for two years in Toronto, from 1985 to 1987, in a lavish all-Canadian production. It grossed $40 million and later went on to tour to full houses across the country. In 1989 similar productions of *Les Misérables* and *The Phantom of the Opera* opened in Toronto for long runs, despite high ticket prices.

Dinner theatres also proved popular, such as at Stage West in Edmonton, Calgary, and Toronto, where a light comedy or musical follows the meal.

Most intriguing of all, perhaps, are the murder mystery events which are staged in restaurants and hotels in different places across Canada, and on train trips and boat cruises. After the "body" has been found, it is up to the sleuths in the audience to uncover the murderer and the motives for the crime.

▷ RELATED ARTICLES: **Drama; Mumming; Radio; Shaw Festival; Stratford Festival; Theatre, Children's** and biographies of the individuals mentioned in the article.

▷ SUGGESTED READING: Eugene Benson and L.W. Conolly, editors, *The Oxford Companion to Canadian Theatre* (1989); Diane Mew, editor, *Life Before Stratford: Memoirs of Amelia Hall* (1989); Betty Lee, *Love and Whiskey: The Story of the Dominion Drama Festival* (1973); Toby Gordon Ryan, *Stage Left: Canadian Theatre in the Thirties, A Memoir* (1981); Anton Wagner, editor, *Contemporary Canadian Theatre* (1985).

■ Theatre, Children's

In children's theatre, the actors are usually adults, although the audience is composed of young people. When all the roles are played by young adults between the ages of about 14 and 19, it may be called "youth theatre."

BACKGROUND

Children's theatre goes back to 19th century pantomime and Punch and Judy shows. Perhaps because the English audience always responded boisterously, a new form of participational theatre emerged in its schools in the early 1960s. The aim of theatre-in-education (or TIE) is always educational. Brian Way, one of the first writers of theatre-in-education plays, wanted his audience to participate in the performance. The children must make choices during the play, and experience the consequences of those choices. One of Way's students, Ken Kramer, founded the Globe Theatre in Saskatchewan.

Children's theatre got its start in Canada later than in the United States. The first children's company, Holiday Theatre in Vancouver, was founded by Myra Benson and Joy Coghill in 1953. The national organization, the Canadian Child and Youth Drama Association (CCYDA), began in 1962. By then, children's theatre had spread right across Canada. In Quebec, Jean-Pierre Ronfard had started Les Jeunes Comédiens. In Manitoba, John

Les Misérables *is one of many Canadian productions supported by David Mirvish, who manages the Royal Alexandra Theatre in Toronto (photo by Pete Ryan/First Light).*

Poster *for Young Peoples' Theatre, Manitoba Company (courtesy Metropolitan Toronto Library).*

Some Canadian Theatres

- *The Centaur Theatre* (1969) is the major English-language theatre in Montreal. It has two stages in the old Montreal Stock Exchange building. The theatre presents many new Canadian plays.
- *Grand Theatre* The Grand Theatre in London, Ont., began as the Grand Opera House in 1881. The building was burned down in 1900 and a new one was built. In 1945, it was purchased by the London Little Theatre, an amateur group. In 1971 this group went professional. The theatre has been beautifully restored.
- *The Manitoba Theatre Centre* (1958) in Winnipeg was the first professional regional theatre in Canada. It was formed by director John Hirsch and others. In the 1960s the Canada Council used it as a model for other theatres to follow. It was copied in other centres throughout North America. It has two stages. The main stage performs well-known dramas to appeal to its large subscription audience. A smaller stage experiments with new Canadian plays.
- *The Neptune Theatre* (1963) in Halifax, N.S., was the first professional theatre in Canada to experiment with a repertory system and to hire a group of actors and designers for a full one-year term. The theatre occupies a renovated vaudeville house.
- *The Tarragon Theatre* (1971) was founded in Toronto by director William Glassco to present new Canadian plays. The theatre has two stages and a training program, with special emphasis on developing new scripts.

Hirsch was producing excellent children's theatre at the Manitoba Theatre Centre. In Nova Scotia, the Mermaid Theatre got its start performing adaptations of Micmac Indian legends. And in Ontario, Susan Rubes started Young People's Theatre (YPT) in 1966.

CANADIAN PLAYWRIGHTS

Many of Canada's best-known playwrights have written children's plays. Early children's classics include Betty Lambert's *The Riddle Machine* and Eric Nicol's *Beware the Quickly Who*. James Reaney wrote *Colours in the Dark*, a poetic play based on children's games. Rex Deverell, the writer-in-residence at the Globe Theatre, wrote *The Copetown City Kite Crisis*. John Lazarus wrote *Babel Rap* about two men arguing over how to build the Tower of Babel. Carol Bolt wrote *Tangleflags* and *My Best Friend is Twelve Feet High*. Recently, she has written *Ice Time*, a play about a girl who was determined to play on a boys' hockey team.

James Reaney's *Names and Nicknames* demonstrates the power of words by creating an atmosphere in which nicknames are used to control others.

AUDIENCE PARTICIPATION

While many plays are written to be experienced quietly in a theatre, other plays encourage the audience to participate in some way. In participation plays, the audience is encouraged to voice opinions, make decisions, or express feelings.

One company that has used participational plays extensively is Carousel Players, founded by Des Davis in 1972. Based in St Catharines, it has performed for more than half a million young people in schools throughout Ontario. The actors invite the children to become members of their group, and question them about their role in the play. Each child finds his or her own way of contributing to the action of the play.

An example of a participatory play is *Almighty Voice* by Len Peterson. Almighty Voice was a Cree Indian outlaw who lived in Saskatchewan in 1895. During the play, each of the five groups become Indians, settlers, or North-West Mounted Police. When Almighty Voice breaks the law by slaughtering a cow which a settler claimed was his, the children who are involved either in protecting him or betraying him to the police must be able to justify their actions.

Children's plays have begun to focus on the real-life problems of children in difficult situations. These plays make strong statements about social problems such as marriage break-up, poverty, racial prejudice, and drug abuse. Children seeing these plays are often stimulated to discuss their own problems.

CHILDREN'S THEATRE FESTIVALS

Children's theatre festivals have become exciting occasions for the sharing of new plays by companies from around the world.

The Vancouver Children's Festival and the International Children's Festival at Harbourfront in Toronto have allowed Canadian children to witness Japan's Kaze No-No, and England's Theatre Centre. It has also presented award-winning Canadian companies, such as Vancouver's Green Thumb Theatre and Toronto's Theatre Direct.

Through this kind of global sharing, children's theatre is becoming more responsive to children's needs. Adults are also learning more about the problems children face at different times in their development. Gradually, both teachers and children are realizing that children's theatre is not just entertainment, but provides powerful, life-giving learning.

▷ RELATED ARTICLE: **Drama.**

▷ SUGGESTED READING: Jane Howard Baker, *A Teacher's Guide to Theatre for the Young* (1978); D. Davis, *Theatre for Young People* (1981); Joyce Doolittle and Zina Barnieh, *A Mirror of our Dreams: Children and the Theatre in Canada* (1979); Anne Masson, *The Magic of Marionettes* (1989).

■ Thelon River

The Thelon River, 904 km long, flows across the Barren Lands of the Northwest Territories into Chesterfield Inlet on the west coast of Hudson Bay. Because of the lushness of vegetation in its valley, it is one of the most important rivers on the Barren Lands. In 1927 a sanctuary was created along the river to protect the muskox from being over-hunted.

■ Thetford-Mines

Thetford-Mines, Que., lies in hilly country about 100 km south of Quebec City. Asbestos was found in the area in 1876, and the community grew when companies began mining in the 1880s. The city is now one of the largest asbestos-producing centres in the world. The population in 1986 was 18 561.

For further information, contact the Greffier, 144 rue Notre-Dame Sud, C.P. 489, Thetford-Mines, Que., G6G 5T3.

Thirteen Colonies

The Thirteen Colonies (also known as the American colonies), were the British colonies that broke away from Britain in 1775 and formed the United States. Situated on the Atlantic seaboard, they were (from north to south) Massachusetts, New Hampshire, Rhode Island, Connecticut, New York, Pennsylvania, New Jersey, Delaware, Maryland, Virginia, North Carolina, South Carolina, and Georgia.

▷ RELATED ARTICLE: **American Revolution.**

Thistle

Thistles are spiny, herb-like plants that sometimes grow over 1.5 m tall. True thistles belong to the genus *Cirsium*, although several other prickly plants are also called thistles. The thistle flower is in the form of a flowerhead and is usually a shade of purple. A few species have white flowers. The flowers produce many small seeds, each with a plume that helps carry it in the wind. The native species do not grow as weeds.

Canada thistle (*C. arvense*) is a species introduced from Europe. It is a common weed of roadsides, fields, and pastures. It is hard to eliminate because of its long and persistent roots. Any small piece of root left in the ground will grow a new plant. The bull thistle (*C. vulgare*) has a flowerhead that looks like a rose-purple shaving brush. It is also a common Canadian weed.

▷ SUGGESTED READING: Clarence Frankton and A. Gerald Mulligan, *Weeds of Canada* (1987).

Thom, Ronald James

Architect (*born in 1923 at Penticton, B.C.; died in 1986 at Toronto, Ont.*). Thom trained as an artist at the Vancouver School of Art and later moved over to architecture. He designed a number of flat-topped steel, glass, and cedar houses in a Japanese style in the area around Vancouver. He also designed the BC Hydro Building. It was one of the first buildings to show its mechanical systems in its overall design and to feature a specific colour scheme – in this case, blue, green, and grey, the colours of Vancouver.

Thom became known across Canada when he won the competition to design Massey College (1963) at the University of Toronto. It is a highly successful building. He moved to Toronto and established his practice under the title of the Thom Partnership. In the 1960s he designed the campus and many of the individual build-ings for Trent University in Peterborough, Ont. He also designed the Shaw Festival Theatre (1973) at Niagara-on-the-Lake, Ont. One of his most challenging projects was the Metropolitan Toronto Zoo (1974), where over 400 species of animals are shown off in pavilions that resemble their own native environments.

Thom always tried to integrate his buildings with their natural setting and with the existing architecture in their neighbourhood. He excelled in designing large projects where many related buildings were grouped on one site. Within his buildings, he gave great attention to colour and to detail, and he often designed the furniture and other interior decorations as well.

Thomas, Dave, *see* SCTV

Thompson

Thompson, Man., is a city lying beside the Burntwood River north of Lake Winnipeg in the rocky Canadian Shield country of central Manitoba. In 1956 large deposits of nickel ore were discovered in the area, which was then quite isolated. A railway line was brought in, a mine was opened and a town quickly appeared. It was named Thompson after the chairman of the mining company, the International Nickel Company (Inco).

During the 1960s demand for nickel boomed and the town grew to a population of over 20 000. Today Thompson is a major regional centre for northern Manitoba and offers a number of recreational facilities. The population of Thompson in 1986 was 14 701.

For further information, contact the City Clerk, City Hall, Thompson, Man., R8N 1S6.

Thompson, David

Explorer and map maker (*born in 1770 at London, England; died in 1857 at Longueuil, Canada East [Que.]*). He was the first European to travel down the Columbia River to the Pacific Ocean. His maps were the first reliable guides to what is now western Canada.

David Thompson came to Canada to work for the Hudson's Bay Company when he was 14 years old. After learning the skills of the surveyor, he left the HBC to join the rival North West Company and became the company's leading mapmaker. One of his first jobs was to survey the border between Canada and the United States from Lake Superior to Lake of the Woods in 1797.

Fur traders were seeking a safe canoe

Stamp commemorating the explorations of David Thompson (courtesy Canada Post Corporation).

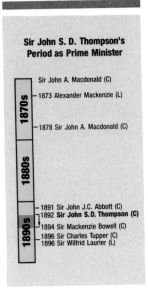

Sir John S. D. Thompson's Period as Prime Minister

1870s
- Sir John A. Macdonald (C)
- 1873 Alexander Mackenzie (L)
- 1878 Sir John A. Macdonald (C)

1880s

1890s
- 1891 Sir John J.C. Abbott (C)
- 1892 Sir John S.D. Thompson (C)
- 1894 Sir Mackenzie Bowell (C)
- 1896 Sir Charles Tupper (C)
- 1896 Sir Wilfrid Laurier (L)

route to the Pacific when Thompson was sent in 1810 to cross the Rocky Mountains and discover where the Columbia River led. After many adventures, he arrived at the mouth of the river in July 1811 to find that American traders had beaten him to the spot. Nevertheless the Columbia became one of the important supply routes of the fur trade.

Thompson retired from the fur trade but continued to work as a surveyor. He located the boundary between Ontario and the U.S. and made charts of parts of the St Lawrence River. Towards the end of his life, Thompson was reduced to surveying city streets for a living and he died in poverty. Along with his maps, his greatest accomplishment was the account he wrote of his explorations in western Canada.

▷ SUGGESTED READING: Stan Garrod, *David Thompson* (1988); James K. Smith, *David Thompson: Fur Trader, Explorer, Geographer* (1971).

■ Thompson, Sir John Sparrow David

Thompson was the second of the four Conservatives who were briefly in office between Sir John A. Macdonald's death (1891) and the beginning of Sir Wilfrid Laurier's Liberal government (1896). Trained as a lawyer, Thompson absorbed information quickly and accurately. He was conscientious and thorough, with a powerful and inquiring mind.

He grew up in Halifax, N.S., where he was raised as a Methodist. In 1870 he married a Roman Catholic, and he was later baptized a Catholic. At the time, Thompson was practising as a lawyer in Halifax, and it says much for his local standing that he did not lose a single Protestant client by changing his religion, although he fully expected to.

POLITICS

Thompson began his political career as a Halifax alderman. In 1877 he moved on from there to become a member of the Nova Scotia Legislative Assembly, and he was briefly premier of Nova Scotia in 1882. His aim had always been to be a judge, and after political defeat in 1882 he was appointed a judge of the Nova Scotia Supreme Court. There he hoped to remain. But in 1885 Sir John A. Macdonald desperately needed new talent for his Cabinet, and Thompson reluctantly agreed to go back into politics. He became minister of justice, and so remained until his death. He was as honest a politician as

Sir John Sparrow David Thompson
4TH PRIME MINISTER OF CANADA

Born: November 10, 1845, Halifax, N.S.
Died: December 12, 1894, Windsor Castle, England
Political Party: Conservative
First Elected: 1877, Legislative House of Nova Scotia; 1885, House of Commons, Ottawa
Chosen Leader: 1892
Period as Prime Minister: December 5, 1892 to December 12, 1894
(PHOTO COURTESY NAC/C-698)

the Conservative Party had seen in many a day. Macdonald leaned on him more and more, and after Macdonald's death (after a short interval of Prime Minister Abbott), Thompson became prime minister in 1892.

The Conservative Party majority was much strengthened under Thompson's regime, but he was not in office long enough to solve such major issues as the Manitoba Schools Question. After barely two years as prime minister, he dropped dead at Windsor Castle, England, of a heart attack. There was no one in the Conservative Party who could quite replace him.

▷ SUGGESTED READING: Peter B. Waite, *The Man from Halifax: Sir John Thompson, Prime Minister* (1985).

■ Thompson, Paul

Theatre director (*born in 1940 at Charlottetown, P.E.I.*). Thompson is one of the most influential figures in modern Canadian theatre. He worked for two years in

Paul Thompson is one of the most influential people in Canadian theatre.

theatre in France before he became director of Toronto's Theatre Passe Muraille (1972-82). He pioneered the idea of the collective drama, in which a group of actors research a theme and, through improvisation, go on to develop both the content and the structure of the play. In his years at TPM, Thompson supervised more than 30 collective creations and dozens of other plays. His most successful collective was *The Farm Show* (1972), which was first produced in a barn in Clinton, Ont., after Thompson and his actors had spent the summer working with local farmers. Other plays include *1837: The Farmers' Revolt* (1973), in which he worked with a writer and his actors in developing the script, and *Maggie and Pierre*, a one-woman show about Prime Minister Trudeau and his wife. In 1987 Thompson became director of the National Theatre School in Montreal, a training school for actors and designers in both English and French.

◼ Thompson River

The Thompson River, 489 km long, is a major tributary of the Fraser River in central British Columbia. The main river is created when the North Thompson and the South Thompson rivers join at Kamloops. The lower part of the river flows through hilly ranching country before merging with the Fraser at Lytton. It is named for the explorer David Thompson.

◼ Thomson, Andrew

Meteorologist (*born in 1893 at Dobbinton, Ont.; died in 1974 at Toronto, Ont.*). Thomson established the science of meteorology in Canada. Meteorology involves research into climate changes, development of improved instruments for gathering data, and a network of research and observation stations. During the 1920s, he studied weather patterns in various parts of the world and he organized a storm-warning system for the South Pacific. Back home in Canada in the 1930s, he established weather-forecasting centres across the country. They were needed, in particular, for the rapidly growing air services that were starting up. Thomson enlarged the system during World War II, when reliable weather information was essential for military aircraft.

After the war, as director of the Meteorological Service of Canada, Thomson oversaw further expansion. He was one of the founders of the World Meteorological Organization, and he served on its executive committee from 1947 until his retirement in 1959.

▷ RELATED ARTICLE: **Meteorology.**

◼ Thomson, Roy Herbert (1st Baron Thomson of Fleet)

Newspaper publisher (*born in 1894 at Toronto, Ont.; died in 1976 at London, England*). The son of a Toronto barber, Roy Thomson built one of the largest newspaper empires in the world. He began work at 14, earning $5 a week as a clerk, and for the next 20 years he struggled to make a living at whatever jobs he could get.

Thomson's breakthrough came when working as a radio salesman in northern Ontario. He had difficulty selling the radios because the programs were broadcast from so far away that people could barely hear them. Thomson bought a radio transmitter, applied for a broadcasting licence, and in 1931 set up his own radio station, CFCH of North Bay, Ont. He followed up with a radio station in Timmins (1933) and another at Kirkland Lake (1934). In 1934 he also bought his first newspaper, the Timmins weekly *Press*. Within three years, he had turned it into a daily paper.

From then on, Thomson's holdings increased rapidly as he added more radio stations and newspapers. In the 1950s he branched into television and then into overseas papers and TV networks. Moving to Britain, he bought the giant Kemsley newspaper chain (1959) and the prestigious *Times* of London (1966). The British made him a baron in 1964. By the end of his life, his investments included oil exploration and many other enterprises. His multi-billion dollar business empire was inherited by his son, Kenneth.

▷ RELATED ARTICLE: **Newspapers.**

▷ SUGGESTED READING: Russell Braddon, *Roy Thomson of Fleet Street* (1965).

Roy Thomson *(artwork by Irma Coucill).*

◼ Thomson, Thomas John

Painter (*born in 1887 at Claremont, Ont.; died in 1917 at Canoe Lake, Ont.*). Tom Thomson worked as a commercial artist at Grip Limited from about 1907 to 1912. His colleagues there were several members of what in 1920 became the Group of Seven. They taught him how to choose his colours and compose his pictures better. He in turn introduced them to Algonquin Park in Ontario. He encouraged them to hike and canoe through the wilderness, which became their subject matter and their inspiration.

Thomson had little formal art training. He was a quick learner, however, with

Tom Thomson *(courtesy NAC/C-17399).*

The West Wind, *1917, is one of Tom Thomson's best-known paintings (courtesy AGO).*

great natural talent. In only five years after he first painted in Algonquin in 1912 he made hundreds of small oil sketches as well as about 30 large paintings. And he enjoyed immediate success. The government of Ontario purchased *Northern Lake* in 1913 for $250, and the National Gallery bought *Northern River* in 1915 for $500 — both high figures at a time when Thomson was earning 75 cents an hour.

Late in 1913 Thomson met Dr James MacCallum, who offered to pay his expenses for a year so he could concentrate on art. Thereafter he spent three seasons a year in Algonquin Park, sometimes working as a forest ranger and tour guide. He returned to Toronto for the winter and lived in a shack behind the Studio Building which Dr MacCallum and Lawren Harris had built for use by artists, mainly the future members of the Group of Seven. Here he reworked some of his sketches of forests, lakes, rocks, and skies into larger canvasses.

On July 8, 1917, Thomson disappeared on a canoe trip. His body was found eight days later. The death of this experienced outdoorsman remains a mystery. He is regarded as one of Canada's greatest painters.

▷ SUGGESTED READING: Ottelyn Addison, *Tom Thomson: The Algonquin Years* (1975); Lorraine Devorski, *Tom Thomson: The Man and His Legend* (1986); W. Little, *The Tom Thomson Mystery* (1977); Joan Murray, *The Best of Tom Thomson* (1986); Kate Taylor, *Painters* (1989); Harold Town and David Silcox, *Tom Thomson: The Silence and the Storm* (second edition, 1982).

■ Thorold

Thorold, Ont., is located in the Niagara Peninsula, next to St Catharines. First settled in the 1780s, it grew rapidly after the opening of the Welland Canal in 1829. The city is named for British politician, Sir John Thorold. Today the economy relies on a variety of industry. The population in 1986 was 16 131.

For further information, contact the City Clerk, 8 Carleton Street South, P.O. Box 1044, Thorold, Ont., L2V 4A7.

■ Thousand Islands

Thousand Islands is the name for a group of over 1500 rocky, wooded islands and islets scattered in the St Lawrence River where it leaves Lake Ontario. The islands extend along an 80 km stretch of the river, and are one of Ontario's favourite vacation areas. The Canada-U.S. border runs down the middle of the river, and islands lie on both sides of it.

The river at this point is rich in fish and waterfowl. Fishing and boating have been popular for more than 100 years. Hotels were built after 1856 and by Confederation in 1867, magnificent summer homes were appearing. Among the most famous is Boldt Castle, an ornate home built by a wealthy New Yorker. Steamboats plied the narrow passages between the islands and cottages began to line the shore.

In 1914 St Lawrence Islands National Park was created to include some of the islands. Today a scenic parkway gives visitors a good view of the area.

▷ SUGGESTED READING: Shawn Thompson, *River Rats: The People of the Thousand Islands* (1989).

In the Northland, *1915. The natural expression and brilliant colour of Thomson's paintings have retained their freshness with generations of viewers (courtesy Montreal Museum of Fine Arts).*

Northern Mockingbird is one of four species of thrasher to nest in Canada (photo by Normand David).

■ Thrasher

There are about 30 species of thrasher (family Mimidae), all of them in the Americas. These birds are known for the variety and power of their song. Some imitate the sounds of other birds. The plumage is a dull grey or brown, and they have a long tail. They live on insects, seeds, and berries. Four species nest in Canada: the Northern Mockingbird (*Mimus polyglottos*), the Gray Catbird (*Dumetella carolinensis*), the Brown Thrasher (*Toxostoma rufum*), and the Sage Thrasher (*Oreoscoptes montanus*). They frequent bushes, hedgerows, and thickets. Only the Northern Mockingbird lives here year-round, but only in parts of southern Canada. The nest is usually built in a tree, thicket, or shrub. Thrashers are aggressive, and chase away any intruders onto their territory.

■ Three Persons, Tom

Champion bronco rider, rancher (*born around 1887 in what is now southern Alberta; died in 1949 at Calgary, Alta*). At the first Calgary Stampede in 1912, Tom Three Persons had the crowds cheering wildly as he rode to a finish on a bucking, rearing, and twisting bronco called Cyclone. Cyclone had rarely before been successfully ridden, though he had been taken on by the world's best cowboys. As a result, Tom Three Persons was declared world bronco-riding champion.

Tom Three Persons was a Blood Indian from Stand Off, Alta. He continued to compete in rodeo events, and he also supplied broncos for rodeos. He had a ranch near Spring Coulee, where he bred racehorses and raised cattle. In 1946 he was badly injured when trying to prevent a colt from breaking out of a corral. He never fully recovered.

▷ RELATED ARTICLE: **Rodeo.**

■ Thrips

A thrip is the common name for insects belonging to order Thysanoptera. Very small insects (0.5-3 mm), they have asymmetrical mouth parts and two pairs of slender wings fringed with long hairs. Colour ranges from yellow to brown to black. The metamorphosis is between a complete one (like a butterfly) and an incomplete one (like a bed bug). They look like adults during their two larval stages, though they are smaller and do not have fully developed wings. In the last stage they are inactive and often enclosed in a cocoon covered in debris. There can be several generations in a year.

There are at least 4500 species of thrips in the world, and 104 of them have been described. Thrips eat plant sap and can transmit disease, thereby posing a serious danger to cultivated plants. They live on fungus, leaves, and under bark, and are particularly abundant on some flowers.

■ Thrush

Members of the large family Muscicapidae, thrushes belong to the sub-family Turdinae, 12 of over 3000 species breed in Canada. Thrushes are widely appreciated as songbirds. In adults, thrushes and the Veery (genera *Hylochichla* and *Catharus*) have a splotched breast; Robins (*Turdus*), brick red; Bluebirds (*Sialia*), blue or reddish; Solitaires (*Myadestes*), grey; and Wheatears (*Oenanthe*), white. The males are usually more brightly coloured than the females. The American Robin (*Turdus migratorius*) is probably familiar to more people than any other bird. It arrives in most parts of the country when bare ground first shows through the snow, and is one of our favourite signs of spring. Robins nest 1.5 to 4.5 m up in trees.

Only one species of Solitaire lives in Canada: Townsend's Solitaire (*Myadestes townsendi*). It is a slender, grey bird, with a long tail rimmed in white, a short bill, a white circle about the eyes, and tan spots on the wings. Some think the Solitaire has one of the most melodious calls of all Canadian songbirds.

Thrushes eat insects, worms, and fruit. Bluebirds nest in cavities or in birdhouses. Robins and Wood Thrushes (*Hilochila mustelina*) nest in trees or bushes and reinforce their nests with mud. They lay three to seven eggs, usually a shade of blue or blue-green. The Solitaire is an exception. It lays eggs that are white with brown spots.

▷ SUGGESTED READING: Earl W. Godfrey, *The Birds of Canada* (1986).

Common Thrip (artwork by Jan Sovak).

Breeding Range of Brown Thrasher ●

Breeding Range of Sage Thrasher ●

Veery (courtesy Macmillan Illustrated Animal Encyclopedia).

Tom Three Persons (courtesy Glenbow Archives/NA-778-7).

■ **Thunder,** *see* **Weather**

■ **Thunder Bay**

Thunder Bay, Ont., is a city at the western end of Lake Superior in the northwest corner of the province. It was created in 1970 when the twin cities of Fort William and Port Arthur joined. Known as the Lakehead, it has long been important as the end of water navigation into the interior of the continent. Two striking features of the surrounding area are Mount McKay to the south, and the massive rock bluff known as Nanibijou, the Sleeping Giant.

Fur Trade The site has been occupied by native peoples for 10 000 years. The name Thunder Bay refers to the thunderbird of Indian myth. The French built the first fur-trade post in 1679, but it was the construction of Fort William by the North West Company (NWC) in 1803 that established the importance of the site. The fort was a rendezvous point where canoes coming down with furs from the interior met canoes travelling inland with supplies from Montreal. Until 1821, when the Hudson's Bay Company and the NWC merged, Fort William was the centre of a trading empire stretching across the continent.

Grain-handling Facilities, *Thunder Bay, Ont. (photo by Hans Blohm/Masterfile).*

Once the fur trade declined, a few settlers remained. Then, after 1870, nearby Prince Arthur's Landing became one end of the Dawson Road, a land-and-water route joining Lake Superior to Winnipeg, Man. Until the railway was built in the 1880s, this was the only route into the West.

Port City When the railway arrived, grain began to flow out of the prairies to Thunder Bay, where it was loaded on ships to be carried down the Great Lakes. With its 15 large grain elevators, the city became one of the world's largest grain ports. The Port of Thunder Bay, operated by the Thunder Bay Commission, handles over 1.7 million tonnes of cargo a

Fort William *was built by the North West Company in 1803 (courtesy Canada Post Corporation).*

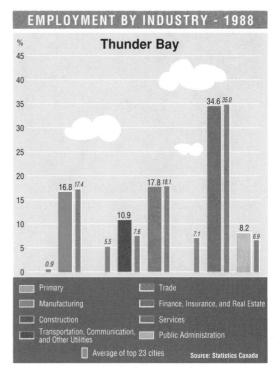

EMPLOYMENT BY INDUSTRY - 1988

Thunder Bay

Primary	Trade
Manufacturing	Finance, Insurance, and Real Estate
Construction	Services
Transportation, Communication, and Other Utilities	Public Administration

Average of top 23 cities   **Source: Statistics Canada**

year, including grain, potash, coal, and iron ore. The economy also relies on the forest industry and a variety of manufacturing.

Thunder Bay is served by two major airlines, and has bus and railway connections. It has four ski resorts, 200 km of groomed ski trails, seven golf courses, and more than 80 racquet sports courts. The Community Auditorium, which opened in 1985, has a performing-arts centre and other cultural facilities. Thunder Bay is the site of Lakehead University. The population in 1986 was 112 272.

For further information, contact the City Clerk, 500 Donald Street East, Thunder Bay, Ont., P7E 5V3.

■ **Thunderbird**

Thunderbird is a powerful supernatural being found in Indian legends throughout North America. He caused thunder by flapping his wings, and lightning by blinking his eyes. He was also a friend and protector of human beings. The Athapaskan peoples in central Canada called him Adee, and told how he flew down from the skies before the Earth was formed, touched the water with his wings, and the land rose from the bottom of the sea. Pictures of the thunderbird are found in Indian art from coast to coast, in early rock carvings (petroglyphs) and rock paintings (pictographs) in Nova Scotia and Ontario, in totem poles and crests on the Northwest Coast, and in contemporary works by artists such as Norval Morrisseau.

▷ SUGGESTED READING: Anne Siberell, *Whale in the Sky* (1982).

■ Thurman, Mark

Illustrator, writer (*born in 1948 at Toronto, Ont.*). Thurman uses drawings to educate children. With Emily Hearn, who writes the text, he produces *Owl* magazine's "Mighty Mites," adventure stories teaching natural science. *Mighty Mites in Dinosaurland* (1981) takes the heroes back in time to learn about the dinosaurs who roamed Alberta's Badlands. He also illustrated Hearn's *Good Morning Franny, Good Night Franny* (1984) and *Race You Franny* (1986), which are stories showing that a physically disabled girl has the same feelings and concerns as other children. Thurman has written and illustrated two series about the problems younger children face. Both series, "Douglas the Elephant" and "Two Pals on an Adventure," in which Albert Alligator joins Douglas, humorously teach such concepts as sharing and accepting disappointments. *Cabbage Town Gang* (1987) is an autobiographical novel about life in a housing project.

■ Ti-Jean

Ti-Jean is a short form of Petit-Jean or Little John, a popular hero in French-Canadian folk stories. Here is one such tale:

There was once a king who had three sons. He decided to give them three tests, to see who should be king. In the first test, he sent them out to find the best horse. They each took a different path through the forest. Finally Ti-Jean came to a cottage where there was a big white cat. Ti-Jean told the cat about the horse and she said: "Take one of my toads. When you get back to the palace it will become a fine horse." So Ti-Jean took the toad and, sure enough, it turned into the best horse his father had ever seen.

The second test was to find the most beautiful piece of cloth. Again the brothers followed different paths and again Ti-Jean consulted the big white cat. "Take one of my walnuts," she said. "When you open it at the palace you will find a fine cloth inside." So Ti-Jean won the second round.

The third test was to find the prettiest girl. Again Ti-Jean went to the big white cat. "I have a spell on me," she explained. "When I marry a prince, I shall become a woman once more." So Ti-Jean returned to the palace with the cat, and the cat turned into the loveliest woman in the land. In this way, Ti-Jean became king.

Thunderbirds by artist Carl Ray, acrylic on canvas (courtesy Confederation College, Thunder Bay).

■ Tibbets, Benjamin Franklin

Inventor (*born in 1813 at Youngs Cove, N.B.; died in 1853 at Scotchtown, N.B.*). Benjamin Tibbets invented a compound steam engine, which enabled ships to run faster and more efficiently. The first of his engines was installed in the paddlewheeler *Reindeer* in 1845. Long after Tibbets was dead, the *Reindeer* was still the fastest boat plying the Saint John River in New Brunswick.

Tibbets had learned the mechanics of steam engines while working at various foundries and machine shops. When he applied for a patent for his engine, he found that it was not the first of its kind in the world. Yet it had considerable impact on shipping in New Brunswick, where Tibbets is honoured as a pioneer of marine engineering. A highly talented man, he would likely have made a greater mark as an inventor had his career not been cut short by tuberculosis, which eventually killed him.

■ Tick

Ticks are parasites who suck blood, mostly from birds and mammals. They belong to class Arachnida of Arthropods. Their cephalothorax is fused with the abdomen, and there is no apparent division between the two. Their mouthparts can clutch and pierce skin. The tips of the front feet bear sensory organs specialized to recognize host vertebrates. Size ranges from 1 to 5 mm. After a meal they may be as large as 20-30 mm.

Ticks can survive several months without eating, sometimes up to a year. The presence of too many ticks can make an animal anemic and susceptible to illnesses or even cause its death. Ticks can leave serious wounds that take a long time to heal. Some ticks transmit Rocky Mountain Spotted Fever to humans. It can be treated with antibiotics. Some 800 species are known around the world and 35 species are in Canada. Fortunately, the Canadian species cause fewer medical problems for their human or animal hosts than those in warmer climates.

Annapolis Tidal Power Plant was the first to transform tidal energy to electricity (courtesy Tidal Power Corporation).

Leonard Tilley had a less successful political career than his famous father (courtesy Provincial Archives of New Brunswick/ P37/126).

■ Tidal Energy

Tidal energy is a renewable source of energy which comes, ultimately, from the force of gravity. Pulled by the Moon, the oceans rise and fall. Where the differences between water levels at high and low tide exceed 5 m or so, tidal energy can be captured in much the same way that the energy of water falling in rivers is captured by hydroelectric dams.

The world's highest and most powerful tides occur in the upper reaches of the Bay of Fundy, which lies between New Brunswick and Nova Scotia. Waters at high tide can be as much as 16 m above those at low tide.

There have been many schemes to harness the Bay of Fundy tides. To test the kinds of turbine-generator proposed for use in the most promising of such schemes, a small tidal power plant (the first in Canada) began producing electricity in 1984. Near Annapolis Royal, N.S., it is capable of generating 20 megawatts of electrical power.

This simple tidal power plant consists of an embankment built across an estuary. Sluicegates permit a gap in the dam to be opened or closed. They are opened while the tide is rising, allowing seawater to flow through. They are closed when the tide is full, storing water in the estuary. The act of opening another set of sluicegates as the tide recedes directs the flow of stored water back into the sea through a turbine. The turbine spins, turning a generator, thus producing electricity. Electricity is generated for several hours, until the tide turns. Then the sea level starts to rise again and the emptied basin is refilled for another cycle of power generation.

▷ RELATED ARTICLES: **Electricity; Energy; Hydroelectricity.**

■ Tides, *see* Ocean

■ Tignish

Tignish, P.E.I., is a village 153 km northwest of Charlottetown. It was first settled in 1799 by a small group of Acadians. Later it attracted many Irish immigrants. In 1896 a disastrous fire swept through the community, destroying 62 homes and businesses. Today most of the village businesses are owned co-operatively. The harvest of Irish moss is important. Tignish's population in 1986 was 960.

For further information, contact the Administrator, P.O. Box 57, Tignish, P.E.I., C0B 2B0.

■ Tiktak, John

Sculptor (*born in 1916 at Kareak, near Whale Cove, N.W.T.; died in 1981 at Rankin Inlet, N.W.T.*). Tiktak spent much of his life as a hunter. In 1958 he moved to Rankin Inlet to work in the nickel mine. About 1961 he started carving in his spare time. He produced small, simplified sculptures representing Eskimo faces, which he sold to tourists as souvenirs. In 1962 the nickel mine closed, and the next year Tiktak began carving full-time. His work, which is more concerned with generalized form and symbolism than most Inuit carving, has been compared to modern European sculpture. Examples of his work are in every museum and major private collection of Inuit art. He was the first Inuit artist to have a major one-man show displaying the best work of his career. It was held at the University of Manitoba in 1970.

▷ SUGGESTED READING: Gallery One-One-One, *Tiktak, Sculptor from Rankin Inlet: A Retrospective Exhibition* (1970).

■ Tilley, Leonard Percy de Wolfe

Premier of New Brunswick (*born in 1870 at Ottawa, Ont.; died in 1947 at Saint John, N.B.*). The son of Sir Samuel Tilley, one of the Fathers of Confederation, he had a less successful career in politics than his famous father. A lawyer, he was elected to the New Brunswick legislature as a Conservative in 1912. In 1925 he joined the Cabinet, and in 1933 he became leader of the party and premier.

It was the middle of the Great Depression. Any government was bound to be unpopular with voters. Tilley's Conservatives went down to defeat in the 1935 election and he left politics to return to the legal world as a judge.

■ Tilley, Sir Samuel Leonard

Politician (*born in 1818 at Gagetown, N.B.; died in 1896 at Saint John, N.B.*). Tilley was New Brunswick's leading Father of Confederation. In the years before Confederation he sat in the New Brunswick legislature (1850-51, 1854-56, 1857-65, and 1866-67). His defeats in the 1850s were caused by his strong stand against alcohol. With a group of Liberals (New Brunswickers called them "the Smashers") Tilley tried to establish prohibition in New Brunswick in 1851-52 and again in 1855-56. Both attempts failed; it was not easy to smash rum drinking in New Brunswick. Recognizing this, Tilley turned his attention to railways and, by 1864, to Confederation. Railways and Confederation were part of the same cause, for Tilley insisted that the union of colonies must be physical as well as political. This meant building a railway to connect the Maritimes with the Province of Canada [Ontario and Quebec].

Tilley had become premier of New Brunswick in 1861, but in 1865 his government was defeated on the Confederation issue, which was temporarily unpopular in New Brunswick. However, he was re-elected in 1866, in time to take part in the final arrangements.

After Confederation, Tilley served as minister of customs in Prime Minister Sir John A. Macdonald's government (1867-73). Tilley was minister of finance after 1878, and in 1879 he brought in the National Policy. In 1885, suffering from ill health, he retired from federal politics and was made lieutenant-governor of New Brunswick.

▷ RELATED ARTICLES: **Confederation; National Policy; New Brunswick.**

▷ SUGGESTED READING: W.S. MacNutt, *New Brunswick: A History 1784-1867* (1963).

■ Timber Trade

Canada's timber industry got its start 200 years ago, after the British conquest of New France. During the French regime, timber was used only for local construction. Little wood was exported, because France had ample forests of its own. England, on the other hand, had recklessly destroyed its domestic forests. It was forced to depend on imported wood for naval and other kinds of construction.

Traditionally, England had purchased the timber it needed from Russia, Sweden, and other countries across the Baltic Sea. During wars, however, this supply could be cut off by its enemies. From the mid-1600s on, England looked to its American colonies as a safe, alternate source of wood. The huge white pines of the New England colonies were particularly valuable, because they could provide the great masts and spars needed for Britain's battleships. When the American Revolution began in 1775, England was forced to turn elsewhere.

The pioneer lumberman William Davidson, of Chatham, N.B., tried for many years in vain to interest England in his timber. Suddenly, in 1779, he was flooded with orders for masts. From about 1795 on, almost all of the masts used by the navy came from either New Brunswick or the St Lawrence Valley.

There was still little market for construction timber. England was still buying it from the Baltic countries. However, in the 1790s England feared that the French, with whom they were at war, might close the Baltic ports to English ships. They looked to Canada as an alternative source. By 1804 the industry had spread from the Maritimes up the St

Sir Samuel Tilley (artwork by Irma Coucill).

Boom Men *at O'Brien logging camp on the shores of Gordon Pasha Lake, B.C. The men pole the logs with pike poles, moving them into large log booms (courtesy NAC/C-79019).*

400-year-old White Pine in northern Ontario. Tall white pines, now rare, were ideal for the masts of the great sailing ships. Wasteful methods almost totally wiped them out (photo by Mike Dobel/Masterfile).

Squaring Pine *at Jocko River, Ont., 1890 (courtesy Archives of Ontario/11778-4).*

Lawrence River to Quebec City. There, the Royal Navy contractors, Scott, Idles and Company, were given a contract to export wood. Settlers as far as Lake Ontario began to send timber down the St Lawrence River. The biggest development was the opening, in 1806, of the greatest white pine country in the world, the Ottawa Valley. White pine, being both strong and workable, was the most sought after of trees.

The founder of the Ottawa Valley industry was Philemon Wright, an immigrant from Massachussets. He established a settlement at Hull, on the Ottawa River. In the summer of 1806 Wright sent the first timber down the Ottawa and the St Lawrence to Quebec City. He had been warned that it could not be done, because of the dangerous rapids. He succeeded by building the timber into rafts. This was the method used to move timber for the next 100 years.

In that same year, 1806, the French emperor Napoleon Bonaparte succeeded in blockading the Baltic timber ports to English shipping. By 1808 England's imports had dwindled to almost nothing. In 1809 the English turned to the British North America colonies for timber. As a result, in 1811, New Brunswick and Nova Scotia

Sailing Ships loading timber at Newcastle, N.B. (courtesy Provincial Archives of New Brunswick).

between them exported nearly 280 000 cubic metres of pine timber, plus 4000 masts. Quebec City dispatched that year over 105 000 cubic metres of pine and oak timber and 23 000 masts. The timber trade rapidly replaced fur as Canada's main export.

The Baltic ports were reopened to English ships in 1812. However, the Canadian trade continued. The British placed heavy tariffs in favour of Canadian wood. Tariffs on Baltic or American timber entering Britain rose to a whopping 65 shillings per fifty cubic feet (1.4 cubic metres) during 1814 to 1821. From 1821 to 1842 the tariff was 55 shillings, while during the same period the tariff on an equal amount of Canadian timber was a mere one shilling.

One of Scott, Idles's young apprentices, William Price, launched his own company in 1816. (It still exists as Abitibi-Price of Toronto, Ont.) He gained control of the Hudson's Bay Company forests up the Saguenay River. He pioneered the exports of "deals." These were three-inch (7.5 cm) spruce planks. They could be sawn to desired size in the sawmills in England.

Most of the wood exported to Britain, however, was "square timber." These were rectangular logs, 12 m long or more. They were squared to a foot (about 30 cm) in diameter with a broad-axe. Square timber was easier to raft and stow on ships than lumber. Like deals, it could be sawn to desired size in England. Square timber makers were selective in the trees they cut. They wanted only the best and tallest trees, and harvested only about 10% of the timber available.

Year after year the trade boomed. Fortunes were made on the Miramichi and Saint John rivers in New Brunswick, on the Saguenay and St Maurice rivers in Quebec, and above all on the Ottawa. Timber was big business. John Egan, a young Irish immigrant who went to work as a clerk in an Ottawa Valley lumber camp, went into business on his own in the 1830s. He took over Philemon Wright's title as "the King of the Ottawa." At the peak of his career he controlled 5200 km² of forest. He sent 55 rafts of square timber down river each summer in the 1840s, and employed 3500 men in his 100 lumber camps.

Timber making was hard, demanding work. Each autumn gangs of "lumberers," as they were called before the term "lumberjack" came into use, went into the woods and built log shanty camps.

They had no stoves. Their fires for cooking, illumination, and for heat during the winter were simple stone hearths in the middle of the floor. There was a hole in the roof for the smoke. They worked six days a week from dawn to dark. They had to make their own amusement, perhaps a bit of fiddle music and storytelling on Saturday night and Sunday. They were too far out in the woods to go to town.

Teams of half a dozen men went out from the shanties each morning. They toppled 30 m trees and hewed them into square timber. The men who felled the trees, with an axe in the early days and later a cross-cut saw, were highly skilled. They could predict precisely where a giant pine would fall. Nevertheless, sometimes there were fatal accidents when the wind caught a toppling tree. Once a tree was down, one man began to chop off the crown and branches. Another made long chalk marks along the edges of the log. Then it was the turn of the most skilful of all, the hewers. They worked with a razor-sharp broad-axe with a 30 cm blade to "hew to the line" and square the log smooth. A third of the tree was wasted in this method. In those days it was thought, wrongly, that the pine would last forever.

In the spring, the logs were made up into rafts for the journey to ports downriver. On rivers of the East Coast, like the Saint John, they were simply lashed together in two tiers of 30 logs to make a "joint." These were fitted together with wooden cross-pieces to make a large raft.

On the Ottawa River, the rapids were more dangerous. A more complicated system had to be used. The basic unit was the "crib," made up of 20 pieces of square

Lumberman's Shanty, Upper Ottawa River, 1871 (courtesy Notman Photographic Archives).

timber. A crib weighed about 40 tonnes. The cribs were coupled to each other like a meccano set, so that they could be swiftly dismantled when necessary. To get around the rapids on the Ottawa River, timber slides, like water slides, were constructed. When the rafts came to these slides they were dismantled. Each separate crib was steered down the watery slope. The whole raft was then reassembled at the bottom.

Some of the Ottawa rafts were half a kilometre long. They carried crews of 20 men who lived in huts on board the rafts. Their meals were cooked over open fires. Some 400 rafts came down the Ottawa each summer. They made a colourful sight, with flags flying and makeshift sails billowing before the westerly breeze on the St Lawrence.

Up to the 1850s, square timber was king. Then the growth of towns in the United States opened a new market for sawn lumber. New men appeared to raise money for sawmills. One of the biggest operators was John Booth. He came to Ottawa and beginning with a little mill he rented, built a vast lumber empire. Booth controlled a forest area larger than Prince Edward Island, and employed 4000 men. To move his wood he built a 1000 km railway from Georgian Bay to the American border. Booth's counterpart in New Brunswick was Alexander "Boss" Gibson, who also built a railway.

By Confederation, 1867, lumber exports to the United States surpassed the square timber trade to the United Kingdom. Ontario had become the largest producer, with 150 steam mills. The logging frontier had been pushed west to the shores of Lake Huron.

Loggers hewing timber in B.C. forest. The man on the right is wielding a broad-bladed "Hudson's Bay" axe (courtesy PABC/ HP 36502).

Life of a Lumberer

"The winter, snow, and frost, although severe, are nothing to endure in comparison to the extreme coldness of the snow-water of the freshets, in which the lumberer is, day after day, wet up to the middle, and often immersed from head to foot.... But notwithstanding all the toils of such a pursuit, those who once adopt the life of a lumberer, prefer it to any other. They are in a great measure as independent, in their own way, as the Indians. After selling and delivering up their rafts, they pass some weeks in idle indulgence, drinking, smoking, and *dashing off* in a long coat, flashy waistcoat and trowsers, Wellington or Hessian boots, a handkerchief of many colours round the neck, a watch with a long tinsel chain and numberless brass seals, and an *umbrella*. Before winter, they return again to the woods, and resume the laborious pursuits of the preceding year."

from John McGregor, British America 1832

Lumberjack

The word "lumber" originated in England. At first, it simply meant the odds and ends stored in a "lumber room." The word came from "lombard room," which was where the international bankers of Lombardy (in Italy) kept their unredeemed pledges. From that came the term "lumberers."

This was what forest workers were called in the 19th century. Eventually the term "lumberjack" was used in eastern Canada in the early 1900s. It was of American origin. Since World War II the term has dropped out of common usage. In B.C., forest workers have always been called loggers.

Joe Montferrand

Joe Montferrand was born in Montreal. He was tall and very strong. He became the amateur boxing champion of Quebec while still a boy, and went to work in the timber trade as a rafting foreman at Bytown. He was known as a man who could run faster, jump higher, and hit harder than anyone else. His battle against a dozen Irish on the bridge across the Ottawa River was exaggerated. The story was retold as one man against 150.

Joe Montferrand was known from the Gaspé to the Ottawa River as the man who implanted the nail marks of his logging boots in a 2.4 m high tavern ceiling by jumping from a standing position. He died at the age of 61, and is buried in Notre Dame des Neiges cemetery in Montreal.

The stories of the mythical Paul Bunyan may have been based on Joe Montferrand.

Logging in Surrey, B.C., 1912 (courtesy PABC/HP-45505).

Logging, like settlement, came later to British Columbia than to the East Coast. It was just getting under way in the 1860s. One of the first lumber camps in B.C. was established by Jeremiah Rogers from New Brunswick. It was on English Bay, in what is now the city of Vancouver. The first sawmills were constructed by an English sea captain, Edward Stamp.

The tremendous size of the trees of coastal B.C. called for new methods of logging. A Douglas fir might grow to 60 m, 1.5 to 3 m around at the base. "Skid roads" of greased logs had to be constructed so that teams of 10 or 12 oxen could move the logs. This was slow work. By the 1890s little steam engines equipped with cables and pulleys took the place of oxen. These engines grew in size until logging sites began to look like outdoor factories. Huge skidders gathered in logs over elaborate "skyline systems," with giant pulleys and kilometres of steel cable. Since there were few coastal rivers big enough to float the great Douglas fir logs, dozens of narrow gauge railways were built.

By the end of World War I in 1918, British Columbia had outstripped all other provinces in lumber production. Its best-known lumberman was H.R. MacMillan. Like all the timber kings, MacMillan was a self-made man. He became a multi-millionaire, selling his lumber from England to Japan. He created the forest products corporation now known as MacMillan Bloedel.

While B.C. "loggers" developed new methods, eastern Canadian "lumberjacks" were busy with a new product that was to revolutionize the industry. Wasteful methods had almost wiped out the white pine. However, the growth of newspapers in the United States created a new demand. Pulp and paper are produced from spruce and fir, which had little use

in earlier days. By the 1920s, pulp and paper replaced lumber as the main export.

The new industry opened up new communities in the northern forests from Newfoundland to the Prairie Provinces, especially in Quebec and northern Ontario. The muscle power of men and horses gave way to power saws, gasoline "skidders" to move the logs, and eventually massive tree harvesters. These monsters can topple half a dozen fir trees with one swipe of their steel claws. University-trained foresters were hired to ensure efficient logging and to guard against the wasteful methods of earlier days. Lumberjacks, now known as forest technicians, make more in a day than their fathers and grandfathers made in a month.

Canada's forest industry is valued at $23 billion per year. It contributes more to the country's trade than agriculture, mining, petroleum, and fisheries combined. As long as continued care is taken in restoring and renewing our forests, forest products will be a source of Canadian wealth in the century to come.

▷ RELATED ARTICLES: **John Rudolphus Booth; Forestry; H.R. MacMillan; William Price.**

▷ SUGGESTED READING: Peter Adams, *Early Loggers and the Sawmill* (1981); Donald MacKay, *The Lumberjacks* (1978).

■ Time

We take time for granted in our daily lives. However, the nature of time itself defies description.

Measuring Time Early humans measured time by the cycles of nature. They noted the rising and setting of the sun, the phases of the moon, and the passing of the seasons. From these came the day, month, and year. The invention of clocks enabled people to divide the day into hours, minutes, and seconds.

Local Time A day is the time between one midnight and the next. Until the late 19th century, people set their clocks to 12:00 when the Sun reached high noon. Thus the time would vary from place to place, according to the movement of the Sun. This became very confusing when the railway moved people quickly from town to town. A conductor on a train might have to keep dozens of clocks. He would set them to the local times of the towns on the route.

Standard Time Sir Sandford Fleming, a Canadian engineer, helped to solve this problem. He and an American divided North America into several time zones. The time would be the same for all places within each zone. The zones would differ

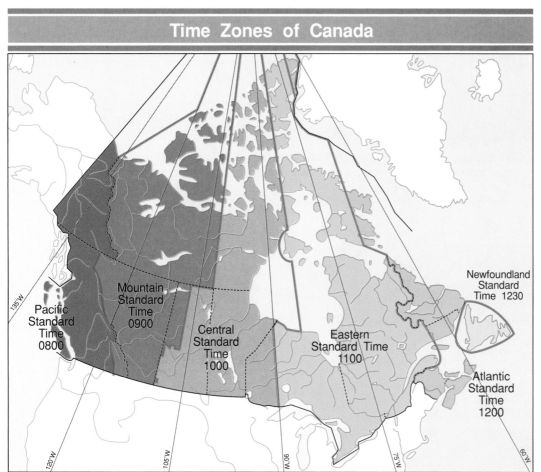

Time Zones of Canada

Pacific
Standard
Time
0800

Mountain
Standard
Time
0900

Central
Standard
Time
1000

Eastern
Standard Time
1100

Atlantic
Standard
Time
1200

Newfoundland
Standard
Time 1230

135 W
120 W
105 W
90 W
75 W
60 W

Standard Time

Noon

6am — 6pm

Midnight

6am becomes 7am

Noon

6am — 6pm

6am

Midnight

Daylight Time

Daylight Saving Time *By shifting the clock one hour ahead, darkness comes one hour later, "saving" more daylight for evening.*

from those on either side by one hour. The system came into use in 1883. North America was divided into the Atlantic, Eastern, Central, Mountain, Pacific, and Yukon (or Alaska) time zones. Later, Canada added a time zone for Newfoundland. When it is noon in Nova Scotia, it is 12:30 in Newfoundland. (Labrador is *officially* on Atlantic time. In *practice* it uses the same time as Newfoundland.) The Yukon later decided to go on Pacific time.

Fleming proposed that this system of Standard Time be adopted around the world. He divided the Earth into 24 time zones, one for each hour of the day. His idea was accepted in 1884.

Many Canadians set their clocks forward by one hour on the first Sunday in April. This "saves" an hour of daylight for later in the day, when most people are awake to enjoy it. Hence, it is called Daylight Saving Time. It was first tried in 1918, but did not come into general use until the 1950s. The clocks are set back to Standard Time on the last Sunday in October. Saskatchewan is the only province that does not use Daylight Saving Time.

Clocks A clock measures time by counting a regular movement or pulse. The pendulum clock, invented about 300

years ago, uses the swinging back and forth of a pendulum. Electric clocks use the vibration of an electrical current. The quartz clock uses the vibrations of a quartz crystal. The most accurate clocks measure the vibrations within atoms, such as those of cesium — a rare metal.

Canadian scientists working at the National Research Council (NRC) built the second cesium clock in 1957. These atomic clocks are extremely accurate. It would take thousands of years for them to gain or lose more than a second. Such accurate time is valuable for scientific research.

The NRC is Canada's official time keeper. It broadcasts a time signal at 1:00 PM Ottawa time every day over the CBC radio network. Anyone can learn the exact time by phoning the NRC at (613) 745-1576 in English, and (613) 745-9426 in French.

▷ RELATED ARTICLE: **Sir Sandford Fleming.**

▷ SUGGESTED READING: Henry Humphrey and Deirdre O'Meara-Humphrey, *When is Now?: Experiments with Time and Timekeeping Devices* (1980); Bobbie Kalman, *Time and Seasons* (1986); Malcolm M. Thomson, *The Beginning of the Long Dash: A History of Timekeeping in Canada* (1978).

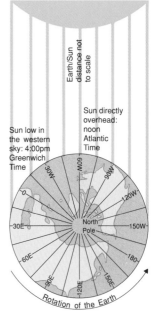

Time of Day *at any place on Earth is determined by the position of the Sun.*

Tlingit spruce-root basket (courtesy UBC Museum of Anthropology).

Timmins

Timmins, Ont., is a city located in northern Ontario, 300 km north of Sudbury. It began in 1912 after the nearby town of South Porcupine burned to the ground. Named for local merchant, Noah Timmins, it grew as the centre of a gold-mining district. The area has produced more gold than any other city in North America. More recently, copper mining and other base metal industries have broadened the economy. The area has the world's largest zinc deposit and is Canada's largest silver producer. In area, Timmins is Canada's largest city. The population in 1986 was 46 657.

For further information, contact the City Clerk, 220 Algonquin Boulevard East, Timmins, Ont., P4N 1B3.

Tipi, *see* Native People: Plains

Tisdale

Tisdale, Sask., is a town situated in east-central Saskatchewan. Founded in 1902, it was first called Doghide after a local creek. In 1904 the Canadian Northern Railway arrived and the name was changed to honour a railway engineer. It is the business centre for a prosperous farming district. The population in 1986 was 3184.

For further information, contact the Town Administrator, P.O. Box 1090, Tisdale, Sask., S0E 1T0.

Titanic

The *Titanic* was the largest passenger liner of its day. Thought to be unsinkable, it set off from England on its maiden voyage across the Atlantic to New York in April 1912. In the darkness of late evening on April 14, the giant ship struck an iceberg about 600 km southeast of Newfoundland. As the 2200 passengers and crew hurried to board the lifeboats, the bow of the crippled vessel filled with water. There was not enough room for everyone in the boats, and as the ship went down many people threw themselves into the frigid water. After two hours and 40 minutes, the *Titanic* slipped beneath the surface. Early the next morning, survivors were picked up by another ship, but by then 1522 lives were lost.

After a long search, a French-U.S. expedition succeeded in locating the wreck of the *Titanic* in September 1985. Since that time, it has been photographed and visited by divers. Artifacts have even been recovered from the sunken hulk, which rests in a deep undersea canyon at a depth of 3798 metres.

▷ SUGGESTED READING: Robert Ballard, *Exploring the Titanic* (1988); Archibald Gracie, *Titanic: A Survivor's Story* (1986); Walter Lord, *A Night to Remember* (second edition, 1963).

Tlingit

The Tlingit lived along the many islands of southeastern Alaska. They were famed as sea-going traders. Some married Athapaskans and moved to the extreme northwestern corner of British Columbia and nearby Yukon. These people are known as Inland Tlingit.

The Inland Tlingit resemble Athapaskans in many ways, but in language, social organization, and ceremonies, they remained Tlingit.

The Inland Tlingit depend on salmon runs of the Taku River, but they also hunt caribou, moose, and other animals. They were divided into two major groups: Wolf and Crow. Membership in either group meant certain obligations, especially concerning feasts.

The Inland Tlingit were exposed to the flood of prospectors that came north to the Klondike Gold Rush in the 1890s. They were stricken by new diseases. Today they number over 1000. *See* **Native People: Northwest Coast.**

Toad

Toad is the name often used for the warty-skinned Amphibians of genus *Bufo*, Order Anura. There are 194 species worldwide. These animals are adapted to live far from water, for their rough skins protect them from drying out. They can easily make great leaps, thanks to their stocky bodies and short, powerful legs. Their hind feet have horny bumps on each side, which help them push off from the ground. However, they are less skilful at swimming than frogs.

The name "toad" is also given to other members of the Bufonidae family (279 species in all), and to members of other families that bear a greater resemblance to typical toads than to true frogs. The

Western Toad (artwork by Jan Sovak).

American Toad (photo by Mary W. Ferguson).

spadefoot toads, for example, found in the Prairie Provinces (2 species), belong to the Pelobatidae family.

Four species of genus *Bufo* live in Canada. These animals have no teeth, but they do have large glands behind the eyes on the head and other warty glands on the body that make their skin poisonous. Toads are usually solitary, but during mating season they gather in large numbers around water sources. Their eggs are laid like necklaces around aquatic vegetation. The tadpoles quickly turn into thousands of baby toads, who come back to land to live, where they eat huge quantities of harmful insects.

▷ SUGGESTED READING: Wyatt Blassingame, *Wonders of Frogs and Toads* (1975); Hilda Simon, *Frogs and Toads of the World* (1975); Edward and Clive Turner, *Frogs and Toads* (1976).

■ Toboggan

A toboggan is a sled used by Inuit, Eastern Woodlands, and Subarctic native peoples for transporting small loads or people over snow. Toboggans were made of two or more thin boards of birchwood, held together by crossboards, with the boards turned up in front and sometimes at the back as well. These runners were shaped either by steaming or by tying the wood in position when it was green. Toboggans were pulled by people or by dogs. Today tobogganing is a popular winter activity across Canada.

■ Tombstones

Tombstones are monuments or markers over a grave. They give the name of the deceased person, with his or her birth date and death date. Sometimes they include other family information and a verse from the Bible or from a poem. Upright tombstones are not allowed in many present-day "memorial parks" or "gardens," and the graves are marked with small flat plaques.

Tombstones are useful in tracing the history of families ("genealogy"). They also show settlement patterns, including the ethnic origin of the people who lived in the area and different waves of immigrants. Often they give information about religious beliefs, epidemics, and race and class divisions. In some cemeteries, people are buried in different sections according to their religion or race, and wealthy families are clustered in higher-priced sections with expensive tombstones.

Tombstones have generally been simple in style, though in the late 19th century they were often ornate and very grand. They were sculptured in marble or granite to resemble angels, cherubs, crosses, and scrolls. Urns symbolized the death of the body, from which the soul rose to heaven; doves represented the Holy Spirit and purity, forgiveness, and peace; flowers indicated beauty and the shortness of life; and the Star of David stood for the Jewish faith.

■ Tornado

A tornado is a windstorm that consists of a mass of whirling air, like a hurricane. However, tornadoes (which are also known as twisters) develop over land, while hurricanes develop over water. Tornadoes are much smaller in size and have a shorter lifespan than a hurricane. They have a different source of energy.

Tornadoes usually begin life as a rotating section on the flank or base of a thunderstorm cloud. A twisting, cloudy funnel of air extends downward from the cloud towards the ground and is met by a twisting debris and dust funnel extending upward from the ground. When viewed from above, tornadoes almost always rotate in a counter-clockwise direction in the Northern Hemisphere, and are associated with low-pressure zones. Their lives are short, rarely as long as an hour, and they are generally small in diameter. A typical tornado leaves a path of damage

Tornado funnel cloud that struck Edmonton July 31, 1987 (photo by Steve Simon/Edmonton Journal).

some 7 km long and less than 100 m wide.

Because of the speed with which a tornado whirls around (its winds can blow at speeds from 100 km/h to 500 km/h) its destructive power can be enormous. Pebbles borne on such high winds can pierce bodies like bullets. Tornadoes can pluck the feathers off chickens, toss railway cars around, and make buildings explode.

Tornadoes occur everywhere in Canada except the Arctic. They are most frequent in southern Ontario and southern Manitoba. They occur during the summer, with activity peaking in late June and early July. They are most likely to occur in the afternoon, and to approach from the West.

A tornado demolished much of downtown Regina on July 30, 1912. The worst tornado in Canadian history was the one that struck Edmonton on July 31, 1987. It killed 27 people, injured over 200, and left over 400 homeless. The tornado caused damage along a 40 km track estimated at over $250 million.

▷ Related Articles: **Climate; Hurricane; Thunderstorm; Wind.**

▷ Suggested Reading: M.J. Newark, *Tornadoes in Canada for the Period 1950-1979* (1983); John Edward Weems, *The Tornado* (1977).

■ Torngat Mountains

The Torngat Mountains are a chain of isolated, rocky peaks running south from the northern tip of Labrador. In the Inuit language, Torngat means "home of the spirits." Nearly completely covered by ice at one time, the barren mountain tops are now capped with over 70 glaciers. Mount Caubvick (known as Mont d'Iberville in Quebec), at 1622 m, is the highest peak in Newfoundland and Quebec. The mountains are broken by narrow lakes and deep fjords from the coast. Vegetation is sparse.

There are no settlements in the mountains, though Inuit fish for char in the fjords each summer.

▷ Related Article: **Mountains.**

■ Toronto

Toronto is the capital city of Ontario and the largest metropolitan area in Canada. Metropolitan Toronto includes the cities of Toronto, North York, Scarborough, York, and Etobicoke, along with the borough of East York. Its population in 1986 was 3 427 168.

Toronto lies along the waterfront near the western end of Lake Ontario. In the 19th century, it grew as the business and government centre of Ontario. After 1900, it extended its influence right across the country. Today, it is the business and manufacturing capital of Canada. It is also a major centre of artistic and cultural activities.

POINTS OF INTEREST

Arts and Recreation
1 Ontario Place
2 Canadian National Exhibition
3 Art Gallery of Ontario
4 Royal Ontario Museum
5 Toronto Zoo
6 Ontario Science Centre
7 Roy Thomson Hall
8 High Park

Education
9 University of Toronto
10 York University
11 Ryerson Institute of Technology
12 Scarborough College

Government and Historical
13 Toronto City Hall
14 Parliament Buildings
15 Old Fort York
16 Black Creek Pioneer Village

Sports
17 Maple Leaf Gardens
18 Skydome
19 Woodbine Racetrack

Metropolitan Toronto

Aerial View of Toronto *The CN Tower and the SkyDome are seen in the centre, Ontario Place in the foreground, next to the old CNE Stadium (photo by Malak, Ottawa).*

HISTORY

Beginnings Toronto takes its name from a Huron word meaning "meeting place." Long before the first Europeans arrived, the site was part of a portage route used by native people to travel between Lakes Ontario and Huron. In the early 1600s, French traders began to use the route, and in 1750 they built Fort Rouillé at the site. The fort was destroyed nine years later, during the Seven Years' War.

After the British took control of Canada, they purchased the land around Lake Ontario from the Mississauga Indians. The purchase included the site of Toronto, for which the Mississauga received a selection of supplies and weapons. The first lieutenant-governor of Upper Canada, John Graves Simcoe, was attracted by the good harbour. He decided to move his capital there from Newark. Construction of the new town, which he called York, was begun in 1793, and the following year York became capital of Upper Canada.

Growth and Development The little town lay on low, marshy ground beside the lake and soon earned the nickname "muddy York." Almost all the buildings were made of wood, including the church and the parliament building. During the War of 1812, American invaders captured York. They looted the houses and burned the parliament building.

Despite such setbacks, York grew steadily. During the early years of the 19th century, large numbers of settlers immigrated to Upper Canada from Great Britain, and York became the business centre for a rich farming district.

Gradually, the town spread north away from the lakefront along its main street,
Yonge Street. Governor Simcoe had planned this road to provide a military route and construction began in 1793. Yonge Street reached Lake Simcoe by 1796 and was later extended farther. Like Dundas Street, which ran westward, it provided settlers with easy access to York. The roads and the harbour on the lake were two of many transportation advantages Toronto has enjoyed over the years.

By 1834, York had a population of over 9000. That year, it became a city, taking its original name, Toronto. The city's first mayor was William Lyon Mackenzie. Mackenzie was a newspaper editor who agitated for reform in Upper Canada. In 1837 he led a rag-tag group of rebels down Yonge Street in an effort to overthrow the government. The rebels fled after only a few shots were fired.

During the 1840s and 1850s, Toronto continued to grow as a port and capital city. The arrival of the railway confirmed its place as a transportation centre. A network of railway lines connected the city with Montreal, New York, Detroit, and Georgian Bay. The railway strengthened the city's grasp on the surrounding area and Toronto quickly outgrew its rivals, Hamilton, Kingston, and Oshawa.

By Confederation in 1867, when Toronto became the capital of the province of Ontario, it was already a leading centre of industry. More and more businessmen built factories there, and this attracted workers looking for jobs. Between 1851 and 1891, the population grew from 30 000 to over 180 000. The main products made in Toronto's factories were farm machinery, clothing, shoes, railway cars, and metal goods.

The 20th Century Hydroelectric power from Niagara Falls was developed in the early 1900s, and this gave a further boost to Toronto's industry by providing factories with cheap electricity. At the same time, the increasing number of banks and

Fort York *as it appeared in 1816 (courtesy Canada Post Corporation).*

University of Toronto *(photo by J.A. Kraulis).*

Toronto *in the 1870s had become a growing centre of industry and commerce (courtesy Metropolitan Toronto Library).*

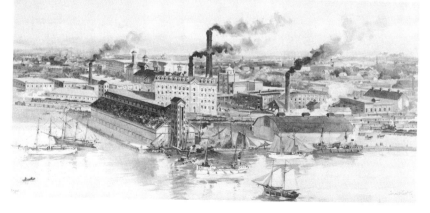

The Archer, *a sculpture by Henry Moore, sits in front of Toronto City Hall (photo by Bill Brooks/Masterfile).*

The CN Tower is *Toronto's most visible landmark. It is a communications tower, restaurant, and viewing platform (photo by J.A. Kraulis).*

Bank Towers *dominate Toronto's skyline (photo by Brian Milne/First Light).*

other services raised Toronto to a national centre of finance, second only to Montreal. As the western prairies filled with farmers, much of their business was done in Toronto.

Meanwhile, more and more people went to live and work in Toronto. Until 1900, the city's population was mainly British in origin. Between 1900 and 1914 a wave of newcomers arrived from a range of European countries. Jews, Italians, Ukrainians, and many others were attracted by jobs in construction and in factories. They settled in their own neighbourhoods with their own friends, churches, stores, and social life.

Another great wave of immigration began in the 1950s. The newcomers included Greeks and Portuguese as well as other Europeans. Since the 1960s, newcomers to Toronto have also included many West Indians and Asians. In recent years, more than one-third of all immigrants to Canada have chosen Toronto as their home.

The population of the city, which had reached 1 million in 1951, rose to 2 million by 1971. During these years, Toronto passed Montreal as the business and financial centre of Canada. Today, many banks and large companies have their head offices in the high-rise towers that mark Toronto's skyline.

THE MODERN CITY

Toronto emerged on a flat plain along the harbour. Governor Simcoe laid out the town in 1793 with a grid of straight lines. As the town grew, this grid was extended. This shore plain has remained Toronto's downtown core. About 4 km north of the lake there is an abrupt rise, which marks the edge of an ancient lake. Settlement spread up and beyond this rise. Today, Toronto extends far east and west of the harbour and well inland.

For many years, the city was cut off from its own lakeshore by a broad zone of railway tracks. Today, this land is being developed, with shops, hotels, apartments, and cultural facilities.

Toronto's skyline is dominated by the CN Tower, the world's tallest free-standing structure (553 m). Nearby is the SkyDome stadium, which was opened in 1989. The most striking modern buildings downtown include the City Hall (1965), the twin towers of Toronto Dominion Centre (1968), Roy Thomson Hall (1982), and the 72-storey First Canadian Place (1975).

Population Toronto is a multicultural city, with people from all parts of the

Kensington Market *in the Italian district of Toronto (photo by Malak, Ottawa).*

world. Many different languages are spoken in Toronto. Whereas the city was once overwhelmingly British, today only about 40% of all Torontonians are of British origin. The second most numerous are the Italians (around 9%). There are said to be more people speaking Italian in Toronto than in Venice, Italy.

Among other large groups are Germans, Poles, Hungarians, Greeks, Portuguese, Slavs, and Chinese. There is a thriving Chinatown in the downtown area, where the street and shop signs are written in Chinese. There are also many people from the West Indies, from the Indian subcontinent, and from Southeast Asia.

Education Toronto's main educational establishments are the University of Toronto, York University, and Ryerson Polytechnic Institute. Others include the Ontario Institute for Studies in Education, the Ontario College of Art, the Royal Conservatory of Music, the National Ballet School, and colleges of applied arts and technology, fashion schools, and so on.

Transportation Toronto's port facilities have been repeatedly improved and the city receives oceangoing ships via the St Lawrence Seaway. By land, a network of major highways, railways, and bus lines converge on Toronto. The railways include "GO" trains, which connect Toronto with nearby suburbs and towns. They are especially useful to commuters who live outside the city but work in it. The major airport, Lester B. Pearson International Airport, is just west of Toronto. It is Canada's busiest airport.

Toronto's subway system is the most extensive in Canada, running north along Yonge Street, east and west along Bloor Street, and northwest along Spadina. Toronto was one of very few cities to main-

Streetcar on Queen Street. Toronto is one of the very few North American cities to keep its street railways. They are very efficient at moving people (photo by Lorraine C. Parow/First Light).

tain its street railway system. There are also bicycle paths and walking routes through the many wooded ravines.

Industry and Commerce Toronto is a major manufacturing city; its factories employ about one-third of all workers in Ontario. The city is the centre of Canada's financial system. All of Canada's major banks have their head offices in Toronto, along with many large companies and brokerage firms. Toronto is also a major centre of book publishing, magazines, English-language film and theatre production, and numerous other activities and businesses.

Communications Toronto's daily newspapers are the *Globe and Mail*, *Toronto Star*, *Financial Post*, *Toronto Sun*, and *Daily Racing Form*. There are several weekly papers, including the French-lan-

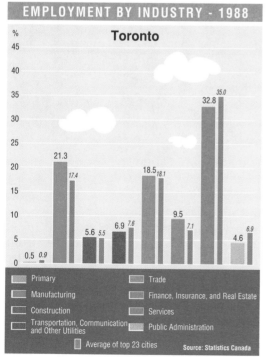

EMPLOYMENT BY INDUSTRY - 1988

Toronto

%									
45									
40									
35								32.8	35.0
30									
25									
20	21.3 17.4				18.5 18.1				
15									
10				9.5 7.1					
5		5.6 5.5	6.9 7.6					4.6 6.9
0	0.5 0.9								

Primary — Trade
Manufacturing — Finance, Insurance, and Real Estate
Construction — Services
Transportation, Communication and Other Utilities — Public Administration
Average of top 23 cities   Source: Statistics Canada

guage *Express*, and there are many ethnic papers and magazines in a wide range of languages.

Culture Toronto is a centre of the performing arts, home of the Toronto Symphony, the National Ballet of Canada, and numerous theatre companies. The major performance centres are Roy Thomson Hall and O'Keefe Centre. A new opera and ballet centre is planned for completion in the 1990s. Among the city's many cultural attractions are the Royal Ontario Museum, the Art Gallery of Ontario, the Ontario Science Centre, McLaughlin Planetarium, Ontario Place recreational area on the lakeshore, and Metro Zoo.

Casa Loma is a bizarre castle built by an eccentric Toronto millionaire (photo by Malak, Ottawa).

Historic sites and museums include Old Fort York (1812-13, restored), Scadding Cabin (oldest house in Toronto), Casa Loma (a castle with underground tunnels), and Black Creek Pioneer Village (a living museum). Heritage buildings include The Grange, a stately old mansion built in 1817, St Lawrence Hall (1850), Osgoode Hall (1857), University College (1859), old City Hall (1899), and Union Station (1927).

Toronto's multicultural character is evident throughout the city in a range of shops, restaurants, and markets, including the lively Kensington Market. Multiculturalism is also the focus of three of Toronto's annual festivals: Metro International Caravan, International Picnic, and Caribana (a West Indian festival with a parade and steel bands).

Each year, more than 2 million people visit the Canadian National Exhibition, the largest annual exhibition in the world. The city's professional sports teams include the Toronto Argonauts (football), Toronto Blue Jays (baseball), Toronto Maple Leafs (hockey), and Toronto Blizzard (soccer). Both the Hockey

Giraffes at the Metro Toronto Zoo (photo by Barry Dursley/First Light).

Eaton Centre, Toronto (photo by J.A. Kraulis).

Canada's Wonderland (photo by J.A. Kraulis).

St Lawrence Hall is one of Toronto's finest historical buildings (photo by Malak, Ottawa).

Hall of Fame and Canada's Sports Hall of Fame are located in Toronto at the Exhibition Grounds.

For further information, contact the City Clerk, City Hall, 100 Queen Street West, Toronto, Ont., M5H 2N2.

▷ SUGGESTED READING: F.H. Armstrong editor, *Toronto of Old* (1987); Roger Boulton, *Toronto* (1990); J.M.S. Careless, *Toronto to 1918: An Illustrated History* (1983); J. Clarence Duff, *Toronto Then and Now* (1984); Edith Firth, *Toronto in Art* (1989); William Kilbourn, *Toronto Remembered* (1984); James Lemon, *Toronto Since 1918: An Illustrated History* (1985); Patricia McHugh, *Toronto Architecture* (1989); Margaret McKelvey and Merilyn McKelvey, *Toronto Carved in Stone* (1989); Joseph Romain and James Duplacey, *Toronto* (1990); Elma Schemenauer, *Hello Toronto* (1986).

■ Toronto Argonauts

The Toronto Argonauts football team take their name from the Argonaut Rowing Club. They took their colours from the double blue of the English universities of Oxford and Cambridge. They won their first Grey Cup in 1914. Led by Lionel Conacher, whom many believe was Canada's greatest all-round athlete, the Argos beat the Edmonton Eskimos in the first East-West Grey Cup game in 1921. Led by Joe Krol and other fine Canadian players they won the Grey Cup in 1933, 1937, 1938, 1945, 1946, 1947, 1950, and 1952. They did not return to the Grey Cup game until 1971, which they lost to Calgary. They returned to the national final in 1982, 1983, 1984, and 1987, winning in 1983. The team moved into CNE Stadium in 1959 and into the SkyDome in 1989.

▷ RELATED ARTICLE: **Football.**

■ Toronto Blue Jays

The Blue Jays joined baseball's American League in 1977. They had their first winning season in 1983. They won their division twice, in 1985 and 1989, losing both times in the final. Over the late 1980s, the Blue Jays had the best regular season record in the American League, but have so far failed to reach the world series.

▷ RELATED ARTICLE: **Baseball.**

▷ SUGGESTED READING: Peter C. Bjarkman, *The Toronto Blue Jays* (1990); Buck Martinez, *From Worst to First* (1985) and *The Last Out: The Toronto Blue Jays in 1986* (1986).

■ Toronto Dance Theatre

The Toronto Dance Theatre is one of the foremost modern-dance companies in Canada. It was founded in 1968 by Patricia Beatty, David Earle, and Peter Randazzo, who were all strongly influenced by the American dancer Martha Graham. Together, they directed the company and choreographed more than 140 highly dramatic works. Many of these dances used scores commissioned from Canadian composers. Since 1981, the award-winning Christopher House has been resident choreographer, and his largely abstract dances have won the company a growing audience. The company has toured successfully in Canada, Europe, the United States, Mexico, Venezuela, and the Orient, and it also runs its own dance school. Many of the dancers have gone on to join some of the leading modern-dance groups in the world. Since 1987, David Earle has been sole artistic director of the company.

Toronto Dance Theatre (photo by Michael Cooper/Toronto Dance Theatre).

■ Toronto Islands

The Toronto Islands are a group of 17 islands in Lake Ontario just offshore from Toronto. Once connected to the shore by a spit of land, the islands were separated in 1858 when a storm washed away the land bridge. Today, the 700 residents commute to the city by ferry. One of the busiest airports in Canada is located on one of the islands.

Toronto Island Ferry carries passengers across the harbour to the islands (photo by Jim Merrithew).

In the 1840s, fishermen's cottages dotted the peninsula. By the 1880s, the islands had grown into a bustling community with elegant resort hotels, a baseball stadium, theatres, beaches, a large amusement park, and hundreds of homes. Torontonians love to spend their weekend afternoons on the islands, picnicking, swimming, and boating. Most of these facilities are now gone, but visitors still flock to the parks and beaches on the islands.

Beginning in the 1950s, the government made plans to evict residents in order to make the islands parkland only. After a long battle, islanders rallied public support and the communities on Ward's and Algonquin Islands were allowed to remain.

■ Toronto Maple Leafs

The Leafs were formed in 1927, when Conn Smythe purchased the Toronto St Pats and renamed them. Despite the hard times of the Great Depression, Smythe managed to finance the building of Maple Leaf Gardens in 1931. He then purchased Frank "King" Clancy from the Ottawa Senators for a large sum of money. The team won its first Stanley Cup in 1932.

Smythe was an ex-military man and he built a team based on his motto "If you can't beat them in the alley, you can't beat them on the ice." The team excelled in the 1940s, but fell to the bottom of the league after a Stanley Cup victory in 1951. "Punch" Imlach rebuilt the team in the late 1950s and won the Stanley Cup in 1962, 1963, 1964, and 1967. The flamboyant Harold Ballard gained control of the club in 1971 and until his death in 1990 subjected Toronto fans to one losing season after another.

▷ SUGGESTED READING: William Houston, *Inside Maple Leaf Gardens: The Rise and Fall of the Toronto Maple Leafs* (1989).

■ Toronto Symphony

The Toronto Symphony orchestra was formed in 1922 by a group of Toronto musicians. It gave its first performance at Massey Hall in 1923. Sir Ernest Macmillan was music director from 1931 to 1956. He was followed by Walter Susskind (1956-65), Seiji Ozawa (1965-69), Karl Ančerl (1969-73), and Andrew Davis (1975-88). Over the years, the orchestra has travelled abroad and made numerous records. In 1982 it moved into Roy Thomson Hall. Gunther Herbig became full-time conductor in September 1990.

■ Tory

In the early 19th century, when British North America was still a collection of colonies, the Tories were the group of politicians who were supporters of the governor and British traditions. Often they were leading members of government. Unlike the Reformers, they did not want any basic changes in the way the colonies were run, and they were especially opposed to responsible government. Today the term is associated with people who are members of the Progressive Conservative Party.

■ Tory, Henry Marshall

Educator and scientist (*born in 1864 at Port Shoreham, N.S.; died in 1947 at Ottawa, Ont.*). Henry Marshall Tory was the most famous Canadian educator of his day, the founder of major universities and research organizations. He was especially known as a champion of science teaching and research. A professor of mathematics at McGill University in Montreal, Tory was sent to British Columbia in 1905 to set up affiliated colleges of McGill at Victoria and Vancouver. These colleges were the basis of the future University of British Columbia and the University of Victoria. Next, Tory helped establish the University of Alberta, serving as president when the university opened in 1908. During the next 20 years, Tory built the U of A into a lively institution with high standards of teaching and research. Meanwhile, in 1917 he organized "Khaki University" for Canadian soldiers in England; in 1919 he helped set up the organization that two years later became Alberta Research Council; and in 1923 he also agreed to act as honorary chairman of the National Research Council (NRC) of Canada.

Tory left Alberta in 1928 and moved to Ottawa to become the first full-time president of the NRC. Between then and his

Totem Pole, "Hole in the Ice," at Kitwancool, B.C. (photo by Karl Sommerer).

Beaver Figures in totem poles of the Haisla people of B.C. (photo by Tom W. Parkin/ Pathfinder).

retirement in 1935, he oversaw the formation of the NRC Laboratories, which he staffed with 50 first-rate scientists. He thus laid the basis of the NRC's worldwide reputation as a major research establishment. Tory was such an enthusiastic educator that even after his retirement he did not retire. At the age of 77 he headed the founding committee of Carleton College in Ottawa, serving as its unpaid president and a lecturer until his death.

▷ SUGGESTED READING: Edward Annand Corbett, *Henry Marshall Tory: Beloved Canadian* (1954).

■ Totem Pole

A totem pole is a carved cedar tree trunk made by some Northwest Coast native peoples. The poles might be 20 m high. They might be house posts inside a longhouse, door posts at the entrance, or freestanding poles in the middle of a settlement. Carvings of crests and helping animal spirits such as the beaver, bear, wolf, whale, raven, eagle, and frog told the history of the entire village or of the families who lived in the house. There were also welcoming poles, and memorials to the dead. The oldest surviving poles date from the 19th century. The art of carving totem poles has been revived by some contemporary artists, such as Bill Reid.

▷ RELATED ARTICLES: **Native People: Northwest Coast; Bill Reid.**

▷ SUGGESTED READING: Marius Barbeau, *Art of the Totem* (1984); Marjorie M. Halpin, *Totem Poles: An Illustrated Guide* (1981); Phil Nuytten, *The Totem Carvers* (1982).

■ Touch-Me-Not

Touch-me-not is the common name for herb-like plants of genus *Impatiens* of the Balsaminaceae family. The nickname "touch-me-not" refers to the ripe fruits that burst open when touched. Impatiens includes hundreds of species found in the temperate regions of Europe and the tropical regions of Asia and Africa. Six species are in Canada, four of them native and two introduced.

A large number of tropical varieties adorn our gardens, greenhouses, and homes. These fragile-looking plants have water-laden stalks and lance-shaped leaves. The numerous five-petalled flowers come in many colours, primarily pink, red, scarlet, orange, and violet. The spotted touch-me-not (*I. capensis*) grows in moist, shady locations throughout Canada. The red-spotted orange flower has a distinctive corolla which is slipper shaped with a long, curved spur.

Seeds spread in a spectacular fashion. All you have to do is lightly pinch the ripe capsules: their walls shrivel up, shooting the seeds far and wide. The sap of the spotted touch-me-not soothes the irritation caused by poison ivy. The Potawatomi Indians made an impatiens-based ointment and used it to treat wounds. They made a yellow dye with the flowers.

■ Tourism

Tourism is a fast-growing industry in Canada. It earns more than $20 billion a year and employs about 600 000 Canadians. It includes services in transportation, accommodation, restaurants, recreation, and entertainment.

There are two types of travellers: business travellers and pleasure travellers. Business accounts for more than half of the tourist industry. It is increasing in volume because more products are being marketed nationally and internationally and because of the popularity of business conferences and conventions.

Pleasure travel is based on Canada's natural scenery, such as the Rockies and Niagara Falls. Visitors are equally interested in such man-made attractions as museums and galleries, theme parks, shopping centres such as the West Edmonton Mall or the Eaton Centre in Toronto, outdoor shows such as the Calgary Stampede, and exhibitions such as Expo

Lower Town, Quebec City. Tourists are attracted to many Canadian cities for their historical or recreational interest (photo by Derek Caron/Masterfile).

67 or Expo 86. Canadians travelling within Canada spend about two-thirds of the total tourist budget. Most foreign visitors come from the United States, followed by Europe, Japan, and Hong Kong. In the next few years, the greatest increase is expected to come from Pacific Rim countries. Still, in 1987, Canadians spent more money ($8.8 billion) in travel outside Canada than all foreign visitors spent ($6.3 billion) in Canada.

History The Canadian Pacific Railway did more than any other entity to attract tourists to Canada, particularly from Europe and the United States. From the late 19th century on, it sponsored an excellent publicity campaign to fill up its steamships, its transcontinental railway, and its hotels. Artists were given free passes on the railway to paint pictures of the Rockies and the lush British Columbia rainforest, and thousands of enticing travel posters were distributed in Canada and abroad.

In 1930 the Tourism Industry Association of Canada was founded as an umbrella organization for businesses engaged in tourism. In 1934 the federal government set up its own tourist agency. Today Tourism Canada is the responsibility of the minister of state for small business and tourism.

▷ RELATED ARTICLE: **Service Industry.**

▷ SUGGESTED READING: E.J. Hart, *The Selling of Canada: The CPR and the Beginning of Canadian Tourism* (1983); Bobbie Kalman, *How we Travel* (1986); Fiona McCall and Paul Howard, *All in the Same Boat* (1988); Veronica Timmons, *Tourism and Travel: Focus Canada, a Guide to Canada's Tourism Industry and Its Careers* (1988).

■ Town, Harold Barling

Artist (*born in 1924 at Toronto, Ont.*). Town is probably Canada's most versatile artist. He has worked in painting, sculpture, drawing, prints, collages, constructions, and murals. He has also written and illustrated books and articles about art. In 1954 he joined Painters Eleven, a group of artists who hoped to introduce abstract art to Toronto. He quickly became the most talked-about member of the group. He does not stay with one style for long, preferring to work on a series of delicate drawings of film stars, for example, and then move on to a different theme. He is a superb designer, and his art is often witty and always full of energy and imagination.

▷ SUGGESTED READING: David Burnett, *Harold Town* (1986).

Toy Horse #163, by Harold Town, gouache on board (courtesy of the artist).

■ Toye, William

Writer, editor (*born in 1926 at Toronto, Ont.*). Toye received a BA from the University of Toronto. He then began to work for Oxford University Press, where he is now editorial director. He entered the field of children's literature because he wanted to publish books for younger readers.

Toye wrote *The St Lawrence* (1959) and *Cartier Discovers the St Lawrence* (1970), both winners of children's literature awards. They are histories that include sections from explorers' diaries. He also wrote several versions of native legends, which were illustrated by Elizabeth Cleaver. The best known of these are *The Mountain Goats of Temlaham* (1969) and *The Loon's Necklace* (1977). Toye has also edited five books, which have won

Travel Agents

Travel agents provide information, plan trips for tourists, sell them tickets, make arrangements for their travel and accommodation, and provide whatever other services are necessary. The minimum educational qualifications is a high-school diploma, but graduates from travel and tourism programs at community colleges are preferred.

Such courses are offered in every province but Prince Edward Island, Nova Scotia, New Brunswick, Manitoba, and Saskatchewan, and usually take two years. Additional on-the-job training is usually provided by the employer. There are about 23 000 travel agents in Canada.

children's literature awards. These include *The Golden Phoenix* (1958), by Marius Barbeau and Michael Hornyansky, and *Tales of Nanabozho* (1963), by Dorothy Reid.

■ Toys and Games

Toys made of found and cast-off items have always been a part of childhood. Pioneer children played jacks with sheep's toe bones, and chased hoops made of old wheel rims. They also had whittled wooden dolls, rattles, and other toys. Games have rules and can be played with friends or alone. There is usually an idea of winning, by beating someone else or the game.

TOYS

In the 1800s, most toys were homemade or imported from Europe or the United States. The first mass-produced toys were made in Canada about 1860. Toys copied grown-up life. Boys played with wooden horses and wagons. Girls played with dolls, miniature furniture, and baby carriages. Rocking horses and blocks were popular with both.

Most children had few toys, because they were poor and had little time to play. Farm children helped with chores and many city children worked in factories.

During World War I (1914-18), toy imports from Europe fell off, and the Canadian toy and games industry expanded. Wooden toys were joined by lead soldiers, brass trumpets, rubber balls, tin tea sets, steel construction sets, rag dolls, and stuffed animals.

The first plastic toys were made in 1940. The plastic interlocking building brick has become a classic. A new type called Zaks was recently developed by the Canadian Irwin Toy Company.

Also in the 1940s, toy sets copying adult activities, such as archery, carpentry, printing, and sewing, were popular.

Dolls have a special popularity, especially with girls. Over the years, Canadi-

Barbara Ann Scott doll was based on the Canadian skating star of 1948. The doll was popular from 1949 to 1955 (courtesy CMC).

Wooden Rocking Horse from Quebec in the 19th century (courtesy Royal Ontario Museum).

***Toy Truck** made in the 1930s (left), racing car (1940s), and transport truck made in Orillia, Ont. (1950s) (courtesy CMC).*

an children have played with dolls made out of wood, wax, porcelain, papier-maché, dried apples, rags, and plastic. Mechanical devices and computer chips have enabled some dolls to walk, talk, and do other tricks. But the most popular dolls continue to be those that can be dressed up and looked after like children.

By 1960, there were 126 Canadian toy-making companies, most located in Quebec and Ontario. In the next few years, large foreign companies (Louis Marx, Mattel, Tonka, Coleco) began making toys in Canada. They soon dominated the industry.

Today, toys are heavily influenced by what is popular on television and in movies. Small plastic characters and accessories from G.I. Joe, Star Wars, and Care Bears, for example, have been very heavily advertised on television and very successful. Toys are now a billion-dollar business in Canada. But there is also a small craft industry producing old-fashioned and ever-popular wooden toys.

GAMES

Team games such as hockey, football, lacrosse, and other sports games are played for fun and in competitive leagues.

Children's Outdoor Games Like children everywhere, Canadian children make games and toys out of things they find. Marbles were homemade out of clay until the early 1900s, when manufactured marbles were imported from Europe.

Most children learn their games in school playgrounds. Hopscotch, hide-and-seek, blindman's bluff, and many other games are almost the same as when they were brought by early settlers from Europe and the United States. Others are new inventions.

Games have been made more up to date and exciting by copying films and televi-

The Munro Company *hockey game was the biggest selling hockey game in the world in the 1950s (courtesy Museum and Archives of Games, University of Waterloo).*

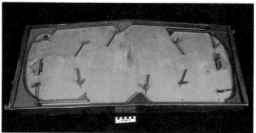

sion. Over time, cowboys and Indians has evolved to cops and robbers and to space invaders.

Indoor Games Many modern indoor games were invented in the 1800s. Charades is a classic. Bagatelle, a game using marbles and wooden targets, has developed into pinball. Some board games are hundreds of years old (such as go, chess, checkers, and backgammon). Many more have been invented in the past 100 years. Some are distinctly Canadian. The Canada Games Company produced a "Canadian" version of Snakes and Ladders called Toboggans and Stairs. From the 1930s to the 1950s, the Munro Company was the world's biggest manufacturer of table-top hockey games. Crokinole games are still made in Ontario.

New Games In the 1970s, fantasy role-playing games, such as Dungeons and Dragons, became popular. Plots combining strategy and luck are made up by the players. Computer technology has led to the invention of video games.

Trivial Pursuit, one of the world's most popular board games, was invented by four Canadians. Its success has encouraged other Canadians to invent Balderdash, QWR (Quick Wit and Repartee), and Scruples.

▷ SUGGESTED READING: Cheryl Atwater, Nancy Haselhan, and Terry Peachey, *Toys* (1988); Edie Kraska, *Toys and Tales from Grandmother's Attic* (1979); Debbie Wager, *Good Toys* (1986).

■ Track and Field

Track and field is a group of sports which includes walking, running, hurdling, jumping, throwing, and combined events (such as decathlon and heptathlon). At the Olympic Games, there are 41 events, 24 for men and 17 for women.

Track and field began with the ancient Greeks, to whom contests were more important than records. Today, it is the headlong pursuit of records that gives the sport much of its fascination.

Organized track and field began in Canada in the 1880s. The sport was tightly controlled to keep a strict code of amateurism. No form of payment was allowed. Also, the men who controlled the sport kept women out until the 1920s on the grounds that it was "unladylike." Today, most of Canada's athletes receive money from the government for expenses. They can also win prize money and receive money for lending their names to products. Canadians have competed successfully at many events.

Sprinters Early in the 20th century, Hamilton's Robert Kerr won gold and bronze medals at the 1908 Olympics. In the 1928 Olympics, Vancouver's Percy Williams captured gold in both the 100 m and 200 m sprints with spectacular leaping finishes. The women's sprint team won the first 4x100 m women's relay at the same games in 1928.

In the next decade Canadian sprinters won six more Olympic medals, but they did not win another until the 1960s when Harry Jerome won an Olympic bronze medal in the 100 m. In 1984 Ben Johnson won a bronze medal in the 100 m and the men's relay and a bronze in the 4x100. Johnson went on to set world records and to win a gold medal in South Korea, but his medal was revoked when he tested positive for a banned drug.

Middle Distance Toronto runner George Orton won Canada's first Olympic gold medal in the steeplechase in Paris in 1900. Bill Crothers, also of Toronto, won a silver medal at the 1964 Olympics in Tokyo. Canadian marathon runners have won Olympic, Pan-American, and Commonwealth Games titles, and have won the Boston Marathon 16 times. Some marathon runners, such as Tom Longboat, Jerome Drayton, and Jaqueline Gareau have become legendary figures in the sport.

Jumping Canada's strongest jumping event has been the high jump. Ethel Catherwood, Duncan McNaughton, Eva Dawes, and Greg Joy have won Olympic medals.

In 1988, despite Dave Steen's dramatic bronze medal in the prestigious decathlon event, Ben Johnson's disqualification cast a pall over Canadian achievements. Drug scandals and a win-at-all costs attitude among the athletes and the general public have driven the sport the farthest it has ever been from the ideals of the ancient Greeks.

▷ SUGGESTED READING: Debbie Brill, *Jump* (1986); Tom McNab, *The Complete Book of Track and Field* (1980).

■ Trade

The word "trade" refers to the exchange of goods or services for either money or other goods and services. It takes place among individuals and business firms in the various cities and provinces of Canada. It also occurs among business firms in different countries. When it is among countries, it is referred to as "international trade." Goods that are sold to other countries are called *exports*. Those that are bought are called "imports."

Why There Is Trade Trade generally occurs because regions or countries tend to produce those goods and services in which they have an advantage over other areas. Such advantages may occur because an area has resources (such as the oil and natural gas reserves in Alberta, the rich ocean fishing grounds in Atlantic Canada, the forests of British Columbia, the metal mines in Ontario and Quebec, and the vast farmlands of the prairies). An area may have advanced research facilities, which enable it to develop new products or to make products for less.

Companies may be able to export goods (that is, sell them abroad) by producing large volumes of a product and thus being able to sell them at a lower price than competitors. This is what is meant by "economies of scale."

Transportation costs may make it cheaper for a region to import a product (that is, buy it from another country) rather than have it shipped over a greater distance from within the same country. For this reason, Ontario buys coal from the United States rather than purchasing it from Alberta or British Columbia — even though Canadian coal has less sulphur in it and would therefore not pollute the environment as much. The cost of shipping the coal by rail all the way across Canada is much higher than bringing it by ship from the U.S.

Comparative Advantage Even if a country is not as efficient as other nations in the production of *any* commodity, it can still take part in international trade. It will be to its benefit to specialize in those products in which its efficiency is least unfavourable. In other words, it would specialize in products in which it has a "comparative advantage" to others. One way it would be able to gain such an advantage is by lowering the price of its currency relative to other countries' currencies. This has the effect of lowering the price of a country's products.

Non-Currency Trade Not all trade involves the exchange of products for currency. Sometimes nations may exchange exports of one type of product for imports of another product. When they do this it is called "barter trade." Also, much trade in the world today is simply shipments of goods between parent firms and their subsidiaries in other countries. In such cases, all that occurs is that the companies record the shipments on their books but no money exchanges hands between them. The best example of this non-currency trade is the shipment of automobiles and parts between Canada and the United States by the large U.S. firms and their subsidiaries in Canada.

Trade Restrictions International trade is sometimes limited by government action in order to protect domestic industries from foreign competition. One way of limiting trade is by restricting imports. The most common form of restriction is *tariffs*. These are taxes placed on imports when they enter a country. They make foreign goods more expensive than similar domestic goods. *Quotas* are another way to restrict imports. They are a type of *non-tariff barrier* to trade. Quotas limit the actual quantity of a product that may be imported from another country.

The major nations of the world have been trying to reduce such barriers to trade through an international organization known as the General Agreement on Tariffs and Trade (GATT). This organization was started in 1948 with just 23 nations (including Canada) participating. Since then the membership has expanded to 96 nations. Seven rounds of negotiations have occurred within GATT, whereby nations have agreed to reduce their tariffs and some other trade restrictions among one another. The eighth round, called The Uruguay Round (because the 1986 organizing meeting was held in Uruguay) is scheduled to be finished by about the end of 1990. If it is successful, then not only will protectionist measures

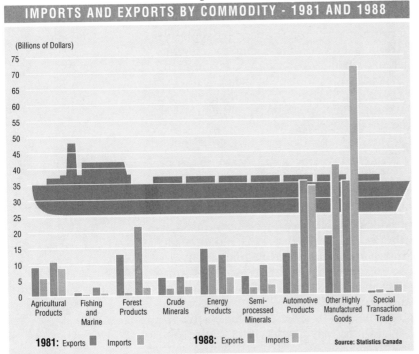

IMPORTS AND EXPORTS BY COMMODITY - 1981 AND 1988

(Billions of Dollars)

75 70 65 60 55 50 45 40 35 30 25 20 15 10 5 0

Agricultural Products | Fishing and Marine | Forest Products | Crude Minerals | Energy Products | Semi-processed Minerals | Automotive Products | Other Highly Manufactured Goods | Special Transaction Trade

1981: Exports Imports   **1988:** Exports Imports   Source: Statistics Canada be reduced on merchandise trade but there will be rules limiting the restrictions which countries can place on trade in services too.

Sometimes nations try to encourage production for export by providing subsidies to firms in the form of grants, loans at below-market interest rates, or exemptions from certain taxes. Or they may attempt to have foreign corporations give their subsidiaries the right to produce a line of products for exporting to world markets. This last procedure is called "product mandating." Other nations may object to these policies and then disputes arise. The GATT is trying to resolve these types of problems as well.

Canada's International Trade Canada is very heavily involved in international trade. Its exports and imports are each equal to about 20% of the total value of all goods and services that are produced in the country.

Although Canada trades with many countries, most of its trade is with the United States. About two-thirds of its commodity imports are from the United States and nearly three-quarters of its exports go there. The European Economic Community (EEC), composed of 12 nations, is Canada's second-largest partner. It supplies about 12% of the nation's imports and buys about 8% of Canada's commodity exports. Japan is Canada's third-largest partner, accounting for about 7% of Canada's merchandise trade.

The largest single item of Canadian foreign trade is "automobiles and parts." It accounts for over one-quarter of all Canadian exports and imports. Its size is the result of a special trade arrangement Canada negotiated with the U.S. in 1965 (the Autopact) which allows for the automobile companies to ship new cars and parts across the border tariff free. Ontario is the centre of this massive industry.

Canada also exports a wide variety of other highly manufactured goods ranging from telecommunications equipment to industrial machinery, office equipment, and petrochemicals. Much of this production is also located in Ontario and, to a lesser extent, in Quebec. However, Canada buys far more highly manufactured goods than it sells.

The products where exports are greatest relative to imports are those based on Canada's supplies of natural resources. These include forest products (lumber, newsprint, and woodpulp), energy products (oil, natural gas, coal, and electrici-

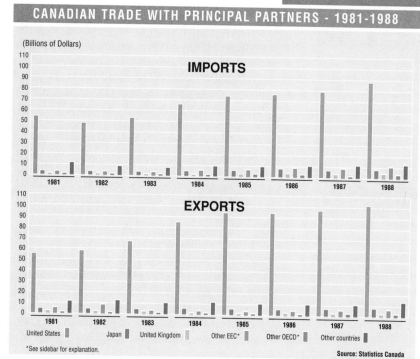

CANADIAN TRADE WITH PRINCIPAL PARTNERS - 1981-1988

(Billions of Dollars)

IMPORTS — 1981, 1982, 1983, 1984, 1985, 1986, 1987, 1988

EXPORTS — 1981, 1982, 1983, 1984, 1985, 1986, 1987, 1988

United States ▪ Japan ▪ United Kingdom ▪ Other EEC* ▪ Other OECD* ▪ Other countries ▪

*See sidebar for explanation.

Source: Statistics Canada

ty), grains and other agricultural products, fish products, and metal and mineral products, such as refined aluminum, copper, nickel, potash, and sulphur. These are all products where Canada has a comparative advantage.

▷ RELATED ARTICLE: **Economics.**

▷ SUGGESTED READING: R.C. Bellan, *Principles of Economics and the Canadian Economy* (sixth edition, 1981).

■ Trades and Labor Congress of Canada

The Trades and Labor Congress of Canada (TLC) was the central federation of trade unions between 1883 and 1956. Founded in Toronto, Ont., it initially attracted unionists from Ontario, but by 1900 the TLC had spread across the country. In politics the TLC was middle-of-the-road, and more radical unions often broke away from it. In 1956 the TLC merged with the Canadian Congress of Labour to form the Canadian Labour Congress.

■ Trail

Trail, B.C., is a city on the Columbia River in the southern interior of the province. It began in 1895 as the site of a smelter to process gold and copper ores from local mines. Production was later expanded to include silver, lead, zinc, and fertilizer. The smelter soon grew to be the largest smelter in the British Empire. The local economy continues to rely on mining. Its population in 1986 was 7948.

For further information, contact the City Clerk, 1394 Pine Avenue, Trail, B.C., V1R 4E6.

Trading Partners *EEC on the graphs refers to the European Economic Community, which includes Belgium, Netherlands, Luxembourg, France, Germany, United Kingdom (which is treated separately on the graphs from other EEC countries), Italy, Spain, Portugal, Greece, Ireland, and Denmark. OECD refers to Organization for Economic Co-operation and Development. It includes Austria, Belgium, Canada, Denmark, France, Germany, Greece, Iceland, Ireland, Italy, Luxembourg, Netherlands, Norway, Portugal, Spain, Sweden, Switzerland, Turkey, United Kingdom, United States and Japan (treated separately on the graphs), Finland, Australia, and New Zealand.*

■ Traill, Catharine Parr

Botanist, author (*born Catharine Strickland in 1802 at London, England; died in 1899 at Lakefield, Ont.*). Before coming to Canada in 1832, she had written about pioneer life, basing her children's novel, *The Young Emigrants* (1826) on letters from friends. She and her husband settled near Peterborough, Upper Canada [Ontario], next to her sister, the novelist Susanna Moodie. She then used her own experience in her writing. A dedicated botanist, she wrote adult works describing Canadian nature and teaching other pioneers how to live in the wilderness. These include *The Backwoods of Canada* (1836) and *The Female Emigrant's Guide* (1854). She also wrote *The Canadian Crusoes* (1852), the first Canadian children's adventure novel. The story of three lost children who survive in the forest, it combines accurate description of the wilderness and practical advice for survival. Her use of the journey to a wilderness setting that tests and matures children set the pattern for later Canadian adventure novels by such writers as Farley Mowat and James Houston.

■ Trakas, George

Sculptor (*born in 1944 at Quebec City, Que.*). Trakas studied for a year at Sir George Williams University in Montreal, Que., before moving permanently to the United States, where he completed his training. His enormous sculptural constructions are examples of environmental art. They are designed to fit into, and become a part of, the room or outdoor site in which they are built. To appreciate a Trakas sculpture it is necessary to walk or climb through it, since Trakas believes that we experience our environment with our bodies as well as our eyes. Most of his work has been commissioned for specific projects or exhibitions. A recent project was a large landscape sculpture on Cap Trinité, Baie d'Éternité, Que.

■ Trans-Canada Highway

The Trans-Canada Highway is a road from St John's, Nfld, to Victoria, B.C. It includes two ferry journeys, one from Newfoundland to the mainland and the other from the mainland to Vancouver Island. (P.E.I.'s section of the Trans-Canada can be reached by ferry from Nova Scotia.) Counting only distance along the road, the Trans-Canada Highway is 7821 km long. This makes it the longest national highway in the world.

An intrepid Englishman, Thomas W.

Trans-Canada Highway (photo by Raymond Giguère).

Wilby, was the first to drive across Canada, in 1912. The trip from Halifax, N.S., to Victoria, B.C., took 52 days. Where there were no roads, Wilby either hoisted his automobile onto a railway flatcar or simply bumped over the railway ties.

An early supporter of a cross-Canada highway was Dr Percy Doolittle. He drove across Canada in 1925.

In 1946, Brigadier R.A. MacFarlane and Kenneth MacGillivray became the first people to drive across Canada by road without resorting to railway tracks. Their journey, from Louisbourg on Cape Breton Island, N.S., to Victoria, B.C., took nine days and they had nine flat tires. The roads they travelled varied greatly in quality.

Four years later, in the summer of 1950, work began on the Trans-Canada Highway. The minimum standards to which it was built were the same across the country. It was at least a two-lane highway, with wide pavement and shoulders, slow curves, gentle slopes and ample clearance room beneath bridges.

Building the highway turned out to be more difficult — and more expensive — than expected. The road had to be protected from avalanches in the Rogers Pass, B.C., where it passes through the Rockies. The 1 km long tunnel through which it passes beneath the St Lawrence River and into Montreal cost $75 million.

The total construction cost, which was shared by the provincial and federal governments, was over $1 billion.

On September 3, 1962, at a ceremony in the Rogers Pass, Prime Minister John Diefenbaker declared the highway open.

▷ RELATED ARTICLE: **Transportation.**
▷ SUGGESTED READING: Wes Rataushy, *Silver Highway* (1988).

■ Transportation

Transportation is the movement of goods

or people from one place to another. Transportation is of particular importance to Canada because of the country's vast size. Great distances must be covered between its mines, farms, forests, and cities. Transportation is also very important to the Canadian economy. Canada exports about one-third of what it produces. Many of these goods, such as timber, grain, and minerals, must move quickly and cheaply if they are to compete with similar products from other nations.

HISTORY IN CANADA

In many ways, the history of Canada is the story of its transportation systems. Until the 19th century, almost all land transportation was done by walking or by wagons pulled by horses or oxen. Ships and smaller vessels moved more easily, with the help of sails or paddles.

The first people came to North America on foot over 10 000 years ago. Although humans walk slowly, they can cover great distances over time. Dogs helped the native people carry their belongings, likely in packs on their backs. Later, dogs were used to pull the travois or dog sleds. In the 18th century, the Plains Indians acquired the horse. Those who lived in forests developed the birchbark canoe, a marvel of speed and lightness. The Haida of the Northwest Coast built oceangoing canoes which they used to hunt whales. But the native people lacked the greatest invention in the history of transportation: the wheel.

Age of Discovery To us, the European sailing ship looks small and flimsy. But it was the wonder of the age. Sails of various shapes caught the wind and allowed the ship to sail in any direction. Improvements in navigation helped the sailors find their way. The first large sailing ship to appear on Canada's shore was likely John Cabot's *Matthew* in 1497. Over the next 450 years sailing ships brought immigrants to Canada and carried fish, fur, timber, and wheat back to Europe.

Early Roads European soldiers and settlers cut the first roads through the Canadian forests. Most were little more than dirt tracks, which turned to quagmires of mud in the rain. A few were paved with logs. Travelling on these roads in a horse-drawn coach was a slow, bone-jarring experience. No traveller's letters or diary would fail to mention their unpleasant ride.

One of the most spectacular roads built in early Canada was the Cariboo Road. It

Stagecoach in 1899 (courtesy National Library of Canada/Rare Book Division).

was built in the 1860s through the rugged mountain country between the Pacific Coast and the Cariboo region of British Columbia, where gold had been discovered. Opened in 1864, the road followed the canyon of the Fraser River, crossing the gorge on wooden bridges, clinging to narrow shelves blasted from the rock walls.

Early Canals Water remained the best means of moving goods in early Canada. Economic activity centered in the ports of Halifax, Saint John, Quebec, and Montreal. Rapids on the St Lawrence prevented further movement towards the Great Lakes. The lakes themselves were separated by Niagara Falls. Improvements were made slowly on the St Lawrence. The Lachine Canal permitted the passage of small vessels by the 1850s.

The first Welland Canal opened in 1829, connecting Lakes Erie and Ontario. An even more impressive accomplishment was the Rideau Canal, which connected the Ottawa River to Lake Ontario. This canal, however, was built for military reasons, not for trade.

The Railways The railway was the greatest revolution in transportation since the invention of the wheel, thousands of years before. Steam-powered locomotives could haul heavy loads over long distances. Canada was quick to embrace the railway. It offered enormous advantages over dirt roads and waterways that froze in winter.

The first railway in Canada opened in

Road Between Kingston and York *(courtesy NAC/C-12632).*

Train of Red River Carts *in the West, 1873 (courtesy PAA).*

Aircraft provide transportation to remote areas of Canada (photo by Pat Morrow/First Light).

1836. In the 1850s, rail lines linked Toronto, Hamilton, and Montreal to U.S. railways in New York and Michigan. The Intercolonial Railway, built in the 1870s, connected Ontario and Quebec with the Maritime colonies. The Canadian Pacific Railway, completed in the 1880s, crossed the prairies and Rocky Mountains and reached the Pacific.

The railways did more than just connect established places. They created new towns and turned towns into cities. By 1900, Canada had one of the longest railway systems in the world.

Automobile Rails are singleminded. They are not practical for everyday movements, from home to work, from farm to town, and so on. Despite the railway, most people still had to cover short distances on foot or in horse-drawn carriages or wagons.

The motor car filled this need for more flexible transportation. The first gasoline-powered car was built in France in the 1860s. It was further perfected by the Germans. But it was the Americans who made it available to everyone through mass production. By 1913, there were over 30 000 cars in Canada.

While the railway required a ribbon of land through the countryside and a large, concentrated patch of ground for its stations and yards, the automobile demanded a vast maze of paved roads. By 1934 Canada had 650 000 km of highways and rural roads. By 1946 the road network spanned Canada. During World War II, the Alaska Highway connected the Yukon and northern B.C. to southern Canada. The Trans-Canada Highway, opened in 1962, was one of the most massive engineering projects ever undertaken. Meanwhile, the automobile transformed Canadian cities with networks of expressways, gas stations, and parking garages.

Air Travel J.A.D. McCurdy was the first person to fly an airplane in Canada, in February 1909. The airplane developed rapidly as a weapon in World War I, and as a means of transport afterwards. Aircraft provided a link to places in the Canadian wilderness that could only be reached before by arduous trips by foot and canoe. Canada's "bush pilots" pioneered this wilderness flying.

As aircraft increased in size and speed, it became practical to move people and light freight, such as mail. Regular passenger service began in the 1930s and has continued to expand down to the present.

TRANSPORTATION IN CANADA TODAY

Canada has an excellent system of transportation. Each system serves a particular need. Some serve a particular area of the country, or a certain economic activity.

Transportation provides more jobs for Canadians than any other activity. It also uses more energy than any other industry. It is one of the biggest customers for steel, cement, aluminum, and other products.

There are five modes of transportation: water, rail, motor carrier, air, and pipeline.

Water Transportation may be separated into three categories: ocean, inland, and coastal.

Ocean transportation has always been very important to Canada. Ships carry raw materials and manufactured goods to customers overseas. About one third of all exports that go by sea move through Vancouver. Montreal, Halifax, Saint John, Churchill, and Quebec City are also important ocean ports.

Oceangoing Ships in Vancouver. About one-third of Canada's ocean cargo is moved through Vancouver (photo by J.A. Kraulis).

The St Lawrence Seaway is the world's greatest inland water route. Great quantities of grain, coal, iron ore, and other goods are moved by lake carriers. The Mackenzie River is an important lifeline to the North.

Coastal water transportation is especially important along the coast of B.C. Great quantities of logs, wood chips, lumber, and chemicals are moved by barge. Sometimes logs are gathered to form a log boom, then pulled by tug. Other logs are moved by large, self-loading barges.

Rail Transportation Canada's railways still move millions of tonnes of bulk cargo, such as coal, potash, grain, and sulphur. Coal often moves in "unit trains," 100 cars long. Railways connect all major Canadian cities and towns. They also reach northward in several provinces: from Sept-Îles to iron-ore deposits in central Quebec; from Toronto northward to James Bay; from Winnipeg to the port of Churchill; from Edmonton to the N.W.T.; from Vancouver into the forests of northern B.C.

Today, passenger rail service is fast disappearing in Canada. VIA Rail Canada, which is responsible for passenger service, records losses of hundreds of millions of dollars.

Motor Carriers Trucks have taken over much of the movement of goods by land. They do not require an airport, track, or waterway. They are flexible in size, from giant trucks which move logs, machinery, and coal, to small delivery trucks which maneuvre in crowded city streets. Almost everything we eat or wear has made part of its journey to us by truck.

Automobiles are the most popular form of passenger transportation. There are about 12 million cars and 16 million drivers in Canada. Canada now has more than 850 000 km of roads and highways.

Air Transportation For long journeys,

Airport in Ottawa, Ont. (photo by Roland Weber/Masterfile).

Canadians prefer to fly. Canada has two major airlines, several smaller carriers, and hundreds of smaller operators. Most communities have some type of air service, whether by aircraft, floatplane, or helicopter. Canadians have led the way in developing aircraft for short city-to-city trips. The Dash 8 and Dash 9 require very short distances for take-offs and landings.

Pipelines Pipelines are the unseen carrier, transporting huge quantities of oil, gasoline, chemicals, and other products over long distances.

Pipelines are expensive to build, but require little maintenance. Canada has one of the most extensive pipeline systems in the world. It is concentrated near the petroleum reserves in Alberta and Saskatchewan, but stretches to eastern Canada and to B.C. as well.

Intermodal Transportation combines two or more transportation modes. "Piggyback" is an example. Goods may be loaded into trucks, transferred to a railway flatcar, and then loaded onto a ship. Trucks themselves can be carried on ferries or ships. This is sometimes called "fishyback" transportation or Ro/Ro (roll on/roll off).

URBAN TRANSPORTATION

As cities grew in size in the late 19th century, it was no longer possible for many people to walk to work. The first attempt to solve the problem was the horse-drawn tram. Toronto had trams in operation by

Railways are still important in Canada for moving bulk goods, such as wheat (photo by Thomas Kitchin).

CPR Maintenance Yards, Calgary. Transportation industries employ a great many Canadians (photo by Rick Rudnicki/Take Stock Inc.).

Pipelines transport huge quantities of oil, gasoline, and chemicals in Canada (photo by Rick Rudnicki/Take Stock Inc.).

Two Kinds of City Transportation, the GO commuter train and cars on the expressway, Toronto (photo by J.A. Kraulis).

Don Valley Parkway, Toronto (photo by Malak, Ottawa).

Commuter on the GO train (photo by J.A. Kraulis).

1845 and Montreal by the 1860s. The system was not ideal. Horses were expensive and polluted the streets. Steam locomotives were unsuitable because they were noisy and dirty and scared the horses.

Urban transportation was revolutionized by the street railway, or streetcar. It was invented in Germany in 1879. One of the first successful examples was built at the Toronto Industrial Exposition in 1885. This short line introduced the trolley pole, which permitted the safe collection of electricity from overhead wires.

The first electric railway line was built in Windsor, Ont., in 1886. Soon most Canadian cities had extensive streetcar service. The streetcar era was over almost as soon as it began, as the automobile offered most Canadians cheap and convenient transportation. Buses also came into use in the 1920s.

After World War II, most Canadian cities tore up their streetcar lines and replaced them with trolley buses. After 1959, only Toronto operated streetcars, which in fact are far more efficient than buses.

In 1954 Toronto opened its Yonge Street subway, which was a major advance in city transportation. Subways carry large numbers of passengers quick-

ly and do not interfere with other traffic.

By the 1950s, the growing number of cars were clogging city streets. Most cities built large expressways to remove cars from local streets. The whole era of expressway building came to a halt in the 1970s because of public protest and the jump in gasoline prices. Cities looked to cheaper, cleaner solutions to transportation problems. Light Rail Transit (LRT) provides most of the advantages of subways at less cost. LRT lines were opened in Edmonton (1978), Calgary (1981), and Vancouver (1986).

LRT Bridge under construction during the extension of the Edmonton LRT line over the North Saskatchewan River, 1989 (photo by McKim Ross).

ROLE OF GOVERNMENT

Government has a long history of involvement in transportation in Canada. The Rideau Canal was built by the British government. Most of the railway lines were either paid for by government or heavily subsidized. Until recently, the federal government owned Canada's largest airline, Air Canada. Provincial governments are responsible for building and maintaining roads. The cost of city transportation systems is often shared between cities and provinces.

Yonge Street, Toronto, 1910 (courtesy Toronto Transit Commission).

The federal government maintains Canada's ports and provides the services of the Canadian Coast Guard.

Transport Canada, a branch of the federal government, is the main government agency involved in transportation.

▷ RELATED ARTICLES: **Aviation; Automobile; Automobile Industry; Ferries; Icebreaker; Pipelines; Railways; St Lawrence Seaway; Shipping; Ships and Shipbuilding; Snowmobile; Trans-Canada Highway;** and "Transportation" sections of the entries on the provinces and territories.

▷ SUGGESTED READING: Mike Hamer, *Transport* (1982); Jane Pachano, *Changing Times: Transportation* (1985); David Paige, *Just About Anything Can be Moved* (1981).

Sarcee Indians *with travois (courtesy McCord Museum of Canadian History).*

■ Travois

A travois is a basic transportation device made by native people on the Plains. Two long poles were tied together with rawhide and attached to an animal's shoulders. A frame or net bag stretched between the poles, and the ends dragged on the ground. Dogs could pull loads of 20 to 30 kg, and horses much larger quantities. Since the poles often doubled as tipi poles, the travois was a sensible means of transportation for a nomadic people.

▷ RELATED ARTICLE: **Native People: Plains.**

■ Treaties

A treaty is an agreement between states that are governed by international law. A general rule of international law is that only the central government can bind a state in a treaty. Thus the federal government alone can commit Canada to international agreements. The Secretary of State for External Affairs, as the minister responsible for foreign relations, recommends when treaty action should be taken by Canada.

Treaties may be either *bilateral*, that is, between two parties, or *multilateral*, that is, between more than two parties. Informal agreements or understandings that are not intended to create legal obligations or which are not entered into by a central government are not regarded as treaties. For example, the provincial governments of Ontario and Quebec have signed a number of educational and cultural arrangements with foreign governments which were not intended to be treaties. The first multilateral treaty signed by Canada was the Treaty of Versailles (1919). The first bilateral treaty signed by Canada independently of Great Britain was the Halibut Fisheries Convention of 1923 with the United States.

▷ RELATED ARTICLES: **Indian Treaties;** and various articles under the names of the treaties (*see* sidebar).

▷ SUGGESTED READING: Peter A. Cumming and Neil H. Mickenberg, editors, *Native Rights in Canada* (second edition, 1972).

■ Tree

A tree is a tall (usually 6 m or higher) plant. It has a single, woody stem (or *trunk*) and a crown of branches. Shrubs are shorter than trees and have numerous stems. Trees are common sights in parks and gardens and cover vast areas of Canada in dense forests.

Trees vary greatly in their characteris-

Major Treaties	
Peace Treaties	
St-Germain,	1632
Breda,	1667
Ryswick,	1697
Utrecht,	1713
Paris,	1763
Paris,	1783
Ghent,	1814
Versailles,	1919
Other Treaties	
Jay's,	1794
Rush-Bagot,	1817
Ashburton-Webster, 1842	
Oregon,	1846
Reciprocity,	1854
Washington,	1871
Bond-Blaine,	1890
Boundary Waters,	1909
Halibut,	1923
Columbia River,	1961

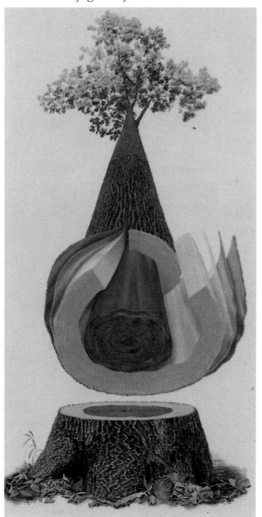

Snow-covered *trees (photo by Chris Bruun).*

Exploded View *of the trunk of a white ash tree, showing the central, dark-coloured heartwood, the sapwood, the inner bark (phloem), and the outer bark (courtesy NMNS/Albert W. Dugal).*

Poplar and Spruce Trees *(photo by Chris Bruun).*

Scots Pine *twig with female cones at the tip. The cross-section of the cone shows the scales and the young ovules. The ovules will develop into seeds after pollination (courtesy NMNS/Albert W. Dugal).*

Pollination *of a female pine cone (courtesy NMNS/Albert W. Dugal).*

tics. Most people are familiar with common kinds of trees from an early age. Trees vary in size all the way up to 100 m, the height of a great Douglas fir. A Douglas fir may be 5 m in diameter and live for 1000 years. Trees are thus the largest and longest living of all living things.

There are two main groups of trees: conifers and broadleaved (or *deciduous*) trees.

Conifers are an ancient group of plants, dating back at least 300 million years. Most conifers live in cool climates. They are often called "softwoods," but this term is not always appropriate. In fact, the softest wood comes from broadleaved trees. Conifers are also called "evergreens," because most of them hold their green leaves year round. The leaves are needle-like. Conifers reproduce through scaly cones. Male and female cones are usually on the same plant. There are ten genera in Canada: firs, cedars, larches, spruces, pines, Douglas firs, hemlocks, junipers, yews, and cypress.

Broadleaves Broadleaved trees normally have flat leaves, and they reproduce by flowering. These trees evolved about 140 million years ago, and they are the dominant plants on Earth. These trees are often called "hardwoods" because of the density of their wood. In the tropics, these trees are evergreen, but in cooler regions, such as Canada, they are *deciduous* (that is, they shed their leaves in fall).

STRUCTURE

Trunk Tree trunks vary in size from massive to delicate. But all contain the same layers. On the outside is the protective bark. Next is the inner bark, or *phloem*, which conducts sugar through to the plant. The inner core conducts water.

A tree grows as long as it is alive, adding a new layer each year. These layers are visible as "rings" when the trunk is cut through. By adding these annual rings, we can calculate the age of the tree.

The phloem carries organic products made by the leaves to the rest of the tree. In the spring, when "sap rises," phloem brings sugar up from the roots. If this inner bark is stripped all the way around a tree, the tree will die.

Roots The root anchors the tree and absorbs moisture. Roots never bear leaves. They may be shallow, in which case the tree may be blown over in a storm. The root system may be far greater in extent than the crown.

Leaves vary greatly in size and shape. They contain a skeleton which connects with the stem. The leaves are the powerhouse of the tree. Each cell contains numerous green *chloroplasts* in which sugars and starch are produced from water and carbon dioxide.

Leaf Section *of a sugar maple (courtesy NMNS/artwork by Marcel Jomphe).*

IMPORTANCE

Trees are basic to all life on Earth. They absorb carbon dioxide and produce oxygen. They provide a home for many animals. Communities of trees (forests) form complex ecosystems which support a wide variety of life. Tree roots hold the soil and their fallen leaves provide organic matter to enrich the soil.

Trees are also of great economic importance, especially to Canada. They support the lumber and pulp and paper industries. In several areas, they produce fruit, such

Trees *are home to many animals, such as this Chipping Sparrow (photo by Normand David).*

as apples and peaches. Finally, trees shape our landscape, protect us, and inspire us with their beauty and grandeur.

▷ RELATED ARTICLES: **Forest; Forest Industries; Natural Regions;** and entries on tree species such as **Beech; Birch; Maple; Oak; Pine; Spruce;** and so on.

▷ SUGGESTED READING: Jean Giono, *The Man Who Planted Trees* (1989); R.C. Hosie, *Native Trees of Canada* (eighth edition, 1979); Jean Lauriault, *The Identification Guide to the Trees of Canada* (1989).

■ Tremblay, Gilles

Composer (*born in 1932 at Arvida, Que.*). With Serge Garant he became a leading figure in Quebec music. He produced the soundtracks for the Quebec pavilion at Expo 67.

Tremblay has composed on commission for Canada's major orchestras, such as the Montreal Symphony Orchestra and the National Arts Centre Orchestra. His compositions are often difficult to perform because of the unconventional techniques they employ. Nevertheless, his reputation is high, not only as a composer, but as a theorist and a teacher. He has influenced a number of younger composers. His music uses not merely normal instrumental sounds but include spontaneous choices made by the players themselves. Tremblay is among the handful of Canadian composers who receive commissions from abroad.

■ Tremblay, Michel

Writer (*born in 1942 at Montreal, Que.*). Raised in a working-class district of Montreal, Tremblay began writing plays in the 1960s. His first work, *Le Train* (1964), won a Radio-Canada prize, but it was really the 1968 production of *Les Belles-Soeurs* which won him sudden fame. Written in "joual," a French urban slang, the play, which presents a harsh portrait of working-class life, raised a storm of controversy. It was later produced in English, like most of Tremblay's plays; no other Canadian playwright has been able to appeal so successfully to audiences in both languages.

As well as his many award-winning plays, Tremblay has written six novels and several musical comedies, radio and television scripts, and songs.

■ Trent Affair

The Trent Affair was an incident that occurred during the American Civil War. In November 1861 a U.S. cruiser stopped a British ship in neutral waters and arrested two Confederate passengers who were on board. The incident brought Britain to the verge of war with the United States, a war that would inevitably have involved the colonies of British North America. *See* **American Civil War.**

■ Trent University

Trent University is in Peterborough, Ont. It has five residential colleges and offers programs in arts and science. It offers interdisciplinary programs (for instance, in Canadian studies, cultural studies, and environmental and resource studies) and teacher education. Specialized graduate programs also exist at Trent.

Trent was founded in 1963. The campus'buildings are award-winning designs of architect Ron Thom. There are over 3300 full-time undergraduate and graduate students. For further information, write the Registrar's Office, Trent University, Peterborough, Ont., K9J 7B8.

■ Trenton

Trenton, Ont., is a city overlooking the Bay of Quinte, just west of Belleville at the mouth of the Trent River. First settled in the 1790s, it grew as a logging and sawmilling centre. Today the economy relies on a mix of light manufacturing. The population in 1986 was 15 311.

For further information, contact the City Clerk, 65 Dundas Street West, P.O. Box 490, Trenton, Ont., K8V 5R6.

■ Trenton

Trenton, N.S., is one of a complex of industrial towns lying south of Pictou near the province's North Shore. Coal mining and steel making were at the heart of the local economy from the 1800s to the

Treeline

The treeline is the zone between the northern forests and the treeless tundra. Despite its name, the treeline is not a definite line, but a band. In parts of Canada, the treeline is a 150 km wide band within which grow both plants of the tundra and small trees, that hug the ground.

The treeline extends across Canada roughly from Inuvik, N.W.T., in the Mackenzie Delta, to Churchill, Man. It then follows the coastline of Hudson Bay down to Attawapiskat, Ont., on James Bay. In Quebec it starts again at the head of James Bay, runs to Ungava Bay, and across to the Labrador coast. North of this natural boundary, there is neither sufficient heat nor moisture for trees to grow. Also, continuous permafrost discourages the growth of trees. There are shrubs instead.

The summits of high mountains are too cold for trees too, and as you climb up such a mountain, you will pass a treeline.

Writer Michel Tremblay (photo by Andrew Danson).

Trinity, Nfld (photo by
J.A. Kraulis).

reach 0.8 m height. Trilliums are typical of deciduous forests like maple bushes.

Eight species of trillium can be found in Canada, most of them in southern Ontario. In 1937 Ontario chose the white trillium (*Trillium grandiflorum*) as its floral emblem. The white flowers appear in April or May, turning pink as they age. The red trillium (*T. erectum*) generally has a bad smell and attracts flies as pollinators. Indians used trilliums for a variety of medicinal purposes.

▷ SUGGESTED READING: James S. Pringle, *The Trilliums of Ontario* (1984).

■ Trinity

Trinity, Nfld, is a community overlooking a large harbour on the west side of Trinity Bay in southeast Newfoundland. Discovered in 1501 on Trinity Sunday by Portuguese explorer Gaspar Corte-Real, Trinity was one of the most important English fishing and trading stations on the island in the 1700s. After 1850 the large merchant companies moved out of Trinity and the community was no longer a major fishing centre. But many of the old buildings remain, giving Trinity the appearance of a 19th-century town. The population in 1986 was 357.

For further information, contact the Town Clerk, P.O. Box 82, Trinity Nfld, A0G 4L0.

■ Trinity Bay

Trinity Bay is a large body of water on the north side of Newfoundland's Avalon Peninsula. The bay has many coves and harbours and is an excellent area for fishing. Many settlements, some of which began as early as the 1600s, dot the shoreline. The first trans-Atlantic cable was laid at Heart's Content in 1866.

■ Trois-Pistoles

Trois-Pistoles, Que., lies on the south shore of the St Lawrence River, 250 km northeast of Quebec City. In the 1500s Basque whalers visited the harbour. More recently the economy of the town has relied on farming and forestry, though whales are becoming important once again as tourists come to watch the giant animals in the St Lawrence. The population in 1986 was 4290.

For further information, contact the Secretary, 5 rue Notre-Dame Est, C.P. 550, Trois-Pistoles, Que., G0L 4K0.

■ Trois-Rivières

Trois-Rivières lies on the north shore of the St Lawrence River, halfway between Montreal and Quebec City. It overlooks

1920s. The town itself was laid out in 1882. When the steel industry went into decline, the period of economic growth ended. The steel industry is still important. The population in 1986 was 3083.

For further information, contact the Town Clerk, P.O. Box 328, Trenton, N.S., B0K 1X0.

■ Trigger, Bruce G.

Anthropologist (*born in 1937 at Preston, Ont.*) Trigger is one of Canada's most respected anthropologists. He began his career by excavating archaeological digs in Egypt and the Sudan, then he joined the anthropology department at McGill University in Montreal in 1964. He is best known for his outstanding history of the Huron people up to the year 1660, *The Children of Aataentsic* (1976). He is also the editor of the volume on the native people of the northeast in the *Handbook of North American Indians*, published by the Smithsonian Institution in Washington, D.C.

■ Trillium

The trillium is a herb-like plant of the lily family (*Liliaceae*). It takes its name from the Latin word for three, an allusion to the way its large leaves and floral pieces are grouped in threes. The flowers range from white to purple. The fruit is usually a red berry. The plant has an underground stalk (rhizome), permitting the colonies to form bright springtime carpets. It may

Trois-Rivières *(courtesy SSC Photocentre/ photo by Michel Gagné).*

the mouth of the St Maurice River, which has played a crucial role in its history.

Trois-Rivières is one of the oldest cities in the province of Quebec. Its name, which in English is Three Rivers, comes from the three arms of the St Maurice River formed by the islands at its mouth. The population of Trois-Rivières in 1986 was 50 122. The population of its metropolitan area was 128 888.

HISTORY

Beginnings In the early 1600s there was an abandoned Algonquin camp at Trois-Rivières. Samuel de Champlain had a *habitation* built there in 1634. This small, fortified settlement served as a trading post where the French bought the furs that native people brought down the river from the interior.

In 1663 the fur-trading settlement was given its own governor and law court. It became the third-most important town in New France, after Quebec and Montreal. But it was far smaller than the other two centres. At the time of the British Conquest in 1760, Trois-Rivières had a population of under 600.

Growth of the City Trois-Rivières grew dramatically in the middle of the 19th century. This was a result of the forest industry that developed in the valley of the St Maurice River. The logs were floated downriver to mills at Trois-Rivières, where they were sawn into lumber and then loaded onto ships for export. Trois-Rivières thrived as a major timber port and as an important administrative centre for the region.

The 20th Century In the early 20th century, dams were built to harness the hydroelectric power of the St Maurice River. This provided the energy for the pulp and paper industry to be developed in the city. By 1930, Trois-Rivières had grown to be one of the world's leading producers of paper products.

The cotton industry also became a major employer. But by the 1960s, both the cotton and the pulp and paper industry had declined. The city's economy came to rely more on a variety of manufacturing jobs, as well as on a growing number of government offices.

THE MODERN CITY

Trois-Rivières today is a mix of old and new. Some prized buildings date back to the time of New France. However, much of the original town was destroyed in a fire in 1908, and modern buildings have risen in its place. High buildings now tower above the cathedral, and a new city hall was built in 1967.

Population The population of Trois-Rivières has always been largely French-speaking. The rapid growth in the early 20th century slowed down during the 1960s. In the mid-1970s, people began to move to nearby suburbs, causing a drop in the population of the city itself.

Education In 1969 a campus of the University of Quebec was established at Trois-Rivières. There is also a medical school, the Trois-Rivières Conservatoire, and a CÉGEP community college.

Transportation Trois-Rivières lies on the main highway between Montreal and Quebec City. It is at the junction of the highway running north to Lac Saint-Jean, and since 1968 it has been linked to the south shore of the St Lawrence by Laviolette Bridge. The city has had its own airport since 1961. VIA Rail also serves the city.

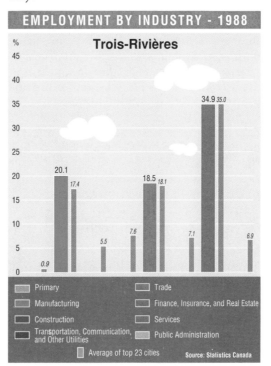

EMPLOYMENT BY INDUSTRY - 1988

Trois-Rivières

%
45
40
35
30
25
20
15
10
5
0

20.1 *17.4*
0.9
5.5
7.6
18.5 *18.1*
7.1
34.9 *35.0*
6.9

Primary
Manufacturing
Construction
Transportation, Communication, and Other Utilities
Trade
Finance, Insurance, and Real Estate
Services
Public Administration

Average of top 23 cities

Source: Statistics Canada

Communications Trois-Rivières has one daily newspaper, *La Nouvelliste*, and one weekly, *La Gazette Populaire*. It has two television stations and three radio stations.

Culture The city is the main cultural centre for the St Maurice region, with art galleries, museums, archives, and a cultural centre. The archaeological museum at the university has a collection of fossils, as well as artifacts relating to the early native and French inhabitants of the region.

The city's most famous historical site is Forges Saint-Maurice, an early iron foundry. It is now a National Historic Park. Audiovisual displays of old Trois-Rivières are also shown at the Manoir Boucher de Niverville, a stone house dating from around 1730.

Each summer, Trois-Rivières hosts a lively festival that includes theatrical shows, street activities, arts and crafts, parades, and fireworks. The city also holds an agricultural exhibition each year, and it is the finishing point of international canoe races that are held on the St Maurice River.

For further information, contact the Greffier, 1325 Place l'Hôtel-de-Ville, C.P. 368, Trois-Rivières, Que., G9A 5H3.

▷ RELATED ARTICLES: **Forges Saint-Maurice; St Maurice River.**

■ Troupes de la Marine

The Troupes de la Marine were troops that served in France's overseas colonies. They were also known as colonial regulars. In Canada there were usually about 30 companies, consisting of 50 men each. By the 1750s, another 20 companies were stationed at Louisbourg. When the system was first established in 1683, the soldiers were all from France. Soon more and more Canadian-born men joined the force so that it became, to a large extent, a *Canadien* army. The soldiers were especially skilled at guerrilla warfare, which they had learned from the native people and which they and their native allies practised with great effect against British settlements.

▷ RELATED ARTICLE: **New France.**

■ Trout

Trout are members of the salmon family. Often confused with char, they can be told by their dark spots on a pale background. They usually live in fresh water, though some live in the ocean but mate in fresh water. There are four species in Canada: the rainbow (*Salmo gairdnerii*) and cutthroat (*S. aquabonita*) come from Europe and California respectively. The Atlantic salmon is also included in the trout group. Mating occurs in cold river water. The eggs develop in the gravel. After hatching, the fry live in the river for a while and then return to a lake or the ocean.

Trout are carnivorous, feeding on insects and small fish. The rainbow trout is the favourite in fish farming. The trout are raised and sold for food or to restock lakes for sport fishing. The fierce brown trout is one of the most difficult to catch.

▷ SUGGESTED READING: Foster Ainsworth, *The Mysteries of Trout Fishing* (1987); Joanne Cole and Jerome Wexler, *A Fish Hatches* (1978); Frederick Wooding, *The Book of Canadian Fishes* (second edition, 1973).

■ Trout, Jennie Kidd

Doctor (*born Jennie Gowanlock in 1841 at Kelso, Scotland; died in 1921 at Los Angeles, California, U.S.*). Trout was the first Canadian woman who was officially recognized as a doctor by being licensed to practise medicine in Canada. She came to Canada as a child and grew up near Stratford, Ont. She decided to study medicine after getting to know Dr Emily Stowe in Toronto. Dr Stowe was practising without a licence at the time because the regulations of the College of Physicians and Surgeons of Ontario made it almost impossible for women to qualify. Jennie Trout, too, had great difficulty, but after graduating in the United States, she took the registration exams of the College, passed, and was duly licensed in 1875.

Trout opened a practice for women and children in Toronto, together with an institute where she gave patients a new form of electrical treatment. She also ran a free clinic for the poor. At the same time, she belonged to numerous women's organizations, including the Association for the Advancement of Women. Most important was the help she gave young medical students by founding the Women's Medical College in Kingston (1883). In 1895 this college joined with the one in Toronto established by Dr Stowe to become the Ontario Medical College for Women. Until 1906, when the University of Toronto finally admitted women medical students, it was the only place in Ontario where women could study to be doctors.

▷ RELATED ARTICLE: **Emily Stowe.**

▷ SUGGESTED READING: Carlotta Hacker, *The Indomitable Lady Doctors* (1974).

Troyes, Pierre de

Soldier (*birth unknown; died in 1688 at Niagara, New France*). De Troyes was a professional French soldier who was posted to New France in 1685. He led a celebrated attack against the English fur traders on James Bay in 1686. The English were expecting an attack from the French, but they thought it would be from the sea. Troyes approached overland across the little-known wilderness south of Hudson Bay. Troyes's force consisted of 30 regular soldiers from France and about 70 locally raised militiamen, who were under the command of young Pierre Le Moyne d'Iberville and two of Iberville's brothers. For three months the party worked its way north, paddling up the Ottawa River and then following the chain of lakes and waterways to Moose River. The men were often near exhaustion as they hauled their boats across portage after portage, but their surprise tactics worked. They successfully captured Forts Moose, Charles, and Albany, as well as a small depot on Charlton Island.

The following year, Pierre de Troyes commanded an equally successful expedition against the Iroquois. He was thought to have a brilliant future in the army, but he died of scurvy after only three years in New France.

▷ RELATED ARTICLE: **Pierre Le Moyne d'Iberville.**

Trucking, *see* Transportation

Trudeau, Pierre Elliott

Trudeau was the first prime minister to be born in the 20th century. He had little experience in government, but his charm, intelligence, and energy appealed to Canadians. Trudeau's years as prime minister were eventful. They are remembered mainly for the fierce, at times violent, struggle between Quebec and the federal government.

Social Critic Trudeau's French-Canadian father was a wealthy businessman. His mother was of Scottish ancestry. He studied law before beginning a career as a professor, writer, and social critic. During the 1950s he joined other young intellectuals to condemn Quebec premier Maurice Duplessis. Duplessis and his party, the Union Nationale, had firmly controlled Quebec politics for a long time. Trudeau criticized Duplessis for corruption and for resisting changes needed to modernize Quebec.

Trudeau also criticized Liberal prime

Pierre Elliott Trudeau
15TH PRIME MINISTER OF CANADA

Born: October 18, 1919, Montreal, Quebec
Political Party: Liberal
First Elected: 1965
Chosen Leader: 1968
Period as Prime Minister: April 20, 1968 to June 4, 1979; March 3, 1980 to June 30, 1984

(PHOTO BY KARSH, OTTAWA)

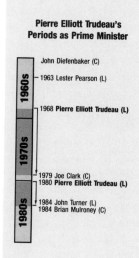

Pierre Elliott Trudeau's Periods as Prime Minister

John Diefenbaker (C)
1960s
- 1963 Lester Pearson (L)
- 1968 Pierre Elliott Trudeau (L)
1970s
- 1979 Joe Clark (C)
- 1980 Pierre Elliott Trudeau (L)
1980s
- 1984 John Turner (L)
- 1984 Brian Mulroney (C)

minister Lester Pearson for agreeing to arm Canada with nuclear weapons. Nevertheless, in 1965, Pearson asked Trudeau to join the Liberal Party and run for Parliament. Trudeau agreed. He was elected and went to Ottawa with his friends Jean Marchand and Gérard Pelletier. Together they were called Quebec's "Three Wise Men."

PRIME MINISTER

Trudeaumania After two years in Ottawa, Trudeau joined the Cabinet as minister of justice. He gained a reputation as a reformer. He brought important changes to laws affecting divorce, homosexuality, and abortion. However, it was a surprise in 1968 when the Liberals chose him leader. Trudeau had been in Parliament less than three years and he was not widely known outside Quebec. He became prime minister April 20, 1968, when Lester Pearson retired.

In the election of 1968, Trudeau took the country by storm. Canadians were entranced by his dynamic, youthful image. "Trudeaumania" swept the country, and carried the Liberals to victory.

Trudeau promised a "Just Society" and a government which would be open to all Canadians. He wanted French Canadians to feel at home in Canada. He utterly rejected the growing movement among French Canadians for an independent Quebec.

In 1969 his government passed the Official Languages Act to promote the use of both French and English.

In October 1970 a terrorist group kidnapped a British diplomat and a Quebec Cabinet minister in Montreal. A few days later the terrorists murdered a Cabinet minister, Pierre Laporte. The governments of Quebec and Canada were thrown into confusion. Trudeau reacted by invoking the War Measures Act to deal with the emergency. Under this law, several hundred people were arrested in Quebec and held for questioning. Soldiers patrolled the streets of Montreal and Ottawa.

Trudeau's actions during the October Crisis are still debated today. Critics charged that he acted ruthlessly and arrogantly. When asked by a reporter how far he would go, he answered "Watch me!" Others defended him for acting decisively in a dangerous situation. In either case, his image of a carefree bachelor was now gone.

Second Term By the 1972 election "Trudeaumania" had disappeared. Many English Canadians resented his policy of bilingualism. Most western Canadians believed that Trudeau had little interest in their problems. Trudeau lost his majority in Parliament. For the next two years, he remained prime minister only with the support of the New Democratic Party.

Third Term Trudeau regained his popularity and won a majority again in 1974. During this time, a new crisis broke out in Quebec. René Lévesque was elected premier of Quebec in 1976. His aim was to negotiate more independence for Quebec. These were also years of economic troubles. Trudeau had won the election largely by promising that he would not put controls on wages and prices. A year later, in 1975, he imposed those controls.

Defeat In 1979 Trudeau and the Liberals were defeated by the Conservatives. Joe Clark became prime minister, and Trudeau announced that he would resign. Three weeks later, a new election was called. The Liberals persuaded Trudeau to remain as leader. In February 1980, he led the Liberals to victory and in March was sworn in as prime minister.

Fourth Term During his last term in office, Trudeau turned his attention again to Quebec. In 1980 the Quebec government held a referendum. A "Yes" vote would give Quebec the right to negotiate with Canada for more independence. Trudeau played an important part in defeating the referendum. He then determined to give Canada a new Constitution and a Charter of Rights and Freedoms. Trudeau always believed in a strong federal government. His battles with the provincial premiers over the new Constitution were widely publicized, but agreement was finally reached. The new Constitution was proclaimed April 17, 1982. However, Quebec refused to be part of the agreement.

Trudeau now devoted more time to international affairs. He visited several countries to try to persuade them to reduce nuclear weapons. He was awarded the Albert Einstein Peace Prize for his work. Trudeau was less successful in other areas. Unemployment and inflation made his government unpopular. His National Energy Program was extremely unpopular in the West.

Retirement By 1984, Trudeau had served longer than any other leader of his time in the Western world. His success in Canadian elections was second only to Mackenzie King's in this century. However, his personal popularity was low. He retired on June 30, 1984 and John Turner took over as prime minister. In retirement, Trudeau joined a Montreal law firm.

▷ RELATED ARTICLES: **Bilingualism; Constitution Act; October Crisis; Quebec: Politics; Separatism; Union Nationale; War Measures Act.**

▷ SUGGESTED READING: Richard Gwyn, *The Northern Magus: Pierre Trudeau and Canadians 1968-1980* (1980); George Radwanski, *Trudeau* (1978); Pierre Elliott Trudeau and Thomas Axworthy, editors, *Towards a Just Society* (1990).

▮ Truro

Truro, N.S., lies 80 km north of Halifax at the head of Cobequid Bay, an extension of the Minas Basin. Acadians lived in the area from about 1700. They were followed by New England farmers who named the site after a town in England. A major railway centre since the 1860s, Truro is at the heart of a thriving farming area. The town has a variety of industries and is the business and service centre for the region. Truro's population in 1986 was 12 124.

For further information, contact the Town Clerk, P.O. Box 427, Truro, N.S., B2N 5C5.

■ Truss, Jan

Writer (*born in 1925 at Stoke-On-Trent, England*). Truss is a teacher who came to Canada in 1957 and whose writing treats serious social and moral questions. Two plays explore issues in Canadian history. *A Very Small Rebellion* (produced 1974) sympathetically portrays the cause of Louis Riel's Metis. *The Judgement of Clifford Sifton* (produced 1974) has conscience, truth, and history challenge the accomplishments of Sifton, who promoted immigration to the West. Her novels emphasize the psychological responses of young people with problems. In *A Very Small Rebellion*, modern Metis youths staging Truss's play learn that they face problems similar to Riel's. In *Jasmin* (1982), winner of the Ruth Schwartz Award, a poor young girl learns to value her artistic talent. Growth in maturity and self-confidence are also central to *Bird at the Window* (1974), *Summer Goes Riding* (1987), and *Red* (1988).

■ Tsimshian

Tsimshian means "people of the Skeena," referring to the Skeena River in B.C. The name is applied to three major native groups: Nishga, Gitksan, and Coast Tsimshian. All speak Tsimshian.

Archaeologists have uncovered cedar villages in the harbour of Prince Rupert dating back 5000 years. Thus the Tsimshian claim one of the oldest heritages in North America. Tsimshian built totem poles and held potlatch feasts to celebrate name giving, accompany a funeral, and other important events. Many present-day Tsimshian families continue the potlatch tradition.

Tsimshian recognize that they belong to one of four major groups: Frog or Raven, Wolf, Eagle, and Killer Whale or Fireweed. A person belongs to the same group as his or her mother and must marry into a different group. Fishing is an important source of income and food. *See* **Native People: Northwest Coast.**

Tsimshian Soul Catcher (courtesy UBC Museum of Anthropology).

■ Tsunami

Tsunami (pronounced "tsoo-nah-me") is the Japanese word for the ocean wave that some earthquakes raise. Such waves, which are sometimes incorrectly called tidal waves, can do enormous damage.

From the centre of an earthquake under the floor of the sea, waves spread out like ripples in a pond. They can travel 900 km per hour. In the deep open ocean they are low (about a metre high). In shallow water, near land, they slow down and rise up, sometimes towering tens of metres. They hit shore with devastating force.

In 1929 an earthquake shook the Grand Banks off Newfoundland. It raised a wave 5 m high when it swept on land, and drowned 27 Newfoundlanders.

Most tsunamis occur in the Pacific, which is ringed by volcanoes and shaken by earthquakes. The tsunami raised by the great Alaska earthquake of 1964 — one of the largest quakes ever recorded in North America — was 7 m high when it crashed into the two communities of Alberni and Port Alberni on the west coast of Vancouver Island. It caused several million dollars' worth of damage.

▷ RELATED ARTICLES: **Earthquake; Ocean.**

▷ SUGGESTED READING: Douglas Myles, *The Great Waves* (1985).

■ Tuberculosis, *see* Epidemics

■ Tuktoyaktuk

Tuktoyaktuk, N.W.T., is on the coast of the Beaufort Sea, near the mouth of the Mackenzie River. The original inhabitants were Inuit who hunted whales. These Inuit died from disease in the late 1800s. The present community began as a port in 1934. The name means "look like caribou" in the Inuit language. The hamlet is a government centre and base for the oil and gas industry in the Arctic.

For further information, contact the Village Manager, Box 120, Tuktoyaktuk, N.W.T., X0E 1C0.

■ Tuna

In Canada, there are four tuna species on the Pacific Coast, six on the Atlantic. Depending on species, these fish of the high seas can weigh 9 to 600 kg. Tuna are often brightly coloured. Their slender fins look like boomerangs. The fine tail has a series of triangular finlets on its upper and lower surfaces, ending in a large, narrow fin. Tuna are excellent swimmers. They move rapidly and can cover long distances without tiring. An internal regulatory system keeps their temperature 10°C higher than that of the water. To get the energy need-

Tundra Plants bloom profusely on the tundra during the brief summer season. Animal life varies with the season. Many species of birds, such as the Snow Goose, Canada Goose, and the Red-throated Loon, nest there in summer, heading back south when fall arrives. The right side of the illustration shows permanent residents such as the Willow Ptarmigan, arctic hare, and muskoxen, all of them well suited to the rigours of winter. Among them, the polar bears prowl the coastline hunting for walrus and seals.

As soon as the snow melts, the tundra is carpeted with flowers. Most of them are brilliantly coloured (such as moss campion, river beauty [willow herb], Lapland rosebay, alpine azalea) because vivid petals more easily absorb the heat. Most tundra plants hug the ground to protect themselves from the wind and cold, either as creepers (such as willow, birch, mountain cranberry) or in little cushion-shaped mounds (such as moss campion, diapensia) (artwork by Claire Tremblay).

ed for their activities, they eat a lot: the equivalent of one-quarter their own body weight each day. They eat crustaceans, octopi, and fish. A major catch in commercial fishing, tuna can be eaten both fresh and preserved. Sports fishermen like to battle tuna on the high sea.

■ Tundra

Tundra is the forbidding, often beautiful land that encircles the northern edges of our planet. It covers about 15% of the Earth's surface. Canada has more tundra than any other kind of vegetation except for the boreal forest. The growing season for plants is extremely short: a mere 750 degree-days at the southern edge of the tundra, to less than 125 degree-days in the Far North. By comparison, southern Ontario has between 1750 to 2500 degree-days. (For definition of degree days, *see* Volume 4, page 323.) The climate of the tundra is harsh, with long, bitterly cold winters and short, cool summers. Beneath the tundra is permafrost. Continuous permafrost inhibits plant growth and prevents deep roots from developing. Trees cannot grow in these conditions.

The plants of the tundra are woody shrubs, herbs, grasses, sedges, lichens, and mosses — all of which hug the ground. Growth is slow, and there are few plant species. Most plants live for more than one year so they must store food to survive over the winter. Because life is so

hard here, the tundra is sometimes known as the Barren Lands, or Barrens. Though in general the tundra is far from lifeless, in the Arctic Archipelago, where the climate is very harsh, plants are more sparse than they are on the mainland. Hillsides more than 100 m or so in height are bare rock.

The tundra is a land of animals such as caribou, muskox, polar bears, arctic fox, and arctic hare. They grow thick, dense coats to insulate themselves from the chill winds and cold of winter. Many species of birds nest in the tundra during the summer, but only a few, such as the Snowy Owl, stay during the winter.

The tundra is a dry land. It is desert-like, with only 100 to 200 mm of precipitation falling each year. Open water is scarce except in low-lying areas where it collects. What water there is on the surface of the land is locked in the form of snow or ice throughout much of the year. In winter, tundra animals must quench their thirst with snow.

▷ RELATED ARTICLE: **Natural Regions.**

▷ SUGGESTED READING: Ian Barrett, *Tundra and People* (1982); Bruce Hiscock, *Tundra: The Arctic Land* (1986); Theodora Stanwell-Fletcher, *The Tundra World* (1952).

■ Tupper, Sir Charles

Tupper was the last of the four Conservatives who served as prime minister in the five years following Sir John A. Macdonald's death. He held office for only ten weeks in 1896, but he had a full political career before that and performed a vital role as a Father of Confederation.

He was trained as a doctor and began to practise medicine in 1843 at Amherst, N.S. In 1855 he was elected as a Conservative to the Legislative Assembly of Nova Scotia, and he served as provincial secretary (1857-60 and 1863-67). He was also premier of Nova Scotia (1864-67).

Tupper was a strong, even reckless, supporter of Confederation. He took part in all three Confederation conferences. In 1866 he succeeded in getting a pro-Confederation resolution passed by both houses of the Nova Scotia legislature. This was a considerable victory, since many Nova Scotians were against Confederation. Tupper was careful not to call an election on the issue in 1866. He waited until Confederation was signed, sealed, and proclaimed; then he had the election. Nova Scotians showed their disapproval by soundly defeating the Conservatives, both in the provincial election and in the first federal election for the new House of Commons in Ottawa. Of the 19 Nova Scotians elected to Parliament in 1867, Tupper was the only Confederation supporter. The other 18 were all anti-Confederates.

AFTER CONFEDERATION

After 1867 Tupper had a long career as a federal Cabinet minister, serving from 1870 to 1873, from 1878 to 1884, and from 1887 to 1888. He had a versatile talent and held a variety of Cabinet positions. A vigorous and aggressive debater, he bore down on his opponents with an impressive power of noise, brass, and argument. Tupper had a considerable memory, a serviceable bad temper, and was generally an unscrupulous debater.

Tupper was Canadian high commissioner to Great Britain from 1884 to 1887 and from 1888 to 1896. He was recalled to political duty in January 1896 because the Conservative government of Mackenzie Bowell was in a perilous condition and was losing support in its own ranks. Tupper took over the leadership of the House of Commons, and at the beginning of May he became prime minister. His immediate challenge was to face a general election, fighting the popular Liberal leader, Wilfrid Laurier. He fought a brave and uphill battle, and he came close to winning. Although Laurier won a majority of seats, Tupper and the Conservatives won a majority of the votes. But they lost the election.

Sir Charles Tupper
6TH PRIME MINISTER OF CANADA

Born: July 2, 1821, Amherst, N.S.
Died: October 30, 1915, Bexley Heath, England
Political Party: Conservative
First Elected: 1855, Legislative Assembly of Nova Scotia; 1867, House of Commons, Ottawa
Chosen Leader: 1896
Period as Prime Minister: May 1, 1896 to July 8, 1896
(PHOTO COURTESY NAC/C-10109)

Sir Charles Tupper's Period as Prime Minister

Sir John A. Macdonald (C)

1870s — 1873 Alexander Mackenzie (L)

— 1878 Sir John A. Macdonald (C)

1880s

1890s — 1891 Sir John J.C. Abbott (C)
— 1892 Sir John S.D. Thompson (C)
— 1894 Sir Mackenzie Bowell (C)
— 1896 **Sir Charles Tupper (C)**
1896 Sir Wilfrid Laurier (L)

Tupper remained in Parliament as Leader of the Opposition until 1901, when he persuaded Robert Borden to replace him. He retired to Vancouver, and in 1913 he moved to England.

▷ RELATED ARTICLES: **Confederation; Political History.**

▷ SUGGESTED READING: Vincent Durant, *War Horse of Cumberland: The Life and Times of Sir Charles Tupper* (1985).

■ Turnbull, Wallace Rupert

Aeronautical engineer and inventor (*born in 1870 at Saint John, N.B.; died there in 1954*). Turnbull invented the variable-pitch propeller, which was hailed as the most important invention in the history of aeronautics. Previously, propellers on airplanes had been fixed at one angle. With Turnbull's propeller, the blades could be adjusted (like changing gears on a car) so that they could be set at different angles for takeoff and landing, and for level flight. The propeller was first flight-tested in 1927. It greatly increased the safety of flying. As well, it allowed heav-

W.R. Turnbull (artwork by Irma Coucill).

ier loads to be carried and thus led to the development of the air transportation industry.

Turnbull was from a wealthy family, and he had a private laboratory at his home in Rothesay, N.B., where he did his research. In 1902, he built the first wind tunnel in Canada. The Saint John airport, Turnbull field, is named in his honour.

▷ RELATED ARTICLES: **Aviation; Invention.**

■ Turner, John Napier

John Turner served as prime minister of Canada for just 80 days, a briefer period than any other prime minister in the 20th century.

From a young age Turner was marked for success. Handsome, charming, and intelligent, he was regarded as a future prime minister from the moment he entered public life. However, as leader of the Liberal party, he failed to win the confidence of Canadian voters.

His father died when John Turner was three years old. He was raised by his mother in Ottawa where she was an economist in the public service. A brilliant student and track star, Turner attended the University of British Colum-

John Turner on radio during his election campaign in 1988 (courtesy Canapress Photo Service/Hans Deryk).

bia and won a Rhodes scholarship to continue his studies in England.

Returning to Canada in 1953, he became a lawyer in Montreal. Lester Pearson brought him into the Liberal party and he won election to Parliament in 1962 when he was just 32 years old. Three years later he joined the Cabinet. Still a junior minister, he seemed to have a bright career ahead of him.

In 1968 Turner made his first run for the leadership of the Liberals, finishing a distant third to Pierre Trudeau. From 1968 to 1972, as minister of justice in the Trudeau government, he sponsored important changes in the legal system.

Early in 1972 Turner became finance minister. Increasingly, he differed with the prime minister over economic policy, and in September 1975 he resigned from the Cabinet, leaving politics altogether a few months later.

Turner returned to the practice of law in Toronto, but it was widely believed that he would return to public life someday. In 1984, the chance came. Trudeau retired and Turner ran for, and won, the Liberal leadership. This also made him prime minister. But in a disorganized election campaign a few months later, he was badly beaten by Brian Mulroney and the Conservatives.

As Leader of the Opposition, Turner was plagued by divisions in his own party. He led the Liberals into the election of November 1988, fighting an emotional campaign against the free-trade policies of the Conservatives. After losing this election, Turner again left politics and returned to private life.

▷ RELATED ARTICLES: **Elections; Free Trade; Liberal Party.**

▷ SUGGESTED READING: Jack Cahill, *John Turner: The Long Run* (1984).

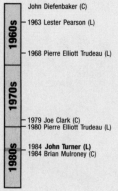

John Turner's Period as Prime Minister

John Diefenbaker (C)

1960s
1963 Lester Pearson (L)

1968 Pierre Elliott Trudeau (L)

1970s

1979 Joe Clark (C)
1980 Pierre Elliott Trudeau (L)

1980s
1984 **John Turner (L)**
1984 Brian Mulroney (C)

John Napier Turner
17TH PRIME MINISTER OF CANADA

Born: June 7, 1929, Richmond, England
Political Party: Liberal
First Elected: 1962
Chosen Leader: 1984
Period as Prime Minister: June 30, 1984, to September 17, 1984
(PHOTO BY GILBERT STUDIOS LTD)

■ Turner Valley

Turner Valley, Alta, lies in the valley of the same name 40 km south of Calgary. It is the site of the first major oil and gas discovery in Alberta (1914). Petroleum development was centered here through the 1930s, but by World War II the field had run down. Today the valley produces little oil. The population in 1986 was 1271.

For further information, contact the Town Administrator, P.O. Box 330, Turner Valley, Alta, T0L 2A0.

■ Turnor, Philip

Fur trader and surveyor (*born about 1751 in England; died about 1800 at London, England*). In 1778 Turnor became the first person hired by the Hudson's Bay Company specifically as a surveyor. His job was to make maps of the inland fur-trading country. Travelling by canoe and on foot in all weather, he mapped trade routes and located the exact position of many landmarks. He also served as master at two trading posts. His maps contributed much information about the little-known interior of what is now Canada.

■ Turtle

Turtles are four-legged reptiles whose bodies are protected by a shell. The shell is made of two parts: the *carapace* covers

Wood Turtle (courtesy Macmillan Illustrated Animal Encyclopedia).

Leatherback Turtle (courtesy Macmillan Illustrated Animal Encyclopedia).

the animal's back and the *plastron* covers its belly. The turtle's backbone and ribs are fused to the carapace. A turtle cannot leave its shell.

There are 14 species of turtle in Canada. They occur only in southern Canada and are most abundant in the Great Lakes region of Ontario. The snapping turtle (*Chelydra serpentina*) has a carapace made of large bony plates. Its plastron is smaller than average, leaving room for its large legs. To make up for this lack of protection, the snapping turtle has strong jaws and defends itself aggressively. Some turtles, like the eastern box turtle (*Terrapene carolina*), have two hinges across the plastron so it can fold up against the carapace. This enables them to cover their head, legs, and tail with the shell. The spiny, softshell turtle (*Trionyx spiniferus*) has a flexible, leathery shell. Canadian turtles are aquatic or semi-aquatic, and live near ponds, marshes, rivers, and lakes. Turtles have no teeth, but they have a strong, sharp beak. Most eat

Spiny Softshell Turtle (courtesy Macmillan Illustrated Animal Encyclopedia).

Some Turtles of Canada: Northwestern Pond (top left), Stinkpot (top right), Snapping (2nd row left), Western Painted (2nd row right), and Leatherback (artwork by Jan Sovak).

Green Turtle (courtesy Macmillan Illustrated Animal Encyclopedia).

Snapping Turtle (courtesy Macmillan Illustrated Animal Encyclopedia).

RCMP at the door of 24 Sussex Drive (photo by Jim Merrithew).

insects, molluscs, and worms. Some also eat plants and fish and scavenge dead animals.

All turtles lay eggs on land, in nests scratched in the ground. The young hatch and fend for themselves. Four marine species have been recorded off Canadian coasts. Marine turtles generally live in warmer waters and lay their eggs on tropical beaches. Turtle meat and turtle eggs of some species are edible, and marine turtles are hunted in many parts of the world. Some species are hunted for their shells to make "tortoise-shell" ornaments.

▷ Suggested Reading: Barbara Froom, *The Turtles of Canada* (1978); Merebeth Switzer, *Turtles* (1985).

Tutchone

The Tutchone are an Athapaskan-speaking group that lives in the southern Yukon. Traditionally, they hunted caribou, moose, freshwater fish, and sometimes salmon. They lived in small, nomadic bands and built shelters of brush or animal skins. The women made hide clothing and decorative birchbark containers. In spring, summer, and fall, families gathered to hunt and fish, and celebrated with songs, dances, and storytelling. In the 19th century they hunted fur-bearing animals for the fur trade. Their culture was drastically changed by the Klondike gold rush in the late 1890s and by the building of the Alaska Highway in 1942. In 1990 the Tutchone and other Yukon Indian groups signed with the federal and Yukon governments a final general agreement on land claims,

within which each of the Yukon bands must still determine its own band-final agreement. *See* **Native People: Subarctic**.

Tweedsmuir, John Buchan, 1st Baron, *see* John Buchan

24 Sussex Drive

24 Sussex Drive in Ottawa, Ont., is the official residence of the prime minister of Canada. The house was built in 1866-68 by Joseph M. Currier, a prosperous mill owner, lumber manufacturer, and member of Parliament. He called it "Gorffwysfa," which is a Welsh word for "place of peace." It occupies a spectacular site on the cliffs overlooking the Ottawa River, within sight of the Parliament Buildings. In 1943 the government expropriated the house, an elegant mansion built in the Gothic Revival style, and had it completely redesigned as a formal, modern residence. Louis St Laurent was the first prime minister to occupy the house. He insisted on paying rent, a custom that continued until 1971. The prime minister also has use of a country retreat at Harrington Lake, just north of Ottawa in Quebec.

▷ Suggested Reading: Maureen McTeer, *Residences: Homes of Canada's Leaders* (1982).

24 Sussex Drive is the official residence of the prime minister (courtesy National Capital Commission).

Twillingate

Twillingate, Nfld, lies on the Twillingate Islands in Notre Dame Bay in northeast Newfoundland. First occupied by prehistoric hunters and fishers, it was used as a fishing station by the French in the 17th century. Later, English fishermen settled the spot, and in the 1800s it became a major centre of the Labrador cod and seal fisheries. The town remains a fishing port and a business centre for the surrounding district. The population in 1986 was 1506.

For further information, contact the Town Clerk, P.O. Box 220, Twillingate, Nfld, A0G 4M0.

■ Two Solitudes

Two Solitudes (1945) is a novel by Hugh MacLennan. The title refers to the lack of communication between the English- and French-speaking cultures in Canada.

Two Solitudes won the Governor General's Award. It is one of the first important 20th-century novels in Canada to deal with the theme of national identity. It has been translated into many languages. For a description of the novel, *see* sidebar in **Literature.**

■ Typhus, *see* Epidemics

Joseph B. Tyrrell was a new breed of scientist/ explorer (courtesy Thomas Fisher Rare Book Library, University of Toronto).

■ Tyrrell, Joseph Burr

Scientist and explorer (*born in 1858 at Weston, Canada West [Ont.]; died in 1957 at Toronto, Ont.*). Joseph Tyrrell was a new breed of explorer, a wilderness traveller who was also a scientist interested in studying the land itself. While working as a surveyor for the Geological Survey of Canada, he explored vast areas of the Canadian West and North. In 1884 he discovered the first dinosaur remains in the area of what is now Drumheller, Alta. He also discovered deposits of coal at Drumheller and at Fernie, B.C.

Later, Tyrrell grew wealthy in the mining business and devoted much of his time to studying the careers of earlier Canadian explorers. The Tyrrell Museum of Palaeontology near Drumheller, Alta, is named in his honour.

▷ RELATED ARTICLE: **Exploration.**

▷ SUGGESTED READING: William Edward Eagan, *Joseph Burr Tyrrell 1858-1957* (1971); Alex I. Inglis, *Northern Vagabond: The Life and Career of J.B. Tyrrell* (1978); Margaret M. Shaw, *Geologists and Prospectors.*

■ Tyrrell Museum of Palaeontology

The Tyrrell Museum of Palaeontology, near Drumheller, Alta., opened in 1985. It has more than 100 000 specimens from all parts of the world in its collection. Some of the fossils are 3.5 billion years old.

In the main gallery there are more than 30 skeleton reconstructions of large dinosaurs including meat-eaters such as *Tyrannosaurus rex* and *Albertosaurus*, and plant-eaters such as *Triceratops*. The museum has a number of audio-visual programs to explain fossil collecting, possible reasons for the extinction of dinosaurs, and other topics.

Visitors can watch fossils being prepared for display through a window into the laboratory. There are also many hands-on activities, a prehistoric garden, and guided hikes in the surrounding Badlands. The museum is named after the scientist and explorer Joseph Burr Tyrrell, who discovered dinosaur remains in the area in 1884. In June 1990, the museum was given royal status and will now be known as the Royal Tyrrell Museum.

For further information, contact the Tyrrell Museum of Palaeontology, Box 7500, Drumheller, Alta, T0J 0Y0.

▷ RELATED ARTICLE: **Dinosaur.**

■ Tyson, Ian, *see* Ian and Sylvia

Edmontonia, an armoured plant-eating dinosaur, displayed at the Tyrrell Museum (courtesy Tyrrell Museum of Palaeontology, Alberta Culture & Multiculturalism).

Albertosaurus standing over Centrosaurus, in the Tyrrell Museum (courtesy Tyrrell Museum of Palaeontology, Alberta Culture & Multiculturalism).

U

Two UFO Sightings

Stephen Michalak, an amateur prospector, claimed that he was able to approach and even touch a hovering UFO that had landed at Falcon Lake, Man., on May 20, 1967. He claims that he heard two human-like voices, and says that he suffered chest and stomach burns from the UFO's exhaust. He had to be hospitalized, and traces of radiation were detected at the site. On July 3, 1967, Warren Smith and two friends observed a UFO speeding across the sky over the Highwood River, Alta. Smith was able to snap two colour photographs of the metallic-looking, saucer-shaped disc.

UFO Landing Pad, St Paul, Alta. A sign at the foot of the stairs leading up to the platform bears the following inspired message: "All visitors from Earth or otherwise are welcome to this territory and to the town of St Paul" (courtesy Victor Post Photography).

■ UFOs

*U*nidentified *F*lying *O*bjects are mysterious objects that are sighted in the sky. The term has replaced the earlier description "flying saucers," since relatively few contemporary reports describe objects that are shaped like saucers.

UFOs have been variously described as space craft from some distant solar system; experimental aircraft that are tested in secret; natural objects, such as the planet Venus, or man-made objects, such as automobile headlights reflected on low-hanging clouds. They may also simply be figments of the imagination.

Simeon Perkins, a Loyalist merchant and resident of Liverpool, N.S., reported what is believed to be the earliest account of a UFO sighting in North America. On October 12, 1796, Perkins reported that three people near New Minas saw a "fleet of ships" fly through the air.

That sighting set the stage for later reports — of which there are thousands in Canada alone. In fact, more reports of UFOs may come from Canada than from any other country. In the early 1950s, two government departments examined reports of sightings. They concluded that the subject was not worthy of scientific study. Reports of sightings sent to the National Research Council are added to a file called "Sightings, non-meteoric." There is no scientific evidence that objects sighted come from outer space.

A UFO landing pad — the world's first — was erected as a Centennial project in 1967 by the townspeople of St Paul, Alta. It resembles a helicopter landing pad and is decorated with the Canadian flag and provincial and territorial flags. The land it stands on has been declared an "international zone."

▷ SUGGESTED READING: Peter Brookesmith, *The Age of the UFO* (1984); John Robert Colombo, *Extraordinary Experiences: Personal Accounts of the Paranormal in Canada* (1989); John Brent Musgrave, *UFO: Occupants and Critters* (1979); Ronald D. Story, *UFOs and the Limits of Science* (1981).

■ Ukrainians

There are 420 200 Canadians of Ukrainian origin. Another 541 100 Canadians have some Ukrainian ancestry. Ukraine is in eastern Europe on the northern shore of the Black Sea. With large expanses of fertile farmland, it has been called "the breadbasket of Europe." Since 1921, most of Ukraine has been part of the Soviet Union. The remainder lies in Poland, Romania, and Czechoslovakia.

THE PIONEERS

Ukrainians settled in Canada in three main waves of migration: 1891 to 1914, 1919 to 1939, and 1947 to 1954. The first wave was set off by Ivan Pylypiw and Wasyl Eleniak, who were villagers from the Ukrainian province of Galicia. They took up land on the prairies in 1891, and the following year Pylypiw returned to Ukraine to collect their families. His stories of the plentiful free land caused many of his neighbours to leave for the prairies too. Many more Ukrainians migrated after 1896, when the Canadian government began to advertise in Ukraine with posters and leaflets. By the time World War I started in 1914, about 170 000 Ukrainians had settled on the prairies. Most were from the western Ukrainian provinces of Galicia and Bukovyna.

These first Ukrainian Canadians were hard-working people with experience of farming, but they were not welcomed by their English-speaking neighbours. English Canadians called them "half-civilized peasants in sheepskin coats" and said they would never fit in because they were too different: they spoke a different language, had different customs, and ate different food.

Faced with this prejudice, Ukrainian families drew closer together, both for companionship and to help one another. Many took land in bloc settlements, farming neighbouring homesteads in one area. There they built community halls and churches, started schools, and tried to create villages like those in their homeland. All three Prairie Provinces had a number of Ukrainian bloc settlements.

In the cities, too, Ukrainians tended to live together in one part of town. A large Ukrainian community developed in the North End of Winnipeg. Saskatoon and Edmonton also came to have large Ukrainian communities. At first, it was mostly single men who lived in the cities. They preferred to look for work there, rather than starting a farm on their own.

The cities also became home for Ukrainians who arrived during the sec-

Poster in Ukraine advertising free land in Canada (courtesy NAC/C-6196).

ond wave of migration, 1919 to 1939. About 70 000 migrated during this period. Nearly all arrived in the late 1920s, when Canada was encouraging labourers from other countries to take work on the railways and as miners and lumbermen. Although their work took them far from the main centres, they eventually made their homes in major cities, especially in Ontario.

THE MODERN ERA

The third wave of migration began after World War II ended in 1945. These people were refugees from displaced persons' camps. They differed from the first two waves in that many of them were professional people with technical skills or university educations. About 34 000 Ukrainians arrived in the years immediately following the war. Since then, migration has slowed to a trickle; the Soviet Union makes it very difficult for people to leave Ukraine.

Most of today's Ukrainian Canadians were born in Canada and speak English as their first language. The majority live and work in towns and cities, especially Edmonton (63 000), Winnipeg (59 000), and Toronto (51 000).

The Ukrainian culture has survived in a wide variety of ways, from food (such as perogies) to customs. Many of the customs are connected with religion. They include Easter ceremonies and the painting of *pysanka* (decorated Easter eggs). They also include the traditional Ukrainian Christmas, which is celebrated on January 6. The two main churches among Ukrainians are the Ukrainian Catholic Church and the Ukrainian Greek Orthodox Church. However, many belong to the Roman Catholic and Protestant churches.

The culture is particularly strong in folk arts. It can be seen in decorated pottery and woodcarving, and in the embroidered clothing that is worn on special occasions. Folk-dancing groups keep up centuries-old dances. They also perform

modern versions of these dances. Traditional songs are kept up by music groups. Ukrainian folk tales and poetry are printed in books and journals. Over the years, there have been more than 500 publications in the Ukrainian language.

Ukrainian Dancers *at the Ukrainian Festival in Dauphin, Man. (photo by Menno Fieguth).*

Because so few Ukrainians have immigrated to Canada since 1960, Ukrainian is spoken far less than it used to be. Most of the young people cannot even understand Ukrainian.

Since language is an important part of any culture, a special effort has been made to prevent the Ukrainian language from dying out in Canada. Many schools in the Prairie Provinces and some schools in Ontario offer classes in the Ukrainian language.

Meanwhile, Ukrainian studies programs in language, literature, and history have been started at several universities, and in 1976 the Canadian Institute of Ukrainian Studies was established at the University of Alberta in Edmonton, Alberta.

▷ RELATED ARTICLES: **Ethnic Group; Immigration; Ivan Pylypiw.**

▷ SUGGESTED READING: Jars Balan, *Salt and Braided Bread: Ukrainian Life in Canada* (1984); Marguerite Burke, *The Ukrainian*

Ukrainian Pioneer Women Cutting Logs (courtesy NAC/C-19134)

Ivan Pylypiw

Pioneer Ukrainian settler (*born in 1859 at Nebyliv, Ukraine; died in 1936 at Northbank, Alta*). Ivan Pylypiw (also written **Pillipiw**) and his friend **Wasyl Eleniak** triggered the first wave of Ukrainian migration to Canada. They were villagers in the Ukrainian province of Galicia. The Canadian settlement scheme sounded so promising that the two Ukrainians decided to check it out themselves. They sold some of their farm animals to pay for their passage and in 1891 took a ship to Montreal and travelled by train across the prairies.

While Eleniak took work in Manitoba, Pylypiw returned to Ukraine to collect their families. He arrived home in 1892 and persuaded many of his neighbours to emigrate too. Pylypiw bought their tickets and arranged their passage, but this brought him into trouble with the authorities in Ukraine. He spent a month in prison before leaving with his family in the spring of 1893. Pylypiw settled on the western prairies, where he took a homestead at Bruderheim, northeast of Edmonton.

St Vladimir's Ukrainian Orthodox Church. *The church was restored to its original form and moved to the Ukrainian Heritage Village at Vegreville, Alta (photo by Michael Breuer).*

Dome *of St Vladimir's Ukrainian Orthodox Church (photo by Michael Breuer).*

Harriet Tubman

Heroine of the Underground Railroad, Tubman was born a slave around 1820 on a plantation in Maryland, U.S. She escaped to Canada and in 1851 settled at St Catharines, Canada West [Ont.] in the Niagara Peninsula. She went back to the American South 19 times to help other slaves escape. Some American slave owners offered a reward of $40 000 for her capture, but she was never caught. More than 300 slaves found freedom in Canada through her efforts *(courtesy University of Western Ontario, Special Collections).*

Canadians (1978); Michael Czuboka, *Ukrainian Canadian, Eh?* (1983); William A. Czumer, *Recollections About the Life of the First Ukrainian Settlers in Canada* (1981); Bohdan S. Kordan and Lubomyr Y. Luciuk, editors, *Creating A Landscape: A Geography of Ukrainians in Canada* (1989); Myrna Kostash, *All of Baba's Children* (1977); Yuri Kupchenko, *The Horseman of Shandro Crossing* (1989); Barbara Smucker, *Days of Terror* (1989); Helen Potrebenko, *No Streets of Gold: A Social History of Ukrainians in Alberta* (1977).

■ Ultramontanism

Ultramontanism was a conservative belief that the Roman Catholic Church in French Canada had the duty and the right to oversee almost every aspect of people's lives, including education, politics, the media, and even day-to-day behaviour in order to strengthen and preserve their Catholic faith.

Its influence was particularly strong in the second half of the 1800s. Ultramontanists' intolerance toward more liberal Catholics who wanted to restrict the range of church authority, led to confrontations. Ultramontanist priests often forbade their parishioners to vote for the Liberal Party, which they considered to be revolutionary and a threat to the authority of the Church.

▷ RELATED ARTICLES: **Bishop Ignace Bourget; Guibord Affair; Institut Canadien.**

■ Umiak

A umiak is a large open boat used by some Inuit in coastal areas for transporting their families and possessions during the summer months, and for hunting, particularly whales. Umiaks range in length from 6 to 10 m, and they are sometimes 1.5 m wide at the centre. The frame is made of driftwood, and it is covered with sealskins or walrus hides that have been sewn together with watertight seams. Some umiaks have sails and others are rowed, mainly by women. They can carry more than 20 people.

The Inuit have used umiaks and the smaller hunting boat or kayak for perhaps 4000 years, but these traditional craft are now largely replaced by manufactured boats from the south.

▷ SUGGESTED READING: E.Y. Arima, *Report on an Eskimo Umiak Built at Ivuyivik, P.Q. in the Summer of 1960* (1963). Stephen R. Braund, *The Skin Boats of Saint Lawrence Island, Alaska* (1988).

■ Underground Railroad

The Underground Railroad was a secret network of people who helped escaped slaves from the southern United States make their way north to Canada. The "railroad" was at its most active between 1840 and 1860.

About 30 000 Blacks are thought to have escaped to Canada by this means. It was a great risk to all those involved. They were passed from one safe house to the next, often travelling at night to avoid capture. Many routes were used, most of them leading to Canada West [Ontario]. Whites and Blacks were involved, including some remarkably brave former slaves who had already arrived safely in Canada but returned to guide other fugitives. The most famous was Harriet Tubman, who was known as "Black Moses" because she led her people to freedom.

▷ RELATED ARTICLES: **Blacks; Josiah Henson; Slavery.**

▷ SUGGESTED READING: Rae Bains, *Harriet Tubman: The Road to Freedom* (1983); George Boyd, *Fugitive Girl* (1977); Anne Petry, *Harriet Tubman: Conductor on the Underground Railway* (second edition, 1971); Barbara Smucker, *Underground Railway* (1977).

■ Unemployment

The unemployed are people who want to work but cannot find paying jobs. In an industrial society such as Canada's, the level of unemployment is one important measure of the health of the economy.

KINDS OF UNEMPLOYMENT

Economists describe four kinds of unemployment:

● *Seasonal unemployment* occurs because of the climate; for example, there are fewer jobs in tourism, fishing, and outdoor construction in winter.

● *Cyclical unemployment* results from the ups and downs of the economy. Jobs increase when the economy is running well and decrease when it is not.

● *Structural unemployment* results from basic changes in the economy; for example, when new technology makes certain jobs outdated.

● *Frictional unemployment* arises from the decisions of individual workers; for example, when they decide to find a new job, or to take a break between jobs.

Statistics Canada defines people as unemployed if they fit the following categories:

● they are available for work

● they have been looking for work in the previous four weeks

● they are not waiting for a new job to begin within the next four weeks.

This means that the unemployment rate

does not include people who have more or less given up looking for work.

Since 1975, the official unemployment rate in Canada has been at least 6.9%; that is, 6.9% of Canadians who want to work could not find jobs. In December 1982, the adjusted rate peaked at 12.8%, the highest since the Great Depression of the 1930s when the rate reached nearly 25%. During the rest of the 1980s the rate declined, but many people argue that the Canadian economy will always have some level of unemployment.

Within this national average, there are many variations. Some regions of the country — Atlantic Canada, for example — usually have higher unemployment than the average. Women are more often jobless than men, and the young more often than older workers.

Individual workers suffer more than just a loss of wages from unemployment. Another serious effect is psychological. Society puts great value on having a job, and much of a person's self-esteem comes from his or her job. Unemployment may result in a loss of confidence and self-respect, and a period of high unemployment may bring higher rates of mental and physical illness.

▷ RELATED ARTICLES: **Economy; Unemployment Insurance.**

▷ SUGGESTED READING: R.C. Bellan, *The Unnecessary Evil: An Answer to Canada's High Unemployment* (1986); Patrick Burman, *Killing Time, Losing Ground: Experiences of Unemployment* (1988); Lois Fletcher, Anthony Ford, and Jim Lotz, *Out of School and Out of Work: Youth Unemployment in Canada* (1971); Kevin B. Kerr, *Youth Employment in Canada* (1985).

■ Unemployment Insurance

Unemployment Insurance is a system of payments made to people who are unemployed. It is run by the federal government. Every employee pays a portion of his or her salary into a special fund, where it joins contributions from the employer and the government. If employees lose their job, they receive regular payments from the fund for a certain length of time to help make the effects of unemployment less severe.

The first attempt to have an unemployment insurance scheme was made by Prime Minister R.B. Bennett in 1935. But the Supreme Court declared that such a plan was the responsibility of the provinces, not the federal government. A change was made to the constitution which gave the federal government the power to introduce a national plan, and it did so in 1940.

Unemployed people may collect payments under the system if they have been working for at least 20 weeks, and if they are actively seeking a new job. In 1989, payments were equal to 60% of their former wage, up to a maximum of $363 per week. Applicants collect payments for a limited number of weeks, depending on how long they were employed and the local rate of unemployment.

In 1989 the federal government announced that it was no longer going to contribute to unemployment insurance. Instead the government is going to use its fund to pay for programs to retrain workers in new skills.

■ Unemployment Relief Camps

Unemployment Relief Camps were created by the federal government in 1932, at the height of the Great Depression. They were to provide housing and shelter for single, jobless, homeless Canadian men. So many of these men were wandering the country looking for work that authorities began to fear they might become a threat to law and order.

Camps were run by the Department of Defence but were staffed by civilians. The men cleared bush, built roads, planted trees, and erected public buildings. In return they received room and board, work clothes, medical care, and pay of 20 cents a day.

Although men were in the camps of their own free will, many were discouraged by the lack of real opportunity they offered. In 1935 this unhappiness boiled over into a strike in the British Columbia camps, resulting in the On To Ottawa Trek.

By the time the last camp was closed in June 1936, 170 248 men had stayed in them.

▷ RELATED ARTICLE: **On To Ottawa Trek.**

■ Ungava Bay

Ungava Bay is a large body of water in-

Relief Project in Hope, B.C., March 1935 (courtesy NAC/ PA-35960).

denting the north coast of Quebec. It has long been occupied by Inuit people who hunt seal and fish for char along the uneven shoreline. The first fur-trade post in the bay was Fort Chimo, built in 1830. Akpatok Island, in the middle of the bay, attracts many polar bears in the summer.

Ungava Bay is frozen from November to June. As with the islands in Hudson Bay and James Bay, the islands in it are part of the Northwest Territories. The name means "far away" in the Inuit language.

(all photos courtesy NMC/CMC).

■ Ungava Peninsula

Ungava Peninsula is the extreme northern portion of Quebec, jutting out into Hudson Strait. Inuit have long lived along the coast, but the rugged, treeless interior does not welcome settlement. Large stores of mineral wealth have been found, but so far they are untapped. In 1950 the meteorite crater named Nouveau-Québec was discovered on the peninsula.

■ Uniforms

Uniforms are clothing and accessories (coats, shirts, trousers, jackets, hats,

Regimental Uniforms of Canada

1. North-West Mounted Police

2. 5th Regiment, Royal Highlanders of Canada, Montreal, Que.

3. 22nd Saskatchewan Light Horse, Lloydminster, Sask.

4. 72nd Seaforth Highlanders of Canada, Vancouver, B.C.

5. 24th Kent Regiment, Chatham, Ont.

6. Governor General's Body Guard, Toronto, Ont.

7. 18th Mounted Rifles, Portage la Prairie, Man.

8. Prince Edward Island Light Horse, Charlottetown, P.E.I.

9. 9th Battalion, Volunteer Militia Rifles of Canada

10. Bombardier, Canadian Field Artillery Hamilton, Ont.

11. Rifleman, 30th Wellington Battalion of Rifles

12. Captain, 64th Régiment de Châteauguay et Beauharnois

belts, shoes, and so on) of a similar style worn by people to show that they belong to the same group. In use since ancient times, uniforms today are worn by such varied groups as post office employees, fire and police officers, security guards, and sports teams, though they are most often associated with the military.

At one time, military uniforms were very colourful in order to be able to tell friends from enemies during the confusion of battle. Most soldiers in the British army, for example, wore bright red. Scottish soldiers could be identified by their kilts, and sailors around the world have traditionally worn uniforms of dark "navy" blue. Uniforms were also designed to show the rank or status of a person within the group, with junior ranks having generally simple rank badges, and more senior people (the officers) more colourful — often gold — rank insignia.

Eventually, brightly coloured uniforms became too easy a target for enemies armed with modern rifles. Today, all armies have adopted combat uniforms that are dull brown, green, grey, or of camouflage patterns to help those wearing them blend in with their surroundings. In some armies, the old colourful uniforms have been kept as special parade dress, and these can be seen at such ceremonies as the changing of the guard on Parliament Hill in Ottawa, Ont., or at Buckingham Palace in London, England.

In Canada, military uniforms until 1968 generally followed British traditions. There were separate styles for the navy, army, and air force, and within the army each regiment had its own particular design to show whether it was infantry, artillery, cavalry, or rifles. From 1968 to 1984 all members of the unified Canadian Armed Forces wore dark green, but today soldiers, sailors, and airmen have separate uniforms.

The most famous Canadian uniforms are probably the *bleu-blanc-rouge* (blue-white-red) of the Montreal Canadiens and the one worn as ceremonial dress by the Royal Canadian Mounted Police (brown stetson hat, scarlet tunic, and wide-legged blue trousers with a yellow stripe).

▷ SUGGESTED READING: David Ross, *Military Uniforms: From the Collection of the New Brunswick Museum* (1980); Jack L. Summers and René Chartrand, *Military Uniforms in Canada 1665-1970* (1981).

■ Union Government

The Union Government was a coalition of Conservatives and Liberals which won the federal election of 1917, during World War I. Earlier that year, Prime Minister Robert Borden announced that his government was going to introduce conscription as a way of raising more troops for the war in Europe. Knowing the measure would be unpopular in Quebec, Borden asked Liberal leader Wilfrid Laurier to join him in a coalition. Laurier refused, but many English-speaking members of the Liberal Party joined Borden to form the Union Government and push conscription through Parliament.

The end of the war in November 1918 destroyed the main reason for coalition and the Union began to break apart. When Borden retired in July 1920, the Union Government died.

▷ RELATED ARTICLE: **Conscription.**

■ Union Nationale

The Union Nationale was a Quebec political party founded in 1935. It formed the government of Quebec from 1936 to 1939, from 1944 to 1960, and from 1966 to 1970. It was a strong supporter of French-Canadian nationalism and of provincial rights.

The Union Nationale's greatest successes came under the leadership of Maurice Duplessis, who was premier of Quebec from 1936 to 1939 and from 1944 to 1959, the year of his death. Duplessis was a conservative traditionalist who was supported by business and by the Catholic Church. He made much use of political patronage to maintain his position.

In 1960 Quebec voters rejected the conservatism of the Union Nationale in favour of the modernizing policies of Jean Lesage's Liberal Party. However, in 1966 they re-elected a Union Nationale government, under Daniel Johnson. Johnson's death in 1968 seriously weakened the party and in the 1970s Quebec nationalists switched their support to the new Parti Québécois.

In the 1980s the Union Nationale was reduced to a small handful of members. In 1989, because it had not paid its debts, the Union Nationale lost its official status as a registered political party.

▷ RELATED ARTICLE: **Maurice Duplessis.**

▷ SUGGESTED READING: Richard Jones, *Duplessis and the Union Nationale Administration* (1983).

■ Unions

Unions are groups of working people organized to protect their rights in the workplace.

Top Ten Unions in Canada, by Membership, 1987	
1. Canadian Union of Public Employees[1]	350 019
2. Food and Commercial Workers[2]	184 120
3. United Steelworkers of America[2]	161 926
4. Public Service Alliance[1]	155 615
5. Canadian Auto Workers[1]	146 094
6. Social Affairs Federation[1]	97 408
7. Quebec Teaching Congress[1]	94 252
8. Teamsters[2]	88 957
9. Service Employees[2]	77 835
10. Ontario Public Service Employees[1]	73 900

[1] Canadian Unions
[2] International Unions
Source: Statistics Canada 71-202

First Unions The first unions were formed in the 19th century. They protected members against financial disaster in times of illness or unemployment. Unions were opposed by employers, and sometimes were formed in secrecy.

In 1872 the federal government passed the Trades Union Act making unions legal. Still, many employers would not allow them. Many bitter strikes were fought before unions won wide recognition.

Today, union members make up about 38% of the non-agricultural workforce; 3.6 million Canadians belong to unions. Membership is greatest in British Columbia and Newfoundland, where about 50% of the workforce belongs to unions.

Most early unions were *craft unions*; that is, they joined all the skilled workers in a particular craft or trade. In the late 1930s, *industrial unions* began to grow in Canada. Industrial unions join all workers in a single industry, whatever their skill. Today the most rapidly expanding section of the union movement consists of public-service unions, made up of government employees (for example, teachers, postal workers, and nurses) at the federal, provincial, and municipal levels of government.

Early in this century, most Canadian workers belonged to unions based in the United States. After World War II, Canadian-based unions became stronger. By 1987, 65% of all union members belonged to Canadian unions.

Unions are mainly interested in the wages and working conditions of their members. But they also become involved in political action. The Canadian labour movement as a whole supports the New Democratic Party, but many union members vote for other parties. In order to explain their position on various issues, unions also organize educational and public-relations activities.

Locals Unions are organized into *locals*, which represent all union members in a particular workplace or a particular local area. Each local elects leaders and holds regular meetings. Union locals, in turn, elect representatives to provincial and national organizations.

In addition, different unions work together in *Labour Councils* which consider questions of interest to the labour movement. Each province also has a provincial *Federation of Labour*, which brings together all unions within the province.

At the national level, unions work together in the Canadian Labour Congress (CLC), formed in 1956. Not all unions belong to the CLC. Some belong to the Canadian Federation of Labour, consisting of all the building trades unions; the Confederation of Canadian Unions, a small group of nationalist unions; and the Quebec-based Confederation of National Trades Unions (Confédération des Syndicats Nationaux).

Unions usually make headlines only when they are involved in strikes. However, most labour disputes are settled peacefully without strikes. Much of the work that unions do is unreported in the media; for example, political lobbying, and workplace health and safety. Today unions play an important role in Canadian economic and political life.

▷ RELATED ARTICLES: **Canadian Federation of Labour; Canadian Labour Congress; Confederation of National Trade Unions; Industrial Relations; Labour; Strikes and Lockouts; Trades and Labor Congress of Canada;** and articles under the different unions.

▷ SUGGESTED READING: Claire Mackay, *Pay Cheques and Picket Lines: All About Unions in Canada* (1989); Kenneth Osborne, *Canadians at Work: Labour Unions and Industry* (1983); Bob White, *Hard Bargains: My Life on the Line* (1987).

■ Unitarians

Unitarians are a religious group founded in central Europe in the 16th century. They spread to England and North America in the 18th and 19th centuries. The first congregation in Canada was formed in 1832 in Montreal, Lower Canada [Quebec]. Today there are 44 Unitarian societies in Canada, with a membership of about 5000.

Unitarians hold various beliefs and emphasize the free use of reason in religious thought. They see themselves as being open to inquiry and to advancing scientific truth. They believe that religion is universal rather than specifically Christian, and they include as members people from various religious traditions.

In 1945, Dr Lotta Hitschmanova and the Unitarian groups across Canada founded the Unitarian Service Committee of Canada. Its formal relationship with the Unitarian Church ended in 1948, but it has expanded to include development programs and aid to countries in Africa and Asia.

▷ SUGGESTED READING: Margaret Gooding, *The Canadians: Adventures of our People, The Unitarian Way* (1984); Philip Hewett, *The Unitarian Way* (1985).

■ United Church of Canada

The United Church of Canada is Canada's largest Protestant church. It has about 2 million members and adherents (people connected with the church who are not formal members).

The church was formed on June 10, 1925, through the union of Canadian Methodists, Congregationalists, and 70% of Canadian Presbyterians. In 1968 a second union brought the Evangelical United Brethren into the church.

Since its beginning, the United Church has declared itself to be "not merely a united, but a uniting church." Over the years there have been discussions concerning union with other churches and closer relations with Roman Catholics. It is active within the Canadian Council of Churches and the World Council of Churches.

The church is run by a General Council which meets every two years. The General Council meetings are attended by delegates from across Canada. Each congregation elects its own "elders" to look after its spiritual concerns and "stewards" to take care of financial matters. Congregations choose their own minister. Women may hold any office in the church. Currently, more than 400 United Church ministers are women. In 1980 Dr Lois Wilson became the first woman Moderator of the United Church. This is the top office of the church and is elected by delegates at the General Council meeting. Lay people (members who are not ordained ministers) may also become Moderator, as in 1968 when Dr Robert MacLure, a medical missionary, was elected to that post.

The United Church has always fought for improvements on social issues such as poverty, housing needs, native rights, labour relations, and prison conditions. It maintains special centres across Canada to help men, women, and youth suffering from unemployment, drug or alcohol addiction, and physical or sexual abuse. It also runs mission boats and hospitals in isolated areas. Its Mission and Service Fund contributes millions of dollars to projects in developing countries around the world.

Sometimes the United Church becomes involved in issues that are not popular with its own members. The latest church statistics show that in 1988 the United Church recorded its sharpest membership decline in ten years. At the end of 1988, church rolls listed 849 401 members, a drop of 14 500 from 1987. Some of this loss of membership has been attributed to a dispute over the ordination of homosexuals. In August 1988 the General Council adopted a policy that all church members, regardless of sexual orientation, can be considered for the ministry. This caused a major controversy within the church that has still not been resolved.

The highest membership in the United Church was recorded in 1965 at 1 064 033.

▷ SUGGESTED READING: Steven Chambers, *Voices and Visions: 65 Years of the United Church of Canada* (1990); Charles Haddon Spurgeon Dawes, *Just Being Around: Reminiscences of a Small Town United Church Minister* (1988); Stuart Geggie and Norma Geggie, *Unto The Hills: A History of the United Church in Canada* (1976); Lois Wilson, *Turning the World Upside Down: A Memoir* (1989).

■ United Empire Loyalists, *see* Loyalists

■ United Farmers of Alberta

The United Farmers of Alberta (UFA) was founded in Edmonton in 1909 to promote policies of benefit to farmers. For many years (1916-31) the organization was led by Henry Wise Wood, a popular champion of farmers' causes.

The UFA sponsored candidates in both the federal and provincial elections in 1921, and a majority of those candidates was elected. The UFA members of Parliament acted as part of the Progressive Party until 1924, when a number of them broke away to form the Ginger Group. In 1932, members of the Ginger Group helped form the Co-operative Commonwealth Federation.

In provincial politics, the UFA formed

the government of Alberta from 1921 to 1935. Its most effective premier was John Brownlee, who led a cautious, rather conservative administration. Health and educational services in the province were improved, and the government tried to meet the financial and marketing needs of the farmers. It was unable to deal effectively with the Depression, however, and in 1935 was defeated by the Social Credit Party.

United Farmers of Canada

The United Farmers of Canada (UFC) was founded in 1926. It was more radical than most farmers' organizations, and during the late 1920s vigorously promoted the idea that the government should take over the marketing of all grain. During the 1930s, it entered politics on a moderate socialist platform, allying itself in 1932 with the Independent Labour Party to form the Farmer-Labour Group. In 1934 this group joined the Co-operative Commonwealth Federation. The UFC was particularly strong in Saskatchewan and Alberta, although its influence declined in the 1950s. During the 1960s, it evolved into the National Farmers Union.

▷ RELATED ARTICLE: **National Farmers Union.**

United Farmers of Manitoba

The United Farmers of Manitoba (UFM) was founded in 1920. It advocated political reforms to make government more responsive to the wishes of the people, and economic reforms to help the farmers. In 1921 it sponsored candidates of the Progressive movement in the federal election, 12 of whom were elected, including T.A. Crerar, the Progressives' first leader. In 1922 the UFM won the provincial election, forming a government led by John Bracken. Interest in political activity declined rapidly among members thereafter. In 1924 the UFM withdrew its support of the Progressives in Ottawa, and in 1928 withdrew from provincial politics as well. Some of the economic reforms advocated by the UFM, like the co-operative marketing of grain, were eventually achieved, but its political reforms were not. In 1939 the UFM became the Manitoba Federation of Agriculture. Today it is called the Manitoba Farm Bureau.

▷ RELATED ARTICLE: **John Bracken.**

United Farmers of Ontario

The United Farmers of Ontario (UFO) was formed in 1914 to promote the interests of farmers in Ontario. In 1919, with over 50 000 members, the UFO entered politics and won the largest number of seats in the provincial election. In coalition with the Independent Labour Party, the UFO formed the government. Led by Premier E.C.Drury, the UFO passed several important measures, including a mothers' allowance, a minimum wage act, and a ban on the sale of liquor. But the government lost support, and in the election of 1923 it fell from power.

The UFO never regained its popularity, and in 1944 it merged with other farm groups to form the Ontario Federation of Agriculture.

▷ RELATED ARTICLE: **E.C. Drury.**

▷ SUGGESTED READING: Charles Murray Johnston, *E.C. Drury: Agrarian Idealist* (1987).

United Farmers of Quebec

The United Farmers of Quebec (UFQ) was a farmers' organization founded in 1920 in an attempt to associate the farmers of Quebec with the United Farmers movement in English Canada. The next year it helped form a farmers' political party, the Progressive Farmers of Quebec. Much of the party's political platform was based on that of the English-Canadian Progressive movement, although it also included some of Henri Bourassa's nationalist ideas. It sponsored 21 candidates in the 1921 federal election, but was able to attract few votes. The UFQ never recovered from this defeat, and by 1924 the organization had given way to the new Catholic Union of Farmers.

United Nations

The United Nations (UN) is a place where representatives of the countries of the world meet to find ways of keeping the peace and acting together to solve national and international problems such as too many armaments and Third World poverty. Its headquarters are in New York, U.S.

Membership The UN, which replaced the League of Nations, was begun on October 24, 1945, with Canada and 50 other members. None of the enemy nations from World War II, such as Japan and Germany, were members at first. Japan joined in 1956, and East and West Germany in 1973. By 1990, there were 160 member countries.

Organization Every UN member is represented in the *UN General Assembly*, a body that meets every year and sometimes in special sessions. Among other functions, the Assembly discusses world problems, makes recommendations, controls the UN budget, and holds elections for many UN positions.

The *UN Security Council* has the main responsibility for the keeping of world peace. It has 15 member countries: five are permanent members (China, France, the United Kingdom, the Soviet Union, and the United States); the other ten are elected by the General Assembly for two-year terms. Canada was elected to the Security Council in 1948-49, 1958-59, 1967-68, 1977-78, and 1989-90.

The vote of nine of the 15 members of the Council is needed before a decision is made. On all important questions, each permanent member has a veto; that is, a vote against an idea by a permanent member means that no action will be taken.

The Security Council looks into and makes recommendations about any problems which its members think threaten peace. Unlike the General Assembly, the Security Council can make decisions that bind all UN members.

The General Assembly recommends and the Security Council appoints the Secretary-General, the chief public servant and spokesperson of the UN. The Secretary-General heads the Secretariat, a large group of administrators from all over the world who help run the UN.

Korean War In 1950, the Security Council (with the Soviet Union absent) decided to send a military force to help South Korea fight back against the invaders from North Korea. Canadian troops were part of the UN force in Korea.

Peacekeeping Usually the Security Council tries to work in peaceful ways — trying to bring quarrelling parties together, encouraging cease-fires, and sending peacekeeping forces to troubled parts of the world.

Peacekeeping is a major UN activity, and Canadians are among the world's best-known peacekeepers. We have contributed soldiers (and sometimes civilians) to every major UN peacekeeping operation. In 1957, Lester B. Pearson was given the Nobel Peace Prize for his part in the UN's dramatic sending of a peace-keeping force to the Middle East at the time of the Suez Crisis.

Economic and Social Co-operation The UN does a great deal of research, helping member governments, and encouraging co-operation between countries in such areas as trade, human rights, and refugees.

Many agencies that promote economic and social co-operation are linked to the UN, such as the International Bank for

Reconstruction and Development (World Bank), the United Nations Educational, Scientific and Cultural Organization (UNESCO), and the World Health Organization (WHO). Although bodies like these largely run their own affairs, they get important assistance from the UN.

Lester B. Pearson at the June 27, 1955, meeting of the United Nations (courtesy United Nations/46731).

CANADA'S PART IN THE UNITED NATIONS

The UN can be very frustrating to those who seek action. It is hard to get so many countries to work together. Canada strongly supported the creation of the North Atlantic Treaty Organization (NATO) in 1949 because we believed that the UN was not doing enough to stop aggression and keep the peace.

UN Peacekeeping operation in Cyprus, 1988 (Canadian Forces Photo/photo by Sgt John Smith).

Even so, Canada has always supported the UN. It is a dangerous world. Co-operation is better than conflict, especially for a smaller power. We believe in peaceful approaches to the world's troublesome problems. We also like the UN because it is a place where many nations come together and we do not feel the power of the United States so strongly.

Right from the beginning, many Canadians have played a big part in the success of the UN. A Canadian was the first head of the WHO. Another set up and led for 20 years the Division of Human Rights in the UN Secretariat. Another was a long-serving judge on the UN court, the International Court of Justice. Yet another was the first Executive Director of the UN Environment Program.

These are just examples, and there have been hundreds of other Canadian employees at the UN over the years, as well as thousands of Canadian peacekeepers who have served around the world.

▷ SUGGESTED READING: Raymond Carroll, *The Future of the United Nations* (1985); Douglas Roche, *United Nations: Divided World* (1984); Harold Woods, *The United Nations* (1985).

■ United Nations World Heritage Site

In 1972, Canada and other member nations of UNESCO (the United Nations Educational, Scientific and Cultural Organization) agreed to recognize and protect places all over the world which have outstanding universal significance because of their natural or cultural values. Such places are called World Heritage Sites.

World Heritage Sites in Canada are designated by UNESCO, but protecting them and maintaining them is left up to the Canadian government or a local government. Through the World Heritage Fund, Canada assists in protecting heritage sites in Canada and elsewhere in the world.

■ United Steelworkers of America

The United Steelworkers of America is one of the largest unions of non-government workers in Canada. It had 160 000 members in 1989. It began in 1936 with an attempt to convince workers in the steel industry to join a union. By 1946 the union was well established and today includes workers from many industries. It is an international union, with headquarters in the United States. The Canadian national office is in Toronto, Ont.

■ Unity

Unity, Sask., is situated in west-central Saskatchewan. It began in 1908 as a railway townsite. The centre of a grain-growing district, it also profits from nearby salt and natural gas deposits. Unity was the site of the first attempt to mine potash in Canada. The population in 1986 was 2471.

For further information, contact the Town Clerk, P.O. Box 1030, Unity, Sask., S0K 4L0.

■ University

A university is an institution of higher education. It takes students who have completed their high-school education and prepares them for degrees.

The first universities originated in Europe in the 12th and 13th centuries. Their courses of study (*curriculum*) consisted of the "Seven Liberal Arts" (arithmetic, geometry, grammar, rhetoric, music, astronomy, and logic). Universities were closely connected with the church, and many of their students became priests and church officials.

In Canada, university education can be traced back to 1663, when Bishop Laval established a seminary for training priests in Quebec City. In 1852 this became Laval University. In English Canada, the first universities were King's College (Windsor, N.S., 1789), Dalhousie (Halifax, N.S., 1818), and McGill (Montreal, Que., 1821). At the time of Confederation in 1867, there were 17 degree-granting institutions in Canada. Thirteen of them were connected with various churches, and most of them had less than 100 students.

By 1939, Canada had 32 universities. Although most were still connected with churches, those that had no religious connection had most of the enrolment. They offered a wide range of programs, including arts, science, medicine, engineering, education, social work, and so on. They had over 35 000 full-time students. These students were mostly male.

Expansion Universities developed rapidly after World War II. The war had shown the importance of the kind of scientific and technical research that universities could provide. The end of the war in 1945 brought 53 000 veterans into universities. Changes in the Canadian economy increased the demand for workers who were better educated. By the 1960s, the post-war "baby boom" also increased the numbers of university-age students.

University education expanded greatly in the 1960s. Enrolment increased to four times that of 1939. Over 18 000 new professors were hired, many from Britain and the U.S., since there were not enough qualified Canadians. Many new universities were built, including Carleton (Ottawa, 1957), York (Toronto, 1959), Waterloo (1959), Victoria (1963), Trent (Peterborough, 1963), and Calgary (1966).

Today there are over 65 universities in Canada, with nearly 500 000 full-time students. Their expenditure is roughly $6.5 billion a year.

Funding The funding of universities has changed over time. By World War II it was realized that private funding was inadequate. In 1951, as a result of the efforts of the Royal Commission on National Development in Arts, Letters and Sciences (the Massey Commission), the federal government began paying grants directly to universities. Education is a provincial responsibility, so this federal funding created some friction. In 1977 the system was changed. The federal government now gives money to the provinces, which are then supposed to use it for both health and education.

Thus, by the 1980s, universities had become very dependent on government funding. This raised problems. Since university education is a major government expenditure, governments argued that they should have a right to control what universities did. Universities replied by defending their traditional claims to freedom and independence. In most provinces, the dispute was dealt with by establishing a University Grants Commission. This is an independent body, which advises governments on university funding.

Independence Universities take their independence seriously. University professors have *academic freedom*, which is the right to research, teach, and publish whatever they choose, provided it meets standards of truth and fairness. They also have the right of *tenure*, which means that they cannot be dismissed or demoted except for incompetence. Thus, they do not have to worry that their jobs will be threatened if they write or say unpopular things. Most decisions within universities are made by academic committees. At the same time, the increasing size, expense, and complexity of universities have given more power to professional managers. Some university professors fear that they are losing their control. As a result, in the 1970s and 1980s, most university staffs organized faculty unions or associations which negotiate collective agreements. The national organization of university professors is the Canadian Association of University Teachers.

Future Today, the major problem faced by universities is lack of funding. Universities and governments are committed to making it possible for all qualified students to attend. However, funding has not kept up with the costs of increasing enrolment and of research expenses so that, by the beginning of the 1990s, universities faced a financial crisis.

▷ SUGGESTED READING: Paul Axelrod and John G. Reid, editors, *Youth, University and Canadian Society: Essays in the Social History of Higher Education* (1989); Dennis Field, Grant Gilchrist, and Nancy Gray, editors, *First Year University: A Survival Guide* (1989); Linda Frum, *Linda Frum's Guide to Canadian Universities* (1989).

■ University College of Cape Breton

The University College of Cape Breton is located in Sydney, N.S. It offers bachelor's degrees in arts, arts community studies, business administration, and science. It also has continuing education and co-operative work-study programs, and offers preparatory programs in engineering, computer science, and physical education.

The university began in 1974 when the Sydney campus of Saint Francis Xavier University and the Nova Scotia Eastern Institute of Technology amalgamated. The College of Cape Breton, as the amalgamation was called, gained university status and assumed its present name in 1982. There are 1200 full-time students. For further information, write the Registrar's Office, University College of Cape Breton, Sydney, N.S., B1P 6L2.

■ University of Alberta

The University of Alberta is located in Edmonton, Alta. It is Canada's second-largest English-language university. It has a wide range of programs, from agriculture to zoology, and from business to sociology. Students receive degrees at the bachelor's, master's, and doctoral levels. It has more than 20 research centres and institutes. The U of A is a leader in a number of areas, such as computing science, microelectronics, engineering, physical education, and fine arts. Faculté Saint-Jean is the only faculty in western Canada where students are taught entirely in French. Students can also get a degree in the new program of native studies.

The U of A was founded in 1906 and classes began two years later. Since then, over 120 000 students have graduated. Its affiliated institutions are St Stephen's College, St Joseph's College, Camrose

---

BA, MA, PhD

● **BA** (*Baccalaureus*) is the first degree. It is given to one who is not yet a master. Our word bachelor (one who is not yet married) comes from the same origin. BA means Bachelor of Arts. There is also BSc (Bachelor of Science), and others.

● **MA** (*Master's*) goes back to when one mastered one's craft. It is a degree above BA.

● **PhD** is the highest degree awarded by a university. It is also called a *doctorate*, and whoever completes it may be called "doctor." The "Ph" refers to philosophy, for in the early days all advanced learning was considered to be philosophy.

Lutheran College, Concordia Lutheran College, and King's College, all in Alberta. Two other affiliated institutions have become autonomous: the University of Calgary and the University of Lethbridge.

The U of A campus is one of the largest and most beautiful in the country. Its first-class facilities attract major international events including the Commonwealth Games and the World University Games.

There are over 25 000 full-time undergraduate and graduate students at the U of A. For further information, write the Registrar's Office, University of Alberta, Edmonton, Alta, T6G 2E1.

▷ Suggested Reading: Walter H. Johns, *A History of the University of Alberta 1908-1969* (1981).

■ University of British Columbia

The University of British Columbia is located in Vancouver, B.C. It has 12 fac-

ulties, ten schools, and more than a dozen institutes and research centres. It offers degree programs at the bachelor's, master's, and doctoral levels. UBC is one of Canada's largest universities, and also one of the country's major research centres. For instance, some of its specializations are forestry, biotechnology, computer science, Pacific Rim studies, fine and performing arts, biomedical imaging, pulp and paper engineering, genetics, and international business research.

UBC was founded in 1908 but did not actually begin operations until 1915. In the interim, denominational colleges affiliated with McMaster, Toronto, and McGill universities provided higher education in the province. UBC's present site, on Point Grey, was selected in 1910 and it moved there in 1925. From 1920 to 1963 Victoria College in Victoria, B.C., was affiliated with UBC. Nowadays, the Vancouver School of Theology, St Mark's College, and Regent College have formal affiliations to the university. There are over 20 600 full-time undergraduate and graduate students. For further information, write the Registrar's Office, University of British Columbia, Vancouver, B.C., V6T 1W5.

▷ Suggested Reading: George Woodcock and Tim Fitzharris, *The University of British Columbia: A Souvenir* (1986).

■ University of Calgary

The University of Calgary is located in Calgary, Alta. It offers bachelor's, master's, and doctoral degrees. Programs are offered in many areas, including arts, fine arts, science, commerce, engineering, education, nursing, medicine, environmental design, law, and social sciences. Its social welfare program is the only one in the province.

The university began in 1946 as a branch of the University of Alberta's Faculty of Education. Called the University of Alberta, Calgary Branch, it moved to its present site in 1960. In 1966 it became a fully autonomous institution. Now, affiliated colleges are Mount Royal College and Medicine Hat College.

There are over 16 800 full-time undergraduate and graduate students at the U of C. For further information, write the Registrar's Office, University of Calgary, Calgary, Alta, T2N 1N4.

■ University of Guelph

The University of Guelph is located in Guelph, Ont. Through its seven academic colleges, it offers degrees at the undergraduate and graduate levels. Programs include arts and science, agriculture and veterinary medicine, family and consumer studies, hotel and food administration, landscape architecture, and engineering.

Although the university was founded in 1964, its roots go back to the 19th century. In 1862 Andrew Smith founded the Ontario Veterinary College, which moved to Guelph in 1922. In 1874 near Guelph, the Ontario Agricultural College was founded as the Ontario School of Agriculture. These two colleges and the Macdonald Institute, which was founded in 1903 to promote domestic science, were affiliated with the University of Toronto. In 1964, however, the three colleges joined to form what is now the University of Guelph.

The university has over 11 000 full-time undergraduate and graduate students. For further information, write the Registrar's Office, University of Guelph, Guelph, Ont., N1G 2W1.

University of King's College

The University of King's College is located in Halifax, N.S. It offers undergraduate degrees in arts, science, and journalism. It is Canada's oldest university. The Anglican Church founded it as a Loyalist college in 1789 at Windsor, N.S. It began granting degrees in 1802. In 1920 a fire resulted in reduced circumstances for the university. It moved to Halifax, and since 1923 it has shared a faculty of arts and science with Dalhousie University.

The university has over 600 full-time undergraduate students. For further information, write the Registrar's Office, University of King's College, Halifax, N.S., B3H 2A1.

▷ SUGGESTED READING: Mark Dewolf, *1789, All the King's Men: The Story of a Colonial University* (1972).

University of Laval

Laval University is located in Ste-Foy, adjacent to Quebec City, Que. It offers many programs through its 12 faculties, nine schools, and three interdisciplinary research centres.

Laval began in Quebec City in 1852. It was the first francophone Roman Catholic university in North America. It was named after Bishop Laval, who had founded the parent institution, the Séminaire de Québec in 1663. In 1876, Laval University founded another campus, in Montreal, which in due course has developed into the University of Montreal. In

University of Laval, Quebec City, was founded in 1852 (courtesy Environment Canada, Parks).

the 1950s, Laval moved into Ste-Foy. The campus combines modern and historic architecture. Recently, Laval University moved back to the historic buildings of the Séminaire de Québec where a second campus has been founded.

There are nearly 23 000 full-time undergraduate and graduate students. For further information, write the Registrar's Office, Laval University, Cité Universitaire, Quebec City, Que., G1K 7P4.

University of Lethbridge

The University of Lethbridge is located in southern Alberta in the city of Lethbridge. It offers undergraduate degrees in arts and science, education, management, fine arts, and nursing. It also offers a master's degree in education. It began as the University Section of what is now Lethbridge Community College. It became an autonomous university in 1967. In 1971 it moved to a 185 ha campus designed by architect Arthur Erickson. The

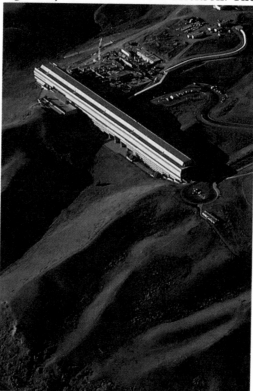

University of Lethbridge, designed by architect Arthur Erickson (photo by J.A. Kraulis).

university's facilities now include the Max Bell Regional Aquatic Centre. It has nearly 2700 full-time undergraduate and graduate students. For further information, write the Registrar's Office, Admissions and Recruitment, University of Lethbridge, 4401 University Drive, Lethbridge, Alta, T1K 2M4.

■ University of Manitoba

The University of Manitoba is located in Winnipeg, Man. It offers programs in many areas through its 20 faculties and schools.

The university was founded in 1877. It was the first institution of higher learning in western Canada. It began with three denominational colleges (St-Boniface, St John's, and Manitoba); other affiliations have occurred throughout the university's development.

There are almost 14 700 full-time undergraduate and graduate students at the University of Manitoba. For further information, write the Admissions Office, University of Manitoba, Winnipeg, Man., R3T 2N2.

■ University of Moncton

The University of Moncton is located on three campuses in Moncton, Edmundston, and Shippagan, N.B. It offers degrees in arts, science and engineering, administration, social sciences, education, and graduate studies. It also has schools of law, forestry, nutrition and family studies, and nursing. Instruction is in French.

The university was founded in 1963 with the amalgamation of three colleges. The campuses are located in the centre of New Brunswick's francophone communities. There are over 4200 full-time undergraduate and graduate students. For further information, write the Registrar's Office, University of Moncton, Moncton, N.B., E1A 3E9.

■ University of Montreal

The University of Montreal is located in Montreal, Que. It has 13 faculties, 60 de-

University of New Brunswick was founded in 1785 as the Provincial Academy of Arts and Sciences (courtesy NAC/ C-23443)

University of Montreal *(photo by Derek Caron/Masterfile).*

partments, schools or institutions, and affiliated schools of commerce and engineering. Its undergraduate and graduate programs cover all disciplines except agriculture and forestry.

The university was founded in 1876. Initially it was a branch of Laval University in Quebec City. It became independent in 1920. Until 1967 it was governed by the Roman Catholic Church. That year the provincial government made it a public, non-denominational institution. There are over 18 200 full-time undergraduate and graduate students, and over 22 200 part-time students at the university. For further information, write the Registrar's Office, University of Montreal, Montreal, Que., H3A 2T5.

■ University of New Brunswick

The University of New Brunswick has campuses in Fredericton and Saint John, N.B. It offers undergraduate and graduate programs in many areas, notably engineering, forestry, science, administration, and arts. The main language of instruction is English, although several courses are offered in French.

The university was founded in 1785 as the Provincial Academy of Arts and Sciences. In 1800 it became the College of New Brunswick, in 1828 King's College, and in 1859 the University of New Brunswick. It was originally based on Anglican ideals, but religious qualifications were abolished in 1846. Women were admitted in 1886. St Thomas University, which offers liberal arts courses, has been associated with the University of New Brunswick since moving from Chatham to Fredericton in 1964.

There are over 7800 full-time undergraduate and graduate students. For further information, write the Registrar's Office, University of New Brunswick, Fredericton, N.B., E3B 5A3.

▷ SUGGESTED READING: Scott Wade, *Behind the Hill* (1967).

University of Ottawa

The University of Ottawa, located in Ottawa, Ont., is Canada's oldest bilingual university. It offers undergraduate and graduate courses. Through its faculties of administration, arts, education, engineering, health sciences (human kinetics, nursing, occupational therapy, physiotherapy), law, medicine, science, and social sciences, and its schools and institutes, it offers a wide variety of programs. In many sectors, teaching is organized in parellel courses in English and French.

The university was founded by the Oblate fathers in 1848. Its original name was the College of Bytown. In 1861 it became the College of Ottawa. It obtained university status in 1866, and assumed its present name at that time. In 1965 it became nondenominational and publicly funded. The faculties of theology and canon law were grouped as the federated St Paul University.

There are nearly 13 000 full-time undergraduate and graduate students. For further information, write the Registrar's Office, University of Ottawa, Ottawa, Ont., K1N 6N5.

University of Prince Edward Island

The University of Prince Edward Island is located in Charlottetown, P.E.I., and is the only university on the Island. It offers undergraduate programs through its faculties of arts, science, and education, and its school of business administration. Students can also study preparatory courses in engineering, agriculture, architecture, dentistry, law, medicine, and veterinary medicine. Since 1986, a doctoral program in veterinary medicine has been offered; UPEI is one of only a few universities in Canada offering such a program.

The university began in 1969. Its antecedents were Prince of Wales College, established in 1834, and St Dunstan's University, which began in 1855. There are now over 2000 full-time students at UPEI. Over 90% of the students come from the Island. For further information, write the Registrar's Office, University of Prince Edward Island, Charlottetown, P.E.I., C1A 4P3.

University of Quebec

The University of Quebec is based in Quebec City. It has campuses in Chicoutimi, Hull, Montreal, Rimouski, Trois-Rivières, and Rouyn. It offers bachelor's, master's, and doctoral degrees in applied and pure sciences, business administration, social sciences, humanities, and arts. Two research institutes, two schools, and a correspondence program complete the U of Quebec's system. Language of instruction is French.

The university was founded in 1968. It was part of the reorganization of Quebec's educational system which took place in the 1960s and 1970s. There are over 27 200 full-time undergraduate and graduate students enroled in the university. Interestingly, there are also over 48 900 part-time students, so University of Quebec's total enrolment makes it one of Canada's largest universities. For further information, write the Registrar's Office, University of Quebec, Quebec City, Que., G1V 2M3.

University of Regina

The University of Regina is located in Regina, Sask. It offers programs in arts, science, fine arts, human justice, journalism, physical activity studies, administration, education, and social work. In some disciplines, a co-operative program alternates studies with paid work experience. Master's and doctoral degrees are offered in some areas. Off-campus registrants may take classes at 30 rural Saskatchewan centres, and television courses are transmitted to Estevan, Moose Jaw, Swift Current, Weyburn, and Yorkton.

The university began in 1911 as Regina College. In 1934 it became affiliated with the University of Saskatchewan in Saskatoon. The first degrees were conferred in 1965. It became an autonomous university in 1974. There are three federated colleges associated with the university: Campion, Luther, and the Saskatchewan Indian Federated College.

There are now almost 5000 full-time undergraduate and graduate students. For further information, write the Communications Office, University of Regina, Regina, Sask., S4S 0A2.

Drake Hall at the University of Regina (photo by Thomas Kitchin).

■ University of Sainte-Anne

Sainte-Anne University is located in Church Point, N.S. It is the province's only francophone university. It offers programs in arts, education, science, business administration, secretarial sciences, and French immersion. It also offers the first two years of a science degree, and diplomas in many programs. Some focus is directed to Acadian language and culture, and to Maritime studies.

The university was founded in 1890 by the Eudist Fathers, a Roman Catholic order. It became non-denominational in 1971. There are over 200 full-time students. For further information, write the Registrar's Office, Sainte-Anne University, Church Point. N.S., B0W 1M0.

■ University of Saskatchewan

The University of Saskatchewan is located in Saskatoon, Sask. It offers most academic programs in arts, science, agriculture, engineering, law, pharmacy, commerce, medicine, education, physical education, nursing, graduate studies, and dentistry. Programs of special interest are agriculture and veterinary medicine, and Indian education and studies.

The university began in 1907, although its roots date from 1879 when the Church of England established Emmanuel College in Prince Albert. Throughout its history the university has had several junior colleges affiliated with it. One of these junior colleges is now the University of Regina.

The University of Saskatchewan has what many consider to be the most beautiful campus in Canada. There are over 13 000 full-time undergraduate and graduate students. For further information, write the Registrar's Office, University of Saskatchewan, Saskatoon, Sask., S7N 0W0.

▷ Suggested Reading: Michael Hayden, *Seeking A Balance: The University of Saskatchewan 1907-1982* (1983).

■ University of Sherbrooke

The University of Sherbrooke is located on two campuses in Sherbrooke, Que. It offers bachelor's, master's, and doctoral degrees in many subjects. Its nine faculties are administration, arts, law, education, physical education and sports, medicine, theology, and science. Students come from across Quebec and overseas. Language of instruction is French.

The university began in 1954. There are over 8600 full-time undergraduate and graduate students. For more information,

Walkway at the University of Toronto (photo by J.A. Kraulis).

write the Registrar's Office, University of Sherbrooke, Sherbrooke, Que., J1K 2R1.

■ University of Toronto

The University of Toronto is Canada's largest English-language university. Located in the heart of Toronto, it offers a wide variety of programs at the bachelor's, master's, and doctoral levels. Throughout its history, the U of T has had many famous students and faculty, including authors, scientists, politicians, historians, educators, lawyers, and business people.

The U of T began as King's College in 1827 and became the University of Toronto in 1850. Affiliated denominational colleges were Trinity College, University College, Victoria College, St Michael's College, Knox College, Wycliffe College, and Emmanuel College. Early faculties were law and medicine, dentistry, and engineering. Today, faculties at the U of T are applied science and engineering, architecture and landscape architecture, arts and science, dentistry, education, forestry, nursing, pharmacy, social work, management, and library and information science. Research institutions to broaden the U of T's international reputation were the Royal Ontario Museum, Connaught Medical Laboratories, and the David Dunlap Observatory. There are now 22 graduate centres and institutes dealing with such areas as biomedical engineering, industrial relations, and transportation.

Today, in addition to the main downtown Toronto campus, the U of T system includes suburban campuses at Scarborough College and Erindale College. New College and Innis College were established in the early 1960s to expand the undergraduate system. The Ontario Institute for Studies in Education is the graduate school of education. The U of T and OISE together have over 34 000 full-

Hart House, University of Toronto (photo by Hartill Associates).

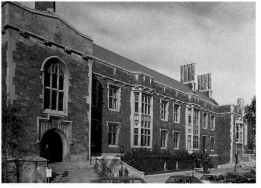

time undergraduate and graduate students. For further information, write the Admissions Office, University of Toronto, Toronto, Ont., M5S 1A1.

▷ SUGGESTED READING: Ian Montagnes and Rudi Christl, *The University of Toronto: A Souvenir* (1984).

■ University of Victoria

The University of Victoria is located in Victoria, B.C. It offers degrees in arts and science, education, law, engineering, fine arts, graduate studies, and human and social development. Unique or special programs include public administration, health information science, child and youth care, and co-operative education. The Faculty of Fine Arts is a group of departments of theatre, creative writing, visual arts, music, and history in art.

The university began as Victoria College in 1903. At first, it was affiliated with McGill University in Montreal. After the University of British Columbia opened in Vancouver in 1915, Victoria College closed for five years. Upon reopening, it was affiliated with UBC until 1963 when it became a fully autonomous university and moved to its present site.

There are over 7400 full-time undergraduate and graduate students. For further information, write the Registrar's Office, University of Victoria, Victoria, B.C., V8W 2Y2.

▷ SUGGESTED READING: Rosemary Neering, *The Story of the University of Victoria and its Origins in Victoria College* (1988).

■ University of Waterloo

The University of Waterloo is located in Waterloo, Ont. It offers undergraduate, graduate, and research programs through the faculties of arts, engineering, environmental studies, human kinetics and leisure studies, independent studies, mathematics, and science. The university has special expertise in the areas of computer science, mathematics, and engineering. It has four church-related colleges affiliated with it.

The university began in 1957 and was provincially chartered in 1959. It offered Canada's first co-operative education program, whereby students alternate four-month terms on campus and on the job.

There are almost 16 000 full-time undergraduate and graduate students. For further information, write the Registrar's Office, University of Waterloo, Waterloo, Ont., N2L 3G1.

■ University of Western Ontario

The University of Western Ontario, located in London, Ont., offers programs in many academic disciplines at the undergraduate and graduate levels. Its faculties include medicine, law, music, graduate studies, business administration, engineering, education, dentistry, library and information science, and journalism. French immersion courses have been offered since 1933. Western also has specialized institutes and research centres.

The university began in 1878 as Western University of London. Founded by the Anglican Church, it became non-denominational in 1908. Its present name was assumed in 1923. Over its development it has been affiliated with several colleges, notably what are now the University of Waterloo and Wilfrid Laurier University.

Western has over 18 000 full-time undergraduate and graduate students. For further information, write the Registrar's Office, University of Western Ontario, London, Ont., N6A 3K7.

■ University of Windsor

The University of Windsor is located in Windsor, Ont. It has 110 undergraduate programs and 44 graduate programs. Windsor's faculties are arts, science, business administration, education, social science, engineering, human kinetics, law, and graduate studies and research. It also has schools that offer programs in performing and visual arts, social work, nursing, and computer sciences.

The university was incorporated by the province of Ontario in 1962, although it began in 1857 as Assumption College. It was affiliated with what is now the University of Western Ontario from 1919 to 1953. There are nearly 8500 full-time undergraduate and graduate students. For further information, write the Registrar's Office, University of Windsor, Windsor, Ont., N9B 3P4.

■ University of Winnipeg

The University of Winnipeg, located in downtown Winnipeg, Man., offers programs in the natural sciences, humanities, and social sciences. The university also offers a graduate program in theology and, in a joint arrangement with the University of Manitoba, provides master's-level programs in history, religious studies, and public affairs.

The University's Collegiate Division, located on campus, provides a Grade 11 and 12 high-school program in day and evening sessions throughout the year. Faculty at the university are involved in research in a variety of fields. Recent in-

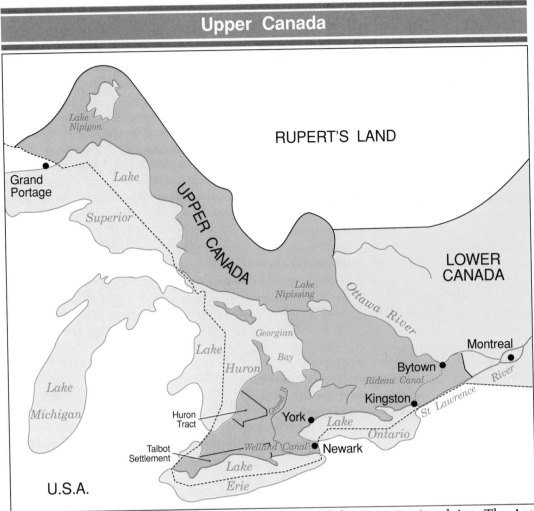

Upper Canada

RUPERT'S LAND

LOWER CANADA

UPPER CANADA

Lake Nipigon

Grand Portage

Lake Superior

Lake Nipissing

Ottawa River

Montreal

Bytown

Georgian Bay

Lake Huron

Rideau Canal

Kingston

Lake Michigan

Grand R.

York

St. Lawrence River

Huron Tract

Welland Canal

Newark

Lake Ontario

Talbot Settlement

Lake Erie

U.S.A.

ternational ventures include remote-sensing projects in Egypt, co-operative arrangements with Ben Gurion University in Israel, and the development of child-care education in Peru.

The annual Manitoba Schools Science Symposium, the largest in Canada, is held on campus each spring. An Enrichment Mini-Course program, held for one week in May each year, allows gifted high-school students to attend the university to study one course in-depth.

The university's roots derive from United College. United was founded in 1938 through the amalgamation of Manitoba College and Wesley College, both of which were established in the late 19th century. United College was for a time affiliated with the University of Manitoba, also in Winnipeg.

The university has over 2900 full-time undergraduate and graduate students. For further information, write the Registrar's Office, University of Winnipeg, Winnipeg, Man., R3B 2E9.

■ Upper Canada

Upper Canada was created in 1791 by the terms of the Constitutional Act. The Act divided the old Province of Quebec into Upper Canada and Lower Canada. Upper Canada was the area of present-day southern Ontario, along the "upper" section of the St Lawrence River. Lower Canada was farther "down" the river. The boundary between the two was the Ottawa River, which today still separates the provinces of Ontario and Quebec. The head of both colonies was the British governor general in Quebec City.

The area of Upper Canada was first settled by the native people. The Huron, Petun, and Neutral lived around Georgian Bay and north of Lake Erie. To the north of them, along the edge of the Canadian Shield, were the Algonquian groups (the Ottawa and the Ojibwa). The French established fur-trade posts near present-day Toronto, Kingston, and Windsor. They also built a mission among the Huron in 1639. After the French defeat in the Seven Years' War (1756-63), the area passed to British hands. From 1763 to 1791, it was part of the old Province of Quebec. Its wilderness remained almost untouched until the end of the American

Upper Canada

Farming during the settlement period involved all the members of the family. In the spring the ground had to be plowed, harrowed, and planted.

For big jobs such as shearing a flock of sheep or building a new house or barn, friends, relatives, and neighbours would gather together for a work bee. When the job was done, everyone sat down to a big dinner and afterward enjoyed dancing.

Craftsmen were very important in the small rural communities. The blacksmith for example would shoe oxen and horses, repair the wheels of wagons and carts, and make tools.

Spring in Upper Canada was a very busy time for the early settlers. They depended on themselves and their communities to provide food, clothing, and shelter.

During the winter season, farmers would clear the land to make new fields. The logs would be hewn for building houses or barns, or taken to the sawmill to be cut into finished lumber. The stumps would be pulled out of the ground, put into piles and burnt to make pot ashes. Lye was made by leaching water through the ashes. It was added to melted tallow and lard to make soap.

Early farmers in Upper Canada usually kept only enough animals to supply themselves with meat, eggs, and dairy products. The only ways to preserve these foods were salting, smoking, and pickling. When the winter's food supply ran low, settlers relied on hunting and crops they had stored.

In the early spring sugar maples were tapped. The sap was collected in buckets and boiled down in large iron pots to make maple syrup and sugar (*artwork by Lewis Parker*).

Revolution, when Loyalist refugees moved to safety across the border.

By 1784, between 5000 and 6000 Loyalists had settled along the St Lawrence River, around present-day Kingston; others settled in the Niagara Peninsula. The Loyalists were soon joined by other American immigrants looking for land, and by 1790 the area had a population of about 10 000.

It was not long before the new immigrants demanded a change in the Quebec Act of 1774. This Act protected the language and religious rights of the French Canadians. The new English-speaking settlers wanted their own government. The solution was to divide Quebec. Lower Canada would still be primarily French. Upper Canada would serve the needs of the Loyalists. Both would continue to be under the authority of the British governor general in Quebec City.

The Constitutional Act gave each colony a lieutenant-governor, an Executive Council, a Legislative Council, and a Legislative Assembly. Only the Assembly was elected. Power was firmly in the hands of the governors and councils, which were responsible not to the Assembly but to the British Crown. Nevertheless, the Assembly had the important power to raise taxes.

In Upper Canada the Act set aside one-seventh of all lands in the province to support the Church of England. Later, another one-seventh of the land was held by the Crown to help support the costs of building roads and other services. These measures would help to keep Upper Canada British, but they would also cause conflict later.

Economy Upper Canada's economy depended on the growing of wheat. Each year, more of the forests were cleared and the harvest of wheat grew bigger. Much of this wheat was shipped to Great Britain and to Lower Canada. Many farmers spent their winters cutting trees. They helped the lumbermen get logs ready to be floated down on the spring floods.

In the Ottawa Valley, the timber trade was the most important activity. The industry grew after Philemon Wright built a sawmill at Hull (across the river from present-day Ottawa) around 1800. It grew further as Great Britain gave special rates to Canadian timber. The timber trade gave rise to a very different society from the rest of Upper Canada. Life in the shanties and on the rafts was rough. The competition, and frequent fights, between the French Canadians and the Irish became legendary.

Upper Canada's economy grew slowly because of its poor transportation system. The St Lawrence River was blocked by rapids near Montreal. Lakes Erie and Ontario were separated by Niagara Falls. The province's roads were quagmires of mud during much of the spring and summer. The French Canadians in the Lower Canada Assembly opposed spending money on canals on the St Lawrence River. The British were willing to build a canal, but they were more concerned with defence than with commerce. The route they chose followed the Rideau River from Kingston to Bytown (the future Ottawa). With its many stone locks and blockhouses, the Rideau Canal was the most expensive project ever undertaken in North America by the British. It was begun in 1826 and opened in 1832.

Upper Canadians had more success with a canal connecting Lakes Erie and Ontario. William Merritt was the driving force behind the Welland Canal. Work began on the canal in 1824. Before it was completed in 1829, it had cost the province a great deal of money. Nevertheless, the canal was a great help to traffic moving between the lakes.

Daily Life The first task that every newcomer to Upper Canada faced was to erect a log cabin and begin to clear the dense forest. Many settlers did not have nails, so wooden pegs were used instead. Windows were covered with paper or cloth. Crops could not be planted among the trees. They needed sunlight, rain, and freshly ploughed earth. Thus, the pioneer family had to cut down the trees and then haul away the logs and burn them. The ashes left by the burning, called potash, were used, or were sold to make soap. As a family cleared more land, it could begin to sell its crops to a nearby town. The pioneer family had to make its own furniture and clothing, and provide its own fuel. Women worked in the fields, tended a vegetable gardens, milked the cows, cooked, washed clothes, and took care of the children. Farm children had little time to play. While there were moments of celebration, life in the backwoods could be very lonely.

Life in cities was more comfortable for the successful merchants. The governor and other British officials lived in pleasant houses and were attended by servants. The British soldiers stationed in the province added greatly to the social life through sporting events and dances.

Population The War of 1812 ended immigration from the United States. Future immigrants came from Great Britain. By 1838, the population had grown to more than 400 000. Settlement stretched from the Ottawa River to the head of the Great Lakes.

As the farms grew in prosperity, local villages emerged. In the village, the farmer could sell wheat, purchase goods at a store, or attend church. In a few years, the village might have a tavern, brewery, school, church, and newspaper, blacksmith shop, and a doctor, lawyer, baker, shoemaker, and tailor. If a village was well located on a river or lake it might flourish.

The largest towns in Upper Canada were Kingston and York. In 1826, Kingston had a population of 3000 and York only 1600. But York was the capital of Upper Canada and was near some of the best land in the province. By 1834, when York was renamed Toronto, it had grown to over 9000 people. Only 20 years later, it had reached over 30 000, while Kingston had only 11 500. York was the political and economic capital of the province.

Politics The first lieutenant-governor of Upper Canada was John Graves Simcoe. He worked to make Upper Canada a model of happiness which would set an example. He moved the capital from Newark (near Niagara Falls, and too close to the American border) to York (the future Toronto). He built roads and set up courts.

Politics began to emerge. The governors continued to choose their councils from among men who thought as they did. This group was later called the Family Compact because it was so closely knit. Those who demanded more power for the elected Assembly were branded as radicals. The War of 1812, in which Upper Canada was invaded by Americans, further made the province suspicious of American ways and consolidated the Family Compact's power.

By the mid-1830s, opposition took two forms. There were moderate reformers, such as Robert Baldwin, who wanted gradual change. Others, such as William Lyon Mackenzie, moved to more extreme positions, demanding an American form of government and separation from Great Britain. In 1837, Mackenzie led a brief rebellion, which was quickly put down by militia and British soldiers.

When Lord Durham came to Canada to investigate the Rebellions of 1837, he spent most of his time in Lower Canada and only visited Upper Canada for a few days. His recommendation that Upper Canada and Lower Canada be reunited was carried out in 1841. Upper Canada became Canada West in the Province of Canada.

▷ RELATED ARTICLE: **Province of Canada.**

▷ SUGGESTED READING: Janet Lunn, *The Root Cellar* (second edition, 1983); Mike Mika and Helma Mika, *United Empire Loyalists: Pioneers of Upper Canada* (1978); Jeanne Minhinnick, *At Home in Upper Canada* (1983); Gary Thomson, *Village Life in Upper Canada* (1988); Wesley B. Turner, *Life in Upper Canada* (1988) and *Album of Upper Canada* (1987).

Upper Canada Village (photo by Malak, Ottawa).

■ Upper Canada Village

Upper Canada Village is an open-air living history museum near Morrisburg, Ont. After building started on the St Lawrence Seaway in 1954, flooding threatened many riverside communities that had been settled since the Loyalists came to Upper Canada, including the War of 1812 battlefield of Crysler's Farm. The government of Ontario decided to move many historic buildings from the areas threatened with flooding to an 800 ha park on the new riverbank.

The preserved buildings became Upper Canada Village. It commemorates the life of pioneer Upper Canadian communities of the mid-19th century. It includes farm buildings, mills and factories, shops, a tavern, school, and doctor's office.

■ Uranium

Uranium, a silvery-white metal, is the heaviest element found in nature. In 1933, when Gilbert LaBine opened Canada's first radium mine — at Port Radium, N.W.T., on Great Bear Lake — uranium was a waste product. A few years later, however, scientists discovered how to extract nuclear energy by splitting uranium

Characteristics of Uranium

Formula: U
Appearance: a silvery-white metal
Properties: heaviest of naturally occurring elements, radioactive
Atomic Weight: 238.04
Uses: producing nuclear energy in reactors and weapons

atoms. During World War II, the United States and its allies joined in a massive effort to build an atom bomb fuelled by uranium. To meet the demand for uranium thus created, mines were opened in the U.S., southern Africa, and Canada.

The demand for uranium dropped in the 1960s, but picked up again in the mid-1970s, stimulated by the development of nuclear power plants for generating electricity. Compared to other Western countries, uranium fuels only a small fraction — about 15% — of the electricity generated in Canada.

Though a minor consumer of uranium, Canada is a major producer. In fact, Canada produces over one-third of the world's uranium and is the leading producer and exporter of uranium in the Western world.

Over 60% of Canada's uranium comes from mines in northern Saskatchewan. One of these mines, at Key Lake, produces more than any other uranium mine in the Western world. The remainder of Canada's uranium is produced from underground mines in the Elliot Lake area of Ontario. The uranium there is less concentrated than that in Saskatchewan.

Uranium is found in an ore, so it must be crushed and milled to separate the uranium from the ore. The uranium is then enriched, undergoes conversion, or it is made into fuel for nuclear power plants. Cameco operates Canada's only uranium refinery, which is located in Blind River, Ont. It also owns a conversion facility in Port Hope, Ont.

Most of Canada's uranium is exported, primarily to the United States, where it is used primarily to generate electricity. Some uranium is processed into the en-

riched form and is again exported.

▷ RELATED ARTICLE: **Nuclear Energy.**

▷ SUGGESTED READING: Lennard Bickel, *The Deadly Element: The Story of Uranium* (1979); Energy, Mines and Resources Canada, *Uraniums in Granites* (1982); Donat Marc LeBourdais, *Canada and the Atomic Revolution* (1959).

■ Uranium City

Uranium City, Sask., lies in the northwest corner of Saskatchewan near the shores of Lake Athabasca. Gold was discovered at nearby Beaverlodge Lake in the 1930s. Then, in 1946, uranium was discovered. As the Eldorado mine went into production, the townsite of Uranium City was established in 1952. It thrived until 1981 when the mine closed. The population in 1986 was 171.

■ Urban Studies

Urban studies is a field that uses the city as an object of study. Sociologists, historians, geographers, planners, and others have contributed to the field. Some of the questions they ask include What forces contribute to the growth of cities? What are the links between urbanization and industrialization? What is the nature of urban society, and how do urban communities relate to each other? How do cities function within a national or regional economy? And how do cities function internally?

Urban studies became important in Canada during the 1970s. The growth of Canadian cities had become intense and a large number of urban problems had begun to appear. The federal government established a Ministry of State for Urban Affairs in 1971 to deal with urban problems at the national level during this period, and many universities set up centres and institutes for studying cities. Some provinces also introduced the study of cities into their high-school curricula, and many books were published on the subject for the university specialist, the general reader, and the college and high-school student.

■ Urbanization

Urbanization is a process by which the population of a region or nation becomes mostly city dwellers rather than country dwellers. People move to cities either because they are attracted by more job opportunities, or because they are forced to leave the countryside because their farms can no longer support them.

In Canada, people are more likely to be drawn to large cities because the variety

Jasper Avenue, Edmonton, in 1890 (top) and 1912. Western cities sprang up almost overnight after the railway arrived (courtesy PAA).

of jobs they will find there is much greater than in small towns or rural areas. When people move to cities, they often develop a different style of life from that which is found in rural areas. Not only do they find greater opportunities for different kinds of employment, but also for entertaining and for expressing themselves. On the other hand, life in big cities is often more impersonal than in rural areas, and it is more difficult to experience a sense of community.

As cities grow a network of urban places develops. Villages, small towns, large towns, and cities are closely linked by economic, political, social, and cultural ties. In Canada's early days, the growth of such a network was closely associated with the growth of industry and the building of the railways. Today, it is usually associated with a large communications network and common media, such as television and newspapers.

As regions become more urbanized, their villages, towns, and cities may become woven together so closely that they operate as one densely settled area. An area of this kind is called a *megalopolis*. The highly urbanized area that extends along the shore of Lake Ontario from Oshawa to Niagara Falls is the largest Canadian megalopolis.

Although areas of this kind are rich in employment opportunities and create a great deal of Canada's wealth, some people suggest that too great a concentration of population in one area creates serious problems. These can include crime, traffic congestion on the highways and at major airports, and the pollution brought about by factories and by the need to dispose of the garbage and sewage of very large numbers of people.

▷ SUGGESTED READING: John N. Jackson, *The Canadian City: Space, Form and Quality* (1973); Bobbie Kalman, *Early City Life* (1983);

Big Bank Towers, Toronto. *Cities exert strong economic power on the surrounding area (photo by J.A. Kraulis).*

Gilbert A. Stelter and Allan Artibise, editors, *The Canadian City: Essays in Urban and Social History* (1984).

Toronto *is Canada's largest city and part of the densely settled area that stretches along Lake Ontario (photo by J.A. Kraulis).*

■ Ursulines

Ursulines are members of a Roman Catholic teaching order of nuns. Canada's first Ursulines arrived from France in 1639. *See* **Marie de l'Incarnation** and **Missionaries.**

■ Utrecht, Treaty of

The Treaty of Utrecht was signed in Utrecht, Netherlands, in 1713. It was one of the treaties ending the War of the Spanish Succession. In North America, France gave up all claim to Rupert's Land and Newfoundland, and agreed to return conquered forts to Britain. Most of Acadia also went to Britain, though France kept part of present-day New Brunswick, Île St-Jean [Prince Edward Island], and Île Royale [Cape Breton Island]. Although the French gave up Newfoundland, French fishermen were allowed to land and dry their fish on the north and west coasts of the island, known as the French Shore.

■ Uzeb

Uzeb is a jazz fusion band which formed in Quebec in 1976. It quickly converted fans and critics to its own blend of jazz, rock, and funk. Uzeb's original philosophy was the creation and continual transformation of jazz fusion where the technical skills of its musicians are equal to their critical vision. This Montreal-based trio is composed of Alain Caron, guitarist; percussionist Paul Brochu; and Michel Cusson, acoustic, electric, and synth guitars. Uzeb's eighth album, *Uzeb Club* (released in 1989), delves a little deeper into the world of avant-garde funk.

Val d'Or

Val d'Or, Que., is located in the forest wilderness of the Abitibi region of western Quebec. The town is a merger of two smaller communities, Val d'Or and Bourlamaque, both founded in the mid-1930s during a feverish gold rush. The economy still relies heavily on two remaining gold mines, which are among the richest in Quebec. Forestry is also important. The population in 1986 was 22 252.

For further information, contact the Greffier, 855 2e Avenue, C.P. 400, Val d'Or, Que., J9S 4B4.

Valdes Island

Valdes Island is one of the Gulf Islands in the Strait of Georgia between Vancouver Island and the southern mainland of British Columbia. About one-third of the wooded island is Indian reserve. It is named for a Spanish explorer of the 1790s. In the late 1920s it was a refuge for the cult leader, Brother Twelve.

Valleyfield

Valleyfield, Que., lies on the St Lawrence River west of Montreal. Until World War II, its most important employers were a paper mill and a large cotton mill. Today it is an important business centre with a variety of manufacturing plants. The original name was Salaberry and though the community came to be called Valleyfield, its official name is Salaberry-de-Valleyfield. The population was 27 942 in 1986.

For further information, contact the Greffier, 61 rue Ste-Cécile, Salaberry-de-Valleyfield, Que., J6T 1L8.

Van Horne, Sir William Cornelius

Railway builder (*born in 1843 at Chelsea, Illinois, U.S.; died in 1915 at Montreal, Que.*). Van Horne was in charge of the construction of the Canadian Pacific Railway (CPR). He began work at age 14 as a telegrapher with the Illinois Central Railroad, and by 1880, he was general superintendent of the Chicago, Milwaukee and St Paul Railroad. In 1881 the Canadian Pacific Railway Company wanted a new general manager to drive construction forward, and Van Horne was appointed on January 1, 1882. His genius and energy were legendary; it was mostly owing to him that the main line across the prairie reached Calgary by the end of the 1883 season. Only two years later, in November 1885, the entire line was completed.

Van Horne thought big. When he became CPR president in 1888, he devised

Van Horne, A Man in a Hurry

Van Horne was a man in a hurry. When one of his engineers, J.H.E. Secretan, suggested a tunnel west of Calgary, Van Horne summoned him to Winnipeg. "Take that damned tunnel out!" he roared. "I'm not here to put in fool tunnels to please engineers! And mind you go up there and do it yourself!" Secretan — one of the best engineers in the business — stopped at the door on his way out. "While I'm up there," he said, "shouldn't I have a few of those mountains moved out of the way too?" Van Horne shook with laughter.

Sir William Van Horne, portrait by Notman & Son (courtesy NAC/PA-171758).

magnificent CPR hotels, such as the Banff Springs in the Rockies and the even more spectacular Château Frontenac in Quebec City. Van Horne insisted that the CPR should also run steamships, and this led to Canadian Pacific ships plying the Pacific and Atlantic oceans.

Van Horne had a rich and varied taste; his art treasures included a collection of Japanese drawings and paintings. He resigned from the CPR in 1899, and during 1900 to 1902 built the first railway across Cuba.

▷ RELATED ARTICLE: **Canadian Pacific Railway.**

▷ SUGGESTED READING: Stephen Mayles, *William Van Horne* (1976); Christopher Moore, *William Van Horne* (1987).

Vancouver

Vancouver, B.C., is the largest city in the province and the third largest in Canada. In 1986 the population of its metropolitan area was 1 380 729. The city is situated in the southwest corner of British Columbia in a magnificent setting of sea and mountains. It occupies a peninsula of land bounded on the north by Burrard Inlet and on the south by an arm of the Fraser River. Its location on the Pacific Ocean has helped it grow into one of the busiest ports in North America.

The city is named for George Vancouver, who explored and mapped the British Columbia coast in the early 1790s.

HISTORY
Beginnings Native people have lived on

Vancouver *lies on the fertile Fraser Delta, at the mouth of the Fraser River. The most heavily settled areas appear in dark blue in this satellite image. The large water inlet to the north is Howe Sound. Much of the delta is marked by patterns of vegetable farms (courtesy Canada Centre for Remote Sensing).*

the site of Vancouver for at least 2500 years. During the 1770s, Spanish and British soldiers began to visit the offshore waters, and in 1792 the British naval captain, George Vancouver, made the first maps of the area.

Settlement began in the 1860s, following the Fraser River gold rush of 1858, which brought thousands of gold miners to mainland British Columbia. There were only a few settlers at first, but logging and sawmilling were begun on the wooded shores of Burrard Inlet, and this attracted more people. During the 1870s, the village of Granville developed. It was also known as Gastown, after a local hotel owner, "Gassy" Jack Deighton.

When the Canadian Pacific Railway was completed in 1885, it ended 20 km farther east, at Port Moody. The railway's general manager, William Van Horne, decided to extend the line to Granville to get the benefit of Burrard Inlet's good harbour. He suggested that Granville be renamed Vancouver, and on April 6, 1886,

the city of Vancouver was formally incorporated.

Growth of the City Two months after becoming a city, Vancouver was burned almost to the ground by a fire which claimed at least 11 lives. The residents quickly rebuilt. Meanwhile, the railway line was extended along Burrard Inlet, and in May 1887 Vancouver received its first passenger train from eastern Canada.

As the West Coast terminus of the transcontinental railway, Vancouver grew steadily. With its excellent harbour, it was a major link in a transportation route that stretched from the Orient to eastern Canada and beyond. Freighters from the Orient unloaded cargoes in Vancouver Harbour and took on wheat, lumber, and minerals that had arrived from various parts of Canada. Passenger liners cruising the world called in at Vancouver. Soon the city replaced Victoria as the main business centre on Canada's West Coast. Vancouver received another boost in 1914 when the Panama Canal was opened, allowing ships to pass easily between the Atlantic and Pacific oceans. Cargo ships from Vancouver could now sail direct to eastern Canada and the United States, and on to Europe.

The 20th Century The ships from the Orient brought immigrants as well as cargo, and by the early years of the 20th century many Chinese, Japanese, and Sikhs were living in Vancouver. They were not welcomed by the majority of the population, who were mostly Canadians of British origin. There were several riots against Asians, in which their businesses and homes were destroyed. After a violent riot in 1907, a series of laws was passed to make it very hard for Asians to immigrate to Canada. The *Komagata Maru*, a ship carrying many Sikhs, was turned away in 1914 after sitting for over two months in Vancouver harbour.

Although life was hard for Vancouver's Asians, they built successful communities in the city. Vancouver's "Chinatown" became one of the largest such communities outside China. Many of the Japanese ran prosperous market gardens. Others operated their own fishing boats. But in 1942, during World War II, Vancouver's Japanese people — like all other Japanese Canadians living on the coast — were forced to move from their homes and go to camps in the interior.

Meanwhile, in the Great Depression of the 1930s, the city had seen social unrest among other groups. Because of Vancou-

ver's mild climate, it attracted the homeless and people who could not find work. In 1935, thousands of unemployed gathered there before setting out on the On To Ottawa Trek. In 1938, there was a month-long sit-in of jobless men, who occupied Vancouver's main post office. The sit-in ended with a violent clash between the police and the protesters, which resulted in a riot.

Despite such problems, Vancouver grew and generally prospered. More and

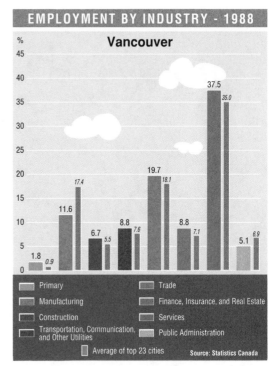

EMPLOYMENT BY INDUSTRY - 1988

Vancouver

Primary 1.8 / 0.9
Manufacturing 11.6 / 17.4
Construction 6.7 / 5.5
Transportation, Communication, and Other Utilities 8.8 / 7.6
Trade 19.7 / 18.1
Finance, Insurance, and Real Estate 8.8 / 7.1
Services 37.5 / 35.0
Public Administration 5.1 / 6.9

Average of top 23 cities   Source: Statistics Canada

Port of Vancouver is the busiest on the Pacific Coast of North America (photo by J.A. Kraulis).

Vancouver

Horseshoe Bay Ferry Terminal
Capilano Lake
District of West Vancouver
District of North Vancouver
Coquitlam Lake
Capilano Suspension Bridge
Lighthouse Park
Lions Gate Bridge
North Vancouver
Indian Arm
Stanley Park
Burrard Inlet
Port Moody
District of Coquitlam
English Bay
BC Place
Pacific National Exhibition
Simon Fraser University
Port Coquitlam
University of British Columbia
Vancouver
B.C.I.T.
Burnaby
New Westminster
Fraser River
District of Surrey
Vancouver International Airport
Sea Island
North Arm Fraser River
Strait of Georgia
Richmond
District of Delta

more businesses located there. New suburbs were built. The port facilities were expanded. By 1963 the port was the largest by tonnage in Canada. By 1986 it produced more jobs in Vancouver than any other business.

In 1986, to mark its centennial, Vancouver hosted Expo 86, a world fair which drew more than 20 million people to the city. The major buildings constructed for Expo have since been adapted for other uses.

THE MODERN CITY

Today's Vancouver is an attractive mixture of old and new. The oldest district is the quaint Gastown, near the waterfront on the south shore of Burrard Inlet. Its 19th-century buildings contain restaurants, boutiques, and nightspots. Farther east is Chinatown, the second-largest Chinatown (after San Francisco's) in North America. The main downtown core lies west of Gastown, between English Bay and Burrard Inlet. Here are high-rise office towers and apartment blocks, and a range of spectacular modern buildings. These include the Provincial Court House, the Robson Square Conference Centre, and Canada Place (which has a roof that looks like a ship's billowing sails). Northwest of downtown Vancouver are Stanley Park and Lions Gate Bridge, leading to the north shore.

False Creek, *Granville Island, Vancouver (photo by Thomas Kitchin).*

Vancouver is surrounded by several municipalities, where many people have moved to take advantage of cheaper housing. Together, these municipalities form the Greater Vancouver Regional District. The district has an elected council, and each community also has its own government.

Population Most of the people are Canadians of British origin, but there are also many other groups, including Canadians of Italian origin and of Asian origin. The Chinese live not only in Chinatown

Vancouver *seen from the south (courtesy Colour Library Books Ltd).*

but throughout the city, participating fully in its life; some are recent immigrants from Hong Kong. There are large numbers of Sikhs and other South Asians, and some families of Japanese origin, though not as many as before the war.

Education Vancouver has two universities, the University of British Columbia (UBC) and Simon Fraser University. Other colleges include B.C. Institute of Technology, the Emily Carr College of Art and Design, and Vancouver Community College.

Transportation Vancouver retains its vital role as a port and as the terminus of transcontinental railways. As well, major highways, including the Trans-Canada Highway, radiate from Vancouver. Vancouver International Airport is a departure point for flights across the Pacific, to the United States, and to South America, as well as to Canadian cities.

Local transport includes ferries to Vancouver Island, the Gulf Islands, and coastal areas. There is also the Seabus (twin-hulled catamarans that are part of Vancouver's public transit system). The transit system includes the SkyTrain, which was built to handle the crowds who came to Expo 86. The SkyTrain is an overhead commuter system called ALRT (Advanced Light Rapid Transit), which runs between the Vancouver waterfront and New Westminster (about 21 km).

Communications There are two daily newspapers, the *Province* and the *Vancouver Sun*. There are also several weekly papers and various specialized journals and ethnic publications. There are 17 radio stations and four television stations.

Culture Vancouver has long been a centre of cultural activity, with a symphony

BC Place *The dome of this sports stadium is held aloft by forced air (photo by J.A. Kraulis).*

Canada Place,
Vancouver (photo by Al Harvey/Masterfile).

Vancouver Law Courts
building, designed by Vancouver native Arthur Erickson (photo by Dick Busher).

orchestra, theatre companies, an opera association, and various art and dance groups. There are numerous galleries and museums, including the Vancouver Art Gallery, the Museum of Anthropology (on the campus of UBC), the Canadian Museum of Flight and Transportation, the H.R. MacMillan Planetarium, the B.C. Museum of Mining, and the Arts, Sciences, and Technology Centre (with hands-on exhibits).

Vancouver has 138 parks, including Stanley Park, which was opened in 1888 and named for Governor General Lord Stanley. The park contains many hectares of dense forest, a zoo, and an aquarium featuring daily shows by resident whales.

Vancouver's sandy beaches and nearby mountains offer a range of opportunities for outdoor recreation. Residents boast that one can go skiing and sailing in the same day. Sports fans can enjoy four professional teams: the British Columbia Lions (football), the Vancouver Canucks (hockey), the Vancouver Canadians (baseball), and the Vancouver 86ers (soccer). The Lions play their home games in BC Place, a huge domed stadium with an air-supported roof.

Annual festivals include those for folk music, sports, and multicultural events such as the celebration of the Chinese New Year. The Vancouver Children's Festival is usually held in May. The Bath-

tub Race across the Strait of Georgia is in July. The Pacific National Exhibition, the second-largest agricultural fair in Canada is held at the end of August each year.

For further information, contact the City Clerk, 453 West 12 Avenue, Vancouver, B.C., V5Y 1V4.

▷ SUGGESTED READING: Barry Bondar, *Vancouver Chronicles: The Story and the Sights* (1986); Plum Lind Johnson, *The 1990 Kids Vancouver Directory* (1989); Eric Nicol, *Vancouver* (1970); Patricia E. Roy, *Vancouver: An Illustrated History* (1980); Elma Schemenauer, *Hello Vancouver* (1986); Terry Stafford, *Matt and Jennie in Old Vancouver* (1986).

■ **Vancouver, George**
Naval explorer (*born in 1757 at King's Lynn, England; died in 1798 at Peter-*

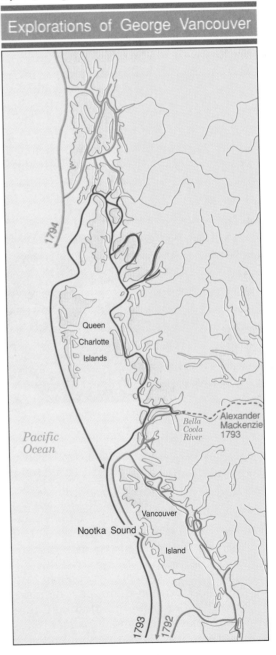

Explorations of George Vancouver

sham, London, England). Vancouver carried out the first thorough charting of the coastline of British Columbia. An officer in the British navy, Vancouver sailed with Captain James Cook on two of his expeditions to the Pacific. In April 1792, Vancouver arrived on the Northwest Coast in command of his own expedition, which was sent to map the coastline between California and Alaska and to deal with Spanish claims on Vancouver Island.

Vancouver spent three summers exploring the coast. Each winter he retreated to the Hawaiian Islands. In his ship, the *Discovery*, he cruised off the present site of Vancouver, B.C., and made painstaking surveys of thousands of kilometres of unknown shoreline. One of his major accomplishments was to show that no Northwest Passage to the Atlantic existed along the coast.

The captain was less successful in his dealings with the Spanish, who refused to give up their possessions on Vancouver Island.

After returning to England in 1795 he spent the remaining years of his life writing an account of his expedition. In his own time, Vancouver's reputation was hurt by a scandal involving the flogging of one of his officers. Today, however, he is recognized as one of history's great navigators.

▷ Related Articles: **Exploration; Nootka Sound Controversy.**

■ Vancouver Art Gallery

The Vancouver Art Gallery was established in 1931. Since 1983, it has occupied the old courthouse building in downtown Vancouver, B.C., which was renovated by architect Arthur Erickson. The collection includes about 5000 paintings, sculptures, photographs, drawings, prints, and videos, and is particularly strong in contemporary Canadian art. One permanent gallery is devoted to exhibiting the works of noted British Columbia artist Emily Carr.

■ Vancouver Canucks

The Vancouver Canucks hockey team joined the National Hockey League in 1970, playing their first game on October 9, 1970. The team entered the same year as Buffalo Sabres. The two teams flipped a coin to see who would get first choice in the amateur draft. Vancouver lost, and the outstanding Gilbert Perrault went to Buffalo. With the sole exception of a surprising advance to the Stanley Cup finals in 1982 (they lost to the New York Islanders), the Canucks have had little success in the standings. They play in the Pacific Coliseum.

■ Vancouver Island

Vancouver Island, 31 285 km², lies off the southwest corner of mainland British Columbia. It is the largest island on the west coast of North America. It is about 460 km long, and anywhere from 50 to 120 km wide.

The isolated west coast of the island is broken by many finger-like inlets cutting deeply into the interior. The coast is generally quite low-lying, while rugged mountains dominate the interior.

The climate, which is generally mild and less rainy than the mainland, attracts many tourists and people looking for a comfortable place to retire. The island is linked to the mainland by several ferries.

Vancouver Island has been occupied by native people for thousands of years. Salish, Nootka, and Kwakiutl Indians are still a prominent part of the population. The first outsiders to arrive were Spanish explorers in 1774, followed by British, Spanish, and French explorers and traders. In the end the British won control.

For years, traders came by boat to collect furs from the Indians, but in 1843 the Hudson's Bay Company built a trading post at the southern tip of the island. This site grew into the city of Victoria, now the capital of the province.

In 1849, Vancouver Island became a British colony, and in 1866 it united with the mainland colony to form the colony of British Columbia.

Chronometer *used by George Vancouver when exploring the Pacific Northwest (courtesy Vancouver Maritime Museum).*

Vancouver Art Gallery *in Robson Square. The gallery was the city's former court house (courtesy Colour Library Books).*

Barkley Sound,
Vancouver Island (photo by John Foster/ Masterfile).

was an alderman in Surrey (1965-68) and mayor (1969-75). After running unsuccessfully for provincial and federal office as a Liberal, he joined the Social Credit Party in 1974, and in 1975 was elected to the British Columbia legislature as the member for Surrey. He served as minister of human resources, municipal affairs, and education between 1975 and 1983. He resigned from politics in 1983, but came back into public life to succeed Bill Bennett as leader of the Social Credit Party in July 1986. He was sworn in as premier in August 1986.

British Columbia became a province of Canada in 1871.

The island is rich in natural resources. Coal mines were opened as early as 1836, and logging was well established by the 1860s. Farming spread through the fertile river valleys and fishermen worked out of many coastal villages. The majority of the population now lives in the southern part of the island in the Victoria-Nanaimo area. However, many smaller communities have grown up around mines, sawmills, and fishing harbours.

Premier Bill Vander Zalm *of B.C. (courtesy Canapress Photo Service).*

Tofino *waterfront, Vancouver Island (photo by Al Harvey/Masterfile).*

▷ RELATED ARTICLE: **British Columbia.**

▷ SUGGESTED READING: Richard Blier, *Island Adventures: An Outdoors Guide to Vancouver Island* (1989); Tim Fitzharris, *The Island: A Natural History of Vancouver Island* (1983).

Vander Zalm has been an outspoken politician, particularly on social issues such as welfare, and moral issues such as abortion. He was sometimes at odds with his party, and faced many resignations over his policies. He was a strong supporter of the free-trade agreement with the United States, and of the Meech Lake Accord.

▷ SUGGESTED READING: Gary Mason and Keith Baldry, *Fantasyland: Inside the Reign of Bill Vander Zalm* (1989); Alan Twig, *Vander Zalm: From Immigrant to Premier* (1986).

■ **Vanderhoof**

Vanderhoof, B.C., is a district municipality in the geographical centre of the province, 100 km west of Prince George. It is named for an American promoter who was hired to attract settlers to the region. Farming and logging are the main activities. The population in 1986 was 3505.

For further information, contact the District Municipal Clerk, P.O. Box 900, Vanderhoof, B.C., V0J 3A0.

Bald Eagle *is a spectacular inhabitant of Vancouver Island (photo by Stephen J. Krasemann/DRK Photo).*

■ **Vander Zalm, Wilhelmus Nicholaas Theodore Marie**

Premier of British Columbia (*born in 1934 at Noordwykerhout, Netherlands*). Bill Vander Zalm's family immigrated to British Columbia in 1947, where he finished high school and went into the nursery business. He developed Fantasy Garden World, a theme park in Richmond, before entering municipal politics. He

Vanier, Georges-Philéas

Governor general (*born in 1888 at Montreal, Que.; died in 1967 at Ottawa, Ont.*). Georges Vanier was one of the most popular people ever to be governor general. He was a World War I hero and a founding officer of the Royal 22nd Regiment (the "Van Doos"). When leading his men into battle, he was seriously wounded and had to have his leg amputated. He won the Military Cross and bar during the war, as well as the Distinguished Service Order.

After the war, Vanier entered the diplomatic service, and represented Canada at the League of Nations and at many international conferences. During 1939-40, he was Canadian minister to France; when France fell during World War II, he returned to Canada. In 1943 he was sent back to England, where he served as Canada's minister to Allied governments in exile. His final diplomatic post was ambassador to France (1944-53).

Vanier became governor general in 1959 and remained in office until his death in 1967. These were difficult years for Canada because of the rise of Quebec separatism. Vanier worked hard to inspire Canadians with a sense of unity and bring them together as one people. His great concern for his country and his efforts on behalf of the Canadian people won him the affection of rich and poor from coast to coast.

▷ SUGGESTED READING: Robert Speaight, *Vanier: Soldier, Diplomat, and Governor General* (1970); Jean Vanier, *In Weakness Strength* (1969).

Varley, Frederick Horsman

Painter (*born in 1881 at Sheffield, England; died in 1969 at Toronto, Ont.*). Varley was the only member of the Group of Seven who painted portraits. He had a good art education in Sheffield and in Belgium, and he worked as a commercial artist when he immigrated to Canada in 1912. He became a Canadian war artist in 1918, and his powerful paintings of the war zone in France express the futility of war. In 1920 he joined in the first exhibition by the Group of Seven, though he did not share the nationalist zeal of the other members. He tried to earn his living as a portraitist, and in 1926 moved to Vancouver to teach at the art college. He made a great impact on his students through his enthusiasm for sketching trips and for oriental art. He painted hundreds of oil and watercolour landscapes around Vancouver in striking and unusual colours. His drawings are also very fine. The De-

John, *oil on canvas, by F.H. Varley (courtesy NGC).*

pression ended his career as a teacher in British Columbia in 1935, and, except for a trip to the Arctic in 1938, he spent the rest of his often unhappy life in Ottawa, Montreal, and Toronto.

▷ SUGGESTED READING: Christopher Varley, *F.H. Varley* (1979); Peter Varley, *Frederick H. Varley* (1983).

Vaudreuil, Philippe de Rigaud, Marquis de Vaudreuil

Soldier and governor of New France (*born in 1643 near Revel, France; died in 1725 at Quebec, New France [Que.]*). Philippe de Rigaud de Vaudreuil was a successful military commander and one of the most popular governors of New France. He arrived in 1687 as commander of the troops, and in the 1690s he conducted campaigns against the Iroquois on behalf of Governor Frontenac. These campaigns brought an end to the wars between the French and the Iroquois, which had been going on for almost 100 years.

Appointed governor of Montreal in 1699, Vaudreuil was promoted to governor of New France in 1703. He held the position until his death 22 years later. During these years, he strove to contain British expansion into the west, where they would threaten France's control of the fur trade. To accomplish this, he was careful to keep on good terms with the Iroquois, as well as forming alliances with other native groups. As a result, French fur traders could travel westward in comparative safety, and this greatly increased the trade. Vaudreuil's fourth son, Pierre, became governor of Louisiana in 1742 and of Canada in 1755.

■ Vaudreuil, Pierre de Rigaud de

Last governor of New France (*born in 1698 at Quebec, New France; died in 1778 at Paris, France*). The son of Philippe de Rigaud de Vaudreuil, he was brought up to be a colonial soldier and administrator like his father. He served as governor of Trois-Rivières 1733 to 1742 and then did an 11-year stint as governor of Louisiana on the Gulf of Mexico.

In 1755, Vaudreuil returned home to take on the position of governor of New France. He was the first Canadian-born person to hold this post, and he was a popular governor. Soon after he took office the Seven Years' War broke out, in which France and Britain fought their final contest for control of North America.

As governor of New France, Vaudreuil was commander-in-chief of the army, but he had little experience of fighting. Moreover, he disliked the senior general sent from France, the Marquis de Montcalm. The rivalry between these two men greatly hindered their conduct of the war, and matters became even worse when, in 1758, Montcalm was promoted over Vau-

Pierre de Rigaud de Vaudreuil was the last governor of New France (courtesy NAC/ C-1243).

dreuil's head and given command of the army.

After Montcalm's death on the Plains of Abraham and the fall of Quebec in 1759, Vaudreuil withdrew to Montreal, where he and General Lévis planned a counterattack. But although Lévis won a victory at Sainte-Foy, near Quebec City, there was little chance of long-term success. Across the Atlantic, France was fighting on many fronts and could not spare the men or supplies that Vaudreuil so desperately needed. In September 1760, he was forced to surrender New France to the British. He spent his last years in France at the family château, having been cleared of any blame for France's loss of its North American Colony.

▷ SUGGESTED READING: Desmond Morton, *Sieges of Quebec* (1984).

■ VE-Day Riots

The VE-Day Riots on May 7-8, 1945, began as a celebration in Halifax, N.S., of the end of World War II in Europe (Victory in Europe). It quickly became a rampage as thousands of military and civilians, mainly sailors, drank, smashed windows, looted stores, and clashed with police. A royal commission blamed naval commanders for not keeping their men under stricter control.

■ Vegetables

Vegetables are edible plants. They are a

Vegetables (artwork by Claire Tremblay).

valuable source of protein, vitamins, minerals, fibre, and carbohydrates. Over 50 different kinds are grown in Canada, but only five or six account for most of Canada's production.

Vegetable crops are more seriously affected by drought than most other crops. Therefore, a source of water for irrigation is necessary.

Relatively few areas of Canada have the moderate climate and long growing season needed to produce vegetables. The main areas are the Fraser Valley, B.C.; irrigated regions of southern Alberta; Red and Assiniboine river valleys of southern Manitoba; southern Ontario and southwestern Quebec; the Saint John River Valley, N.B.; the Annapolis Valley of N.S.; and almost the whole of P.E.I.

The potato is by far the most widely cultivated vegetable in Canada. The Atlantic region concentrates heavily on potatoes. Ontario ranks first in vegetable production among the provinces.

■ Vegetation Regions, *see* Natural Regions

■ Vegreville

Vegreville is an Alberta town located 100 km east of Edmonton. The first settlers were mainly French Canadians in the 1890s and the town is named for a priest, Father Valentin Vegreville. When the Canadian Northern Railway arrived in 1905, the town was moved to a new site, some 8 km northeast. Both French and Ukrainian influences were seen from the start in the churches, schools, and community halls. The Ukrainian Pysanka Festival is a major event. The town's famous giant Easter egg (called a pysanka) was dedicated by the queen in 1975. Vegreville is the centre of a rich farming area. Its population was 5276 in 1986.

Pysanka Monument in Vegreville, Alta (photo courtesy Victor Post Photography).

Harvesting Celery, Holland Marsh, just north of Toronto (photo by Malak, Ottawa).

■ Verchères, Marie-Madeleine Jarret de

Heroine (*born in 1678 at Verchères, New France; died in 1747 in New France*). In 1692, when she was 14, Madeleine de Verchères defended her family against an Iroquois attack. Along with other settlers, she was working in the fields when the onslaught began. Her parents were away from home, and she acted with both speed and courage as she fled to the fort and then took charge of its defence.

Verchères later wrote an account of the events that played up her own heroism. She became more dramatic with each retelling. The lone Iroquois who tried to catch her became 45 in later versions.

Madeleine de Verchères has gone down in history as a heroine, when in fact she was probably no braver than many other young women of her day. Nevertheless, her story has helped inspire others with courage in times of danger.

▷ SUGGESTED READING: Richard A. Boning, *Soldier Girl* (1975); Janet Grant, *Madeleine de Verchères* (1988).

■ Verigin, Peter Vasilevich

Doukhobor leader (*born in 1859 at Slavyanka, Russia; died in 1924 near Grand Forks, B.C.*). Known as Peter the Lordly, Verigin (also spelled Veregin) was the first leader of the Canadian Doukhobors, a religious group that immigrated to Canada from Russia in 1898-99. Verigin was chosen as leader in 1886 while the Doukhobors were still in Russia. He was immediately arrested. The Russians viewed the Doukhobors as dangerously disloyal because their religious beliefs prevented them from swearing allegiance to the czar.

Peter Verigin was sent to exile in Siberia in 1887, but in 1902 he was allowed to join his people on the Canadian prairies. To gain full ownership of the land they had been granted on the prairies, the Doukhobors were required to

take a Canadian oath of allegiance. Verigin was against such an oath, and in 1908 he led his followers to a large stretch of land he had bought them in British Columbia. There he established a prosperous self-contained community of about 5000 Doukhobors. But some Doukhobors were jealous of his power. He died in a mysterious accident. On October 29, 1924, he was killed by an explosion which ripped through a railway carriage in which he was travelling.
▷ RELATED ARTICLE: **Doukhobors.**

■ Vernon

Vernon, B.C., is a city at the north end of Okanagan Lake in the south-central interior. It was a camp on the fur-trade trail before missionaries made the first settlement in the 1840s. Fruit growing, still an important activity, began in the 1890s. The city was incorporated in 1892. Today it is the business centre for the North Okanagan Valley and is popular with skiers and summer tourists. Kalamalka Lake and Swan Lake are nearby. The city is named for a pioneer settler and government official, F.G. Vernon. The population in 1986 was 20 241. For further information, contact the City Clerk, 3400 30th Street, Vernon, B.C., V1T 5E6.

■ Verrazzano, Giovanni da

Giovanni da Verrazzano (courtesy NAC/C-17525).

Explorer (*born about 1485 near Florence, Italy; died about 1528 in the West Indies*). An Italian by birth, Verrazzano was sailing under the French flag when he reached America in 1525. He cruised along the coast between Florida and Newfoundland and showed that there was no water passage through the new continent. On another voyage four years later, he landed on a Caribbean island and was killed by the natives.

■ Versailles, Treaty of

The Treaty of Versailles was one of the peace treaties that ended World War I. It was signed on June 28, 1919, at Versailles, near Paris, France. The treaty imposed a heavy penalty on Germany, blaming it for causing the war. It took away much German territory, and required Germany to pay costly war damages.

Canada had little voice in making the terms of the treaty. However, it was an important step for Canada in gaining full independence from Britain. Prime Minister Robert Borden insisted that Canada have a place at the peace table. It was the first treaty that Britain did not sign on behalf of Canada. The two people who signed the treaty for Canada were the

Peter Verigin (courtesy NAC/C-8882).

minister of justice, C.J. Dougherty, and former Alberta premier Arthur Sifton.

■ Vesak, Norbert

Choreographer (*born in 1936 at Port Moody, B.C.*). He was choreographer of the Vancouver Playhouse in 1964 and has since created ballets for many different companies in North America. In the early 1970s he devised two popular works for the Royal Winnipeg Ballet: *The Ecstasy of Rita Joe*, based on George Ryga's play about contemporary Indian society, and *What to do till the Messiah Comes*, which won a gold medal for choreography at the Varna International Ballet Competition in Bulgaria in 1980. He is noted for the lavish visual effects from many different media which he includes in his works.

■ Veterinary Medicine

Veterinary medicine deals with health and disease in animals.

Most veterinarians set up their own practice. Some work for governments to help control or prevent animal diseases and ensure the safety of food. University veterinarians teach and do research. Most work in Canada's colleges of veterinary medicine.

Pets There are several million pets in

Canada. The veterinarians who specialize in treating pets almost always set up their own clinics or hospitals. They deal mainly with dogs and cats, but also treat rabbits, mice, gerbils, birds, fish, and so on. Animal patients require medical care that is often similar to what humans require.

An animal hospital requires similar equipment to a hospital for humans. It usually includes equipment for surgery, laboratory diagnosis, X-rays, and so on.

Farm Animals In farming areas, veterinarians deal mostly with domestic animals raised for food, such as cattle, pigs, goats, chickens, and turkeys.

Farm animals are often raised in large numbers in close quarters. Under such conditions, infectious diseases can occur and spread rapidly, especially those affecting the lungs and intestinal tract.

Veterinarians seek to prevent all forms of disease by using vaccinations and safe drugs. They also advise farmers on how to feed and raise the animals. Today's veterinarians use computers to keep track of the health of the animals.

Work and Recreation Animals Animals perform little work in Canada today. A few horses may pull farm equipment. Dogs that herd sheep, pull sleds, guard, do police chores, and help people with impaired sight or hearing are cared for by small-animal veterinarians.

Most horses are used for recreation and sports. They are prone to injuries related to these activities. Some veterinarians specialize in horses, which are prone to lameness and breathing difficulties.

Fur and Wool Sheep are the only important producers of wool in Canada, although muskoxen produce a high-quality fibre, called *qivit*.

Disease control is important in fur farming, where large numbers of animals, such as mink and fox, are raised in confinement. Veterinary services are very important to these industries.

Wildlife Veterinary medicine is taking an active interest in health and disease in Canada's wildlife. Wild animals are good indicators of the spread of certain animal and human diseases, such as rabies. Many of the bison in Wood Buffalo National Park have tuberculosis. Veterinarians have been called in to help decide if these animals should be destroyed.

Zoo animals are especially prone to disease because they live in an artificial environment together with many other animals. Canada's zoos employ veterinarians full- and part-time.

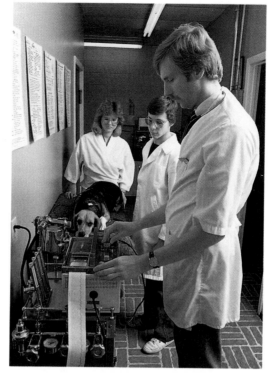

Veterinarian and patient (courtesy Alberta Career Development).

Laboratory Animals are widely used in medical research. The care and humane use of these animals have grown in importance as the public is more concerned about animal welfare. The use of laboratory animals has led to important medical breakthroughs, such as the theory of germs and the discovery of insulin (a drug to treat diabetes).

Education There are four veterinary colleges in Canada. Ontario Veterinary College, in Guelph, Ont., is Canada's oldest (dating from 1862). Until 1963, it was English Canada's only veterinary college.

Atlantic Veterinary College was established in 1983 at Charlottetown, P.E.I. The first students graduated in 1990.

The Faculty of Veterinary Medicine at the University of Montreal is located at St-Hyacinthe, Que. It is the only French-language veterinary college in North America. The Western College of Veterinary Medicine was established at Saskatoon, Sask., in 1963. It serves the four western provinces and the North.

In general, six years of training are required to earn a veterinary degree. The first woman graduated in 1928. Today, more than half the graduates are women. There are about 6000 professional veterinarians working in Canada.

▷ SUGGESTED READING: K. Aspinwall, *First Steps in Veterinary Science* (1976); Fern Brown, *Behind the Scenes at the Horse Hospital* (1981); Sally Haddock, *The Making of a Woman Vet* (1985); William Jaspersohn, *A Day in the Life of a Veterinarian* (1978).

Zoo animals, such as this emu, require special veterinary care (photo by Stephen Homer/First Light).

Vickers, Jonathan

Tenor (*born in 1926 at Prince Albert, Sask.*). Jon Vickers is probably the greatest dramatic tenor of the late 20th century. He has sung at the highest level the major roles of all operatic repertoires.

Vickers remembers singing at a Christmas concert when he was three years old. He sang through school and in church choirs and in operetta productions. He took voice lessons in Winnipeg and moved to Toronto for voice lessons and stage training at the Royal Conservatory of Music. In 1951, he sang the tenor solos in the Toronto Mendelssohn Choir's annual performance of Handel's *Messiah*.

In 1956 his international career began when the American mezzo-soprano Regina Resnick sang Bizet's *Carmen* with the fledgling Canadian Opera Company, and Vickers sang Don José opposite her. On her recommendation he landed roles in New York, from where he went on to London and then in 1958 he made his debut at Bayreuth, Germany, as Siegmund in Wagner's *Die Walküre*.

Vickers has sung at all the great opera houses. He made two recordings of perhaps his most famous role — Verdi's Otello. Vickers also recorded two of his most important roles — Aeneas in Berlioz's *The Trojans* and Peter in Britten's *Peter Grimes*. In 1986 Vickers recorded a superb collection of songs by Canadian composers for the Canadian Music Centre's label, Centredisc.

Victoria

Victoria is the capital of British Columbia. It occupies a peninsula overlooking Juan de Fuca Strait at the southern end of Vancouver Island. It is about 100 km by water south of Vancouver on the mainland. Greater Victoria includes 12 communities: Saanich, Oak Bay, Esquimalt, Central Saanich, North Saanich, Sidney, View Royal, Colwood, Langford, Metchasin, Victoria, and Sooke. The population of Greater Victoria in 1986 was 265 380, making it the 14th-largest city in Canada.

The city is named after Queen Victoria, who was the reigning British monarch when Victoria was founded.

Victoria appears as a dark blue area on the southern tip of Vancouver Island. The city's mild climate and beautiful setting attract many retired people. The pink and yellow areas are logging scars (courtesy Canada Centre for Remote Sensing).

Victoria

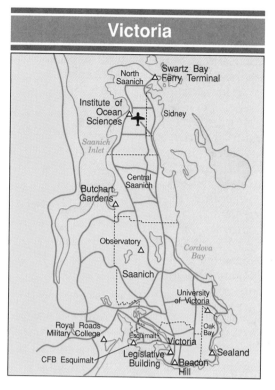

HISTORY

Beginnings Coast Salish people first occupied the site of Victoria. In 1843, James Douglas of the Hudson's Bay Company founded Fort Victoria there as the company's new Pacific Coast headquarters. The headquarters had been farther south, in the Oregon Territory on the mainland; but that territory was soon to be taken over by the United States, so Douglas was sent to choose a site farther north. He chose the spot on southern Vancouver Island because of its protected harbour.

Victoria remained a small fur-trading community with very few settlers until 1858, when a ship crowded with gold miners entered the harbour. The miners were on their way to the British Columbia mainland to pan the rivers, which they had heard were rich with gold. During the gold rushes that followed, Victoria

Victoria in 1865, looking north on Wharf Street (courtesy Victoria City Archives).

boomed as a supply centre for the miners.

Capital City When the colony of Vancouver Island was created in 1849, Victoria became its capital. It remained the capital until 1866, when Vancouver Island and the British colony on the mainland were united as one colony called British Columbia. For the next two years, the united colony's capital was New Westminster, on the mainland. But in 1868 the capital was moved back to Victoria, and Victoria remained the capital when British Columbia became a province of Canada in 1871.

Growth of the City Victoria was incorporated as a city in 1862, and in 1865 the British made the harbour at nearby Esquimalt a naval base for their ships. This spurred Victoria's growth. As well as a government centre, the city was the major shipbuilding, banking, and business centre on Canada's West Coast.

Victoria's development suffered a blow in the 1880s when the Canadian Pacific Railway decided not to carry its new railway line across Georgia Strait to Vancouver Island. Instead of Victoria being the Pacific terminus of the railway, the line ended on the mainland, at Vancouver. From then on, Vancouver began to surpass Victoria as a business centre. However, Victoria remained the centre of government, and Esquimalt remained an important naval base. As the years passed, Victoria became a major tourist town, attracting visitors precisely because it was not a huge modern city. It still kept much of its old-world charm.

Statue of Queen Victoria, for whom the city of Victoria is named, outside the Legislature Building (photo by J.A. Kraulis/Masterfile).

Legislature Building at night, Victoria (photo by J.A. Kraulis).

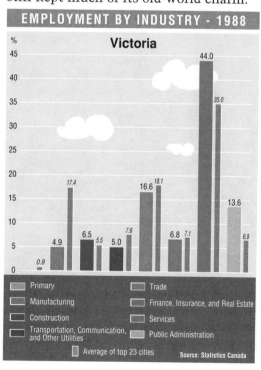

EMPLOYMENT BY INDUSTRY - 1988

Victoria

Industry	%
Primary	0.9
Manufacturing	4.9
Construction	6.5
Transportation, Communication, and Other Utilities	5.5
Trade	16.6
Finance, Insurance, and Real Estate	6.8
Services	44.0
Public Administration	13.6

Average of top 23 cities

Source: Statistics Canada

Victoria, B.C. (photo by Malak, Ottawa).

Butchart Gardens, near Victoria (photo by Malak, Ottawa).

THE MODERN CITY

Victoria grew up around its inner harbour, and today this is the focus of the downtown area. Two of the city's most historic buildings overlook the harbour: the provincial legislature (completed 1898) and the Empress Hotel (1908), a famous railway hotel and Victoria landmark. Victoria is said to be the most "British" city in Canada, and it preserves this image, with its double-decker buses, teashops, and other British touches.

Population The percentage of people of British origin is higher in Victoria than in any other Canadian city. The population is also older. Many Canadians over 65 choose to retire to Victoria.

Education The principal educational establishments are the University of Victoria, Royal Roads Military College, the Victoria Conservatory of Music, and Camosun College. There is also the Lester B. Pearson College of the Pacific, a notable international college.

Transportation The BC Ferry Corporation runs services between Victoria and mainland British Columbia; there are also ferries and steamships to American towns. Major national and international airlines call at Victoria International Airport, connecting Victoria with the principal Canadian cities, as well as with other countries. Highways and railways connect Victoria with other parts of Vancouver Island.

Communications Victoria has one daily newspaper, the *Times Colonist*, and two weekly papers. It has four radio stations and one television station.

Culture The Victoria Symphony Orchestra and the Bastion Theatre are the main centres of the performing arts. The principal galleries and museums are the Provincial Museum and Art Gallery of Greater Victoria; others include Craigflower Manor and the Classic Car Museum. Also of interest are the Dominion Astrophysical Observatory, Fort Rodd Hill National Historic Park, and Butchart Gardens. The Victoria Folkfest International festival is normally held in June, and the Victoria Classic Boat Festival in September.

For further information, contact the City Clerk, 1 Centennial Square, Victoria, B.C., V8W 1P6.

▷ RELATED ARTICLE: **British Columbia.**

▷ SUGGESTED READING: Barry Bondar, *Victoria Chronicles: The Story and the Sights* (1986); Barry F. King, *Victoria Landmarks* (1989); Michael Kluckner, *Victoria: The Way it Was* (1986); Terry Reksten, *More English than the English: A Very Social History of Victoria* (1986); Elma Schemenauer, *Hello Victoria* (1986).

■ Victoria Cross

The Victoria Cross (VC) is the Commonwealth's highest medal for bravery in battle. It was created by Queen Victoria in 1856 and was first awarded in 1857. It is awarded only very rarely and only for exceptionally brave deeds. Only 1351 people have ever been honoured with the medal. Of these, 94 were Canadians.

Queen Victoria introduced the medal to reward bravery during the Crimean War of 1854 to 1856 against Russia. Canada's first VC winner was a hero of that war, Alexander Dunn. The bronze from which all the medals have been made was taken from one of the Russian cannons captured by the British during the Crimean War. After 1902 the VC could be awarded if the person died while performing the act of bravery. The youngest Canadian and the second youngest in the British Empire to receive the VC was 17-year-old Thomas Ricketts of Newfoundland, who received it during World War I. For articles on some of Canada's most famous VCs, *see* separate entries on **William Barker; William Bishop; Alexander Dunn; William Hall; Andrew Mynarski;** and **George Pearkes**.

▷ RELATED ARTICLE: **Medals.**

▷ SUGGESTED READING: Douglas A. Melville, *Canadians and the Victoria Cross* (1987); John Swettenham, *Valiant Men: Canada's Victoria Cross and George Cross Winners* (1973).

■ Victoria Island

Victoria Island, 217 291 km², is the second-largest island in Canada. It lies in the Arctic Ocean just north of mainland North America. It is treeless and rugged, its rocky plains and uplands broken by wandering rivers and many lakes. In many places, the coastline rises in bold cliffs.

The island was occupied by ancestors of the Inuit thousands of years ago. When explorers first arrived, they named the inhabitants the Copper Inuit because they were using raw copper to make tools and weapons. The island was named in 1839 after Britain's Queen Victoria. In the 1920s, trading companies built posts on the coast to collect white fox furs from the Inuit. Today, Cambridge Bay and Holman, N.W.T., are the main settlements.

■ Victoriaville

Victoriaville, Que., lies in the hill country south of the St Lawrence River between Sherbrooke and Trois-Rivières. Once just a small railway station, it has grown recently into a major manufacturing centre, known for producing clothing, furniture, and metal products. Its name honours Queen Victoria. The population in 1986 was 21 587.

For further information, contact the Greffier, 1 rue Notre-Dame Ouest, C.P. 370, Victoriaville, Que., G6P 6T2.

■ Vigneault, Gilles

Singer, songwriter, poet, publisher (*born in 1928 at Natashquan, Que.*). After graduating from Laval University in 1953, Vigneault held a variety of jobs in teaching and broadcasting in the late 1950s. At the same time, he was writing poetry and songs reflecting his profound affection for his native province. In 1959, he founded his own publishing house, Les Éditions de l'Arc, to distribute his work, and the next year he began performing his own songs. Although his singing career developed satisfactorily, his reputation at home and abroad was established by the success of his song, "Mon Pays" (1964), which became virtually an anthem for Québecois. Vigneault shares with Félix Leclerc much of the credit for reviving the Quebec *chanson*, reinforcing its distinctive character, and providing it with a universal appeal. He has been one of Quebec's most successful and most honoured artists and cultural ambassadors.

■ Vikings, *see* Norse

■ Ville-Marie

Ville-Marie was the name that Maisonneuve and his party gave to the small missionary settlement they established on Montreal Island in 1642. As the settlement grew into a major fur-trading town, the name Ville-Marie was gradually replaced by the name Montreal (which had originated with Jacques Cartier). Today, Ville-Marie is recalled in such buildings as Place Ville Marie, the high-rise office complex and shopping mall in downtown Montreal. *See* **Montreal.**

■ Villeneuve, Gilles

Racing driver (*born in 1950 at Chambly, Que.; died in 1982 at Zolder, Belgium*). Villeneuve was Canada's most successful high-speed racer.

Villeneuve began by racing snowmobiles and used his earnings to enter car races. He broke his leg at a race at Mossport, Ont., in 1974 but was highly successful in 1975 and 1976. He joined the famous Ferrari team on the world circuit and won his first race at Montreal in 1979. He won 6 of the 67 races he drove for Ferrari and was runner-up one year as the world's finest Grand Prix driver.

Villeneuve was killed in a race at the Belgian Grand Prix following a collision at 250 km/hr. Montreal's Grand Prix circuit is named in his honour.

▷ SUGGESTED READING: Gerald Donaldson, *Gilles Villeneuve* (1989).

■ Vimy Ridge

Vimy Ridge was a battle fought Easter weekend, 1917, in northern France during World War I. German soldiers occupied the long, low ridge, which allowed them to fire down on Allied troops below. The

Victoria Cross *(courtesy NMC/K71-95).*

Lt Fred Campbell, *awarded the Victoria Cross in World War I. The ghostly reflection is a flaw in the photograph (courtesy NAC/C-11195).*

The Refrain of "Mon Pays"

Mon pays ce n'est pas un pays c'est l'hiver
Mon jardin ce n'est pas un jardin c'est la plaine
Mon chemin ce n'est pas un chemin c'est la neige
Mon pays ce n'est pas un pays c'est l'hiver.

My country is not a country, it is winter
My garden is not a garden, it is a plain
My road is not a road, it is the snow
My country is not a country, it is winter.

Canadian Machine Gunners dig in on Vimy Ridge, France, 1917. The desolate landscape was created by years of artillery bombardment. The military victory at Vimy Ridge cost over 10 000 Canadian casualties (courtesy NAC/PA-1017).

Canadian Corps was given the job of driving the enemy from the ridge. It was the first battle in which the Canadian Corps fought as a unit. After weeks of planning, the Canadians attacked, and in five days of heavy fighting achieved a major victory, at a cost of over 10 000 dead and wounded. A monument to Canadian soldiers who died at Vimy now stands atop the ridge.

▷ RELATED ARTICLE: **World War I.**

▷ SUGGESTED READING: Pierre Berton, *Vimy* (1987); Jim Matresky and Bill Larkin, *World War I* (1986).

■ Violet

Violets are annual or perennial herb-like plants of the violet family (Violaceae). Violets can be divided into two groups: stemless ones, whose leaves and flower stalks emerge separately from the soil, and ones with stems (*caulescent*) bearing the leaves and flowers. Pansies are well-known ornamental violets, but the African violet cultivated in so many homes is *saintpaulia*, belonging to another family (Gesneriaceae).

In Canada, we have 35 native species in the woods, prairies, and marshes. Most species produce two types of flowers. The first appears in spring and is purple, white, blue, or yellow. It produces a scented nectar that attracts insects, thereby ensuring pollination. The second type of flower appears later in summer. These green flowers have no petals and do not open; they are self-fertilizing and produce many seeds enclosed in a capsule. The hooded or purple violet (*V. cucullata*), which flowers in May and June, was named the floral emblem of New Brunswick in 1936. It is abundant in eastern Canada, especially in woods. Leaves and petals of violets are edible. "Candied violets" make an unusual decoration for cakes and desserts.

■ Virden

Virden, Man., lies on the Trans-Canada Highway, 25 km from the Saskatchewan border. It began in 1882 as a railway construction camp. As farm settlers moved into the area, Virden grew as a business centre for the district. In the 1950s, oil was discovered nearby and the population of the town doubled. The area still produces more than 40% of the province's oil output. The population in 1986 was 3054.

For further information, contact the Town Secretary, P.O. Box 310, Virden, Man., R0M 2C0.

■ Vireo

Vireos are members of the bird Family Vireonidae. They are greyish green above and white (usually with yellow) below. They are hard to tell apart. The bill is hooked at the tip. Their silhouette is somewhat stockier than that of the warbler, and their head and bill are stronger, when seen high up in the foliage.

Red-eyed Vireo (courtesy Macmillan Illustrated Animal Encyclopedia).

Vireos are mostly found in the tropics in the Western Hemisphere and eight of the 43 known species migrate to Canada in spring. The song of most vireos is often quite monotonous, as if some were endlessly calling "vireo, vireo," all day long. They have a distinctive cup-shaped nest that hangs suspended from a fork in the branch of a tree by its rim (most other birds' nests are supported from the bottom). They lay three to five spotted eggs which incubate for 12 to 16 days. The Red-eyed Vireo (*Vireo olivaceus*) is the most widespread; the Warbling Vireo (*V. gilvus*) is the most urbanized and its song most like that of a Purple Finch. Vireos eat mostly insects, but also berries.

■ Volcano

A volcano is a hole or opening in the crust of the Earth through which molten rock (*magma*), gases, and ash erupt. The mountain formed by accumulation and cooling of lava, ash, and other volcanic products is also called a volcano.

Most people think of a volcano as a cone-shaped mountain. In fact, there are many kinds of volcanoes. They erupt in different ways to produce different landforms. Large volumes of *lava* (molten rock that emerges at the surface) erupt relatively quietly from fissures in the Earth's crust and build broad shields, like the volcanoes of Hawaii, the great lava plateaus of Iceland, or the enormous volcanic fields that are on the ocean bottoms. Magma may explode violently to produce ash and cinders, which accumulate rapidly around the volcanic vent to form the familiar cones.

Eruptions of lava and ash may take place over many hundreds and thousands of years. Their products accumulate to form huge, majestic mountains (called *stratavolcanoes*), such as Mount St Helens of the Cascades Range in the northwestern United States. Many of the ancient, eroded volcanoes that form parts of the mountain ranges of British Columbia are of this type.

Volcanic Cinder Cone in northwestern B.C. The lava flow dates back about 200 years, the most recent in Canada (photo by Tom Parkin/ Pathfinder).

Where are Volcanoes Formed? There are about 800 active volcanoes on Earth, and some 500 more are potentially active (*dormant*). About 60 volcanoes erupt each year. About three-quarters of the active volcanoes are arranged in huge arcs around the margins of the Pacific Ocean. This almost continuous chain of arcs, known as the Pacific "ring of fire," stands above deep fractures in the Earth's crust which mark the boundaries between huge, rigid plates. Geologists believe that the skin of the Earth is divided into plates, which are continuously in motion. For example, the Pacific Ocean rides on the giant Pacific Plate that is colliding with and passing under the North American Plate. Rocks melt at great depth beneath these plate junctions, producing magma, which rises toward the Earth's surface and erupts to form volcanoes.

Mt Edziza, B.C., shows the familiar cone shape of a volcano (photo by J.A. Kraulis).

Magma also leaks out at the surface to form volcanoes where the Earth's crust is being torn apart. For example, a gigantic, underwater volcanic range, known as the mid-Atlantic Ridge, marks a long fissure stretching from Iceland to south of Tristan da Cunha (an island in the south Atlantic). Along this range volcanoes are probably erupting all the time. Iceland is the only major part of the ridge that has grown above sea level. Hundreds of volcanoes lie in the ocean basins.

Volcanoes in Canada More than 100 volcanoes have erupted in the western part of the mountains of British Columbia and the Yukon since the last ice age. The most recent eruption took place about 200 years ago near Terrace, B.C. Although most volcanoes in southern British Columbia have not erupted in living memory, they were created by the same forces that formed Mount St Helens. Some of these volcanoes may come to life again in the future.

The Canadian Shield contains some of the most ancient volcanoes on Earth. It has over 150 volcanic belts (now deformed and eroded to nearly flat plains), ranging from 600 to 2800 million years old. These volcanic belts are rich in minerals and contain most of Canada's major gold deposits.

Volcanoes are the windows through which scientists may look into the innards of the Earth. From volcanoes they can study the shifting layers of the Earth's crust, and the processes that transform

Volcanic Landscape in B.C. (photo by J.A. Kraulis).

Meadow Vole (courtesy Macmillan Illustrated Animal Encyclopedia).

molten material into solid rock. Volcanoes have also contributed to the conditions that enabled life to emerge on our planet. They have provided the air that all Earth creatures breathe.

▷ RELATED ARTICLES: **Earthquake; Plate Tectonics.**

▷ SUGGESTED READING: Fred M. Bullard, *Volcanoes of the Earth* (1976); Ellen Curran, *Mountains and Volcanoes* (1985); Kathryn Allen Goldner and Carole Garbuny Vogel, *Why Mount St Helens Blew Its Top* (1981); Patricia Lauber, *Volcano: The Eruption and Healing of Mount St Helens* (1982); Hershell H. Nixon, *Volcanoes: Nature's Fireworks* (1978).

■ Vole

Voles and lemmings belong to the same sub-family of rodents. This is the largest family of mammals in North America, with 70 species. The small, round-headed voles have protruding dark eyes, ears that do not extend much beyond the fur, and generally short, hairy tails. Many species are commonly called field mice, but they live also in forests, prairies, and tundra. Some apparently never move more than 100 m from their birth site, but others may repeatedly swim across as much as 2 km of ocean to reach neighbouring islands.

Voles do not hibernate and although they are most active at night they may be active at any hour, in any season. They eat mainly plants. The appearance of the first green vegetation in spring stimulates mating. The gestation period is usually only three weeks, so two to four litters per season are common. If hot, dry weather suppresses the growth of green vegetation, breeding may cease. As females may mature sexually in only three weeks, the vole population can increase rapidly. Voles form an important component of the food web, as they are eaten by nearly every species of predatory bird and mam-

Southern Red-backed Vole (artwork by Jan Sovak).

mal. In the wild, few live to be a year old.

■ Volkoff, Boris Vladimirovich

Dancer, choreographer (*born Boris Vladimirovich Baskakoff in 1900 at Schepotievo, Russia; died in 1974 at Toronto, Ont.*). Volkoff founded Canada's first ballet company. He studied at the Bolshoi dance school in Moscow and worked as a character dancer in Russia, China, and the United States. He came to Canada in 1929 and found work as a dancer and ballet master at a movie theatre in Toronto, where he organized live entertainment between films. He was also choreographer of ice ballets for the Toronto Skating Club for 14 years.

In 1930 Volkoff established the Boris Volkoff School of Dance, where he quickly became known as a teacher and choreographer and built up a keen audience. In 1936 his dancers won a medal at the Berlin Olympics. In May 1939 he launched the Boris Volkoff Ballet Company. One of its best-known works was *The Red Ear of Corn* (1949), which Volkoff choreographed to a score he had commissioned from Canadian composer John Weinzweig. He was also one of the founders of the Canadian Ballet Festival in 1948, which brought dancers and choreographers together in different cities for the six years of its existence. When the National Ballet of Canada was founded in 1951, Volkoff handed his studio and some of his dancers over to the young company.

■ Volleyball

Volleyball is a sport played by two teams of six players each which face each other across a net. The net is placed at 2.43 m for men and 2.24 m for women. The goal is to strike the ball over the net so that it hits the floor in the opponents' court.

Volleyball developed in the United States in the late 19th century. It has become a highly competitive sport around the world and has been an Olympic sport since 1964. Canadian teams qualified for the Olympics in 1976 and 1984. The men's team scored victories over the Soviet team in 1984 and later finished fourth at the 1984 Olympic Games.

▷ SUGGESTED READING: Robert Bratton and Christopher E. Lefroy, *Volleyball Skills and Game Concepts: Beginner to Advanced* (1986); William B. Black, *Better Volleyball* (1978); Bernthold Frohner, *Volleyball: Game, Theory and Drills* (1989).

■ Voltigeurs Canadiens

The Voltigeurs Canadiens was a light infantry corps recruited by Charles de Salaberry in Lower Canada in 1812. The Voltigeurs were the heroes of the Battle of Châteauguay during the War of 1812. The Voltigeurs were disbanded in 1815, after the end of the war, but there is a modern regiment named after them: Les Voltigeurs de Québec.

▷ RELATED ARTICLES: **Charles de Salaberry; Battle of Châteauguay; War of 1812.**

■ Voting

Voting is the process by which people choose their representatives at elections. The candidate who wins the highest number of votes is declared elected, even though he or she may not have a majority of all votes cast. Since 1874 in Canada, voting in federal elections has been conducted by secret ballot. This protects voters from attempts to influence them, for instance, by threats or bribery. Compared to many countries, Canada has a good record of voting. At federal elections, around 70% of those entitled to vote usually do so. However, at municipal and school board elections the figure is usually very much smaller.

▷ RELATED ARTICLE: **Elections.**

▷ SUGGESTED READING: Linda Granfield, *Canada Votes: How We Elect Our Government* (1990); John Ricker, John Saywell and Alan Skeoch, *How Are We Governed in the 80s?* (1982).

■ Voyageur

A voyageur was one of the colourful characters of the fur trade. Originally, voyageurs were merchant-traders who carried goods to the native people to trade. Later, the term came to refer to all participants in the trade, and especially to the men who paddled the canoes across the continent. *See* **Fur Trade.**

■ Vulture

Vultures are birds of prey of the Cathertidae family, which includes all seven American species. Two species are found in Canada: the Turkey Vulture (*Cathartes aural*) and the Black Vulture (*Coragyps atratus*).

The Turkey Vulture has a small, bald head, a strongly hooked bill, and wings whose span can reach almost 2 m. It glides and circles for long distances high in the sky. Its weak feet are unable to capture living prey, for it is a scavenger like other vultures. It has a black body, a distinctive red head, white bill, and silver-grey underside to its wings. It lives in dry, open land, cultivated fields, and woods. The female does not build a nest, but lays her two eggs in a sheltered spot such as a cave, abandoned building, or tree trunk. Incubation lasts 30 to 41 days.

The vulture is a useful bird because it gets rid of dead animals that might otherwide cause disease.

▷ SUGGESTED READING: Victoria Cox and Stan Applebaum, *Nature's Flying Janitor* (1974); Ann Warren Turner, *Vultures* (1973).

White Mud Portage on *the Winnipeg River. The voyageurs adapted the birchbark canoe from the native people. It was sturdy and light enough to carry, or "portage" around rough water (painting by Paul Kane/ courtesy NGC).*

Breeding Range of Turkey Vulture

Voyageurs at Dawn, *painting by Frances Ann Hopkins. The overturned canoes make temporary shelters for the men (courtesy NAC/C-2773).*

Wabana

Wabana, Nfld, lies at the north end of Bell Island in Conception Bay. It grew up around the iron-ore mines which opened in the 1890s and continued in production until 1966. Though the population dropped drastically at that time, Wabana remains the major town on the island. The population in 1986 was 4057.

Waddington, Miriam

Writer, poet (*born in 1917 at Winnipeg, Man.*). She published her first volume of poetry, *Green World*, in 1945. *The Second Silence* (1955) and *The Season's Lovers* (1958) follow the same themes of nature and society. Apart from many books of poetry, including *The Visitants* (1981) and *Collected Poems* (1986), Waddington is also author of a critical study of A.M. Klein (1970) and editor of *The Collected Poems of A.M. Klein* (1974). She has also written short fiction: *Summer at Lonely Beach and Other Stories* (1982).
▷ Suggested Reading: Peter Stevens, *Miriam Waddington and her Works* (1984).

Wagner, Barbara Aileen

Figure skater (*born in 1938 at Toronto, Ont.*). Wagner and her partner Robert Paul (*born in 1937 at Toronto*) formed the outstanding Canadian figure-skating team of the late 1950s and early 1960s. They started skating together in 1952. They placed sixth in the 1956 Olympic Games and won the world championship in 1957. In 1960 Olympics at Squaw Valley, California, they won the gold medal. All seven judges awarded them first place. They skated professionally until 1964. Wagner became a coach and teacher.

Wainwright

Wainwright, Alta, 200 km southeast of Edmonton, became a railway divisional point in 1908 and was named for railway executive William Wainwright. Oil and gas finds made in 1922 continue in production. The town is the centre of a large

Morgan the Magnificent, *by Ian Wallace, was inspired by the writer's love of the circus (courtesy Ian Wallace/ Groundwood Books/ Douglas & McIntyre).*

Noce canadienne *("French-Canadian Wedding"), oil on canvas by Horatio Walker. Walker's favourite subject was the daily life of the country people. At the peak of his popularity, he was one of the world's highest-paid painters (courtesy Musée du Québec/photo by Patrick Altman).*

agricultural area. Camp Wainwright is the spring training area for the Canadian military. The population in 1986 was 4665.

Walker, Horatio

Painter (*born in 1858 at Listowel, Canada West [Ont.]; died in 1938 at Ste-Pétronille, Que.*). Walker received his early training at the Notman-Fraser photographic studio in Toronto during 1873-75 before moving to New York in 1878. In 1881 he visited France, where he was greatly impressed by the work of Jean François Millet, a popular painter of French peasant life. Inspired by Millet's example, Walker spent the rest of his life producing similar paintings of French-Canadian habitant life. He often set his scenes of country life against a background of glowing skies. Though considered sentimental by today's tastes, at the peak of his reputation, he was one of the world's highest-paid artists. One of his paintings, *Oxen Drinking*, was bought for the National Gallery of Canada for $10 000, an enormous sum at the time.
▷ Suggested Reading: David Karel, *Horatio Walker* (1986).

Wallace, Ian

Writer and illustrator (*born in 1950 at Niagara Falls, Ont.*). He grew up in a family of storytellers and began drawing and painting while very young. He graduated from the Ontario College of Art in 1974 and took a job with Kids Can Press. His first book, *Julie News*, appeared in 1974. *The Sandwich* and *The Christmas Tree House* followed in 1975 and 1976.

The idea for *Chin Chang and the Dragon's Dance* (1984) came to Wallace as he watched a Chinese parade. Chin is frightened that he will make mistakes during his first dragon's dance. He runs away, but meets an old lady who helps him to find the courage to join the ceremony. Remembering how he once had rescued an injured sparrow, Wallace created *The Sparrow's Song* (1986), the story of Katie and her brother Charlie, who adopt an orphaned bird and later set it free. Wallace's love of circuses led to *Morgan the Magnificent* (1987), the adventure of a little girl who sneaks away to the circus and walks the high wire.

Wallace's illustrations help to portray the emotions and ideas in each story. The decorative borders in *Chin Chang* suggest Chinese ceremonies. Green, the colour of nature, is dominant in *The Sparrow's Song*. The pictures in *Morgan* are in the style of circus posters and wagons.

Walnut (artwork by Claire Tremblay).

■ Wallaceburg

Wallaceburg, Ont., lies beside the Sydenham River in southwestern Ontario near the United States border. Settled in the 1830s, it grew as a lumbering and shipbuilding centre. After 1900, glass making and sugar-beet growing became important. Sugar beets have declined but glass products are still important in the local economy, along with metal goods, plastics, auto accessories, and the canning of farm products. The town is named for Scottish patriot Sir William Wallace. The population in 1986 was 11 367.

■ Walleye

The walleye is a freshwater species of the perch family. It is found almost everywhere in Canada, from the eastern side of the Rockies to the mid-North Shore of Quebec. The walleye has a long body, pointed mouth, and slightly forked tail. It has two dorsal fins, one spiny and one soft-rayed. Its large, protruding eyes allow it to see well at night and in murky water. Walleye are *carnivorous* (meat eaters), feeding mainly on other fish but also insects, crustaceans, and amphibians.

In spring, they spawn on sand or gravel of large streams, rivers, and lakes. As adults they are prey for pike and muskellunge; the young are eaten by various species of fish. They are taken in both commercial and sport fishing. Their white, flaky, flesh is very tasty.

▷ Suggested Reading: Frederick Wooding, *The Book of Canadian Fishes* (1973).

■ Walnut

Walnuts (*Juglans*) and hickories (*Carya*) are trees belonging to the walnut family (Juglandaceae). In Canada, walnut trees are now found only around the Great Lakes, the St Lawrence River, and in southern New Brunswick. But 50 000 years ago, when the climate was much warmer, they were found throughout North America, even in Alaska and Greenland.

Walnut trees have very large leaves (20-30 cm long), divided into numerous leaflets: 11 to 17 in the case of the butternut (*J. cinerea*), 15 to 23 in the black walnut (*J. nigra*). They produce nuts with an edible kernel, surrounded by a hard shell wrapped in a soft hull. The butternut hull yields a yellow or orange dye, and the black walnut, a brownish black dye. Black walnut wood has many excellent properties: it is hard, heavy, strong, and resists decay. It does not twist or shrink with age. It is used for high-quality furniture and for veneers for cabinet work. Gun butts and stocks are usually made of Black walnut. Commercial plantations have been established in southern Ontario and Quebec to meet market demand. Butternut is primarily in demand for its nuts. Native people used to extract an oil from the nuts which they used for medicinal purposes. Squirrels bury the nuts in the ground as winter approaches, thereby helping them germinate and contributing to the spread of walnut trees.

■ Walrus

The walrus (*Odobenus rosmarus*) looks very much like a huge sea lion but is different enough to be placed into its own family, Odobenidae. It has a streamlined

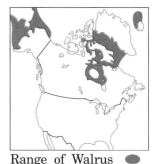

Range of Walrus ●

Walrus male and female. *The walrus's wrinkled skin covers a thick layer of fat which provides insulation against the cold arctic waters (artwork by Pieter Folkens).*

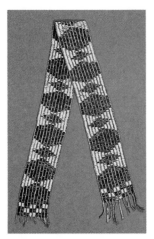

Wampum Belt (courtesy NMC/CMC/575-620).

Dorothy Walton was a badminton champion but excelled in tennis and other sports as well (courtesy NAC/ PA-50308).

body, powerful, short limbs, and a small head. The wrinkled skin, frequently more than 25 mm thick, is underlain by a thick layer of fat which provides insulation and buoyancy. The two upper canine teeth are enlarged into ivory tusks.

Walrus males can be 3.5 m long and weigh more than 1000 kg. They often lounge together on the rocks or on ice floes. Males usually form groups apart from the females.

Walrus are awkward on land, but in water dive and swim with ease. They feed mostly on molluscs, which they harvest from the ocean floor. They mate beneath the surface of the sea in February and March, near the end of the arctic winter. A great deal of subsurface vocalization is associated with their courtship. The huge neck of the males has air sacks that can be inflated, allowing the walrus to produce loud, resonant, bell-like sounds both on the surface and under the water.

After about 366 days, a single young, covered by a thin coat of silvery hair, is delivered on an ice floe. The young walrus is nursed for almost two years and the mother often carries it on her back while swimming.

Inuit once hunted walrus for their meat, oil, and skin, which were used to cover boats that were very resistant to puncture by ice. European whalers decimated walrus populations for oil and ivory between 1650 and the early 1900s. Today some are still taken by the Inuit, mostly for the ivory, which is used in carvings. Protection from commercial exploitation has led to greater numbers of some local populations. Their only natural predators, besides humans, are killer whales and polar bears.

▷ SUGGESTED READING: Laima Dingwall, *Walrus* (1986).

■ Walton, Dorothy Louise
Badminton champion (*born MacKenzie in 1909 at Swift Current, Sask.; died in 1981 at Toronto, Ont.*). From high school

on, Walton showed exceptional ability in a wide range of sports. At the University of Saskatchewan, where she studied economics, she was on 14 sports teams, including swimming, field hockey, tennis, badminton, and track and field. She was the first female student to be awarded the oak shield as the university's outstanding athlete.

She eventually moved to Toronto, and in 1935 won the Ontario badminton championship. In the next few years, she won title after title, becoming the champion female badminton player of North America. In 1939 she won the All-England badminton championship, which made her world champion. She held the title until 1947.

Meanwhile, Walton also shone as a tennis star. Between 1924 and 1931, she won 54 tennis titles in western Canada, and in the late 1930s she ranked as one of Canada's six best female tennis players. In the Canadian Press poll of 1950, she was voted one of Canada's six leading female athletes of the half-century.

■ Wampum
Wampum were prized by native people in eastern Canada. They were used to record treaties, settle disputes, and make peace. They were made of white and purple shells that were traded inland from the Atlantic coast. The shells were threaded on strings or woven into belts, often with intricate designs that had a precise meaning. In the fur trade they were sometimes used by Europeans as a trade good or as a form of currency.

▷ SUGGESTED READING: R. Fadden, *Wampum Belts* (1983).

■ Wapiti
The wapiti, or American elk (*Cervus elaphus*), is the second-largest deer in the family Cervidae. In Europe it is called the red deer. Adult males may weigh as much as 500 kg. The animal's Shawnee Indian name, *wapiti*, means "white rump" — and indeed, its brown coat bears a light patch on the rump. Males bear magnificent antlers.

Today wapiti are found from southern Ontario, across the parkland belt, to the foothills and alpine pastures of the western provinces. Wapiti often migrate. They live in both coniferous and deciduous forests, brushlands, grasslands, and even alpine tundra. In summer, the cows and calves group together, while the bulls form separate bands. During the rut, dominant bulls defend a harem of up to 20

Wapiti Bulls will defend a harem of up to 20 cows during rut (photo by Thomas Kitchin).

Range of Wapiti ●
park herds ○
introduced ·

cows and their calves from other bulls. After the rut, most of the males depart and the females, plus a few males, gather into large herds, sometimes of as many as 1000, led by a mature female. Males more than two years old usually form smaller separate herds. The cow-calf herds dissemble in spring when the females depart to bear their young alone. A single young is typically born in late May or June. Although males are capable of breeding as yearlings they do not often get a chance to do so.

The wapiti is the noisiest of the deer family, and its bugling can be heard for 1.5 km. Wapiti are very adaptable feeders. In summer, they eat sedges and grasses, and even mushrooms. In fall, those within the deciduous forest eat great quantities of fallen leaves. During winter, they paw through snow for forage, and also browse on twigs. When food is very scarce, the bark of large aspens and even the needles of Douglas fir, juniper, and pine may be eaten.

Hunters prize the wapiti as a trophy. Increasing numbers are being raised on game ranches for antlers, which are used to prepare a tonic in many Asian countries; hides, which are the source of excellent buckskin; and meat. Wapiti respond well to management, and are either reoccupying traditional ranges or expanding their range in many parts of Canada. The main natural predators include black and grizzly bears, wolves, cougars, and, to a lesser extent, coyotes and lynxes.

▷ SUGGESTED READING: Pamela Martin, *Elk* (1985).

War Brides

War brides are women who married members of the Canadian military overseas during World War II, then came to Canada after the war to join their husbands. By the end of 1946, 47 783 wives had come to Canada, most from Great Britain. The government gave the war brides free passage to their new homes in Canada, along with food and medical care on the boats and trains.

▷ SUGGESTED READING: Joyce Hibbert, *The War Brides* (1978); Peggy O'Hara, *From Romance to Reality* (1983).

War Crimes

War criminals are people who break internationally agreed-upon rules against the making of war or the mistreatment or murder of civilians and prisoners of war. Kurt Meyer, a German army officer, was sentenced to death for crimes against Canadian prisoners in World War II, but this was changed to life imprisonment, and he was released after several years in prison. German and Japanese leaders were convicted of war crimes at Nuremberg, Germany, and Tokyo, Japan, from 1945 to 1947. Some World War II criminals escaped, of course, and it was sometimes wondered if they had made their way to Canada. On February 7, 1985, the Government of Canada set up a Commission of Inquiry on war criminals under Judge Jules Deschênes to find out whether there were German war criminals in Canada, when and how they got in, and what could be done to deal with them.

The commission made its report on December 30, 1986, after looking at the files of more than 800 alleged war criminals. It recommended legal action against 20 Canadian residents, and that the government continue to investigate approximately 200 other files. In most cases the commission said that the accused was either not living in Canada or that there was no solid proof that he or she had participated in war crimes. In May 1990, Imre Finta was acquitted after he was tried for war crimes.

▷ SUGGESTED READING: Margaret Baldwin, *The Boys Who Saved the Children* (1982); Eva Brewster, *Vanished in Darkness: An Auschwitz Memoir* (1984); Barbara Rogasky, *Smoke and Ashes: The Story of the Holocaust* (1988).

War Measures Act

The War Measures Act became law in 1914, the year World War I began. It was designed to give the federal government power to deal with domestic and international emergencies. Under the War Measures Act, for example, the government could censor the media, arrest people on the suspicion that they had committed a crime, imprison people without trial, ignore Parliament, control communications and transportation, and generally

Time Line: War of the Austrian Succession

Major engagements in North America:
- **1744** French troops from Louisbourg invade Nova Scotia. They seize Canso but fail to take Annapolis Royal
- **1745** A combined British and New England force captures Louisbourg. Soldiers from New France raid Saratoga and other frontier settlements in the British colonies
- **1748** Treaty of Aix-la-Chapelle formally ends the war. Louisbourg is returned to the French

A Mere Matter of Marching

"The acquisition of Canada this year ... will be a mere matter of marching, and will give us experience for the attack of Halifax the next, and the final expulsion of England from the American continent."

Thomas Jefferson, U.S. President, August 1812

adopt dictatorial powers. Such powers are usually thought to be necessary in times of war, when a country obviously faces an emergency. In World War I, for example, the government used the War Measures Act to intern people whom it suspected of disloyalty, to censor some newspapers and close some publications down altogether on the grounds that they were unpatriotic, and to declare strikes and certain kinds of meetings illegal. Similar powers were used in World War II.

The federal government can use the War Measures Act during peacetime if it fears that the country is in danger. In October 1970, for example, the government declared that a state of "apprehended insurrection" existed in Quebec and that an armed rebellion was about to take place. This fear was the result of the activities of the Front de Libération du Québec, which kidnapped a British diplomat (James Cross) and assassinated a Quebec Cabinet minister (Pierre Laporte). Later these fears turned out to be greatly exaggerated but at the time, in October and November 1970, over 450 Quebec citizens were arrested and imprisoned simply because they were thought to be security risks.

Opponents of the War Measures Act have argued that it was very dangerous to give any government such sweeping power. They saw the Act as a threat to democracy. A government could not use the War Measures Act unless Parliament approves, but critics point out that in the parliamentary system the government automatically has a majority.

Criticisms of the War Measures Act led the federal government to repeal it in 1988 and to replace it with the Emergencies Act.

▷ RELATED ARTICLE: **October Crisis.**

▷ SUGGESTED READING: Denis Smith, *Bleeding Hearts, Bleeding Country: Canada and the Quebec Crisis* (1971); David J. Riseborough, editor, *Canada and the French* (1975).

■ War of the Austrian Succession

The War of the Austrian Succession was a European war lasting from 1739 to 1748. It spread to North America (1744-48), where it was known as King George's War. Britain and France were on opposing sides. The main developments affecting Canada are shown in the table. The war ended in a stalemate which satisfied neither side. It was followed by an uneasy peace, which lasted barely six years before fighting again broke out in North America between France and England.

▷ RELATED ARTICLE: **Seven Years' War.**

▷ SUGGESTED READING: George F.G. Stanley, *New France: The Last Phase 1744-1760* (1968).

■ War of the Spanish Succession

The War of the Spanish Succession, also known as Queen Anne's War, was a general European war in which France and Britain were on opposing sides. It lasted from 1702 to 1713.

As usual, the war was fought in North America as well as Europe, and there was local raiding between Acadia and the New England colonies. French forces led by d'Iberville destroyed the English settlement at Bonavista in Newfoundland (1704) and captured St John's, also in Newfoundland (1708). The British captured Port-Royal (1710), a victory that brought them control of Acadia. The British also attempted to invade Quebec, but their invasion fleet was wrecked in the St Lawrence River in 1711. The war ended with the Treaty of Utrecht, in which France gave up all claims to Hudson Bay and Newfoundland. France also ceded most of Acadia to Britain. However, the French retained much of present-day New Brunswick, along with Île Saint-Jean [Prince Edward Island] and Île Royale [Cape Breton Island].

▷ RELATED ARTICLES: **Acadia; Pierre Le Moyne d'Iberville.**

▷ SUGGESTED READING: Dale Miquelon, *New France 1701-1744* (1987).

■ War of 1812

The War of 1812, which lasted from June 1812 to December 1814, was an important milestone in Canadian history, a fight for survival against American invasion. Officially, the war was between the U.S. and Great Britain, but it focused on Britain's North American colonies rather than on Britain itself. Most of the fighting took place in the border regions between the U.S. and Upper and Lower Canada [Ontario and Quebec].

CAUSES OF THE WAR

A major cause of the war was American anger that U.S. ships were being stopped and searched by the Royal Navy. Britain was in the midst of the Napoleonic Wars against France, and it had declared a naval blockade to prevent any shipping from taking supplies to France. To enforce the blockade, the British stopped and searched ships from neutral countries. Many of these ships were American. The British also claimed the right to seize any deserters from the Royal Navy that they found on the ships. In 1807 they took four

War of 1812

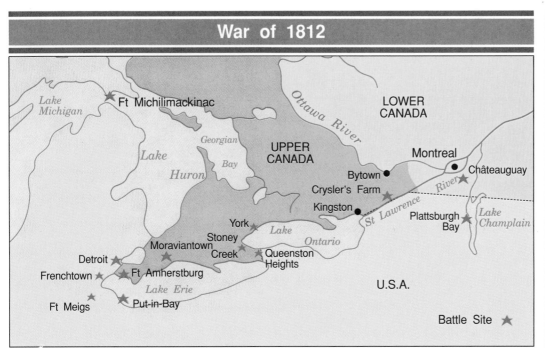

seaman from the American frigate *Chesapeake*, assuming that they were British deserters. But two of the men were American. This caused such an outcry in the United States that the two were later returned to the U.S. with an apology. But the British refused to give up their practice of boarding and searching neutral ships on the high seas and forcing deserters back into the Royal Navy.

This alone would likely not have led to war, but the U.S. Congress was dominated by a group of men known as "War Hawks." The War Hawks were mostly from the western and southern states. They wanted to expand into the Indian Territory of the Ohio Valley. The native people of the Ohio Valley traded with British merchants from Montreal, buying the guns with which they fought to protect their territory. The War Hawks intended to stop this trade by driving the British out of Canada. Like many other Americans, they believed that it was the "manifest destiny" of the United States to take over all of British North America. Here was their chance to do so.

The declaration of war was made on June 18, 1812. Less than a month later, an American army crossed the Detroit River and invaded Upper Canada.

THE FIGHTING

The Americans thought it would be easy to conquer Canada — just "a matter of marching." They did not expect much opposition. In Upper Canada, about four-fifths of the inhabitants were American in origin, most of them recent arrivals

who had moved north because of the cheap land available. In Lower Canada most of the people were of French origin. The Americans expected both groups to rise up and join them, eager to free themselves from British rule. But this is not what happened. Instead, settlers of all origins fought to protect their homeland. They wanted to remain under British rule.

The brunt of the fighting was borne by professional British soldiers stationed in Canada. They were supported by Canadian militiamen and also by native troops. The native fighters included Chief Tecumseh and others from the Ohio Valley, and Mohawks from the Grand River in Upper Canada and from Caughnawaga in Lower Canada.

The initial invasion was quickly beaten back, thanks to the bold action of General Isaac Brock, who was in charge of military and civil affairs in Upper Canada. Brock's forces won three successive victories in 1812 — at Michilimackinac, Detroit, and Queenston Heights. This gave a great boost to morale early in the war, when it was most needed.

For the next two years the warfare continued, with each side gaining some territory and losing some. Most of the fighting took place in the Niagara Peninsula and on Lakes Ontario and Erie. It spread as far south as Washington, which the British attacked in 1814, and there was a campaign in Lower Canada in 1813. The war also affected the British colonies on the Atlantic, where adventurous sea captains became licensed privateers, preying on

Time Line: War of 1812

● **1812**
June 18 U.S. declares war on Great Britain
July 12 American army crosses the Detroit River into Upper Canada
July 17 The British capture Michilimackinac
Aug 16 The British lay siege to Detroit. Americans surrender without a fight
Oct 13 The British, led by Brock and General Roger Sheaffe, repulse an American invasion at Queenston Heights. Brock is killed
● **1813**
Apr 27 American fleet on Lk Ontario captures York [Toronto], burning the Parliament Building
May-Dec Americans take Fort George but are driven back at the battles of Stoney Creek (June 6) and Beaver Dams (June 24)
Sept 10 American navy defeats British at Put-In-Bay on Lake Erie
Oct 5 Battle of Moraviantown. British retreat, leaving Tecumseh and his native warriors to face the American attack.
Tecumseh is killed
Oct-Nov American advance on Montreal defeated at Châteauguay (Oct 26) by Colonel Charles de Salaberry, and at Crysler's Farm (Nov 11) by Colonel Joseph Morrison
● **1814**
July Americans again invade Niagara peninsula but defeated at Lundy's Lane (July 25)
Aug British troops land near Washington, D.C., and burn the White House and Capitol
Sept The British, led by Sir George Prevost, strike south, but are defeated at Plattsburg on Lake Champlain
Dec 24 Treaty of Ghent ends the war and restores the boundaries to their positions at the beginning of the war

American merchant ships and keeping a proportion of the profits.

RESULTS OF THE WAR

The war ended in a stalemate with neither side being the winner. The Treaty of Ghent, signed in Belgium on December 24, 1814, returned all conquered territory, so that the situation was the same as it had been in 1812. The big difference was that the people in the British colonies, especially Upper and Lower Canada, had gained a sense of nationhood. Together, they had fought to repel an invader, and this gave them a new pride and caused them to think of themselves as Canadians, identifying with the land in which they lived rather than in the countries they had come from.

The major events of the war are given in the timeline on the previous page. There are also separate articles on the battles of Beaver Dams; Châteauguay; Crysler's Farm; Lundy's Lane; Queenston Heights; and Stoney Creek.

▷ RELATED ARTICLES: **Sir Isaac Brock; Laura Secord; Tecumseh.**

▷ SUGGESTED READING: Pierre Berton, *The Invasion of Canada 1812-1813* (1980) and *Flames Across the Border, 1813-1814* (1981); Barbara and Heather Bramwell, *Adventures at the Mill* (1963); Mary Beacock Fryer, *Battlefields of Canada* (1986); J. Mackay Hitsman, *The Incredible War of 1812: A Military History* (1965); Barbara Mitchell, *Cornstalks and Cannonballs* (1980); Gregory Sass, *Redcoat* (1985); George F.G. Stanley, *The War of 1812: The Land Operations* (1983); Wesley B. Turner, *The War of 1812* (1982).

■ Warbler

In North America, warbler applies to brightly coloured songbirds of the Wood-warbler subfamily in the Emberizidae family that also includes sparrows, meadowlarks, blackbirds, and others. The Old World subfamily of warblers is in a different family of birds (Muscicapidae). In Canada they are represented only by

Black-and-White Warbler (courtesy Macmillan Illustrated Animal Encyclopedia).

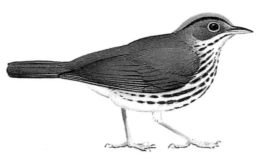

The Ovenbird hunts for insects along the ground (courtesy Macmillan Illustrated Animal Encyclopedia).

Yellow Warbler (artwork by Claire Tremblay).

kinglets and the Blue-grey Gnatcatcher. Thirty-seven of the 125 species of warblers breed here.

These are the birds that win the keenest attention from birdwatchers in spring, when the males are at their vivid best, with splashes of yellow, red, orange, blue, or green, and a whole range of patterns. Many species have bright yellow markings and sometimes are referred to as wild canaries. They lose their brilliant plumage in fall, taking on a more discreet appearance. Their delicate bill is well adapted to catching insects in a variety of situations: the Ovenbird (*Seiurus aurocapillus*), on the ground; the Black-and-white Warbler (*Mniotilta varia*), on branches and trunks of trees; the Black-throated Blue Warbler (*Dendroica caerulescens*), on shrubs or saplings; and the Yellow-rumped Warbler (*D. coronata*), on evergreen trees. These birds are very useful, particularly whenever there is a spruce budworm infestation.

The nest is usually cup-shaped, though the Ovenbird builds one shaped like an oven (hence its name). Many suffer greatly from the predations of the Brown-headed Cowbird (*Molothrus ater*), which lays its eggs in warbler nests. Only the Yellow Warbler (*D. petechia*), which then builds a new nest over the old one, can fight back against this parasitism.

▷ SUGGESTED READING: Mary MacPherson, *Birdwatch: An Introduction to Birding for Young People* (1988).

■ Ward, Maxwell William

Airline pioneer and businessman (*born in 1921 at Edmonton, Alta*). Max Ward grew up in Edmonton, served with the Royal

Canadian Air Force in World War II, and then became a bush pilot, flying between Yellowknife, N.W.T., and Peace River, Alta. In 1946 he bought an airplane and formed his own airline, Polaris Charter Company Ltd, which he operated single-handedly, acting as pilot, ground crew — everything. Based in Yellowknife, it was the forerunner of Wardair, which became Canada's largest charter airline.

Ward formed Wardair in 1953 as a northern service. His planes were the first seen in some of the North's most remote communities. In 1962 he began charter flights abroad, having moved his head office to Edmonton. Wardair became a major charter airline, offering a wide variety of package tours and overseas holidays. In addition, it competed with Air Canada and Canadian Airlines International on the busiest scheduled runs between Canadian cities. In 1989 the company became part of Canadian Airlines International.

■ Wardair, *see* Aviation; Max Ward

■ Ware, John

Rancher (*born in 1845 near Georgetown, South Carolina, U.S.; died in 1905 near Brooks, Alta*). John Ware was a well-known rancher in the southwestern prairies around the turn of the century. Tough and very strong, he was greatly admired by his neighbours, who viewed him as "one of the best-natured and most obliging men in the country."

Ware had been born a slave on a planta-

John Ware and his family (courtesy Glenbow Archives/NA-263-1).

tion in South Carolina, and after slavery was abolished in the United States he became a cowboy in Texas. In 1882 he came to Canada on a cattle drive, staying on to work as a cowboy in the foothills country southwest of Calgary. In 1890 Ware started his own ranch in the foothills, and ten years later he moved to a larger ranch along the Red Deer River, east of Brooks. He died there as a result of an accident when his horse tripped in a badger's hole and fell heavily, rolling on him.

▷ SUGGESTED READING: Grant MacEwan, *John Ware's Cow Country* (1960).

■ Wars, *see* American Civil War; Armed Forces; Fenians; Iroquois; Korean War; North-West Rebellion; October Crisis; Peacekeeping; Spanish-American War; Rebellions of 1837; Red River Rebellion; Seven Years' War; War of 1812; War of the Austrian Succession; War of the Spanish Succession; World War I; World War II.

■ Wartime Elections Act

The Wartime Elections Act was passed in 1917 during World War I. It gave women serving in the armed forces and close female relatives of men in the forces the right to vote in federal elections. This was the first step to granting all Canadian women the federal vote.

At the same time, the Act took away the vote from large numbers of immigrant men who had been born in countries that were at war with Canada. Even if they had become citizens, most were denied the vote unless their citizenship dated back to before 1902. *See* Women's Suffrage.

■ Wasp

Wasps, like bees and ants, belong to Order Hymenoptera. They have a narrowing at the base of the abdomen ("wasp-waist"). Some have a social structure (hornets, paper wasps, yellowjackets), others are solitary and often parasitical (gall and spider wasps), and others miniscule (chalchids).

Wasps are widespread in Canada: we have well over 1500 species. They are yellow, red, blue, white, and black. Their size varies from less than 1 mm to 30 mm. The yellowjackets live in colonies and eat insects, fruit, and nectar. They are aggressive and, unlike bees, can sting repeatedly for they do not lose their stingers after use. Spider wasps catch spiders that they paralyse by injecting them with venom from their stinger. They imprison the spider in a small hole dug in the ground, and lay an egg on top. The spider will be slowly devoured by the larva. Gall wasps are

Max Ward served with the air force and worked as a bush pilot before founding his own airline, Wardair (courtesy Wardair International).

Thread-waisted Wasp

Paper Wasp (artwork by Jan Sovak).

usually black and very small (4-8 mm). They parasitize plants, causing the appearance of the characteristic gall. Some species of wasp parasitize insect larvae or eggs, and are used for the biological control of certain pests.

▷ SUGGESTED READING: John Reynolds, *Bees and Wasps* (1974).

■ Water

Water is a liquid compound of hydrogen and oxygen. Its chemical formula is H_2O. Pure water at sea level freezes at 0°C and boils at 100°C.

Water covers almost 75% of the surface of the Earth (photo by Bill Brooks/Masterfile).

Water is the most abundant liquid on Earth. In liquid or in the form of ice, it covers almost 75% of the surface of the Earth. It is also present in the atmosphere in the form of vapour. It makes up most of the living tissues in our bodies.

Water is essential to life. Because of the life it supports, it provides us with food. In Canada, it is used to generate electricity. It is used for transportation and irrigation and is essential to many industries.

Water moves continuously through the environment in what is called the *water cycle* (*see* diagram, Volume I, page 109). Water is heated by the sun and evaporates from the oceans, lakes, and land surfaces. Movements of air may carry the water vapour over great distances. The water falls

The Water Cycle circulates water as liquid and vapour through the atmosphere, ground, and oceans (photo by Al Harvey/Masterfile).

back to Earth in the form of precipitation, and runs into streams and rivers which flow into oceans and lakes, thereby completing the cycle.

In most of the world, about two-thirds of the water on the land surfaces evaporates. Because Canada is a cold country, less than 40% of the water evaporates. Much of it is held in the form of ice. Canada has an immense reserve of fresh water. Canada has 9% of the world's supply of fresh water.

Groundwater Two-thirds of the world's fresh water is found underground. Groundwater is held in the tiny spaces in soil or in cracks in the rock.

When this water accumulates, it forms an *aquifer*. Aquifers are the sources of wells and springs. Groundwater is extremely valuable in parts of Canada for irrigation or use by cities and towns.

Bottled groundwater, known as "spring water" or "mineral water" is bought by many Canadians to replace drinking water from taps. It is generally safer to drink than surface water because it has been naturally filtered by the ground. However, these waters are also being polluted by chemicals and sewage.

Water Distribution Water resources are unevenly distributed across Canada. Alberta accounts for almost half the water used in Canada. It has over 60% of the irrigated land in Canada. However, Alberta has only 2.2% of the supply of water. Saskatchewan also requires large quantities of water for irrigation.

Manitoba, Ontario, and Quebec have abundant supplies of water. The major problem in these areas is the *quality* of the water. Much of it is polluted by industry or by sewage.

Drought A drought occurs when there is a below normal supply of water, in the form of precipitation, streamflow, or

% of Fresh Water by Province	
	%
Newfoundland	4.5
Prince Edward Island	0.0
Nova Scotia	0.4
New Brunswick	0.2
Quebec	24.4
Ontario	23.5
Manitoba	13.5
Saskatchewan	10.8
Alberta	2.2
British Columbia	2.4
Yukon	0.6
Northwest Territories	17.7
	100.2*

* does not add up to 100% because of rounding

Icefields, St Elias Mountains, Yukon. Much of Canada's water is held in the form of ice (photo by J.A. Kraulis).

Irrigation *equipment sprays water on crops near Brooks, Alta (photo by Jim Merrithew).*

groundwater. Droughts are natural events and can occur anywhere. However, droughts more seriously threaten areas where the annual water supplies are barely adequate to meet water demands. In Canada, southern Saskatchewan and the Interior valleys of British Columbia suffer frequent drought.

Water Distribution Systems The movement of water from its sources to its users requires a complex system. Water is moved to irrigate crops by a network of canals, pumps, and pipes. The system required to distribute water to city users is even more intricate. It requires pumping stations, treatment plants, reservoirs, and pipes. Water is not always taken from the nearest source. The city of Winnipeg, for instance, gets its water from Shoal Lake in the Lake of the Woods, 160 km away.

While Canada has great water resources, Canadians are also among the highest users in the world. Care and conservation are required to maintain the quality of the water. Society also faces a number of conflicting demands on water. The Fraser River, for example, has a potential to produce hydroelectricity. However, the dams required would destroy the salmon run. So far, those protecting the fishery have prevented the dams being built.

▷ RELATED ARTICLES: **Environment; Ice; Lakes; Oceans; Rivers.**

■ Water Flea

Water fleas are tiny, freshwater crustaceans of order Cladocera. They are found in abundance in pond water. There are about 400 species in the world. To swim, the water flea (*Daphnia pulex*) sweeps its antennae in up-and-down strokes that propel it along. It feeds on phytoplankton and organic detritus that it catches in the hairs on its appendages. During unfavourable conditions, the water flea can remain dormant. In Canada,

researchers are studying the possibility of raising water fleas for use as fish food.

■ Water Lily

The water lily (*Nymphaea*), with its huge white or pink flowers, is certainly the most beautiful of all water plants. It opens in morning and closes in the afternoon. The flowers of the pond lily (*Nuphar*), yellow and smaller, seem never to open fully. In both cases, the huge rounded, floating leaves provide rafts where frogs can sunbathe.

The pond lily is much more common and grows farther north than water lilies. In summer, the best place to see a moose is near a pond lily colony. The plant's large root systems (called *rhizomes*) contain starch, like potatoes, and are favourites of the moose. They are also very nutritious. Beaver and muskrat also like pond lily and water lily leaves and rhizomes, but ducks eat only the seeds. The Indians ate both rhizomes and seeds, and made use of the plants' medicinal properties.

White Water Lily (photo by William Reynolds).

Other members of this family of aquatic plants include the water-shield (*Brasenia*), which has a characteristic envelope of gelatin surrounding all its submerged parts.

▷ SUGGESTED READING: Charles O. Masters, *Encyclopedia of the Water Lily* (1974).

■ Water Pollution, *see* Pollution

■ Water Transportation, *see* Transportation

■ Waterfall

A waterfall is a sudden drop in a river or stream. Waterfalls are often found in mountainous terrain, where the course of a river is steep and turbulent. They may result from some great disruption in the land, such as an earthquake, the upward movement of the land, or the action of a glacier. Niagara Falls, for example, was

Takakkaw Falls *Many people consider Takakkaw to be Canada's highest waterfall. It drops a total of 503 m into the Yoho River. Its longest vertical drop is 254 m, second only to Della Falls. By comparison, Niagara Falls drops 57 m (photo by Bill Brooks/ Masterfile).*

Montmorency Falls *(photo by John deVisser).*

Falls and Location	Vertical Drop (m)
Della Falls Della Lake, B.C.	440
Takakkaw Falls Daly Glacier, B.C.	254
Hunlen Falls Atnarko River, B.C.	253
Panther Falls Nigel Creek, Alta	183
Helmcken Falls Murtle River, B.C.	137
Bridal Veil Falls Bridal Creek, B.C.	122
Virginia Falls South Nahanni River, N.W.T.	90
Montmorency Falls Rivière Montmor-ency, Que.	84
Ouiatchouan Falls Rivière Ouiatchouan, Que.	79
Churchill Falls Churchill River, Nfld	75
Brandywine Falls Brandywine Creek, B.C.	61
Niagara Falls (Horseshoe Falls) Niagara River, Ont.	57

Helmcken Falls on the Murtle River, B.C., has carved a deep cauldron in the rock (photo by J.A. Kraulis).

created when the glacial ice retreated some 10 000 years ago. Tidal falls are formed where a river empties into the ocean over a rock shelf. At low tide, the river falls over the drop into the ocean. At high tide, the flow is reversed as the ocean waters are higher than the river. The most famous example of a tidal falls in Canada is the Reversing Falls on the Saint John River in the city of Saint John, New Brunswick.

If there is a series of short drops, it is called a *cascade*. If it is more gradual, it forms a *rapids*. Some of the notable rapids in Canada are on the South Nahanni Riv-er, N.W.T., on the Fraser River, B.C., and on the St Lawrence River near Montreal, Que.

Life of a Waterfall Over time, the pow-er of moving water will erode rock. The greater the flow, the faster the erosion. For example, Niagara Falls has been cut-ting through its channel at roughly 1.2 m per year. Since it was created about 10 000 years ago, it has cut a deep gorge, some 11 km long. This rapid erosion is caused by the huge volume of water pouring over Niagara.

In time, these great falls will turn to rapids. In some very high falls, erosion is much slower because the flow of water is small and much of it turns to mist on the descent. The world's highest waterfall, Angel Falls in Venezuela (979 m high), is an example.

Canadian Waterfalls The highest wa-terfall in Canada, and the tenth highest in the world, is Della Falls (440 m high), in British Columbia. Niagara Falls (57 m) is one of the largest waterfalls in the world, measured by the volume of water that passes over it. Other great waterfalls in Canada include Churchill Falls (75 m) in Labrador, which generates huge amounts of power through its deep gorge; Mont-morency Falls (84 m), in Quebec, which is known for its beauty; and Virginia Falls (90 m) in the N.W.T., one of the wildest and most beautiful waterfalls in the world.

Alexandra Falls, near Hay River, N.W.T. (photo by Hälle Flygare).

Importance Waterfalls were very im-portant to early settlers, who harnessed their power to drive their mills. However, they were also obstacles to the canoes and boats that carried Canada's early trade. Canals had to be built to bypass rapids at Sault Ste Marie and on the St Lawrence River and the falls at Niagara (the Well-and Canal).

Today, many of Canada's waterfalls provide electric power. While many of the highest falls lie deep in the wilderness and are seldom seen, those that can be reached, such as Niagara, attract millions of visitors to their spectacle.

Niagara Falls (photo by Michel de Sablière/ Canapress Photo Service).

■ Waterfowl

The term "waterfowl" is used to describe birds of the Family Anatidae. It includes ducks, geese, and swans. Forty-nine species of waterfowl are found in Canada. They are most abundant in the boreal forest areas of North America. All are water birds. They have flattened, round-tipped bills, webbed feet, and waterproof plumage over a heavy layer of down. Waterfowl are generally strong fliers. In spring and fall they usually travel in large flocks, following north-south migration patterns called "flyways." They often build their nests near water by plucking up plant material from around the nest. Many nests are lined with down and three to 12 eggs are incubated by the female. Ducks usually lay more eggs than geese or swans. When the female leaves the nest before incubation, she covers the eggs with down plucked from her lower breast.

Waterfowl were some of the first birds to be domesticated and have been hunted as food for thousands of years. Today, they are threatened in some areas by the destruction of wetlands. Many small ponds and swamps are filled in for agricultural use, destroying areas used for feeding and nesting. Many suffer from lead poisoning after eating lead shot. It is ingested with the many seeds that some ducks strain from the mud. The Labrador Duck is a species that became extinct in the late 1800s before much was known of its life history.

▷ SUGGESTED READING: John P.S. Mackenzie, *Waterfowl* (1988).

■ Waterloo

Waterloo, Ont., is the smaller of the twin cities, Kitchener-Waterloo. The two cities are not separated by any natural boundary, yet they have developed separately.

Waterloo was first settled by Mennonites in 1806. It became a village in 1857, a town in 1876, and a city in 1947. The town remained heavily German until the late 1940s. The Seagram distillery prospered in the 1870s. Other industries include insurance, furniture, and music.

The population increased fivefold from 1948 to 1981. The German population dropped and the city spread into suburbs. Nevertheless, the strong sense of community remains. The city contains two universities, Wilfrid Laurier and Waterloo. The population was 58 718 in 1986.

For further information, contact the City Clerk, 100 Regina Street South, P.O. Box 337, Waterloo, Ont., N2J 4A8.

■ Waterton, Betty

Writer (*born in 1923 at Oshawa, Ont.*). Waterton moved to British Columbia when she was a child. She worked as a reporter and TV artist. She published her first children's book in 1978. Her books are of two types: stories of young people overcoming problems, and humorous adventures of funny characters. In *A Salmon for Simon* (1978), a native boy feels unhappy because he is the only member of his family who cannot catch a fish. *Pettranella* (1980) is about a 19th-century immigrant girl who finds happiness in her new home in Manitoba. *Mustard* (1983) is about a very large puppy which annoys everyone until it rescues a drowning kitten. Three books, *Quincy Rumpel* (1984), *Starring Quincy Rumpel* (1986), and *Quincy Rumpel, P.I.* (1988) are about a zany girl and her family.

■ Waterton Lakes National Park

Waterton Lakes National Park (505 km²) lies on the U.S. border in the southwest corner of Alberta. Canada's fourth national park, it was established in 1895. There are no foothills in this area of the Rocky Mountains as a result of the Lewis Overthrust, so the prairies abruptly end at the Rocky Mountains. The mountains make up most of the park but the prairies are also represented. The park was joined with Montana's Glacier National Park in 1932 to form the world's first international peace park. Alberta's first oil well was drilled along Cameron Creek in 1902. Although that area was outside the park boundary at the time, it is now within the park and is a national historic site. The chateau-style Prince of Wales Hotel overlooks Upper Waterton Lake.

For further information, contact the Superintendent, Waterton Lakes National Park, Waterton Lakes, Alta, T0K 2M0.

Waterfowl include ducks, geese, and swans. All are adapted to the water, with webbed feet and waterproof plumage. The illustration shows, from top left and then in a circle to the right: *Green-winged Teal, Northern Pintail, Mallard, Whistling Swan,* and *Canada Goose* (artwork by Claire Tremblay).

Carthew Summit, looking over alpine meadows and spruce forests in Waterton Lakes National Park (photo by Cliff Wallis).

▷ SUGGESTED READING: Heather Anne Pringle, *A Guide to Waterton Lakes National Park* (1986).

■ Watson, Homer Ranford

Painter (*born in 1855 at Doon, Canada West [Ont.]; died there in 1936*). Watson found the subject matter for his finest paintings in the countryside around Doon, now a suburb of Kitchener, where he lived most of his life. He began drawing and painting as a boy, inspired, perhaps exclusively at first, by the illustrated magazines of the day. Later, from 1874 to 1876, when he lived briefly in Toronto and visited New York, he received what little instruction he ever had. Although largely self-taught, he had no difficulty gaining acceptance as an artist. His paintings of the rural landscape of southern Ontario, the trees, fields of grain, grazing animals, and old buildings, led to comparisons with European masters such as John Constable. At the peak of his career, at the end of the century, he had become one of the few Canadian painters to achieve an international reputation.
▷ SUGGESTED READING: Muriel Miller, *Homer Watson: The Man of Doon* (1988).

■ Watson, Patrick

Television producer and writer (*born in 1929 at Toronto, Ont.*). Watson's many skills include writing, producing, film-making, and flying an airplane. His best-known book is the thriller, *Alter Ego* (1978). He has also performed on stage in his own version of *The Book of Job* (1984).

Watson is best known for his television work, particularly as a producer and host of the popular Canadian Broadcasting Corporation (CBC) public-affairs program, "This Hour Has Seven Days." From October 1964 until it was cancelled by the CBC in May 1966, this program attracted a wide audience for its entertaining yet thoughtful coverage of a variety of topics. He was the host of "The Watson Report" (1976-81) and "Venture." In 1989 Watson won acclaim for his impressive ten-part series, "The Struggle for Democracy." That year he was appointed chairman of the CBC.

■ Watson Lake

Watson Lake, Y.T., lies on the Alaska Highway near the Yukon-British Columbia border. When the highway was built in the 1940s, the community moved a short distance from the lake to the road. Named after a pioneer settler, the town is the centre of a large forest industry. Its population in 1986 was 826.

For further information, contact the Town Manager, P.O. Box 590, Watson Lake, Y.T., Y0A 1C0.

■ Wawa

Wawa, Ont., is a town located between Sault Ste Marie and Thunder Bay. It is located in the Township of Michipicoten, the second-oldest registered place in Ontario. Wawa is famous for the large monument of a Canada Goose on the highway at the entrance to the town. Wawa's primary industries are iron-ore mining, which supplies the Algoma Steel plant in Sault Ste Marie, gold mining, and tourism. Wawa was originally a fur-trade post. The population was 3972 in 1986.

For further information, contact the Town Clerk, 16 Main Street, Webbwood, Ont., P0P 2G0.

■ Waxman, Albert Samuel

TV and movie star (*born in 1935 at Toronto, Ont.*). Al Waxman is one of Canada's most familiar and successful actors. He studied acting in New York and performed in some Hollywood films. From 1975 to 1980 he was the title character in the Canadian Broadcasting Corporation's popular television comedy "King of Kensington," for which he won an ACTRA award in 1976. He has also starred in the American TV series "Cagney and Lacey."

Al Waxman

He supports a number of charitable organizations and is often active in their fund-raising campaigns.

■ Waxwing

Waxwings belong to the Bombycillidae family. Two of the three species inhabit Canada: the Bohemian Waxwing (*Bombycilla garrulus*) and the Cedar Waxwing (*B. cedrorum*). These are small, brownish birds, with a black mask about the eyes. They bear a crest, and the tip of several wing feathers are red and waxy. The tip of the tail is yellow. Gregarious and tree-dwelling, they flock to wherever they find berries. Sometimes they eat so much they are too heavy to take flight again, and laze about on the branches. Along with the berries they love so much, they also eat insects. The female sits on three to six eggs. Both species are migratory. The Bohemian Waxwing passes the winter in southern Canada and the northern United States; the Cedar Waxwing winters anywhere from southern Canada near the U.S. border, to Panama.

▷ SUGGESTED READING: Tim Fitzharris, *Wild Birds of Canada* (1989).

Comedians Johnny Wayne (left) and Frank Shuster (courtesy NAC/CBC Collection/ 12438).

■ Wayne and Shuster

Wayne and Shuster is a comedy team made up by John Louis Wayne (*born in 1918 at Toronto, Ont.*) and Frank Shuster (*born in 1916 at Toronto, Ont.*). Wayne and Shuster met at high school in Toronto, where they performed together in the annual revues. They continued their act at the University of Toronto and, after they enlisted in World War II, they were popular entertainers on The Army Show. On their return, they began to work in radio and, by 1947, they had their own program on the Canadian Broadcasting Corporation. Later, Wayne and Shuster performed their skits on television, in-cluding a clever take-off on the assassination of Julius Caesar. They were particularly successful in the United States, and TV host Ed Sullivan invited them to appear a record-breaking 67 times on his prime-time show. But they have always lived in Toronto, and have resisted many offers of fame south of the border.

■ Weasel

The name "weasel" is used to describe a family of mammals, Mustelidae. All members of this family have anal glands that produce a stinking liquid. The weasel family includes marten, fisher, otter, skunk, and others.

The name "weasel" also refers to three particular members of the weasel family: the long-tailed weasel (*Mustela frenata*), the ermine or short-tailed weasel (*M. erminea*), and the least weasel (*M. nivalis*). The long-tailed weasel is the largest of the three and the least weasel is the smallest.

In summer, all weasels have brown upper parts; the sides range from creamy white to orangeish. In winter all Canadian weasels are white except for a black tail tip in long-tailed weasels and ermines. Weasels are widely distributed across the tundra, taiga, and prairies. They eat small mammals, birds, eggs, and insects. A few weasels are trapped in winter for their white pelts, but foxes, coyotes, birds of prey, and domestic cats undoubtedly kill more than are trapped.

The ermine and long-tailed weasel mate in July and August, but the least weasel may mate at any time of the year. Implantation of the embryos is delayed in the long-tailed weasel and ermine until March or April. Birth follows implantation by three to four weeks. Gestation in the least weasel lasts 35 days. A single an-

Breeding Range of Cedar Waxwing ●

Breeding Range of Bohemian Waxwing ●

***Bohemian Waxwing** (courtesy Macmillan Illustrated Animal Encyclopedia).*

***Black-footed Ferret** is a member of the weasel family. It is likely the rarest land mammal in North America (artwork by Todd Telander).*

***Short-tailed Weasel,** or ermine, turns white in winter in snowy regions of Canada (artwork by Claire Tremblay).*

Fisher is a solitary member of the weasel family. It is secretive and seldom seen (artwork by Todd Telander).

Long-tailed Weasel feeds on mice, pocket gophers, prairie dogs, rats, and chickens when it can break into a farmer's yard (artwork by Todd Telander).

Least Weasel is the smallest carnivore in North America, hardly bigger than the mice it hunts (artwork by Todd Telander).

Ermine (also called the short-tailed weasel) are extremely curious, bold creatures. They are excellent climbers and often pursue squirrels in trees (artwork by Todd Telander).

Satellite View of a cyclonic storm system (courtesy Masterfile).

nual litter of four to eight young is typical for long-tailed weasels and the ermine. Least weasels usually bear four to five young in each of two to three litters per year. All weasels are born naked with closed ears and eyes. The eyes of least weasels do not open until the young are 30 days old. Male weasels are attracted to the females within a short time after they give birth. The males frequently help provide food for the young.
▷ SUGGESTED READING: Bill Ivy, *Weasels* (1985).

■ Weather

Weather is the state of the atmosphere at a certain time and place. The general characteristics of weather during a certain period in a particular area are called the *climate* of the area.

No-one can fail to notice that the weather is changing continuously: from hot to cold, still to windy, the changing pattern of clouds, rain, snow, sleet. Weather has a profound effect on our lives. A farmer's crops need the right combination of sun and rain to grow and ripen. Frost, hail, and severe storms can destroy plants. Rain, snow, fog, ice, and high winds affect travel. Tornadoes and hurricanes can spread destruction and cause loss of life.

ELEMENTS OF WEATHER

Weather develops in the Earth's atmosphere. There are three main ingredients that produce all the weather we know.

Solar Radiation represents 99.9% of the energy that heats the Earth. Sunlight does not heat all areas of the Earth equally. Because the angle at which sunlight strikes the Earth varies, the tropics gain more heat than the polar regions. It is this unequal heating that drives the oceans and creates the winds. In an endless attempt to reach an energy balance in the atmosphere, heat is transported from the tropics towards the poles, while cool air moves southward. These movements of air create our changing weather.

Everyone knows from experience that the temperature usually rises and falls during the day. After reaching a maximum in mid-afternoon, the temperature falls until sunrise the following day. The control of this daily cycle is, of course, the Sun. As the Sun angle increases, the intensity of sunlight also rises. During the arctic winter the maximum temperature is not influenced by the Sun, since it is below the horizon.

Water Water vapour makes up only a small fraction of the atmosphere, from almost 0% to 4% by volume. Nevertheless, water vapour is the most important gas in the atmosphere when it comes to understanding weather. Water is circulated through the environment by the *water cycle* (*see* illustration Volume II, page 109). Water from the oceans is constantly evaporating into the atmosphere. A much smaller amount evaporates from lakes and moist land surfaces.

Water vapour contains vast amounts of energy (called *latent heat*). It takes a considerable amount of heat to turn liquid

Water Vapour is the most important gas in the atmosphere when it comes to understanding weather (photo by Wilhelm Schmidt/Masterfile).

water into a gas. When water vapour condenses back to liquid water, it releases this heat into the atmosphere. Latent heat can be carried thousands of kilometres. Thus energy absorbed over the Pacific Ocean may fuel a storm over Alberta.

Humidity is the general term to describe the amount of water vapour in the air. The most common way of describing humidity is by relative humidity. This is the ratio of the air's water vapour content compared with the maximum amount of water vapour that could be absorbed by the air at the same temperature. For example, at 25°C, the maximum moisture that could be absorbed by the air is 20 grams per kg. If the air actually contains 10 grams per kilogram, the relative humidity is 10/20, or 50%.

Tiny droplets of water or crystals of ice form *clouds*. Clouds are one of the most familiar features in the sky. They are of great interest to meteorologists because they provide a visible indication of what is going on in the atmosphere.

Clouds are classified by their appearance and height. *Cirrus* clouds are high, white, thin, and wispy. *Cumulus* clouds

Clouds form a straight edge in this Chinook Arch in Alberta (photo by Mark Tomalty/Masterfile).

range from small "puffy" clouds to massive thunderstorms. They often have the shape of a cauliflower. *Stratus* clouds are flat sheets that cover much or all of the sky. Each of these types can be classified by their height: high (*cirro*) and middle (*alto*). There is no single word to identify a low cloud.

Air Pressure Normal variations in air pressure are generally not noticed by human beings (except perhaps some who suffer from migraine headaches). Nevertheless, they are important in providing changes in our weather. The difference, or variation, in air pressure from place to place is the cause of wind.

Air pressure is the force of the atmosphere pressing down on the Earth. That is why pressure decreases as you go up in the atmosphere. There is less air overhead at higher elevations. It is this change is pressure that you can feel in your ears when travelling down or up a very long steep hill or when flying.

Temperature has a great effect on air pressure because cold air is denser than warm air, meaning that the same amount of air occupies a smaller volume.

Pressure differences are very important, because air tends to move from high pressure to low pressure. This can be observed when a valve is opened on an inflated tire. The pressure is higher inside the tire than out, and the air rushes out.

The unequal heating of the Earth in the tropic and polar regions sets up pressure differences. The hot air of the tropics is lighter and rises. The cool air of the polar regions is heavier and sinks. The result is a global circulation of air. Thus air moves out of the polar regions and into the tropical regions. If this were the only force at work, we would expect the winds to flow north and south. However, this movement is complicated by the fact that the Earth spins on its axis. This spinning causes an east/west curve of wind direction. In southern Canada, the winds are westerly (from the west).

In addition to these global patterns of winds, there are many types of local winds. They arise for the same reason: temperature differences that result from the unequal heating of the Earth's surface. These differences cause pressure differences. One of the most familiar local winds is the sea breeze. Land is heated more rapidly during the day than water. As a result, the air above the land becomes warmer and hence less dense, creating a low pressure area.

Cumulus clouds rising near Fergus, Ont. These clouds often produce thunderstorms (photo by John Foster/Masterfile).

Fog at Cape Enrage, on the Bay of Fundy (photo by Mike Dobel/Masterfile).

Ice Fog demonstrates the effect of unequal heating as water vapour rises from the warmer water and turns to ice crystals in the colder air (photo by John deVisser/Masterfile).

Freezing Rain on power lines, Bonshaw, P.E.I. (photo by Barrett & MacKay/Masterfile).

Snowstorm in Ontario (photo by John Foster/ Masterfile).

Fronts occur where warm and cold air masses meet. The diagram shows how powerful updrafts along a cold front create towering cumulus clouds, which often result in thunderstorms.

The cooler (denser) air over the water then blows onto the land to replace the rising warmer air. Local winds can also be the result of land features affecting the large-scale wind flow. Winds can be very strong near mountains, hills, or valleys as a large amount of air attempts to move through a small area or around an obstacle. (The same "tunnelling" effect occurs between tall buildings.)

WEATHER PATTERNS

Anyone living in southern Canada has experienced hot summer heat waves and frigid winter cold waves. In the first case, the hot spell might come to an abrupt end, marked by thunderstorms, followed by several days of cool relief. In the second case, cloudy skies and snow may replace the clear, frigid skies and temperatures may climb. In both cases, the weather patterns and their abrupt changes are caused by the movement of large bodies of air, called *air masses.*

There are four main air masses that affect Canada's weather. The *Arctic Air Mass* originates in the snow-covered regions of northern Canada. It is cold and dry. In winter, it moves southward, carrying cold, dry weather to southern Canada and sometimes as far south as the Gulf of Mexico.

There are two main *Maritime Polar Air Masses*. They form over the oceans in northern regions. They are cool and moist, but relatively mild during the win-

ter because of the higher temperatures of the ocean surfaces. One sweeps in from the Pacific bringing clouds and showers. When it advances inland, it encounters the western mountain ranges. The mountains force the air upwards and it releases its moisture as rain or snow. The air mass from the Atlantic affects the weather of the Atlantic Provinces. In winter, this "north-easter" brings freezing temperatures and rain. In summer, it brings pleasant weather.

The fourth important air mass forms over the Gulf of Mexico and southern oceans. This *Maritime Tropical Air Mass* is warm or hot and very humid. During winter, it seldom ventures north. In summer, it brings hot, humid conditions most often to eastern Canada.

FRONTS AND SEVERE WEATHER

The line where warm and cold air masses meet is called a *front*. The word "front" comes from a military term for when two armies meet, and indeed the meeting of air masses is sometimes violent.

Fronts separate air masses of different density. One is warmer and often higher in moisture than the other. Above the ground, the surface of the front slopes upward, so that warmer (lighter) air lies over cooler air. Usually, the air on one side of the front is moving faster than the air on the other side. This causes one air mass to collide with the other. In all cases, the warmer, lighter air is forced upward.

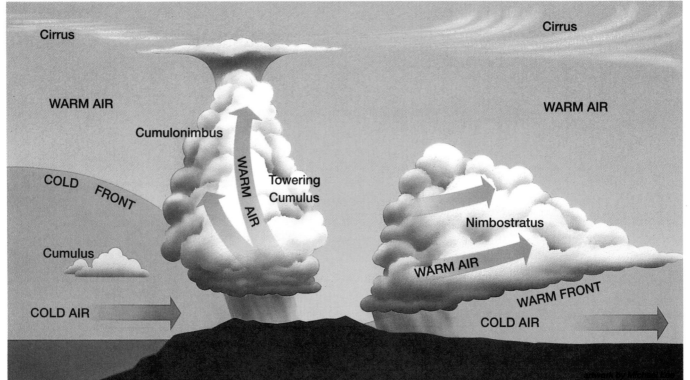

Cirrus

WARM AIR

Cumulonimbus

WARM AIR

Towering Cumulus

Cirrus

WARM AIR

Nimbostratus

COLD FRONT

Cumulus

WARM AIR

COLD AIR

WARM AIR

WARM FRONT

COLD AIR

Leading Edge *of a cold air mass (photo by Daryl Benson/Masterfile).*

When cold air moves into a region formerly occupied by warm air, the zone is called a *cold front*. When cold air retreats and is replaced by warmer air, the leading edge of the warmer air mass is called a *warm front*. Friction tends to slow the surface of a cold front more than its position aloft. Consequently, a cold front is steeper than a warm front. This, combined with the fact that cold fronts move faster than warm fronts, accounts for the usually more violent nature of cold-front weather.

Cyclones *are the circulation of the air around an area of low pressure (courtesy NASA/ Masterfile).*

Cyclones A cyclone is the counterclockwise circulation of air around an area of lower pressure. The word is also used incorrectly to refer to tornadoes or hurricanes. Cyclones frequently develop along a front between two air masses. In North America, this commonly means polar air from the north meeting tropical air from the south. This creates a circular movement of air. This movement can be simulated by holding a pencil in the palms of your hands and moving your right hand forward. Cyclones move along in a wave-like pattern. They may or may not develop severe weather.

Thunderstorms are caused by powerful up-and-down movements of air. As cold

Lightning, *Awenda Provincial Park, Ontario (photo by Bill Ivy).*

air advances into regions of warm, moist air, the warmer air is forced upward. This upward movement may be increased by daytime heating of the Sun. As the moist air soars, it forms the billowy, cauliflower shape of a *cumulonimbus* cloud.

When the cloud reaches a certain height, it spreads from side to side, creating a flat, anvil shape. Rain begins to fall, producing strong downdrafts. The cloud bursts, releasing its moisture in a torrent. Sometimes the updraft carries an ice crystal repeatedly upward, gathering layers of ice until a hailstone forms. A thunderstorm releases its terrific energy in just a few hours.

Thunderstorms are responsible for all severe local storms. Their high winds damage crops and property. Heavy rains lead to flash floods. Lightning ignites forest fires and poses a severe danger to people. Most thunderstorms in Canada occur in late afternoon, May to September. They are most common in southwestern Ontario, which receives about 30 to 50 per year.

Tornado Under certain conditions, a thunderstorm will develop into a tornado. A tornado is a violently rotating column of air in contact with the ground. Tornadoes are most often spawned along the cold front, or squall line, of a cyclone. The greater the contrast between the cold arctic air and the warm, humid air, the more intense the storm and the greater the chance of a tornado.

The exact conditions that produce tornadoes are not known. It is believed that tornadoes are more likely to occur when a layer of cold air aloft traps a thunderstorm below, making it more compressed and violent. The average tornado measures

Hurricane Allen *over the Gulf of Mexico, 1980, from a satellite image. The spiral formation of the hurricane is clearly visible (courtesy NOAA/ Science Photo Library/ Masterfile).*

Weather Reports are *often accompanied by satellite images, such as this one (below) produced by the Meteorology Division at the University of Alberta. The information was collected from a satellite on June 11, 1990. Wind arrows, coastlines, and provincial boundaries have been added.*

The image shows the counterclockwise circulation around a Low which covered most of western Canada. It brought warm, moist air northward, and caused bands of very heavy rain in B.C. and Alberta, threatening to flood several communities.

Edmonton is shown by a square and Calgary by a dot (courtesy University of Alberta, Meteorology Division).

Tornado *(photo by Howie Bluenstein/Masterfile).*

about 150 to 600 m across and travels across the land at about 45 km per hour. Wind speeds within the tornado reach up to 450 km per hour.

Tornadoes cause severe damage to homes, buildings, and crops. Their fantastic winds have hurled railway cars through the air like toys and shot pieces of wood through solid metal.

Because tornadoes are so short-lived, they are very difficult to forecast. Meteo-rologists are able only to describe situations in which tornadoes *may* occur. In these cases, they issue *tornado watches*. When a tornado has actually been sighted, a *tornado warning* is announced.

Hurricanes are the greatest storms on Earth. Most average about 600 km across and generate winds over 115 km per hour. Hurricanes form over tropical oceans in late summer. Fueled by the intense heat, the warm, moist air is sucked upward and drawn into an ever-tightening spiral. As the air moves towards the centre of the storm, the speed of the winds increases. This is similar to when a figure skater starts to spin with arms extended. When the arms are pulled inward, the spin becomes faster and faster.

Hurricanes wreak great damage when they strike land, but because they rapidly lose their power over land, they seldom reach Canada. An exception was Hurricane Hazel which struck Toronto in 1954, causing flooding and several deaths.

Blizzards may occur in any region of Canada, except southwestern B.C. The prairie and Atlantic provinces are most frequently affected. A blizzard is part of a low-pressure storm system. It is created as mild air from the south is rapidly displaced by a cold front sweeping from the north or west. Blizzards sweep from west to east. They create high winds, snow, and low visibility. They block highways and rail lines, bring down electric power lines, strand motorists, and kill livestock.

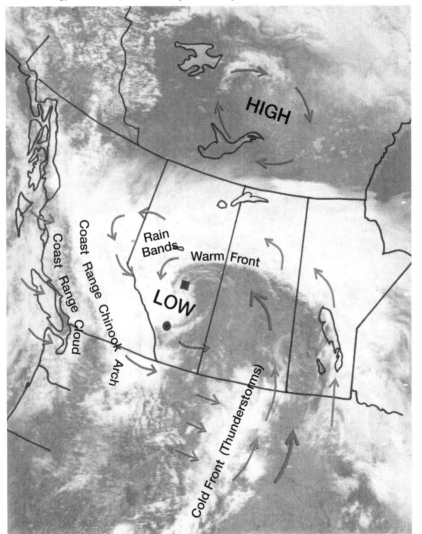

Early Snowstorm, *Alberta (photo by Freeman Patterson/Masterfile).*

WEATHER FORECASTING

Weather forecasts try to predict the weather that will occur at some future time. It is a complex science. The movement of air masses is complicated by the spinning of the Earth, landscape features such as mountains and bodies of water, and other factors.

Meteorologists (those who study the weather) use several stages in forecasting the weather. First they observe what is happening at many places. They analyse the data from their observations. Using mathematics and computers, they project their picture into the future. From this picture they try to predict the temperature, humidity, wind, and precipitation.

Improvements in technology in the 1960s and 1970s improved forecasts. Today, forecasts extend five days into the future. Meteorologists who are interested in a shorter time range (one or two days) can often forecast by observing the sky, cloud formations, wind conditions, air pressure, and so on.

Weather observations in Canada come from balloons released at many locations, satellites, radar, aircraft, and ships. There are over 100 automatic weather stations operating from northern locations, lighthouses, and elsewhere. The data from these observations are analysed in the Canadian Meteorological centre in Montreal. The data are then fed to meteorologists in the form of a series of weather maps. The results are passed on to the public in weather forecasts. Many radios contain a special weather band, which provides information 24 hours a day.

▷ RELATED ARTICLES: **Blizzard; Chinook; Climate; Cloud; Hurricane; Precipitation; Tornado; Wind;** and the "Climate" section of the entries on the provinces and territories.

▷ SUGGESTED READING: Terence Dickinson, *Exploring the Sky by Day: The Equinox Guide to Weather and the Atmosphere* (1988); John Farrand Jr, *Weather* (1990); Reuben A. Hornstein, *The Weather Book* (1980); Sandra Markle, *Weather, Electricity, Environmental Investigation* (1982); Valerie Wyatt, *Weatherwatch* (1989); David Suzuki, *Looking at Weather* (1988).

■ Weaving

Weaving is an ancient craft. Baskets were woven by hand out of grasses, roots, and twigs long before looms were invented. Spinning was first used to make ropes and fishing lines out of tough, woody fibres. Then finer fibres were used to create yarn.

Basketry techniques were gradually replaced by a simple loom. "Warp" threads were stretched taut from one end of the loom to the other. "Weft" threads were interlaced through them. In this way, cloth was made.

Early settlers brought well-developed weaving skills to Canada. Using their "homespun" material, they made blankets, clothes, and other items.

With the Industrial Revolution, looms developed into bigger and more complicated forms that could create cloth at great speed. Textile mills became a principal industry in Quebec. But few mills have kept up with the introduction of computer technology, and the industry is now in decline.

Weaving as a craft has gained popularity since the 1960s. There are now about 8000 weavers in Canada. Soft hand-spun, hand-dyed wools are just one of the materials they use for beautiful one-of-a-kind creations. Most weavers continue to make traditional, useful objects. Others create hangings and tapestries.

Several native people have long been expert weavers. They weave by hand, without a loom. The Nootka on Vancouver Island create grass and cedar baskets. The Inuit make lidded baskets out of lime grass, often with soapstone knots. Most famous are the blankets made by the Chilkat.

▷ SUGGESTED READING: Dorothy K. Burnham and Harold B. Burnham, *The Comfortable Arts: Traditional Spinning and Weaving in Canada* (1981) and *Handweaving in Pioneer Canada* (1971); Robert Leclerc, *Creative Weaving* (1971) and *Warp and Weave* (1979).

■ Webb, Phyllis

Writer (*born in 1927 at Victoria, B.C.*). Educated in Vancouver and Montreal, her first book of poems *Even Your Right Eye* (1956) was followed by *The Sea is Also a Garden* (1962) and *Naked Poems* (1965). Her poems are clear, simple, and elegant. She has described poetry as "the dance of the intellect in the syllables." In 1964 she began a career in broadcasting at the Canadian Broadcasting Corporation in Toronto, and returned to the West Coast in 1969. Her later collections are *Selected Poems 1954-65* (1971), *Wilson's Bowl* (1980), *Sunday Water* (1982), and *The Vision Tree* (1982), which won a Governor General's Award. *Talking* (1982) is a selection of broadcast pieces and reviews, including essays on the creative process.

■ Webster, John Edgar (Jack)

Journalist and broadcaster (*born in 1918 at Glasgow, Scotland*). As a broadcaster, Jack Webster became the champion of the underprivileged against the authorities in British Columbia. He immigrated to Canada in 1947 and worked on the *Vancouver Sun* until 1953. He joined the radio station CJOR with his program *City Mike*, and quickly established his reputation as a hard-hitting investigator and interviewer. He is best known for his "open-line" shows, first on radio (1963-78) and then on television (1978-87), where he supported the rights of the elderly and of re-

Modern Weavers *use hand-spun, hand-dyed wools for beautiful one-of-a-kind creations (courtesy Canadian Crafts Council).*

tarded children, and worked to improve the legal aid system in the province. Today he appears on the TV show "Front Page Challenge."

■ Weeds

Weeds are plants that grow where we don't want them: in lawns, flower beds, and, above all, in farmers' fields. With the exception of thistles, nettles, fleabane, and poisonous plants, weeds are usually harmless. The problem arises when they appear among cultivated plants and choke them out. Most weeds are annuals, since perennials are eliminated with yearly effort. Annuals produce more seeds than perennials, and the least desirable plants do it best. Their most annoying characteristic is that their seeds remain capable of germination for many years: they can patiently await the day when they will be brought back to the surface before demonstrating they are still around. It is therefore not enough to weed a field once if you want to eliminate these plants for the long term. The ground contains enough seeds to keep us scratching away for years! Some weeds have long roots and can grow a new plant from any small root fragment. They also tend to grow faster than cultivated plants. Furthermore, they survive bad weather that kills others.

Farmers have looked on herbicides (which kill weeds) as one of the world's great inventions, along with insecticides and other pesticides. Their enthusiasm is steadily turning to caution, however, because such powerful substances are not without their unwanted side effects. Just as microbes develop an ability to withstand antibiotics, some weeds are adapting to herbicides. Farmers therefore quite rightly look for ways to replace them, for example with insects or diseases that attack only the unwanted species.

▷ SUGGESTED READING: Clarence Frankton and Gerald Mulligan, *Weeds of Canada* (1987); Adam F. Szczawinski, *Edible Garden Weeds in Canada* (1988).

■ Weightlifting

Weightlifting features two events. In the *snatch*, the athlete lifts the bar up to arm's length in one continuous motion. In the *clean and jerk*, the athlete lifts the bar to his shoulders, then "jerks" it overhead. Medals are awarded in each event at different bodyweights. Weightlifting has been an Olympic sport since 1896.

The greatest figure in Canadian weightlifting was strong-man Louis Cyr.

His feats included lifting 250 kg with one finger and lifting 1967 kg on his back — claimed to be the greatest weight ever lifted by one human being.

In formal competition, G. Gratton won a silver medal at the 1952 Olympic Games. Doug Hepburn won the world championship in 1953 and Jacques Demers won a silver medal at the 1984 Olympic Games.

After a series of scandals in the 1980s, relating to drug use, the sport was in disrepute.

▷ SUGGESTED READING: Franco Columbo, *Weight Training for Young Athletes* (1979); R.F. Fodor, *Competitive Weightlifting* (1978).

■ Weights and Measures

Measurements are used daily by almost everyone. They may be casual, as an estimated time it took to get to school. They might be of extreme accuracy, as required in scientific experiments. We watch to see that our cars do not exceed the speed limit, buy meat by its weight and cost per kilogram, dress according to the temperature outside, and cook by setting the temperature of an oven.

Humans have used measurements for thousands of years. They became particularly important after people began to exchange or to buy and sell goods. Many thousands of measuring systems developed to make trading easier. Until recently, Canada used a system, called the Imperial (or English) system, that dated back to ancient times. Ancient people measured things by comparing them to the length of certain parts of the body. The Romans used the *unica* for the width of a thumb. This became the "inch" in the English system. Twelve *unica* equaled a *foot*, or the length of a person's foot. Three feet equaled a *yard*, which was the distance from a man's nose to the tip of the middle finger on his outstretched arm.

Draughtsman uses a micrometer to measure a pipe attachment (photo by Jim Merrithew).

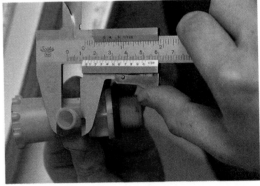

Science and technology demanded greater accuracy in measurement. This resulted in *standards* being set for measurements. Standards were also required to reduce cheating in trade and to help government collect taxes. The International Bureau of Weights and Measures (BIPM) was established in 1875. Canada became a full member in 1907.

Today, science and industry require extremely accurate measurements. For example, a car or an aircraft may be assembled from parts made in several different countries. These parts must be very exact in measure if the machine is to be properly assembled.

Since 1971, Canada has been converting to the metric system, or Système International (SI). The SI relies mostly on the decimal system (calculated in tens). SI is now in general use although many non-SI units are kept for special purposes.

The SI is steadily made more accurate. For example, for a long time, a second was defined as one-86 400th of a day. In 1968 it was based on the frequency of radiation between certain energy levels of the cesium-133 atom. In Canada, the National Research Council makes measurements that require the utmost precision.

▷ RELATED ARTICLE: **Metric System.**

▷ SUGGESTED READING: Gerald J. Black, *Canada Goes Metric: An Introductory History of Measurement* (1974).

◼ Weinzweig, John

Composer (*born in 1913 at Toronto, Ont.*). The most influential Canadian composer-teacher of his generation, Weinzweig studied in Toronto, but found his real direction in the 20th-century music courses at the Eastman School in Rochester, New York. His encounters there with the rhythmic music of Stravinsky (*The Rite of Spring*) and the 12-tone music of Alban Berg interested him deeply. In the second movement of his first *Suite for Piano* (1939) he became the first Canadian to use a 12-tone row. That same year he began teaching at the Toron-

to Conservatory of Music and his classes there (and later at the University of Toronto) introduced the Schoenberg system to Canadian students. In some 40 years of teaching he dominated the trend of Canadian composition through his own work and the work of his pupils, who include Robert Aitken, Murray Schafer, Harry Somers, and many others.

In his own music, Weinzweig wrote film scores and incidental music for radio dramas, where he could experiment widely. After 1945, however, he composed only concert music.

By bending the austere 12-tone system to his will and even to his whim, Weinzweig has kept his music alive.

◼ Welfare

Welfare is the name for payments made under a variety of plans by governments. They attempt to provide people who receive them with a basic minimum standard of living. Payments are based on individual or family income, number of children, and other similar standards. *See* **Social Security.**

◼ Welland

Welland, Ont., lies on the Welland Canal, which links Lakes Ontario and Erie across the Niagara Peninsula. The town grew up after the canal was opened in 1829. When hydroelectric power arrived from Niagara Falls after 1900, it became a significant manufacturing centre.

Welland now boasts large iron, steel, and electrical equipment industries. The population in 1986 was 45 054.

For further information, contact the City Clerk, City Hall, 411 East Main Street, Welland, Ont., L3B 3X4.

◼ Welland Canal

The Welland Canal crosses the Niagara Peninsula of southern Ontario. Port Weller is on the Lake Ontario side. Port Colborne is on the Lake Erie side. The canal is 42 km long and covers a height difference of 99.4 m. The canal bypasses

John Weinzweig at 70 (courtesy Metropolitan Toronto Library).

Composer John Weinzweig (photo by Ruth Kaplan).

Welland Canal is an important link in the St Lawrence Seaway (photo by John Reeves/Masterfile).

Welland Canal Locks *These twin locks can raise one ship while another is lowered (photo by Thomas Kitchin).*

Niagara Falls and the turbulent Niagara River.

The canal has seven lift locks and one guard lock, and is crossed by 11 lift-bridges, three tunnels, and one high-level bridge. In an average year, about 4000 ships pass through the canal, about 1000 of which are oceangoing.

The first Welland Canal opened in 1829. It was largely promoted by St Catharines businessman William Hamilton Merritt. It has been rebuilt and expanded several times since. Numerous communities and industries are located along the canal.

▷ RELATED ARTICLES: **Canals; William Hamilton Merritt.**

■ Wells, Clyde Kirby

Premier of Newfoundland (*born in 1937 at Buchans Junction, Nfld*). Wells became premier in 1989, after leading Newfoundland's Liberal Party to victory in the provincial election. It was a major turnaround, for the Liberals had been out of office for 17 years.

The son of a freight handler, Wells graduated from Dalhousie University Law School in 1962. His abilities drew the attention of Premier Joseph Smallwood, who persuaded him to run for the Liberal Party. Elected in 1966 when he was still in his twenties, Wells was made minister of labour in Smallwood's Cabinet, but he resigned from the Cabinet after two years because he disagreed with government policies. In 1971 he resigned from politics and resumed his career as a lawyer.

Wells returned to politics in 1987 when he was elected leader of the Newfoundland Liberals. Although his party won the 1989 election, he personally failed to win a seat (losing by just 101 votes to his Conservative opponent). However, he won handily in a by-election.

Almost immediately, Wells drew na-

Clyde Wells *(photo by Jim Merrithew).*

tional attention because he took a strong stand against the Meech Lake Accord, which had been agreed to by his predecessor, Brian Peckford.

As other premiers opposed to the accord gave their consent, attention focused more and more on Wells during a series of intense meetings in June 1990. Wells did not agree to sign the accord. He agreed only to submit it (with its new revisions) to the legislature of Newfoundland for its approval. This he did not do, because, he said, of events in Manitoba, which were delaying approval, and of the refusal of the federal government to extend the deadline. The accord died in June 1990.

■ Welsh

Welsh people come from Wales, in the British Isles. About 23 000 Canadians are of Welsh origin, and a further 127 000 have some Welsh in their ancestry. In 1612 a Welsh naval officer, Thomas Button, sailed in the Canadian Arctic searching for the Northwest Passage. In 1617 Sir William Vaughan sent some Welsh settlers to Newfoundland in an attempt to start a colony there, but it did not last. The explorer David Thompson was of Welsh origin, and so was Elizabeth Simcoe, wife of the first lieutenant-governor of Upper Canada [Ontario].

From the late 18th century on, there was a steady flow of Welsh among the immigrants arriving from the British Isles. The largest single group came not from Wales but from Patagonia in South America. For 35 years, they had lived in a Welsh colony at the southern tip of Argentina, and in 1902 they moved to Saskatchewan.

The Welsh settled in all provinces, especially in mining areas. Many had been coal miners in Wales, and they continued the same work in Canada. In religion, they were mostly Methodist or Presbyterian. Some worked as missionaries.

Recent Welsh immigrants have a wide variety of backgrounds. The majority live and work in the cities, especially in Ontario and British Columbia.

The Welsh people have kept their language and customs, despite centuries of close association with England. Some Welsh Canadians can speak Welsh, and many sing Welsh songs and hymns. The Welsh are famous for their choral music. They have kept this tradition in Canada, forming Welsh choirs and music groups. Most major Canadian cities have a St David's Society, named after the patron saint of Wales. These societies organize special festivals, such as the Eisteddfod, a celebration of music, song, and poetry. They also celebrate St David's Day on March 1.

▷ RELATED ARTICLES: **Ethnic Origin; Immigration.**

▷ SUGGESTED READING: Carol Bennett, *In Search of the Red Dragon: The Welsh in Canada* (1985).

■ West Coast Trail

The West Coast Trail is a wilderness hiking trail, 77 km long, along the southwest coast of Vancouver Island. The trail was first built to help rescuers reach shipwrecked sailors along this isolated coastline. It is now part of Pacific Rim National Park.

■ West Edmonton Mall

West Edmonton Mall is cited in the Guinness Book of World Records as the largest shopping mall in the world. It is eight city blocks long and three blocks wide and it contains more than 800 stores and services, including amusement parks, aquariums, movie theatres, a chapel, a hotel, and a nightclub. There is an NHL-sized skating rink, a water park, submarines, and a replica of Columbus's ship, *Santa Maria*. Sixteen thousand people work in the mall, which has become a tourist attraction.

Caribana is a West Indian celebration held each year in Toronto (photo by Malak, Ottawa).

■ West Indians

West Indians are from Jamaica, Haiti, Trinidad and Tobago, and other islands and territories in the Caribbean. Although the majority are of African ancestry, they include people of Asian origin. *See* **Ethnic Origin.**

▷ SUGGESTED READING: Velma Carter and Levero Carter, *The Black Canadians: Their History and Contribution* (1989).

■ Western Settlement

Between the years 1870 and 1920, European settlers changed the western prairies forever. The native people, who had inhabited the area for thousands of years, were swept aside in only a few generations. In their place came immigrants from all over the world. The open grasslands were ploughed under and gave way to wheat fields. The tens of millions of bison that once roamed freely were mostly gone by the 1870s. Along the iron rails of the railway, towns popped up, almost overnight.

NATIVE PEOPLE OF THE PLAINS

Several native cultures had successfully adapted to the environment of the West by the time that the Europeans arrived. There were five major groups. The most easterly of these groups were the Ojibwa, who lived in the forest area between Lake Superior and Lake Winnipeg. They spoke a similar language to their northern neighbours, the Cree. These Algonkian peoples had developed the birchbark canoe and the snowshoe, and lived in conical tipis made of animal skins. The Assiniboine, who lived on the great plains south of the Cree, spoke Siouan, a completely different language. They had followed the bison herds for thousands of years. The Blackfoot, Piegan, and Blood, who were Algonkian-speaking peoples, also lived by hunting the bison. They lived in the prairie region of present-day Alberta. The last group, the Chipewyan, lived in the forest area north of the Cree and Blackfoot; they were an Athapaskan-speaking people.

Contrary to what the Europeans of the time believed, the native people were not poor. They had achieved a rich life, carefully adapted to the forests and plains. Trading was an important part of the life of the native people, so it was natural that they began to trade with the Europeans when they arrived.

Because the territories of the Ojibwa and Cree lay between the western tribes and the French and English traders, these groups became important "middlemen" in the trade. They imposed tolls on those passing through. The Cree, for example, might pay 14 beaver pelts to the English for a gun and sell it to the Blackfoot for 50 pelts.

THE EUROPEANS

The Fur Trade The Europeans arrived in the West from two directions. The first European to see the prairie was a young fur trader, Henry Kelsey, who walked there from Hudson Bay. The French came from eastern Canada, by canoe. The ex-

Advertisement for men needed to help harvest grain in western Canada (courtesy NAC/C-56088).

Settling the Prairie

The immigrants' first view of the prairie was often a shock. Few were prepared for the vast openness of the "bald" prairie. They had never seen a country without trees.

The first task was to find a homestead. The most attractive land was along the rivers, but much of that land was taken by the 1880s. The immigrants tended to look for land that was familiar to them. For example, many settlers chose land because it had trees. Once a group, such as the Ukrainians, settled in an area, future settlers of the same group would come there. It was very important to have neighbours that you could talk to.

The second task was to build a shelter. Often settlers had to use the only material available to them to build a house — prairie sod. The most important task was to make a waterproof roof, which was very difficult with sod and grass. The progress of a family was marked by the speed with which they were able to abandon their "soddy" and build a frame house.

Perhaps the greatest hardship was homesickness. People had lost their sense of place, which was especially painful for people whose lives had been centered on their villages. As one Ukrainian wrote:

All is different in you,
  Canada
The plants, the birds
  and all the animals —
Sadness and dreariness, as in a grave.
Nothing to see that
  is dear to me
save the lone cranberry, the only plant
That took our roots —
  beloved cranberry!

Red River Carts by the North Saskatchewan River, 1871. The Metis were pushed westward by the rush of settlers from the east (courtesy NAC/PA-138573).

plorer La Vérendrye and his family built a series of posts from Lake Superior to Lake Winnipeg in the 1730s and 1740s and began the trade that carried furs to Montreal. The Hudson's Bay Company (HBC) opened the door from the north, via Hudson Bay, building their posts at the mouths of the rivers.

After the fall of New France, the North West Company (NWC) took up the trade from Canada and pushed it far inland. The cutthroat trader Peter Pond was the first to reach Lake Athabasca. In 1793, Alexander Mackenzie followed the Peace River into British Columbia and reached the Pacific Ocean. Thus it was the fur traders who opened the West and who built the first European outposts there. In 1821, the HBC bought out the NWC, and claimed the trading rights over the entire Northwest.

As the number of Europeans grew in the inland posts, the need for food increased. The Assiniboine, in particular, began to supply the posts with pemmican and fresh meat. A Scottish aristocrat, Lord Selkirk, developed a scheme to settle the area around Red River with farmers from Scotland. The settlement would provide a new opportunity for poor Scots and would supply the fur traders with food. The first families arrived in 1812, and they struggled to survive through droughts, grasshopper plagues, and disease.

The farmers had a further problem. They were resented by the original inhabitants of Red River, particularly a new group, the Metis.

Emergence of the Metis

The Metis people were the children of European traders who had married native women. The term usually refers to those who spoke French, although many were the children of English-speaking fathers.

The Metis had developed a way of life that combined their two heritages. They settled around Red River part of the year, and followed the bison for the hunt. They saw themselves as a "new" nation in the West and were close allies of the North West Company. The Metis and the Red River settlers had many unpleasant encounters. In the worst incident, near Seven Oaks in 1816, 21 colonists and one Metis were killed.

Disappearance of the Indian Way of Life

The Plains Indians underwent an extraordinary upheaval in a very short period of time. While the fur trade brought new prosperity, the killing of larger numbers of bison threatened a way of life that had supported them for some 10 000 years. As more animals were killed for food and then for a market for buffalo robes in the United States, the numbers reached dangerously low levels. In one year alone, about 100 000 bison were slaughtered.

The native people had no immunity to European diseases, which struck them with disastrous results. Smallpox, measles, and whooping cough killed perhaps 90% of the people in some bands. It is thought that half the Assiniboine and one-third of the Cree died of the new diseases. Another deadly enemy was the whisky trade which disrupted native life. Yet more were killed in wars that were made deadly by European guns. In one battle by the Oldman River, some 300 Cree were killed by Blackfoot warriors.

By the 1870s, the bison had almost disappeared. Many native groups were reduced to starvation. Their only hope of survival was to rely on aid from the Canadian government. One by one, the western tribes signed treaties and turned over rights to their land in return for small parcels of land, called reserves, food, and small annual payments of money. Within a generation, the proud, independent western tribes were confined to reserves, every aspect of their lives controlled.

The West Becomes Part of Canada

Canada purchased the Northwest from the HBC in 1870. The Metis feared that their rights to own land and sit in the government would not be honoured by the Canadians. Their resistance, under their leader Louis Riel, led to the Red River Rebellion of 1869-70, and the North-West Rebellion of 1885 (*both described in separate entries*). The result of the first up-

Homesteading in Alberta in the 1890s

The North-West Mounted Police arrived first.

Then came the ranchers. During the 1880s, cowboys rode the range, rounded up cattle and branded young stock in the ranch corrals.

Many people came by horse and wagon, or set out overland from the nearest train station to their land. Gradually, gangs of workers moving through the west in work camps pushed their noisy, steam-driven "track layers" in all directions to lay steel rails on top of a bed of "sleepers" or "ties."

The first settlers faced a huge expanse of prairie with few neighbours and no roads. Staking out a claim on a quarter section (64 ha) homestead, each family began by breaking the sod with ploughs. Log walls and sod roofs were used for homes, barns, and granaries. Later, neighbours helped build better houses with sawn lumber and other materials which could be brought in from railway townsites.

Both men and women worked on any task that needed doing. Most families had the help of horses, oxen, or mules.

Many ranchers and settlers developed windmill-powered wells to provide water. Steam engines like the "Countess of Dufferin" first powered the trains, fueled by wood or coal. Smaller steam engines powered the threshing operations separating the grain from the straw.

At sidings or townsites, the landmarks of the new age were the massive grain elevators that collected the wheat, oats, barley, and other products of the prairie harvest brought on wagons from a multitude of farms for transportation out by train (*artwork by Lewis Parker*).

Ivan Lupul's Ukrainian home at Wostok, Alta (courtesy Glenbow Archives/NA-949-97/ RCMP Museum, Regina).

Poster advertising free farms in western Canada (courtesy NAC/C-63478).

rising was the formation of the West's first province, Manitoba, in 1870. Many Metis, fearful that they would have no place in the new province, left Red River and moved farther west.

To support its claim to the West and to keep good relations with the native people, the Canadian government formed the North-West Mounted Police in 1873. The "Mounties" played an important role in the history of the West. Rival traders, including many American whisky traders, moved onto the prairies after the HBC lost the right to keep them out. This led to a brief period of lawlessness, which ended when the NWMP arrived. They also performed many other duties, including delivering mail, collecting taxes, and providing medical services.

The West was changed forever by the arrival of the Canadian Pacific Railway at Winnipeg in 1882. It pushed on past Calgary by 1883. Canada now had the means to move settlers to the prairies. Most of the land was free, costing only a $10 fee for registration. Settlers were given full ownership after three years, provided that they had ploughed and planted some of their land and had built a shelter. Land could also be bought for only $1 per acre.

Despite the railway and free land, settlement was very slow. Canada simply was not well-known to Europeans, and immigrants chose the United States, Australia, South America, and other places ahead of the Canadian West. The only groups to come in large numbers were the Mennonites, Icelanders, and French

Trekking from Moose Jaw, Sask. (courtesy NAC/C-4988).

Canadians. These groups provided a flow of immigrants, but not the flood that the Canadian government had hoped for. The only area that was successfully settled was the foothills region of present-day Alberta. The cattle trade prospered on the rangelands that had once fed the bison. Ranching began there in the 1870s when an American cattleman drove cattle north from Montana. By 1885, there were 50 ranches and some 60 000 cattle.

The Flood Tide The period from 1897 to 1930 is one of the most dramatic in Canadian history. The population of the West exploded, from 400 000 to 2.4 million. A vast agricultural society was settled on the plains which was made up of people of strikingly different origins. What had caused this change?

First, Canada became better known to Europeans as a result of a huge advertising campaign. Thousands of ads and brochures praised western Canada as the "Last Best West." Second, the western lands of the United States, once the prime destination of Europeans, had all been settled. Third, more jobs were available in the West in the coal industry, lumber, and railway construction.

Finally, research by Canadian scientists played an important role. They developed new ways of cultivating the prairie, which was once thought to be too dry to grow wheat. Researchers also found new breeds of wheat. The most popular strain of wheat, Red Fife, took too long to grow and was often killed by frost. In 1904, many farmers lost their crops to frost. A few years later, researchers introduced Marquis wheat, which matured earlier. In 1910, a year after Marquis was available, the prairie crop doubled from what it had been only five years before.

At the centre of the campaign to settle the West was the minister of the interior, Clifford Sifton. In particular, he had encouraged groups such as the Ukrainians to come to Canada. Many Canadians argued that these immigrants would not fit into Canadian society, but Sifton argued that their experience would help them survive better than many others.

The stories of the western homesteaders, who braved the prairie winters and the loneliness of the open plain, are part of Canada's imagination. However, the days of pioneer life in log shacks and sod huts were short. While in theory every homesteader began with the same opportunity, soon a society emerged that had the same divisions as elsewhere, with those wealthier farmers and ranchers on top.

Birth of Western Towns Although the homesteader was the heart of western settlement, prairie life quickly centered around the towns. Here the homesteaders' wheat was stored in the familiar grain elevators, to be loaded onto the railway cars. Almost every major western town was born with the railway, although a few were located at the site of a former fur-trade post: for example, Winnipeg and Edmonton. Calgary began as a NWMP post. Along with Saskatoon and Regina, these towns provided education, finance, newspapers, blacksmith shops, religion, health care, and trade.

By 1905, growth of the West justified the formation of two new provinces: Alberta and Saskatchewan. Edmonton won out over its rival, Calgary, to become capital of Alberta. Regina was made capital of Saskatchewan over rival claims by Saskatoon and other towns.

Winnipeg was for a long time the foremost city in the West, reaching a population of 157 000 by 1911. Life in Winnipeg was typical of western cities. Wealthy businessmen (mostly English Canadians) lived very comfortably in the finest areas of town. Across the vast railway yards, in the North End, immigrant families lived in crowded, grimy rooming houses. They struggled to work and to survive. They were easy prey to disease and suffered from the attitude of the English majority, who feared and hated them because they were different. For the immigrants and for the ruling class, the sooner they learned English and took on "British" values, the better. Later generations — and Canadian society itself — have come to appreciate that the life of western Canada is rich because of the many origins of its people.

▷ RELATED ARTICLES: **Dominion Lands Act; Ethnic Group; Homesteading; Immigration; Native People: Plains; North-West Territories, 1870-1905; Red River Colony; Red River Rebellion; Clifford Sifton;** and the "History" section of the entries **Alberta; Manitoba; Saskatchewan.**

▷ SUGGESTED READING: Barry Broadfoot, *The Pioneer Years 1895-1914* (1976); Graham Leslie Brown and Douglas Hall Fairbairn, *Pioneer Settlement in Canada 1763-1895* (1981); Tony Cashman, *An Illustrated History of Western Canada* (1971); Maryanne Caswell, *Pioneer Girl* (1964); Edna Jaques, *Prairie Born, Prairie Bred: Poetic Reflections of a Pioneer* (1979); Dave McIntosh, *When the Work's All Done This Fall: The Settling of the Land* (1989); Rosemary Neering, *In the Pioneer Home* (1978).

Wawota, Sask. The first prairie towns sprang up like cardboard cutouts on the flat prairie (courtesy Saskatchewan Archives Board/R-3293).

◼ Westport

Westport, N.S., is a fishing village on Brier Island off the tip of Digby Neck on the west coast of Nova Scotia. First settled by Loyalists in 1783, it is known particularly for cod and pollock fishing. It was the hometown of Joshua Slocum, the first person to sail alone around the world (1895-98). Westport's population in 1986 was 350.

For further information, contact the Village Clerk, P.O. Box 1203, Westport, N.S., B0V 1H0.

◼ Westville

Westville, N.S., is a mining town 8 km from New Glasgow. Coal was discovered in 1866 and until World War I the town boomed. However, the demand for coal declined, the mines closed and today most residents work in nearby towns. The population in 1986 was 4271.

◼ Wetaskiwin

Wetaskiwin, Alta, 70 km south of Edmonton, owes its name to the nearby Peace Hills where a treaty between the Cree and Blackfoot was made in 1867. The word is Cree for "hills (or place) of peace." The city was founded in 1891 as a siding on the Calgary-Edmonton Railway. It developed into a wheat-farming

Interior of Harvey School, near Vulcan, Alta. Teachers gave lessons in cleanliness, which they presented as a "British" virtue. Throughout the school system there was a strong emphasis on British values and British achievements. Children from central Europe were made to speak English at school and were punished if they spoke their own language (courtesy Glenbow Archives/NA-748-41).

and cattle-ranching centre. The population in 1986 was 10 071.

For further information, contact the City Clerk, P.O. Box 6266, 4906 51 Street, Wetaskiwin, Alta, T9A 2E9.

■ Weyburn

Weyburn, Sask., is a city beside the Souris River in southeast Saskatchewan. It was founded in 1902 with the arrival of a group of American settlers, and grew as the centre of a rich farming district. Since the 1950s, oil production also has been important. The population in 1986 was 10 153.

For further information, contact the City Clerk, City Hall, P.O. Box 370, Weyburn, Sask., S4H 2K6.

■ Whale

Whales are marine mammals, members of the Order Cetacea. Thirty-three species are found in the oceans bordering Canada. There are two sub-orders of whales. The Odontoceti have teeth and a single blowhole, and the Mysticeti are toothless but have baleen, or whalebone, forming a set of horny plates that acts as a sieve, and two blowholes.

The Odontoceti feed on fish and squid while the Mysticeti filter plankton and small fish with their baleen. The migratory whales move north in spring and south as winter approaches. Gestation lasts ten to 12 months and the females give birth in warm waters.

Humans have hunted whales since the 12th century. Unfortunately, hunting has decimated many whale populations. The bowhead whale (*Balaena mysticetus*), the northern right whale (*Eubalaena glacialis*), the humpback whale (*Megaptera novaeangliae*), and the blue whale (*Balaenoptera musculus*), the largest animal in the world, are now all listed as endangered species. Canada banned commercial whaling in its waters in 1972. Native groups still harvest some annually. Whale-watching cruises are now available so that people may see these magnificent mammals in their natural environment.

▷ RELATED ARTICLES: **Beluga Whale; Mammals.**

▷ SUGGESTED READING: Anne Cameron, *Orca's Song* (1987); Cynthia D'Vincent, Delphine Haley, and Fred A. Shape, *Voyaging with the Whales* (1989); Donna K. Grosvenor, *The Blue Whale* (1977); John Lien and Steven K. Katona, *A Guide to the Photographic Identification of Individual Whales* (1990); Mark Shawver, *Whales* (1985); Seymour Simon, *Killer Whales* (1978) and *Whales* (1989).

■ Whaling

Whaling has been against the law in Canada since 1972, but for 400 years it was an important activity on all the ocean coasts. Whales were valued for their meat and for the oil contained in their thick blubber. This oil was used as fuel for lamps, as a lubricant, and in a wide variety of products, from margarine to shoe polish.

Some species of whales have long pieces of baleen, or whalebone, in their mouths, which they use to filter their food. Baleen is very flexible. Before plastic was invented, it was used to stiffen clothing, and make carriage wheels, luggage, and many other things. Taking oil and baleen together, a single whale could be worth tens of thousands of dollars.

In Canada, the first whalers were the Inuit and some groups of Indians who hunted the animals for food. The first people to catch whales in order to sell their products were the Basques (from the Bay of Biscay area in Europe), who had whaling stations in the Strait of Belle Isle in the 1500s. Later, Americans, Britons, and Norwegians cruised the Atlantic and Pacific coasts in search of the huge mammals. But nowhere was the hunt as important as it was in the Canadian Arctic. Beginning early in the 1700s, dozens of vessels from Britain and the United States arrived each year on the arctic coast to chase bowhead whales.

The hunt ended about 1914 in the Arctic, but it continued in other coastal areas of Canada until the 1960s. Today, only Indians and Inuit are allowed to kill whales, and then only for local use.

Hunting Techniques In the early days, whalers used open boats and hand-held harpoons and lances to chase their prey. The harpooner thrust his weapon deep into the animal's back. Then the boat crew hung on for their lives while the maddened whale dragged them at high speed across the ocean. Soon the wounded whale tired and the whalers moved in for the kill. Afterwards, they towed the carcass back to the main ship, or to a station on shore.

By the end of the 19th century, hunters were armed with harpoon guns that shot explosives into the whales. The number of animals killed began to increase. After 1925, huge factory ships processed every part of the dead animal into saleable products. Hunters used aircraft and sonar to locate the whales, then pursued them in high-powered catcher boats. By the late

Whales of Canada

Grey Whale

Minke Whale

Pacific White-Sided Dolphin

Dall's Porpoise

Harbour Porpoise

Humpback Whale

Killer Whale

Long-Finned Pilot Whale

Northern Right Whale

White-Beaked Dolphin

Atlantic White-Sided Dolphin

Bowhead Whale

Stejneger's Beaked Whale

Sei Whale

Northern Bottlenose Whale

Narwhal

Fin Whale

Blue Whale

Beluga

Sperm Whale

Cuvier's Beaked Whale

artwork by Pieter A. Folkens

1930s, whalers were killing 50 000 animals a year.

In 1946 the International Whaling Commission (IWC) was formed to control the slaughter. The killing of some species was banned completely. Quotas were set to control the killing of the rest. This protection saved Canadian whale species which seemed to be on the verge of extinction. Nevertheless, Canada withdrew from the IWC in 1982 because it was unhappy with some of the IWC's policies. Canada continues to ban all commercial whaling in its waters.

▷ SUGGESTED READING: Dorothy Harley Eber, *When the Whalers were Up North: Inuit Memories from the Eastern Arctic* (1989); Daniel Francis, *A History of World Whaling* (1990); W.A. Hagelund, *Whalers No More* (1987); Roderick Haig-Brown, *The Whale People* (1962); Bobbie Kalman, *Arctic Whales and Whaling* (1988); Robert McNally, *So Remorseless a Havoc* (1981); Farley Mowat, *A Whale for the Killing* (1977).

■ Wheeler, Anne

Filmmaker and writer (*born in 1946 at Edmonton, Alta*). Wheeler was an actress before she started making films in 1971. She joined the National Film Board's prairie region in the 1970s as a documentary filmmaker. In 1981 she made *A War Story*, based on her father's diaries as a Japanese prisoner of war.

She now makes feature films. Although they are often about people's problems, they usually have an optimistic outlook. Most stories are set in the prairies, where Wheeler lived until moving to B.C. in 1990. *Loyalties* (1986) is about friendship between an immigrant Englishwoman and an Indian woman. In *Cowboys Don't Cry* (1988), a young boy has to learn to grow up after his mother dies. *Bye Bye Blues* (1989) is based on Wheeler's mother's experience during World War II.

Filmmaker Anne Wheeler (photo by Daniel Dutka).

■ Wheeler, Lucile

Alpine skier (*born in 1935 at Montreal, Que.*). Until Lucile Wheeler made her stunning breakthrough in the late 1950s, no Canadian skier had ever won a medal at the Winter Olympics and no North American skier had ever won the world championships. It was almost taken for granted that Europeans would carry off the top prizes.

Wheeler's parents ran a ski lodge in the Laurentian Hills of Quebec. On skis from the age of two, she showed such talent that she was given special coaching. She was Canadian junior ski champion when she was 12, and she first competed in the world championships at the age of 14.

In 1956 she came third in the downhill event at the Olympics in Cortina, Italy, winning a bronze medal. Her victory in the world championships was in 1958, when she won both the downhill and the giant slalom. Wheeler's success sparked a new enthusiasm for Canadian skiing and was followed by further triumphs by Canadian female skiers.

▷ RELATED ARTICLES: **Nancy Greene; Anne Heggtveit; Skiing**.

■ Whelk

Whelk is the common name for several species of snail-like molluscs. There are more than 4000 species all over the world, probably all carnivorous. Some are edible, such as the flavourful waved whelk (*Buccinum undatum*) on the east coast of Canada. Whelks have a well-defined feeding canal and a shell with a horny covering over the entrance. They range in size from less than 1 cm to over 20 cm.

Certain species of whelk lay their eggs in large rounded masses. Some of the eggs are eaten by the developing larvae, which ensures their survival and growth before they hatch. Whelks are bottom-feeders and scavengers, and can easily be caught with bait.

■ Whitby

Whitby, Ont., is a lakefront town, 48 km east of Toronto. In the 19th century, it was one of several towns along Lake Ontario that drew trade down from the surrounding interior to its fine harbour. One local politician was William Lyon Mackenzie, leader of the Upper Canadian Rebellion in 1837, who used to hold radical meetings in the town square. By the end of the century, Whitby had been surpassed as a business centre by larger towns. The population of Whitby in 1986 was 45 819.

■ White Pass

White Pass is a pass through the mountains on the border between northern British Columbia and Alaska. During the Klondike gold rush in the late 1890s, thousands of gold-seekers from the south struggled over the pass to reach Dawson City. A railway was built across the pass (1898-1900) and today a highway crosses it as well.

▷ RELATED ARTICLE: **Klondike Gold Rush**.

■ White Rock

White Rock, B.C., is a seaside resort area 48 km southeast of Vancouver. A small cottage community developed in the early 1900s, centered on the lovely beach. The city was incorporated in 1959 when it separated from the neighbouring municipality of Surrey. The name comes from a white rock on the beach used as a navigation maker. White Rock's population in 1986 was 14 387.

For further information, contact the City Clerk, City Hall, White Rock, B.C., V4B 5C6.

■ Whitefish

Whitefish are fish of the Northern Hemisphere, a sub-family of the Salmonidae. There are 18 species found all over Canada: 14 species of Coregonus (including 11 species of Ciscos, five of which are only in the Great Lakes), three species of Prosopium, and one species of Stenodus. The inconnu is the largest whitefish.

Whitefish are usually freshwater fish, though some populations live in the ocean but reproduce in fresh water. Their mouths are oriented toward the underside, allowing them to feed on the invertebrate organisms found on lake bottoms. Ciscos eat primarily plankton. Several spines on the branchial arch create a strainer that catches the organisms. The inconnu eats fish.

Lake whitefish (*Coregonus clupeaformis*) were once the most important freshwater fish for commercial purposes in Canada, but pollution and overfishing have reduced catches. Sports fishermen have little interest in them, despite their delicious flesh. Even today, however, they are a major item in the diet of indigenous peoples. In Newfoundland and Labrador, capelin, of the smelt family, are also known as whitefish.

▷ SUGGESTED READING: Department of Fisheries and Oceans, *Freshwater Fishes of Canada* (1985).

■ Whitehorse

Whitehorse is the capital of the Yukon Territory. It lies in the south-central Yukon, about 100 km north of the British Columbia border.

With a population of 15 199 in 1986, Whitehorse is the largest community in Canada above 60°N lat.

Whitehorse spreads across a number of plateaus beside the Yukon River at the point where paddle wheelers coming up the river from Dawson City could go no farther because of the Whitehorse Rapids. Settlement really began in 1900 when the White Pass and Yukon Railway arrived over the mountains from Skagway, Alaska. For many years the railway was

the most important employer and was a major transporter of goods and people.

A brief boom in copper mining in the early 20th century resulted in the growth of the population of Whitehorse. World War II brought new prosperity with an airfield being built, along with an oil pipeline, an oil refinery, and the Alaska Highway. Whitehorse was the supply and transport base for all this activity.

After the war the good economic times continued. The territorial capital was moved from Dawson to Whitehorse in 1953 and the city became the centre for administration, communication, and transportation.

In the 1980s the Yukon mining industry went into a slump and the railway shut down. But Whitehorse was able to weather this threat to its future because of a growing tourist industry, based on wilderness recreation and the spectacular natural scenery of the Yukon. Mining, government administration, secondary manufacturing and supply, retail and commercial services are now the mainstays of Whitehorse's economy.

For further information, contact the Chief Administration Officer, 2121 Second Avenue, Whitehorse, Y.T., Y1A 1C2.
▷ RELATED ARTICLES: **Klondike Gold Rush; Yukon Territory.**
▷ SUGGESTED READING: Elma Schemenauer, *Hello Whitehorse* (1986).

■ Whiteshell Provincial Park
Whiteshell Provincial Park (675 840 km²)

Whitehorse is the capital and largest centre in the Yukon Territory (photo by John deVisser).

Whitehorse Rapids are so named because when they rise up, they resemble the mane of a white horse. They gave their name to the city of Whitehorse (courtesy Canadian Circumpolar Institute, University of Alberta).

is a wilderness of forest and lake, 105 km east of Winnipeg, Man., at the Ontario border. Archaeologists say that native people have lived in the area for 5000 years. For many years, fur traders passed through the park via the Winnipeg River. Cottage development began in the 1920s, and the park was established in 1961. Today, Falcon and West Hawk lakes are resort centres. Visitors to the park enjoy canoeing, hiking, horseback riding, water sports, skiing, and snowmobiling.

For further information, contact the Department of Natural Resources, Regional Services, Whiteshell Region General Delivery, Rennie, Man., R0E 1B0.

■ Whitton, Charlotte

Mayor of Ottawa and social worker (*born in 1896 at Renfrew, Ont.; died in 1975 at Ottawa, Ont.*). As mayor of Ottawa in the 1950s and 1960s, Charlotte Whitton was the first woman to be mayor of a city in Canada. Fearless and energetic, she never minded stirring up a storm if she felt the cause was worthwhile. She began her public life as a social worker and became director of the Canadian Welfare Council (1926-41). One of her many concerns during these years was to get trained and qualified people looking after young immigrants and neglected children. After leaving the council, she worked as a freelance lecturer and journalist until 1950, when she entered Ottawa city politics as an alderman. She was

Charlotte Whitton

Charlotte Whitton often urged women to play a greater role in public life, though she knew this required great determination. She once said that if a woman wanted to be thought half as good as a man, she had to perform twice as well. "Luckily, it's not difficult," she added.

Charlotte Whitton campaign poster (courtesy NAC/Historical Researches Branch).

YOU PUT ME IN
"THEY" PUT ME OUT

PUT ME IN AGAIN
Charlotte Whitton — Capital Ward

mayor of Ottawa (1951-56 and 1960-64) and then continued as alderman until 1972.

▷ SUGGESTED READING: Patricia T. Rooke and R.L. Schnell, *No Bleeding Heart: Charlotte Whitton, A Feminist on the Right* (1987).

■ Who Has Seen the Wind

Who Has Seen the Wind (1947) is a novel by W.O. Mitchell. It is the story of Brian O'Connal between the ages of four and 12. He grows up in a small southern Saskatchewan town during the Depression of the 1930s. The death of his father and his relationships with his family and friends help him to understand about life. Three important symbols are the town, the prairies, and the wind. The town stands for human activities; the prairies for the power of nature; and the wind for the unseen forces that affect life. The book is one of the most popular Canadian novels of all time. It has been translated into many languages and was made into a movie.

Whooping Crane (artwork by Jan Sovak).

■ Whooping Crane

The Whooping Crane (*Grus americana*) belongs to the crane family. It is a large, migratory bird, the largest bird in Canada (about 1.4 m long). It is pure white, except for the black tips to its wings and a red face. It looks like a heron, but differs by the large feathers covering its rump and tail, and by its outstretched neck in flight. Its nest of marsh vegetation is usually placed in shallow water. The two eggs are incubated for 34 to 35 days; typically only one of the two young survives.

Today the bird is an endangered species. Its nesting grounds in the interior grasslands of North America have been replaced by agriculture. It is now found only in the freshwater bogs of Wood Buffalo National Park in Alberta, where it nests, and in the salt marshes of the Aransas National Wildlife Refuge in Texas where it winters. It can be seen between these two points during migration. The population is estimated at approximately 160 birds and the steps being taken to ensure its survival seem to be meeting with some success.

▷ SUGGESTED READING: Robin Doughty, *Return of the Whooping Crane* (1990); Lorle Harris, *Biography of a Whooping Crane* (1977); Faith McNulty, *Peeping in the Shell: A Whooping Crane is Hatched* (1986).

■ Widmer, Christopher

Physician and surgeon (*born in 1780 at High Wycombe, England; died in 1858 at Toronto, Canada West [Ont.]*). Widmer was known as "the father of surgery in Upper Canada." An army surgeon who was posted to Upper Canada in 1814, he settled in York [Toronto] when he retired in 1817, and became the driving force in organizing the medical profession there.

In a pioneering community such as Upper Canada, it was all too easy for unqualified people to call themselves doctor and prescribe "cures" to the sick. Widmer made sure that only people who were properly licensed could legally practise medicine. Together with a handful of British-trained doctors, he set up the Medical Board of Upper Canada (1819) and other authorizing bodies. He oversaw the training of medical students and encouraged the formation of Upper Canada's first medical schools. For more than 20 years he was the senior medical officer at York General Hospital (the future Toronto General Hospital) which was built under his leadership and received its first patients in 1829. There was hardly an aspect of medicine in Upper Canada that Widmer did not influence in some way. Meanwhile, he gained a formidable reputation as a brusque and no-nonsense character, who was "known for his bad language and good surgery."

▷ RELATED ARTICLE: **Medicine.**

■ Wiebe, Rudy Henry

Writer (*born in 1934 near Fairholme, Sask.*). A child of Soviet immigrant Mennonite parents, Wiebe studied at the University of Alberta in Edmonton and in West Germany. He has taught at the University of Alberta since 1967. His first novels, *Peace Shall Destroy Many* (1962), *First and Vital Candle* (1966), and *The Blue Mountains of China* (1970), are about the struggle to live with moral and spiritual values that are no longer the norm in modern society. Wiebe's Christian vision, a product of his Mennonite upbringing, is committed to this quest.

The next three works, *The Temptations of Big Bear* (1973), winner of a Governor General's Award, *The Scorched-Wood People* (1977), and a novella called *The Mad Trapper* (1980), are set in historical times. In the Indian novels, Wiebe attempts to find the Indian point of view in western Canada in the last part of the 19th century. Each concerns a colourful figure in Canadian history: Chief Big Bear, Louis Riel, and Albert Johnson. His most recent novel, *My Lovely Enemy* (1983), is set in contemporary Edmonton, and has human love as its theme. Wiebe has also produced three collections of short stories and a play, *Far as the Eye Can See* (1977). He has also edited several anthologies of short stories.

▷ SUGGESTED READING: W.J. Keith, editor, *A Voice in the Land: Essays By and About Rudy Wiebe* (1981); Susan Whaley, *Rudy Wiebe and His Works: Essays on Form, Context and Development* (1986).

■ Wieland, Joyce

Artist and filmmaker (*born in 1931 at Toronto, Ont.*). Wieland trained at Central Technical School in Toronto. She lived in New York from 1962 to 1972 and then returned to Canada. She works in many different art forms — painting, drawing, sculpture, construction, quilting, embroidery, and films. She is passionately concerned with women's issues, the environment, and Canadian nationalism, and treats her themes with wit and imagination. In her experimental film, *Rat Life and Diet in North America*, gerbil political prisoners escape to Canada and celebrate flower festivals, only to have their

Whooping Crane and Chick (courtesy Environment Canada/Parks, Prairie Region).

Rudy Wiebe *Many of Wiebe's books deal with moral and spiritual struggles (photo by Jorge Frascara).*

Flight Into Egypt, *oil on canvas by Joyce Wieland (copyright Joyce Wieland/Vis*Art Inc.).*

haven invaded by the United States. In the wall-hanging *The Water Quilt*, flaps of embroidered arctic flowers cover pages from a book warning Canadians of American plots to exploit their northern resources. Her paintings range from large, richly coloured abstracts to small-scale representational works full of mythical figures. She has received commissions for public art — in the Toronto subway system and in the National Science Library in Ottawa.

▷ Suggested Reading: M. Fleming, L. Lippard, and L. Rabinovitz, *Joyce Wieland* (1987).

■ Wigwam

A wigwam is a conical or dome-shaped house used by the native hunters of the Eastern Woodlands. Similar to the tipi of the Plains people, the wigwam had a framework of poles covered by birchbark or woven reed mats. One or more holes in the roof allowed the smoke from the fire to escape. Because wigwams were easy to build and take down, they were well suited to nomadic groups.

▷ Suggested Reading: Bonnie Shemie, *Houses of Bark: Tipis, Wigwams and Longhouses* (1990).

■ Wild Animals I Have Known

Wild Animals I Have Known, published in 1898, is a collection of animal stories by Ernest Thompson Seton. When Seton decided to write his first book for children, he used his skills as a writer, artist, and careful student of nature. The wild animals he described were those he had observed while growing up in Ontario. He gives accurate accounts of their habits and he treats them as heroes. Each animal character in the book is the best of its spe-

Wildflowers *(photo by J.A. Kraulis).*

cies. Lobo the wolf is the strongest and most cunning; Molly Cottontail, the bravest in protecting her young; Silverspot the crow, the wisest of his kind. Seton believed that animals had rights and should be treated with dignity. He felt that when they were killed by human beings, their deaths were tragic.

Wild Animals I Have Known was one of the most popular Canadian books of the early 20th century and was translated into 15 languages.

■ Wild Rice

Wild rice (*Zizania*) grows with its roots in water. It belongs to the same family (Gramineae) as white rice, which originated in Asia, has been cultivated for over 5000 years, and feeds much of the world's population. The very long grains of wild rice, black on the outside, are a gourmet treat for anyone lucky or patient enough to gather them. Wild rice grows on the edges of waterways in central and eastern North America, in 0.5 to 2.5 m of water. The plants look a bit like corn, both in silhouette and size (up to 3 m), with separate male and female flowers. The female flowers, which produce the grains, are found above the yellow or red male flowers. The grains do not all mature at the same time and fall off once ripe.

The native people harvested wild rice by bending the stalks over their canoe and shaking the heads of grain, and repeating the whole operation a little later on. Today much of the wild rice we see in grocery stores is harvested with machines. The dried grains must then be gently roasted to remove their husks.

Wherever wild rice grows abundantly, as in the Great Lakes region, it constitutes a major item in the Indian diet. And wherever wild rice is ripening you'll also find ducks, diving for the grains that have fallen to the lake or river bottom.

▷ Suggested Reading: S.G. Aiken, *Wild Rice in Canada* (1988).

■ Wildflowers

Wildflowers are called "wild" because they grow without our help, and "flowers" because they have coloured petals and a pleasing appearance. They are usually herb-like plants with showy flowers. Of the 4000 known species of flowering plants in Canada, about three-quarters may be called wildflowers. Others flower more discreetly than the rest: for example, the grasses, sedges, and rushes, are plants pollinated by the wind. They do not need to attract insects with lovely colours, perfume, nectar, or nourishing pollen. The seductive measures aimed at insects often meet our human criteria for beauty, but not always. Since bees cannot see red, this colour is rare in wildflowers. Trillium, on the other hand, gives off a wonderfully meaty odour so as to attract pollinating flies.

Wildflowers grow everywhere. The most widespread flowers are found in the boreal forest. Most flowers in deciduous forests take full advantage of spring, blooming before leaves appear on the trees. Mountains, dunes, rocks, and tundra all offer plenty of light and space — but wind, cold, and lack of moisture as well. In the most hospitable plant environments, a sunlit prairie for example, with plenty of water and good drainage, plants compete fiercely: the winners are not necessarily the most beautiful, but the healthiest, most aggressive, and most dominant.

▷ SUGGESTED READING: Tim Fitzharris, *Wildflowers of Canada* (1987); Gloria Keleher, *Wildflowers* (1985); George W. Scotter and Halle Flygare, *Wildflowers of the Canadian Rockies* (1986).

Wildflowers *in Kluane National Park (photo by Pat Morrow).*

■ Wildlife Conservation

Wildlife conservation is the protection of wild animals and their habitat. Often this means protection against the activities of people.

Human activities, such as hunting, farming, and the spread of industry, make it hard, and sometimes impossible, for some kinds of wild animals to survive.

Threats to Wildlife The first European settlers found abundant wildlife in Canada. The fisheries and fur-bearing animals were, in fact, Canada's first resources. The settlers believed that in such a vast land, wildlife was unlimited. This was soon proven untrue. European guns made hunting far more destructive. In the 1820s bison numbered in the millions on

the western prairie. By the late 1870s they were almost exterminated by hunting. Also by then, hardwood forests had been destroyed, and hunters had wiped out the Passenger Pigeon.

The Europeans also changed the way the native people used wildlife. Tradi-

Wildflowers: ① milkweed, ② buttercup, ③ bunchberry, ④ heal-all, ⑤ chicory, ⑥ goldenrod, ⑦ blue-eyed grass, and ⑧ blue flag (artwork by Claire Tremblay).

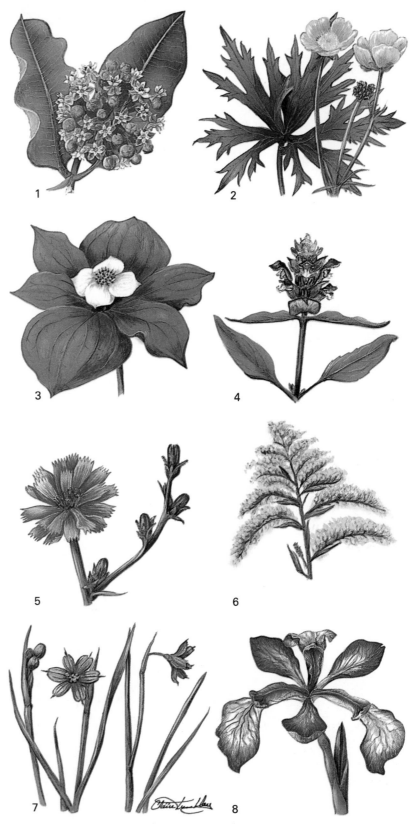

Biologists place a radio transmitter on a caribou, B.C. (photo by Thomas Kitchin).

Caribou Wildlife is a treasure that belongs to all Canadians (photo by Brian Milne/First Light).

Beaver were once threatened in parts of Canada before conservation measures were taken (photo by Brian Milne/First Light).

Moose Cow and Calf The main threat to Canada's wildlife is the destruction of their habitats (photo by Thomas Kitchin/First Light).

tionally the native people of Canada depended on wildlife, such as beaver and caribou, for food and clothing. After Europeans arrived, the natives began to kill these animals in greater numbers in order to trade their furs.

Today the main threat to wildlife is no longer hunting or trapping, but the destruction of the habitat. Society's need to produce food, to mine, or to cut down the forests is often in conflict with the long-term conservation of wildlife.

Conserving Wildlife Concern for threatened wildlife slowly gained support in the late 19th century. Between 1900 and 1960 the killing of wildlife was banned in some parts of Canada. Areas in which hunting was forbidden, called sanctuaries or parks, were established. In 1887, the first bird sanctuary in North America was established at Last Mountain Lake in Saskatchewan. Some migrating ducks, geese, swans, and other birds nest here; others stop off during migration to rest and feed. Similarly, the Thelon Game Sanctuary was established in the Northwest Territories in 1927 mainly to protect muskoxen, but grizzly bears also benefit. Other animals that have benefited from these measures are sea otters,

wapiti, pronghorn, and antelope.

Canada's parks are very important in the preservation of wildlife. Banff National Park was established in 1885. It was not originally created to protect wildlife and wildlife habitat, but these have become one of its main purposes. Wood Buffalo National Park, on the border of Alberta and the Northwest Territories, was established to preserve the bison, and the park also provides a safe nesting ground for the rare Whooping Crane. There were only 21 of these birds left in the world in 1941. When their nesting grounds were discovered in the park, efforts were made to protect them. There are now about 160 of the birds.

Not only areas of land, but also areas of water have been set aside for wildlife. One example is Fathom Five National Marine Park at Tobermory, Ont. Some island sanctuaries for seabirds have been established, for example, Funk Island off Newfoundland and Bylot Island in the Arctic Archipelago.

Wildlife Preserves are areas of land or water set aside to protect wildlife. Some preserves, for example, the Creston Valley Interpretation Centre in British Columbia combine protection with educational facilities.

The organization Ducks Unlimited Canada has secured nearly 7 million ha of waterfowl habitat across Canada. Bird sanctuaries are found from Sable Island, off the Atlantic coast of Nova Scotia, to Polar Bear Pass on Bathurst Island in the Far North.

Preserves are sometimes threatened by campers and hikers. There may be pressure to permit logging, oil drilling, or mining. There are also dangers from pollution. Thus, setting aside a preserve is only a beginning.

Government Agencies The federal government carries on two kinds of wildlife management. The first concerns fisheries and marine mammals, such as seals. Canada's Department of Fisheries and Oceans limits the harvest of these sea resources to maintain a healthy population. The second kind of management concerns birds, mammals, and other animals. Migratory birds are protected by federal law. Land wildlife is protected mainly by provincial law.

The main federal agency engaged in conservation is the Canadian Wildlife Service, an agency of Environment Canada. It was created to manage and conduct research on migratory birds and other in-

ternationally significant wildlife, such as polar bears and the Porcupine herd of barren-ground caribou, which migrates between the Yukon and Alaska. It has created 45 national wildlife areas and about 100 migratory bird sanctuaries across Canada.

Canadian Wildlife Service scientists study, among many other things, the numbers of different species of mammals. They recommend regulations to control hunting. They band birds, and thus map migration routes. They work to restore the numbers of rare and endangered animals, such as the Whooping Crane and the swift fox.

Wildlife Conservation Organizations

A number of private, non-profit organizations in Canada work to conserve wildlife. They include the following:

• The Canadian Nature Federation represents individuals, many conservation and naturalist groups across Canada. It runs a mail-order service offering books and materials on nature and the environment, and publishes the magazine *Nature Canada*.

• The Canadian Wildlife Federation is active in educating people about wildlife. It distributes fact sheets on Canada's endangered species and a magazine, *Ranger Rick*, for young people.

• Ducks Unlimited Canada works to protect upland and wetland habitats for waterfowl and other wildlife. It has kept some 7 million ha of land across Canada for these uses. The land is made available by the landowners.

• The Nature Conservancy of Canada works to save areas of importance to plants or animals from destruction, usually by buying land.

• World Wildlife Fund (Canada) supports conservation projects across the country and raises money to help endangered species from extinction.

Why Should We Conserve Wildlife?

Wildlife is part of the natural environment, which makes up the balance of nature. This balance is crucial to the survival of people as well as of wildlife. We must not forget that we have the same needs for clean air, water, and food that mammals, birds, and other animals have.

Wildlife is also a source of food for many Canadians. It is, in particular, part of the way of life of Canada's native people and forms an important part of their cultural heritage.

Wildlife is a source of enjoyment for campers, hikers, photographers, bird-

Feeding Birds at Jack Miner's Bird Sanctuary near Kingsville, Ont. (photo by Malak, Ottawa).

watchers, and many others. It is also part of the heritage of Canada and conservation is the responsibility and concern of all Canadians.

▷ SUGGESTED READING: David Day, *Noah's Choice: True Stories of Extinction and Survival* (1990); Janet Foster, *Working for Wildlife: The Beginning of Preservation in Canada* (1978); Clive Roots, Andrew Allentuck, and Celia Godkin, *Endangered Species: Canada's Disappearing Wildlife* (1987); Philip Whitfield, *Can the Whales be Saved?* (1989).

■ Wilfrid Laurier University

Wilfrid Laurier University is located in Waterloo, Ont. It offers undergraduate degrees in many disciplines, and master's degrees in arts and science, business and economics, and social work. It has a doctoral program in social work.

The university began in 1911 as the Waterloo Lutheran Seminary of Canada. In 1960 Waterloo Lutheran University was chartered, joining the seminary and Waterloo College, which had been founded in 1924. The university became nondenominational and assumed its present name in 1973, although Waterloo Lutheran Seminary remains affiliated. There are over 5050 full-time undergraduate and graduate students. For further information, write Institutional Relations, Wilfrid Laurier University, Waterloo, Ont., N2L 3C5.

■ Willan, Healey

Composer (*born in 1880 at Balham, London, England; died in 1968 at Toronto, Ont.*). Willan was born and trained in late-19th century England. In his heart, his music, and his ways he remained an Englishman all his long life. Yet he lived in Canada for the last 55 years of his life and he became one of the most influential musicians in the country. He arrived in 1913 to teach theory at the Toronto Conservatory. He later (1937-50) taught counterpoint and composition at the University of Toronto. Many of Canada's most distinguished musicians were his pupils.

Willan himself composed in a late-19th century style influenced by the Englishmen Parry and Elgar and by the great continental masters Brahms, Wagner, and Tchaikovsky. Willan's opera *Deirdre* (1934-35) was the first Canadian-composed opera to be produced by the Canadian Opera Company.

To most Canadians, Willan's most important music was for the church. At St Mary Magdalene church, Toronto, he had complete authority over every musical aspect of the service. From 1921 until his death, Willan chose or composed the music, played the organ and trained the choir. His music circulated widely in other Canadian churches. He composed the homage anthem for the Coronation of Elizabeth II ("O Lord, Our Governor," 1953). On July 9, 1989 in Toronto, Elizabeth, the Queen Mother, unveiled a plaque in Willan's honour to be installed on the front wall of the Church of St Mary Magdalene.

▷ RELATED ARTICLE: **Music.**

▷ SUGGESTED READING: Frederick Clarke, *Healey Willan: Life and Music* (1983).

Percy Williams won gold medals in the two most prestigious Olympic track and field events: the 100 m and 200 m sprints (courtesy Canada's Sports Hall of Fame).

■ Williams, James Miller

Pioneer of the oil industry (*born in 1818 at Camden, New Jersey, U.S.; died in 1890 at Hamilton, Ont.*). The first producing oil well in North America was dug by James Miller Williams at Oil Springs (near today's Petrolia, Ont.) in 1857. That same year, Williams set up North America's first oil-refining plant to process and sell the oil from his well.

Williams had settled in Upper Canada [Ontario] in 1840 and had built up a carriage-making and railway car company at London and Hamilton. Ever ready to try something new, he started searching for petroleum in the 1850s. After digging unsuccessfully near London, he made his historic strike at Oil Springs in 1857. The well he dug there produced up to 100 barrels of oil a day.

Williams followed up with further wells, founding the Canadian Oil Company with a group of associates. As well as digging for oil, Williams was probably the first person in the world to drill for oil — digging down to bedrock and then drilling into the rock itself (though this claim has also been made for the American oil pioneer E.L. Drake).

▷ RELATED ARTICLES: **Oil; Petroleum.**

■ Williams, Percy Alfred

Sprinter (*born in 1908 at Vancouver, B.C.; died there in 1982*). Williams suffered from rheumatic fever when he was a child. Despite a damaged heart, he became an outstanding runner. At the 1928 Olympic Games in Amsterdam, Holland, he blazed to victory in the 100 m and 200 m sprints. Because the sprint events are the most glamorous in all track and field, Williams was the sensation of the Olympic Games. He remained unbeaten in a series of indoor races against the world's best. Williams' double gold remain the most brilliant achievement by any Canadian in track and field competition.

■ Williams Lake

Williams Lake, B.C., is a city in the Cariboo country of the central interior 552 km northeast of Vancouver. It is the business centre of a ranching area. Recently, forestry has become the most important economic activity. Government agencies, mining, and tourism also help diversify the economy of the area. The city is named after a local Indian chief. The population in 1986 was 10 280.

For further information, contact the City Clerk, 450 Main Street, Williams Lake, B.C., V2G 1N3.

■ Williston Lake

Williston Lake, 1761 km², is the largest lake in British Columbia. In the Rocky Mountain Trench, it is a man-made lake, created in 1968 when a hydroelectric dam was built on the Peace River. It is located in the northeast corner of the province and is named for a former politician. Pulp mills and sawmills support an active forest industry.

■ Willow

Willows (*Salix*), like poplars (*Populus*), belong to the willow family (Salicaceae). They are usually recognized by their long, narrow leaves and their male and female flowering catkins. Only a few of the 75 species found in Canada are trees; the others are shrubs that either stand upright or hug the ground. These latter are particularly abundant in the Arctic. Mosses and lichens often virtually cover their branches and stems.

Willows are a major source of food for mammals and birds, especially the Willow Ptarmigan. Farther south, willows are usually found at water's edge, where they help stabilize the banks. Willows flower early in spring, and are thus a great favourite of bees and other insects that gather the nectar from their flowers. The weeping willow (*S. babylonica*), with its drooping branches, is a European species familiar all over Canada. We also cultivate the basket willow (*S. viminalis*), which produces a large quantity of slender, flexible branches used in the wickerware industry. Willow bark contains

Arctic Willows (photo by Barry Griffiths/ Network).

salicin, a substance similar to salicylic acid, which is used as a painkiller.

■ Willson, Thomas Leopold

Inventor (*born in 1860 at Princeton, near Woodstock, Canada West [Ont.]; died in 1915 at New York City, U.S.*). "Carbide Willson," as he was called, invented a process for making bulk calcium carbide and acetylene gas from a mixture of lime and coal tar. This was in 1892, and it was the beginning of today's massive carbide industry. Willson established his own carbide plant at Merritton, Ont., and he also shared his expertise with other carbide-producing companies. Meanwhile, he was one of the earliest promoters of hydroelectricity. It was partly because of his efforts that Canada asserted its right to use power from Niagara Falls. Willson's enthusiasm for electricity dated back to his teenage years, when he invented an electric dynamo. He experimented in many areas and took out some 70 patents in Canada during his lifetime.

▷ RELATED ARTICLE: **Invention.**

■ Wilson, Eric Hamilton

Author (*born in 1940 at Ottawa, Ont.*). The son of an RCMP officer, he lived in various parts of Canada as a child. He received a BA from the University of British Columbia in 1963 and a teacher's certificate the following year.

In nearly a dozen Tom and Liz Austen mysteries, beginning with *Murder on the Canadian* (1976), Wilson has tried, he says, "to combine the adventure of the Hardy Boys with the true detection of an Agatha Christie novel." Each book teaches interesting facts about a different Canadian setting. Some also explore serious issues. For example, *Terror in Winnipeg* (1979) is about industrial pollution, and *The Kootenay Kidnapper* (1983) warns children about trusting strangers.

Wilson's teenage detectives are more

Willow (artwork by Claire Tremblay).

Illustration from Green Gables Detectives by Wes Lowe (with permission of Collins Publishers).

believable than his villains or his plots. Neither superheroes nor geniuses, they often make serious mistakes before solving a mystery.

■ Wilson, Ethel

Author (*born in 1888 in South Africa; died in 1980 at Vancouver, B.C.*). After her mother died in 1898, Wilson was sent to England and later to Vancouver to live with her grandmother. *The Innocent Traveller* (1949) is based on this experience. Her first published novel, *Hetty Dorval* (1947), did not appear until she was 59 years old. *The Equations of Love* (1952) is a volume of two novellas in which Wilson continues to probe female characters in moral dilemmas. Her most acclaimed work, *Swamp Angel* (1954) is again about a woman who must make difficult choices. Her last novel, *Love and Salt Water* (1956), explores her favourite theme of human relationships. Her short stories are collected in *Mrs. Golightly and Other Stories* (1961).

▷ SUGGESTED READING: Mary McAlpine, *The Other Side of Silence: The Life of Ethel Wilson* (1988); Beverly Mitchell, *Ethel Wilson and Her Work* (1984).

■ Wilson, John Tuzo

Earth scientist (*born in 1908 at Ottawa, Ont.*). When he was a student, he spent a summer helping a geologist in northern Canada and learned to love rocks. He switched from physics to geology at the University of Toronto, and in 1930, when he was 22 years old, he became the first person in Canada to graduate from university with a degree in geophysics — the science that studies the behaviour and structure of the Earth.

He went on to study in England and the United States. Then he went to work for the Geological Survey of Canada. In 1946 he became a professor of geophysics at the University of Toronto.

Wilson became well known in the world of science for providing new answers to old questions about how big features of the Earth, such as glaciers, mountains, oceans, and continents, came to be.

In the 1960s, he helped bring about a revolution in earth sciences. He and a few other pioneers convinced other scientists that the surface of the Earth is made up of rigid slabs called plates. Wilson showed where the edges of these plates were, and how they are moving. All earth scientists today agree on these ideas, which are part of what is called the theory of plate tectonics.

Michael Wilson (courtesy Canapress Photo Service).

For 11 years, starting in 1974, Wilson ran the Ontario Science Centre in Toronto. He has received many honours and prizes.

▷ RELATED ARTICLE: **Plate Tectonics.**

■ Wilson, Lois

First woman Moderator of the United Church of Canada (*born in 1927 at Winnipeg, Man.*). Lois Wilson was ordained a minister of the United Church in 1965. During the next 15 years, she shared team ministries in Winnipeg, Thunder Bay, Hamilton, and Kingston, before serving as Moderator of the United Church (1980-82). She then took on the post of co-director of the Ecumenical Forum of Canada (1983-89), an organization involving many different religious groups. In 1983 she also became one of the seven presidents of the World Council of Churches (WCC), the first Canadian ever to be a president of the WCC. She has long been concerned about major world issues, such as peace and the need to relieve the desperate poverty in many countries. Her role in tackling such problems has been recognized with many honours, including the Pearson Peace Medal, which she received in 1985. In 1989 she published her autobiography, *Turning the World Upside Down.*

■ Wilson, Michael Holcombe

Minister of finance (*born in 1937 at Toronto, Ont.*). Michael Wilson interrupted a successful career in the investment business to run for Parliament as a Conservative candidate in 1979. After service in the brief Joseph Clark administration of 1979-80, he made an unsuccessful bid for the Conservative Party leadership in 1983. A year later, he was named finance minister in the new government formed by Brian Mulroney. As minister, he supported free trade and promised tax reforms. An intelligent, hard-working, and highly regarded individual, his economic policies favoured less government involvement in the economy. His most controversial measure was the GST (Goods and Services Tax).

■ Wind

Winds are horizontal currents of air. They are named by the point of the compass from which they blow. Canada sprawls across the mid-latitude belt where west winds, continually circling the globe at high altitude, dominate the weather. Sweeping Canada from west to east, the prevailing westerlies are the reason it normally takes longer to fly from Halifax,

N.S., to Vancouver, B.C., than from Vancouver to Halifax. Although the winds are mainly from west to east, they often meander from north to south.

In essence, wind is the motion of air over the surface of the Earth. Air does not move in a straight line from high pressure to low pressure areas because it is deflected by the Earth's rotation. In the Northern Hemisphere, moving air tends to swing to the right; in the Southern Hemisphere, to the left. This deflection effect — named for Coriolis, the 19th-century French mathematician who first described it — creates the circular vortices, the rotating wind systems that dominate the weather at the Earth's surface in the mid-latitudes.

These winds show up clearly in satellite photographs, looking like whirlpools in the atmosphere. They are the circular feature labelled "L" for low on weather maps (see Volume V, page 234).

Low-pressure zones rotate counterclockwise in the Northern Hemisphere and are also known as depressions or, technically, cyclones. There are also high-pressure zones, known as anti-cyclones, which rotate clockwise in the Northern Hemisphere.

There are also local winds that bear no relation to the large-scale pattern of pressure displayed on weather maps, though they are still controlled by local pressure patterns. These include the mountain slope and valley breezes that occur in the interior of British Columbia, and the land and sea breezes that occur in coastal areas and near the Great Lakes.

The latter winds occur because water stores and releases heat more sluggishly than land. This means that over land, the air becomes cooler and heavier at night than over a nearby sea or lake. A land breeze results, as the heavier air moves out from over the land to over the water. During the day, the cooler air is over the water, from where it blows towards the land — a sea breeze.

With an average annual wind speed of 35 km per hour, higher than anywhere else in the country, Resolution Island in the Northwest Territories is about the windiest spot in Canada.

▷ RELATED ARTICLES: **Blizzard; Chinook; Climate; Hurricane; Thunderstorm; Weather.**

▷ SUGGESTED READING: Caroline Roaf, *Wind* (1968); Laurence Santrey, *What Makes the Wind?* (1982); Jean-Pierre Verdet, *The Air Around Us: The Sky Never Stays the Same* (1986); Lyall Watson, *Heaven's Breath: A Natural History of the Wind* (1984).

■ Wind Energy

Wind energy is the energy contained by moving air. Air moves when it is heated by sunshine. Wind energy is thus a form of solar energy.

Next to the muscles of humans and animals, the wind was the earliest of natural energy sources to be harnessed. For more than 1000 years, humans have used windmills — devices with blades that spin in the wind — to harness this energy. Windmills have been in use in Canada since Europeans settled here; the French built the first windmills in Canada, in the 17th century, using them mainly to grind grain.

The advantages of the wind as an energy source are that it is free, inexhaustible, and non-polluting. The main disadvantage of wind energy is that it is unpredictable. Wind energy was thus often used for jobs such as grinding grain or pumping water, jobs which did not have to be done at fixed times but could wait until the wind is blowing.

Contemporary windmills, known as wind turbines, capture the wind's energy in order to drive generators of electricity, not pumps or grindstones. Water pumps are usually driven by small, slow-turning wind turbines. But electricity generators spin rapidly, and so too do the new wind turbines, both small and large, which researchers in Canada and other countries are now perfecting.

There are two basic kinds of high-speed wind turbines. The first kind resembles an aircraft propeller and spins around a horizontal axis. The second kind spins around a vertical axis. Canadian researchers have concentrated on this second kind of wind turbine. Named after its inventor, the Darrieus wind turbine looks like an eggbeater. The energy such systems capture is converted into electricity when the wind is blowing. It is then added to a power grid also supplied with electricity generated from other, more reliable, but more expensive, sources. There

Vertical Wind Turbine Canadian research concentrates on this type of turbine, which spins around a vertical axis (photo by Rick Rudnicki/ Take Stock Inc.).

The Beaufort Scale

Admiral Beaufort of the Royal Navy devised a scale for measuring wind, based on its effect on water or land.

Beaufort 0 is *calm*, when the sea is like a mirror. In a *fresh breeze* (5) there are moderate waves at sea and small trees begin to sway. At 10, called a *storm*, heavy seas slam into ships and trees are uprooted on land. A hurricane is Beaufort 12.

Winds reach gale force when it is difficult to walk against the wind (photo by Hans Blohm/Masterfile).

Old Windmill *near Tompkins, Sask. (photo by G.J. Harris).*

are many isolated communities in Canada where conventional energy sources such as diesel fuel are expensive and where strong winds blow. Such communities are located on the arctic islands, the East and West coasts, the western shore of Hudson Bay, and in the southern portions of Alberta and Saskatchewan. Electrical utilities in a number of provinces are experimenting with wind energy systems in such communities.

In 1986, for example, the world's largest Darrieus wind turbine began operation near Cap-Chat, Que. Experts-Conseils Shawinigan Inc., an engineering firm, erected and runs this prototype machine, which evolved from a small model tested by the National Research Council. It is 96 m tall and can generate up to four megawatts of electrical power.

▷ RELATED ARTICLES: **Electricity; Energy.**
▷ SUGGESTED READING: Ed Catherall, *Wind Power* (1981); Sean McCutcheon, *Wind Energy* (1981).

■ Windigo

Windigo is the most evil figure in legends told by the Algonquian-speaking Indians of Canada. He could appear as an Indian brave breathing fire, or as a supernatural creature with a heart of ice. Sometimes he ate his victims, and at other times he frightened them into madness.

▷ SUGGESTED READING: John Robert Colombo, editor, *Windigo: An Anthology of Fact and Fantastic Fiction* (1982); Howard Norman, *Where the Chill Came From: Cree Windigo Tales and Journeys* (1982).

■ Windmill, Battle of

The Battle of Windmill, November 12, 1838, was a raid into Upper Canada by members of the American-based Hunt-

ers' Lodges. Led by Colonel Nils Von Schoultz, the Hunters occupied a windmill and several nearby stone buildings near Prescott as part of their attempt to liberate Upper Canada from what they believed to be British tyranny. They were overcome by a large Canadian force and surrendered after four days.

▷ RELATED ARTICLE: **Hunters' Lodges.**

■ Windsor

Windsor, Nfld, is in central Newfoundland next to Grand Falls. With the construction of a pulp and paper mill at Grand Falls in 1909, Windsor grew up nearby. From the beginning, its economy has been tied to that of its larger neighbour. Its population in 1986 was 5545.

For further information, contact the Town Clerk, P.O. Box 220, Windsor, Nfld, A0H 2H0.

■ Windsor

Windsor, N.S., is a town 60 km northwest of Halifax, at the mouth of the Avon and St Croix rivers. First settled by Acadians

Windigo, painting by Norval Morrisseau (courtesy Glenbow Museum).

Windigo

One day in a particularly cold winter, Windigo was hungry. He went to a village and frightened the people with his blazing eyes and his blood-curdling cries.

He ate their food, then turned them into beavers and began to eat them too. With every bite he grew taller and more hungry, so he left to find another group to eat.

When Big Goose returned, he found the village empty. At first he thought a war party had destroyed it, but then he saw Windigo's huge footprints in the snow. He asked the Great Spirit Manitou for help, and soon he too became a giant. Big Goose followed the footprints until he found Windigo beside a large lake. They hurled mountains, rocks, and glaciers at each other, until finally Windigo was dead. Then all the beaver Windigo had eaten were released and came back to the village in their proper shape as people.

in 1684, and called Pisquid, it was renamed Windsor in 1764 when wealthy people from Halifax received land grants there. With the arrival of Loyalists in the 1780s, the town became a bustling business centre. During the 1800s the economy thrived, with sawmills, cotton mills, a plaster mine, and other factories.

Today, much of that activity is gone, and Windsor is mainly a residential community. A major tourist attraction is the fine home of Thomas Haliburton, 19th-century author of the Sam Slick stories. The population in 1986 was 3665.

For further information, contact the Town Clerk, P.O. Box 158, Windsor, N.S., B0N 2T0.

■ Windsor

Windsor, Ont., is Canada's southernmost city. It lies in the extreme southwest corner of Ontario where the Detroit River flows out of Lake St Clair. Detroit, Michigan, is across the river, and more travellers enter Canada from the U.S. through Windsor each year than any other point of entry. The city is part of the 15th-largest metropolitan area in the country, with a population in 1986 of 253 988. It is known as the "automotive capital" of Canada.

Early Settlement Around 1700 the French built a fort at Detroit. A small number of French settlers began to take up land across the river in what would become Windsor. These pioneers were joined by English-speaking Loyalists in the 1780s. A village grew up around the dock for the ferry to Detroit and in 1836 it took the name Windsor.

At first, Windsor grew as the business centre of a farming district. The growth of industry began in 1858 when Hiram Walker built a distillery in nearby Walkerville (now part of Windsor). Walker's distillery became famous for its Canadian Club whisky. In 1904 the Ford Motor Company went into production next door to the distillery and it was not long before several car makers were located in Windsor.

The 20th Century The auto industry was the key to the city's growth and economic prosperity. In 1928 the population was five times larger than it had been just 20 years earlier. Most of the people came to work in the auto plants.

The Great Depression of the 1930s dealt a terrible blow to the auto industry and many people lost their jobs. But the setback was temporary, and today Windsor is Canada's fifth-largest manufacturing centre.

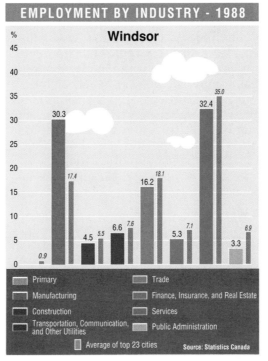

EMPLOYMENT BY INDUSTRY - 1988

Windsor

Industry	Windsor %	Average of top 23 cities %
Primary	0.9	
Manufacturing	30.3	17.4
Construction	4.5	5.5
Transportation, Communication, and Other Utilities	6.6	7.6
Trade	16.2	18.1
Finance, Insurance, and Real Estate	5.3	7.1
Services	32.4	35.0
Public Administration	3.3	6.9

Source: Statistics Canada

Windsor has always had close ties to Detroit. A railway tunnel connected the two cities under the river in 1910. Auto traffic can cross over the river on the Ambassador Bridge (1929), which is the longest suspension bridge between two countries in the world, or under the river through the Auto Tunnel (1930). Many Windsor residents work in Detroit. Each year the cities celebrate an International Freedom Festival, which ends with a huge fireworks display. Windsor still has a sizeable French population. It is an official bilingual district, with French schools, television, and radio.

Today, Windsor offers a variety of sights and entertainment. Visitors can tour the Hiram Walker Historical Museum or the Willistead Manor, an historic mansion. The Art Gallery features permanent and travelling displays. The University of Windsor is located in the city.

For further information, contact the City Clerk, 350 City Hall Square, P.O. Box 1607, Windsor, Ont., N9A 6S1.

■ Windsor Strike

The Windsor Strike, lasting from September to December 1945, pitted auto workers in Windsor, Ont., against the Ford Motor Company. After more than a year of negotiations, workers went on strike to force the company to deal with their union, the United Automobile Workers. The company had police help to break through picket lines. But workers blockaded the factory by filling the streets around it with parked cars.

The strike ended when both sides agreed to arbitration by Ivan Rand, a judge of the Supreme Court. Rand condemned both sides in the dispute, but his report supported a key demand by the workers: that because all workers benefited from a contract negotiated by the union, all should pay union dues whether they were members of the union or not. This was called the compulsory checkoff, and it was widely applied in other industries.

▷ RELATED ARTICLES: **Strikes and Lockouts; Unions.**

■ Winkler

Winkler, Man., is southwest of Winnipeg near the United States border. It began in 1892 as a railway siding on land owned by a merchant and politician named Valentine Winkler. Blessed with ideal conditions, the area blossomed into one of Manitoba's finest farming districts and Winkler grew to be the regional business and industrial centre. The population in 1986 was 5926.

■ Winnipeg

Winnipeg is the capital of Manitoba. Called the "Gateway to the West," it lies on the flatlands near where the Canadian Shield levels out onto the western prairie. This location made Winnipeg the jumping-off point for the settlement of the West and for many years the business capital of the region. With a population of 594 551 in 1986, it is the fourth-largest city in Canada.

BOOMTIME

The founder of Winnipeg was Henry McKenney, a hotel keeper from Upper Fort Garry, centre of the Red River Colony. In 1862 he opened a general store away from the fort at a point beside the Red River where a cart trail headed off in-

Corner of Portage and Main, *Winnipeg, 1872. This famous street corner is still the heart of Winnipeg (by permission of the British Library).*

to the prairie. Many people laughed at McKenney for choosing such an isolated spot, but today it is the corner of Portage Avenue and Main Street in downtown Winnipeg, the most famous intersection in Canada.

The name Winnipeg was first applied to the tiny settlement in 1866. The name comes from a Cree expression meaning "murky water." In 1873, Winnipeg became a city and capital of the new province of Manitoba, which had been created in 1870.

Growth was slow until the arrival of the Canadian Pacific Railway in the early 1880s and the flood of farm settlers onto the prairie which followed. Winnipeg was the stopover point for almost all the newcomers arriving in western Canada, many of whom chose to stay in the city. In the years before 1914, the population skyrocketed and many businesses and factories opened their doors. Prairie grain flowed through Winnipeg on its way east to market. It was a boom never equalled by any other Canadian city.

DIVIDED CITY

As a result of its rapid growth, Winnipeg became a divided city. In the north, beyond the railway tracks, was the "North End." This was a neighbourhood of crowded homes and tenements where immigrants and working people lived because it was inexpensive and close to their jobs in the factories and rail yards.

The North End was neglected by the government. It was not properly served with water and sewage and many homes were overcrowded. As a result, health conditions were poor; more people died of typhoid fever because of bad water in Winnipeg than in any other city in North America. Since 1919, Winnipeggers have had a supply of pure water from Shoal Lake, about 100 km away.

Wealthier residents lived in the South End of the city. They were mainly of British, Canadian, or American background and they distrusted the newcomers on the other side of the tracks. Different languages, religions, and customs all led to a lack of understanding between the two groups.

By the 1950s, immigrants were taking an equal place in Winnipeg society. This change is symbolized by the election of Stephen Juba, a Ukrainian-Canadian, as mayor in 1956. Today Winnipeg is proud of its lively mix of different ethnic groups. One group which has not joined the mainstream is the native people who come to the city from their reserves and often are not able to find jobs or support.

ECONOMY

The boom period ended with World War I. Following the war, in 1919, Winnipeg was crippled by a massive general strike, the most famous labour dispute in Canadian history. The Panama Canal, newly opened, allowed grain to be shipped to Europe via Vancouver and much of the crop was diverted away from Winnipeg. Worse yet, the city was plunged into a business depression which did not end until the outbreak of World War II.

After World War II, Winnipeg entered a period of steady growth. It continues to be the most important city in Manitoba; more than half the population of the province lives there, and industry in the city produces over 80% of the province's manufactured goods.

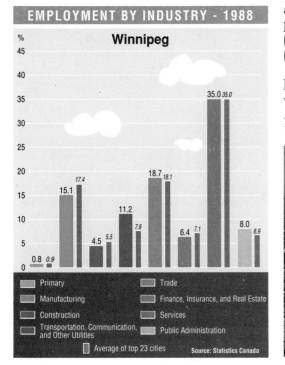

EMPLOYMENT BY INDUSTRY - 1988

Winnipeg

	%
Primary	0.8 / 0.9
Manufacturing	15.1 / 17.4
Construction	4.5 / 5.5
Transportation, Communication, and Other Utilities	11.2 / 7.6
Trade	18.7 / 18.1
Finance, Insurance, and Real Estate	6.4 / 7.1
Services	35.0 / 35.0
Public Administration	8.0 / 6.9

Average of top 23 cities

Source: Statistics Canada

But Winnipeg's role in the prairie region as a whole has become less important since the 1950s. With the discovery of new resources such as oil and potash, Calgary, Edmonton, and Regina began to claim their share of economic activity. Winnipeg no longer stands alone as "first city" of western Canada.

CULTURE

The city has long been one of Canada's thriving cultural centres, producing many fine writers and performing artists. It is home to the world-acclaimed Royal Winnipeg Ballet, along with a symphony orchestra, and a theatre centre. Two universities serve the community — the University of Manitoba and the University of Winnipeg. More than 65 different amateur sports are played in Winnipeg. In professional sports, the Blue Bombers (football), the Jets (hockey) and the Fury (soccer) are widely known.

The historic warehouse district in the heart of the city has recently been redeveloped.

Winnipeg Flood, 1950.
The threat of these disastrous floods, which occur periodically as the Red River overflows, has been greatly reduced by a series of flood canals (courtesy PAM).

Winnipeg *(photo by Malak, Ottawa).*

Royal Canadian Mint, Winnipeg (photo by Todd Korol/First Light).

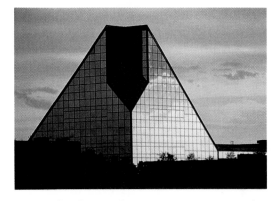

Winnipeg General Strike North Main Street in May or June 1919 (courtesy Goodall Photos).

For further information, contact the City Clerk, Civic Centre, Winnipeg, Man., R3B 1B9.

▷ RELATED ARTICLES: **Royal Winnipeg Ballet; Winnipeg General Strike.**

▷ SUGGESTED READING: Alan Artibise, *Winnipeg: An Illustrated History* (1977); Harry Gutkin with Mildred Gutkin, *The Worst of Times, The Best of Times: Growing up in Winnipeg's North End* (1987); Elma Schemenauer, *Hello Winnipeg* (1986).

■ Winnipeg Blue Bombers

The Blue Bombers football team was formed in 1930 as the Winnipeg Rugby Club. In 1935, it became the first western team to win the Grey Cup. The following year its name was changed to its present name. It reached the national final in 1937, 1938, 1939, and 1941, winning the last two. In 1957, a successful era began under coach Bud Grant. In ten seasons (1957-66), the Blue Bombers played in six Grey Cup games, winning four (1958, 1959, 1961, 1962). Since then the team has won two other cups, in 1984 and 1988.

▷ RELATED ARTICLES: **Football; Grey Cup.**

Marchers in support of the strike leaders leaving Market Square and passing city hall, 1919 (courtesy NAC/C-34022).

■ Winnipeg General Strike

The Winnipeg General Strike lasted from May 15 to June 25, 1919. It began when about 30 000 Winnipeg workers left their jobs in support of building and metal workers who wanted the right to form a union. It was Canada's most dramatic general strike, and it came at a time when workers across the country were organizing to fight massive unemployment and rising prices. Winnipeg was paralysed by the strike. Factories closed. Streetcars stopped running. Telephones did not ring. The mail stopped. Even the police voted to support the strikers, though they stayed on the job.

Employers organized to fight the strike as the Citizens' Committee of 1000. They believed the strike was not a labour dispute, but a revolution against established authority. The federal government agreed, and feared to see the conflict spread to other cities. Troops were rushed to Winnipeg, and special police were sworn in to replace those in sympathy with the strikers.

Before dawn on June 17, government agents arrested six strike leaders and hustled them off to jail. Four more were arrested shortly after. On June 21, when demonstrators attacked and burned a streetcar to protest what they regarded as strike breaking, police fired on the crowd, killing one man and wounding several others. "Bloody Saturday" ended with the city under military patrol. Fearing more violence, workers decided to call off the strike. In return, the government promised to name a royal commission to study labour conditions.

The ten arrested men were R.B. Russell, John Queen, George Armstrong, R.E. Bray, A.A. Heaps, William Ivens, William Pritchard, R.J. Johns, Fred Dixon, and J.S. Woodsworth. All but Woodsworth, Heaps, and Dixon were convicted of conspiracy and given jail terms from six months to two years.

▷ Suggested Reading: A. Balawyder, *The Winnipeg General Strike* (1967); David Jay Bercuson, *Confrontation at Winnipeg: Labour, Industrial Relations and the General Strike* (1974); Geoffrey Bilson, *Goodbye Sarah* (1981).

■ Winnipeg Jets

Organized hockey in Winnipeg dates back to the mid-1890s. In fact, the Winnipeg Victorias captured the Stanley Cup in 1896 and 1901. The Jets were founded as a member of the World Hockey Association in 1972. They lured Bobby Hull, the world's best player, away from the Chicago Black Hawks of the National Hockey League. With several brilliant Swedish players, the Jets won the league championship (Avco Cup) three times. The Jets joined the National Hockey League in 1979, but part of the price they paid was the loss of many of their best players. In their second season, they set a modern-day record for the fewest wins, nine.

The Jets have since enjoyed success in the regular season but have failed to advance in the Stanley Cup playoffs.

■ Winnipeg River

The Winnipeg River, 813 km long, flows out of Lake of the Woods across southeast Manitoba to empty into Lake Winnipeg. During the fur-trade period, canoe brigades heading west from Lake Superior travelled on its churning waters. Voyageurs had to make 26 portages where the river was too rough for canoe travel. When settlers arrived in Manitoba, the river was harnessed to produce electrical power. The first power plant was begun in 1902; today there are six hydroelectric stations on the river. Whiteshell Provincial Park is on the route of the Winnipeg River.

■ Wintergreen

Like mint, wintergreen (*Gaultheria procumbens*) was used to flavour candies and chewing gum. The substance responsible for this delicious taste is methyl salicylate, now produced synthetically as wintergreen flavouring. It is chemically related to aspirin (acetylsalicylic acid). Wintergreen has the same medicinal properties as aspirin for easing pain, rheumatism, and colds. Applying wintergreen to the skin can have a wonderful effect on rheumatism, but prolonged use will irritate the skin and may even cause poisoning.

The wintergreen is a small plant with shiny, oval leaves, white bell-shaped flowers, and delicious, edible red berries. It grows mostly in eastern Canada. Native groups knew its medicinal properties and made much use of it. The creeping snowberry (*G. hispidula*) resembles it only in taste. It has white fruit and very tiny leaves on wiry stems that trail across the moss. Three species of *Gaultheria* grow in western Canada, including the alpine wintergreen (*G. humifusa*).

The name "wintergreen" comes from the fact that its leaves and fruit survive winter very well. The great botanist, Linnaeus, named *Gaultheria* in honour of Jean-François Gaulthier (1708-56), naturalist and king's physician in New France, who was interested in botany and wrote about wintergreen.

■ Wintering Partner

Wintering partners were traders who passed the winter in the interior of the continent collecting furs from the native people. In the summer they travelled down to meeting places such as Fort William on Lake Superior. There they met with their merchant partners to exchange the furs for trade goods and other supplies for the next season.

▷ Related Article: **Fur Trade.**

■ Witch Hazel

Witch hazel is the common name for trees and shrubs of Genus *Hamamelis*. Canada has only one native species: witch hazel (*H. virginiana*), found in eastern Canada from southeast Ontario to Nova Scotia. The Chinese witch hazel (*H. mollis*), was introduced long ago and is used as an ornamental plant in several regions of the country.

Witch hazel is a small tree, 5 m high. It has also been called "winter bloom" since it flowers late in fall when there is sometimes already snow on the ground. Its yellow flowers turn into fruit that remain on the branches until the following autumn. Once mature, they burst and propel their

Witch Hazel is a small tree which flowers in late fall (artwork by Claire Tremblay).

two black seeds some 2 m from the tree. This is why they are also called "snapping hazel."

Witch hazel is known for its medicinal properties. An oil extracted from its leaves, branches, and bark is used in aftershave lotions because it helps slow the flow of blood. It is also used to soothe burns and rashes caused by insect bites or fleabane.

■ Witches

When we hear the word "witch," most people think of an ugly, old woman who casts spells and rides a broomstick across the night sky on Halloween. Witches of this kind are found only in superstition and in popular art.

A modern witch is any man or woman who claims to be a pagan, who belongs to a coven, or circle, of other witches, and who worships natural powers and forces. The worship revolves around a ritual and a practice called witchcraft, or *wicca*. Modern witches do not worship the devil; that is left to satanists. But they do practise magic, white magic rather than black magic, and they attempt to influence natural and supernatural forces and to help and heal people.

In the eyes of the early missionaries and explorers, the pagan practices of the native peoples appeared to be a form of witchcraft. In 1771, Samuel Hearne recorded the legend of the Coppermine Witch, the female guardian of the mineral deposits along the Coppermine River, N.W.T. In 1809, near the Columbia River, David Thompson described his meeting with "a lady conjuress...well dressed, of twenty-five years of age," who painted half her face black and cast spells.

New France had its share of witches. A miller named Daniel Vuil was accused of casting spells to influence the affections of a young and beautiful woman. Claiming she was plagued with spirits, she was committed to the care of a convent. In 1662 Vuil was executed for witchcraft. Then there was Jean-Pierre Lavallée, the sorcerer of Île d'Orléans. In 1711, it is said, this semi-legendary figure saved the island in the St Lawrence River from the English by conjuring up a dense fog which caused the invaders' ships to run aground or withdraw.

There were also reports of witchery in Upper Canada [Ontario] in the 19th century. The "Witch of Plum Hollow" is the way people described Elizabeth Barnes. Curious men and women flocked to Plum Hollow in Leeds County to test Mrs Barnes's "second sight" and "sixth sense," and it is said they were seldom disappointed. Residents of Long Point on Lake Erie referred to John F. Troyer as a "witch-doctor." The pioneer settler was certainly a practitioner of herbal and homeopathic medicine, but he was neither a qualified doctor nor a practitioner of witchcraft. In fact, he lived in fear and dread of witches, even constructing a "witch-trap" to protect himself from their power!

There is no proof that traditional witchcraft really works, yet there does exist a great deal of anecdotal evidence that people are affected by their beliefs. If there is a lesson to be learned from the study of witchcraft, it is that the power of belief and suggestion is a potent force indeed.

▷ SUGGESTED READING: Edna Barth, *Witches, Pumpkins and Grinning Ghosts: The Story of Halloween Symbols* (1972); Georgess McHargue, *Meet the Witches* (1984).

■ Wolf

The wolf (*Canis lupus*) is the largest wild member of the dog family. The wolf is similar in appearance and size to a large German Shepherd dog, though it is leaner and has longer legs and much bigger feet. Wolves have a long, bushy tail with a black tip.

Wolves vary widely in colour, from white to coal black. They are most frequently greyish. The coat consists of coarse, outer guard hairs and a short, soft underfur. The foot pads of northern wolves are protected by stiff tufts of hair. Males are larger than females. A large grey wolf male might weigh 45 kg. Northern wolves tend to be bigger.

Social Behaviour Wolves are pack animals. They live in groups of three to seven, with a dominant male and a breeding

Wolf Family All members of the pack feed and protect the pups (artwork by Jan Sovak).

Range of Wolf ●

Grey Wolves *Wrestling is one kind of social behaviour that helps relieve tension in the pack (photo by Peter McLeod/First Light).*

bitch. Wolves live in dens in the breeding season, under a shelf of rock or in a burrow abandoned by a badger or some other expert digger.

The pack protects and feeds the nursing mother. Lower ranked members of the pack may "babysit" the pups when the parents are away hunting.

The wolf has a complex social life. Each has its own place in the pack, which is displayed every time wolves meet by tail wagging, caressing, romping, wrestling, and dozens of other gestures. A dominant wolf stands erect, holds its tail high, and points its ears up and forward. A lower ranked wolf crouches, holds its tail between its legs, and lowers its ears. As a result of these rituals, there is very little aggression within the pack. Outsiders, however, may be dealt with ruthlessly.

The wolf's howl, a long, quivering wail, is to human ears one of the most melancholy sounds in nature. It is not known why wolves howl.

Hunting Wolves possess a very keen sense of smell and hearing. All their major prey can outrun them, though wolves have astonishing stamina. The pack hunts together, responding to signals from the dominant member. They take

Two-month-old Grey Wolves *(photo by Peter McLeod/First Light).*

turns chasing the prey, in order to tire it or they may split up and chase the victim into an ambush.

Packs occupy a fixed home range and travel along set paths, which they mark with urine. Wolves feed on moose, caribou, wapiti, deer, mountain sheep, and sometimes muskoxen. They also hunt smaller game in summer.

Wolves and Humans No other wild animal stimulates the same interest as the wolf. It was, and still is, revered by some Indian groups, who admire its cunning. However, the wolf is a hated and feared animal in many societies. This is seen even in fairy tales, such as Little Red Riding Hood, and in legends such as the werewolf. As a result, wolves have been hunted relentlessly for sport or from sheer malice. Bounties were paid for wolves in North America for 300 years. They have been eliminated from all the settled parts of North America. They are most common in wilder northern regions.

Yearling *male grey wolf (photo by Peter McLeod/First Light).*

The reported cases of wolves attacking humans are extremely rare. In fact, wolves are shy and very wary of people. Most experts believe that the domestic dog is descended from the wolf. The two are genetically identical and can be interbred.

▷ RELATED ARTICLE: **Dog.**

▷ SUGGESTED READING: R.D. Lawrence, *In Praise of Wolves* (1987); Dawn Richardson, *Smoke* (1985); Judy Ross, *Wolves* (1985); Candace Savage and Paul Mech, *Wolves* (1988).

Wolves *vary in colour from white to coal black (photo by Robert Lankinen/First Light).*

■ Wolfe, James

British army officer (*born about 1727 at Westerham, England; died in 1759 at Quebec, New France.*). The son of a colonel in the Royal Marines, Wolfe joined his father's regiment when he was 13. He transferred to the infantry in 1742, served in Scotland and continental Europe, and during the Seven Years' War

General James Wolfe
(courtesy NAC/C-3916).

was sent to North America. There, in 1758, he drew attention when taking part in the assault on the French fortress of Louisbourg. Assigned to lead the main British assault onto the beaches west of Louisbourg, he encountered heavy musketry and artillery fire. Nevertheless, he led his men ashore through the surf and established a foothold on the beach. During the rest of the siege he showed himself to be an efficient and active officer, with the result that he was put in charge of the large British force that was sent to take Quebec City the following year.

The Siege of Quebec, June-September 1759 The British fleet bearing Wolfe's army arrived off Quebec late in June. But capturing Quebec was to be no easy matter, for the walled city stood high on the cliffs above the St Lawrence River. Wolfe had planned to land his troops downstream and advance up the north shore. The French had anticipated this, and the downstream shore of the river was strongly defended.

For two months, Wolfe camped with his army on Île d'Orléans, trying to make up his mind what to do. A downstream landing near Montmorency Falls in July was easily beaten back by the French. As the weeks passed, sickness swept through the British ranks, greatly reducing the army's strength.

Meantime, Wolfe vented his frustration by having his men pillage and burn the surrounding countryside, killing any habitants who showed resistance.

To add to his troubles, Wolfe quarrelled with his senior officers. They disliked his cold manner and were frustrated by his

Colonel Garnet Wolseley led the army expedition to Red River in 1870 *(courtesy NAC/C-20658).*

indecision. It was they who eventually suggested the plan of attack — to slip up-river past Quebec and mount a surprise assault from the rear. The British crept up the cliffs during the night of September 12-13 and assembled on the plains the next morning. Wolfe was mortally wounded in the following battle.

▷ RELATED ARTICLES: **Plains of Abraham, Battle of the; Seven Years' War;** and the articles on the French officers Louis-Joseph de Montcalm, Pierre de Vaudreuil, and François-Gaston de Lévis.

▷ SUGGESTED READING: Christopher Hibbert, *Wolfe At Quebec* (1959); Joseph Schull, *Battle for the Rock: The Story of Wolfe and Montcalm* (1960).

■ Wolfville

Wolfville, N.S., lies on the Minas Basin, 75 km northwest of Halifax. First settled by Acadian farmers in the 1600s, it later welcomed immigrants from New England. Shipbuilding was important at the natural harbour nearby. Acadia University was established in 1829 and Wolfville is now a quiet university town with little industry. The population in 1986 was 3277.

For further information, contact the Town Clerk, P.O. Box 418, Wolfville, N.S., B0P 1X0.

■ Wollaston Lake

Wollaston Lake, 2681 km^2, lies in the forests of northeast Saskatchewan. Used for many years by fur traders travelling between the Churchill River and the Mackenzie River, it was named for an English chemist, William Hyde Wollaston.

■ Wolseley, Garnet Joseph (1st Viscount Wolseley)

Soldier (*born in 1833 near Dublin, Ireland; died in 1913 at Menton, France*). Colonel Wolseley was a British army officer stationed in Canada from 1861 to 1870. He was chosen to lead the expedition to the Red River Colony in the summer of 1870. Although he arrived in August, after the departure of Louis Riel and other perceived insurgents, he handled this difficult assignment so well that he was made a knight. Later in his career he was put in charge of other expeditions on Britain's behalf. Among these was his expedition up the Nile River in 1884-85. By then he was General Wolseley. He ended his career as Field Marshal Lord Wolseley, Commander-in-chief of the British army.

▷ RELATED ARTICLES: **Nile Expedition; Red River Expedition.**

■ Wolverine

The wolverine (*Gulo gulo*) is the largest land member of the weasel (Mustelidae) family. In Europe and Asia it is called the glutton. It resembles a bear cub, since it is 80 to 110 cm long and weighs 11 to 16 kg. Because of this resemblance, and because it often applies a stinking scent to any leftover food it cannot consume, wolverines are sometimes called skunk-bears.

It is dark brown with two lighter stripes that extend along the flanks from the shoulder to the base of the tail. The wolverine lives on the tundra and taiga and is active day and night throughout the year. It eats small mammals, carrion left by bears or wolves, birds, fish, fruit, roots, and on occasion, prey as large as caribou or moose.

Wolverine (artwork by Jan Sovak).

The female bears a single annual litter of one to five young between March and mid-April. The young stay with their mother for a year. Wolverines are rarely killed by wolves; humans are their chief enemy. Trappers prize wolverine fur, which is preferred for parka trim because it resists frost more than other furs. Only very scattered populations exist in eastern Canada today. Wolverines are more numerous in the West and North. The wolverine may live ten years in the wild. The fierce, solitary wolverine is featured in many Indian legends.

▷ SUGGESTED READING: Paige Dixon, *The Loner: A Story of the Wolverine* (1978).

■ Woman's Christian Temperance Union

The Woman's Christian Temperance Union (WCTU) was formed in 1874 in Ontario. It was the leading women's society in Canada's temperance movement. Founder Letitia Youmans made it a nationwide organization in 1885. The WCTU campaigned against drinking and attempted to get the sale of alcoholic bev-

erages banned in Canada. Since drunkenness was seen as the cause of many social ills, including wife beating and other violence in the home, the WCTU attacked these problems too. It campaigned for reforms that would give women more control over their lives. This included getting women the right to vote; the WCTU was one of the groups that fought for women's suffrage (the right to vote).

Thousands of Canadian women supported the WCTU during the late 19th and early 20th centuries. During World War I, the organization achieved its two main aims: prohibition (which outlawed the making and selling of alcoholic beverages) and women's suffrage. Membership dropped off after the war, and today the WCTU has only about 2500 members throughout Canada.

▷ RELATED ARTICLE: **Prohibition.**

■ Women's Movement

Since the 1960s, women in Canada have worked together to make life better and fairer for the 51% of our population that is female. The women's movement includes many people, many concerns, and many points of view, but there is common agreement on the goal, which is to bring about full equality between men and women.

The Constitution Act (1982) contains two statements guaranteeing equality between the sexes. Section 15.1 of the Charter of Rights and Freedoms, after stating that "every individual is equal before and under the law and has the right to the equal protection and equal benefit of the law," goes on to forbid discrimination on the basis of sex, among other grounds. Then for good measure, and because women lobbied actively for it, the Charter also has Section 28, which reads: "Notwithstanding anything in the Charter, the rights and freedoms referred to in it are guaranteed equally to male and female persons." This gives Canadian women one of the strongest endorsements of their right to equality anywhere in the world.

Why are these explicit guarantees necessary? Aren't men and women equal now, whatever may have been the case in the past? It is true that few formal barriers remain to women's full and equal participation in every sphere of life. All around us we see women broadcasters, bus drivers, letter carriers, police officers, and even a handful of engineers. The news stories about "the first woman such-and-so in Canada" are becoming rare, and will

Range of Wolverine ●

Letitia Youmans

Letitia Youmans (1827-96) was born in Hamilton Township, Upper Canada (Ontario). She founded her first temperance group at her home in Picton, Ont., after visiting the United States and meeting prominent members of its women's temperance movement. Over the next few years, she travelled in many parts of Canada to encourage women to start local temperance societies, and in 1885 she drew all these branches together to form a national Woman's Christian Temperance Union, of which she became president. She retired in 1889, and in 1893 she published her autobiography (*courtesy NAC/C-5084*).

Parachute Riggers, *oil on canvas by Paraskeva Clark (courtesy Canadian War Museum/ NMC/14086).*

soon disappear. But younger Canadians may not know that these are very recent developments, and represent long years of argument and struggle to establish the rights of girls and women to shape their lives according to their own aspirations and values.

Probably the biggest changes to Canadian women's lives since the end of World War II have to do with education, paid work, marriage, and the family. These three spheres are closely intertwined, and reflect the great changes in the Canadian economy during this century. While many of these changes have benefited women, there have been some costs as well. The majority of Canadian women now work outside the home for most of their adult lives; yet women continue to do most of the housework and childcare. Men, too, will have to change their traditional family and work roles if fairness to women is to prevail.

For many Canadians, education is the key to a secure and fulfilling future. Over the past two decades, women have made up most of the increases in university and college enrolments. In 1960, about one-third of university students was female. In 1987, women made up 55% of university undergraduates. Between 1971 and 1987, the proportion of master's degrees earned by women doubled, from 22% to 45%. Women's share of doctorates more than tripled from 9% to 29%. Of course, only a small minority of Canadians study for post-graduate degrees. Nevertheless, the changes are dramatic, and show that young women now realize how impor-

tant it is that our society be able to draw on the talents and skills of women doctors, lawyers, scientists, administrators, writers and business leaders.

Women in the Labour Force Most women, like most men, do not work in the higher paid professions, but work for wages in industry or services, or run their own business or farm. Here, the discrepancy between men's and women's economic opportunities and rewards is very marked. The vast majority of women — over 80% — work in only three fields: clerical, service, or sales occupations. These tend to be non-unionized, low paying, and insecure; they may also involve part-time work, in which women predominate. Because they may interrupt their work-life to raise children, or simply because of the lingering prejudice against women managers, only a small fraction of senior positions in any field is occupied by women.

As a result of these and many other factors, women on average earn far less than men: in 1987, full-year, full-time women workers earned 66% of what their male counterparts earned. This is an improvement since 1971, when women earned 60 cents on the "male" dollar. Still, it is no wonder that many more women than men face poverty in their old age; that single-parent households headed by women (which is over 80% of the total) are poorer than those headed by men; and that when couples are deciding who should stay home to look after the children, it usually makes economic sense for it to be the woman.

Despite all these considerations, Canadian women continue to move into the labour force. In 1951, only 11.2% of all

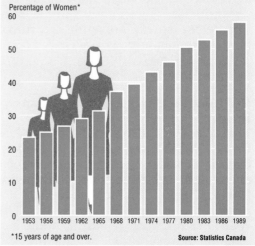

PARTICIPATION OF WOMEN IN THE LABOUR FORCE - 1953-1989

Percentage of Women*
60

*15 years of age and over.   **Source: Statistics Canada**

married women in Canada worked for pay. Few women with small children took jobs or followed professions, partly because society frowned upon working mothers, and partly because pay scales for women were about half those paid to men. By 1975, 41.6% of all married women worked outside the home, rising to 59.1% in 1988. By the late 1980s, mothers with young children were more likely to have a job than to be full-time homemakers.

It seems likely that this is a decisive change in the way Canadian girls and women see their lives. Although they may intend to marry and have children, they also expect to share the breadwinner role with their husbands, and to be prepared, if necessary, to support themselves and their children.

Marriage and Family Patterns These changed expectations are closely tied in with changes in marriage and family patterns. On average, women are marrying later and are having fewer children than their mothers and grandmothers did. In the 1950s, the average age of first-time brides was 21; in 1988, it was 25. Instead of four children, which was the norm in the late 1950s, the typical Canadian woman now has less than two. (When we talk of a birth-rate of 1.7 children per woman, the current rate in Canada, we are describing an average over the whole population.) Women who are intent on finishing their education or establishing themselves in a job may decide to postpone having their first child until they are in their late 20s or later. This is now possible because of the invention of the contraceptive pill, and the widespread acceptance of family planning, both of which happened only in the 1960s.

Proposals for Change The persistence of the earnings gap between men and women, and the tendency of women to cluster in a narrow range of occupations rather than spread more or less evenly with men among all fields, have led to new ideas about discrimination. We now understand that there are many taken-for-granted habits and structures that end up favouring men over women, without anyone intending to be unfair. Thus we look for ways in which this unintended discrimination works against women's equality, and then try to find fairer ways to organize affairs so that women are not harmed.

Out of these new ideas have come many forward-looking proposals for change: paid parental leave, better day care, more flexible work patterns, special training for women to enter trades or take on management responsibilities, and equal pay for work of equal value. These are some of the issues around which many women activists are now organizing, in labour unions, through the media, and in lobbying or electing politicians.

Politics is another area where we can see the effects of discrimination that is part of the system. When Canadian women got the vote at the end of World War I, everyone assumed that equality between the sexes would soon follow. Yet from 1916 to the late 1960s only a handful of women were elected to Parliament, or to provincial legislatures. As a result, needed changes to the law were slow in coming. Recently, all political parties have started to seek out good women candidates, but it is still more difficult for women than for men to combine the demands of family and a political career. In 1990, only 40 of 294 seats in the House of Commons in Ottawa were held by women, and the proportions in most provincial legislatures were no higher, and in some cases even lower.

Law Even though few of our lawmakers have so far been female, the impact of the women's movement on the interpretation of the law has recently begun to appear. Nearly half of current law school students are female, and many are developing new perspectives on the law, showing how laws have placed unfair burdens on women. Of the nine Supreme Court judges in Canada in 1990, three were women.

An important recent development is that some male and female judges in Canada are learning to understand equality in a new way. This new view of equality argues that treating men and women exact-

AVERAGE EARNINGS OF WOMEN AND MEN - 1967-1988

Source: Statistics Canada

ly alike in all cases is not fair to women. They argue that there are important differences between the sexes and that remedies are sometimes required to overcome long-term disadvantages.

The most fundamental differences between women and men are related to sexuality and reproduction. In the 1970s and 1980s, issues like sexual harassment, sexual assault, pornography, wife battering, child abuse, and incest received serious public attention. Many people in the women's movement believe that as long as there continues to be such widespread violence against women, there cannot be equality between the sexes.

Women's capacity to bear children is another key element in sexual equality. Many people argue that in order to avoid unwanted pregnancies, girls and women must have the ability to refuse sexual relations, or to insist on the use of effective contraception, and this cannot happen as long as women are dependent on men. Finally, for many but not all Canadian women, the right to access to a safe, medical abortion is a strongly held belief.

The Future For many women who have long been active in the women's movement, the changes and improvements in women's lives often seem to happen very slowly. However, many ideas that seemed revolutionary a generation ago are now familiar to a wider public, and seem less surprising and dangerous than they once did. In addition, women's studies in schools, colleges, and universities have given young people a chance to study these ideas, and see how they apply to their lives. Through the many discussions about sexual equality that take place in the media, the classroom, and among friends and families, the groundwork is being laid for the eventual acceptance of full equality between the sexes.

Making the promises in Canada's Charter of Rights and Freedoms come true will take time and goodwill. But equality among all people, regardless of their sex, race, or other personal characteristics, is a noble goal, and one well worth working for.

■ Women's Organizations

Women's organizations have played an important part in Canadian social life. There are many different types, but their purposes are the same: to offer mutual support, assistance, education, and social contact to women of all ages and needs. They recognize that there is strength in numbers, and that individual problems can often find solutions among sympathetic and like-minded people who share common goals and interests.

Some women's organizations have a long history. Examples are the Young Women's Christian Association (founded in 1895), the National Council of Women (1893), Girl Guides (1910), and Canadian Girls in Training (1915). Other groups that have had large memberships over the years are Women's Institutes, Business and Professional Women's Clubs, and the Canadian Federation of University Women. Farm women, women teachers and artists, women in unions, and women in political parties have all formed committees, auxiliaries, or caucuses to deal with women's concerns, which tend to get overlooked when memberships or executives of organizations are dominated by men, as is often the case.

Some organizations are national in scope, others are local or regional. At the national level, the National Action Committee on the Status of Women (NAC) was founded in 1971 to push for government action on the many recommendations contained in the 1970 *Report* of the Royal Commission on the Status of Women. NAC is an umbrella organization that relates to over 500 member groups across Canada. Through NAC, more than 3 million Canadian women keep in touch with current issues of concern to women, and express women's viewpoints on important public matters, ranging from social welfare to constitutional reform to the needs of native, immigrant, or rural women. Its counterpart in Quebec is the Fédération des femmes du Québec (1966).

Women's groups have often been effective politically, campaigning tirelessly for such issues as nuclear disarmament and peace, the crisis in farming communities, day care, rape crisis, and abortion laws. Recently, the National Association for Women and the Law and the Legal Education and Action Fund joined together to bring new understanding of equality and discrimination into our laws and court judgements. Women's groups also ensured that women's equality rights would be entrenched in our Canadian Charter of Rights and Freedoms (Sections 15 and 28).

Older organizations tend to have a formal structure, with an executive and regular monthly meetings. Groups that formed in the 1970s and after have often experimented with more flexible structures and procedures. They may be called centres, collectives, or ad hoc working groups rather than clubs or associations.

■ Women's Suffrage

"Suffrage" is the right to vote in political elections. Men began to vote in elections in Canada in 1791. For the next 100 years, only men could be politicians and only men were allowed to vote. It was generally accepted (by most women as well as men) that politics, like medicine and law, was a male profession.

Attitudes changed during the second half of the 19th century as a few women began to enter the professions that had been formerly thought of as part of the male "sphere." Further pressure came from women's organizations that were working to bring about social reforms, such as laws to curb alcohol abuse or to improve working conditions for factory women. To get the desired reforms, women had to have the vote to influence politicians.

The first Canadian group to press for women's suffrage was the Toronto Women's Literary Club, formed by Emily Stowe in 1876. The club changed its name to Toronto Women's Suffrage Association in 1883, becoming the Canadian Suffrage Association in 1907. After Emily Stowe's death in 1903, her daughter Augusta Stowe-Gullen carried on the leadership.

In western Canada, the suffrage movement began early in the 1890s among Manitoba settlers from Iceland and at Winnipeg's Woman's Christian Temper-

Manitoba Equal Suffrage Club, 1900 (courtesy PAM/N10675).

ance Union (WCTU). As in eastern Canada, the suffrage groups held meetings and demonstrations, and sent petitions to the government. Progress was slow until 1911, when Nellie McClung arrived in Winnipeg. A fiery public speaker, McClung soon emerged as the West's leading "suffragette." In 1912, she helped organize the Political Equality League (PEL), a Winnipeg group backed by the WCTU and the Icelandic Women's Suffrage Association, and also by labour and farm groups. The PEL kept up a forceful campaign, gathering an increasing number of supporters.

By this time a large number of men, including some politicians, had declared their support for women's right to vote. During World War I, thousands of women took on the jobs of men who had joined the armed forces. Others risked their lives overseas as doctors or nurses. Meanwhile, petitions and referendums in Canada proved that the suffrage movement had widespread support. In January 1916 Manitoba passed a law that granted women the vote. It was soon followed by other provinces (see table, page 268, Volume V). These laws permitted women to vote in provincial elections, but did not apply to federal elections. The federal vote came in two stages. There was the Wartime Elections Act of 1917, which gave the

Nellie McClung, Alice Jamieson, and Emily Murphy (courtesy PABC/HP39854).

Whooping Cranes in *Wood Buffalo National Park (photo by E. Kuyt).*

vote to women serving in the forces and to female relatives of men in the forces. Finally, there was the Women's Franchise Act of 1918, which permitted all women citizens aged 21 and over to vote in federal elections after January 1919.

▷ SUGGESTED READING: Catherine L. Cleverdon, *The Woman Suffrage Movement in Canada: The State of Liberation 1900-1920* (second edition, 1974); Linda Kealey, editor, *A Not Unreasonable Claim: Women and Reform in Canada 1880s-1920s* (1979); Valerie Knowles, *First Person: A Biography of Cairine Wilson, Canada's First Woman Senator* (1988); Helen K. Wright, *Nellie McClung and Women's Rights* (1980).

■ Wood, Henry Wise

Farm leader (*born in 1860 at Monroe City, Missouri, U.S.; died in 1941 at Calgary, Alta*). A wheat farmer in Alberta, Wood spearheaded the struggle of western farmers for a fair share of the country's wealth. He was educated as a church minister in his native Missouri. Wood took up farming instead, though he was a religious man all his life. In 1905 he moved to Alberta where he bought a wheat farm.

Wood believed strongly in the need for farmers to organize, to promote their own interests. From 1916 to 1931, he was president of the United Farmers of Alberta (UFA). When the UFA formed the government of Alberta in 1921, Wood was asked to be premier, but he declined.

Wood had his own theory of government. He wanted to replace political parties with groups based on the kind of work members did. In this way, farmers would have their own representatives in Parliament, as would miners, factory workers, and other occupations. The idea was called group government, but it never gained wide acceptance.

During the 1920s, Wood worked for the creation of wheat pools to sell western grain at a fair price for farmers. A powerful speaker and a tireless worker, Wood was a leading voice in the farm movement of the 1920s and 1930s.

▷ RELATED ARTICLE: **United Farmers of Alberta.**

▷ SUGGESTED READING: William Kirby Rolph, *Henry Wise Wood of Alberta* (1950).

■ Wood Buffalo National Park

Wood Buffalo National Park (44 807 km²) is Canada's largest national park. Three-quarters of it lies in Alberta in a vast area of the boreal forest. The rest is in the Northwest Territories. Its main waterway is the Peace River, which meanders through the park for 200 km. The delta formed by the meeting of the Peace and the Athabasca rivers is one of the largest inland deltas in the world. Its bewildering jumble of lakes, marshes, meadows, and narrow channels is a perfect home for birds and animals.

The park was created in 1922 to preserve the remaining herd of wood bison, which at one time was reduced to only 300 animals. The Canadian government also moved a herd of plains bison here in 1925 and 1928. Today there are over 4000 bison in Wood Buffalo National Park. The park is also home to wolves, bears, and other mammals. Another rare occupant of the park is the Whooping Crane, North America's tallest bird. There were only 21 left in 1941. It was not until 1954 that a bush pilot discovered its breeding grounds in the northern part of Wood Buffalo National Park. Today the Whooping Crane is still endangered; there are only about 160 in the wild.

For further information, contact the Superintendent, Wood Buffalo National Park, P.O. Box 750, Fort Smith, N.W.T., X0E 0P0.

■ Wood Mountain

Wood Mountain (1013 m) lies in the southwest corner of Saskatchewan near the United States border. The treed slopes were settled by Metis after 1870, and both the Hudson's Bay Company and the North-West Mounted Police built posts. In 1876, Sitting Bull and his Sioux warriors sought refuge in the area after the Battle of the Little Bighorn. The mountain became part of a provincial historic park in 1965.

■ Woodcock

The American Woodcock (*Scolopax minor*) belongs to the same family as sandpipers and snipes (Scolopacidae). It is very stocky with a short neck and tail and a very long bill. The tip of the bill is extremely sensitive, functioning like an antenna to detect the earthworms the bird loves to eat. Its large eyes are placed high on its bulky head.

In mating season, the male spirals high into the sky and zigzags back towards the ground. He seems to be singing as he goes, but in fact it is the sound of wind passing through the feathers on his wings. Female birds' wings also produce the sound. The woodcock is a nocturnal and secretive bird that nests in damp woods and ditches in southeastern Canada to Florida. It usually winters in the southeastern United States and along the Gulf of Mexico.

■ Woodcock, George

Author and literary journalist (*born in 1912 at Winnipeg, Man.*). George Woodcock is one of Canada's most wide-ranging and productive writers. He grew up in England, where he wrote for and edited magazines. He returned to Canada in 1949. Ten years later he founded the magazine *Canadian Literature* and remained its editor until 1977. Woodcock has written more than 60 books on such varied subjects as history, poetry, travel, literary criticism, and biography. His political history of *Anarchism* (1962) is a classic in its field; so is the study of his friend George Orwell, *The Crystal Spirit* (1966), which won a Governor General's Award. Woodcock's many books on Canadian subjects include *Gabriel Dumont* (1975), *Faces from History* (1978), *The Canadians* (1979), and *The Century That Made Us: Canada 1814-1914* (1989). He has also written two volumes of autobiography: *Letter to the Past* (1982) and *Beyond the Blue Mountains* (1987).

■ Woodenware

Woodenware, or "treen" as it is also called, is the name for simple wooden objects with a practical purpose. Few of the treen objects once common in Canada survive today. They have worn out, rotted away, or been burnt.

Early settlers used wood to replace household and farm items. Wood was strong, easily worked, and usually available. In Europe these items would have been made of other materials, such as iron, glass, silver, or earthenware.

Pioneers used the long winter evenings to make spoons, breadboards, bowls, rolling pins, pitchforks, and many other tools. They took great care to choose the proper wood-working technique. Hollow objects might be chiselled. Handles might be turned on a lathe. Curved or round objects might be shaped by using steam and clamps.

It was also important to choose the right kind of wood. Hardwoods were chosen when the object had to be strong and long lasting. For example, ash absorbs shock, and so was perfect for axe and hammer handles.

Burls (lumpy growths on tree trunks) were prized for making bowls. A burl is hard to work, but has an unusual and beautiful grain. It is also water-resistant and seldom splits.

Softwoods were used when speedy production was more important than durability. Spoons could easily be whittled out of softwood. Kitchen utensils were normally made of pine, because it is light, odourless, and tasteless.

With the coming of the Industrial Revolution, the use of hand-crafted woodenware quickly declined. Mass-produced objects were cheaper and more practical.

The recent revival of crafts has renewed interest in woodenware. Treen and burl bowls, along with butter presses and maple sugar molds, are again being made by Canadian craftspeople.

■ Woodpecker

Woodpeckers are climbing birds. There are 204 species of them, 14 in parts of Canada. Seven species are found across Canada: Pileated Woodpecker (*Dryocopus pileatus*), Downy Woodpecker (*Picoides pubescens*), Hairy Woodpecker (*P. villosus*), Northern Three-toed Woodpecker (*P. tridactylus*), Black-backed Woodpecker (*P. articus*), Northern Flicker (*Colaptes auratus*), and Yellow-bellied Sapsucker (*Sphyrapicus varius*). Others have a more limited range in southern or western Canada and are much rarer.

Woodpeckers are very well adapted for climbing trees. They have short legs, strong claws on their toes, and a tail with straight feathers used to brace the bird against the trunk. They also have a very long tongue that catches the insects they find in infested tree trunks. They swoop while flying. Their plumage, sometimes striped, is usually black and white with some red or yellow. The Pileated Woodpecker has a red crest.

Breeding Range of American Woodcock ●

Wooden Bowl made *from a burl (courtesy Royal Ontario Museum).*

Yellow-bellied Sapsucker (photo by Wayne Lankinen/DRK Photo).

Downy Woodpecker (photo by William Reynolds).

Most species eat insects found in trees, some look for ants in the soil. Sapsuckers bore a series of tiny holes in trees and then drink the sap that drips out. Woodpeckers dig holes in trees for nests. They lay two to eight eggs and both parents take care of the nest. Sometimes starlings manage to take over a freshly dug woodpecker hole. The drumming sound you sometimes hear far off in the forest is made by the woodpecker.

▷ Suggested Reading: Adrian Forsyth, *The Nature of Birds* (1988).

■ Woodstock

Woodstock, N.B., nestles in the valley of the Saint John River, 103 km upstream from Fredericton. Settled first by Loyalists, it grew in the 19th century as the site of several small mills and factories. It is named for a town in England and is the oldest incorporated town in the province. The population in 1986 was 4549.

For further information, contact the Town Clerk, P.O. Box 1059, Woodstock, N.B., E0J 2B0.

■ Woodstock

Woodstock, Ont., lies beside the Thames River in southwestern Ontario, 140 km from Toronto. It began in the 1830s as a farming centre, named for a town in England. Then it began to attract a variety of manufacturers, until by 1900 it was

James Shaver Woodsworth (courtesy NAC/C-55449).

known as "The Industrial City." The economy continues to rely on manufacturing, as well as business from the surrounding farm district. Woodstock's population in 1986 was 26 386.

■ Woodsworth, James Shaver

Minister, social worker, first leader of the Co-operative Commonwealth Federation (*born in 1874 at Etobicoke, Ont.; died in 1942 at Vancouver, B.C.*). As a young boy, Woodsworth settled with his family in Manitoba where he studied to become a Methodist minister. Moved by the poverty of so many city dwellers, he went to work among immigrants in a poor district of Winnipeg. Woodsworth was a follower of Social Gospel, a social reform movement in the church. "To really save one man," he wrote, "you must improve the community in which he lives."

Socialist and Pacifist Woodsworth was a socialist and a pacifist. During World War I, he opposed Canada's support for the war. When his church supported the conflict, he quit the ministry and took a job on the docks in Vancouver loading freight.

In 1919 Woodsworth arrived in Winnipeg at the height of the General Strike. He threw himself behind the strikers. He was arrested along with other strike leaders, but his case never came to trial.

Politician After the strike, Woodsworth helped to organize a new political party, the Independent Labour Party of Manitoba. In the 1921 election, he won a seat in the House of Commons for a Winnipeg riding. For the next 20 years he was undefeated in elections.

In Parliament, Woodsworth joined with a small group called the Ginger Group, composed of radical farm and labour members of Parliament. When the Depression struck, he was one of the founders of the Co-operative Commonwealth Federation (CCF), a new socialist political party. He became the first leader of the new party.

At the outbreak of World War II, Woodsworth found himself at odds with his party. He was still a pacifist and wanted Canada to remain neutral. But the CCF did not favour neutrality and Woodsworth was shunted aside as leader. When the vote came in Parliament, he was the only MP to oppose the declaration of war.

In 1940 Woodsworth won his last election. He died in 1942, respected to the end for his fierce devotion to his principles.

▷ Suggested Reading: Kenneth McNaught, *J.S. Woodsworth* (1980).

◼ Woodward Family

Charles Woodward (1842-1937) was the founder of the Woodward's chain of department stores. He moved to Vancouver from Ontario and opened his first store there three months after his arrival in 1892. The store did well, for Woodward was determined to provide everything working people needed — from shoes to groceries — and he sold the goods at reasonable prices. A hard worker who was committed to his business, he was a millionaire by the 1920s. In 1926, he opened a branch store in Edmonton, Alta.

William Culham Woodward (1885-1957) and *Percival Archibald Woodward* (1890-1968) were the two sons (from a family of nine children) who followed their father into the business. Percival specialized in merchandising, while William's specialty was finance. William succeeded his father as president of Woodward's Ltd in 1937. He was a major influence in British Columbia and served as lieutenant-governor of the province from 1941 to 1946.

Charles N.W. "Chunky" Woodward (1924-1990) was William C. Woodward's son. He took over as president in 1956. During the following years, he greatly expanded the business, increasing the number of stores from six to more than 20. Chunky had many other interests other than department stores, and he retired in 1985 so that he could devote more time to ranching. He owned Canada's largest cattle ranch, the Douglas Lake Ranch, in British Columbia.

Chunky's sons, John and Christopher Woodward, are both vice-presidents and directors of the company. By the early 1980s, Woodward's Ltd was having financial difficulties, partly because of competition from other stores and partly because of the economic recession at that time. At the end of 1989, in an effort to solve the problems, the Woodwards stepped aside from the business which had been run by the family for four generations. A new management team took office, though members of the Woodward family continue to sit as directors on the board.

▷ SUGGESTED READING: Douglas E. Harker, *The Woodwards* (1976).

◼ Work, *see* Labour

◼ Workers' Compensation

Workers' compensation is a plan to provide payments and medical care to workers who suffer injuries on the job or develop serious illnesses as a result of working conditions. The plan is administered by the different provinces, and covers up to 80% of all Canadian workers. Recipients are paid from a fund provided by employers and receive a portion of their usual salary.

Ontario introduced the first workers' compensation plan in Canada in 1914. Prior to that time, workers suffering injuries on the job had to sue their employers. Because they had to prove that the accident was the fault of the employer, not many workers won compensation in the courts. The government plan does not try to discover who is at fault; payments are made regardless.

Following the Ontario example, similar plans were introduced in Nova Scotia (1915), British Columbia (1916), Alberta and New Brunswick (1918), Manitoba (1920), Saskatchewan (1929), Quebec (1931), Prince Edward Island (1949), and Newfoundland (1950, but it had a plan in existence from 1908).

Workers' compensation does not reduce the risks faced in the workplace, but it does help to reduce the hardship caused by injury or illness.

◼ Workers Unity League

The Workers Unity League (WUL) was a federation of trade unions supported by the Communist Party of Canada during the Great Depression of the 1930s. It found its membership among less-skilled workers and the unemployed. It led several strikes during the early 1930s. The WUL disbanded in 1935 when communists decided it was better to work within non-communist unions than to be in competition with them.

◼ Working-Class History

Working-class history is the history of all Canadians who earn their living in the form of wages and salaries. Often it is the study of trade unions and labour strife. However, important as unions are, only a portion of Canadian workers belong to them. As a result, working-class history must include the study of working people in their families, their communities, and their jobs.

Rise of the Working Class A large working class emerged in Canada during the 19th century with the spread of industrialization. Until that time, most people were self-employed. They supported themselves by farming, fishing, or producing goods in small workshops. The family was the centre of the economy and

every member played a part in the production of goods.

Industrialization changed the way work was organized. Workers came together in large factories. The use of complex machinery increased. Early factories were poorly lit, dirty, noisy, and dangerous. More and more, machines set the pace of work. Each worker had a task to repeat over and over again. Work became more efficient, but it was less rewarding for the individual. Instead of being self-employed, most people worked for someone else.

In the early years of industrialization, children as young as ten years old worked in the mills and factories. They were set to work at simple jobs and were paid very little. They worked to help their families make ends meet. Early in the 20th century, laws were passed to remove children from the factories and put them in school. By World War I, most provinces had laws regulating child labour.

Women filled many jobs in the new factories, especially in the textile industry. However, the leading occupations for women were as servants and housekeepers in the homes of the wealthy. They also worked as secretaries, receptionists, and typists in offices, and ran small businesses. By 1900, women were working as teachers and nurses and were fighting their way into medical and law schools. But equality came slowly, and most

women made less money and had fewer work opportunities than men.

THE LABOUR MOVEMENT

Strikes and labour unrest go back a long way in Canadian history. The first recorded strike for better wages occurred in 1794 when a group of fur traders at Rainy River [Ontario] went on strike. Workers often stopped work to protest low wages or poor working conditions.

Realizing that unity brought strength, workers organized the first unions. Often they were illegal. Members went to jail or were fined, and soldiers were called in to break up strikes. Despite this opposition, unions spread, especially among skilled workers.

In 1872 the Trade Unions Act made unions legal. That same year thousands of workers in Ontario and Quebec paraded through the streets in support of reducing the working day from 12 to nine hours.

Knights of Labor march, King Street, Hamilton, 1885 (courtesy NAC/PA-103086).

Local unions joined together to form larger organizations. One of the most successful was the Knights of Labor, an American organization that came to Canada in 1881. Strongest in Quebec, Ontario, and B.C., the Knights attracted more than 16 000 members by 1882. In 1883 the Knights helped to form the Trades and Labor Congress of Canada, which went on to become Canada's main national forum for labour.

Parades and rallies on Labour Day, the first Monday in September, began to be celebrated in 1872. Labour Day was declared a national holiday in 1894. In 1900, the federal government created a Department of Labour in Ottawa. In 1909 William Lyon Mackenzie King became its first minister.

World War I After 1900, with the general improvement of economic conditions, union membership grew rapidly. Many of the unions were based in the

---

Time Line: Working-Class History

- **1794** First strike among fur traders at Rainy River [Ont.]
- **1872** Trade Unions Act; Nine-Hour Movement; Labour Day celebrations begin
- **1881** Knights of Labor come to Canada
- **1883** Trades and Labor Congress of Canada is formed
- **1894** Labour Day becomes an official National holiday
- **1900** Department of Labour is established
- **1919** One Big Union is formed; Winnipeg General Strike
- **1930s** Great Depression. In 1933, 25% of all wage earners are jobless
- **1945** The Rand Formula brings compulsory deduction of dues

Workers in a textile plant, around 1908 (courtesy City of Toronto Archives/James Collection 137).

United States, with branches in Canada. American unions attracted Canadian workers because of their size and wealth. In Quebec the Catholic Church organized unions for its worker members.

The number of strikes increased in the pre-war period. Wages were only one issue. Workers also protested working conditions and the use of new machinery, which was robbing them of their skills and independence.

During World War I membership in unions continued to grow. At the end of the war strike activity increased everywhere in the country. The cost of living rose, and the return of many soldiers meant that there were fewer jobs to go around. Workers believed that the end of the war would bring a new era of equality and prosperity. Instead, they found their situation unimproved.

By 1919 union membership stood at 378 000. More than 300 strikes took place across the country in 1919. The most dramatic one was the Winnipeg General Strike, joined by about 30 000 people. But this period of unrest did not improve things for most workers. Economic hard times brought wage cuts and unemployment. The recession lifted in the mid-1920s, but generally speaking labour was in retreat during the decade.

Great Depression During the Great Depression of the 1930s, unemployment was worse than ever. At the peak of the crisis, in 1933, about 25% of all wage earners were jobless. Large numbers of unemployed men wandered across the country, hopelessly seeking work. Under the Department of National Defence, the federal government created work camps where single men received room and board and 20 cents a day.

The Depression did not really lift until the outbreak of World War II in 1939. The army offered jobs to the unemployed. The war effort created a demand for goods and munitions. The wheels of Canadian industry began to turn again.

During the war, the federal government tried to limit the power of unions. Ottawa imposed wage limits and restricted the right to go on strike. But workers opposed these measures. At war's end, they won the right to join the union of their choice. As well, employers had to deal with unions chosen by their employees. Another important change was the so-called Rand formula, which required all workers to pay union dues, whether they belonged to a union or not.

LABOUR AND POLITICS

Many improvements in working conditions came about because of labour's involvement in politics. The first workers' candidate was elected to Parliament in 1872.

There were labour parties in the different provinces which elected members to all levels of government. Since the 1930s, most labour candidates have found a home in the Co-operative Commonwealth Federation and its successor, the New Democratic Party.

Labour used its political power to support the rise of the welfare state during the 1930s and 1940s. Measures such as unemployment insurance, workers' compensation, and family allowance helped to protect working people from the effects of illness and unemployment. After World War II, the welfare state continued to expand.

In the post-war period, a major development has been the growth in the number of Canadians who work for the federal, provincial, or city governments. By the 1970s, about one in five employees worked in government. Today, three of the four largest unions in Canada represent public servants. Most Canadian workers now belong to Canadian, not American, unions.

At the same time, there was a shift in the kind of work that most Canadians performed. At the end of the 19th century, most workers were employed in farming, logging, and mining. Then, industrialization increased the number of jobs in manufacturing. Finally, within the last few decades, the majority of Canadians found work in the service industries; that is, they provide services instead of making products.

Another major change since World War II has been a dramatic increase in the number of women workers. In April 1990 women made up 45% of the workforce. As a result, workers are increasingly interested in issues such as maternity leave, child care, and equal pay for men and women.

The post-war years brought a period of growing prosperity for most Canadians. Working people enjoy a better standard of living than ever before, but at the same time, unemployment continues to plague the economy in parts of the country.

▷ RELATED ARTICLES: **Child Labour; Immigrant Labour; Industrialization; Knights of Labor; Labour; Labour Force; Nine-Hour Movement; Strikes and Lockouts; Unemployment; Unemployment Relief Camps; Unions.**

Workman, Joseph

Psychiatrist (*born in 1805 near Lisburn, Ireland; died in 1894 at Toronto, Ont.*). Joseph Workman was a pioneer in the treatment of mental illness. A graduate in medicine from McGill University in Montreal, Que., he was appointed superintendent of the Provincial Lunatic Asylum in Toronto in 1854. For more than 20 years, this kindly man directed the affairs of the asylum, taking a personal interest in each patient. This in itself was a novelty, for most 19th-century mental institutions were more like jails than hospitals, and little if anything was done to help the patients. Workman thought up projects and games to amuse those in his care. He read to them, chatted to them, listened to them, and generally made the asylum a far happier place. His work inspired others to take a scientific approach to treating the mentally handicapped.

▷ RELATED ARTICLE: **Charles K. Clarke.**

World War I

World War I, August 4, 1914 to November 11, 1918, involved all the world's great powers and many other countries as well.

Great Britain, France, Russia, and other countries fought Germany, Austria-Hungary, and Turkey. Canada sided with the mother country, Great Britain, from the first day of the war, and the United States joined the war effort against Germany in 1917.

An estimated 65 million men served in their countries' armed forces during the war; almost half that number were killed or wounded. This senseless slaughter was one of the reasons for the setting up of a League of Nations in 1919 to help maintain the peace and avoid another mistake like World War I.

The Treaty of Versailles (signed with Germany in 1919) was the most important of the peace treaties. Many Germans felt it was too harsh, and Adolf Hitler used resentment against it in his rise to power in the 1930s.

For a nation of only about eight million, Canada made a huge contribution to the war. Exports of food and ammunition helped fuel the Allied war effort. Over 600 000 men served in the Canadian

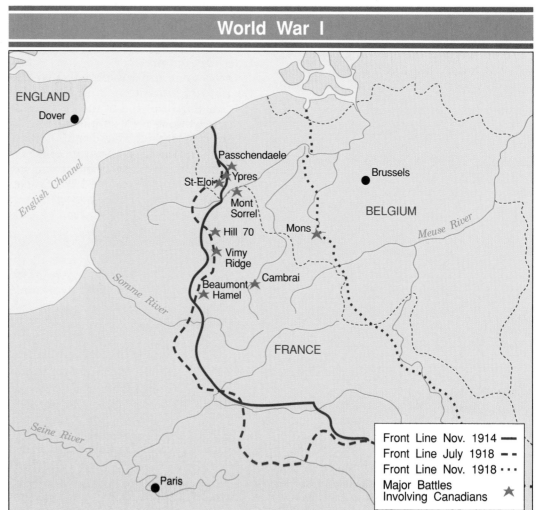

World War I

Front Line Nov. 1914 ——
Front Line July 1918 – – –
Front Line Nov. 1918 ·····
Major Battles Involving Canadians ★

Canadian Troops in France (courtesy City of Vancouver Archives).

army, and the Canadian Corps became one of the war's finest fighting units, winning a great victory at Vimy Ridge in 1917 and leading the final Allied charge through the German line in 1918. 60 661 soldiers died. 21 000 Canadians went into the British flying services; a large number of those trained in Canada; some of the great air aces of World War I were Canadian. Even the tiny navy made an impact, doing valuable convoy and anti-submarine work.

Prime Minister Robert Borden had a long, difficult war. The economy presented many problems, and the government ended the war with a national debt five times greater than what it had been in 1914. There were also, by war's end, shortages of food and fuel, and restrictions and strikes. "Temporary" income tax was introduced for the first time in 1917, and it has stayed to this day. The biggest controversy, however, was over conscripting young men to fight. The French Canadians and some English Canadians did not want conscription, but Borden forced it through in 1917.

In return for Canada's sacrifices, Borden demanded that the British allow him a part in high-level decisions about the war and the peace treaty that came out of it. He sat with the mighty at the Imperial War Cabinet of 1917 and 1918 in London and at the 1919 Peace Conference in Paris, and Canada's status as an independent nation certainly increased. But the Canadian representatives signed the peace treaty only after the British prime minister had already signed it for the entire British Empire, Canada included. That showed that Canada had a long way to go before it would be recognized as a truly independent country.

World War I left the country with thousands of dead, a big national debt, divisions between different cultures and

classes, and more government in their lives than Canadians had ever known. The war also gave many Canadians a better sense of themselves, a stronger feeling that we could do more by and for ourselves. This "nationalism," unfortunately, was not shared by all Canadians. The war, after all, had been a British war, and few French Canadians could accept being forced to share in that.

▷ RELATED ARTICLES: **Armed Forces; Foreign Relations; Versailles, Treaty of.**

■ World War II
World War II began September 3, 1939, when Britain declared war on Adolf Hitler's Germany after Germany invaded Poland, Britain's ally.

World War II was a "total war." Unprecedented numbers of civilians as well as soldiers died: well over 20 million soldiers and at least 13 million civilians.

Even before the war was over, the two allies, the United States and the Soviet

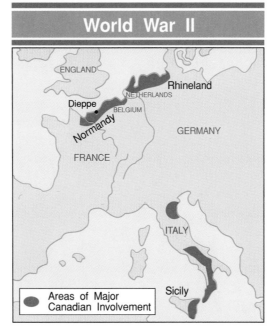

Colonel William Barker was credited with fighting 60 air battles (by permission of the British Library).

Time Line: World War II (1939-41)

● **1939**
Sept 3 Great Britain and France declare war on Germany
Sept 10 Canada declares war on Germany
Dec First Canadian Division lands in Britain. The British Commonwealth Air Training Plan is established
● **1940**
June Nazi, Fascist, and Communist groups are declared illegal in Canada, and their leaders are jailed
Nov The Trans-Atlantic Ferry Service begins to fly planes, men, and supplies from Canada to Britain
● **1941**
Aug Canadian Women's Army Corps established
Oct Two Canadian infantry divisions are sent to Hong Kong
Nov First Canadian Army is established in Britain with Lt Gen A.G.L. McNaughton in command
Dec Canada declares war on Japan.
Hong Kong surrenders to the Japanese; Canadian troops are taken prisoner. Japanese Canadians in B.C. are finger-printed and given identity cards

Normandy Canadian soldiers faced bitter fighting in the landing on the beaches of Normandy (courtesy NAC/PA-122765/photo by G. Milne).

Union, were at each other's throats. The rivalry of the two new "superpowers" would dominate the next four decades and more.

Canada Enters the War Canada waited one week after the British declared war on Germany in September 1939 before entering the war at the mother country's side. Prime Minister W.L. Mackenzie King, who was in power through all of the war, wanted to make it clear that this was a Canadian decision, freely made. The Canadian tie to Britain was still strong, however, and it was that tie that caused Canada to go to war.

Unlike Sir Robert Borden in World War I, King did not travel in search of a voice in high-level decision-making about the war. He preferred to stay at home, trying to keep English and French Canadians together and to avoid conscription for overseas service. King finally brought in conscription in 1944, but he had tried so hard to prevent it that most francophones did not turn against his Liberals after the war.

Army The Canadian army did not see action until 1942, when it took part in the poorly planned and disastrous raid on Dieppe, France. In 1943 the 1st Division joined the Allied attack on Sicily and took part in the advance up the Italian mainland. In spring 1944, Canadians under E.L.M. Burns played a leading role in breaking through the Hitler Line. Altogether 92 700 Canadians served in Italy; 5764 were killed.

First Canadian Army played a costly part in the Normandy Invasion on June 6, 1944. The first wave ashore encountered fierce opposition. The Canadians played a leading part in the breakout from the beaches. First Canadian Army cleared the German fortresses along the coast and fought a bitter battle to open the Scheldt

Anti-submarine Warfare *in the North Atlantic during World War II. Depth charges dropped from the Canadian destroyer explode underwater (courtesy NAC/PA-133246).*

River. On March 10, 1945, Canadians pushed the Germans back over the Rhine and liberated the east and north Netherlands. Some 237 000 Canadians served in this campaign; 11 336 were killed and many more wounded.

Air Force The Canadian air force trained thousands of Allied airmen under the British Commonwealth Air Training Plan. Large numbers of Canadians served in Britain's Royal Air Force. Almost 10 000 Canadians were killed in the bombing raids over Germany. Canadian airmen also served in North Africa, Italy, and South East Asia. Some 232 600 men and 17 000 women served in the Royal Canadian Air Force; 17 100 were killed.

Navy The tiny Royal Canadian Navy mushroomed during the war. By war's end it had 471 vessels. Canada's main

de Havilland Factory *during World War II (courtesy Boeing Canada).*

War Conference, March 1941. Canadian general A.G.L. McNaughton (left) and British leader Winston Churchill study a military map at Canadian headquarters (courtesy NAC/ PA-119399).

Liberation of the Netherlands by Canadians (courtesy NAC/PA-131566).

task was to protect the troop and supply ships crossing the Atlantic from German submarines. During the war, the navy sank 29 enemy subs and lost 24 vessels, with 2024 fatalities.

Home Front Canada made a huge industrial contribution to the war. A great variety of guns, ships, aircraft, and some 815 000 military vehicles were made. Britain could not hope to pay for all of it, so Canada financed most of it. During the war, Canada gave Britain some $3 billion in assistance.

Canada had no effective part in directing the war, though King played host to two high-level meetings at Quebec City.

The financial cost of the Canadian war effort was astronomical, amounting to perhaps over $20 billion. The tragic loss of Canadian lives was 42 042. Many more were injured or disabled or mentally or emotionally scarred by their experiences.

The war drew Canada closer to the United States, and made many Canadians worry that we were not so free after all. In addition, after the war, Canada found itself allied to the United States in its conflict with the Soviet Union. The "cold war" had begun, and Canada would soon find itself, for the first time in its history, on the firing line.

▷ RELATED ARTICLES: **Armed Forces; Canadian-American Relations; Dieppe; Foreign Relations; Normandy; World War I.**

▷SUGGESTED READING: Ken Bell, *The Way We Were* (1988); Geoffrey Bilson, *Hockey Bat Harris* (1985); J.L. Granatstein and Desmond Morton, *A Nation Forged in Fire: Canadians and the Second World War 1939-1945* (1989); Kit Pearson, *The Sky is Falling* (1989); Ruth Roach Pierson, *They're Still Women After All: The Second World War and Canadian Womanhood* (1986); Ben Wicks, *No Time to Wave Good-bye* (1988) and *The Day They Took the Children* (1989).

■ **Worms,** *see* **Annelida**

■ **Wrangel Island**

Wrangel Island lies in the Arctic Ocean north of Russia. No one lives on the island, but in 1914 it was a refuge for the crew of a Canadian ship, the *Karluk*, wrecked during a scientific expedition. Before they were rescued, members of the crew claimed the island for Canada. At the urging of Vilhjalmur Stefansson, the government tried to assert this claim, but dropped the matter after Russia objected.

■ **Wren**

Wrens are little birds of the Troglodytidae family. They have pudgy bodies and a tail that is usually tilted upwards when they sit. They have strong voices for their size, but not very melodious ones.

The most northern species, the Winter Wren (*Troglodytes troglodytes*), is also found in Europe, but the other 58 species live only in the Americas. Of our eight species, four are found in a few limited regions of the West and in areas of southern Ontario.

The other wrens live in very differing habitats: forests for the Winter Wren; shrubby, broad-leaved urban areas for the House Wren (*T. aedon*); marshes for the Marsh Wren (*Cistothorus palustris*); wet and grassy marshes for the Sedge Wren (*C. platensis*).

The House Wren happily occupies any birdhouse you offer it and brightens up the neighbourhood. The male will even build nests in several birdhouses, so that his beloved will have a choice — a favourite trick of the wren. The nest is usually domed and closed. Wrens lay five to eight eggs. The cry of the Winter Wren is one of the longest among songbirds, lasting a full five to six seconds. It is also one of the most piercing.

▷ SUGGESTED READING: Earl W. Godfrey, *The Birds of Canada* (1986).

■ **Wrestling**

Wrestling matches have been held for thousands of years. Today, there are three official styles: Greco-Roman, with holds

Marsh Wren (top) and House Wren (courtesy Macmillan Illustrated Animal Encyclopedia).

Spring, *sculpture in sumac wood, by Florence Wyle (courtesy AGO/ collection of Mr Jennings Young).*

above the waist only; freestyle, which allows wrestlers to use any part of their body; and Sambo, which allows moves from the martial arts.

In wrestling, the emphasis is on speed and strength. There are no points for defence but only for attack. A match consists of two 3-minute rounds. It may end before the 6-minute term in the event of a fall or other circumstances.

Canadians have excelled at freestyle wrestling. Olympic medal winners include D. Stockton (silver, 1928), Jim Trifunov (bronze, 1928), M. Letchford (bronze, 1928), D. McDonald (silver, 1932), Joe Schleimer (bronze, 1936), Bob Molle (silver, 1984), and Chris Rinke (bronze, 1984).

Professional Wrestling is more entertainment than sport, with an emphasis more on spectacle than on physical skill. It is often a drama of good versus evil, while the "referee" looks helplessly on. Nevertheless, the matches are highly popular and physically demanding. Canadian wrestler Yukon Eric lost an ear in a grudge match with "Killer Kowalski." Other popular Canadian professional wrestlers include world champions "Whipper Billy" Watson, Gene Kiniski, Edouard Charpentier, and Maurice "Mad Dog" Vachon.

■ Wright, Philemon
Pioneer of the Ottawa Valley timber industry (*born in 1760 at Woburn, Massachusetts, U.S.; died in 1839 at Hull, Lower Canada [Que.]*). Wright led a group of American settlers from Massachusetts in 1800 to establish a farming community on the banks of the Ottawa River, where the city of Hull now stands. At that time the Ottawa Valley was a wilderness. Wright and his people were among the first settlers. He soon found that farming produced little cash in such a remote place. To add to his earnings, in 1806 he rafted the first timber down the Ottawa River, thereby opening up one of the world's greatest timber-producing regions.

For a quarter of a century, Wright and his sons, Ruggles and Tiberius, ran the biggest logging outfit in the Ottawa Valley. He appears to have been an overly ambitious businessman, however, for he was often in financial difficulty. He was a progressive farmer and stock breeder, and a member of the Legislative Assembly of Lower Canada. A writer at the time called him "a man in constant motion, teaching and being taught — a true pioneer."

■ Wyle, Florence
Sculptor (*born in 1881 at Trenton, Illinois, U.S.; died in 1968 at Newmarket, Ont.*). Trained at the Art Institute of Chicago, Wyle settled in Toronto with sculptor Frances Loring in 1913. They were soon accepted in the art community and known affectionately as "The Girls." They co-operated on a series of bronze sculptures showing women as farm and munitions workers during World War I. In the 1920s, Wyle completed busts of her friends in the Group of Seven, F.H. Varley, Lawren Harris, and A.Y. Jackson. She was regarded by contemporaries as Canada's finest academic sculptor, particularly of small-scale studio works. She worked mainly with the human figure, and over the years her style changed from detailed realism to stylized simplicity. Since she could not afford to cast many of her sculptures in bronze, most of them remain in painted plaster.

■ Wynne-Jones, Tim
Author (*born in 1948 at Cheshire, England*). He grew up in Kitimat and Vancouver, B.C., and Ottawa, Ont. He studied at Waterloo and York universities. He then worked as a book designer, rock singer, teacher, book reviewer, and writer. His first book, *Odd's End* (1980), an adult novel, won the Seal First Novel award. He has written two other adult novels and six books for children.

Madeline & Ermadello (1977) is about a little girl and her imaginary playmate. *Zoom at Sea* (1983) and *Zoom Away* (1985) are based on his own cat. They tell of its fantastic adventures at sea and at the North Pole. In both stories, the cat begins his travels in the magical, mysterious house of his human friend, Maria. The two books were illustrated by Ken Nutt. *Mischief City* (1986) is a collection of poems about Winchell, his family, and his imaginary friend, Maxine. The hero of *I'll Make You Small* (1986) bravely enters the house of his mean old neighbour and makes a friend of the unhappy man. *Architect of the Moon* (1988) tells about David's journey into the sky where he builds up the Moon with his toy blocks.

In his children's books, Wynne-Jones deals with two main themes: the power of imagination and the value of friendship. Madeline, David, and Zoom have wonderful adventures by using their imaginations. In *I'll Make You Small*, Roland learns that a person must learn to understand someone else if real friendships are to grow.

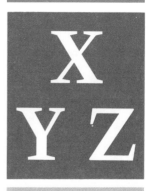

XY Company

The XY Company (XYC) was a fur-trade company based in Montreal. It competed with the North West Company (NWC) and the Hudson's Bay Company between 1798 and 1804. Its name refers to the mark used to identify its goods. It was created by some Nor'Westers who broke away from the larger company, but after a period of bitter rivalry the XYC merged with the NWC again. *See* **Fur Trade**.

Yachting

Yachting is the sport of racing sailing craft. Competitors must follow a course, marked by buoys. A wide variety of craft is used, from small dinghies to elegant oceangoing vessels with large crews.

Olympic yachting has six classes: Tornado (crew of two), Flying Dutchman (vessels of 174 kg, crew of two), 470 class (188 kg, crew of two), soling (crew of three), Finn (crew of one), and Tempest (crew of two).

Yachting Race, Halifax, in 1850. The Halifax Yacht Club, founded in 1837, is the oldest active yachting club in Canada (courtesy NGC).

In Canada, yachting began in Halifax, Kingston, and Toronto, and by 1892 had spread to Victoria. The Canada Cup races were established in 1895 as a challenge series between yachts from Canada and the U.S. on the Great Lakes. The Americans dominated the races until the Canadian yacht *Evergreen* won in 1978, and Canadians have continued to have success since then.

Canadian sailors won silver and bronze medals in the 1936 Olympics and bronze medals in soling in 1972. In the 1988 Olympics, Frank McLaughlin and John Miller won a bronze medal in the Flying Dutchman class. Canada also competes in the America's Cup for 12 m yachts.

Yarmouth

Yarmouth, N.S., overlooks an excellent harbour at the western tip of Nova Scotia. Called "Port Fourchu" by the French, who colonized it in the 1600s, the site was settled by New Englanders from the 1760s. The town grew as a shipbuilding centre, until by 1879 Yarmouth was home to the second-largest fleet of ships in Canada. Today the economy relies on fishing and a mix of light industries. Yarmouth is the business centre of southwestern Nova Scotia and is linked by a ferry service to Maine, U.S. The population in 1986 was 7617.

For further information, contact the Town Clerk, Court House, 403 Main Street, Yarmouth, N.S., B5A 1G3.

Yarrow

Yarrow is the common name for more than 200 species of herb-like plants of genus *Achillea* of the daisy family (Compositeae). The genus name *Achillea* was chosen to honour the Greek hero Achilles who is supposed to have used these plants to heal his warriors' wounds.

Three species are found in Canada. The most widespread is the common yarrow (*A. millefolium*), a perennial plant that may measure 30 to 100 cm high. Its velvety, finely divided, alternating leaves look like carrot leaves. Its white flowers form umbrella-shaped flowerheads at the end of the stalk. The whole plant gives off a lovely aroma. Common yarrow grows everywhere in Canada — in fields, dry spots, and by roadsides. The Québecois nickname is "turkey grass," since early people fed it to turkeys. Yarrow has been used through the ages to bring down fever, and for problems with the liver, stomach, and intestines.

Common Yarrow grows across Canada in grassy places and roadsides (artwork by Claire Tremblay).

Yeast

Yeast is a group of one-celled fungi with at least 450 known species. Those microscopic fungi multiply either through cell division, or by putting forth buds that quickly attain the size of the mother cell and in turn put forth buds of their own. The best-known yeast is *Sacchoromyces cerevisiae* (common bread, brewing, and wine yeast), used for leavening and brewing for thousands of years. When added to bread dough, this yeast turns the small quantity of sugar (glucose) produced by the hydrolysis of the starch into alcohol and carbon dioxide. The alcohol evaporates during cooking, while the bubbles of carbon dioxide form the holes in the bread. Louis Pasteur discovered the role of yeasts in fermentation.

Other species have been used in biotechnological processes: treatment of woodpulp wastes, production of food and fodder yeast, and so on. Yeasts may act to

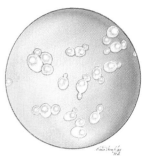

Yeasts multiply by budding and by cell division (artwork by Claire Tremblay).

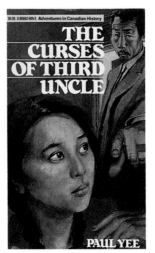

The Curses of Third Uncle, *cover illustration for the book written by Paul Yee (courtesy James Lorimer & Co.).*

Yew (ground hemlock) are conifers, though they do not have scaly cones. The fruit is attractive but poisonous (artwork by Claire Tremblay).

help food spoil. Although not as widely distributed as bacteria, yeasts occur in terrestrial and aquatic environments worldwide, in association with plants and animals. They are particularly abundant in the upper levels of orchard and vineyard soils and occur naturally on many fruits.

▷ SUGGESTED READING: Bernice Kohn, *Our Tiny Servants, Molds and Yeasts* (1962).

■ Yee, Paul

Writer (*born in 1956 at Spalding, Sask.*). Yee's parents were Chinese immigrants who died soon after he was born. He was sent to Vancouver, B.C., and grew up in and near Chinatown. His Aunt Lilian introduced him to Chinese oral traditions. In high school, Yee became interested in his Chinese-Canadian identity. At university he specialized in Canadian history. He has worked as an archivist for both the cities of Toronto and Vancouver, his chief task being to preserve multicultural heritage and history.

Yee's writing explores the way people struggle to achieve an identity. He tries in particular, "to give visible minorities images of themselves not commonly found in mainstream mass media." Yee's work for children includes *Teach Me to Fly, Skyfighter* (1983), four linked stories of contemporary life, and an historical adventure mystery novel, *The Curses of Third Uncle* (1986). His writings for adults include poetry and short stories, and the sumptuous *Salt Water City: An Illustrated History of Chinese in Vancouver* (1988).

■ Yellowhead Pass

The Yellowhead Pass, elevation 1131 m, is the route followed by the Canadian National Railway across the Continental Divide. It lies on the British Columbia-Alberta border in the Rocky Mountains, 24 km west of Jasper, Alta. It was a minor fur-trade route from the 1820s, and is named after an early trader. A major highway also crosses the pass. It was designated a national historic site in 1985.

■ Yellowknife

Yellowknife is the capital and largest city in the Northwest Territories. It lies on the flat northern shore of Great Slave Lake, 965 km north of Edmonton. It is the jumping-off point for travel down the Mackenzie River to the Arctic coast. It is only 440 km south of the Arctic Circle.

Yellowknife's name comes from the fact that the local native people used knives with yellowish copper blades. The site became a fur-trade post in 1789, as a result of Alexander Mackenzie's visit, but a settlement did not develop until 1934 when gold mining began in the rocks along the lakeshore. The two gold mines at either end of the city are still crucial to the local economy.

Yellowknife consists of two neighbourhoods. Old Town is the original mining town by the lake; New Town is a more modern district laid out in the late 1940s, a short distance inland. The population is a mixture of Dene, Inuit, Metis, and whites.

Yellowknife is linked to Edmonton by the Mackenzie Highway. Named capital of the territories in 1967, the city is a major government centre; about one-third of the residents work in government jobs. There are two weekly newspapers; one appears twice weekly, and one twice a month. Yellowknife has three radio stations and two television stations.

"Folk on the Rocks," a lively open-air concert that features Dene, Inuit, and other performers from Canada and the United States, is held in late July. Other events include those in June, when the northern days are at their longest, such as the "Midnight Sun Golf Tournament" and "River Mad Daze." The population in 1986 was 11 753.

For further information, contact the Administration Officer, Yellowknife, N.W.T., X1A 2N4.

▷ SUGGESTED READING: Elma Schemenauer, *Yellowknife* (1986).

■ Yew

Though yews (*Taxus*) are conifers, they have no scaly cones. Their fruits contain a single seed surrounded by red flesh. Though the fruits are very attractive, the seeds are poisonous.

Two yew species are native to Canada: the ground hemlock (*T. canadensis*), found from Manitoba eastward, and the western yew (*T. brevifolia*), in British Columbia. The ground hemlock, a shrub whose branches practically lie on the ground, forms in damp, shaded woodlands. The leaves are flat, soft needles and grow all over the branches.

Yew wood is strong and supple and it has long been used for archers' bows. Even Robin Hood was probably able to carry out his exploits thanks to a bow made from the common European yew (*T. baccata*). Yew wood is used for paddles, tool handles, and sculptures. Many species of birds, including grouse, eat yew fruit without any problem. They digest the flesh but excrete the seed, thus helping the species spread.

■ YMCA/YWCA

The YMCA (Young Men's Christian Association) and YWCA (Young Women's Christian Association) are independent but closely associated organizations. They have similar histories, share the same ideals, and often occupy the same building.

The YMCA's first North American branch was in Montreal, Canada East [Quebec], in 1851. The first YWCA branch in Canada was in Saint John, N.B., in 1870. The YWCA became a national association in 1895; the YMCA, in 1912.

The associations were created to give physical and spiritual help to young, single, men and women who were moving to the cities in search of work. At first, they had strong links to the Protestant churches. Then, as now, cities were often dangerous for young people who were alone and poor. The YM/YWCAs were safe places to make friends and enjoy activities. They also provided cheap beds and meals. Modern YM/YWCAs serve people of all ages, races, religions, and walks of life. Their programs include sports, training, youth camps, and adult education.

In 1988, more than 2 million Canadians made use of YM/YWCA services.

■ Yoho National Park

Yoho National Park (1313.1 km²) lies in the Rocky Mountains to the west of Banff National Park, just across the Alberta border in British Columbia. Created in 1886, it is named from a Cree word meaning "awe," referring to the soaring mountain peaks which dominate the park. Takakkaw Falls (254 m) is Canada's second-highest waterfall. Kicking Horse Pass is the route through the mountains used by both the Canadian Pacific Railway and the Trans-Canada Highway. The park contains the Burgess Shale, a rare deposit of fossils.

For further information, contact the Superintendent, Yoho National Park, P.O. Box 99, Field, B.C., V0A 1G0.

▷ RELATED ARTICLE: **Parks.**
▷ SUGGESTED READING: David M. Baird, *Yoho National Park* (1962).

■ York Boat

York boats were large, open boats used by the Hudson's Bay Company to carry supplies on major rivers and lakes of the interior fur country. They handled more cargo than traditional bark canoes, and were less easily damaged. The boats, pointed at

York Boats *were durable boats used to transport furs by the Hudson's Bay Company (courtesy Hudson's Bay Co. Archives/PAM).*

both ends, were propelled by oars or by sail, and had a crew of six to eight men. They were first used in 1749, but came into common use around 1800 and lasted in service until the 1920s.

▷ RELATED ARTICLE: **Fur Trade.**

■ York Factory

York Factory, at the mouth of the Hayes River and close by the mouth of the Nelson River, was the most important Hudson's Bay Company (HBC) trading post on Hudson Bay during most of the fur trade. Most of the company's trade with the western interior of Canada passed through York Factory. York boats, which carried the goods on the rivers and lakes of Manitoba, were named for York Factory. Founded in 1684, it is the oldest permanent European outpost in the province of Manitoba.

York Factory was a frequent target for French attacks on the HBC fur trade. New France's great soldier, Pierre Le Moyne d'Iberville, captured it in 1694 and in 1697, and France held it until 1713. In

Kicking Horse River *in Yoho National Park, B.C. (photo by Pat Morrow/ First Light).*

1782 it was captured and burned by the Comte de Laperouse, but it was later rebuilt.

The HBC post at York Factory closed in 1957, and the federal government's National Parks branch took over the site in 1968. Some of the York Factory buildings remain, but erosion by the river is destroying the site.

York University

York University is located on two campuses in Toronto, Ont. It offers full- and part-time degree programs at undergraduate and graduate levels. Among its special facilities are the Centre for Research in Experimental Space Science and the LaMarsh Research Program on Violence and Conflict Resolution. It operates several programs with the University of Toronto, including the Joint Centre on Asia Pacific Studies and the Joint Program on Transportation. Osgoode Law School, founded in 1862 and the major legal institution in Canada, is affiliated with York University.

York began in 1959. Instruction is mainly in English, but Glendon College offers bilingual programs. There are nearly 20 300 full-time undergraduate and graduate students. For further information, write the Registrar's Office, York University, Downsview, Ont., M3J 1P3.

Yorkton

Yorkton, Sask., lies in the rich prairie farm belt of southeast Saskatchewan. It began in 1882 when a group of farmers from York County in Ontario settled in the district. When the railway passed close by in 1889, the village moved to its present location. Many European immigrants later arrived, especially Ukrainians and Doukhobors. Today, Yorkton retains its importance as a business centre for the surrounding district. Points of interest include a branch of the Western Development Museum, the Godfrey Dean Cultural Centre, and the dome paintings of St Mary's Ukrainian Catholic Church. Yorkton's population in 1986 was 15 574.

For further information, contact the City Clerk, City Hall, P.O. Box 400, Yorkton, Sask., S3N 2W3.

Young, George

Swimmer (*born in 1910 at Toronto, Ont.; died in 1972 at Niagara Falls, Ont.*). One of the finest long-distance swimmers of his day, Young won numerous racing titles in Canada while he was still a teenager. The exploit for which he is most famous, the swimming of the channel be-

Church in Yorkton, Sask. (photo by Richard Vroom).

tween Catalina Island and mainland California, took place when he was 17. He was one of 100 entrants, and the only one to finish the race. He completed the 48 km swim in 15 hours, 45 minutes, winning a $25 000 prize.

Young, Sir John, Baron Lisgar

Governor general (*born in 1807 at Bombay, India; died in 1876 at Bailieborough, Ireland*). Young was the second governor general of Canada, serving from 1869 to 1872. Sir John A. Macdonald considered him the ablest of all the governors general under whom he had served.

Several important events took place during his term in office. The Treaty of Washington was signed with the United States in 1871. The Hudson's Bay Company's territory of Rupert's Land was transferred to Canada in 1870; and two new provinces, Manitoba (1870) and British Columbia (1871), entered Confederation. The most important event was the Red River Rebellion, led by Louis Riel, in 1869-70. In an effort to help resolve the crisis peacefully, Young used the governor general's power to proclaim an amnesty for the Red River rebels on December 6, 1869. But although the rebels would not be prosecuted for any acts before that date, the amnesty did not cover the execution of Thomas Scott in March 1870, the most controversial event of the rebellion.

Young, Neil

Singer, songwriter, guitarist (*born in 1945 at Toronto, Ont.*). During the 1960s, Young worked in Winnipeg coffeehouses and Toronto folkclubs. While in Winnipeg, he met people such as Steven Stills, Richie Furay, and Joni Mitchell. While in Toronto, he formed a band called the Mynah Birds with bassist Bruce Palmer . In 1966 Neil drove his Cadillac hearse to Los Angeles with Palmer and formed one of rock's greatest bands, Buffalo Springfield, with Stills, Furay, and Dewey Martin. Palmer was ultimately replaced by Jim Messina. During the Buffalo Springfield era, Young wrote such classics as "Broken Arrow" and "Mr. Soul." The group split up in 1968.

Young went solo, and in 1969 released the album *Neil Young*. This was followed the same year by *Everybody Knows This Is Nowhere*, recorded with his band Crazy Horse. In the early 1970s, Young joined Crosby, Stills, and Nash. The group made the album *Déjà Vu*, as well as hit singles "Woodstock," "Teach Your

Children," and "Our House." The group then disbanded. Young returned to a solo career and recorded such hit albums as *After The Goldrush* (1970), *Harvest* (1972), and *Rust Never Sleeps* (1979). In 1988 Neil Young and the Bluenotes recorded *This Note's For You*. Young's father is the writer Scott Young.

▷ SUGGESTED READING: Scott Young, *Neil and Me* (1984).

■ Young, Scott

Writer and columnist (*born in 1918 at Glenboro, Man.*). Young served in the navy during World War II and has had a distinguished career in journalism in Winnipeg and Toronto. He has been a newspaper and television columnist, a sports writer, and an editor. He holds several awards, including the 1958 National Newspaper Award for sports writing, and the 1963 Wilderness Medal for his television documentary, "The Opening of the West."

Young's writings encompass sports, history, biography, and even mystery adventure. His adult books include *Hockey is a Battle: Punch Imlach's Own Story* (1969), *War on Ice* (1976), *Hello Canada: The Life and Times of Foster Hewitt* (1985), and *Gordon Sinclair: A Life ... and Then Some* (1987). Of special interest is his *Neil and Me* (1984), the moving story of his son, Neil Young, the rock star and songwriter.

Young's work for children includes *The Clue of the Dead Duck* (1962), a mystery; *Hockey Heroes Series* (1974); and a trilogy of hockey novels that captures the thrill of action on the ice and celebrates the value of sports: *Scrubs on Skates* (1952, revised 1985), *Boy on Defence* (1953, revised 1985), and *A Boy at the Leafs' Camp* (1963, revised 1985).

■ Young Offenders

Young offenders once faced the same treatment and penalties as adults. This harsh practice was later changed so that young children, particularly those under seven years of age, were considered incapable of crime.

From 1908 to 1984, youths were governed by the Juvenile Delinquents Acts. Its approach, as stated in the Act, was to treat every juvenile delinquent "not as a criminal, but as a misguided and misdirected child — needing aid, encouragement, help and assistance."

The Young Offenders Act was passed by Parliament in April 1982, and came into effect in 1984. It has two goals: to protect the public from the unlawful behaviour of young people, and to encourage those who have committed an offence not to commit another. This law applies to youths who are 12 years old or older and under 18. These age limits are controversial. Some consider them too high, and others consider them too low.

Children under 12 who commit criminal acts cannot be charged, although police still have a role to play in dealing with them, along with agencies such as the Children's Aid Society.

The Young Offenders Act sets out the process to be followed and the sentences (called *dispositions*) that a judge can give to a young offender who has committed a criminal offence.

The Act allows for the following dispositions:
● an absolute discharge;
● a fine of up to $1000;
● probation for up to two years;
● or one of the following orders: to pay money to any person whose property has been damaged (*compensation*); to return property to the rightful owner (*restitution*); to perform personal services for the victim; to perform work in the community; or to seek treatment in a hospital or other similar facility.

Most cases involving young offenders are heard in a separate youth court. However, youths 14 years or older charged with serious offences, such as murder, may be transferred to adult court. Trial and sentencing take place there and adult penalties may be applied.

The challenge of how best to respond to a young person's needs is still under study, and further changes to the law may occur. The present law offers many opportunities for rehabilitation. For many young offenders, sentences make them realize that illegal behaviour has serious consequences. For a smaller number, crimes are part of a pattern of more serious difficulties, such as drug abuse or family violence.

The Young Offenders Act has several safeguards. Every youth has the right to consult a lawyer; the government will provide a lawyer at the youth's trial if the youth is unable to obtain one. The court may hold hearings to review dispositions and may modify the disposition to ensure that it remains appropriate. The media may not publish information that will identify the young offender, except in limited circumstances. Records of young offenders are not able to be looked at after a crime-free period ranging from two to five years. Every province may set up "alternative measures" programs. This usually means that first-time offenders who commit less serious offences can be handled without the formal court process.

■ Ypres, Battle of

Ypres was the first major battle to involve Canadian soldiers in World War I. On April 22, 1915, the Germans launched a surprise attack. They sent clouds of poisonous chlorine gas rolling toward Allied trenches near Ypres, Belgium. Panicking, unable to breathe, soldiers fled from the front lines. In a week of fierce fighting they endured more gas attacks, a heavy artillery barrage, and wave after wave of enemy soldiers attacking their positions. The Canadian soldiers held the line. Their tenacity prevented a German breakthrough.

▷ RELATED ARTICLE: **World War I.**

■ Yukon Field Force

The Yukon Field Force, formed 1898, was sent to the Yukon at the height of the Klondike gold rush to help the Mounted Police maintain order and to stress that the Yukon was Canadian territory. Consisting of just over 200 men, the field force was composed of soldiers from the Canadian militia. Half left the Yukon in 1899, and the remainder in 1900. *See* **Gold Rushes.**

■ Yukon River

The Yukon River, 3185 km long, is the second-longest river in Canada. It begins at the northern British Columbia border, flows north across the Yukon Territory into Alaska, then continues in a west-

Yukon River carves a beautiful valley across the northern landscape (photo by Brian Milne/ First Light).

ward arc to empty into the Bering Sea.

The winding river valley may have been the route followed by the first people to come into America thousands of years ago. Native people still occupy the valley, relying on trapping and hunting for their livelihood. The first outsiders to arrive were fur traders, followed by gold prospectors during the great Klondike gold rush of the late 1890s.

For three months of the year the river is free from ice all the way to Whitehorse. Steamboats plied the river between 1866 and 1955.

The majestic river valley is too far north for farming, and its forests are too stunted for logging, so it remains sparsely populated. However, more and more tourists are attracted by the scenic beauty of the wilderness.

■ Yukon Territory

The Yukon is one of Canada's two northern territories. Situated between the U.S. state of Alaska and the Northwest Territories, it lies farther west than any other part of Canada. Most of the territory lies west of the longitude of Vancouver, B.C. Whitehorse is the capital of the Yukon Territory.

The Yukon takes its name from the Kutchin Indian name for the "great river" that flows through much of the territory. Because of the Klondike gold rush of 1897-99, people throughout the world identify the Yukon with gold miners, snow, hardship, Mounted Police, dance-hall women, and colourful characters from the poems of Robert Service. In fact, almost everything most outsiders know about the Yukon is connected with the gold rush. But of course there is more to the Yukon than that one brief episode in its history. Although the Yukon is a fairly new part of Canada in some respects, it can also be viewed as the oldest part of the country. It was the first part of Canada to be inhabited by people.

LAND AND WATER

Geology The Yukon is mainly in the Western Cordillera, the great mountain chain that forms the western margin of North America. In Yukon, the cordillera consists of a series of hills and mountain ranges running roughly northwest to southeast, separated by valleys and plateaus. The most spectacular of these ranges is the St Elias range in the extreme southwest part of the territory. It contains Mount Logan (5951 m), the highest mountain in Canada. In the north lies the

Arctic Coastal Plain, a much more level, treeless area that slopes gently down to the Arctic Ocean. Continuous permafrost underlies much of the Yukon, causing problems with road and building construction.

Three main geologic events shaped much of the landscape of the Yukon. The first occurred 175 million years ago when an oceanic plate rode over the North American plate, to form most of the present landmass. The boundary of the two plates runs northwest from Teslin Lake across the Yukon and into Alaska.

Most of the present mountain ranges, such as the Selwyn, Cassiar, and Mackenzie Mountains, began to form during this period.

About 100 million years ago, a second plate, the Pacific plate, collided with the North American plate. This time the denser Pacific plate plunged beneath the lighter North American plate, creating the St Elias Mountains. The process has continued to the present day, and accounts for the earthquakes that are sometimes felt in southwest Yukon.

During the last ice age, the southern and eastern portions of the territory were heavily glaciated, and glaciers still cover many of the highest peaks, mainly in the St Elias Mountains. Much of northern and west-central Yukon escaped glaciation. This is the largest unglaciated area in Canada. The present landforms largely reflect glaciation or the lack of it. In glaciated areas, mountains tend to be jagged and rough, and valleys are broad and U-shaped with thick gravel deposits and occasional lakes covering their floors. In unglaciated areas, mountains are rolling and smooth, with little bedrock exposed, and valleys are narrow. Deposits of black organic muck, which have been exposed by miners in the Klondike area near Dawson, contain bones of large mammals

Glaciers feed many of the streams and rivers of the Yukon (photo by Robert Semeniuk/First Light).

Yukon Territory

Facts about the Yukon Territory

Created as a Territory:	June 13, 1898
Motto:	none
Floral Emblem:	Fireweed
Origin of Name:	Kutchin Indian name meaning "great river"
Capital City:	Whitehorse
Government:	*Territorial:* Commissioner, Executive Council, Legislative Assembly. The number of members of the Legislative Assembly (MLAs) is 16 *Federal:* Represented in the Senate of Canada by one senator; in the House of Commons by one member of Parliament (MP)
Population:	23 504 (1986), 0.1% of total population of Canada. Yukon's population is 64.7% urban, 34.5% rural, and 0.8% Indian Reserve
Area:	483 450 km² (of which 4480 km² is lakes and rivers); 4.8% of Canada
Main Products:	*Mining:* zinc, lead, gold *Trapping:* marten, lynx, muskrat, wolverine *Forestry:* lumber, logs
Time Zone:	Pacific Standard Time
Parks:	*National:* Kluane, Northern Yukon *Territorial:* Herschel Island and 44 territorial campgrounds *Land and Water Reserved for Conservation:* With no logging, mining, or hunting allowed: 6.7%

Highest Points:		
	Mount Logan	5951 m
	Mount St Elias	5489 m
	Mount Lucania	5226 m
	King Peak	5173 m
	Mount Steele	5073 m
Lowest Point:	Sea level at Arctic Ocean	
Largest Lakes:	Teslin Lake*	381.0 km²
	Tagish Lake*	354.6 km²
	Kluane Lake	306.0 km²
	Lake Laberge	213.9 km²
	Kusawa Lake	140.0 km²
	(* not entirely in the Yukon)	

Languages: (1986)				
	English	88.2%	Kaska (Nahani)	0.5%
	French	2.4%	Dutch	0.5%
	German	1.7%	Tutchone	0.4%
	Ukrainian	0.5%	Other	5.8%

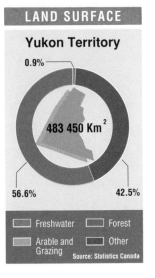

LAND SURFACE

Yukon Territory

0.9%

483 450 Km²

56.6%   42.5%

☐ Freshwater   ☐ Forest
☐ Arable and   ☐ Other
   Grazing
Source: Statistics Canada

Yukon Territory

Scale

0   100   200
kilometres

Capital city   ✪

National park   ☐

Road   —

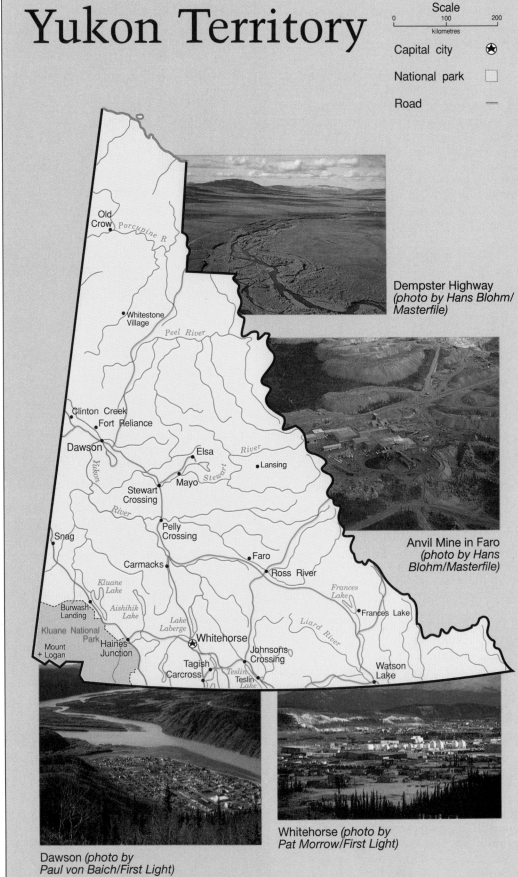

Old Crow

Porcupine R.

Whitestone Village

Peel River

Clinton Creek
Fort Reliance

Dawson

Elsa   *River*
              Lansing
Mayo   *Stewart*

Stewart
Crossing

Yukon

Pelly
Crossing

River

Snag   Faro

Carmacks   Ross River

Kluane Lake   *Frances Lake*

Burwash   *Aishihik Lake*   Frances Lake
Landing   *Liard River*

Kluane National Park   *Lake Laberge*

Mount + Logan   Haines   Whitehorse   Johnsons
                 Junction   Crossing

Tagish   Watson
Carcross   *Teslin*   Lake
           Teslin
           Lake

Dempster Highway
(photo by Hans Blohm/ Masterfile)

Anvil Mine in Faro
(photo by Hans Blohm/Masterfile)

Whitehorse *(photo by Pat Morrow/First Light)*

Dawson *(photo by Paul von Baich/First Light)*

such as the woolly mammoth, which became extinct at the end of the last ice age.

Water Over two-thirds of the territory is drained by the Yukon River system, which also drains part of British Columbia and much of Alaska. This great river rises in northern British Columbia and flows 3185 km through the Yukon and Alaska to its mouth on the Bering Sea. Before the hydroelectric dam was built north of Whitehorse, the Yukon River could be navigated from its mouth almost to its source.

The northeastern part of the Yukon is drained by the Peel River system; the southeastern is drained by the Liard. Both these rivers flow into the Mackenzie River and the Arctic Ocean. The Yukon has a number of glacial lakes, none of them very large.

Yukon River *system drains the water from over two-thirds of the Yukon (photo courtesy First Light).*

CLIMATE AND WEATHER

Although parts of the Yukon are less than 100 km from the Pacific Ocean, mountains block the mild Pacific air from the territory for much of the time. The Yukon therefore has a continental sub-arctic climate, with long, cold, dry winters and short, dry, warm summers. Sometimes in winter, Pacific air does penetrate into the southwest corner of the territory, bringing mild spells to the Whitehorse region. The northern Yukon, however, gets little relief from severe cold in winter. The average maximum January temperature at Dawson is -27°C; the minimum is -34°C. For Whitehorse, the January figures are -16°C (maximum) and -25°C (minimum). This is not much different from Winnipeg, 1300 km farther south, where the average January temperature is -14°C (maximum) and -24°C (minimum).

Because of its northern location, the Yukon has very short days in winter, balanced by very long days in midsummer. Though the Arctic Circle lies some distance north of Dawson, the "midnight sun" can be seen in late June from the Dome (the large hill behind the city). The Yukon is quite dry. Average annual precipitation at Dawson is 306 mm; at Whitehorse, 261 mm. The growing season ranges from 45 to 75 days.

NATURAL REGIONS

The natural regions of the Yukon correspond very closely to its geological areas. The mountains are part of the Boreal and Tundra Cordillera regions. The steeply sided slopes of the mountains in the Tundra Cordillera region support a typical tundra vegetation: lichens, mosses, low shrubs, sedges, and herbs. Although all of the Yukon except the Southern Arctic Region lies south of the treeline, most of the territory is at too high an elevation and the permafrost is too widespread to support much tree growth.

The forested areas of the Boreal Cordillera region lie mostly south of Dawson, particularly in the river valleys. Only about 16% of the territory has a thick cover of boreal forest. The main tree

Sphagnum Moss *provides ground cover over much of the Yukon (photo by Pat Morrow/ First Light).*

World's Largest Icefields *outside the polar regions, in Kluane National Park (courtesy Colour Library Books Ltd).*

Minus 40°C *in the Yukon (photo by Pat Morrow/ First Light).*

Record Temperatures

The highest temperature recorded in the Yukon was 36.1°C, at Mayo in 1969.

The lowest temperature recorded was -63°C, at Snag (near Kluane Lake) in 1947. This is the coldest temperature that has ever been recorded in Canada.

Natural Regions of Yukon Territory

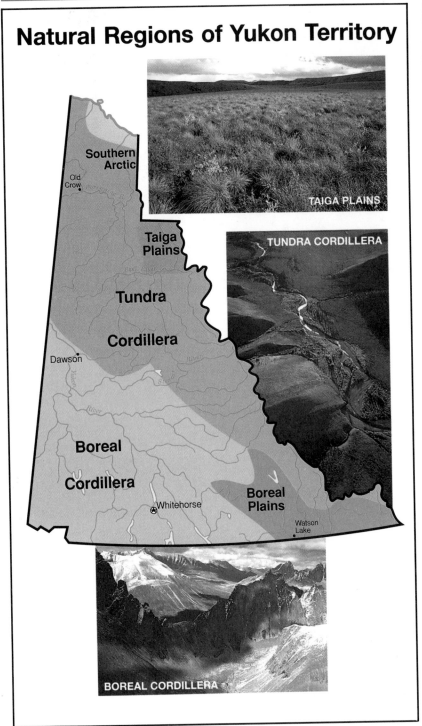

Southern Arctic

Old Crow

Taiga Plains

Tundra

Cordillera

Dawson

Boreal

Cordillera

Whitehorse

Boreal Plains

Watson Lake

TAIGA PLAINS

TUNDRA CORDILLERA

BOREAL CORDILLERA

Trees have a difficult time growing in much of the Yukon because of the high elevation and permafrost (photo by Pat Morrow/First Light).

Photos by Brian Milne/ First Light (Taiga Plains), Brian Milne/First Light (Tundra Cordillera), Brian Milne/First Light (Boreal Cordillera).

species are spruce, birch, poplar, and lodgepole pine. In areas where the ground thaws deeply in summer, spruce trees can grow as high as 35 m.

In the north, the Southern Arctic Region has a ground cover of lichens, grasses, mosses, and sedges, together with low bushes such as dwarf willow and birch and Labrador tea.

In parts of the territory that were not glaciated there are plants that occur nowhere else in the Canadian North. There are even plants that might be con-

sidered exotic; the Yukon contains at least six species of wild orchids. In the southern part of the territory a certain amount of agriculture is possible, particularly growing hay for horses.

WILDLIFE

Wildlife is abundant in the Yukon. Moose are found throughout the territory and are a common summer sight along lakeshores and in swamps. Mule deer occupy the southern half of the territory. There are large herds of both barren-ground and woodland caribou. Grey wolves are found throughout forest, in both alpine and tundra areas. Black bears are common in the lowlands and grizzly bears are distributed throughout.

Muskoxen occasionally wander into the northwestern Yukon from Alaska.

There are also wapiti (elk), mountain sheep, and mountain goats. The lynx inhabit dense forest areas, and wolverines are found in both forest and tundra areas. Fourteen different mammal species are trapped for fur.

There are 19 species of birds of prey. The endangered Peregrine Falcon is now increasing in number, and the Bald and Golden Eagles are fairly common. Grouse and ptarmigan are common. Southern and central Yukon are major migration

Ogilvie Mountains *Much of the vegetation of the Yukon is determined by the mountainous terrain (photo by Brian Milne/First Light).*

Male Grey Wolf *(photo by Peter McLeod/First Light).*

corridors for waterfowl. Sandhill Cranes, swans, ducks, and geese are found in large numbers. Old Crow Flats and the wetlands of the north slope are important breeding grounds.

Lake trout, pike, grayling, inconnu, and whitefish are found in lakes and streams. Salmon swim up from the ocean to spawn in the upper Yukon River and in the Tatshenshini River.

The Yukon is too cold for reptiles, and amphibians are limited to the wood frog and the western toad (in the extreme south).

Migrating Caribou *(photo by Pat Morrow/First Light).*

NATURAL RESOURCES

Mining The Yukon's chief natural resource has long been its mineral wealth. The promise of gold lured tens of thousands of people to the Yukon at the end of the 19th century. For many years, gold was the primary mineral produced, but today, there are other minerals, such as zinc and lead, of equal importance. Substantial amounts of silver and small amounts of copper, cadmium, and antimony have also been produced.

There are two types of gold mined in the Yukon, placer and hard rock. Placer gold is found as flakes or nuggets in sand and gravel along creeks and rivers. It is

mined by a variety of means from shovels to large earth-moving equipment. The sand and gravel are dug up and put into a sluice box that separates the gold. The other type of gold is mined by conventional mining techniques.

Large amounts of placer gold were found in August 1896 in creeks near where Dawson later developed. This started what became known as the Klondike gold rush. Today, gold is still mined in the Klondike area, mainly by individual prospectors. In 1989, there were two active hard rock mines and over 200 placer mines in the Yukon. The most important centre of mineral production in the Yukon is now the lead-zinc mine of Curragh Resources Inc. at Faro. There is also a gold mine at Ketza River owned by Canamax Resources Inc.

The fact that mineral production is so important to the Yukon economy poses a problem to the territory. It makes the whole economy very vulnerable to world metal prices and other economic forces. This was shown when the Faro mine closed in 1982. The population of Faro dropped from 1652 in 1981 to only 400 in 1986, and the White Pass and Yukon Railway, whose main business was carrying the mine's ore, shut down operations. In 1985 the mine was bought by Curragh Resources Inc. and was reopened the following year. The population of the town has since returned and the Yukon's economy revived. The boom-and-bust cycles of the territory's economy, however, are harmful to its long-term development.

Forestry The forest resources of the territory are very important locally for logs (for housing, poles, and posts), lumber, and fuel. Much of the forest production goes to lumber mills in the southeastern Yukon near Watson Lake. The Yukon is the last area in Canada where the forest resources are managed by the federal government.

Tourism is one of the Yukon's chief sources of revenue. The main drawing card for the over 200 000 tourists who visit each year is the rugged, unspoiled wilderness. The number of tourists that come each year is over eight times the resident population of the territory. In 1989 tourists spent over $50 million in the Yukon.

Fishing trips and guided hunting are popular with some visitors. For many people, Dawson and its reminders of the gold rush are the main attraction. Many of the historic buildings are being pre-

Bull Moose *(photo by Thomas Kitchin/First Light).*

Lead-zinc Mine *at Faro reopened in 1986, giving a boost to the Yukon economy (photo by Pat Morrow/First Light).*

Dawson *Many of the historic buildings have been restored to their condition at the time of the gold rush (photo by Bill Brooks/Masterfile).*

Hikers *are drawn to the Yukon's remote wilderness. This scene is in Kluane National Park (photo by J.A. Kraulis/Masterfile).*

Gold Mining *still continues on a small scale in the Yukon (photo by Brian Milne/ First Light).*

Mount St Elias, *in Kluane National Park, which has been declared a World Heritage Site (photo by Pat Morrow/First Light).*

served and restored by the federal and territorial governments. Some private restoration has also been carried out. Gold-bearing creeks in the area are still being worked, and one of the old dredges has been preserved as a national historic site. The Bear Creek mining camp is another national historic site in the area.

Other attractions include hiking, camping, and the Interpretive Centre at Kluane National Park. The Yukon's native people participate in the tourist industry through guiding, and through the sale of crafts, parkas, and other goods. There are also native-owned tour companies, wilderness outfitters, and other businesses.

Conservation The Yukon has two national parks (Kluane and Northern Yukon) and one territorial park (Herschel Island). Kluane National Park, in the southwestern corner of the territory, has been declared a United Nations World Heritage Site. It is dominated by the St Elias range and is famous for its spectacular scenery, massive glaciers, and wildlife. It is the domain of Dall's sheep and mountain goats, as well as grizzly bears and other animals.

Northern Yukon National Park is an important migration route for the Porcupine herd of barren-ground caribou and a major waterfowl area. It is also home to black, grizzly, and polar bears. Herschel Island includes archaeological sites of early native people, and a whaling settlement. There are two wildlife sanctuaries in the territory: Kluane, an extension of Kluane National Park, and MacArthur, south of Mayo.

ECONOMY

There is very little manufacturing or agriculture in the Yukon. The economy is mainly based on mining and tourism, supported by trapping and some forestry. The largest employer is government, which also plays an important stabilizing role in the economy. One-third of the em-

ployed people work for one of the three levels of government. Other important industries for employment are transportation, trade, and accommodation and other services.

Trapping The fur trade is the oldest industry in the Yukon. For almost 150 years, trapping has played a small but important role in the territory's development. There is a wide range of furbearing animals found in the Yukon. The large mammals include polar bear, grizzly, moose, and caribou. Smaller mammals include beaver, fox, muskrat, mountain goat, and the rare Dall's sheep. The cyclical nature of animal populations, in addition to other factors, means that some years are better than others for trappers. For example, in 1984 the value of fur production was only $737 000. The next year, it was $1.3 million. The value of fur production in the Yukon for 1988 was $1.4 million. Lynx and wolverine pelts are most valuable, but marten and wolf pelts also bring in a good price.

Subsistence Economy It is difficult to assess the value that the native people's hunting and fishing have on the local economy. A large part of the diet of the Yukon's people, the native people in particular, is filled by "country food" (that is, fish and game). This is worth many thousands of dollars to the territory's economy.

POPULATION

Before the coming of Europeans, there were three distinct groups of native people in the Yukon. In the far north of the territory, along the Arctic coast, lived a population of Inuit, perhaps as many as 2500. Because of diseases imported from the south, particularly by whaling crews around 1900, almost all these people were dead by 1930. Today, there are no Inuit living permanently in the Yukon.

Whitehorse *About two-thirds of the Yukon population lives in Whitehorse (photo by Pat Morrow/First Light).*

The major native groups of the Yukon are members of the Athapaskan language family, related to the Dene people of the Mackenzie Valley. In the north of the territory, in the region centered around Old Crow, are the Kutchin people. South of them are the Han (to the west) and Northern Tutchone (to the east). In the southern part are the Southern Tutchone (in the west), the Tagish and Inland Tlingit (in the centre), and the Kaska (in the southeast). The Inland Tlingit are not Athapaskan, but are related to the Coast Tlingit.

Today, native people make up only 20% of the Yukon's population. Most people are Canadians of European origin. A large number are single men who have come to take well-paying jobs and may leave after a few years. Most of the non-natives live in communities, especially Whitehorse. With a population of over 15 000, it houses about two-thirds of the entire population of the Yukon.

TRANSPORTATION AND COMMUNICATION

Transportation The Yukon's one railway, the White Pass and Yukon Railway, was completed in 1900. It runs from Skagway in Alaska to Whitehorse. It closed in

Dempster Highway *(photo by Brian Milne/First Light).*

1982. (The Skagway-Fraser section reopened for tourist traffic in the summer of 1988, but its freight operations remain closed.) Before World War II, the main transportation route in the territory was the Yukon River. Regular steamboat service operated between Dawson and the railhead at Whitehorse during the navigation season, from May to late October, depending on the weather. During the winter, a sleigh-coach service operated between the two centres until 1951. In 1942, during World War II, the Alaska Highway was built between British Columbia and Alaska. It ran through the Yukon and thus gave Yukoners easy access to the south. In 1979 the Dempster Highway was completed from near Dawson northeast to Inuvik, N.W.T. In 1981 a highway was officially opened to link Whitehorse and Skagway, Alaska, giving the Yukon direct road access to the Pacific.

Yukon River Ferry *(photo by Brian Milne/First Light).*

Today, nearly every community in the Yukon (except Old Crow) is joined to the national road network by all-weather roads. There are 4480 km of highways. Each community also has an airport or landing strip. Air B.C., Canadian Airlines International, and several regional carriers operate regularly scheduled flights out of Whitehorse. Charter aircraft are important for reaching small communities.

Communications The Yukon has one daily newspaper, the *Whitehorse Star*, and one twice-weekly paper, *Yukon News*. There are four radio stations and no TV stations. CBC-TV is available in all communities through satellite and relay stations. Cable systems and satellite broadcast systems also provide additional channels to 12 communities.

EDUCATION

Education is the responsibility of the Government of the Yukon. In 1989-90 there were 25 elementary and secondary

Charter Aircraft *serve many northern communities (photo by Robert Semeniuk/First Light).*

Helicopter *used to reach northern mining camps (photo by Brian Milne/First Light).*

Population of Major Communities (1986)	
Whitehorse*	15 199
Dawson	896
Watson Lake	826
Faro	400
* city	

Population Growth	
Year	Population
1901	27 219
1911	8512
1921	4157
1931	4230
1941	4914
1951	9096
1961	14 628
1971	18 388
1981	23 075
1986	23 504

Beaver Creek

Beaver Creek, near the Yukon's border with the American state of Alaska, is Canada's most westerly community.

White Pass and Yukon Railway connects Whitehorse to the Pacific Coast. Today, it only carries tourists (photo by Robert Semeniuk/First Light).

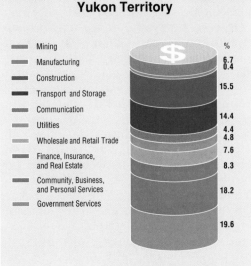

GROSS DOMESTIC PRODUCT BY INDUSTRY - 1984

Yukon Territory

Industry	%
Mining	6.7
Manufacturing	0.4
Construction	15.5
Transport and Storage	14.4
Communication	4.4
Utilities	4.8
Wholesale and Retail Trade	7.6
Finance, Insurance, and Real Estate	8.3
Community, Business, and Personal Services	18.2
Government Services	19.6

Source: Input-Output Division, Statistics Canada

Yukon Legislature Chamber (courtesy Canadian Circumpolar Institute, University of Alberta).

S.S. Klondike is a national historic site. The S.S. Klondike was one of the last sternwheelers used. Now restored to its 1940s condition, it sits on the bank of the Yukon River at Whitehorse (courtesy Environment Canada, Canadian Parks Service/F. Cattroll).

schools in the territory, with over 4000 students registered. Whitehorse is the home of Yukon College, which has learning centres in 11 communities. It offers a variety of technical programs as well as university-level courses.

CULTURE

The MacBride Museum in Whitehorse has modern interpretive exhibits on Yukon history, prehistory, and natural history. The national historic site in Dawson has a collection of more than 80 structures relating to Klondike history. Other museums include Keno (mining), Burwash (native history and wildlife), and Teslin (Tlingit culture) and are also open during the summer. The Yukon Arts Council supports artists and arranges exhibitions and concerts in schools and small communities. The territory is home to a number of artists, including Ted Harrison, whose paintings have been exhibited across Canada.

Historic Sites The S.S. Klondike National Historic Site in Whitehorse commemorates the importance of river transport in the Yukon. Sternwheelers like the

S.S. *Klondike* travelled the Yukon River from the late 1860s to the mid-1950s.

The Klondike National Historic Sites at Dawson commemorates the Gold Rush. The Palace Grand Theatre is a reconstruction of the luxurious 1899 original, where gold-rush entertainment is featured during the summer. The old Post Office, Harrington's Store Exhibit, and the goldfield's Gold Dredge #4 offer insights into the past.

Robert Service's cabin is also in Dawson. It was the home of the poet who wrote such well-known gold-rush poems as "The Shooting of Dan McGrew."

SPORT AND RECREATION

Most of the recreational activity in the Yukon comes from the residents and communities themselves. Baseball, made popular by the construction crews that built the Alaska Highway, is a common summer sport. The Yukon Sourdough Rendezvous in February features snowshoe races and flour-packing contests. Dawson's Discovery Days in August is a celebration of the gold rush. Whitehorse hosts the Yukon Championship Dog Race in February and the International Curling Bonspiel in March.

GOVERNMENT AND POLITICS

The Yukon Territory was created as a separate political unit by Act of Parliament in 1898, when it was formed from the northwestern part of the North-West Territories. It was made a separate territory because of a sudden increase in population, the result of many people thronging to the Klondike gold rush.

At first, the Yukon was governed by a commissioner (appointed by the federal government) and an appointed council consisting of the five leading officials in the territory: the judge, the gold commissioner, the registrar, the legal adviser, and the superintendent of police. In 1900 two elected members were added to the council. The number was increased to five in 1902, equal to the number of appointed members. That same year, the territory received a member of Parliament, elected by adult male British subjects who had 12 months' residency in the territory. The makeup of the council changed over the years, and at one time it was abolished for a year because of a drop in population.

Today, the Yukon government consists of an appointed commissioner, a five-member Council, and an elected Legislative Assembly of 16 members. The Assembly has had party politics since 1978

Government Leaders Since 1978

Leader	Party	Term
Chris Pearson	Con	1978-85
Willard Phelps	Con	1985
Tony Penikett	NDP	1985-

Con=Conservative
NDP=New Democratic Party

when the Progressive Conservatives won 11 of the 16 seats. The leader of the party with the most members has been known as the *premier* since 1989 and is also the president of the Executive Council. He or she has a similar role to a premier of a province but with less power, for the Yukon is still a territory, not a province.

Unlike provincial governments, the Yukon government does not have control of its natural resources, except for fish and wildlife. The federal government controls resources, and it receives the revenue from resource development.

As well as electing members to their territorial government, the people of the Yukon elect one member to the House of Commons in Ottawa. Their current member (in 1990) is Audrey McLaughlin, who is also leader of the federal New Democratic Party. Yukoners are represented in the Senate of Canada by one appointed senator.

HISTORY

The First People Yukon and Alaska were the first parts of North America to be occupied by human beings. People first came here from Asia across the land bridge that existed where the Bering Strait now is. It is not known when this occurred, but humans were definitely in the Yukon well over 12 000 years ago, hunting caribou, bison, and woolly mammoth.

The ancestors of today's Yukon Indian people were living in the Yukon by at least 8000 BC. They were hunter-gatherers. They derived everything they needed for food and clothing from the caribou and other animals, and from the wild plants of the Yukon.

Long before the first European arrived in the Yukon, the region's native people had learned of their existence and had received trade goods through native traders. Russians moved onto the Alaska coast in the late 18th century, and it was not long before their trade goods went inland to the Yukon. Along with these goods went diseases to which the Yukon Indians had no resistance. Long before the Yukon In-

dians saw a European face-to-face, large numbers of them had died from smallpox and other diseases carried to the interior by other natives.

Explorers, Traders, and Missionaries
The first European actually to set foot in the Yukon was John Franklin, who travelled and explored along the territory's Arctic coast in 1825. In the same year, the Yukon's western boundary was set at 141°W by a treaty signed between Great Britain and Russia. The real European presence in the Yukon dates from the 1840s, when Hudson's Bay Company traders arrived from the Mackenzie Valley to set up fur-trade posts at Fort Frances (1842, the first HBC post in the Yukon), Fort Youcon (1847, actually in Alaska), and Fort Selkirk (1848).

The next Europeans to arrive were Anglican missionaries. The first was the Rev. William Kirby, who came to Fort Youcon in 1861. Then, in 1865, Bishop William C. Bompas arrived at Fort Simpson to begin a 40-year career in which he devoted himself to the spiritual needs of the Yukon's people.

After the missionaries came explorers and surveyors. In 1860 to 1862 Robert Kennicott surveyed the animal life of the Yukon River valley on behalf of the Smithsonian Institution. Frederick Schwatka explored the region in 1883 for the American army, giving it several of its geographical place-names. In 1887 to 1888 George M. Dawson, assistant director of the Geological Survey of Canada, and William Ogilvie, a Dominion Lands surveyor, explored the Yukon region for the Canadian government. Ogilvie established the location where the Canadian-American boundary crossed the Forty Mile River.

In 1872 the first men arrived specifically for the purpose of finding gold. The first real strike was made in the Forty Mile district in 1886, and by the end of that year there were nearly 300 people wintering there. In 1894 another good find was

Time Line: Yukon

- More than 12 000 years ago, first native people arrive from Asia
- **1825** John Franklin explores Arctic coast
- **1840s** Hudson's Bay Company traders establish fur-trade posts in the Yukon
- **1896** George Carmack and his companions make their big gold strike in the Klondike
- **1897-99** Klondike gold rush brings tens of thousands of people to the Yukon
- **1898** Yukon Territory is created, governed by a federally appointed commissioner and Council, with the capital at Dawson
- **1900** White Pass and Yukon Railway is completed
- **1942** The Alaska Highway is built
- **1951** Yukon Legislative Council is increased to five elected members (later increased to 16); but the appointed commissioner still holds power
- **1953** Capital is moved from Dawson to Whitehorse
- **1979** Power is transferred from the commissioner to the leader of the majority group in the Council (government leader)
- **1979** The Dempster Highway is completed
- **1989** Audrey McLaughlin, MP for the Yukon, becomes leader of Canada's New Democratic Party

Fort Selkirk *(courtesy Aerocamera Services Inc., Orangeville, Ont.).*

made at Circle City, just across the Alaska boundary. By then there were as many as 1000 gold miners in the upper Yukon Valley.

In 1894 two members of the North-West Mounted Police were sent to the Yukon to maintain order, and a further 20 arrived the following year. Thus, when the Klondike gold rush began, the police were already in the territory to enforce Canadian law.

The Klondike Gold Rush The great find was made on August 16, 1896 (commemorated in the Yukon every year by "Discovery Day," a territorial holiday). Three men, George Carmack, Skookum Jim, and Tagish Charley, looking for gold on a creek running into the Klondike River, found gold lying in the cracks of the rocks, "thick between the flaky slabs, like cheese in sandwiches." When they arrived in Forty Mile to register their claims, nearly every man in the Yukon took off on the run to stake a claim. The town of Dawson, located on swampy land where the Klondike River flowed into the Yukon, about 25 km from the gold creeks, mushroomed overnight.

The main gold rush began in 1897, for almost a year passed before word of the strike reached the "outside," as Yukoners called the rest of the world. When two ships reached Seattle and San Francisco in July 1897, one of them carrying over $1 million in gold, people from Canada, the U.S., and many parts of the world, were swept up by the excitement. Thousands quit their jobs and rushed to the Yukon, even though few knew exactly where it was.

During 1898-99, Dawson swelled to a population of 16 000 to 18 000, and was for a time the largest city in Canada west of Winnipeg. Although there were plenty of saloons and dance halls, it was a very law-abiding city. The North-West Mounted Police ran it with a firm hand. No one was allowed to carry a handgun, and bad characters were often simply told

to get out of the territory. There were fewer than 200 members of the NWMP in the Yukon, and 200 men of the Yukon Field Force to help them maintain order. The police, commanded first by Charles Constantine and then by the famous Sam Steele, were determined that the largely non-Canadian population of the Yukon would obey Canadian laws.

The native people of the Yukon were largely untouched by the gold rush. Race prejudice kept them from jobs in the mines or in the settlements, and most of them preferred to maintain their way of life as hunters and trappers in the bush. However, some earned a little money by cutting wood for the river steamers or providing meat to the miners.

Whaling Far to the north, in a little-known part of the Yukon, a smaller but equally dramatic event occurred in the 1890s. In that decade Herschel Island, in the Beaufort Sea off the Yukon's Arctic coast, became the centre of an important whaling industry. Whaling ships from San Francisco used the island as a wintering place, spending the summer hunting bowhead whales in the Beaufort Sea. Good prices for whale oil and baleen (flexible material from the whale's mouth that was used for buggy whips and corset stays) made each whale worth between $10 000 and $15 000. Between 1890 and 1914, over $14 million worth of whales were killed in the region. Complaints from missionaries that the Inuit were being harmed and Canadian sovereignty ignored led to the arrival in 1903 of a two-member detachment of the Mounted Police to enforce the law. The whaling industry, however, did not end until World War I, when the increasing use of petroleum and the scarcity of whales made it unprofitable.

The 20th Century Although the Klondike gold rush lasted only a couple of years, gold mining continued. There was still gold in the creeks, though it was not concentrated enough to attract individual mining. It needed heavy equipment, such as dredges, for the mining to be worthwhile. Consequently, gold-mining companies were formed. They were run by men such as Joe Boyle, "the King of the Klondike." Meanwhile, the romance of the Yukon was kept alive by the poetry and novels of Robert Service, who worked as a bank clerk in the territory, and in the novels of Jack London.

The population shrank steadily, despite finds of other minerals, such as cop-

Routes to the Gold Rush

There were several routes to the Klondike, as the gold-bearing region around Dawson was called.

The easiest was by steamer up the Yukon River from the Bering Sea to Dawson, but this could cost as much as $1000.

The cheapest and most direct route was by boat up the Inside Passage off the coast of British Columbia to Skagway, then over either the Chilkoot Pass or White Pass to Lake Bennett, at the source of the Yukon River; and then down the river to Dawson. The trouble with this route was that all the miners' supplies had to be carried by back over the passes. The Mounted Police would not let anyone into the Yukon without a year's supplies. So the miners had to make as many as 50 trips up the Chilkoot Pass, bent over under heavy loads. (This was the scene captured in the famous photographs of the pass. *See* photos pages 37 and 38, Volume III.)

Armed Escort carrying $400 000 worth of gold from the Klondike Gold Rush (courtesy PAA/ P-7118).

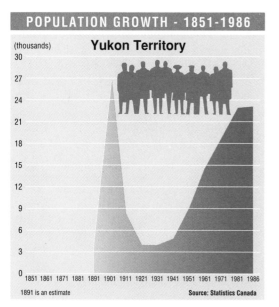

POPULATION GROWTH - 1851-1986

Yukon Territory

(thousands)

30
27
24
21
18
15
12
9
6
3
0

1851 1861 1871 1881 1891 1901 1911 1921 1931 1941 1951 1961 1971 1981 1986

1891 is an estimate   Source: Statistics Canada

Tony Penikett *(Yukon government leader) and Nick Sibbeston (N.W.T. government leader) air their concerns about the Meech Lake Accord (courtesy Canapress Photo Service).*

per, lead, and zinc. During World War I, hundreds of young men left the Yukon to join the army. In October 1918, when the steamship *Princess Sophia* sank in a snowstorm off Skagway, more than 300 people were drowned, many of them Yukoners. By 1921, the Yukon's population had reached a low point of about 4100, of whom 1500 were native people.

In the years between the two world wars, the Yukon was almost forgotten by the rest of Canada and the world. World War II, however, turned the spotlight of attention on the Yukon once more when in 1942 the Alaska Highway was built from Dawson Creek, B.C., to Fairbanks, Alaska, running across the southern part of the Yukon Territory. Thousands of U.S. servicemen and civilian labourers came to the Yukon. Whitehorse, which had been a sleepy transportation town before the war, saw its population grow by four times in the space of a few months. New airfields and new communication facilities were built. All levels of Yukon society were disrupted. The native people were hit by a devastating series of epidemics in 1942, as the new road ended the isolation which had previously kept them relatively safe from communicable diseases.

Until World War II, Dawson had been the Yukon's most important community, but the growth of Whitehorse as the hub of the Alaska Highway tilted the balance in its favour, for there was no road connecting Dawson to the Alaska Highway. In 1953 Whitehorse replaced Dawson as the capital city of the Yukon.

After World War II, the Yukon changed dramatically. Previously, the federal government had spent as little money as pos-

sible in the North, but after 1945 there was a complete about-face. Money began to flow into the North, first as part of federal social programs, such as unemployment insurance, and as payments and special grants. In the 1960s, the federal government began to develop historic sites in Dawson. More recently, it has entered into negotiations with the Yukon's native people for the settlement of their land claims. At the same time, the territory has gained more self-government, and is less as a half-forgotten colony of the federal government.

▷ RELATED ARTICLES: **Martha Louise Black; Joe Boyle; Klondike Gold Rush; Kluane National Park; Native People: Arctic; Native People: Subarctic; Old Crow Plain; Robert Service; Whaling.**

▷ SUGGESTED READING: Ken Coates and W.R. Morrison, *Land of the Midnight Sun: A History of the Yukon* (1988); Harry Gordon-Cooper, *Yukon Yarns: True Tales of the Yukon* (1989); Allan Duncan, *Medicine, Madams and Mounties: Stories of a Yukon Doctor* (1989); Ted Harrison, *Children of the Yukon* (1988); J.W. Paterson, *Ghost Towns of the Yukon* (1977).

■ **Zeidler, Eberhard Heinrich**

Architect (*born in 1926 at Braunsdorf, Germany*). Zeidler believes that architecture is an art which combines technology with the expression of feeling. He does not try to hide the structural and mechanical elements in his buildings, but rather incorporates the steel trusses, air ducts, and communication systems into his overall design. As a result, his projects often resemble a child's giant construction toy, though they are made attractive inside by his use of bright colours, interior courtyards, and fountains and shrubs. He expects that his buildings will have to change over time to meet constantly changing needs, but he wants them to be happy, joyful places.

Zeidler was trained at the famous Bauhaus in Weimar, East Germany, and he immigrated to Canada in 1951. He is now a principal with the Toronto-based Zeidler Roberts Partnership. His many high-profile projects include Ontario Place (1971), a theme park built on three artificial islands on the Toronto waterfront, the McMaster University Health Sciences Centre (1972) in Hamilton, Ont., the Eaton Centre (1981) in Toronto, the Walter C. Mackenzie Health Sciences Centre (1986) in Edmonton, and Canada Place for Expo 86 in Vancouver. He has received many prestigious awards for his work.

Characteristics of Zinc

Formula: Zn
Appearance: a bluish white metal
Properties: of medium hardness, with a melting point of 419°C
Atomic Weight: 65.37
Uses: a coating for iron or steel products such as pipes; small electrical appliances, tools, car doors, window handles; dry-cell batteries; roofing; alloyed into brass and German silver

Zookeeper with a young Bald Eagle, Metropolitan Toronto Zoo (photo by Stephen Homer/First Light).

Japanese Macaque and babies at Metropolitan Toronto Zoo. Zoos are important sources of research which may help preserve threatened species in the wild (photo by Stephen Homer/First Light).

■ Zinc

Zinc is a medium hard metal. Its chief use is to coat iron or steel products, such as ventilating pipes, so that they do not rust. Putting on a coat of zinc is known as galvanizing. Zinc is also used to make parts such as door and window handles for cars. Mixed with copper it becomes brass, a material used in pipes and other products. Canada is the world's largest producer and exporter of zinc. In 1987, Canadian mines produced about 1158 million kg of zinc, worth just over $1.5 billion. This zinc came from mines in every province of Canada except for Alberta, Nova Scotia, and Prince Edward Island.

▷ RELATED ARTICLE: **Metals and Metallurgy.**

■ Zola, Meguido

Writer, professor (*born in 1939 at Cairo, Egypt*). Born to Jewish parents escaping the Nazis, he was raised in Africa. He studied in France and England. He is now a professor of education at Simon Fraser University in Vancouver.

Zola's writing reflects his multicultural background. His retellings of traditional Jewish stories, *A Dream of Promise* (1980) and *Only the Best* (1981), are about characters who discover that the valuable treasure they have long sought is within themselves. *Moving* (1983), a novel about Mennonites, shows that life often requires change. Zola's *Nobody* (1983), written with Angela Dereume, is about three native children's tricks on their mother, and *My Kind of Pup* (1985), about a mischievous dog.

Zebras at the Metropolitan Toronto Zoo (photo by Malak, Ottawa).

■ Zoo

Zoos are collections of living animals, usually for public display. Zoos have existed for thousands of years, but only recently have they been devoted to science and education. The rising concern over the disappearance of wild animals has given greater importance to zoos. Meanwhile, a concern with the treatment of animals has forced zoos to show that they are concerned with the kind of research that benefits the animals themselves and their survival in the wild. In Canada, zoos are bound by a code of ethics.

There are over 55 zoos in Canada, including aquariums, where fish and other marine animals are displayed. Many have school programs, interpretive talks, camps, and workshops. Canada's largest zoo is the Metropolitan Toronto Zoo, with 106 species of mammals, 144 species of birds, and many other species. Some 1.3 million people visit each year. About 1.2 million visit the Stanley Park Zoological Gardens in Vancouver and another 950 000 visit the Vancouver Public Aquarium. The Calgary Zoo in Calgary, Alta, receives about 800 000 visitors (many more when the famous pandas from China stayed there). It has 88 species of mammals and 136 species of birds.

■ Zoology

Zoology is the study of animal life. It is often thought of as one of the main branches of biology (botany being the other). However, such divisions have blurred over time as it has been proven that the same principles apply to all living things.

We now know that the conditions that support life on Earth are found nowhere else in our solar system. The Earth's atmosphere provides essential gases, such as oxygen, while at the same time screening out harmful rays that would destroy life. Zoologists study how life evolved on Earth, how and where animals live, and how they interact with one another and their environment.

History Zoology became a science in the 17th century. Through observation and experiments, the English scientist William Harvey explained how blood circulates in an animal's body. Most of his research was performed on deer.

In the 19th century, Charles Darwin developed the theory of evolution, which is still the central concept in biology. He showed that species have come and gone on Earth and that one species gives rise to another. It is still not known, however, *how* species change, and this remains an exciting field of research.

The invention of the microscope revealed a microscopic world to biologists. They discovered that cells are the building blocks of all living things. They began to understand the process of reproduction, and that all animals begin as a single cell and go through various stages of development. The greatest advances in the 20th century came in genetics. Zoological studies contributed greatly to the unfolding of the code of life, through the discoveries of genes and of DNA.

Classification Zoologists have tried to bring order to the enormous variety of living things through a system of classification. It was first devised by Swedish scientist Carl von Linné, who is also known by his Latin name, Carolus Linnaeus. Linnaeus used two Latin words to describe living things. He used Latin because it was a language shared by all educated people of Europe at the time. The first term, he called *genus*, which referred to a group of similar living things. The second term, the specific name, defines *species* within the genus. The two names together form the species name. Thus the genus *Canis* refers to a group of similar animals, including wolves, foxes, and dogs. Wolves are the species *Canis lupus*, while dogs are the species *Canis familiaris*.

Today, zoologists use a more complex system of classification. It is based on the principle, first stated by the French naturalist Georges Buffon, that all living forms are related to each other. Similar genera are grouped in *families*. Similar families make up *orders*. Similar orders form *classes*. Similar classes make up a *phylum*. Similar phyla are grouped into *kingdoms*. Thus, the classification of human beings would be as follows:

- Species: *Homo sapiens*
- Genus: *Homo*
- Family: Hominidae
- Order: Primates
- Class: Mammalia
- Subphylum: Vertebrata
- Phylum: Chordata
- Kingdom: Animalia

Biologists now recognize five kingdoms, where once there were only two: Animalia (animals) and Plantae (plants). Now they also recognize Monera (bacteria), Protista (some types of algae), and Fungi (molds and mushrooms).

When most people think of animals, they think of fishes, birds, and mammals. Yet 97% of all the animals alive on Earth today are invertebrates (no backbone), such as earthworms, butterflies, and snails. Each of these types of animals is studied by zoologists. The vertebrates are of particular interest, as they are to the public. They are the largest animals: fierce hunters, speedy runners, and long-distance fliers. They also show complex behaviour.

Animal Biology Zoologists study how animals find and ingest food, how they find water, and how they defend territories. Unlike plants, animals move, sometimes over great distances. Zoologists study the movements of herds of caribou or the migrations of birds over thousands of kilometres. Much of this work is extremely important for wildlife conservation. Zoological studies are also essential for the proper running of zoos and aquariums, and for medical research.

Habitats Every animal has its *habitat*, its place in the environment. It also has its *niche*, or role in the community of living things. For example, a red squirrel eats flowers, mushrooms, and other forest plants. In turn, it transports their seeds through the forest, helping with reproduction.

Lion in the Metropolitan Toronto Zoo (photo by Lorraine C. Palow/First Light).

Lead Sled Dog shows its dominance through its body language (photo by Barbara Brundege and Eugene Fisher).

Thick-billed Murres take off from a cliff on Bylot Island (photo by Barbara Brundege and Eugene Fisher).

Zoologists study how energy "flows" through the environment. The links between the berries and plants on the arctic tundra and the birds that feed on them and the foxes that feed on the birds are called a *food chain*. This concept helps to explain, for example, how insecticides can build up to deadly levels as they are passed on through the food chain.

Animal Behaviour Zoologists' studies of behaviour include studying how animals learn and communicate. A honeybee can tell other bees where to find honey through an elaborate dance. A wolf signals its dominance over others by raising its tail, pointing its ears, and baring its teeth. Humans communicate through speech. Studies in all these areas have shown that animals are as diverse in their behaviour as in their forms.

ZOOLOGY IN CANADA

John Cabot's report of vast populations of fish off the coast of Newfoundland raised the first zoological interest in Canada. The study of the fisheries continues in Canada down to today. These studies are of enormous importance to help the industry prevent overfishing.

Many Canadians have contributed to zoology through their studies of insects, parasites, and the environment. Most of this research is carried on in universities, research institutes, and museums. The public can gain a better understanding of the animal kingdom by visiting one of the museums across Canada. The National Museum of Natural Sciences is located in Ottawa. The Royal Ontario Museum is in Toronto. All provinces have museums and zoos. The Biological Survey of Canada is collecting a description of as many animals as possible.

▷ RELATED ARTICLES: **Amphibians; Biology; Birds; Dinosaurs; Fish; Insects; Lizards; Mammals; Reptiles; Snakes;** and other entries on individual animal species.

■ Zouaves

Zouaves were infantrymen serving in the pope's army in Italy. Between 1868 and 1870, seven contingents of Canadians enroled as Zouaves to help defend the pope when Giuseppe Garibaldi was trying to conquer Rome. They came from almost every parish in Quebec, spurred on by Bishop Ignace Bourget of Montreal and other staunch supporters of the pope. On their return to Canada, the Zouaves formed an association which still exists.

■ Zurakowski, Janusz

Test pilot (*born in 1914 at Ryzawka, Russia*). Zurakowski learned to fly gliders while he was in high school. In 1935 he joined the Polish air force. When Germany invaded Poland in 1939, he escaped to England. There he became a fighter pilot with the Royal Air Force (RAF).

Zurakowski first flew as a test pilot while with the RAF. He immigrated to Canada in 1952. On December 18, 1952, he became the first pilot to fly a Canadian-designed aircraft faster than the speed of sound. This was during a test flight of the CF-100. In March 1958 he also test-flew the Canadian-designed Avro Arrow, reaching a speed of 1600 km per hour on its seventh flight.

Test Pilot Janusz Zurakowski after the first flight of the Avro Arrow, *March 1958 (courtesy NAC/C-61731).*

INDEX

When to Use the Index The index is a handy way to find information in the encyclopedia. For example, if you want to find out about dinosaurs, you would first turn to the article called **Dinosaur**. However, dinosaurs may also be discussed in other entries in the encyclopedia as well. The index can help you locate these entries.

The index will also help you find information on subjects that *do not* have their own articles, for example, the dome-headed dinosaur.

How to Use the Index

a) *Finding an Article Title* All subjects that have their own articles are listed in the index. They are always in **boldface type** and are followed by a volume number (also in boldface) and page number(s). Each page is divided by imaginary lines into four sections. The capital letter after the page number tells you where on the page to begin looking, as follows:

A	C
B	D

The reference to the article **Dinosaur** looks like this:

volume number ↘   ↙ page number
article title→**Dinosaur 2**-29D←page section

Often article titles are followed by one or more **sub-entries**. These point you to more information in different articles, as in the following example:

> **Dinosaur 2**-29D
> **Dinosaur Provincial Park 2**-34C
> **Fossil 2**-198A, **2**-198B

b) *Finding a Subject Entry* Subject entries (that is, subjects that do not have their own article) are in light type. They are *not* followed by volume and page numbers. For example, the entry on the dome-headed dinosaur looks like this:

> dome-headed dinosaur
> **Dinosaur 2**-31D

The light type tells us that there is not a separate entry on the dome-headed dinosaur. However, there is information on this creature in the article **Dinosaur**, which is located in volume 2, on page 31, in section D.

c) *Illustrations* (*pictures, maps, graphs, boxes, charts, tables*) are noted in the index only if they are found somewhere other than in an article of the same name. For example, pictures of a deer in the article **Deer** would *not* be listed in the index. However, there is a picture of a deer in the article **Forest**.

> **Deer 2**-13B
> **Forest 2**-185C (*picture*)

A page reference followed by "with box," "with *picture*," and so on, means that there is both an illustration and information in the text on the same page.

d) *Cross-references* A *See also* listing leads you to other headings in the index where more entries on your topic are listed.

> **Mining 3**-211B. *See also*
> **Metals and Metallurgy; Mineral**

A *See* reference contains no information itself but sends you to another listing in the index.

> Delaney, Marshall. *See* **Fulford, Robert Marshall Blount**

e) *Alphabetical Order* Headings in this index are in word-by-word alphabetical order, as they are in the encyclopedia.

H

N

Q

R

T

U

Z

Abbreviations Used For Illustration Sources

AGO	Art Gallery of Ontario
ASC/CMC	Archaeological Survey of Canada/Canadian Museum of Civilization
CBC	Canadian Broadcasting Corporation
DIAND	Department of Indian and Northern Affairs
EMR	Energy Mines & Resources Canada
NAC	National Archives of Canada
NFB	National Film Board of Canada
NGC	National Gallery of Canada
NMNS	National Museum of Natural Sciences
NMC/CMC	National Museums of Canada/Canadian Museum of Civilization
PAA	Provincial Archives of Alberta
PABC	Provincial Archives of British Columbia
PAM	Provincial Archives of Manitoba
PMA	Provincial Museum of Alberta
RCMP	Royal Canadian Mounted Police Archives

The Junior Encyclopedia of Canada

Designed by Roberge Hoffman Young Graphic Design Inc., Edmonton

*Composed and typeset at Printing Services, University of Alberta
in 10.5 point Trump Medieval*

Colour separations by R.P.J. Litho, Montreal

*Printed by Imprimerie Ronalds,
A division of Quebecor Printing Inc., Montreal*

*Paper (60 lb Rolland ST-101)
manufactured by Rolland Inc., St. Jérôme, Quebec*

Bound by The Bryant Press Ltd, Toronto

*Cloth (Millbank Linen)
manufactured by Columbia Finishing Mills, Cornwall, Ontario*

Slipcases by Torham Packaging, Toronto

Cartons designed and manufactured by Kruger Manufacturing, Toronto

Packaging by Britman Industries, Oshawa, Ontario